$\mathcal{W}$ELLNESS

CREATING A LIFE
OF HEALTH AND FITNESS

Jerrold S. Greenberg
University Of Maryland

George B. Dintiman
Virginia Commonwealth University

with **Barbee Myers Oakes**
Wake Forest University

Allyn and Bacon

Boston • London • Toronto • Sydney • Tokyo • Singapore

Senior Series Editor: Suzy Spivey
Editor-in-Chief: Sean W. Wakely
Marketing Manager: Quinn Perkson
Production Administrator: Mary Beth Finch
Editorial-Production Service: Thomas E. Dorsaneo
Electronic Composition: Dayle Silverman
Text Designer: Wendy LaChance/*By Design*
Cover Administrator: Linda Knowles
Cover Designer: Studio Nine
Composition and Prepress Buyer: Linda Cox

Copyright © 1997 by Allyn & Bacon
A Viacom Company
Needham Heights, MA 02194-2310

Internet: www.abacon.com
America Online: Keyword: College online

Portions of this material appeared in Greenberg, Dintiman, and Oakes, *Physical Fitness and Wellness*,
copyright © 1995 by Allyn and Bacon.

Library of Congress Cataloging-in-Publication Data
Greenberg, Jerrold S.
       Wellness: creating a life of health & fitness/ by Jerrold S. Greenberg and George B.
Dintiman.
             p.   cm.
       Includes bibliographical references and index.
       ISBN 0-205-26078-0
       1. College students—Health and hygeine. 2. Health.
I. Dintiman, George B. II. Title.
     RA777.3.G74   1994
     613.7—dc20   94-16503
                                                                                         CIP

Printed in the United States of America
10 9 8 7 6 5 4 3 2 1   01 00 99 98 97 96

Dedication

This book is dedicated to the memory of our loved ones who encouraged us to be healthy: David Greenberg and Gladys Blough Dintiman

Contents

7 PRINCIPLES OF EXERCISE 139

8 CARDIORESPIRATORY FITNESS 161

9 MUSCULAR ENDURANCE, MUSCULAR STRENGTH, AND FLEXIBILITY 193

viii ✦ Contents

12 PREVENTING HEART DISEASE 301

13 PREVENTING CANCER 317

14 EXPLORING EXERCISE INJURIES AND PREVENTING INJURY, ILLNESS, AND DISEASE 343

15 DESIGNING A PROGRAM
UNIQUELY FOR YOU: A
LIFETIME OF WELLNESS   **389**

*A*PPENDICES

Preface

*I*N RECENT YEARS there has been what some might call a health and fitness revolution, or perhaps the word *revelation* is more appropriate. Increasingly, health professionals and the lay public have become more aware of the benefits of health-related behavior on the length and quality of life. On college campuses, this revelation is evidenced by the greater number of "wellness" courses and the increasing numbers of students enrolling in these courses. To accommodate this interest in wellness, some colleges have combined the content usually taught in physical fitness classes and the content usually taught in personal health classes into a course called "Wellness" or some comparable term. Recognizing this movement, and realizing there are but a few texts devoted to wellness, we have written this book, *Wellness: Creating a Life of Health and Fitness,* that can be taught in such a course.

We discuss topics typically taught in fitness courses, such as principles of exercise, cardiorespiratory fitness, muscle strength and endurance, flexibility, and the like. But we also discuss topics usually reserved for personal health courses, such as stress, sexuality, alcohol and other drugs, nutrition and weight control, and cancer and coronary heart disease. In other words, this book contains an array of valid information sufficient for you to become healthy and fit or to maintain your present state of health and fitness if they are adequate.

SPECIAL FEATURES

In addition to the more traditional approaches to the topics of health, fitness, and wellness, we have addressed some issues that are often neglected. For example, aware that researchers have found knowledge of wellness insufficient in itself to motivate people to become healthy and fit and to maintain an adequate lifelong level of wellness, we include a chapter entitled "Behavioral Change and Motivational Techniques." The well-researched strategies covered in this chapter are further described throughout the text in examples of how they might be used to overcome barriers to wellness. Most chapters have a **Behavioral Change and Motivational Strategies** box describing obstacles specific to that chapter's content that can interfere with achieving wellness, and behavioral change strategies that can be employed to overcome these obstacles.

Another of this book's unique features developed as we were researching this book. We were disturbed by the misconceptions about health, fitness, and wellness we encountered. Given the popularity of health, fitness, and wellness, it is not surprising that many individuals should pose as the latest gurus of wellness. Unfortunately, too many of these self-proclaimed gurus are not adequately trained nor qualified to teach about health, fitness, or wellness. The result is that misconceptions are presented as, and believed to be, fact. For this reason we include a **Myth and Fact Sheet** box in each chapter. These boxes present general misconceptions related to the content of the chapter and correct these myths with factual information.

Perhaps the most important feature of this book is the boxed material entitled **Improving Your Community**. Each of us is a member of several different communities. We reside in a city, in a county, in a state, and in a country. We are part of a college or university community and are residents of a worldwide community living on the planet Earth. All too often wellness courses, as well as personal health and fitness courses, emphasize readers' responsibilities for their own health and the health of their immediate families. Ignored, however, are the responsibilities readers have to others with whom they share a common interest—their larger "families"—to contribute to their wellness. Not so here! The **Improving Your Community** boxes encourage readers to feel responsibility to others in their communities; and they suggest numerous ways in which readers can use the content presented in each chapter to make the lives of other people more "well"—that is, healthier, more fit, and more satisfying.

Last of all, we are concerned with helping students see the relevance of the content in each chapter to their own lives. Consequently, we include three student-centered activities per chapter. Each **Lab Activity** engages readers in the content and encourages them to make improvements in their health and fitness behaviors as a result of what they find out about themselves.

We have presented the information needed to engage in a life of wellness. We provide techniques that can be used to motivate and encourage continued participation in a wellness lifestyle. And, we have done so in a way that recognizes the responsibility readers have to the well-being of the communities in which they reside. The use of this book to achieve health, fitness, and high-level wellness is now up to each reader. We will feel no greater satisfaction than if we have succeeded in improving the lives of our readers throughout the country by having written this book. Make our day—be well.

SUPPLEMENTS

Instructor's Manual and Test Bank with Transparency Masters and Video Guide

This comprehensive supplement provides everything a fitness instructor will need to teach from this exciting new text. Included in the Instructor's Manual section are chapter outlines, objectives and summaries, key terms and concepts, lecture and lab activity outlines, discussion questions, suggested student activities, supplementary readings, and supplementary videos and other media materials. The Test Bank provides 50 questions for each chapter with multiple choice, true-false, fill-in, and essay type questions to choose between. A computerized version of the test bank is available to adopters in both IBM and Macintosh formats.

Video Material

A specially edited videotape provides an exciting means for enhancing classroom discussion. This unique videotape includes segments on such relevant topics as eating disorders, yoga, disabled aerobics, a wellness dorm, men's nutrition, and osteoporosis exercises. A video user's guide can be found in the Instructor's Manual that provides a description of each video segment, suggested classroom use for each segment, tie-ins with the text material, and discussion questions for each segment.

ACKNOWLEDGMENTS

We would like to thank the following reviewers for the thoughtful criticism and valuable suggestions they provided: Harry Duval, University of Georgia; Coach Michael Manley, Anderson University; Joseph T. Lopour, Southern Utah University; Larry Durstine, University of South Carolina; Joe Smith, University of Alabama; Robert Case, Sam Houston State University; Dr. Mary Mahan, Miami Dade Community College; Peggy McDonald, Central Piedmont Community College; Andrew Paterna, Manchester Community Technical College; Carol Christensen, San Jose State University; Dr. Christine L. Wells, Arizona State University; Robert Rothstein, Miami Dade Community College; Dr. Pat Vehrs, University of Houston; and Linda Halbert, University of North Carolina, Charlotte.

In addition, we owe a debt of gratitude to the people at Allyn and Bacon who committed themselves to the careful review, editing, and production of this book. In particular, we wish to thank Suzy Spivey, Senior Series Editor; Thomas E. Dorsaneo, Production Editor; and Mary Beth Finch, Production Administrator. They provided us with valuable insight and guidance in all phases of the creation of this book, from the first written word to the last details of organization, design, illustration, and production.

Finally, our families have provided us with the support that all authors need. They were there to bounce ideas off of, to console and to cajole (whichever happened to be needed at the time), and to provide a haven of love to which we could retreat. Although we have come to expect these things from our families, we nevertheless would like to take this opportunity to acknowledge that we probably do take them for granted too often and announce loudly for all to hear: Thanks for being there!

*H*EALTH, *W*ELLNESS, AND *P*HYSICAL *F*ITNESS

*C*hapter *Objectives*

By the end of this chapter, you should be able to:

1. Define and differentiate between health, wellness, and physical fitness.
2. Describe the importance of health, wellness, and physical fitness.
3. Cite similarities between health, wellness, and physical fitness.

*S*EVERAL YEARS HAD passed—five to be exact—since Rodney and I last saw each other. I was looking forward to catching up on old times. When I asked the standard, "How have you been?" Rodney replied that he had never felt better. He had taken up jogging and was now running 50 miles a week. He had given up cigarette smoking, become a vegetarian, and had more confidence than ever.

In spite of his reply, I needed further assurance. He looked like death warmed over. His face was gaunt; his body emaciated. His clothes were baggy, creating a sloppy appearance. He had an aura of tiredness about him.

"How's Cynthia?" I asked.

"Fine," Rodney replied. "But we are no longer together. She just couldn't accept the time I devoted to running, and her disregard for her own health was getting on my nerves. She is still somewhat overweight, you know, and I started viewing her differently when I became healthier myself."

Inez was a college athlete. Her basketball team always had a winning record, and she was a major reason they were so good. Still, that was long ago. Today Inez is in her 50s, and an automobile accident has left her without the use of her legs. But she still participates in sports. She plays wheelchair basketball in her leisure time and coaches a community center soccer team on the weekends. She may not be able to run a mile, but she certainly can shoot foul shots. She may not be able to demonstrate a soccer kick, but she sure can motivate the girls she coaches.

Figure 1.1 ✦ The Health-Illness Continuum

Perfect Health   Health   Illness   Death

You may know an Inez, a Rodney, or someone like them. Are they healthy? This is a complicated question, one that this chapter explores, first by defining health, wellness, and physical fitness, and then by differentiating among them.

HEALTH

What do you mean when you think of health? If someone told you Aaron was really healthy, what picture of Aaron would you have in your mind? If you were asked to elaborate on your health, what would you say? We will help you answer that question, but first try listing five ways in which you could improve your health.

We are willing to bet you listed ways to improve your physical health. You probably listed ways to prevent contracting heart disease, such as eating less fatty foods or exercising more, or ways to prevent cancer by not smoking cigarettes and getting regular checkups. Yet physical health is not the total picture; other components of health that are just as important. These include:

1. **Social health** This is the ability to interact well with people and the environment, to have satisfying interpersonal relationships.

2. **Mental health** This is the ability to learn and grow intellectually. Life's experiences as well as more formal structures (for example, schools) enhance mental health.

3. **Emotional health** This is the ability to control emotions so that you feel comfortable expressing them and you can express them appropriately. Conversely, it is the ability to refrain from expressing emotions when it is inappropriate to do so.

4. **Spiritual health** This is a belief in some unifying force, which will vary from person to person but will have the concept of faith at its core. Faith is a feeling of connection to other humans, of a purpose to life, and of a quest for meaning in life.

So health is not just caring for your body. It concerns your social interactions, mind, feelings, and spirit. Often we decide to give up health in one area to gain greater health in another. For example, when you decide you're just not up to exercising today, you may choose to improve your emotional health (to seek relaxation) at some expense to your physical health. When you decide to study instead of spending time with your friends, you may be choosing mental over social health. We make decisions like these about our health all the time even though we do not express them in these terms.

To identify the strengths and weaknesses of the components of your health, complete Lab Activity 1.1: Identifying Your Health Strengths and Weaknesses at the end of this chapter.

Now you can appreciate that physical health is just one component of overall health. **Health** then is an individual's total physical, social, emotional, mental, and spiritual status, and health is separate and distinct from illness (see Figure 1.1).

In Figure 1.1 the continuum is a dotted, rather than a solid, line. Each dot is made up of the five health components (see Figure 1.2), and therefore everyone has some degree of health no matter where he or she is located on the continuum.

WELLNESS

Imagine that each health dot, as depicted in Figure 1.2, is a tire on the vehicle in which you travel through life. If the tire is properly inflated, you will have a smooth ride; if it is not, the ride will be bumpy. The same is true for your *health tire*. If you do not pay enough attention to your health and all its components, improving (inflating) them when you can, you will experience conditions that make life more difficult and dissatisfying. For example, if you do not exercise frequently enough or properly, you may become fatigued easily or susceptible to various illnesses.

If you overdo any one component of health at the expense of the others, you may wind up with a tire like the one in Figure 1.3. That tire is *out of round*

Figure 1.2 ✦ A Single Health-Illness Continuum Dot

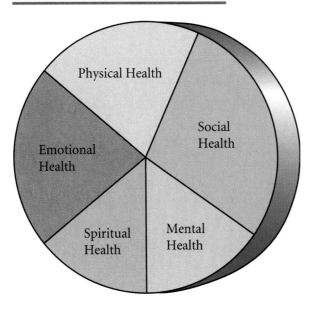

quately inflated and balanced, paying attention to and improving all aspects of health without exaggerating any one. Inez, the other person we introduced at the beginning of this chapter, could not use her legs, but she participated in physical activity at the level at which she was capable. She even learned about soccer so she could coach a community center team. Inez probably possessed a higher level of wellness than did the physically advantaged Rodney. That is why you need to focus on your social, mental, emotional, and spiritual health as you read this book. We will help you do that by regularly presenting the health and wellness implications of the content discussed.

and will not provide a smooth ride. That health tire has expanded physical health to the detriment of the other aspects of health. Here is where Rodney, introduced at the beginning of this chapter, comes to mind. He expanded his physical health but was no longer married and looked terrible. He had no time for friends (social health), reading (mental health), or enjoying nature or participating in religious traditions (spiritual health). Even though he was more physically fit, he was not arguably healthier. Furthermore, he did not possess a very high level of wellness. We refer to **wellness** as having your health tire *in round,* that is, having the components of health ade-

PHYSICAL FITNESS

Physical fitness is defined differently by different people. In this text, it is defined as the ability to meet life's demands and still have enough energy to respond to unplanned events. There are five basic components of physical fitness: cardiorespiratory endurance, muscular strength, muscular endurance, flexibility, and body composition. Participation in sports activities that can improve these fitness components often requires certain motor skills. Consequently, motor skills (such as agility, balance, coordination, power, speed, and reaction time) are often included in physical fitness programs. It *is* possible to develop the five basic components of physical fitness without proficiency in these and other motor skills. That is why someone who is not a natural athlete can still be extremely fit.

Cardiorespiratory Endurance

To engage in physical activity, even breathing, requires oxygen. Without oxygen, it would be impossible to burn the food you need for energy. To supply oxygen to the various parts of the body requires a transport system. The body's transport system consists of lungs, heart, and blood vessels. When you breathe, you inhale air that contains oxygen into the lungs. The lungs absorb oxygen into their blood ves-

Figure 1.3 ✦ An Asymmetrical Dot on the Health-Illness Continuum

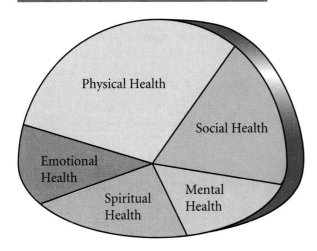

Health The total of your physical, social, emotional, mental, and spiritual status.

Wellness Having the components of health balanced and at sufficient levels.

sels and transport it to the heart where it is pumped out through other blood vessels to all parts of the body. The more efficiently and effectively you transport oxygen, the greater your cardiorespiratory endurance (*cardio* for heart and *respiratory* for lungs and breathing)—the ability to supply and use oxygen, over a period of time and in sufficient amounts, to perform normal and unusual activities.

Muscular Strength and Endurance

The maximal pulling force of a muscle or a muscle group is called **muscular strength**. The ability of a muscle to contract repeatedly or to sustain a contraction is called **muscular endurance**. Lifting a load or moving an object depends on muscular strength. Doing that repeatedly over time requires muscular endurance. In spite of tremendous cardiovascular endurance, without sufficient muscular strength or endurance you may not be able to do the things you wish to do.

Muscular Flexibility

The range of motion around a joint, or more simply the degree to which you can move your limbs with grace and efficiency, is **flexibility**. Flexibility is important in performing exercise efficiently, safely, and enjoyably. Without adequate flexibility you might not be able to stretch far, might overstress a muscle or ligament, and might even feel uncomfortable moving. Flexibility is probably the component of physical fitness that is most overlooked; yet the con-

Exercising outdoors is an invigorating way to enhance spiritual health while at the same time improving physical health. (Photo courtesy of the Aspen Hill Club.)

sequences of ignoring flexibility can be injury, pain and discomfort, and poor health.

Body Composition

Your body contains some parts that are made up of fats and others that are not. The fat component is usually referred to as **fat weight**, and fat in relation to the body as a whole is referred to as **percent body fat**. The nonfatty component is called **lean body mass**. **Body composition** is the relationship between these two components. In the past, people relied on height-weight charts to evaluate body composition. We now realize that someone can weigh many more pounds than a chart based on height says is appropriate but still have good body composition. This can happen because the person is muscular and has a good deal of lean body mass. Conversely, someone at just the right weight according to a height chart could in actuality be overweight because of too much fatty tissue and not enough lean body mass.

Health Objectives for the Nation

Figure 1.4 compares the major causes of death in 1900 and today. Heading the 1900 list are diseases

---

Muscular strength The amount of force a muscle can exert for one repetition.

Muscular endurance A muscle's ability to continue submaximal contractions against resistance.

Flexibility The range of motion around a joint or the ability to move limbs gracefully and efficiently.

Fat weight The weight of your body fat.

Percent body fat The percentage of your body weight made up of fat.

Lean body mass The nonfatty component of your body.

Body composition The relationship between your fat weight and your lean body mass.

Figure 1.4 ✦ Comparison of Causes of Death, 1900 and Today

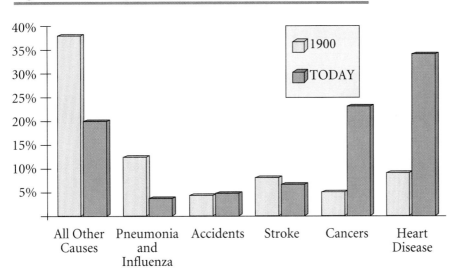

that are passed from one person to another or that are the result of unsanitary practices (tuberculosis, pneumonia, influenza). Increased knowledge led to legislation that has, for the most part, drastically reduced the incidence of these diseases through the development of proper waste disposal and sewage systems, quarantine, and other community actions to prevent their spread.

The killers of today do not lend themselves to such remedies. These conditions (heart disease, cancer, and stroke) are more the result of lifestyle than of a microorganism. In a democratic society, we cannot legislate lifestyle. For significant decreases to occur in these diseases, people must voluntarily change unhealthy behaviors (cigarette smoking, lack of regular physical activity, lack of proper amounts of sleep,

Exercise is something that we all need to fit into our schedules. If Presidents, who work more than 15 hours a day, can find time to exercise, perhaps you can too! (Photos courtesy, from left to right, the White House, the Aspen Hill Club, and the Jimmy Carter Library.)

Table 1.1 ✦ National Health Objectives Specific to Physical Fitness and Wellness

The following are objectives related to health, wellness, and physical fitness. The objective and the baseline condition, the status of the behavior or condition when the objective was written, are presented here.

OBJECTIVE	BASELINE
1. Reduce coronary heart disease deaths to no more than 100 per 100,000 people.	135 per 100,000
2. Reduce overweight to no more than 20 percent of people aged 20 and older and no more than 15 percent of adolescents aged 12 through 19.	26 percent for people aged 20 through 74 and 15 percent for adolescents aged 12 through 19
3. Increase to at least 30 percent the proportion of people aged 6 and older who engage in light to moderate physical activity for at least 30 minutes per day.	22 percent of people aged 18 and older are active at least 30 minutes five or more times per week and 12 percent are active seven or more times per week
4. Increase to at least 20 percent the proportion of people aged 18 and older and to at least 75 percent the proportion of youths aged 6 through 17 who engage in vigorous physical activity that promotes the development and maintenance of cardiorespiratory fitness three or more days per week for 20 or more minutes per occasion.	12 percent for people aged 18 and older and 66 percent for youth aged 10 through 17
5. Reduce to no more than 15 percent the proportion of people aged 6 and older who engage in no leisure-time physical activity.	24 percent for people aged 18 and older
6. Increase to at least 40 percent the proportion of people aged 6 and older who regularly perform physical activities that enhance and maintain muscular strength, muscular endurance, and flexibility.	None available
7. Increase to at least 50 percent the proportion of overweight people aged 12 and older who have adopted sound dietary practices combined with regular physical activity to attain an appropriate body weight.	30 percent of overweight women and 25 percent of overweight men for people aged 18 and older
8. Increase to at least 50 percent the proportion of children and adolescents in 1st through 12th grade who participate daily in school physical education.	36 percent
9. Increase to at least 50 percent the proportion of school physical education class time that students spend being physically active, preferably engaged in lifetime physical activities.	27 percent
10. Increase the proportion of worksites offering employer-sponsored physical activity and fitness programs.	Worksite with 50 to 99 employees, 14 percent; with 100 to 249 employees, 23 percent; with 250 to 749 employees, 32 percent; with more than 749 employees, 54 percent
11. Increase community availability and accessibility of physical activity and fitness facilities.	Hiking, biking, and fitness trails—1 per 71,000 people; public swimming pools—1 per 53,000 people; park and recreation open space—1.8 per 1,000 people
12. Increase to at least 50 percent the proportion of primary care providers who routinely assess and counsel patients regarding the frequency, duration, type, and intensity of physical activity practices.	Counseling routinely provided for 30 percent of sedentary patients

Source: From *Healthy People 2000: National Health Promotion and Disease Prevention Objectives,* U. S. Department of Health and Human Services, 1991, Washington, DC: U.S. Government Printing Office, DHHS Publication No. (PHS) 91-50212.

The National Institutes of Health (NIH) is an important branch of the federal government concerned with the health and wellness of Americans. NIH conducts research, provides treatment, and organizes educational programs and instructional materials to respond to various health issues. (Photo courtesy the National Cancer Institute)

abuse of alcohol and other drugs, eating foods high in saturated fats, and so forth). Medical researchers estimate that 20 percent of the risk for heart disease, cancer, and stroke can be attributed to heredity, another 20 percent to environmental factors, 10 percent to inadequate health care, and an alarming 50 percent to unhealthy lifestyles.

Recognizing the need to encourage the adoption of healthy lifestyles, the Surgeon General of the United States developed health goals for the nation. The first national health goals were distributed in 1979 and 1980. More recently, goals for the year 2000 have been announced. Examples of national health objectives related to health, wellness, and physical fitness appear in Table 1.1.

To assess the risk of ill health associated with your lifestyle decisions, complete Lab Activity 1.2: Assessing Your Health Risk at the end of this chapter.

𝒲HAT'S IN IT FOR YOU

Although there are no guarantees, the potential benefits of maintaining your health and wellness are fairly obvious: *You will live longer and you will live better.* That is, you will not die prematurely of coronary heart disease, lung cancer, or stroke. Further, as you age you will not be limited by disabilities caused by an unhealthy lifestyle. You will be muscularly able to perform job responsibilities, cardiovascularly able to climb stairs and walk reasonable distances, and emotionally and socially healthy enough to effectively interact with other people. Add to this mix the spiri-

tual health benefits of a worldview that you are connected to something larger than yourself—for example, nature, or a higher power, or your children and grandchildren and generations to come—and you can see the advantages of maintaining a healthy lifestyle likely to lead to high-level wellness.

The Benefits of Physical Activity

Physical fitness also has identifiable benefits. A friend of ours likes to kid that he gets his exercise serving as a pallbearer at the funerals of his jogger friends. Aside from just being contentious, he is expressing an important point. Exercise itself will not guarantee a long life. Heredity sets limits on how long you will live, but within these limits is a range. Regular physical activity of sufficient duration and intensity can help you reach your upper limits. This is demonstrated in the studies of Harvard alumni by Paffenbarger and colleagues (1986). Paffenbarger found that mortality rates were lower for physically active alumni. By age 80, the amount of additional life attributed to adequate exercise, compared with sedentariness, was between one and two plus years.

The multiple risk factor intervention trial (MRFIT) study involved over 12,000 men and also found that the men most physically active lived longer than the least physically active. Furthermore, the MRFIT study indicated that *any* activity (not just vigorous activity) of 30 minutes, five times a week, decreased the risk of coronary heart disease, although more exerting physical activity was more protective. Another study found that death rate increased as fitness level decreased. Two of the major reasons for lower death rates in exercisers can be explained by our knowledge that exercise can help prevent coronary heart disease and cancer, the first and second leading causes of death in the United States. Researchers have found an increase in natural killer (NK) cell activity among people who exercised as seldom as once per week. NK cells help prevent cancer.

Physical activity can both prevent illness and disease and help rehabilitation. In this way, it enhances physical health. Since we will discuss the relationship between physical activity and health in more detail elsewhere in this book, suffice it to say here that among the illnesses and diseases that physical activity can help prevent are the nation's leading killers: heart disease, cancer, and stroke. And this sort of activity can help prevent, and serve as a treatment for, hypertension (high blood pressure), itself a major cause of heart disease and stroke.

One reason that physical activity is so helpful in preventing and treating various conditions is that it

Myth and Fact Sheet

Myth	Fact
1. When we speak of health, we mean physical health.	1. Health consists of more than just physical health. It includes social, emotional, mental, and spiritual health as well.
2. Wellness is synonymous with health.	2. Wellness means having the five components of health in balance. No single component should be exaggerated at the expense of any other.
3. Someone who can run a long distance is physically fit.	3. Someone who can run a long distance may not possess upper body muscular strength or muscular endurance or may not be flexible enough.
4. Because the leading killers are the result of unhealthy lifestyles, there is little the U.S. government can do to make people healthier.	4. The U.S. government developed national health objectives to encourage individuals to adopt healthier lifestyles and thereby live longer, better quality lives.
5. There is not much you can do about how you feel about yourself, your self-esteem.	5. If you become physically fit, you will feel better about yourself, and your self-esteem will improve.

helps people control their weight. Overweight, obesity, and malnutrition are implicated in numerous states of ill health. These conditions are also related to the amount of cholesterol in the blood (serum cholesterol) that can clog arteries leading to the heart or brain, thereby resulting in a heart attack or stroke. Some cholesterol, however, is actually helpful since it picks up blood fats and deposits them outside of the body. This *good* cholesterol is called high-density lipoprotein (HDL). Exercise increases the amount of HDL in the blood. It also decreases the amount of bad cholesterol (low-density lipoprotein [LDL]) that accumulates on the blood vessel walls and can eventually block the flow of blood to the heart and other body parts.

In addition, regular exercise can be an extremely effective means of managing stress. In this way, it improves emotional health. As we will discuss in chapter 4, stress changes the body so it is prepared to respond to a threat. It is geared up for some physical reaction. Exercise uses the built-up stress by-products and the body's preparedness to do something physical. The result is a sense of stress relief. Exercise also enhances the production of brain neurotransmitters (endorphins) that make you feel better and less stressed.

The rehabilitative benefits of exercise are almost notorious. It wasn't too long ago that people needing surgery or women giving birth were restricted to a hospital bed for days, sometimes weeks. That is no longer the case. The benefits of physical activity in recuperating from many conditions are now well recognized. Take the case of an individual who had a triple bypass operation in which three of the blood vessels supplying the heart were found to be obstructed. The obstructed sections were bypassed with blood vessels grafted from his legs. Shortly after the operation, the patient was expected to get out of bed and walk around. Although he was nervous at first, he soon learned that physical movement helped him get back to his regular routine. His muscular strength returned sooner then he expected, his blood circulation was enhanced by muscular contractions forcing pressure on the blood vessel walls, and his mood improved dramatically.

Physical activity can even help elderly people live longer and postpone the effects of aging. As people get older, they become susceptible to conditions that can restrict their activities, even to the extent that they become dependent on others to tie their shoes, transport them, and buy them food. A life of regular physical activity can postpone this dependency by providing elders with the necessary muscular strength and endurance, cardiorespiratory endurance, and flexibility to manage their own affairs. Several national health objectives speak to the needs of the elderly. The baseline figures that follow refer to the state of affairs that existed at the time the objectives were written. The national health objectives specific to the elderly include:

Objective	Baseline
1. Increase the years of healthy life to at least age 65.	Overall, 62 years; African Americans, 56; Hispanics, 62; people aged 65 and older, 12.
2. Reduce to no more than 90 per 1,000 people the proportion of all people aged 65 and older who have difficulty performing two or more personal care activities, thereby preserving independence.	111 per 1,000.
3. Reduce the proportion of people aged 65 and older who engage in no leisure-time physical activity to no more than 22 percent.	43 percent.

These people are enhancing their social health while engaging in a moderate physical activity. Perhaps their social health is more important to them at this time. What do you think? (Photo courtesy The Aspen Hill Club.)

Physical activity has additional benefits that are often overlooked. For example, several researchers have found that physically fit workers are absent from the job less frequently. In addition, people who are physically fit are less apt to experience depression and are more likely to feel in control of their lives.

Physical activity can also improve spiritual health. For example, when you are exercising outdoors, you have the opportunity to experience nature and all its wonders—to feel the rush of air on your face and the heat of the sun on your skin, to hear the sound of the birds and of the wind rustling through the leaves, and to sense the exhilaration of your body performing physical movement. In this way, you can feel connected—body, mind, and spirit—to a unifying force. And if you engage in physical activity with other people, you improve your social health while improving all the other components of health.

occur for several reasons. First, regular exercise helps maintain body weight and develop a desirable body image. Feeling good about how your body looks and feels will translate into feeling good about yourself.

Second, physical activity often provides challenges that are faced and overcome. That is one of the advantages of competitive sports activities. Being successful at these challenges will give you confidence to face other challenges in your life. And yet not all challenges are mastered. Physical activity also allows you to fail to meet the challenge but recognize that life goes on. You have probably heard someone say that you cannot hit a home run if you do not step up to the plate. When you bat, however, you can also strike out. So what? Striking out, or trying and failing, can be an effective learning and growth experience. When you fail, you can learn what you need to adjust to become better.

Self-Esteem and Physical Activity

Physical activity also has the potential of giving you more confidence and making you feel better about yourself. This is known as **self-esteem**. These benefits

Self-esteem The amount of regard you hold for yourself, the amount of value you place on yourself.

Physical activity can be fun and improve self-esteem if approached in the right way. Starting when young and when attitudes are being formed is most desirable. (Photo courtesy The Aspen Hill Club.)

Finally, physical activity improves endurance and strength. This allows you to perform activities more effectively and for longer periods of time. Being able to perform in this way can make you more confident and less likely to avoid events that are physically challenging. The result will be greater self-esteem and, as a result, better emotional health.

YOUR PERSONAL HEALTH AND WELLNESS PROFILE

The first step in achieving the benefits of a healthy lifestyle is to assess where you begin this journey. What is your level of health now? Where are you in relation to high-level wellness? Which components of physical fitness do you want to maintain and which do you want to improve? We help you conduct such an assessment in the next chapter. In addition, throughout this book we include health questionnaires, wellness scales, physical fitness tests to evaluate components of fitness, and even measures of psychological factors (such as self-esteem) related to health and wellness decisions. We also provide lab activities in each chapter that are designed to help you learn more about yourself and about health, wellness, and physical fitness. By the time you finish reading this book, you will have enough information about yourself to plan an effective wellness program, one that is based on your personal health and wellness profile and that will meet your personal health and wellness goals.

Just being concerned with your own health and wellness is not enough. You live in a community—actually, various communities. You are part of your college's community, the community of your city or town, those of your state and the United States, and the world. As such, you also have a responsibility to contribute to the health and wellness of the communities to which you belong. It is for this reason that we provide suggestions for how you can contribute to bettering your community in an **Improving Your Community** box, like the one on page 11, in each chapter.

While gardening may not be the key exercise for improving cardiorespiratory fitness, it contributes to other components of fitness and can enhance social and spiritual health. (Photo courtesy the National Cancer Institute.)

Improving Your Community

Promoting Health

You can contribute to the health of your community, nation, and world in numerous ways. Here are a few suggestions for how you might accomplish this goal:

1. Help to improve the spiritual health of your community by volunteering to clean up nature paths and areas that are conducive to a sense of something larger than oneself. You could also participate in church or synagogue programs concerning health matters (for example, AIDS education programs).

2. Clean up the neighborhood in which you live. Pick up litter, paint murals on walls of buildings that are unattractive (perhaps they are abandoned), or plant flowers in dirt-filled areas.

3. Lobby restaurant owners to include heart-healthy (low-fat) foods and low-salt foods on their menus and identify these with symbols. In this way you will be helping your neighbors eat more healthfully.

4. Participate in food drives for your neighborhood's homeless people, volunteer to help collect supplies for earthquake victims, or walk in patrols designed to discourage drug dealers from setting up drug markets.

5. Join an organization, such as Big Brothers or Big Sisters or the Foster Parent Program, which can use your time or financial contributions to help children in need.

6. Help to collect funds for, acquire supplies for, or coach a team for the Special Olympics (mentally disabled children and adults).

7. Write legislators to encourage improvements that will make your world healthier. For example, write local politicians to install a traffic light at a dangerous intersection, or write your senator to support national laws that make discrimination illegal, or write the White House to insist foreign aid be provided to peoples of countries in desperate need. ✦

SUMMARY

Health

Health consists of five components: physical, social, mental, emotional, and spiritual. Physical fitness is but one component of physical health, albeit an important one.

In the past, most people in the United States died from conditions that were passed from one person to another or were the result of unsanitary practices. Tuberculosis and pneumonia are examples. The federal and state governments responded by passing legislation that eliminated these unsafe practices and effectively reduced deaths from these conditions. Today, most deaths are the result of lifestyle practices such as cigarette smoking, lack of exercise, inadequate sleep, and poor nutrition. Changes in these practices are up to individuals; governments cannot legislate these changes.

The federal government has developed national health objectives, however, to publicize and encourage healthier lifestyles and attempt to reduce death and disability from lifestyle diseases and illnesses. Several of these objectives are specific to physical fitness and physical activity, and numerous others are tangentially related.

Wellness

Wellness is maintaining the components of health in sufficient amounts and in balance with one another. An ideal state of wellness is one in which no single component of health is emphasized at the expense of any other component.

Physical Fitness

Physical fitness encompasses cardiorespiratory endurance, muscular strength, muscular endurance, muscular flexibility, and body composition. It also includes the motor skills of agility, balance, coordination, power, speed, and reaction time.

What Physical Fitness Can Do for You

Physical activity can improve physical health by decreasing LDLs (bad cholesterol) and increasing HDLs (good cholesterol), by preventing or reducing high blood pressure, by helping to maintain desirable weight and lean body mass, and by preventing some cancers.

Physical activity can also improve emotional health by helping to manage stress, spiritual health by focusing on nature and bodily sensations, and social health by exercising with other people. In addition, physical activity can help diminish and postpone the effects of aging and aid in recuperation from illnesses and medical procedures. Furthermore, physical activity can make you feel more confident and thereby improve your self-esteem. It can also improve self-esteem by helping to maintain recommended body weight and a desirable body image, and by providing challenges that develop confidence and the realization that, even if the challenges are not successfully overcome, significant learning occurs. Self-esteem is also enhanced when endurance and strength are developed so you can perform daily activities effectively and for longer periods of time.

REFERENCES

Blair, S. N., Kohl, H. W., Paffenbarger, R. S., Clark, D.G., Cooper, K. J., & Gibbons, L. W. (1989). Physical fitness and all-cause mortality: A prospective study of healthy men and women. *Journal of the American Medical Association*, 262; 2395–2401.

Brandon, J. E., & Lofton, J. M. (1991). Relationship of fitness to depression, state and trait anxiety, internal health locus of control, and self-control. *Perceptual and Motor Skills* 73; 563–568.

Donahue, R. P., Abbott, R. D., Reed, Q. M., & Yano, K. (1988). Physical activity and coronary heart disease in middle-aged and elderly men: The Honolulu heart program. *American Journal of Public Health* 78; 683–685.

Krucoff, C. (1992, January 14). Exercise and cancer: Moderate activity may help reduce risk of some tumors. *Washington Post Health*, p. 16.

Kusaka, Y., Kondou, H., & Morimoto, K. (1992). Healthy lifestyles are associated with higher natural killer cell activity. *Preventive Medicine*, 21; 602–615.

Leon, A. S., & Connett, J. (1991). Physical activity and 10.5 year mortality in the multiple risk factor intervention trial (MRFIT). *The International Journal of Epidemiology*, 20; 690–697.

Paffenbarger, R. S., Hyde, R. T., Wing, A. L., & Hsieh, C.-C. (1986). Physical activity, all-cause mortality, and longevity of college alumni. *New England Journal of Medicine*, 314; 605–613.

Rakowski, W., & Mor, V. (1992). The association of physical activity with mortality among older adults in the longitudinal study of aging. *Journal of Gerontology*, 47; M122–M129.

Shepard, R. J. (1989). Nutritional benefits of exercise. *Journal of Sports Medicine*, 29; 83–90.

Steinhardt, M., Greenhow, L., & Stewart, J. (1991). The relationship of physical activity and cardiovascular fitness to absenteeism and medical care claims among law enforcement officers. *American Journal of Health Promotion*, 5; 455–460.

Tucker, L. A., Aldana, S. G., and Friedman, G. M. (1990). Cardiovascular fitness and absenteeism in 8,301 employed adults. *American Journal of Health Promotion*, 5; 140–145.

Lab Activity 1.1

Identifying Your Health Strengths and Weaknesses

INSTRUCTIONS: *On this chart, list your strengths and weaknesses for each of the five components of health. Once you have done that, develop a plan for maximizing your strengths and minimizing your weaknesses. This means that you should find ways to use your strengths to make them even more influential on your health and to eliminate health weaknesses or decrease their negative effects on your health. Once you put your plan into action, you will become healthier and achieve a higher level of wellness.*

COMPONENT	STRENGTHS	WEAKNESSES
Mental health		
Physical health		

Component	Strengths	Weaknesses
Social health		
Spiritual health		
Emotional health		

Lab Activity 1.2

Assessing Your Health Risk

INSTRUCTIONS: *The U.S. government developed this questionnaire to help people assess their health behavior and risk of ill health. Notice that this questionnaire has six sections. Complete one section at a time by circling the number corresponding to the answer that describes your behavior. Then add the numbers you have circled to determine your score for that section. Write your score on the line provided at the end of each section.*

✦ Cigarette Smoking

	Almost Always	Sometimes	Almost Never
1. I avoid smoking cigarettes.	2	1	0
2. I smoke only low-tar and low-nicotine cigarettes, or I smoke a pipe or cigars only.	2	1	0

Your Cigarette Smoking Score: _____

✦ Alcohol and Drugs

	Almost Always	Sometimes	Almost Never
1. I avoid drinking alcoholic beverages, or I drink no more than one or two a day.	4	1	0
2. I avoid using alcohol or other drugs (especially illegal drugs) as a way of handling stressful situations or my problems.	2	1	0
3. I am careful not to drink alcohol when I am taking certain medicines (for example, medicine for sleeping, pain, colds, and allergies).	2	1	0
4. I read and follow the label directions when I use prescribed and over-the-counter drugs.	2	1	0

Your Alcohol and Drugs Score: _____

✦ Eating Habits

	Almost Always	Sometimes	Almost Never
1. I eat a variety of foods each day, such as fruits and vegetables, whole-grain breads and cereals, lean meats, dairy products, dry peas and beans, and nuts and seeds.	4	1	0
2. I limit the amount of fat, especially saturated fat, and cholesterol I eat (including fats in meats, eggs, butter, cream, shortenings, and organ meats such as liver).	2	1	0
3. I limit the amount of salt I eat by not adding salt at the table, avoiding salty snacks, and making certain my meals are cooked with only small amounts of salt.	2	1	0
4. I avoid eating too much sugar (especially frequent snacks of sticky candy or soft drinks).	2	1	0

Your Eating Habits Score: _____

✦ Exercise and Fitness

	Almost Always	Sometimes	Almost Never
1. I maintain a desired weight, avoiding overweight and underweight.	3	1	0
2. I do vigorous exercise for 15 to 30 minutes at least three times a week (examples include running, swimming, and brisk walking).	3	1	0
3. I do exercises that enhance my muscle tone for 15 to 30 minutes at least three times a week (examples include yoga and calisthenics).	2	1	0
4. I use part of my leisure time participating in individual, family, or team activities that increase my level of fitness (such as gardening, bowling, golf, or baseball).	2	1	0

Your Exercise and Fitness Score: _____

Lab Activity 1.2 *(continued)*
Assessing Your Health Risk

✦ **Stress Control**	Almost Always	Sometimes	Almost Never
1. I enjoy the school or other work I do.	2	1	0
2. I find it easy to relax and express my feelings freely.	2	1	0
3. I recognize early, and prepare for, events or situations likely to be stressful for me.	2	1	0
4. I have close friends, relatives, or others with whom I can talk about personal matters and call on for help when it is needed.	2	1	0
5. I participate in group activities (such as church/synagogue or community organizations) or hobbies that I enjoy.	2	1	0

Your Stress Control Score: _____

✦ **Safety**	Almost Always	Sometimes	Almost Never
1. I wear a seat belt while I am riding in a car.	2	1	0
2. I avoid driving while I am under the influence of alcohol and other drugs. I also avoid getting in a car with someone driving who is under the influence of alcohol or other drugs.	2	1	0
3. I obey the traffic rules and the speed limit when I am driving and ask others to do so when I am a passenger in a car with them.	2	1	0
4. I am careful when I am using potentially harmful products or substances (such as household cleaners, poisons, and electrical devices).	2	1	0
5. I avoid smoking in bed.	2	1	0

Your Safety Score: _____

✦ Your Health Score

After you have totaled your score for each of the six sections, circle the number in each column below that matches your score for that section of the test.

CIGARETTE SMOKING	ALCOHOL AND DRUGS	EATING HABITS	EXERCISE AND FITNESS	STRESS CONTROL	SAFETY
10	10	10	10	10	10
9	9	9	9	9	9
8	8	8	8	8	8
7	7	7	7	7	7
6	6	6	6	6	6
5	5	5	5	5	5
4	4	4	4	4	4
3	3	3	3	3	3
2	2	2	2	2	2
1	1	1	1	1	1
0	0	0	0	0	0

✦ Interpreting Your Score

Scores of 9 or 10 are excellent! Your answers show you are aware of the importance of this area to your health. More important, you are putting your knowledge to work by practicing good health habits. Even so, you may want to consider areas where your health habits can be improved.

Scores of 6 to 8 indicate that your health practices in this area are good, but that there is room for improvement. Look again at the items you answered with "sometimes" or "almost never." What changes can you make to improve your score?

Scores of 3 to 5 mean your health risks are showing! You should ask your instructor for more information about the health risks you are facing. Your instructor will probably be able to help you decrease these risks. An exception is the cigarette smoking section for which a score of 3 to 4 is excellent. Review your responses to the cigarette smoking items to better interpret their meaning.

Scores of 0 to 2 for all sections except the cigarette smoking section mean you may be taking serious, unnecessary risks with your health. Maybe you are not aware of the risks and what to do about them. Consult with a health expert or your instructor to improve your health. For the cigarette smoking section, scores of 0 to 1 mean you may be taking unnecessary risks with your health. Review your responses to these items to better interpret their meaning.

Lab Activity 1.3

Changing a Health Behavior

INSTRUCTIONS: *Consider that your decision to perform a certain behavior is a function of forces—forces that pull you in the direction of performing the behavior and forces that push you away from performing the behavior. It then stands to reason that if you want to perform a certain behavior, you maximize forces pulling you in that direction and minimize forces pushing you in another direction. Likewise, if you do not want to engage in a certain behavior, you would maximize forces pushing you away from that behavior and minimize forces pulling you in the direction of the behavior. This activity gives you the opportunity to use forces to control a health, wellness, or physical fitness behavior.*

1. In the space provided below, write in a health, wellness, or physical fitness behavior that you want to adopt. For example, you might want to eat a nutritionally balanced diet or participate regularly in an exercise program.

    _____

    _____

    _____

2. List those forces working in favor of you engaging in this behavior:

    a. _____

    b. _____

    c. _____

    d. _____

    e. _____

3. For each of the forces working in favor of you engaging in this behavior, cite one way you can maximize that particular force. For example, you might plan to eat with a friend who also wants to eat a nutritionally balanced diet, or you might join an exercise club to encourage you to exercise regularly.

   a. _____

   b. _____

   c. _____

   d. _____

   e. _____

4. List those forces working against you engaging in this behavior:

   a. _____

   b. _____

   c. _____

   d. _____

   e. _____

5. For each of the forces working against engaging in this behavior, cite one way you can minimize that particular force. For example, you might specifically plan not to eat with a friend whose diet consists of a lot of junk food.

   a._____

   b. _____

   c. _____

   d. _____

   e. _____

You might want to consider doing the same thing for a behavior you wish to eliminate from your life (for example, smoking cigarettes). In that case you would want to minimize forces encouraging you to smoke and maximize forces encouraging you not to smoke.

2

DETERMINING *Your* *Wellness* PROFILE

Chapter Objectives

By the end of this chapter, you should be able to:

1. Understand how your current behavior may or may not be keeping you healthy.

2. Measure and analyze your health and fitness appraisal scores and identify areas where improvement is needed.

3. Indicate when it is appropriate to obtain a medical examination prior to beginning an exercise program.

4. List the components of a good medical examination.

KIM'S EXCUSE FOR avoiding any discussion about her "wellness" is one voiced by many university students: "I get enough exercise in my daily routine and part-time department store job and cope very well with the rigors of college life." Kim feels that her health habits are satisfactory since she is only a "social" drinker, doesn't do drugs except to help her stay up late during exam time, cooks her own meals, and tends to be careful around campus, especially at night. Kim recently told a friend, "I am already fit. Why should I waste my time exercising?" One way for Kim to find out if she is practicing a healthy lifestyle and is physically fit is to complete the battery of tests described in this chapter to see if she can score in the average or above-average category on each item.

This chapter provides Kim with the opportunity to complete both a health and fitness appraisal and develop a complete wellness profile. Although she may feel quite indestructible at the age of 20, health choices followed in the past and made in the near future will play a large role in determining her future quality of life, free from injury and illness. The self-administered tests in this chapter will either confirm her concept of a healthy lifestyle or identify risk areas that will eventually threaten her well-being. Kim's test results will also provide her with a chance to stop, assess her current lifestyle, and take positive action.

THE HEALTH APPRAISAL

The U.S. government has become increasingly interested in our health-related behavior. You see, when you adopt what are called health "risk factors"—for example, smoking cigarettes, abusing drugs, or mismanaging stress—you will need to use the medical care system more than otherwise. The more that system is used, the higher the cost of health care will be. When this cost becomes high, governmental support services are called into play: Medicare, Medicaid, social services. The result is that taxes increase, inflation plagues the country, and the economy is thrown into turmoil.

The federal government believes that helping you to maintain your health—and prevent or postpone illness—can have beneficial financial implications for the nation as a whole. For that reason, governmental agencies have been enlisted—most notably, the Office of Disease Prevention and Health Promotion (ODPHP)—to encourage Americans to adopt healthy behaviors. The ODPHP has developed a questionnaire that measures the degree to which people are behaving in healthy or unhealthy ways. If you have not completed this *health behavior questionnaire,* which appears in chapter 1 (Lab Activity 1.2), please take a moment to do so now. The interpretation of your scores can be found at the end of the questionnaire. If you have taken the test, take a moment to review your scores.

THE MEDICAL EVALUATION

There is an abundance of literature regarding the need for medical evaluation before beginning a program of regular exercise. There are also a number of areas of disagreement among experts concerning the components of such a medical evaluation, who should receive one, and even whether an evaluation is necessary at all. These viewpoints will be presented as

Blood lipid analysis Examination and study of the fats present in the blood.

Electrocardiogram (ECG) A tracing of the electrical currents involved in the cycles of a heart beat.

Graded exercise test (stress test) Test designed to monitor the electrical activity of the heart; it is performed by walking on a treadmill that is slowly being elevated to increase the work load.

objectively as possible to help you make a decision about your need for such an examination.

The Need for a Medical Evaluation

Most physicians indicate that a physical examination is necessary for individuals over the age of 40, those with symptoms of heart disease or other medical ailments, and those who have previously been sedentary. Some physicians favor a comprehensive exam; others prefer only general screening.

The recommendations of the American College of Sports Medicine (ACSM) provide sound information related to the health, status, and age of the participant (see Table 2.1). They classify individuals who may undergo exercise testing into three categories:

1. **Apparently healthy** Those who appear to be in good health and have no major coronary risk factors.

2. **Individuals at higher risk** Those who have symptoms suggestive of heart disease, pulmonary or metabolic disease, or at least one major coronary risk factor.

3. **Individuals with disease** Those with known cardiac, pulmonary, or metabolic diseases.

The National Heart, Lung and Blood Institute (NHLBI) advises that most people under 60 years of age do not need a medical examination prior to beginning a gradual and sensible exercise program. Their rationale is based on the realization that sedentary living is a far more dangerous practice than exercising without a physician's approval, that many people will not take the time to secure an examination, and that a recommended medical exam is nothing more than another excuse to avoid exercise.

Certainly it is desirable for everyone to have a complete medical examination before their physical fitness evaluation and the start of a new exercise program to increase safety and aid in the exercise prescription. It is also a generally accepted fact that certain categories of people face some risk when engaging in fitness programs without a medical examination.

Components of the Ideal Medical Evaluation

Although the exact contents of the ideal evaluation depend on the history and symptoms of each individual, common areas include a medical history that asks questions about your own and your family's history of diabetes and coronary heart disease and asso-

Table 2.1 ✦ Guidelines for Exercise Testing

	APPARENTLY HEALTHY		HIGHER RISK[1]		
	Younger ≤ 40 years (men) ≤ 50 years (women)	*Older*	*No symptoms*	*Symptoms*	*With Disease*[2]
Medical exam and diagnostic exercise test recommended prior to					
Moderate exercise[3]	No[5]	No	No	Yes	Yes
Vigorous exercise[4]	No	Yes[6]	Yes	Yes	Yes
Physician supervision recommended during exercise test					
Sub-maximal testing	No	No	No	Yes	Yes
Maximal testing	No	Yes	Yes	Yes	Yes

[1]Persons with two or more risk factors or symptoms.
[2]Persons with known cardiac, pulmonary, or metabolic disease.
[3]Moderate exercise (exercise intensity 40 to 60% VO_{2max})—Exercise intensity well within the individual's current capacity and can be comfortably sustained for a prolonged period of time, i.e., 60 minutes, slow progression, and generally noncompetitive.
[4]Vigorous exercise (exercise intensity > 60% VO_{2max})—Exercise intense enough to represent a substantial challenge and which would ordinarily result in fatigue within 20 minutes.
[5]The "no" responses in this table mean that an item is "not necessary." The "no" response does not mean that the item should not be done.
[6]A "yes" response means that an item is recommended.

Source: From *Guidelines for Exercise Testing and Prescription,* 4th ed. (p. 7), 1991 American College of Sports Medicine, Philadelphia: Lea & Febiger.

ciated risk factors such as hypertension, stress, smoking, eating habits, current activity level, and physical disabilities. If symptoms indicate the need, the examination may also include measurement of blood pressure, listening to the heart and lungs, determining resting pulse rate, chest X-ray, **blood lipid analysis**, a resting **electrocardiogram (ECG)**, and a **graded exercise test (stress test)**.

The results of this medical evaluation should be discussed with the patient, and any restrictions on physical activity or fitness testing should be identified at that time. Remember that the fact that your physical activity may have limits does not mean you should avoid exercise. This book provides you with a number of sound exercise choices that will meet your fitness needs without endangering your health.

THE FITNESS APPRAISAL

In addition to the medical evaluation, it is also important to appraise your present level of physical fitness, to monitor your body's response to exercise, to determine your initial fitness level, to prepare your individualized program, and to monitor your progress. You can easily assess each major component of fitness: cardiorespiratory endurance, muscular strength and endurance, flexibility, and body composition.

During your fitness appraisal, stop any test immediately if you begin to feel chest pains, faintness, or dizziness; develop an excruciating headache; or cannot get enough air. If you notice any other disturbing sensations, do not complete the test. If any of these signs appears, consult a physician to determine their causes. It may be that your fitness level is so low that your body cannot handle strenuous activity, or a medical problem may exist. To avoid endangering your health and eliminate worry, it is important to have the problem diagnosed.

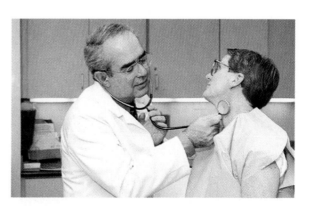

A medical evaluation may be necessary before beginning an exercise program. (Photo courtesy of the George Washington University Medical Center.)

Table 2.2 ✦ 1.5-Mile Run Test (time in minutes)

		AGE (YEARS)					
Fitness Category		13–19	20–29	30–39	40–49	50–59	60+
I. Very poor	(men)	> 15:31	> 16:01	> 16:31	> 17:31	> 19:01	>20:01
	(women)	> 18:31	> 19:01	> 19:31	> 20:01	> 20:31	> 21:01
II. Poor	(men)	12:11–15:30	14:01–16:00	14:44–16:30	15:36–17:30	17:01–19:00	19:01–20:00
	(women)	16:55–18:30	18:31–19:00	19:01–19:30	19:31–20:00	20:01–20:30	21:00–21:31
III. Fair	(men)	10:49–12:10	12:01–14:00	12:31–14:45	13:01–15:35	14:31–17:00	16:16–19:00
	(women)	14:31–16:54	15:55–18:30	16:31–19:00	17:31–19:30	19:01–20:00	19:31–20:30
IV. Good	(men)	9:41–10:48	10:46–12:00	11:01–12:30	11:31–13:00	12:31–14:30	14:00–16:15
	(women)	12:30–14:30	13:31–15:54	14:31–16:30	15:56–17:30	16:31–19:00	17:31–19:30
V. Excellent	(men)	8:37–9:40	9:45–10:45	10:00–11:00	10:30–11:30	11:00–12:30	11:15–13:59
	(women)	11:50–12:29	12:30–13:30	13:00–14:30	13:45–15:55	14:30–16:30	16:30–17:30
VI. Superior	(men)	< 8:37	< 9:45	< 10:00	< 10:30	< 11:00	< 11:15
	(women)	< 11:50	< 12:30	< 13:00	< 13:45	< 14:30	< 16:30

Note: < means *less than*; > means *more than*.

Source: From *The Aerobics Program for Total Well Being,* by K. H. Cooper. Copyright 1982 by K. H. Cooper. Used by permission of Bantam Books, a division of Bantam Doubleday Dell Publishing Group, Inc.

Cardiorespiratory Assessment

All sound exercise programs place primary emphasis on cardiorespiratory endurance. The publicity surrounding the benefits of exercise for the nation's leading killer (heart disease), whether justified or not, is probably responsible for the emphasis on improving the functioning of the heart, circulatory system, and lungs. Exercise that overloads the **oxygen-transport system** (aerobic activity) leads to an increase in cardiorespiratory endurance and the muscular strength and endurance of some large muscle groups.

The 1.5-Mile Test You can assess your cardiorespiratory endurance using the 1.5-mile test either indoors or outdoors. It is relatively simple to measure off a 1.5-mile course on a track or other flat area where you can run or walk. Your objective is to complete the distance as quickly as possible by running, walking, or combining the two. Consult Table 2.2 to

determine your cardiorespiratory fitness rating based on your time. Record both your time and rating in Lab Activity 2.2: Your Physical Fitness Profile at the end of this chapter.

The Harvard Step Test This test provides an alternate assessment method that accurately identifies your cardiorespiratory fitness level. To complete the **Harvard step** test, secure a sturdy 18-inch bench or stool and a wristwatch with a second hand, and then follow these procedures:

1. Step on the bench first with one foot and then the other until you are standing erect with the knees unbent. Then step down with

> **Oxygen-transport system** The ability of the body to take in, deliver, and use oxygen at the tissue level during physical activity.
>
> **1.5-mile test** Field test designed to measure cardiorespiratory endurance (aerobic fitness).
>
> **Harvard step test** Test designed to measure cardiorespiratory endurance (aerobic fitness).

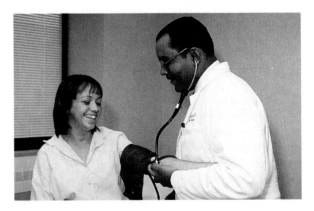

Blood pressure screening may be part of a medical evaluation. (Photo courtesy of the George Washington University Medical Center.)

Myth and Fact Sheet

Myth	Fact
'1. A physical examination isn't necessary for college students who are feeling all right.	1. It is quite common for young adults to feel good yet still have high blood pressure and/or high blood cholesterol. These "silent" killers afflict adults of all ages and are only detected through regular checkups. Although you may have no reason to suspect them, ailments may be detected in their early stages when treatment is most effective.
2. Weekend party drinking and the occasional use of drugs is perfectly safe.	2. Even monthly episodes of drinking that always result in intoxication and behavior problems are a sign of alcohol abuse that may lead to serious health problems in the future. Alcohol and drug use is never safe. Recreational use of any drug imposes immediate health concerns due to behavior problems or an overdose reaction since it is often impossible to judge the potency of illicit drugs or the way you will react when drugs are combined with alcohol or other drugs.
3. Fitness testing will make me too sore to function the next day.	3. When sedentary people complete tests that require maximum effort, they do experience considerable soreness the next day. The areas of soreness show which muscles you have not been using. Many college instructors eliminate the problem of soreness by using a two- to three-week preconditioning program before performing any maximum-effort fitness testing.
4. I know enough about my fitness level already and do not need to be tested.	4. You may have a good feel for some aspects of your physical fitness. On the other hand, standardized tests may be just what you need to compare yourself to others of your age and to highlight the areas in which you need the most improvement. Test results often provide strong motivation for individuals to begin an exercise program.
5. The 1.5-mile test for cardiorespiratory endurance is too dangerous.	5. The test is not dangerous if it is performed properly. If you have been inactive for more than a year or have never engaged in aerobic exercise, you have several choices. First, you can skip the 1.5-mile test, assume that your cardiorespiratory fitness rating is poor, and choose a beginner's aerobic exercise program that allows you to progress slowly and safely to higher levels. Second, you can undertake a two- to three-week preconditioning program of walking and jogging to prepare yourself for the 1.5-mile test. Finally, you can choose to stop and walk during any or all of the test, as long as you give it your best effort.
6. I'm fit enough. Too much exercise will cause athlete's heart and jeopardize my health.	6. "Athlete's heart," or "sporterz," is a term used by a Swedish researcher who detected enlarged heart muscles among skiers in 1899. As the years passed, the term gained momentum and was used incorrectly to refer to an abnormally large heart brought on by exercise. Because of this myth, some people actually became concerned that exercise would damage their hearts and result in disability or death. Aerobic exercise does develop the heart muscle more fully and cause it to become heavier and larger. It also causes the heart to pump more blood per beat (stroke volume) and per minute (cardiac output) and to become a more efficient organ. Cardiac changes that occur from aerobic exercise are both natural and healthy, and it is highly unlikely that proper aerobic exercise would cause damage to a healthy heart.

one foot followed by the other to return to the starting position.

2. Step at a cadence that will result in 30 such repetitions each minute (one every 2 seconds) for 4 (females) or 5 (males) minutes.

3. At the end of the 4- or 5-minute period, sit down.

4. After waiting exactly 1 minute, take your pulse or have a partner take your pulse for 30 seconds, and record that number.

5. Wait an additional 30 seconds before taking your pulse once again for a 30-second period, and record that number.

6. Repeat step 5 in 30 seconds. You will now have taken your pulse between 1 and 1 1/2 minutes, 2 and 2 1/2 minutes, and 3 and 3 1/2 minutes after completing the step test.

7. Using the total of the three pulse counts, compute the formula:

The Harvard Step Test is one way to determine your cardiorespiratory endurance. It involves stepping up and down repeatedly and then measuring the pulse rate to determine how fast the heart recovers. (Photo courtesy of the United States Tennis Association.)

$$\text{index} = \frac{\text{duration of exercise in seconds} \times 100}{2 \times \text{sum of the 3 pulse counts in recovery}}$$

8. Determine your cardiorespiratory fitness level from the scale below:

Below 55	Poor
55–64	Low average
65–79	Average
80–89	Good
90 and above	Excellent

Record your appraisal on Lab Activity 2.2: Your Physical Fitness Profile.

Muscular Strength Assessment

In the laboratory, muscular strength, the absolute maximum force that a muscle can generate, is measured using elaborate and expensive equipment. Dynamometers, cable tensiometers, and force transducers and recorders have all been used this way. One problem with such methods is the need to test numerous muscle groups to obtain an accurate measure in the legs, the abdomen, and the arms. These muscles cover such diverse body parts, however, that you can safely assume their levels of muscular strength are representative of total body strength.

You can also measure the strength and endurance of practically any muscle group by using free weights or a variety of weight machines. In some cases, you can test yourself; in others, such as the 1-RM testing using barbells, you will need a *spotter* to assist you throughout the movement.

1-RM (Repetitions Maximum) Testing Free weights are commonly used to determine your **1-RM** (maximum amount of weight you can lift one time) for a particular muscle group.

The *bench press* and *shoulder press* will accurately measure the strength of your triceps, pectoralis, and deltoid muscles; the *arm curl* measures bicep muscle strength, and the *leg press* will determine the strength of the quadriceps muscle group. For each test, a weight is selected that can be lifted comfortably. Additional weight is then added in subsequent trials until the weight is found that can be lifted correctly just one time. If the weight can be lifted more than once, additional weight is added until a true 1-RM is determined. Approximately three trials with a two- to three-minute rest interval between each are needed to determine the 1-RM for each muscle group. Since the resistance to be overcome in 1-RM testing is heavy, it is important to use one or two spotters to

Table 2.3 ✦ Optimal Strength Values for Various Body Weights (based on the 1-RM test)

Body weight (lb)	BENCH PRESS		SHOULDER PRESS		BICEPS CURL		LEG PRESS	
	Male	Female	Male	Female	Male	Female	Male	Female
80	70	60	55	40	40	30	160	120
100	85	70	70	50	50	35	200	150
120	105	85	80	60	60	40	240	180
140	125	100	95	65	70	50	280	210
160	145	115	110	75	80	60	320	240
180	160	125	120	85	90	65	360	270
200	180	140	135	95	100	70	400	300
220	200	155	150	105	110	75	440	330
240	225	170	160	115	120	85	480	360

Note: Data in pounds; obtained on Universal Gym apparatus; applicable ages 17 to 30.

Source: Reprinted with the permission of Macmillan College Publishing Company from *Health and Fitness Through Physical Activity,* by M. Pollock, J. Wilmore, and S. Fox III, 1978, New York: Macmillan College Publishing Company. All rights reserved.

protect you from injury by taking over the barbell should you be unable to complete the lift. See chapter 9 for an explanation of the proper technique for these tests.

Record your scores on Lab Activity 2.2: Your Physical Fitness Profile. You can also use Table 2.3 to compare your strength to others of similar age in the bench press, shoulder press, biceps curl, and leg press.

Muscular Endurance Assessment

There is a great difference between muscular endurance and muscular strength, and therefore among the kinds of tests that apply to these components. Strength tests determine the maximum amount of weight that can be moved one time, whereas endurance tests measure continuous work by determining the total number of times a specific weight can be moved. It is important to evaluate the muscular endurance of your arms, shoulders, and abdominal area by completing the *pull-up* or *bar dip* (men), *flexed-arm hang* (women), and the *sit-up* (men and women). After completing these tests, remember to record your scores on the Lab Activity 2.2.

Abdominal Endurance Testing Although it is difficult to obtain a pure, isolated measurement of the abdominal region, the 60-second *bent-knee sit-up test* is one of the best tests available. To test yourself, as-

sume a supine position with arms folded across your chest, knees bent at a 90-degree angle with both feet flat on the floor and in front of your buttocks. The feet should be anchored by a partner who grasps your ankles. You may do several practice sit-ups prior to the official testing session. At the "go" command, begin a series of rapidly executed bent-knee sit-ups. Your partner will count each correct repetition, eliminating those containing any procedural infraction such as failing to reach the vertical sitting position, lifting the feet from the floor, or not returning to the starting position with the middle of the back touching the floor. Consult Table 2.4 to evaluate your performance.

Arm and Shoulder Muscular Endurance You can complete the *pull-up test* for men by grasping an adjustable horizontal bar with your palms facing away from the body. Now raise your body until your chin clears the top of the bar, then slowly lower yourself to a full hang without any pause as many times as you

1-RM The maximum amount of weight that can be lifted at one time.

Table 2.4 ✦ Norms for the 60-second Bent-Knee Sit-up Test

COLLEGE FEMALES	PERFORMANCE STANDARDS	COLLEGE MALES
51 or above	Excellent	60 or above
46 to 50	Good	50 to 59
33 to 45	Average	34 to 49
21 to 32	Low	26 to 33
0 to 20	Poor	0 to 25

Improving Your Community

Working for a Smoke-Free Society

The association between tobacco use and disease has been strongly established. The controversy is over: Tobacco use in any form is without a doubt the leading cause of preventable death and disability in the United States. Unfortunately, many American teenagers and adults continue to smoke or use smokeless tobacco. We must all continue to help our community and society become smokeless. Here are some things you can do:

1. Adopt a smoke-free lifestyle and set an example for your friends, colleagues, and fellow students.

2. Join the movement to discourage tobacco use in the United States. Make your dormitory, apartment, or house completely smoke-free by eliminating ashtrays, matches, and designated smoking areas. If you work for a private company, ask your human resources or personnel department to encourage antismoking programs and to eliminate cigarette machines and ashtrays in the workplace. Discourage individuals from smoking in every way possible.

3. Organize free informational programs to help people stop smoking through your church or temple, fitness or wellness club, school, or workplace.

4. Work with young people in group sports, day camps, or other activities, such as Girl Scout and Boy Scout groups, and encourage them to discourage the use of tobacco among their families, friends, and communities.

5. Effectively use the power of peer pressure to encourage friends and family to stop smoking. Get friends, siblings, parents, and other relatives to express their concern directly to the smoker about her or his tobacco use.

6. Actively support programs and legislation aimed at monitoring and discouraging tobacco advertising.

7. Support the American Lung Association, the American Cancer Society, and the American Heart Association. These organizations offer effective programs to help people stop using tobacco. Check your phone book for their addresses and phone numbers. ✦

can. Your body must return to a stretch position (elbows locked) each time. Deliberate swinging, resting, or leg kicking is not permitted. Table 2.5 will help you evaluate the strength and endurance of your arms and shoulders.

The *modified pull-up* for women closely resembles the pull-up for men. An adjustable horizontal bar is grasped with your palms facing away from the body at a level that is just even with the base of the sternum (breastbone). Your body is now placed under the bar until a 90-degree angle is formed at the point where the arms and the chest join. Only the heels support the weight of the lower body. One point is scored each time your chin is pulled over the bar and the body returns to the support position with the arms fully extended.

The *bar dip test* is used to determine the strength and endurance of the triceps and shoulder girdle. Using parallel bars, begin in a straight-arm support position close to the bar ends. The idea is to lower

Table 2.5 ✦ Scoring of Pull-ups, Modified Pull-ups, and Dips

PERFORMANCE STANDARDS	PULL-UPS (NO.)	MODIFIED PULL-UPS (NO.)	BAR DIPS (NO.)
Excellent	13 or above	30 or above	20 or above
Good	10 to 12	25 to 29	15 to 19
Average	5 to 9	16 to 24	7 to 14
Poor	0 to 4	0 to 15	0 to 6

your body slowly until your arms form a 90-degree bent-arm position. After reaching this position, attempt to straighten your arms until you return to the starting position.

Flexibility Assessment

Flexibility is an important component of fitness. It involves the ability to move the body throughout a range of motion and stretch the muscles and tissues around skeletal joints. The *shoulder reach, trunk flexion*, and *trunk extension* tests provide an excellent indication of body flexibility. Use Table 2.6 to help evaluate your flexibility.

Shoulder Reach From a standing position, raise your right arm and reach down behind your back as far as possible. At the same time, reach up from behind with the left hand and try to overlap the palm of the right hand. Have a partner measure, in inches, how much the fingers on your right hand overlap the fingers of the left hand. If you overlap, place a plus sign in front of the amount of overlap on the Lab Activity 2.2: Your Physical Fitness Profile sheet; if the fingers of your right and left hand do not touch, place a minus sign in front of the amount of the gap. If the fingers of one hand just barely touch those of the other, give yourself a score of zero. Repeat this test with the arms reversed; that is, the arm that first reached down over the shoulder will now reach up from behind the back.

Trunk Flexion To measure the ability to flex your trunk and to stretch the back of your thigh muscles, remove your shoes and sit with your legs straight and your feet flat against a box positioned against a wall. Place a ruler on top of the box. Place one hand on top of the other so the middle fingers are together and the same length. While your partner keeps your knees from bending, lean forward and place your hands on top of the box. Slide your hands along the measuring scale as far as possible without bouncing and hold that position for at least three seconds. Repeat the test two more times and record your highest score to the nearest inch on Lab Activity 2.2. Your score is the number of inches beyond the edge of the box you can stretch (use a plus sign in front of that value) or the number of inches short of the edge of the box you can reach (use a minus sign in front of that value). If you can reach only to the edge of the box, give yourself a score of zero.

Trunk Extension To determine the flexibility of your back, lie on the floor face down with a partner applying pressure on your upper legs and buttocks. Clasp your hands behind your neck, raise your head and chest off the ground as high as possible, and hold that position for three seconds. Ask your partner to measure the distance to the nearest inch between your chin and the floor. Enter this value on Lab Activity 2.

Nutritional Assessment

Numerous IBM- and Apple Macintosh-compatible software programs are available to analyze your dietary intake accurately over a three- to seven-day period. Regardless of the software program you choose, it will be necessary to record your dietary intake (food and drink) carefully over a three- to seven-day period, making note of portion sizes, brand names of products whenever they are available, specific fast food products, and other specific information that you will code later according to the specifications of the software manual. It is also possible to provide a fairly accurate analysis of your nutritional habits by completing Lab Activity 10.2: Do You Meet the U.S. Government Dietary Recommenda-

Table 2.6 ✦ Flexibility Interpretations

	SHOULDER REACH (RUP/LUP)	TRUNK FLEXION	TRUNK EXTENSION
For men			
Above average	6+/3+	11+	15+
Average	4–5/0–2	7–10	8–14
Below average	Below 4/below 0	Below 7	Below 8
For women			
Above average	7+/6+	12+	23+
Average	5–6/0–5	7–11	15–22
Below average	Below 5/below 0	Below 7	Below 15

Behavioral Change
and Motivational Strategies

Roadblock	Behavioral Change Strategy
Like many other men and women, you may not like undergoing a medical examination. The setting may make you feel so uncomfortable and embarrassed that you will do almost anything to avoid it.	These feelings are quite natural. Fortunately, there are ways to make the experience less traumatic. Consider calling your physician and say that you want to begin an exercise program and would feel better knowing that there are no medical contraindications. Your physician may know enough about your medical history to give you the green light over the phone. If not, make an appointment with your physician to have the tests you want completed, and make it clear that these are the only tests you need at this time and that you are not interested in other examination procedures.
You may detest running and would never choose that form of aerobic exercise. In fact, the mere thought of running 1.5 miles to complete the aerobic test may be a turn-off and destroy your motivation to begin a program.	Many people dislike running as a form of exercise. Fortunately, there are other valuable aerobic choices as beneficial as jogging or running. You also can assess your cardiorespiratory endurance without running. Review the Harvard Step test described in this chapter. Find a bench and complete the test in your gym. Many step classes at fitness centers use this method as a complete workout. You can complete the test alone. If you dislike physical tests, avoid both the 1.5-mile and Harvard Step tests, and select an aerobic exercise program that has a beginner's level and slowly progresses toward more advanced fitness.
You are self-conscious about the amount of fat on your body and do not want anyone to measure you with skinfold calipers.	This is a common concern, and you have the right to avoid such tests of body composition. Consider some options that will still provide you with some type of assessment. 1. Borrow a skinfold caliper for an hour or two and ask a relative or a close friend to take the measurements. 2. Find equipment to perform hydrostatic (underwater) weighing. A school physical education or biology department might have this kind of equipment. Then you need only put on a bathing suit and submerse yourself in water. 3. Avoid any specific test of body composition, and apply your own *pinch an inch* method to various body parts. If you are pinching an inch, you are now aware that you possess too much fat in that area. If this occurs in more than two areas, it is an indication that your total body fat is too high.
List other roadblocks you are experiencing that seem to be reducing the effectiveness of the fitness assessment phase of your program. 1. _____ 2. _____ 3. _____	Now list the behavior change strategies that can help you overcome these roadblocks. Read ahead in chapter 3 for help with behavior change and motivational techniques. 1. _____ 2. _____ 3. _____

Figure 2.1 ✦ Nomogram for BMI

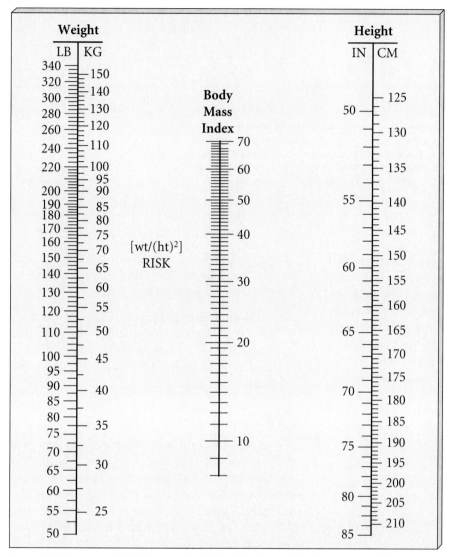

tions at the end of chapter 10. This lab activity will also help you identify major food and fluid intake problems as well as factors contributing to your control of body weight and fat.

Body Composition Assessment

Numerous tests are available to measure your body's composition. Height-weight charts, discussed in chapter 11, are perhaps the least accurate method of providing an indication of associated health risks except for the very obese individual. Three practical tests—body mass index, waist-to-hip ratio, and skinfold measures—provide an accurate assessment of your body composition and the associated health risks

based on body fat content. Record your scores on the Lab Activity 2.2.

1. **Body mass index (BMI)** provides a more sensitive indicator of body composition and health risks than body weight. You can determine your BMI using Figure 2.1 by placing a "dot" at your

> **Body mass index (BMI)** A method of determining overweight and obesity by dividing body weight (in kilograms) by height (in meters) squared; this method is considered superior to height-weight table ranges.

Table 2.7 ✦ BMI Values for Men and Women

	MEN	WOMEN
Underweight	< 20.7	< 19.1
Acceptable weight	20.7 to 27.8	19.1 to 27.3
Overweight	27.8	27.3
Severe overweight	31.1	32.3
Morbid obesity	45.4	44.8

Source: From the 1983 Metropolitan Life Insurance Company tables, designed by B. T. Burton and W. R. Foster, Health Implications of Obesity, an NIH Consensus Development Conference, 1985, *Journal of the American Dietetic Association,* 85, pp. 1117–1121. Copyright 1983 by Metropolitan Life Insurance Company. All rights reserved. Reproduced by permission.

exact height in inches in the column to the rightt and another dot at your exact weight in pounds in the column to the left, drawing a straight line to connect the two dots, and recording the number where the line intersects the vertical column in the middle. Keep in mind that weights and heights are determined without clothing. A body mass index greater than 27.2 for men or 26.9 for women indicates a need for weight reduction. Traditional weight tables and the BMI provide only rough estimates of what people should weigh.

Example: A college woman 5 feet, 6 inches tall and weighing 185 pounds will have a BMI of about 31.0.

2. **Waist-to-hip ratio** provides an indication of the way you store fat. Obese people who tend to store large amounts of fat in the abdominal area, rather than around the hips and thighs, are at higher risk for coronary heart disease, high blood pressure, congestive heart failure, strokes, and diabetes. To provide an accurate and practical indicator, the waist-to-hip ratio test was devised by a panel of scientists appointed by the National Academy of Sciences and the Dietary Guidelines Advisory Council for the U.S. Departments of Agriculture and Health and Human Services. If the waist-to-hip ratio is 1.0 or higher in men or .85 or higher in women, the panel recommends weight loss.

Example: John has a 40-inch waist and a 38-inch hip. His ratio of 1.05 (40 ÷ 38) is indicative of increased risk for disease.

3. **Skinfold measures** at various sites on the body provide an accurate indicator of your percent of body fat. The four-site skinfold test described in chapter 11 is designed for both college men and women.

Conclusion

Your wellness profile is complete. You can now evaluate your physical fitness in absolute terms (Are you satisfied with your levels of each component?) or in relative terms (Are you happy with how you compare with others?). Wellness requires information. Where are you now? Where do you want to be? How can you get there? Now that you have identified your current fitness level, you can decide on what goals you need to set for yourself. For example, if you are not satisfied with your cardiorespiratory fitness, read the remainder of this book with a view toward improving that component. You can do the same for muscular strength and endurance, flexibility, or body composition. This book contains the means for you to be successful at enhancing your level of physical fitness. All you need to do is apply them. Always keep in mind that improving one aspect of your health or fitness should not result in the decline of another component. It is important to strive for balance in all components of physical fitness.

SUMMARY

The Health Appraisal

Although physical fitness is extremely important, it is only one aspect of wellness. The health decisions you make about use of tobacco (smoking and smokeless), use of alcohol and other drugs, eating habits, stress control, and your personal safety are also key factors that make up your wellness profile. Your health appraisal scores can highlight potential problem areas that may occur in the future if you continue to practice unhealthy behaviors.

The Medical Evaluation

Not all experts agree whether everyone starting an exercise program should obtain a medical evaluation. Even when there is agreement in this area, experts may disagree concerning exactly what the examination should entail. We recommend that a medical examination is necessary after the age of 45 and at any age when identifiable risk or disease is present. The contents of the evaluation depend on the age of the patient and the symptoms present and may include taking a medical history, measurement of blood pressure, listening to the heart and lungs, determining resting pulse rate, having a chest X-ray, administering a resting ECG and a graded exercise test, and administering blood tests for blood fats and the ratio between high- and low-density lipoproteins.

We also feel that all readers should decide whether they need a medical examination before they start exercise testing and an exercise program based on their knowledge of their personal health, present physical fitness level, and medical history.

The Fitness Appraisal

The ideal physical fitness appraisal should include measures of cardiorespiratory endurance, muscular strength and endurance, flexibility, and body composition. Specific tests are available that allow the individual to obtain an accurate assessment in each of these areas: cardiorespiratory endurance can be measured by the 1.5-mile test or the Harvard step test; muscular strength by the bench press, arm curl, and leg press; muscular endurance by sit-ups, bar dips, and pull-ups or the flexed-arm hang; flexibility by the shoulder reach, trunk flexion, and trunk extension tests; nutritional analysis through the use of numerous software programs or by manually recording and analyzing dietary intake; and body composition by determining your BMI, waist-to-hip ratio, or skinfold measures at four specific sites. For an accurate evaluation of your level of physical fitness, it is important to give your best effort on each test, while staying alert to physical signs of overexertion. See Tables 2.8 and 2.9 for sample assessments.

Table 2.8 ✦ An Assessment Example: 42-year-old Bill

Bill has been sedentary for most of his adult life. Now, approaching the coronary-prone years, he has decided that an ounce of prevention is worth a pound of cure. Consequently, Bill spoke with his physician about beginning a regular program of exercise. His physician classified Bill in the C category of the American College of Sports Medicine's guidelines for exercise testing because Bill was over 35 years old, physically inactive, and was without coronary heart disease or its risk factors. As a result, Bill needed a complete medical exam. Bill related his medical history as part of this examination: There was little coronary heart disease in his family; there were a few cases of hypertension, but most family members had lived well into their eighties. He was not currently ill or taking any medication, did not smoke, and had no physical disabilities of which he was aware. His physician tested Bill's blood pressure (135/85), took his pulse (80), listened to his lungs and heart, took a chest X-ray, tested his blood for blood fats and for the ratio of high- and low-density lipoproteins, and administered a resting electrocardiogram and a stress test. All these procedures determined Bill to be within normal limits.

Bill's physician then recommended he consult with a fitness expert and gave him the telephone number of the local university physical education department. Bill was referred to the fitness program conducted at the university, and an appointment was made for him to be screened.

Table 2.8 ✦ An Assessment Example: 42-year-old Bill *(continued)*

The screening consisted of Bill's completing a 1.5-mile run/walk on the track to determine his cardiorespiratory endurance; several weight-lifting one-repetition maximum tests to determine his muscular strength; sit-ups and pull-ups to determine his muscular endurance; shoulder reach, trunk flexion, and trunk extension tests to determine his degree of flexibility; skinfold tests to determine his degree of body fat; and the Illinois agility run to determine how much agility he possessed. The results of these tests were as follows:

1. **Run/walk:** 14 minutes, 10 seconds (fair)
2. **1-RM tests**
   Bench press: 130 pounds (below average)
   Standing press: 90 pounds (below average)
   Curl: 65 pounds (below average)
   Leg press: 325 pounds (average)
3. **Sit-ups:** 30 (below average)
4. **Pull-ups:** 2 (below average)
5. **Shoulder reach:** 2/0 inches (below average)
6. **Trunk flexion:** 5 inches (below average)
7. **Trunk extension:** 6 inches (below average)
8. **Skinfold:** 18% (average body fat)

Based on these results, Bill's exercise program emphasized cardiorespiratory endurance (by beginning a walking program, progressing to run/walks, and leading up to jogging); development of greater upper body strength (with bench press, standing press, and curl exercises with low weights progressing to greater weights); muscular endurance (sit-ups beginning with just the head and shoulders lifting off the ground and progressing to the whole upper body lifting, with increasing repetitions, and pull-ups beginning with flexed-arm hangs); and flexibility (with hamstring, shoulder and chest, and spine and waist stretches).

Source: From *Physical Fitness: A Wellness Approach,* by J. S. Greenberg, 1989, Englewood Cliffs, NJ: Prentice-Hall.

Table 2.9 ✦ An Assessment Example: 66-year-old Joan

Joan was older than Bill, and her fitness profile differed in some respects. Her physician classified Joan in the D category of the American College of Sports Medicine's guidelines for exercise testing because she was asymptomatic, physically inactive, had no coronary diseases, but did have a high cholesterol level and elevated blood pressure readings. Joan's medical history was without incident except for her 20-year-old cigarette smoking habit, and her screening revealed only the concern for her hypercholesteremia and hypertension.

She too was put in touch with the local university's physical fitness program. When tested, her results were:

1. **Run/walk:** 21 minutes (poor)
2. **Sit-ups:** 31 (below average)
3. **Shoulder reach:** 3 inches (average)
4. **Trunk flexion:** 8 inches (average)
5. **Trunk extension:** 16 inches (average)
6. **Skinfold:** 32% (above-average fat)

Table 2.9 ✦ An Assessment Example: 66-year-old Joan *(continued)*

It was determined to withhold the muscular strength testing at this time, since the concern was to devise a program to respond to the hypercholesteremia and the hypertension. Consequently, an aerobic exercise program would be needed, and to develop one required a determination of Joan's present endurance fitness. It was decided to test flexibility as well, since the program the fitness experts had in mind had a tendency to decrease flexibility.

The analysis of Joan's fitness testing concluded she needed to develop cardiovascular and muscular endurance and decrease her body fat. Her flexibility was fine.

Based on these findings, a program was developed to get Joan jogging. Jogging has a tendency to burn up calories, strengthen muscles, improve the ratio of high- and low-density lipoproteins, and decrease blood pressure. Since Joan's run/walk test placed her in the poor category, she was instructed to walk four days a week for a distance that did not exhaust her (perhaps 1.5 miles initially) and gradually work up to a slow jog after several weeks or months. When she could begin jogging would be determined by how Joan felt walking and her heart rate response.

Prior to jogging, however, Joan was instructed to walk some and jog some of her route. The program then progressed gradually from walking, to walking some and jogging some, to jogging. Joan was told that even if she stayed at the walking stage and could do that while maintaining her target heart rate, she would be benefitting physically.

In addition to the walk/run program, Joan was instructed on which stretches to do before and after each exercise session to maintain a satisfactory level of flexibility.

Since it has been found that regular exercisers tend not to smoke cigarettes, it was hoped that Joan would give up her habit. In particular, aerobic exercise is incompatible with cigarette smoking. However, to be sure of responding to Joan's high cholesterol and blood pressure, her physician recommended she enroll in a stop-smoking program and put her in touch with a registered dietitian who would develop a diet for her.

All things considered, Joan was well on her way to taking greater control of her health. With the support of loved ones, the fitness program personnel, the dietitian, the stop-smoking staff, and her physician, we can expect that Joan's health will soon improve—especially if she is committed to that goal.

Source: From *Physical Fitness: A Wellness Approach,* by J. S. Greenberg, 1989 (Englewood Cliffs, NJ: Prentice-Hall.

ℛEFERENCES

Ainsworth, B., et al. (1993). Validity and reliability of self-reported physical activity satatus. *Medicine and Science in Sports and Exercise,* 25, 92-98.

American College of Sports Medicine. (1991). *Guidelines for exercise testing and prescription* (4th ed.) Philadelphia: Lea & Febiger.

Bouchard, C., et al. (Eds.) (1994). *Physical activity, fitness and health.* Champaign, IL: Human Kinetics.

Dintiman, G. B., Ward, B., & Tellez, T. (1997). *SportSpeed II.* Champaign, IL: Human Kinetics

Dintiman, G. B., Davis, R., Stone, S., & Pannington, J. (1989). *Discovering lifetime fitness: Concepts of exercise and weight control* (2nd ed.). Champaign, IL: Human Kinetics.

Greenberg, J., Dintiman, G., & Oakes, B. (1995). *Physical fitness and wellness.* Boston, Allyn & Bacon.

Hatfield, F. (ed.). (1991). *Fitness: The complete guide.* Santa Barbara: International Sports Science Association.

Lamb, D., & Murray, R. (Eds.). (1988). *Perspectives in exercise Science and sports medicine. Prolonged exercise.* Indianapolis: Benchmark.

Lee, R., & Nieman, D. (1993). *Nutritional assessment.* Madison, WI: Brown and Benchmark.

Miller, D. (1994). *Measurement by the physical educator: Why and how.* (2nd ed.). Madison, WI: Brown and Benchmark.

Lab Activity 2.1

Determining the Reasons for Choosing or Not Choosing Exercise and High-Level Wellness

INSTRUCTIONS: *Join a group of six to eight classmates in a separate section of the room, forming as many small groups as necessary for the class size. Complete the following steps:*

1. Students in each small group are divided into two areas: those who exercise and those who do not.

2. The exercisers and nonexercisers each prepare a list (using a 3-by-5-inch card) of the main reasons they choose to exercise or choose not to exercise on a regular basis.

3. Students in each group now reverse their roles, using the list made up by the other group to "defend" the reasons for exercising or not exercising (the active group is defending inactive behavior and the inactive group is defending active behavior).

   Each group is allowed three minutes to present their case. A two-minute rebuttal follows each presentation.

4. The session ends by returning the 3-by-5 cards to the appropriate group and allowing each group to present a summary of their true beliefs.

✦ Results

Each student is now asked to respond, in writing, to the following questions:

Did anyone become more sensitive to the issues of the other side?

Was it helpful to learn how students with opposite values view students on the other side?

List two arguments presented by the opposing group that you feel have some merit.

List two ways you can be more supportive and encouraging to those with an opposing view about exercise.

Lab Activity 2.2

Your Physical Fitness Profile

INSTRUCTIONS: *As you complete each test, place your score where indicated. Consult the tables on standards for each test, and check the appropriate rating in the column to the right. Summarize your fitness profile by completing section VII.*

✦ **I. Cardiorespiratory fitness**

    A. 1.5-mile test

        Score _____

        Rating (check one)

        _____ Very poor

        _____ Poor

        _____ Fair

        _____ Good

        _____ Excellent

        _____ Superior

    B. Harvard step test

        Index _____

        Rating (check one)

        _____ Poor

        _____ Low average

        _____ Average

        _____ Good

        _____ Excellent

✦ **II. Muscular strength**

    A. Bench press

        Amount lifted _____

        Rating (check one)

        _____ Optimal

        _____ Above optimal

        _____ Below optimal

B. Standing press

Amount lifted _____

Rating (check one)

_____ Optimal

_____ Above optimal

_____ Below optimal

C. Curl

Amount lifted _____

Rating (check one)

_____ Optimal

_____ Above optimal

_____ Below optimal

D. Leg press

Amount lifted _____

Rating (check one)

_____ Optimal

_____ Above optimal

_____ Below optimal

✦ **III. Muscular endurance**

A. Abdominal

Number of sit-ups _____

Rating (check one)

_____ Excellent

_____ Good

_____ Average

_____ Low

_____ Poor

B. Arm and shoulder

Number of pull-ups or dips _____

Rating (check one)

_____ Excellent

_____ Good

_____ Average

_____ Poor

✦ **IV. Flexibility**

A. Shoulder reach

Score in inches _____

Rating (check one)

_____ Above average

_____ Average

_____ Below average

Lab Activity 2.2 *(continued)*
Your Physical Fitness Profile

    B. Trunk flexion

        Score in inches _____   Rating (check one)

                                                                      _____ Above average

                                                                      _____ Average

                                                                      _____ Below average

    C. Trunk extension

        Score in inches _____   Rating (check one)

                                                                      _____ Above average

                                                                      _____ Average

                                                                      _____ Below average

✦ **V. Nutrition**

    A. List the deficiency areas identified:

✦ **VI. Body composition**

    A. Body mass index (BMI) _____   Rating (check one)

                                                                      _____ Underweight

                                                                      _____ Acceptable weight

                                                                      _____ Overweight

                                                                      _____ Severe overweight

                                                                      _____ Morbid obesity

    B. Waist-to-hip ratio _____   Rating (check one)

                                                                      _____ High; weight loss indicated

                                                                      _____ Normal

C. Percent of body fat _____

Rating (check one)

_____ Very low fat

_____ Low fat

_____ Ideal fat

_____ Above ideal fat

_____ Over fat

_____ High fat

✦ **VII. Summary**

A. List those components of physical fitness for which you rated

1. Above average

2. Average

3. Below average

Lab Activity 2.3

A Quick Practical Assessment of Body Composition

INSTRUCTIONS: *It is a simple task to assess your body composition without sophisticated testing equipment. Often, this is all that is needed to determine whether you are in need of a regular exercise program and/or calorie reduction to lower your percentage of body fat. Complete each of the following steps to examine your body in a number of different ways.*

1. **Height** (add 1 in. to your height without shoes)

   Weight (in clothes; add 3 lb for women, 5 for men to unclothed weight)

   Frame Size Wrap your thumb and middle finger around your right wrist to determine your frame size: Large frame (thumb and middle finger do not meet), Medium frame (thumb and middle finger just do touch), and Small frame (thumb and middle finger overlap).
   Compare your weight to the suggested ranges for your height and frame size on the Metropolitan height-weight table in Chapter 11.

2. **Pinch an inch**—Lie flat on your back before using the thumb and index finger of your right hand to firmly grasp the skin and underlying adipose tissue to the right of your umbilical area, the thigh, back of upper leg, buttocks, hip, and back of upper arm. List the areas to the right where you were able to pinch more than an inch.

3. **Ruler Test**—Lie flat on your back and place a ruler across your stomach from one hip bone to the other. Does the ruler lie flat or create an angle?

4. **Waist-hip Ration**—Complete the waist-hip ratio test described in this chapter. Measure both at the widest point. Does your ratio place you at a low, moderate, or high health risk?

✦ **Results**

   What did you learn about your body? Keep in mind that some fat is desirable. A minimum of 3 percent for men and 12 percent for women is considered essential to health. Does it appear that you possess enough extra fat to impose a health risk? Compare your results later with the skinfold tests described in chapter 11.

BEHAVIORAL CHANGE AND MOTIVATIONAL TECHNIQUES

Chapter Objectives

By the end of this chapter, you should be able to:

1. Discuss the importance of psychosocial lifestyle factors such as locus of control, social support, and self-esteem in deciding on a wellness program.

2. Describe several techniques that researchers have demonstrated to be effective in helping people achieve their wellness goals.

3. List several means of improving the chances of maintaining a wellness program once one has been started.

4. Modify a wellness program in the face of obstacles so it need not be interrupted.

THE COMEDIAN HENNY Youngman tells of a man who told his psychiatrist, "Doc, I have a guilt complex," to which his doctor replied, "You ought to be ashamed of yourself!" We do not want to shame you into regularly engaging in health- and wellness-enhancing activities. That would be dysfunctional, something like a physical education instructor who makes physical activity so distasteful that students are repelled by exercise for the remainder of their lives. Instead we want you to appreciate the benefits of being healthy and well and then to decide for yourself whether to engage in health-promoting behaviors. If you decide to do that, we can show you how to begin a program and the best way to continue participating in it over an extended period of time.

PSYCHOSOCIAL FACTORS TO CONSIDER

To plan a wellness program you need to know something about yourself: about your motivations, about your perceptions of the amount of control you have over your life, about the degree to which you associate with other people, and about the confidence you have in yourself. This chapter makes the importance of this information clear.

Locus of Control

Some people believe they can control events in their lives. This construct is called one's **locus of control.** People who believe this construct possess an internal locus of control or *internality.* People who do not believe in the construct possess an external locus of control or *externality.*

Externals believe that the course of their lives is a matter of luck, fate, or chance, or of what powerful others do. This is more than merely an academic distinction. If you do not believe you control events in your life, you are apt to adopt a laissez-faire attitude. Relative to physical fitness, you might believe that whether you are in good shape is a function of luck or of genetic makeup. There is no sense in engaging in an exercise program if you do not control your fitness level.

Internals believe that what they get is, for the most part, a result of what they do. Therefore internals will probably learn a good deal about exercise and physical fitness and plan a program in which they can participate. An internal locus of control is very important if you are serious about achieving wellness and maintaining it. Complete Lab Activity 3.1: Locus of Control Assessment at the end of this chapter to determine your locus of control. If you score as an external, make a list of the parts of your life that you influence. Then read that list daily to change your focus. In addition, take some measure-

ments before beginning a wellness program (for example, your pulse rate and weight), and measure those variables again after engaging in your program for several weeks. The change will reinforce the notion that you can influence your body and mind rather than resigning yourself to being a victim of your habits or of your genetic makeup.

Social Isolation

We all need to interact with other people. Researchers have found that the social support we have actually helps prevent us from getting ill and enhances the quality of our lives. Conversely, not having significant others with whom to share our joys and sorrows causes ill health or **social isolation.** Refer to Lab Activity 3.2: Alienation Assessment at the end of the chapter for a social isolation scale that will help you determine whether this is a problem for you.

If you find you need to improve your social network, structure your wellness program accordingly. Consider joining an exercise club, Weight Watchers, a

Having friends who encourage you can be an important part of achieving high-level wellness. (Photo courtesy of the Aspen Hill Club.)

Locus of control The degree to which you believe you are in control of events in your life.

Social isolation The lack of other people with whom to discuss important matters relevant to your life.

Body cathexis Physical self-esteem, how highly you regard your physical self.

health spa, the YMCA or YWCA, or Jewish Community Center, or enrolling in a college health course. You might meet people there with whom you can become friendly. Participation in organized sports (at levels suited to your skill and experience) can also provide an opportunity to meet people. Playing in leagues and tournaments (team as well as individual) is another avenue for alleviating social isolation. You should not ignore your social self when structuring your fitness program. To do so is to endanger your health and wellness.

Self-Esteem

What you think of yourself, no matter whether that perception is accurate, influences your health, wellness, and physical fitness. If you do not think well of yourself, you might not believe you can become healthy and fit. You may lack confidence, think you are genetically inferior, or think you have so far to go that beginning a wellness program is futile.

For example, what you think of your body, your bodily self-esteem (sometimes called **body cathexis**), will affect your health and fitness. Lab Activity 3.3: Body Self-Esteem Assessment at the end of this chapter is a scale to help you determine your bodily self-esteem.

There are probably parts of your body with which you are satisfied and parts with which you are dissatisfied. Be proud of those parts about which you scored 4 or 5 in Lab Activity 3.3. Let others know how proud of them you are, but not in a boastful way. Do not fret about those parts of your body to which you assigned a 1 or 2 value. You can improve them, at least many of them, and thereby feel better about yourself. For example, if you are dissatisfied with your waist, you can do exercises to strengthen the muscles in your waist. We discuss these in the chapter on muscular strength and endurance. There are even strategies that are useful for those body parts you assigned a 1 or 2 value that cannot be changed, such as your nose. These are body parts about which you need to become more accepting. One effective way of doing this is to recognize that things could be worse. Volunteering for an organization that caters to the needs of the physically challenged or the socioeconomically disadvantaged can help you put your concern about your nose, for example, in proper perspective.

STRATEGIES FOR ACHIEVING YOUR WELLNESS GOALS

There is a good deal of research identifying effective ways of achieving your wellness goals. Before the appropriate techniques can be applied, however, you must first identify the goals.

Goal Setting

In determining your wellness goals, adhere to these guidelines.

Just as racers have the finish line in sight, so should you when establishing wellness behavior change goals. Those goals should be obtainable and progress toward them should be periodically assessed. (Photo courtesy of the Aspen Hill Club.)

Be Realistic Jorge was playing tennis with a friend one pleasant summer day. The sun was out, the birds were chirping, and the water in the creek alongside the tennis court was gently caressing the rocks as it moved downstream. You couldn't ask for a better day, that is, unless you were Jorge. His game was off. "Enough is enough," Jorge thought when he netted still another backhand. Before anyone realized what was happening, his tennis racket flew over the fence, above the trees beyond, and landed in the middle of the creek. When last seen, the racket was heading downstream, never again to be used.

Some of you may know a Jorge, or you may be one. The problem is in being realistic. Some of us are has-been athletes expecting to perform at the level we could when we were younger and practiced daily. Others of us are never-beens with grand delusions and dreams that will never be fulfilled. Do not fall into either trap when setting your wellness goals. Be realistic about what you can attain and the time it will take you to attain it. If your goals are unobtainable, you will become frustrated and give up on health and wellness altogether.

In fact, it is wise in the beginning to set goals that are easy to achieve. In that way, when you do attain them, you will reinforce healthy behavior and be more likely to achieve subsequent goals.

Periodically Assess Once you decide on your wellness goals, periodically assess how you are meeting those goals. If you conclude that you are making progress in an appropriate amount of time, keep doing what you are doing. If your assessment indicates problems meeting your goals, it is time to make adjustments. Maybe you need to exercise longer, more intensely, or more frequently. Maybe you need to ingest fewer calories or meditate more often. Without periodically assessing your program, you will not identify changes that are needed to help you achieve your wellness goals.

Behavioral Change Techniques

Among the more effective techniques you can employ in meeting your wellness goals are the use of social support, contracting, reminder systems, gradual programming, tailoring, chaining, and covert techniques.

Social Support This is just another way of saying you need other people to encourage and help you. It is much easier to adopt a habit of eating nutrition-

If family members engage in physical activity together, they are improving their physical health at the same time they are enhancing their social and spiritual health.

ly, or any habit for that matter, if you are encouraged by others. If you can get someone else to eat nutritionally with you, to ask you daily whether you have eaten healthy foods, or to buy you a healthy snack periodically, you will be more apt to stick with your regimen. To begin, make a list of people you think would be willing to assist you and discuss with them how they can help.

Contracting One way to use social support is to develop a contract to achieve a certain wellness goal and to have it witnessed by someone else. If that person then helps you periodically to assess your progress, you will be more likely to be successful. Figure 3.1 is a sample of an effective contract. It identifies the *behavior goal*, the *date* when it should be achieved (and assessed), and the *reward* for achieving the goal as well as the *punishment* for not achieving it. Rewards can be going to the movies, buying something you have wanted for a long time, or a night free of school work. Punishments might include not watching television for a week or not eating your favorite snack for several days. Although rewards are more effective than punishments in controlling behavior, punishments have a place as well. Contracts have been found to work best when there is a witness, but they can also be effective if you merely contract with yourself.

Reminder Systems One way to remember things is to make a note of them. Reminder notes will help you remember to exercise, especially if you leave the notes in places where you cannot miss them, for example, on the bathroom and refrigerator doors or on the

Figure 3.1 ✦ Fitness Contract

I _____ desire to improve my physical fitness
(your name)

because _____ .
(the reason)

I have decided I intend to _____
(your goal)

by _____ . If I achieve this goal, I will reward myself
(date)

by _____ . If I do not achieve my
(the reward)

goal, I will punish myself by _____ .
(the punishment)

_____   _____
(your signature)   (today's date)

_____   _____
(witness signature)   (today's date)

bathroom mirror. You can also use notes in appointment books and calendars as reminders.

Gradual Programming Too often, people who have never exercised regularly or who have not exercised regularly for some time expect to be able to run a mile in under four minutes. Less obvious, but no less unrealistic for many people, is the goal of exercising every other day when they have been sedentary for years or that of exercising intensely when they have not done so for a while. Giving up the sedentary life "cold turkey" may be extremely difficult. If it is, do not fret. Instead use a graduated plan in which you start slowly and gradually increase both frequency and intensity. In fact, to prevent injury, fitness experts recommend graduated plans even for those who are already highly fit. For example, runners are warned not to increase their distance by more than 10 percent a week, and weight trainers not to increase the weight they lift by more than 5 percent.

You can even use graduated plans to study more, to change your eating habits, or for other behaviors you have been meaning to change. For example, if you want to better manage the stress you experience, and decide to engage in a relaxation technique regularly, you might begin by meditating once every other day. Your goal would be to work up to meditating twice a day, every day. However, you would be work-

ing up to that goal gradually. Similarly, if you wish to decrease your caloric intake from 2,800 calories per day to 1,800 calories per day, you might start off with a daily average of 2,400 calories the first week, 2,000 calories the second week, and 1,800 calories (your goal) the third week.

Tailoring No two people are alike. This is not the most provocative of statements, yet people sometimes act as though they do not know this simple fact. When you adopt a wholesale exercise program, for example, designed for a group, without adjusting that program to your own needs and circumstances, you are increasing the likelihood you will soon stop exercising regularly. Some people are free to exercise in the mornings, others in the evenings. Some people are in better physical condition than others. People vary in their choice of meal-times. Some are more committed to exercise than others. We could go on and on, but the point is that any wellness program must be tailored to the individual. We will present numerous health, wellness, and physical fitness activities in later chapters, but you must choose which ones to do and when, how frequently, and how intensely to do them for your program to be successful.

Chaining In chaining, one behavior is linked to a previous one and that to a previous one, and so on, like links in a chain. You can use chaining to help achieve your wellness goals. To adopt a behavior, such as exercising regularly, you want to have as few links as possible between the decision to exercise and actually engaging in a fitness activity. To demonstrate, let us look at two people, U. R. Wrong and I. M. Right.

U. R. Wrong decides to exercise at about 5:30 in the afternoon. So U. R. rushes home and starts gathering exercise clothes. In one drawer are gym shorts and socks. In another drawer is a shirt. Sneakers are under the bed in another room. Then U. R. looks for the car keys since he needs to drive to the track to jog. The track is 10 minutes away. On the way there, U. R. realizes the car needs gas and stops to get some. Finally, U. R. arrives at the track and is ready to exercise.

I. M. Right decides to exercise at the same time of day. However, I. M. prepares beforehand. All the clothes needed for later are left on the bed in the morning. I. M. decides to run around the neighborhood instead of the track, so that all that is required at 5:30 P.M. is to come home, dress, step outside the front door, and exercise.

If we consider each behavior needed to exercise as a link in a chain, we see that U .R. Wrong has many more links. The more links, the more difficult it is to exercise, and the more likely it is not to happen. The trick is to decrease the links for a behavior you want to adopt and to increase the links for a behavior you want to give up (for example, cigarette smoking).

Covert Techniques Some people are so inactive or so busy that it is difficult for them to engage in regular exercise or other health or wellness activities. Three techniques can help these people change behavior without requiring them to do anything physically. These are called *covert techniques.*

1. **Covert rehearsal** This procedure requires that you imagine yourself engaging in a health or wellness behavior. Your image must be vivid; notice all the details (what you are wearing, the weather, the location), smell the atmosphere, feel the bodily sensations, and so on. Being able to imagine yourself exercising, for example, makes it more likely that you will actually exercise. You will have desensitized yourself to the image of you exercising so that seeing yourself exercising will not seem foreign to you.

2. **Covert modeling** For some of us, even imagining ourselves exercising is difficult. It is just not

us. If that is the case with you, there is still hope. First identify someone else you *can* envision exercising. Next imagine, as vividly as you can, that person exercising. Once that image is clear in your mind, substitute yourself for that person. Model the image of you exercising after the image of that person exercising. After a while, it will be easier for you to think of yourself as a potentially regular exerciser, and it will be more likely that you will actually become one.

3. **Covert reinforcement** When you can imagine yourself exercising, it is a good idea to reward yourself for it. The use of another image as a reward is called *covert reinforcement.* Usually a pleasant image is used as a reward (a day at the beach, a calm lake) and is allowed to surface and be focused on only after the goal image is successfully accomplished.

These same techniques can be applied to numerous health and wellness behaviors.

Ⓜ️AINTAINING YOUR WELLNESS PROGRAM

Once you have begun a wellness program, the trick is to maintain it. In addition to the methods already described, here are additional suggestions for keeping at it.

Material Reinforcement

Behavior that is rewarded tends to be repeated. Consequently, if you want to exercise regularly, reward yourself when you do. Material rewards can take many forms. For example, you might treat yourself to a trip to the beach to show off your newly toned body. Or you might buy yourself an article of clothing you have been eyeing for some time.

Social Reinforcement

Peer group pressure need not be limited to negative influences. We can use such pressure to encourage and reward desirable behavior. Take a moment to list five people whose opinions you value. Then enlist them as social reinforcers to inquire about your wellness behavior and to pat you on the back if you report behaving in a healthy way regularly. After a while, healthy behaviors will become part of your lifestyle, and you will no longer need to be rewarded for continuing.

When making behavioral changes, it is best to acquire the support of others. The encouragement other people can give you can help achieve your wellness goals. (Photo courtesy Metro Orthopedics & Sports Therapy)

Joining a Group

One of the reasons Weight Watchers, Inc., is so effective in helping people lose weight is that it employs group support and positive peer pressure. It is often easier to accomplish your goals if you are working with others. You can join a health club, a local YMCA or YWCA, or a Jewish Community Center. Or you can organize a group of friends to exercise together at a predetermined time. You can even enroll in a health education class at a local university or community college, or in a community program. Any group involvement will increase the likelihood of your maintaining a health and wellness program.

Boasting

Many people, while they were students, have had the experience of having two tests returned the same day, one on which they did well and the other on which they did not. They complained about the poor grade for days, while ignoring the test on which they did well. Many of us react this way. We relive negative experiences by repeatedly thinking about them, by being embarrassed about them over and over again, or by feeling inadequate in other ways. For positive experiences, such as getting an A on a test, we exhibit false modesty and say, "It was nothing." We would

do better to learn from our mistakes and let them go and to relive our positive experiences and even boast about them. Of course, you do not want to be obnoxious or to be perceived of as being conceited. Yet if you run three miles daily and someone asks how far you usually run, rather than say, "Only three miles," you might say, "I'm proud to say that I run three miles regularly." Boasting in this way will help reinforce your wellness behavior.

Self-Monitoring

By observing and recording your own behavior, you will know that your health and wellness program is having a positive effect, that it is moving toward your goal. Remember not to expect immediate dramatic results. Assuming your goal is realistic, accept small gains. Do not expect more rapid change than is warranted. Eventually, with persistence, you will successfully attain your goal. When you see slow but steady progress toward your goal, you will be encouraged to maintain the program.

Making It Fun

If the wellness program you designed is not fun, you selected the wrong activities. If it is not fun at least most of the time, you will not continue it for very long. We present so many options in this book that you should be able to find activities that accomplish your goals while providing enjoyment. All you need to do is be selective. Think about your choices carefully, and seek help from others when that is necessary.

$\mathcal{M}$AINTAINING WELLNESS UNDER DIFFICULT CIRCUMSTANCES

If you maintain a wellness program long enough, you will undoubtedly encounter obstacles. We have selected five such obstacles to demonstrate how, if you are serious, your program need not be interrupted. These obstacles are traveling, being confined to a limited space, being injured, being busy, and having visitors.

Traveling

If you travel often, you should consider that when you develop your program. For example, rather than joining a local health club, you would be wise to join one with facilities throughout the country so you can exercise when you are in other cities. YMCAs and YWCAs, Jewish Community Centers, and some nationally franchised health clubs have

facilities throughout the United States. In addition, select activities that take regular travel into account. You would be better off jogging, for example, than playing tennis. Jogging requires little by way of equipment or facilities and does not involve obtaining a partner. To summarize: The factors to consider if you travel often are equipment, facilities, and dependence on other people.

Being Confined to a Limited Space

If there are times when you are confined to a limited space (for example, if you are a student studying for final examinations and seldom leaving your dormitory room), you need not abandon your physical fitness or wellness program. If you have access to an exercise room, you might be fortunate enough to have treadmills, steppers, ski machines, stationary bikes, or rowers at your disposal. Since that is unlikely, you can exercise without ever leaving your office or room. For example, you can run around the room. Be sure not to run in one place since that might cause too much strain on your legs and knees. Running around the room can respond to your need for cardiorespiratory endurance.

Alternatively, you can purchase a jump rope and use it in your room. You can even do some of the flexibility exercises described in chapter 9 or perform isometric muscular strength activities. **Isometric**

If you really want to maintain your wellness, nothing can stop you! These resourceful exercisers are training indoors for downhill skiing. (Photo courtesy of the Aspen Hill Club)

Maintaining a wellness program is possible, even in the face of obstacles. This couple is using a special stroller to take their baby on a jog. (Photo courtesy of RunAbout, Inc.)

contractions consist of exerting a force that is equal to, or less than, that required to move an object. Therefore, the object does not move, there is no movement in the joint, and there is no change in the length of the muscle. For example, if you push against a wall, that is an isometric contraction. You can also do isotonic activities. **Isotonic contractions** consist of movement at the joint and changes in the length of the muscle. For example, if you lift weights, you are engaged in isotonic contractions. It needn't be a barbell or other weight-lifting equipment that

you use. Lifting any object of sufficient weight to offer resistance will suffice. You might also be able to find someone else who also feels confined, to exercise with you. For example, rather than pushing against a wall, you might be able to push against each other and thereby create the resistance you require (see Figure 3.2).

Being Injured

If you exercise long enough, you will inevitably experience an injury of some sort. As with any other obstacle, you can always use such an injury as an excuse not to exercise. On the other hand, you can almost always find a way to exercise around the injury. For example, injury to your leg may preclude jogging but not swimming, and one to your shoulder may eliminate a regular racquetball game but not jogging. For most injuries, common sense will dictate what you can and cannot do. For more serious fitness

Figure 3.2 ✦ Improving Muscular Strength with a Partner

Isometric contraction Force applied to an immovable object that does not result in muscle shortening.

Isotonic contraction Shortening of the muscle in the positive phase and lengthening during the negative phase of an action.

Improving Your Community

Promoting Healthy Behavior

Now that you know how to manage your behavior, you can help other people in your community manage theirs. Here are some suggestions for how you might be able to contribute to the health of your community by helping people manage their unhealthy behaviors.

1. Volunteer to work with a group of students at a local high school or at your college who wish to quit smoking cigarettes. You can teach them how to use behavioral contracts, social support, or tailoring to quit smoking.

2. Offer to lecture to members at a senior citizens' center, YMCA, or Jewish Community Center on how to use behavior change strategies to manage unhealthy behaviors (for example, eating junk food). If you are able, you could offer to visit with the audience periodically to see how effectively they are using the behavioral change techniques and what adjustments may be necessary.

3. Lobby public health officials to make improvements in the community that encourage healthy behaviors. For example, you might meet with the

town parks and recreation supervisor and ask that more bike paths be built. Or you might lobby the safety commissioner to place lights in parks so they can be used after dark. These activities may lead to actions that make it easier for people in the community to behave in a more health-enhancing way.

4. You could conduct a communitywide survey (local or even statewide) to determine which health-related behaviors people find most difficult to manage. Then you can develop a program to help community members change these irksome and unhealthy behaviors. For example, you might produce posters (with the assistance of the campus art department) that you distribute for store owners to display. These posters would describe how to use behavioral change techniques to manage unhealthy behavior. Or a local radio or television station might allow you to air a public service announcement you develop with the assistance of the campus communications department that describes how to use behavioral change strategies effectively. ✦

injuries, however, consult a professional for advice. By doing so you might prevent further damage or prolonged recovery.

Being Busy

"I don't have time to exercise, or meditate, or pay attention to what I eat. I'm too busy," sounds out like a battle cry from some people. Yet when even busy schedules are dissected, there is always enough time for participation in wellness activities. The problem is that people decide to use this time for other activities, such as watching television, partying, or talking on the telephone. It may make sense to use your time in this way. But you must realize that is your decision to make, and as with all decisions, you can change it if you so choose.

It seems self-destructive to say you value health and fitness but to take a long lunch instead of a short lunch and a short workout or to meet your friends at

the local watering hole instead of exercising. You can find time to exercise if you really value health and fitness. In fact, exercise can rejuvenate you, make you more efficient, and provide just the break you need, both physically and mentally.

We do not mean to imply that no adjustments are necessary during particularly busy times. The operative word here, however, is *adjustment*. With the proper adjustment, you can maintain your program and resume your normal activities when the busy period passes.

Having Visitors

Suppose a friend comes to stay with you. What happens to your wellness program? Although visits from friends or relatives can encourage healthy behaviors, especially if guests eat well or exercise regularly, such visits usually interfere with your pro-

Myth and Fact Sheet

Myth	Fact
1. There are some situations in which you really have no control.	1. You have some control in all situations, even if it is only control over your own feelings and reactions.
2. Some people are born to value physical activity and others to abhor it.	2. Everyone can find some physical activity that they enjoy and that can be the basis of an effective fitness program.
3. The reason people do not achieve their wellness goals is because they do not work hard or long enough.	3. People may not achieve their wellness goals because their goals are unrealistic or unobtainable.
4. When trying to change a behavior, it is best to work at changing by yourself so you do not embarrass yourself in front of other people.	4. It is a good idea to involve other people to help you change a behavior because they can provide both support and peer pressure so you are more likely to be successful.

gram. You can use several strategies to maintain your wellness activities during visits. For example, if visitors are regular exercisers, there is no problem. Just exercise at the same time they do. If your visitors do not exercise regularly, help them organize short trips they can take while you exercise. Sightseeing trips are ideal. If other relatives or friends are nearby, perhaps they can entertain your visitors while you exercise. What is required is some ingenuity, rather than interruption of your health, wellness, and fitness routine.

SUMMARY

Psychosocial Factors to Consider

To plan a wellness program, you need to know certain things about yourself. These include your locus of control, the degree to which you feel socially isolated, and your level of self-esteem (in particular, your bodily self-esteem).

Locus of control is your perception of the amount of control you exert over events in your life. If you believe you have a great deal of control, you have an internal locus of control. If you believe you have little control, you have an external locus of control.

People who are socially isolated are susceptible to illness and disease. Wellness programs can be organized to respond to social needs as well as to physical ones.

What you think of yourself and your body has significant influence on your health and wellness. Body cathexis is the esteem in which you hold your body and bodily functions. Fitness programs can improve self-esteem while they improve more traditional fitness components.

Strategies for Achieving Your Wellness Goals

Among the more effective strategies for achieving your wellness goals are goal-setting and behavioral-change techniques. When you are determining wellness goals, be realistic about what is possible and periodically assess your progress toward meeting your goals. Behavioral-change techniques that can be used to help you achieve your goals include developing social support, contracting with yourself and others, reminder systems, gradual programming, tailoring, chaining, and the covert techniques of rehearsal, modeling, and reinforcement.

Maintaining Your Wellness Program

Strategies to use to maintain your wellness program include material and social reinforcement, joining a group, boasting, self-monitoring, and making your program fun.

Maintaining Wellness under Difficult Circumstances

Periodically there will be obstacles to maintaining your wellness program. Among these are traveling, being confined to a limited space, being injured, being busy, and having visitors. In spite of these and other obstacles, adjustments can prevent interruption of your program. All that is required is a little ingenuity and determination to continue behaving in healthy ways.

Lab Activity 3.1

Locus of Control Assessment

INSTRUCTIONS: *Circle the answers that best describe your beliefs.*

1. a. Grades are a function of the amount of work students do.

   b. Grades depend on the kindness of the instructor.

2. a. Promotions are earned by hard work.

   b. Promotions are a result of being in the right place at the right time.

3. a. Meeting someone to love is a matter of luck.

   b. Meeting someone to love depends on going out often in order to meet many people.

4. a. Living a long life is a function of heredity.

   b. Living a long life is a function of adopting healthy habits.

5. a. Being overweight is determined by the number of fat cells you were born with or developed early in life.

   b. Being overweight depends on what and how much food you eat.

6. a. People who exercise regularly set up their schedules to do so.

   b. Some people just don't have the time for regular exercise.

7. a. Winning at poker depends on betting correctly.

   b. Winning at poker is a matter of being lucky.

8. a. Staying married depends on working at the marriage.

   b. Marital breakup is a matter of being unlucky in choosing the wrong marriage partner.

9. a. Citizens can have some influence on their governments.

   b. There is nothing a citizen can do to affect governmental function.

10. a. Being skilled at sports depends on being born well coordinated.

    b. Those skilled at sports work hard learning the skills.

11. a. People with close friends are lucky to have met people with whom to be intimate.

    b. Developing close friendships takes hard work.

12. a. Your future depends on whom you meet and on chance.

    b. Your future is up to you.

13. a. Most people are so sure of their opinions that their minds cannot be changed.

    b. A logical argument can convince most people.

14. a. People decide the direction of their lives.

    b. For the most part, we have little control over our futures.

15. a. People who do not like you just do not understand you.

    b. You can be liked by anyone you choose to like you.

16. a. You can make your life a happy one.

    b. Happiness is a matter of fate.

17. a. You evaluate feedback and make decisions based on it.

    b. You tend to be easily influenced by others.

18. a. If voters studied nominee's records, they could elect honest politicians.

    b. Politics and politicians are corrupt by nature.

19. a. Parents, teachers, and bosses have a great deal to say about your happiness and self-satisfaction.

    b. Whether you are happy depends on you.

20. a. Air pollution can be controlled if citizens get angry about it.

    b. Air pollution is an inevitable result of technological progress.

To determine your locus of control, give yourself one point for each listed response:

ITEM	RESPONSE	ITEM	RESPONSE	ITEM	RESPONSE
1	a	8	a	15	b
2	a	9	a	16	a
3	b	10	b	17	a
4	b	11	b	18	a
5	b	12	b	19	b
6	a	13	b	20	a
7	a	14	a		

Scores of 10 or above indicate you believe you are generally in control of events that affect your life, an internal locus of control. Scores below 10 indicate you believe you generally do not have control of events that affect your life, an external locus of control.

Lab Activity 3.2

Alienation Assessment

INSTRUCTIONS: *For each statement, place a letter in the blank space provided:*

A = strongly agree   D = disagree
B = agree   E = strongly disagree
C = uncertain

_____ 1. Sometimes I feel all alone in the world.

_____ 2. I do not get invited out by my friends as often as I would like.

_____ 3. Most people today seldom seem lonely.

_____ 4. Real friends are as easy as ever to find.

_____ 5. One can always find friends if one is friendly.

_____ 6. The world in which we live is basically a friendly place.

_____ 7. There are few dependable ties between people anymore.

_____ 8. People are just naturally friendly and helpful.

_____ 9. I do not get to visit friends as often as I would like.

You have just completed a scale measuring a concept called *social isolation,* which is the lack of significant others (friends, relatives, and so forth) in whom to confide. To score this scale, record the number of points indicated for each of your responses:

Question 1:	A = 4	B = 3	C = 2	D = 1	E = 0
Question 2:	A = 4	B = 3	C = 2	D = 1	E = 0
Question 3:	A = 0	B = 1	C = 2	D = 3	E = 4
Question 4:	A = 0	B = 1	C = 2	D = 3	E = 4
Question 5:	A = 0	B = 1	C = 2	D = 3	E = 4
Question 6:	A = 0	B = 1	C = 2	D = 3	E = 4
Question 7:	A = 4	B = 3	C = 2	D = 1	E = 0
Question 8:	A = 0	B = 1	C = 2	D = 3	E = 4
Question 9:	A = 4	B = 3	C = 2	D = 1	E = 0

The average score for male undergraduates is 11.76 and for female undergraduates is 14.85. If you scored below the average, perhaps you should consider physical fitness activities that involve other people. In that way, you will be responding to your need for developing a social network while becoming physically fit.

Source: From "Alienation: Its Meaning and Measurement," by D. G. Dean, 1961, *American Sociological Review* 26, pp. 753–758. Used by permission.

Lab Activity 3.3

Body Self-Esteem Assessment

INSTRUCTIONS: *Using the scale, place the number alongside each body part or body function that represents your feelings about that part of yourself.*

✦ Scale

1. Have strong feelings and wish a change could somehow be made
2. Do not like, but I can put up with
3. Have no particular feelings one way or the other
4. Am satisfied with
5. Would not change, consider myself fortunate

✦ Body Part or Function

_____ hair	_____ appetite	_____ shoulder width
_____ hands	_____ fingers	_____ energy level
_____ nose	_____ waist	_____ shape of head
_____ wrists	_____ ears	_____ body build
_____ back	_____ weight	_____ ankles
_____ chin	_____ profile	_____ height
_____ neck	_____ chest	_____ eyes
_____ arms	_____ lips	_____ skin texture
_____ hips	_____ teeth	_____ forehead
_____ legs	_____ voice	_____ health
_____ feet	_____ posture	_____ face
_____ knees	_____ facial complexion	

✦ Scoring

Now sum up the point values you assigned and divide the sum by 33. Your score should fall between 1 and 5. If your score is below 2.5, you do not hold your body in high esteem. If your score is above 2.5, you do think well of your body. In particular, look at those items you assigned a 1 or a 2. Those are the parts of your body or bodily functions which you think are most in need of improvement. Concentrate on making those parts or functions better and you will think better of your body.

4

Stress Management and Wellness

Chapter Objectives

By the end of this chapter, you should be able to:

1. Define stress, stressor, and stress reactivity.
2. List sources of stress and differentiate between distress and eustress.
3. Describe the bodily changes that occur when a person experiences stress.
4. Manage stress by using coping mechanisms at various levels of the stress response.
5. Use time management techniques to free up time for wellness activities.
6. Detail the role of exercise in the management of stress.

Emilio's wife died last year, and he grieved long and hard for her. He felt that her death was unfair (she was such a kind person), and a sense of helplessness crept over him. Loneliness became part of his days, and tears became the companions of his late evening hours. There were those who were not even surprised at Emilio's own death just one year after his wife's. They officially called it a heart attack, but his friends know he died of a broken heart.

You probably know some Emilio's—people who have died or become ill from severe stress with seemingly little physically wrong with them. That is what stress can do. You will soon learn how stress can actually change your body to make you susceptible to illness and disease or other negative influences. Contrary to what some people might tell you, it is not all in your mind. You will learn how you can prevent these negative consequences from occurring and how exercise plays a role in that process.

𝒮TRESS-RELATED CONCEPTS

Even the experts do not agree on the definition of **stress**. Some define it as the stimulus that causes a physical reaction (such as being afraid to take a test), while others view it as the reaction itself (for example, increases in blood pressure, heart rate, and perspiration). For our purposes in this text, we define stress as a combination of the cause (**stressor**) and the physical reaction (**stress reactivity**). The significance of these definitions is not merely academic. It is important to consider a stressor as having the potential to result in stress reactivity but not necessarily to do so.

A demanding, fast-paced job can cause a great deal of stress if you let it. (Photo courtesy of Cable News Network.)

Common Stressors

There are biological stressors (toxins, heat, cold), sociological stressors (unemployment), philosophical stressors (deciding on a purpose in life), and psychological stressors (threats to self-esteem, depression). Each has the potential to result in a stress reaction.

We all encounter stressors in our daily lives. You may have stressors associated with school (getting good grades, taking exams, or having teachers think well of you); with work (too much to do in a given amount of time, not really understanding what is expected of you, or fear of a company reorganization); with family (still being treated as a child when you are an adult, arguing often, lack of trust); or with your social life (making friends, telephoning for dates). Even scheduling exercise into your already busy day may be a stressor.

Stress Reactivity

When a stressor leads to a stress response, several changes occur in the body. The heart beats faster, muscles tense, breathing becomes rapid and shallow, perspiration appears under the arms and on the forehead, and blood pressure increases. These and other changes prepare the body to respond to the threat (stressor) by either fighting it off or running away. That is why stress reactivity is sometimes called the **fight-or-flight response**. Although many people consider the fight-or-flight response harmful, it is only bad for you if it is inappropriate to fight or run away, that is, when it is inappropriate to do something physical.

For instance, if you are required to present a speech in front of your class, you cannot run from the assignment (you will fail the class if you do so) and you cannot strike out at the professor or your class-

mates. It is in these situations, when you do not or cannot use your body's preparedness to do something physical, that the stress reaction is unhealthy. Your blood pressure remains elevated, more cholesterol roams about your blood, your heart works harder than normal, and your muscles remain tense. That, in turn, can lead to various illnesses, such as coronary heart disease, stroke, hypertension, and headaches. At this point, pay attention to your body, particularly to your muscle tension. If you think you can drop your shoulders, that means your muscles are unnecessarily raising them. If your forearm muscles can be relaxed, you are unnecessarily tensing them. This wasted muscle tension—since you are not about to do anything physical—is the result of stress and can cause tension headaches, backache, or neck and shoulder pain. Lab Activity 4.1: Experiencing Stress Reactivity at the end of this chapter provides you with an activity to identify how your heart reacts to stress.

Stress The combination of a stressor and stress reactivity.

Stressor A stimulus that has the potential to elicit stress reactivity.

Stress reactivity The physical reaction to a stressor that results in increased muscle tension, heart rate, blood pressure, and so forth.

Fight-or-flight response A physiological reaction to a threatening stressor; another name for stress reactivity.

Psychosomatic Illnesses or diseases that are either worsened or develop in the first place because of the body changes resulting from an interpretation of thoughts.

Psychosomatic Disease

When built-up stress products (for example, increased heart rate and blood pressure) are chronic, go unabated, or occur frequently, they can cause illness and disease. These are called **psychosomatic**, from the Greek words *psyche* (the mind) and *soma* (the body). That does not mean these conditions are all in the mind; instead it means that there is a mind-body connection causing the illness. An example is the effect of stress on allergies. Stress results in fewer white blood cells in the immunological system which, in turn, can lead to an allergic reaction (teary eyes, stuffy nose, itchy throat). That is because it is the white blood cells that fight off *allergens* (the substances to which people are allergic); fewer of them will make a person more susceptible to an allergic reaction.

To determine to what degree you experience physical symptoms of stress complete Table 4.1. If your score indicates excessive physical stress symptoms, pay particular attention to the stress management techniques described later in this chapter.

A MODEL OF STRESS

Stress can be better understood by considering the model depicted in Figure 4.1. The model begins with a *life situation* occurring that is *perceived as distressing*. Once it is perceived this way, *emotional arousal* (anxiety, nervousness, anger) occurs that, in turn, results in *physiological arousal* (increased heart rate,

blood pressure, perspiration). That can lead to negative *consequences* such as psychosomatic illness, low grades at school, or arguments with family and friends.

Now let us see how the model operates in a stressful situation. Imagine you are a college senior and that all you need to graduate this semester is to pass a physical fitness class. Imagine further that you fail this class (life situation). You might say to yourself, "This is terrible. I will not be able to start work. I must be a real dummy. What will all my friends and relatives think?" In other words, you view the situation as distressing (perceived as distressing). That can result in fear and insecurity about the future, anger at the physical-fitness instructor, or worry about how friends and family members will react (emotional arousal). These emotions can lead to increased heart rate, muscle tension, and the other components of the stress response (physiological arousal). As a result, you can develop a tension headache or an upset stomach (consequences).

It is as though a road winds its way through the towns of Life Situation, Perceived as Stressful, Emotional Arousal, Physiological Arousal, and Consequences. And that means that, as with any road, a roadblock can be set up that interferes with travel. Remember, a stressor only has the potential to lead to stress. A roadblock can prevent that stressor from proceeding to the next "town." That is the very essence of stress management; that is, setting up roadblocks on the stress model to interfere with travel to the next level.

Using the example of failing a physical-fitness

Exercise is particularly useful as a means of managing stress. (Photo courtesy of the Aspen Hill Club.)

Table 4.1 ✦ Physical Stress Symptoms Scale

Indicate how often each of the following effects happens to you either while you are experiencing stress or after exposure to a significant stressor. Respond to each item with a number between 0 and 5, using the scale that follows:

0 = Never	2 = Every few months	4 = Once or more each week
1 = Once or twice a year	3 = Every few weeks	5 = Daily

Cardiovascular Symptoms

_____ Heart pounding   _____ Heart racing or beating erratically

_____ Cold, sweaty hands   _____ Headaches (throbbing pain)   Subtotal _____

Respiratory Symptoms

_____ Rapid, erratic, or shallow breathing   _____ Shortness of breath

_____ Asthma attack   _____ Difficulty in speaking because of
                                             poor breathing control   Subtotal _____

Gastrointestinal Symptoms

_____ Upset stomach, nausea, or vomiting   _____ Constipation

_____ Diarrhea   _____ Sharp abdominal pains   Subtotal _____

Muscular Symptoms

_____ Headaches (steady pain)   _____ Back or shoulder pains

_____ Muscle tremors or hands shaking _____ Arthritis   Subtotal _____

Skin Symptoms

_____ Acne   _____ Dandruff

_____ Perspiration   _____ Excessive dryness of skin or hair   Subtotal _____

Immunity Symptoms

_____ Allergy flare-up   _____ Common cold

_____ Influenza   _____ Skin rash   Subtotal _____

Metabolic Symptoms

_____ Increased appetite   _____ Increased craving for tobacco or sweets

_____ Thoughts racing or difficulty sleeping   _____ Feelings of anxiety or nervousness   Subtotal _____

Overall Symptomatic Total (add all seven subtotals) _____

What Does Your Score Mean?

0 to 35   Moderate physical stress symptoms
A score in this range indicates a low level of physical stress manifestations, hence minimal overall probability of encounter with psychosomatic disease in the near future.

36 to 75   Average physical stress symptoms
Most people experience physical stress symptoms within this range. It is representative of an increased predisposition to psychosomatic disease but not an immediate threat to physical health.

76 to 140 Excessive physical stress symptoms
If your score falls in this range, you are experiencing a serious number and frequency of stress symptoms. It is a clear indication that you may be headed toward one or more psychosomatic diseases sometime in the future. You should take deliberate action to reduce your level of stress.

Source: From *Investigations in Stress Control* (pp. 101–105), by R. J. Allen and D. Hyde, 1980, Minneapolis: Burgess.

Figure 4.1 ✦ A Model of Stress

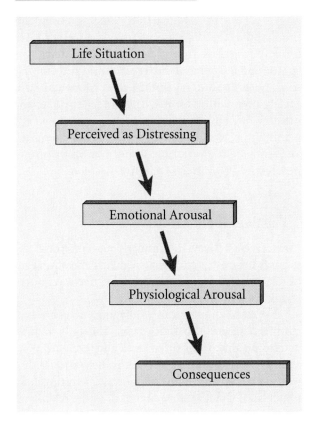

class again, imagine that your reaction was, "It's not good that I failed this course, but I still have my health and people who love me. They'll help me get through this." In this case, the life situation is not perceived as distressing. Consider this change in perception a roadblock preventing emotional arousal. Without emotional arousal, there will be no physiological arousal and no negative consequences. In fact, there might even be positive consequences. Maybe failing the course will result in your studying extra hard the next time with the benefit of learning much more about physical fitness and becoming more fit than you would have been otherwise. In that instance, rather than experience distress you have experienced **eustress**. That is stress that results in personal growth and positive outcomes.

ℰXERCISE'S UNIQUE CONTRIBUTION TO STRESS MANAGEMENT

Exercise is a unique stress-management intervention since it can be plugged in at many levels on the stress model. It is a life situation intervention when you give up stressful habits (for example, cigarette smok-

ing) because they interfere with your exercising. When you make friends through participating in a training program, you may also be using exercise as a life situation intervention since loneliness and social isolation may be remedied.

Exercise can be a perception intervention as well. The brain produces neurotransmitters (endorphins) during exercise, and their euphoric, analgesic effect serves to relax the brain and the rest of the body. That relaxed state helps us perceive stressors as less stressful.

Exercise is also an emotional arousal intervention. During exercise, we focus on what we are doing and away from our problems and stressors. It can therefore be relaxing to engage in physical activity. Furthermore, numerous research studies have found that exercise enhances well-being. It reduces feelings of depression and anxiety while increasing the sense of physical competence. The result is a higher level of self-esteem. And exercise can use up the built-up stress by-products and the body's preparedness to do something physical. Consequently, it can also be a physiological arousal intervention.

It is because of its unique ability to be plugged into all the different levels of the stress model that exercise is particularly useful as a means of managing stress. Be careful, however, to exercise in ways recommended in this book rather than inappropriately. Whereas exercise is an excellent stress-management coping mechanism, if it is done incorrectly, it can result in injury or discomfort. In that case, it will be a stressor rather than a stress reliever. And if exercise in itself is not your cup of tea but you participate anyway because you know it is good for you, you can still make it more pleasant. Exercise with a friend. Listen to music while you are exercising. Engage in physical activity outdoors in a pleasant setting, listening to the birds chirp and the wind rustling through the leaves. These and other accommodations can make your exercise more pleasing and, therefore, make you more likely to maintain your program.

𝓜ANAGING STRESS

To manage stress you need to set up roadblocks at each level of the stress model.

Eustress Stress that results in personal growth or development and, therefore, the person experiencing it is better for having been stressed.

The Life Situation Level

At the life situation level, you can make a list of all your stressors, routine ones that occur regularly and unusual ones that are often unanticipated. Then go through the list trying to eliminate as many of them as you can. For example, if you jog every day but find jogging stressful, try a different aerobic exercise or vary exercises from day to day. If you commute on a crowded highway and often become distressed about the traffic and construction slowdowns, try taking a different route. If you often argue with a friend and the associated stress interferes with your work, see the friend less often or not at all. By habit, you probably tolerate many stressors that can be eliminated, thereby decreasing the stress in your life.

The Perception Level

You can perceive or interpret stressors that cannot be eliminated as less distressing. One way to do that is called **selective awareness**. In every situation there is some good and some bad. Choosing to focus on the good, while not denying the bad, will result in a more satisfying and less distressing life. For example, rather than focusing on the displeasure of standing in line at the checkout counter, you choose to focus on the pleasure of being able to do nothing when your day is usually so hectic.

Consider the story about a female college student who wrote her parents that she was in a hospital after having fallen out of her third-floor dormitory window. Luckily, she landed in some shrubs and was only temporarily paralyzed on her right side (that explained why her handwriting was so unclear). In the hospital, she met a janitor, fell in love with him, and now they are planning to elope. The reason for elop-

ing is that he is of a different religion, culture, and ethnic background and she suspected her family might object to the marriage. She is confident, though, that the marriage will work since her lover learned from his first marriage not to abuse his spouse and the jail term he served reinforced that lesson. She went on to say in the letter, "Mom and Dad, I really am not in a hospital, have not fallen out of any window, and have not met someone with whom I am planning on eloping. However, I did fail chemistry and wanted you to be able to put that in its proper perspective." Now that is selective awareness.

The Emotional Arousal Level

An excellent way to control your emotional responses to stress is to engage regularly in some form of relaxation. Some of the more effective ways of relaxing are described in this section.

No research allows us to diagnose which relaxation technique is best for you. The only way to determine that is to try several and evaluate their ability to make you feel relaxed. To help you do that we have provided a relaxation technique rating scale (Table 4.2). Use it after you try each of the relaxation techniques.

Progressive Relaxation With **progressive relaxation**, you first tense a muscle group for 10 seconds, all the while paying attention to the sensations that are created. Then relax that muscle, paying attention to that sensation. The idea is to learn what muscular tension feels like so you will be more likely to recognize it when you are experiencing it and to be familiar with muscular relaxation so that, when you are tense, you can relax those muscles. It is called *progressive* because you progress from one muscle group to another throughout the body.

Autogenic Training The relaxation technique called **Autogenic training** involves imagining your arms and legs are heavy, warm, and tingly. When you are able to imagine that, you are increasing the blood flow to those areas. This precipitates the relaxation response. After the body is relaxed, think of relaxing images (a day at the beach, a park full of trees and green lawn, a calm lake on a sunny day) to relax the mind.

Body Scanning Even when you are tense, some part of your body is relaxed. It may be your thigh or your chest or your hand. The relaxation technique called **body scanning** requires you to search for a relaxed

---

Selective awareness A means of managing stress by consciously focusing on the positive aspects of a situation or person.

Progressive relaxation A relaxation technique in which you contract, then relax, muscle groups throughout the body.

Autogenic training A relaxation technique in which you imagine your arms and legs are heavy, warm, and tingly.

Body scanning A relaxation technique in which you identify a part of your body that feels relaxed and transport that feeling to another part of your body.

Table 4.2 ✦ The Relaxation Technique Rating Scale

To determine which is most effective for you, try each relaxation technique presented in this chapter and evaluate it by answering these questions, using this scale:

1 = Very true

2 = Somewhat true

3 = I'm not sure

4 = Somewhat untrue

5 = Very untrue

1. It felt good.

2. It was easy to fit into my schedule.

3. It made me feel relaxed.

4. I handled my daily chores better than I usually do.

5. It was an easy technique to learn.

6. I was able to shut out my surroundings while I was practicing this technique.

7. I did not feel tired after practicing this technique.

8. My fingers and toes felt warmer after trying this relaxation technique.

9. Any stress symptoms I had (headache, tense muscles, anxiety) before doing this relaxation technique disappeared by the time I was done.

10. Each time I concluded this technique, my pulse rate was much lower than it was when I began.

Now sum up the values you responded with for a total score. Compare the scores of all the relaxation techniques you try. The lower the score, the more appropriate a particular relaxation technique is for you.

Source: From *Comprehensive Stress Management,* 5th edition (pp. 140–141), by J. S. Greenberg, 1996, Dubuque, IA: Wm. C. Brown.

body part and transport that feeling to the tenser parts of your body. That can be done by imagining the relaxed part as a fiery, hot ball that you roll to the tenser parts of your body. The more you practice this technique, the more effective you will become with it. This is true with all relaxation techniques.

Biofeedback This technique involves the use of an instrument to mirror what is going on in the body and to report the results back to the individual. Biofeedback instrumentation can measure and *feed back* to the person numerous physiological parameters: temperature, blood pressure, heart rate, perspiration, breathing rate, muscle tension, brain waves, and many others. One interesting aspect of biofeedback is that individuals can control these previously thought-to-be involuntary responses once the measure has been reported back to them. The physiological parameters already enumerated in this paragraph can be increased or decreased with biofeedback training. Since the body and the mind are connected, changes in either can effect changes in the other. Consequently, when a person is taught to decrease heart rate and muscle tension, for example, the psychological states of anxiety and nervousness may also be decreased.

Lab Activity 4.2: Measuring the Effects of Meditation teaches meditation, which is another effective relaxation technique. Complete this lab activity at the end of the chapter to determine the effectiveness of meditation for you.

The Physiological Arousal Level

To manage stress once your body is prepared to do something physical requires engaging in some physical activity, which can range from the obvious to the obscure. Running around the block as fast as you can will use the stress by-products and do wonders for your disposition. Dribbling a basketball up and down the court mimicking several fast breaks, serving 30 tennis balls as hard as you can, biking as fast as you can, or

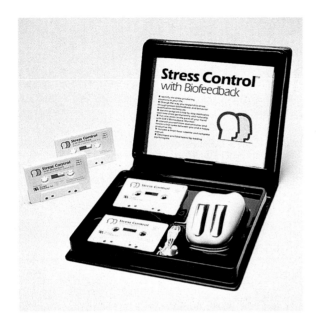

Many companies manufacture biofeedback equipment. This is a galvanic skin response machine that measures perspiration associated with stress. (Photo courtesy of Thought Technology, Ltd.)

swimming several laps at breakneck speed, as well as other tiring exercises, can also relieve stress. Still, you need not engage in formal sports activities to relieve stress at this level on the model. You can simply punch your mattress or pillow as hard and as long as you can. You will not hurt them nor yourself, but you will feel better.

TYPES A AND B BEHAVIOR PATTERNS AND THE EXERCISER

Researchers have discovered a **behavior pattern (Type A)** related to the subsequent development of coronary heart disease. Type A people are aggressive and competitive, never seem to have enough time, do two or more things at once (this is called being *polyphasic*), are impatient, and become angry easily. **Type B behavior pattern** seems to be protective of the development of coronary heart disease. Type B people exhibit no free-floating hostility, always seem to have enough time to get things done and if they do not do so they are not worried, are more cooperative than competitive, and are concerned with quality rather than quantity (it is not how fast they run but whether they enjoy their run).

Recent research has clarified the relationship between Type A and coronary heart disease. It ap-

pears that the hostility is the trait of major concern. People who tend to become angry easily are more apt to develop coronary heart disease than are others.

Our friend Jorge, mentioned in an earlier chapter, characterizes the Type A exerciser. If you remember, on a sunny, windless day, Jorge was playing tennis when he hit one too many backhands that went awry. Losing control, he threw his racket over the fence, over several trees, and into the creek alongside the court. As the racket floated downstream never to be seen again, Jorge was at a loss about what to berate more severely, his tennis skills or his temper. This aggressiveness and hostility are classical characteristics of Type A behavior.

Type A exercisers are aggressive (they may smack their golf clubs into the ground when they hit a shot off target), hostile (they may accuse their opponents of cheating), competitive (losing may be more than they can bear); and they evaluate themselves by numbers (how many matches they won rather than whether they played well or had fun participating). If you see yourself as a Type A, think about a change. Use the behavioral change techniques and strategies presented in chapter 3 to become more Type B. You may be healthier, and you will probably be happier.

TIME MANAGEMENT: FREEING UP TIME FOR WELLNESS

To manage stress, you need to set aside time. To exercise regularly and engage in other health-promoting activities, you also need to set aside time. Since stress can capture your attention, energy, and time, it can interfere with your wellness regimen. After all, stress can be a threat to your physical self or to your self-concept. Who can blame you for postponing or canceling wellness activities such as exercise to manage that threat? This section shows you how to organize your time better so you have plenty of time for exercise, managing stress, and the myriad of other wellness activities you need, and choose, to do.

To be serious about using time-management strategies you need to realize that:

1. Time is one of your most precious possessions.

2. Time spent is gone forever.

3. You cannot save time. Time moves continually and it is used, one way or another. If you waste time, there is no bank where you can withdraw the time you previously saved to replace the time wasted.

Myth and Fact Sheet

Myth	Fact
1. Stressful events of necessity cause stress and a stress reaction.	1. Stressful events only have the potential to cause a stress reaction. They need not do so if they are interpreted as nonstressful.
2. There is really nothing that can be done about stress. It is just a normal part of living.	2. There are many ways to manage stress so it does not make you ill or interfere with the satisfaction you derive from living.
3. Exercise is stressful because of the toll it takes physically.	3. Exercise is an excellent way of managing stress since it responds to every level of the stress model.
4. You should try to eliminate all stress from your life.	4. There is an optimal level of stress that results in joy and stimulation and encourages your best performance. Therefore, you need some stress to make life worth living.

4. To come to terms with your mortality is to realize that your time is limited. None of us will live forever, and none of us will be able to do everything we would like to do.

You can *invest* time to free up (not to save) more time than you originally invested. Then you will have sufficient time to use the stress-management techniques presented in this chapter and plenty of time to participate in a regular wellness program. The techniques we will now describe will help you to do that. As you read the following suggestions for better managing your limited time, try to apply these techniques directly to your situation. Most of these techniques you will want to incorporate into your lifestyle; others you will decide are not worth the effort or the time.

Assessing How You Spend Time

As a first step, analyze how you spend your time now. To do this, divide your day into 15-minute segments as shown in Table 4.3. Record what you are doing every 15 minutes. Review this time diary and total the time spent on each activity throughout the day. For example, you might find you spent 3 hours socializing, 4 hours eating meals, 3 hours watching television, 1 hour doing homework, 2 hours shopping, 2 hours listening to music, 6 hours sleeping, and 3 hours on the telephone as shown on the example in Table 4.4. Evaluate your use of time as shown in Table

4.4, and note in the *adjustment* column that, even though study time is increased by an hour, the other adjustments would free up 6.5 hours a day. That would leave plenty of time to exercise.

A good way to actually make the changes you desire is to draw up a contract with yourself that includes a reward for being successful. Refer to chapter 3 for the most effective way to develop such a contract.

Prioritizing

One important technique for managing time is to prioritize your activities. Not all of them are of equal importance. You need to focus on those activities of major importance to you, and only devote time to other activities after the major ones are completed. One of the major activities for which you should prioritize your time is exercise.

To prioritize your activities, develop A, B, C lists.

Type A behavior pattern A constellation of behaviors that makes individuals susceptible to coronary heart disease.

Type B behavior pattern A combination of behaviors that seem to protect people from contracting coronary heart disease, i.e., lack of hostility, anger, aggression; cooperativeness; focusing on one task at a time.

Table 4.3 ✦ Daily Activity Record

TIME (A.M.)	ACTIVITY	TIME (P.M.)	ACTIVITY
12:00		12:00	
12:15		12:15	
12:30		12:30	
12:45		12:45	
1:00		1:00	
1:15		1:15	
1:30		1:30	
1:45		1:45	
2:00		2:00	
2:15		2:15	
2:30		2:30	
2:45		2:45	
3:00		3:00	
3:15		3:15	
3:30		3:30	
3:45		3:45	
4:00		4:00	
4:15		4:15	
4:30		4:30	
4:45		4:45	
5:00		5:00	
5:15		5:15	
5:30		5:30	
5:45		5:45	
6:00		6:00	
6:15		6:15	
6:30		6:30	
6:45		6:45	
7:00		7:00	
7:15		7:15	

Table 4.3 ✦ Daily Activity Record *(continued)*

Time (A.M.)	Activity	Time (P.M.)	Activity
7:30		7:30	
7:45		7:45	
8:00		8:00	
8:15		8:15	
8:30		8:30	
8:45		8:45	
9:00		9:00	
9:15		9:15	
9:30		9:30	
9:45		9:45	
10:00		10:00	
10:15		10:15	
10:30		10:30	
10:45		10:45	
11:00		11:00	
11:15		11:15	
11:30		11:30	
11:45		11:45	

On the A list (Table 4.5) place those activities that *must* get done, that are so important that not to do them would be very undesirable. For example, if a term paper is due tomorrow and you have not typed it yet, that gets on your A list.

On the B list (Table 4.6) are those activities you would like to do today and need to get done. If they don't get done today, however, it would not be too terrible. For example, if you have not spoken to a close friend and have been meaning to telephone, you might put that on your B list. Your intent is to call today, but if you don't get around to it, you can always call tomorrow or the next day.

On the C list (Table 4.7) are those activities you would like to do if you get all the A- and B-list activities done. If the C-list activities never get done, that is no problem. For example, if a department store has a sale and you would like to go browse, put that on your C list. If you do all of the As and Bs, you can go browse.

In addition, make a list of things not to do. For example, if you tend to waste your time watching television, you might want to include that on your not-to-do list (Table 4.8). In that way, you will have a reminder not to watch television today. Other time wasters should be placed on this list as well.

Other Ways to Free Up Time for Wellness

There are numerous other time-management strategies you can use to make time for wellness activities.

Say No Because of guilt, concern for what others might think, or a real desire to engage in an activity, we often have a hard time saying no. A, B, C lists and

Table 4.4 ✦ Summary of Daily Activities

ACTIVITY NEEDED	TOTAL TIME SPENT ON ACTIVITY	ADJUSTMENT
Socializing	3 hours	1 hour less
Eating meals	4	1 hour less
Watching television	3	1.5 hours less
Doing homework	1	1 hour more
Shopping	2	1 hour less
Listening to music	2	1 hour less
Sleeping	6	None
On telephone	3	2 hours less

prioritizing your activities will help identify how much time remains for other activities and make saying no easier.

Delegate to Others When possible, get others to do things that need to be done but that do not need your personal attention. Conversely, avoid taking on chores that others try to delegate to you. This does not mean that you use other people to do work you should be doing or that you do not help out others when they ask. What it means is that you should be more discriminating regarding delegation of activities. Another way of stating this is not to hesitate to seek help when you are short on time and over-

loaded. Help others when they really need it and when you have the time available to do so.

Give Tasks the Once-Over Many of us will open our mail, read through it, and set it aside to act on it later. This is a waste of time. If we pick it up later, we have to familiarize ourselves with it once again. As much as possible, look things over only once.

Use the Circular File How many times do you receive obvious junk mail and, in spite of knowing what is enclosed in the envelope and that you will eventually throw it all out anyhow, still take the time

Table 4.5 ✦ A. List of Activities for Today

LIST ONLY THOSE ACTIVITIES ON WHICH YOU MUST SPEND TIME TODAY.

1. _____

2. _____

3. _____

4. _____

5. _____

6. _____

7. _____

8. _____

9. _____

10. _____

Table 4.6 ✦ B. List of Activities for Today

LIST THOSE ACTIVITIES ON WHICH YOU WOULD LIKE TO SPEND TIME TODAY BUT THAT COULD WAIT UNTIL TOMORROW.

1. _____
2. _____
3. _____
4. _____
5. _____
6. _____
7. _____
8. _____
9. _____
10. _____

Table 4.7 ✦ C. List of Activities for Today

LIST THOSE ACTIVITIES TO WHICH YOU WILL DEVOTE TIME TODAY ONLY IF AND AFTER YOU HAVE COMPLETED ALL **A** AND **B** ACTIVITIES.

1. _____
2. _____
3. _____
4. _____
5. _____
6. _____
7. _____
8. _____
9. _____
10. _____

to open it and read the junk inside? You would be better off bypassing the opening and reading part, and going directly to the throwing out part. That would free up time for more important activities, such as exercise.

Limit Interruptions Throughout the day you will be interrupted. Recognizing this fact, you should actually schedule times for interruptions. That is, don't make your schedule so tight that interruptions will throw you into a tizzy. On the other hand, try to keep these interruptions to a minimum. There are several ways you can accomplish this. You can accept phone calls only between certain hours. You can also arrange to have someone take messages so you can call back later, or you can use an answering

Table 4.8 ✦ Not-to-Do List of Activities for Today

LIST THOSE ACTIVITIES ON WHICH YOU WILL AVOID SPENDING TIME TODAY.

1. _____
2. _____
3. _____
4. _____
5. _____
6. _____
7. _____
8. _____
9. _____
10. _____

Behavioral Change
∼∽∼ *and Motivational Strategies* ∼∽∼

Many things might interfere with your ability to manage stress. Here are some barriers (roadblocks) and strategies for overcoming them.

Roadblock	Behavioral Change Strategy
You may have a lot to do with little time to get it all done. Term papers are due, midterm or final exams are approaching, you are invited to a party, you are expected to attend a dinner celebrating your sister's birthday, your team is scheduled for an intramural game, and your professor is holding a study session.	When responsibilities are lumped together, they often seem overwhelming. Use the behavioral change strategy of *divide and conquer.* Buy a large calendar, and schedule the semester's activities by writing on the calendar when you will perform them, when you will do library research for term papers, when you will begin studying for exams, and when you will read which chapters in which textbooks. Do not forget to include nonacademic activities as well. For example, write your intramural team's schedule and times of parties or dinners to attend on the calendar. You will soon realize that you have plenty of time. You just need to get organized. That realization will go a long way in relieving unnecessary stress.
You are not accomplishing your fitness objectives and because of that you feel distressed. You are not running as fast as you would like to run, nor are you lifting the amount of weight you would like to lift, doing the number of repetitions you would like to do, losing the amount of weight you would like to lose, or participating in aerobic dance classes.	Use *goal-setting* strategies outlined in chapter 3. Set realistic fitness goals, give yourself enough time to achieve them, and make your workout fun. If you are distressed because your goals seem elusive, perhaps they are. Maybe they are too difficult to achieve or too difficult to achieve in the amount of time you have allotted. If you are injuring yourself regularly, perhaps your fitness program is too difficult or too intense. Use *gradual programming* and *tailoring* to devise a program specific to you and to the level of fitness you presently possess.
You try to relax but you cannot. Your thoughts seem nonstop. Your body becomes fidgety. You are anxious to move on to do something that needs doing. Finding the time to engage in a relaxation technique is impossible. You are just too busy.	Use *material reinforcement* to encourage the regular practice of relaxation. Every time you set aside time to relax, reward yourself with something tangible. You might put aside a certain amount of money or buy a healthy snack. Another behavior change technique that could help is *boasting.* Be proud of taking time to relax and share that feeling of pride with friends. That will make you feel good and more likely to engage in that relaxation technique again. You will also need to assess periodically your relaxation method. Use Table 4.2 to help you perform this assessment. You will find that some relaxation techniques are more effective for you than others, so you will learn which ones to use regularly.
List roadblocks interfering with your ability to manage stress.	Cite behavioral-change strategies that can help you overcome the roadblocks you just listed. If you need to, refer back to chapter 3 for behavioral-change and motivational strategies.
1. _____	1. _____
2. _____	2. _____
3. _____	3. _____

Improving Your Community

Reducing Stress

College students taking a a health course most frequently learn about how to eliminate stressors from their lives and how to manage the stress they cannot completely eliminate. What they don't usually learn, however, is how they can control the stressful effects they themselves may have on other people. Without realizing it, you too may be a stressor to many of the people in your life. Perhaps you are causing another student to sleep less soundly by leaving your stereo on late at night. Maybe you compete too aggressively on an intramural volleyball team that was established more for fun and exercise than for competition. It's possible that you are pressuring someone you are dating to have sex with you. Whatever the situation, you should be aware that the stress you make for these people is just as likely to make them ill as any other form of stress.

If you could figure out when and how you create stress for other people, you can adjust your behavior to eliminate much stress. Imagine the effect on our soociety if we all changes our behavior to eliminate much of our stress. Imagine the total effect on our society if we all changed our behavior in such a way as to get rid of the stress we were causing others!

Here's how you can make a start at this:

1. Ask people you interact with on a regular basis to list the ways that you make them feel stressed. You could start with friends, classmates, professors, and family.

2. Next ask these people to rank the ways that you "stress them out" according to severity; that is, which of your behaviors creates the most stress, the next most stress, and so on.

3. Then brainstorm at least three ways you can change your behavior to diminish or eliminate the stress for the first two items in each list.

4. Now choose the behavior change you think would most reduce the stress you create for the people around you. Try these behavior changes. If it works, treat yourself to a small gift! If it doesn't, try the other changes you brainstormed until you find ones that work.

Congratulate yourself for your social consciousness. Your interest in decreasing the stress in society by diminishing the stress you create for other people is to be applauded. ✦

machine. Do the same with visitors. Anyone who visits should be asked to return at a more convenient time, or you can schedule a visit with them for later. If you are serious about making better use of your time, you will adopt some of these means of limiting interruptions.

Recognize the Need to Invest Time The bottom line of time management is that you need to invest time initially in order to free it up later. We often hear people say, "I don't have the time to organize myself the way you suggest. That would put me further in the hole." This is an interesting paradox. If you are so pressed for time that you believe you do not even have sufficient time to get yourself organized, that in itself tells you that you are in need of applying time-management strategies. The investment in time devoted to organizing yourself will pay dividends by allowing you to achieve more of what is really important to you. After all, what is more important than your health and wellness? And what better way is there to achieve health and wellness than freeing up time for regular regular exercise and other health-promoting activities.

SUMMARY

Stress-Related Concepts

Stress can be defined as a combination of the cause (stressor) and the physical reaction (stress reactivity). A stressor has the potential to result in stress reactivity, but does not necessarily do so. Whether it does depends on how the stressor is perceived or interpreted. Stressors can take a variety of forms: biological (toxins, heat, cold), sociological (unemployment), philosophical (deciding on a purpose in life), or psychological (threats to self-esteem or depression).

When a stressor leads to a stress response, several changes occur in the body. The heart beats faster, muscles tense, breathing becomes rapid and shallow, perspiration appears under the arms and on the forehead, and blood pressure increases. These and other changes make up the fight-or-flight response.

When built-up stress products (for example, increased heart rate and blood pressure) are chronic, go unabated, or occur frequently, they can cause illness and disease. These psychosomatic conditions consist of a mind-body interaction that causes the illness or makes an existing disease worse.

A Model of Stress

A model to better understand stress and its effects begins with a life situation occurring that is perceived as distressing. Once the situation is perceived this way, emotional arousal occurs (anxiety, nervousness, anger), which in turn results in physiological arousal (increased heart rate, blood pressure, muscle tension, perspiration). This can lead to negative consequences such as psychosomatic illness, low grades at school, or arguments with family and friends. The essence of stress management is to set up roadblocks on the stress model to interfere with travel to the next level.

The goal, however, is not to eliminate all stress. Certainly, some stress (distress) is harmful. On the other hand, some stress is useful since it encourages peak performance, or eustress.

Exercise's Unique Contribution to Stress Management

Exercise is a unique stress-management intervention since it can be plugged in at many levels on the stress model. It is a life situation intervention when you give up stressful habits because they interfere with exercising. It is a perception intervention when

your brain produces neurotransmitters during exercise that make you feel relaxed. It is an emotional arousal intervention when you focus on the physical activity and ignore problems and stressors. And it is a physiological arousal intervention when you use the built-up stress by-products by doing something physical.

Managing Stress

Managing stress involves interventions at each of the levels of the stress model. At the life situation level, you can assess routine stressors and eliminate them. At the perception level, you can use selective awareness. At the emotional arousal level, you can do progressive relaxation, autogenic training, body scanning, biofeedback training, and meditation, and at the physiological level, you can exercise regularly.

Types A and B Behavior Patterns and the Exerciser

People who are aggressive, competitive, never seem to have enough time, do two or more things at once, are impatient, and become angered easily exhibit Type A behavior patterns. Type As are prone to coronary heart disease, with the most harmful characteristic being free-floating hostility. Type B people, who exhibit no free-floating hostility, always seem to have enough time to get things done, are more cooperative than competitive, and are concerned with quality rather than quantity, seem to be protected from developing coronary heart disease.

Time Management: Freeing Up Time to Exercise

Time cannot be saved, but you can free up time by being more organized. Some effective time-management strategies include assessing how you spend time so you can make sensible adjustments, prioritizing your activities, learning to say no so you do not take on too many responsibilities, delegating tasks to others, looking things over only once, avoiding spending time on junk mail, and limiting interruptions. Time invested in applying time-management strategies will pay off in terms of freeing up time for such important activities as regular exercise.

Lab Activity 4.1

Experiencing Stress Reactivity

INSTRUCTIONS: *While seated in a comfortable position, determine how fast your heart beats at rest using one of these methods. (Use a watch that has a second hand.)*

1. Place the first two fingers (pointer and middle finger) of one hand on the underside of your other wrist, on the thumb side. Feel for your pulse and count the number of pulses for 30 seconds.

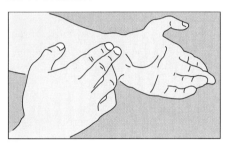

2. Place the first two fingers of one hand on your lower neck, just above the collar bone; move your fingers toward your shoulder until you find your pulse. Count the pulse for 30 seconds.

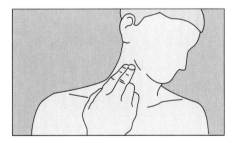

3. Place the first two fingers of one hand in front of your ear; move your fingers until you find a pulse. Count the pulse for 30 seconds.

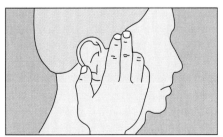

Multiply your 30-second pulse count by two to determine how many times your heart beats each minute while you are at rest. Now close your eyes and think of either someone you really dislike or some situation you experienced that really frightened you. If you are recalling a person, think of how that person looks and smells and what he or she does to incur your dislike. Really feel the dislike, do not just think about it. If you recall a frightening situation, try to place yourself back in that situation. Sense the fright, be scared, vividly recall the situation in all its detail. Think of the person or situation for one minute and then count your pulse rate for 30 seconds, as you did earlier. Multiply the rate by two and compare your first total with the second.

Most people find that their heart rates increase when they are experiencing stressful memories. This increase occurs despite a lack of any physical activity; the very thoughts increase heart rate. This demonstrates two things: the nature of stressors and the nature of stress reactivity.

Source: From *Comprehensive Stress Management,* 5th ed. (p. 10), by J. S. Greenberg, 1996, Dubuque, IA: Wm. C. Brown.

Lab Activity 4.2

Measuring the Effects of Meditation

INSTRUCTIONS: *Learning how to meditate is easy. Just close your eyes and repeat the word* calm *or* one *or some other relaxing word in your mind every time you exhale. Make sure not to eat anything or ingest a stimulant beforehand. Stimulants such as caffeine or nicotine will interfere with your ability to relax. Do this for 20 minutes but recognize that no one can stay focused on a word for that long. As soon as you realize your mind has wandered, just return to repeating the relaxing word as you did before.*

To measure whether meditation has a relaxing effect on you, follow these instructions:

1. Using one of the techniques presented in Lab Activity 4.1: Experiencing Stress Reactivity, determine your resting pulse rate per minute. Place that number in the space below marked "Pulse Rate before Meditating."

2. After determining how fast your heart beats at rest, meditate for 20 minutes. Be sure not to set an alarm clock since it will speed up your heart rate when it goes off. Merely look at your watch when you think 20 minutes has passed.

3. After meditating, determine your pulse rate per minute again. Place that number in the space marked "Pulse Rate after Meditating."

Pulse Rate before Meditating _____

Pulse Rate after Meditating _____

Difference in Pulse Rate _____

Most people find their heart rate decreases after meditating (or engaging in any other relaxation technique). That finding should not be unexpected since we know that one of the effects of relaxation is to slow down the heart.

Lab Activity 4.3

College Schedule of Recent Experience

One theory of stress considers it a consequence of the need to adapt to various life events. The more significant life events one experiences, the more stress, and the more stress, the more likelihood there is of stress-related illnesses developing. The scale below measures the amount and degree of significant life events you have experienced recently and your chances of developing a stress-related illness as a result.

INSTRUCTIONS: *On the answer sheet following this list, write in the number of times during the past 12 months you have experienced each of the following life events.*

1. Entered college.

2. Married.

3. Had either a lot more or a lot less trouble with your boss.

4. Held a job while attending school.

5. Experienced the death of a spouse.

6. Experienced a major change in sleeping habits (sleeping a lot more or a lot less or a change in part of the day when asleep).

7. Experienced the death of a close family member.

8. Experienced a major change in eating habits (a lot more or a lot less food intake or very different meal hours or surroundings).

9. Made a change in or choice of a major field or study.

10. Had a revision of your personal habits (friends, dress, manners, associations).

11. Experienced the death of a close friend.

12. Have been found guilty of minor violations of the law (traffic tickets, jaywalking, etc.)

13. Had an outstanding personal achievement.

14. Experienced pregnancy or fathered a pregnancy.

15. Had a major change in the health or behavior of a family member.

16. Had sexual difficulties.

17. Had trouble with in-laws.

18. Had a major change in the number of family get-togethers (a lot more or a lot less).

19. Had a major change in financial state (a lot worse off or a lot better off than usual).

20. Gained a new family member (through birth, adoption, older person moving in, etc.)

21. Changed your residence or living conditions.

22. Had a major conflict in or change in values.

23. Had a major change in church activities (a lot more or a lot less than usual).

24. Had a marital reconciliation with your mate.

25. Were fired from work.

26. Were divorced.

27. Changed to a different line of work.

28. Had a major change in the number of arguments with spouse (either a lot more or a lot less than usual.

29. Had a major change in responsibilities at work (promotion, demotion, lateral transfer).

30. Had your spouse begin or cease work outside the home.

32. Had a marital separation from your mate.

32. Had a major change in usual type and/or amount of recreation.

33. Had a major change in the use of drugs (a lot more or a lot less).

34. Took a mortgage or loan *less* than $10,000 (such as purchase of a car, TV, school loan, etc.)

35. Had a major personal injury or illness.

36. Had a major change in the use of alcohol (a lot more or a lot less).

37. Had a major change in social activities.

38. Had a major change in the amount of participation in school activities.

39. Had a major change in the amount of independence and responsibility (for example: for budgeting time).

Lab Activity 4.3 *(continued)*
College Schedule of Recent Experience

40. Took a trip or a vacation.

41. Were engaged to be married.

42. Changed to a new school.

43. Changed dating habits.

44. Had trouble with school administration (instructors, advisors, class scheduling, etc.).

45. Broke or had broken a marital engagement or a steady relationship.

46. Had a major change in self-concept or self-awareness.

✦ College Schedule of Recent Experience

Answer and Scoring Sheet

First, for the number corresponding to each of the life events listed on the previous pages, indicate the number of times (1, 2, 3, etc.) that the particular event has occurred in your life during the past 12 months then multiply each item by the indicated weight and total the scores.

1. _____ x 50 = _____   **13.** _____ x 40 = _____

2. _____ x 77 = _____   **14.** _____ x 68 = _____

3. _____ x 38 = _____   **15.** _____ x 56 = _____

4. _____ x 43 = _____   **16.** _____ x 58 = _____

5. _____ x 87 = _____   **17.** _____ x 42 = _____

6. _____ x 34 = _____   **18.** _____ x 26 = _____

7. _____ x 77 = _____   **19.** _____ x 53 = _____

8. _____ x 30 = _____   **20.** _____ x 50 = _____

9. _____ x 41 = _____   **21.** _____ x 42 = _____

10. _____ x 45 = _____   **22.** _____ x 50 = _____

11. _____ x 68 = _____   **23.** _____ x 36 = _____

23. _____ x 36 = _____   35. _____ x 65 = _____

24. _____ x 58 = _____   36. _____ x 46 = _____

25. _____ x 62 = _____   37. _____ x 43 = _____

26. _____ x 76 = _____   38. _____ x 38 = _____

27. _____ x 50 = _____   39. _____ x 49 = _____

28. _____ x 50 = _____   40. _____ x 33 = _____

29. _____ x 47 = _____   41. _____ x 54 = _____

30. _____ x 41 = _____   42. _____ x 50 = _____

31. _____ x 74 = _____   43. _____ x 41 = _____

32. _____ x 37 = _____   44. _____ x 44 = _____

33. _____ x 52 = _____   45. _____ x 60 = _____

34. _____ x 52 = _____   46. _____ x 57 = _____

Subtotal = _____   Subtotal = _____

Total Life Change Score = _____

◆ Interpretation

Classify the number of life events you experienced in the past 12 months into one of the following categories:

Category	Score
Mild	0–499
Moderate	500–999
Excessive	1,000 or above

Research findings indicate that those who experience only mild life changes have approximately a 30 percent chance of becoming ill as a result of the stress associated with those life events, whereas those who experience moderate life changes have a greater chance of becoming ill. And those who experience excessive life changes have the greatest chance of developing significant health problems as a result. The higher the score—that is, the more life changes and the accompanying stress associated with them—the greater the likelihood of developing an illness as a result.

Lab Activity 4.3 *(continued)*
College Schedule of Recent Experience

✦ Analysis

Answer the following questions to understand the effects of the stress you experienced from life changes and what you can do to prevent this stress from resulting in illness.

1. Based on your scores on the College Schedule of Recent Experience, what can you conclude about the likelihood of the recent life changes you have experienced placing you at risk for health problems?

2. Can the life changes you experienced be grouped into categories; for example, school-related, family-related, or social?

3. Some stress researchers believe that the hassles you experience daily—albeit minor in nature—have an even greater effect on your health than do major life changes. What hassles do you encounter routinely? What can you do to eliminate some of these hassles?

4. To eliminate all stressful events would make life boring and routine, thereby stressful. However, to encounter too much stress can be unhealthy. Judge the amount of stress you experience from life changes. Is it too much? Is it too little? Is it just right? What adjustments do you need to make in the level of stress you experience from changes in your life?

5

HOW CHEMICALS AFFECT WELLNESS

Chapter Objectives

By the end of this chapter, you should be able to:

1. Differentiate between drug use, misuse, and abuse and give examples of each.

2. Describe the prevalence of alcohol on college campuses and make suggestions for drinking responsibly.

3. Cite methods used by colleges to control alcohol on their campuses.

4. Describe the prevalence of tobacco use and its effects on the body.

5. Describe strategies to quit smoking and/or to make smoking less harmful.

6. List drugs used to enhance athletic performance and discuss their safety and effectiveness.

THE THOMAS AND the Lopez families both experienced a very difficult year. Glenn Thomas was diagnosed with angina (pain in the chest due to constricted coronary arteries) and started taking nitroglycerin pills periodically. His wife, Barbara, contracted a sinus infection in February and was prescribed antibiotics. In May her gynecologist recommended she begin regular doses of estrogen to replace her body's decreased production of estrogen caused by menopause. Their son, Clark, was diagnosed with attention deficit disorder, and his pediatrician put him on the drug Ritalin.

The Lopezes were no more fortunate. Felipe decided that he needed assistance to stop smoking and was encouraged by his doctor to wear a nicotine patch. Flore Lopez was diagnosed with high blood pressure and instructed to take hypertension medication daily. And Melinda, the Lopez's teenage daughter, was found to be anemic and began taking an iron supplement each day.

More than ever before, drugs—prescription and nonprescription—are available to treat medical and psychological conditions, thereby improving the quality of our lives. Without these drugs, the Thomases and the Lopezes would not feel as well each day and would probably either live shorter lives or have their activities limited.

You, too, are a drug user; we all are. In fact, America is a drug-taking society. And, in many respects, it is fortunate that we are. Think about the important drugs we use:

1. Vaccines that provide protection from diseases that can wipe out whole societies.

2. Antibiotics that control previously fatal bacterial diseases.

3. Oral contraceptives that help some people plan families and that have a profound, though controversial, effect on our society.

4. Tranquilizers that allow people with mental illness to function.

For all the good that has come from drugs, many people believe that U.S. society has become too reliant on medication and mood-altering substances. Too often the remedy for anxiety is a tranquilizer, the response to a headache is an aspirin or some other painkiller, the answer to a problem is alcohol, and social occasions are more stimulating with cocaine.

DRUG USE, MISUSE, AND ABUSE

You will soon see that differentiating between drug use, misuse, and abuse is not as easy as it at first appears. Start this section by listing the last ten times you can remember taking a drug.

Drug Use

Your list probably includes an occasion when you were ill and took either a drug prescribed by your physician or one available over the counter. Perhaps you had a strained muscle from exercising and took aspirin or ibuprofen to control the inflammation and pain. If you used this drug properly, it probably

> **Drug use** The proper use of a drug.
>
> **Drug misuse** The inappropriate use of a legal drug.
>
> **Drug abuse** The use of an illegal drug or the use of a legal drug for purposes other than those it was intended for.
>
> **Cirrhosis** A scarring of cells of the liver that is associated with the excessive use of alcohol.

helped you overcome your illness. In fact, this drug might have been so important to your health that if you had not used it, you may have gotten even more ill. For example, if you contract pneumonia and do not take the antibiotic prescribed for you, you might die. This is **drug use**; that is, when drugs are used as they are recommended to be used and for the purposes for which they were recommended.

Drug Misuse

Unfortunately, some people ruin a good thing. They take too many aspirin tablets in too short a period of time, or ingest ibuprofen without drinking enough fluids. The result could be intestinal problems such as bleeding stomach caused by damage to stomach tissue. When a legal drug is used inappropriately, it is **drug misuse**.

Drug Abuse

When an illegal drug is used or when a legal drug is used for purposes other than for what it was intended, that is **drug abuse**. Typical drugs of abuse include marijuana, cocaine, heroin, anabolic steroids, and amphetamines. These drugs are often taken for the euphoria they produce rather than for any medical or physiological reason. Legal drugs that are sometimes abused include Demerol (meperidine), Dilaudid (hydromorphine), and Darvon (propoxyphene). These drugs are prescription pain relievers that are sometimes sold illicitly for their narcotic effects.

Drugs That Are Difficult to Categorize

Although the differentiation between drug use, misuse, and abuse may at first appear clear, a number of drugs and drug usages are difficult to categorize. For example, how would you classify the use of tobacco products? They are legal but cause the body harm. What about the use of alcoholic beverages? In this case, the amount of drug used (the dosage) might dictate its categorization. And in which category would you place the use of over-the-counter diet remedies? They, too, can be taken in excessive amounts or in place of changes in eating and exercise habits.

Space dictates that we limit our discussion of drugs and fitness, and the effects of drugs on health and wellness. Consequently, we have chosen to discuss only the more prevalent drugs or those with direct application to physical fitness.

ALCOHOL

Studies indicate that 64 percent of young adults aged 18 to 25 are current consumers of alcohol, and in general almost half of men (46 percent) and a quarter of women (25 percent) are heavy drinkers who average four or more drinks daily. Drinking starts even earlier. Thirty-one percent of high school seniors report that most or all of their friends get drunk at least once a week. This situation is probably not dissimilar to what occurs on college campuses throughout the United States (see Table 5.1). Alcohol is the drug of choice on college campuses and leads to too many accidents, fights, suspensions and expulsions from school, injuries, and even death. All of this occurs in spite of the legal drinking age in many states having been returned to 21 in recent years.

People drink for many reasons: to relax, to be sociable, to have something to do with their hands during social occasions, and to decrease inhibitions and become less shy. When drinking is limited, alcohol-related problems usually do not occur. When too much alcohol is ingested in too short a period of time, is taken with other drugs or medications, or is combined with events requiring coordination and speedy reflexes (such as driving an automobile), serious consequences can result.

Alcohol's Effects

Alcohol affects the body in many different ways. It results in blood vessels in the head dilating, which can lead to headaches. It also increases heart rate and blood pressure while constricting (narrowing) the blood vessels supplying the heart. And when the liver is subjected to excessive doses of alcohol over a period of time, it too can be damaged. **Cirrhosis** of the liver is a condition to which alcoholics are prone; it is irreversible and sometimes leads to death. Malnutrition, cancer (of the liver, esophagus, nasopharynx, and lar-

---

Table 5.1 ✦ Facts and Figures on College Students and Alcohol

The U.S. Department of Health and Human Services reports these statistics pertaining to college students and alcohol:

- Of the current student body in the United States, between 2 and 3 percent will eventually die from alcohol-related causes, about the same number that will get advanced degrees, masters and doctorate degrees combined.

- For the over 12 million college students in the United States, the annual consumption of alcoholic beverages totals well over 430 million gallons. To visualize this, imagine an Olympic-sized swimming pool filled with beer, wine, and distilled spirits. In a single year, the student body of each college in the country drinks the equivalent of one pool.

- Over half of all college students participate in drinking games that involve the consumption of extremely high quantities of alcohol. The average amount consumed in these games is between 6 and 10 drinks in a short period of time.

- Approximately 35 percent of all college newspaper advertising revenue comes from alcohol advertisements.

- Fraternity members drink more frequently and more heavily than other college students.

- Depending on the particular study, between 53 and 84 percent of college students get drunk at least once a year. Between 26 and 48 percent get drunk once a month.

- College administrators believe alcohol is a factor in 34 percent of all academic problems and in 25 percent of dropouts.

- Almost half of college athletes who drink admit that their use of alcohol has had a harmful or slightly harmful effect on their athletic performance.

Source: From *Prevention Resource Guide: College Youth*, U.S. Department of Health and Human Services, 1991, Washington, DC: DHHS Publication No. (ADM) 91-1803.

ynx), endocrine and reproductive problems, neurological disorders, and mental illness are but a few other potential effects of the abuse of alcohol.

How to Take Control of Your Drinking

As you can see in Table 5.2, alcohol can significantly impair your physical functioning. To be physically fit, be healthy, and possess a high level of wellness all require either abstaining from ingesting alcohol or drinking responsibly. That means limiting the amount of alcohol ingested to no more than one drink containing no more than 0.6 fluid ounces of alcohol per hour (the amount your liver can metabolize in an hour), drinking only when it is appropriate and never when you are driving, and refraining from drinking when you need good judgment.

And yet, saying no to alcohol is often easier said than done. Imagine that your friends drink alcohol every time you socialize. Either they go to a bar near campus, bring in beer and sit around and drink, or attend a party where alcohol is available. If you do not drink, they will think you are strange. You fear they might not want anything more to do with you. What can you do?

You can adopt any of the following strategies:

1. Take one drink and nurse it for a long time to limit the amount of alcohol you ingest.

2. Tell your friends you are taking medication that prohibits you from drinking.

3. Invite someone else to join you who also does

Although it is a social custom for friends to share a drink together, too much alcohol can lead to dependence and a range of illnesses. (Photo courtesy of the National Cancer Institute.)

not want to drink. With company it will be easier to withstand peer group pressure.

4. Practice refusal skills in which you assertively tell your friends that you prefer not to drink.

Table 5.2 ✦ Effects of Blood-Alcohol Level (BAL) on Functioning

BAL	EFFECTS
Less than .03	Reflexes, sensory function generally intact, but subtle changes can be detected with sensitive tests.
.03–.05	Greater impairment of judgment, reflexes, and coordination; alterations of sensory perception; changes are enough to alter driving skills but not enough to be illegal in the United States; occurs after consuming the equivalent of 2 oz of 86-proof spirits, 8 oz of wine, or two 12-oz beers.
.05–.15	Judgment, reflexes, and coordination usually impaired measurably; blood levels above .1 are sufficient for a charge of legally impaired driving; the equivalent of 6 oz of 86-proof spirits, drunk quickly, is enough to produce a blood level of .15.
.15–.40	Moderate to severe intoxication with deteriorating judgment, reflexes, and coordination; aggressive behavior often develops, followed by progression to lethargy, sedation.
.40–.60	Severe intoxication; individual usually sleeps and arousal is difficult; blood levels of approximately .5 or more are liable to produce coma and death.

Source: From *The Nurse, Pharmacology, and Drug Therapy,* 2nd ed., by Marshal Shlafer, 1993. Copyright 1993 by Addison-Wesley Publishing Company. Reprinted by permission.

Improving Your Community

Insisting on the Responsible Use of Alcohol

Many experts consider alcohol to be the most problematic drug in our society. It certainly is the most pervasive and might be described as epidemic on college campuses. However, there are things you can do to improve the health of your immediate environment and the wider society in which you live as it relates to alcohol. For example:

1. Support alcohol-free parties and gatherings on your campus. Suggest several nonalcoholic beverages that could be served instead of beer, wine, or hard liquor. If some alcoholic beverages are nevertheless going to be served, suggest snacks that aren't salty and, therefore, don't increase thirst.

2. Whenever going out with friends to a place where alcohol is served, insist that the person driving not drink. If no one else volunteers to be the designated driver, you assume the role.

3. During discussions by politicians about budget matters—local, state, or national—advocate that revenue be raised by increasing taxes ("sin taxes") on alcohol. That will have the effect of both discouraging the excessive use of alcohol and of placing the responsibility for funding the health care system on a segment of the population that can be expected to use it more often.

4. Encourage campus administrators to meet with local bar owners to educate them about their responsibilty for actions by students who become inebriated in their bars. Request that bar owners and bartenders refuse to serve alcohol to someone who has obviously had too much to drink.

5. Educate any pregnant relatives or friends about the potential effects of alcohol consumption on the health of the fetus.

6. Support politicians who advocate sufficient funding for alcohol treatment and alcoholism prevention programs. ✦

Do so without turning them off by not being judgmental. For example, you might say, "You can drink if you like but I would prefer not to." You might have to say this several times for your friends to believe you mean it, but once they do, they will usually accept your decision.

If you do decide to drink, follow these guidelines:

1. Drink in moderation.

2. Never drink on an empty stomach. Food in your stomach will slow down the absorption of the alcohol.

3. Never drink when you are taking medication.

4. Never ingest alcohol in combination with other drugs.

5. Drink slowly.

6. Dilute your drinks with water or a mixer.

7. Do not drink and eat salty or spicy foods at the same time. The salts and spices will make you thirsty, and you will drink more.

Too many people have a problem with alcohol. To determine whether you have a problem with alcohol, complete Lab Activity 5.1: Signs of Alcoholism at the end of this chapter.

Alcohol on College Campuses

A number of strategies have been developed in response to the problems created by alcohol on college campuses. These include, but are not limited to, the following:

1. Some universities have offered dry bars. That is, bars that only serve nonalcoholic beverages. Then students can gather and meet as they do at alcoholic bars but with neither the pressure nor the opportunity to ingest alcohol. An example is the University of Maryland's Dry Dock.

2. Some universities have offered hangover-free Friday mornings that include music and dancing.

3. A national organization has formed to educate students about how to drink responsibly, how to help friends who have been drinking from experiencing problems (such as driving

drunk), and how to control their own drinking. This organization, funded by the alcohol industry, is called BACCHUS (Boost Alcohol Consciousness Concerning the Health of University Students) and is now present on many campuses across the United States.

4. College theater groups have presented skits educating students regarding responsible use of alcohol. An example is Wellesley College's Alcohol Information Theater (Project WAIT).

5. Sporting and other events on campuses that once boasted of having kegs of beer are refraining from the alcohol connection. An example is George Washington University where they used to have a "Miller's Rocks the Block" party with free beer, T-shirts, and hats distributed. Now, although the beer distributors are still present on the George Washington campus, they no longer provide beer; instead, they sponsor a superdance for muscular dystrophy.

6. On some campuses, college administrators have prohibited beer kegs at parties and require that food and soft drinks be served where beer is available. Such a policy was begun at Roanoke College in Virginia.

Table 5.3 ✦ Alcohol-Related Groups, Organizations, and Programs for College Students

Al-ANON Family Groups, Inc. World Service Office P.O. Box 862, Midtown Station New York, NY 10159 212-254-7230 1-800-344-2666	**Center for Science in the Public Interest** 1875 Connecticut Avenue, NW, #300 Washington, DC 20009 202-332-9110	**The Marin Institute for the Prevention of Alcohol and Other Drug Problems** 24 Belvedere Street San Rafael, CA 94901 415-456-5692
Alcohol Policies Project Center for Science in the Public Interest 1875 Connecticut Avenue, NW, #300 Washington, DC 20009 202-332-9110	**The Coalition of (Campus) Drug and Alcohol Educators** 250 Arapahoe, Suite 301 Boulder, CO 80302 303-443-5696	**National Interfraternity Conference** 3901 West 86th Street Suite 390 Indianapolis, IN 46268 317-872-1112
Alcoholics Anonymous (AA) World Service, Inc. 468 Park Avenue, South New York, NY 10016 212-686-1100	**Commission on Alcohol and Other Drugs of the American College Personnel Association** Central Michigan University Mt. Pleasant, MI 48859 517-774-3381	**National Organization of Student Assistance Programs and Professionals (NOSAPP)** 250 Arapahoe, Suite 301 Boulder, CO 80302 800-972-4636
American College Health Association 15879 Crabbs Branch Way Rockville, MD 20855 301-963-1100	**Health Promotion Resources** 509 University Avenue St. Paul, MN 55103 1-800-782-1878	**Network of Colleges and Universities Committed to the Elimination of Drug and Alcohol Abuse** Office of Educational Research and Improvement U.S. Department of Education 555 New Jersey Avenue, SW Washington, DC 20208-5644 202-357-6265
American College Personnel Association Central Michigan University Mt. Pleasant, MI 48859 517-774-3381	**Integrated Substance Abuse Consultants (INSAC)** P.O. Box 7505 Arlington, VA 22205 703-237-3840	
American Council on Education One Dupont Circle Washington, DC 20036 202-466-5030	**Nar Anon Hotline** 800-780-3951 **National Association of Student Personnel Administrators** One Dupont Circle, Suite 330 Washington, DC 20036 202-293-9161	**Peterson's Drug and Alcohol Programs and Policies** Dept. 9377 P.O. Box 2123 Princeton, NJ 08543 800-338-3282
Campuses Without Drugs, Inc. National Office 2530 Holly Drive Pittsburgh, PA 15235 412-731-8019		

7. Universities such as William and Mary College, the University of Virginia, James Madison University, and Louisiana State University have instituted dry fraternity and sorority rushes.

8. At the University of Maryland, campus-area alcohol retailers have begun a program entitled SUDS (Students Understanding Drinking Sensibly). They distribute SUDS T-shirts and buttons, train local bartenders, and arrange for local police officers to have breathalyzers available for those drinkers who voluntarily choose to have their blood-alcohol levels tested.

What is your campus doing to respond to both the pressure to drink and the problems resulting from the consumption of alcohol? If you decide to become proactive, you can obtain assistance from the organizations listed in Table 5.3.

𝒯OBACCO

Another too prevalent drug is tobacco and its products. These include cigarettes, cigars, pipes, and chewing tobacco. The U.S. government estimates that tobacco use is responsible for one of every six deaths in the United States and is the most preventable cause of death and disease in our society. Tobacco use is the major risk factor for heart and blood diseases; chronic bronchitis and emphysema; cancers of the lung, larynx, pharynx, oral cavity, esophagus, pancreas, and bladder; and other problems such as respiratory infections and stomach ulcers. Cigarette smoking accounts for approximately 390,000 deaths each year, including 21 percent of coronary disease deaths, 87 percent of lung cancer deaths, and 30 percent of all cancer deaths. Smokers of more than two packs of cigarettes a day are 15 to 25 times more likely to die of lung cancer than people who never smoked.

Smoking Rates

It is estimated that by the late 1990s smoking rates for women will exceed those for men. Presently, 32 percent of men and 27 percent of women aged 20 and older smoke cigarettes. Overall, 29 percent of the people in the United States smoke. Most people start smoking regularly when they are young, before the age of 20. If that same percentage of the 70 million children in the United States start smoking and continue smoking cigarettes as adults, at least 5 million of them will die of smoking-related diseases.

Smokeless Tobacco

Smokeless tobacco includes primarily moist or dry snuff and chewing tobacco. It is used by almost 7 per-

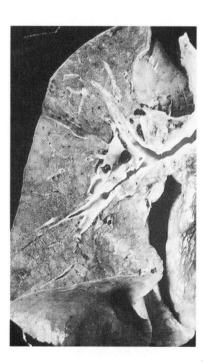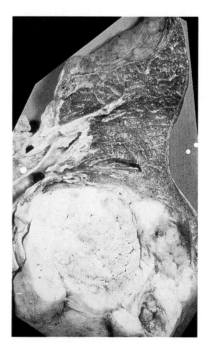

Smoking can cause severe damage to the lung. Photograph A shows a normal lung. Photograph B is a lung with cancer. Photograph C shows a lung with damage to the air sacs, a condition called emphysema.

cent of males aged 12 through 17 and 9 percent of males aged 18 through 24. Smokeless tobacco users are quite susceptible to oral cancer, with long-term snuff users being 50 times more likely to develop oral cancer than nonusers. Adolescent males make up the great majority of new users of smokeless tobacco (only 1 percent of females use it). They may see their favorite athlete (usually a baseball player) chew tobacco and emulate that behavior.

Tobacco's Effects on the Body

Tobacco affects the body in many ways. The nicotine in tobacco stimulates the central nervous system and therefore increases the heart rate. Tobacco use also constricts blood vessels, increases blood pressure, destroys air sacs in the lungs, and increases the production of hydrochloric acid in the stomach. The result is shortness of breath; upset stomach; cold and clammy fingers and toes; the development of heart disease, hypertension, stroke, emphysema, and/or digestive disorders; and lung and other cancers.

Why People Use Tobacco Products

Before reading further, complete Lab Activity 5.2: Why Do You Smoke? at the end of this chapter. If you are not a smoker, complete the lab activity by guessing how most smokers would respond to the statements presented.

The purpose of tobacco advertising is to sell tobacco products. And they do a pretty good job of it as the statistics presented above prove. In our search to be desirable, envied, "cool," and admired we are taught to emulate the people depicted in the tobacco product ads. They are handsome and pretty, they are smiling and obviously happy, and they appear wealthy enough to have fine furniture and expensive clothing.

There are other reasons people use tobacco products. They provide something to do with the hands. Best friends or parents may smoke, so their behavior is copied. It is *antiauthority* (schools and workplaces disallow it and parents often object) and, therefore, "cool" to do. It relieves boredom and is psychologically relaxing for some people, in spite of it being a central nervous system stimulant. It substitutes for food and can be used to control weight.

How to Quit

Researchers have found that the best way to quit smoking is simply to quit. That might sound simplistic, but what usually happens is that smokers try to

Tobacco use contributes to heart disease, high blood pressure, cancer, emphysema, and numerous other illnesses, and is one of the largest causes of disease in the United States. (Photo courtesy of the National Cancer Institute.)

quit when they are not really committed to doing so. Eventually they get to a point when they are well motivated and during that next attempt are successful. That is why it is difficult to cite any one program that is better than another. The key ingredient in any program is the motivation and seriousness of the smoker wishing to quit.

Imagine you smoke cigarettes and cannot seem to quit. They relax you after dinner and give you something to do with your hands during social occasions. You have tried to quit many times without any success. Do not give up. There are strategies you can employ that are effective.

You can write a *contract* using the form in chapter 3 with the goal being to decrease the number of cigarettes you smoke progressively over several weeks until you quit altogether. A friend or relative can witness the contract and check on your progress at predetermined intervals.

You can also use *chaining*. In this case you want to increase the links in the chain leading to smoking. For example, you can take your pack of cigarettes and place it in a sock. Then wrap the sock with masking tape and place it in a locked draw as far away from where you usually smoke as possible (perhaps upstairs if you tend to smoke downstairs). Next, take the key to the drawer and place that in the other sock, wrap it with masking tape, and deposit it in a drawer far away from the drawer in which the pack of cigarettes is located. Now to smoke, you have to go through a bunch of inconveniences. Compare this to just reaching into your pocket or pocketbook and lighting up almost without thinking.

Here are some other suggestions that can help motivated smokers stop smoking or at least lessen the harm they expose themselves to:

- Smoke only one cigarette per hour and eventually taper down.
- Smoke exactly half as many cigarettes each week as you did the week before.
- Inhale less and with less vigor, avoiding deep inhalation.
- Smoke each cigarette only halfway.
- Remove the cigarette from your mouth between puffs.
- Smoke slowly.
- Smoke brands with low tar and nicotine content.
- Place unlighted cigarettes in your mouth when you have the urge to smoke.
- Switch to a brand you dislike.
- Put something else in your mouth when you want a cigarette (for example, chewing gum, fruit, hard candy).
- Exercise regularly so you do not smoke out of boredom.
- Develop the sense of wanting to do well by your body.
- Spend time in places where smoking is prohibited.
- Brush your teeth directly after every meal.
- Alter your behavior pattern. For example, avoid friends who smoke for several weeks after quitting and substitute another activity for smoking after dinner.
- Remind yourself frequently why you quit smoking.
- Use the other behavior change techniques discussed in chapter 3 to quit smoking.

MARIJUANA

Marijuana continues its controversial history of use and abuse in the United States. The use of marijuana as a recreational drug has been trivialized since the 1960s. A renewed interest in its legalization is taking place once again, largely due to claims for its therapeutic benefits, wide margin of safety, somewhat minor potential for abuse, and the inability of law enforcement agencies to eliminate production and

distribution. As a result, marijuana is still viewed as a mild substance and one of the least addicting illicit drugs. Although marijuana use by high school seniors declined rapidly from 1979 to 1992, an upward swing occurred in 1993, suggesting the acceptance of the drug by adolescents. Currently, marijuana is the number one illicit drug of choice in the United States.

Marijuana smoking primarily affects the central nervous system to alter mood, coordination, memory, and self-perception. Use can cause euphoria and paranoia, drowsiness and sedation, and hallucinations. Smoking a few cigarettes daily can also impair pulmonary function. Many 20-year-old smokers of hashish and tobacco have been diagnosed with lung damage comparable to a heavy tobacco smoker over 40 years of age. Marijuana also affects the cardiovascular system, increases the probability of developing a rare form of leukemia in babies whose mothers smoke it, and impairs, and may retard, fetal growth. Although outright physical addiction involving obsessive drug-seeking and drug-taking behavior is rare, psychological dependence involving an attachment to the euphoric effects of the THC content in marijuana is not.

Marijuana has been shown to be effective in treating nausea and vomiting in patients undergoing chemotherapy and stimulating appetite in patients with advance AIDS. Unauthorized use includes treatment to reduce intraocular (eye) pressure, as an antiasthmatic drug, a muscle relaxant, antiseizure, antidepressant, and analgesic drug.

In some states, marijuana is one of the largest cash-producing crops. Although law enforcement agencies appear to be having little effect, many young users and distributors discover too late that the law in their state has not relaxed and still imposes heavy penalties (fines and considerable jail time) for possession and distribution. It may appear that "everyone is doing it" and that "it is safe in the privacy of your home or room," as college students have often said, but the truth is that this recreational drug can ruin your life. It can result in your expulsion from college, heavy fines, and a felony on your record. Complete Lab Activity 5.3: Marijuana Statutes in Your State to become familiar with the specific marijuana laws in your state. Help classmates understand the tremendous risks involved with the use of marijuana.

DRUG-TAKING TO ENHANCE ATHLETIC PERFORMANCE

Athletes are competitive by nature. They try hard to beat someone else at their sport or, competing against themselves, strive to do better than they have ever done before. It stands to reason they would want whatever edge they can get. This desire to perform at their best has led some athletes to a search for drugs that can enhance performance. Among these drugs are anabolic steroids, caffeine, amphetamines, and cocaine.

Anabolic Steroids

So you want to be strong? So you want to run faster than you ever thought you could? Well, forget about all the work of weight training or exercise that makes you perspire. Try steroids. In today's quick-weight-loss, quick-fitness, quick-everything society, why not engage in quick bulking up? As we shall soon see, the answer to that question is no. The use of anabolic steroids is quite dangerous.

Anabolic steroids made the news when Olympic world-record-holder Ben Johnson was disqualified from receiving a gold medal for winning the 100-meter sprint at the 1988 Olympic Games. When he was routinely tested just after the race, Johnson tested positive for a steroid. The death of former professional football player Lyle Alzado of cancer, which was attributed to anabolic steroid use in an attempt to gain strength, also fueled the publicity about these drugs.

Anabolic steroids are derivatives of the male sex hormone testosterone. They are prescribed as treatment for anemia and growth problems and as an aid in recovery from surgery. A black market has developed, however, and steroids are illegally used to increase body weight and muscle mass, gain power, and increase strength.

Steroids can be taken in pill form or injected directly into the bloodstream. It is not unusual for steroid users to take more than one steroid at a time, believing that by doing so the effect will be hastened or enhanced. This is called *stacking.*

Steroid users place themselves at risk for liver cancer, high blood pressure, heart disease, sterility, and increased hostility. In men steroid use can lead to atrophied testicles, prostate cancer, and breast growth. In women it can result in menstrual irregularities, a deepening of the voice, decreased breast size, baldness, and facial hair growth. In both men and women, anabolic steroid use can lead to clogging of the arteries, eating compulsions, and increased aggressiveness.

The American College of Sports Medicine (ACSM) states that anabolic steroid use is contrary to the rules and ethical priciples of athletic competition, and that they deplore its use by athletes. Athletes and non-athletes of all ages are generally aware of the tremendous health risks from information provided by coaches, parents, and magazines. And yet, almost 5 percent of high school seniors, not to mention other students and athletes, use anabolic steroids illegally.

Suppose, in the gym in which you work out, there are many men and women your age who look fantastic. The men are chiseled. Their muscles are round and hard, and they do not have an inch of fat on them—or so it seems. The women are curved to perfection. They have muscles in all the right places and are round where they should be round. Upon inquiring, you learn they take steroid drugs. Without the drugs, you are told, they would not look so good. You would love to look like they do and are tempted to try these drugs. How can you overcome this temptation?

You can always use *selective awareness.* Instead of focusing on how good you could look if you took steroids, concentrate on their potential effect on your liver, your sexual organs (atrophied or shrunken testicles if you are a male and menstrual irregularities if you are a female), and the threat they pose to your life. Imagine you could be the most chiseled corpse ever, without any life to enjoy the perfect body.

You could also use *covert modeling.* After watching someone weight train who looks good and does not take steroids, close your eyes and imagine you are doing just what you observed the other person doing. Smell the smells, hear the noise, see the sights, and so forth. Make it vivid. Refer back to chapter 3 for other ways to take charge of your behavior.

Caffeine

Coffee tea, chocolate, and soft drinks contain **caffeine,** a stimulant drug. Caffeine can activate the brain, thereby decreasing drowsiness and fatigue. It

Lyle Alzado blamed his years of steroid use for his brain cancer, which eventually caused his death. (Photo courtesy of Cable News Network.)

Myth and Fact Sheet

Myth	Fact
1. Beer will not get you as drunk as hard liquor will.	1. It is the alcohol that is responsible for inebriation. You can ingest just as much alcohol from beer as you can from other sources.
2. Drinking alcohol is relaxing.	2. A small amount of alcohol initially acts as a stimulant. Larger amounts depress the central nervous system. The feeling of relaxation, however, is because the brain is deadened. The price paid is that other bodily functions are depressed as well, such as the ability to think well or be coordinated. The result can be accidents or poor decisions that result in injury or ill health.
3. Anabolic steroids is safe if you know what you are doing.	3. Steroid use in any form and any pattern is an unhealthy choice capable of causing serious damage to your body.
4. Being physically fit and possessing a high level of wellness means never using drugs.	4. We all use drugs. We take prescribed antibiotics, we buy over-the-counter cold remedies, and we ingest aspirin or ibuprofen when our muscles ache. The key is to use safe drugs safely, as they were intended to be used.

also increases heart and breathing rates. In addition, caffeine serves as a stimulant for skeletal muscles and enables the body to use fatty acids for energy better. The result is an increase in physical work output. That is why caffeine has been suggested as an aid to physical fitness and athletic activities.

Caffeine consumption as an adjunct to physical activity, however, is not recommended because caffeine can have serious side effects. Depending on the dosage, caffeine can result in irregular heartbeat, hyperactivity, headache, insomnia, an increase in low-density lipoprotein (LDL) which is associated with coronary heart disease, and low-birth-weight when consumed by pregnant women.

Amphetamines

As central nervous system stimulant drugs, **amphetamines** result in increased heart rate, blood pressure, rate of breathing, and blood sugar and in high arousal levels. It is this psychological arousal effect, along with the physiological arousal effects, that disguises muscle fatigue so greater work output can occur.

Amphetamines should not be used to increase work output for several reasons. First, there is no evidence to show that their use enhances athletic performance. In fact, they may even interfere with athletic performance by increasing hyperactivity when more controlled physical responses are needed. Second,

amphetamine users often become dependent on these drugs and, to come down from an amphetamine high, resort to taking barbiturates. This yo-yo drugging effect can be quite dangerous. Not enough people know that barbiturates are extremely addictive and that withdrawing from them without medical supervision can be deadly.

Cocaine

Another drug people take to improve physical performance or for "recreational" reasons is **cocaine.**

Anabolic steroids Drugs that are derivatives of the male sex hormone testosterone; sometimes used illegally by those desiring to increase their body size, speed, or strength.

Caffeine A stimulant drug present in coffee, tea, and colas and other soft drinks that have not been decaffeinated.

Amphetamines Drugs that stimulate the central nervous system, increasing heart rate, blood pressure, and other body processes.

Cocaine A drug that stimulates the central nervous system and that can cause tremors, rapid heartbeat, and harmful psychological effects.

Behavioral Change
and Motivational Strategies

Many things might interfere with your healthy use of chemical substances. Here are some barriers (roadblocks) and strategies for overcoming them.

Roadblock	Behavioral Change Strategy
You want to quit smoking but you are afraid you will gain weight. Your looks are important to you. Therefore, you decide not to stop smoking in order to look better.	The U.S. Public Health Service reports that 60 percent of women and 47 percent of men say they continue to smoke because they are afraid of gaining weight. And yet most smokers do not gain weight when they quit. In fact, only one third gain weight, another one third stay the same weight, and the rest actually lose weight. Even when weight gain does occur, it is usually minimal and certainly worth the health benefits of not smoking.
Weight gain is only one of the excuses smokers use for not quitting. Others include, "The air is polluted anyway, I might as well smoke," and, "It's too late to quit, I've been smoking too long."	Knowledge can go a long way in dispelling these myths. The truth is that the U. S. Public Health Service advises that even in heavily polluted urban areas, the concentrations of pollutants in the air are tiny in comparison with the concentrations of them in cigarette smoke. Regarding smoking for a long time, it is never too late to prevent a serious disease. After you quit, your chances of dying from smoke-related diseases gradually decreases until they are close to those of people who have never smoked.
You have an important examination next Tuesday so you plan to stay up all Monday night studying. Around 1:00 A.M. Tuesday however, you start feeling drowsy so you think about drinking something with a large amount of caffeine to keep going. You realize, though, that a large amount of caffeine can make your heart beat irregularly, give you a headache, and increase the LDL in your blood.	Of course, the best strategy is to plan to study for several nights rather than pulling an all-nighter. But, given that you did not follow this advice, you can use selective awareness to focus on the benefits you will derive from getting some sleep. It will make your learning more efficient since you will not be drugged, it will be healthier, and you will be more alert during the examination. A few hours of sleep can do wonders for your performance. You can also focus on the negative aspects of ingesting a lot of caffeine. After all, who wants to subject themselves to heart problems? A bad grade on an examination is better than a bad electrocardiogram (ECG).
List roadblocks interfering with your using chemicals appropriately.	Now cite behavioral change strategies that can help you overcome the roadblocks you just listed. If you need to, refer back to chapter 3 for behavioral change and motivational strategies.
1. _____	1. _____
2. _____	2. _____
3. _____	3. _____

Cocaine can be snorted through the nose, smoked as crack, or injected. It, too, can increase work output by the nature of its stimulating effect on the central nervous system. It also produces a euphoria that disguises fatigue.

Aside from cocaine being illegal, however, it can result in dire consequences. It can cause tremors and rapid heartbeat; raise blood pressure dangerously high to the point of threatening stroke; lower the effectiveness of the immune system, thus subjecting its users to various illnesses; and decrease appetite, resulting in malnutrition. In addition, it can cause acute anxiety, confusion, and depression. In a few cases, *cocaine psychosis* has occurred in heavy users, leading to delusions and violence.

*S*UMMARY

Drug Use, Misuse, and Abuse

When drugs are used as they are recommended and for the purposes for which they were recommended, that is drug use. When a legal drug is used inappropriately, that is drug misuse. When an illegal drug is used or a legal drug is used for purposes other than those for which it was intended, that is drug abuse.

Alcohol

Alcohol is the most prevalent drug on college campuses. It is so widely used that it is estimated that between 2 and 3 percent of the current college student body will eventually die from alcohol-related causes. Between 53 and 84 percent of college students get drunk at least once a year, and between 26 and 48 percent get drunk once a month.

Alcohol dilates blood vessels in the head thus causing headaches; narrows the blood vessels supplying the heart; damages cells in the liver; often leads to malnutrition, endocrine, and reproductive system problems; and can cause cancer in several body sites.

Drinking responsibly means not getting inebriated by limiting the amount of alcohol ingested to no more than one average-sized drink (0.6 fluid ounces) an hour, drinking only when appropriate, never drinking and driving, and refraining from drinking when good judgment is needed. To control drinking, drink in moderation, never drink on an empty stomach, never drink when taking medication, never ingest alcohol in combination with other drugs, drink slowly, dilute drinks, and do not eat salty or spicy foods when drinking.

Tobacco

Tobacco use is the most preventable cause of death in the United States. It is the major risk factor for heart and blood diseases; chronic bronchitis and emphysema; cancers of the lung, larynx, pharynx, oral cavity, esophagus, pancreas, and bladder; and other problems such as respiratory infections and stomach ulcers.

Tobacco use constricts blood vessels, increases blood pressure, destroys air sacs in the lungs, and increases the production of hydrochloric acid in the stomach. The results are shortness of breath; upset stomach; cold and clammy fingers and toes; the development of heart disease, hypertension, stroke, emphysema, and digestive disorders; and lung and other cancers.

To quit, or cut down on, smoking, smoke only one cigarette an hour, smoke only half the cigarette, inhale less, smoke slowly, smoke brands you dislike, place unlighted cigarettes in your mouth when you get the urge, exercise regularly as a divergence, and spend time in places where smoking is prohibited.

Marijuana

Marijuana use is increasing after a 14-year decline among young adolescents. A more relaxed attitude toward the drug appears to be a direct result of increased therapeutic use, a so-called wide margin of safety, and low potential for abuse and physical addiction. Numerous health and behavior hazards have been associated with the regular smoking of marijuana. Although attitudes toward use of marijuana are changing, the law has not. Marijuana is still considered an illicit drug, and using it can result in substantial penalties in many states, such as expulsion from college, loss of a job, and fines and prison terms for users and distributors.

Drug-Taking to Enhance Athletic Performance

Among the drugs taken in an attempt to improve on athletic performance are anabolic steroids, caffeine, amphetamines, and cocaine. None of these are effective in this regard and all of these drugs present a serious threat to health.

Anabolic steroids subject the user to liver cancer, high blood pressure, heart disease, sterility, and increased hostility. In men it can lead to atrophied testicles, prostate cancer, and breast growth. In women it can result in menstrual irregularities, a deepening of the voice, decreased breast size, baldness, and facial hair growth. In both men and women, anabolic steroid use can lead to clogging of the arteries, eating compulsions, and increased aggressiveness.

Caffeine is a stimulant. It increases heart and breathing rates, enables skeletal muscles to use fatty acids for energy more efficiently, and decreases fatigue and drowsiness. Caffeine, however, can have serious side effects depending on the amount ingested. It can result in irregular heartbeats; hyperactivity; headache; insomnia; an increase in LDL, which is associated with coronary disease; and low-birth-weight babies when it is consumed by pregnant women.

Amphetamines and cocaine are also stimulants. They can create feelings of psychological and physiological arousal. However, they are drugs on which people can become dependent, and they can cause serious cardiac problems that can even result in death.

ℛEFERENCES

American Cancer Society. (1995). *Cancer facts and figures–1995.* Atlanta: American Cancer Society.

Avis, H. (1996). *Drugs and life* (3rd ed.). Madison: Brown & Benchmark.

Carrol, C. R. (1996). *Drugs in modern society* (4th ed.). Madison: Brown & Benchmark.

Robert H. Coombs, R. & Ziedonis, D. (eds.) (1995). *Handbook on drug abuse prevention: A comprehensive strategy to prevent the abuse of alcohol and other drugs.* Boston: Allyn & Bacon.

Hanson, G., & Venturelli, P. J. (1995). *Drugs and society* (4th ed.). Boston: Jones and Bartless.

Institute for Health Policy, Brandeis University. (1993). *Substance abuse: The nation's number one health problem.* Princeton: Robert Wood Johnson Foundation.

Koop, C. E. (1988). *The health consequences of smoking: Nicotine addiction,* a report of the Surgeon General. Washington, DC: U.S. Government Printing Office.

National Center for Health Statistics. (1993). *Health, United States, 1992.* Hyattsville, MD: U.S. Public Health Service.

National Institute on Alcohol Abuse and Alcoholism. (1993, October). Alcohol and nutrition. *Alcohol Alert* no. 22, PH 346.

Oakley, R. & Ksir, C. (1996). *Drugs, society, and human behavior* (7th ed.). St. Louis: Mosby.

Objectives. (1991). Washington, DC: U.S. Government Printing Office, Pub. No. (PHS) 91–50212.

Physicians' Desk Reference (48th ed.). (1994). Montvale, NJ: Medical Economics Data Production.

U.S. Department of Health and Human Services. *Healthy People: National Health Promotion and Disease Prevention.*

U.S. Department of Health and Human Services, Office of the Inspector General. (1991). *Youth and alcohol: A national survey—Drinking habits, access, attitudes, and knowledge.* Washington, DC: National Clearinghouse for Alcohol and Drug Information.

U.S. Environmental Protection Agency and U. S. Department of Health and Human Services. (1993). *Respiratory health effects of passive smoking: Lung cancer and other disorders,* a report of the EPA, NIH Publication No. 93–3605. Bethesda, MD: National Institutes of Health.

Lab Activity 5.1

Signs of Alcoholism

INSTRUCTIONS: *Answer each of the questions below. Then read the interpretation section to find out what your score indicates about you and symptoms of alcoholism.*

Yes	No	
_____	_____	Do you ever drink too heavily when you are disappointed, under pressure, or have had a quarrel with someone?
_____	_____	Have you ever been unable to remember part of the previous evening even though your friends say you did not pass out?
_____	_____	Has a family member or close friend ever expressed concern, or complained, about your drinking?
_____	_____	Do you often want to continue drinking after your friends say they have had enough?
_____	_____	When you are sober, do you sometimes regret things you did or said while you were drinking?
_____	_____	Are you having financial, work, or school and/or family problems as a result of your drinking?
_____	_____	Has a physician ever advised you to cut down on drinking?
_____	_____	Do you eat very little or irregularly at times when you are drinking?
_____	_____	Have you recently noticed that you cannot drink as much as you used to?
_____	_____	Have any of your blood relatives ever had a problem with alcohol?

✦ Interpretation

Any "yes" indicates you may be at greater-than-average risk for alcoholism. More than one "yes" may indicate the presence of an alcohol-related problem or alcoholism and the need for consultation with an alcoholism professional. To find out more, contact the National Council on Alcoholism and Drug Dependence in your area.

Source: These questions have been excerpted from "What Are the Signs of Alcoholism? The NCAAD Self Test," published by the National Council on Alcoholism and Drug Dependence, Inc. For a copy of this brochure, please send $.50 to NCAAD, 12 West 21 St., New York, NY, 10010.

Lab Activity 5.2

Why Do You Smoke?

INSTRUCTIONS: *Here are some statements made by people to describe what they get out of smoking cigarettes. If you are a smoker, how often do you feel this way when smoking cigarettes? If you are not a smoker, how often do you think smokers feel this way when they smoke? Perhaps responding to these questions, even if you do not smoke cigarettes, will help you better understand why other people smoke. Circle one number for each statement.* **Important: Answer all statements.**

		Always	Frequently	Occasionally	Seldom	Never
A.	I smoke cigarettes in order to keep myself from slowing down.	5	4	3	2	1
B.	Handling a cigarette is part of the enjoyment of smoking it.	5	4	3	2	1
C.	Smoking cigarettes is pleasant and relaxing.	5	4	3	2	1
D.	I light up a cigarette when I feel angry about something.	5	4	3	2	1
E.	When I have run out of cigarettes, I find it almost unbearable until I can get them.	5	4	3	2	1
F.	I smoke cigarettes automatically without even being aware of it.	5	4	3	2	1
G.	I smoke cigarettes to stimulate me, to perk myself up.	5	4	3	2	1
H.	Part of the enjoyment of smoking a cigarette comes from the steps I take to light it up.	5	4	3	2	1
I.	I find cigarettes pleasurable.	5	4	3	2	1
J.	When I feel uncomfortable or upset about something, I light up a cigarette.	5	4	3	2	1
K.	I am very much aware of the fact when I am not smoking a cigarette.	5	4	3	2	1
L.	I light a cigarette without realizing I still have one burning in the ashtray.	5	4	3	2	1
M.	I smoke cigarettes to give me a "lift."	5	4	3	2	1
N.	When I smoke a cigarette, part of the enjoyment is watching the smoke as I exhale it.	5	4	3	2	1

	Always	Frequently	Occasionally	Seldom	Never
0. I want a cigarette most when I am comfortable and relaxed.	5	4	3	2	1
P. When I feel "blue" or want to take my mind off cares and worries, I smoke cigarettes.	5	4	3	2	1
Q. I get a real gnawing hunger for a cigarette when I haven't smoked for a while.	5	4	3	2	1
R. I've found a cigarette in my mouth and didn't remember putting it there.	5	4	3	2	1

✦ Scoring

1. Enter the numbers you have circled in the test questions in the spaces below, putting the number you have circled for question A over line A, for question B over line B, and so on.
2. Add the three scores on each line to get your totals. For example, the sum of your scores over lines A, G, and M gives you your score on *Stimulation*; lines B, H, and N give the score on *Handling*, etc.

Totals

$\underline{\quad} + \underline{\quad} + \underline{\quad} = \underline{\qquad}$
A   G   M   Stimulation

11 or above suggests you are stimulated by the cigarette to get going and keep going. To stop smoking, try a brisk walk or exercise when the smoking urge is present.

$\underline{\quad} + \underline{\quad} + \underline{\quad} = \underline{\qquad}$
B   H   N   Handling

11 or above suggests satisfaction from handling the cigarette. Substituting a pencil or paper clip or doodling may aid in breaking the habit.

$\underline{\quad} + \underline{\quad} + \underline{\quad} = \underline{\qquad}$
C   I   O   Pleasurable relaxation

11 or above suggests you receive pleasure from smoking. For this type of smoker, substitution of other pleasant habits (eating, drinking, social activities, exercise) may aid in eliminating smoking.

$\underline{\quad} + \underline{\quad} + \underline{\quad} = \underline{\qquad}$
D   J   P   Crutch: tension reduction

11 or above suggests you use cigarettes to handle moments of stress or discomfort. Substitution of social activities, eating, drinking, or handling other objects may aid in stopping.

$\underline{\quad} + \underline{\quad} + \underline{\quad} = \underline{\qquad}$
E   K   Q   Craving: psychological addiction

11 or above suggests an almost continuous psychological craving for a cigarette. "Cold turkey" may be your best method of breaking the smoking habit.

$\underline{\quad} + \underline{\quad} + \underline{\quad} = \underline{\qquad}$
F   L   R   Habit

11 or above suggests you smoke out of mere habit and may acquire little satisfaction from the process. Gradually reducing the number of cigarettes smoked may be effective in helping you to stop.

Scores can vary from 3 to 15. Any score of 11 or above is *high*; any score of 7 and below is *low*.

Source: National Clearinghouse for Smoking and Health (USPHS).

Lab Activity 5.3

Marijuana Statutes in Your State

Marijuana has a controversial history of use and abuse among college students. In the past, recreational use in the United States has been trivialized and is further complicated by studies showing some significant benefits of marijauna smoking in the field of medicine. In some states, authorized use includes the management of pain, treatment of extreme nausea and vomiting associated with cancer chemotherapy, antiemetic treatment of cancer patients, and appetite stimulation for advanced AIDS patients suffering from anorexia. Numerous other unauthorized benefits include uses for glaucoma, asthma, and as a muscle relaxant, antidepressant, analgesic, and antiseizure treatment.

Marijuana is still perceived to be a mild substance and one of the least seriously addicting drugs available to college students. It is also the most widely used illicit drug. A significant decline in use by teenagers during the mid-1980s to 1991 has now reversed and taken an upward swing. Efforts to eliminate both production and distribution have failed and rekindled fires of discussion about legalization, in spite of the abundance of information indicating marijuana use produces adverse effects on the central nervous system, respiratory system, cardiovascular system, as well as sexual performance and reproduction.

INSTRUCTIONS: *Although penalties for possession and distribution vary, law enforcement agencies still vigorously prosecute both users and distributors in the United States in spite of the often casual attitude of college students toward maintaining their "stores" for an occasional hit.*

1. Examine the laws in the 11 states described below to obtain a "feel" for existing criminal charges brought against users and distributors.
2. Call a drug abuse hotline in your area and ask for a copy of the marijuana law in your state and locality.
3. Prepare a short report on your findings and present this information to your class. Post the law on dormitory and other bulletin boards around your campus.

✦ **Marijuana Statutes in 11 U. S. States That Have Decriminalized Marijuana Possession to Some Degree**

California:
Possession: Up to 1 oz, up to $100 fine; more than 1 oz, up to 6 months/$500.
Cultivation: 16 months–3 years.
Sale: 2–4 years

Colorado:
Possession: Up to 1 oz in private, up to $100; in public, up to 15 days/$100; 1–8 oz, up to 2 years/$500; more than 8 oz, 1–2 years.
Cultivation or sale: Any amount, 2–4 years.

Maine:
Possession: Up to 1.5 oz, for personal use, up to $200; 1.5 oz–2 lb, up to 1 year/$1,000; 2–1,000 lb., up to 5 years/$2,500; 1,000 lb and up, up to 10 years/$10, 000.
Cultivation or sale: Up to 1.5 lb, up to 1 year/$1,000; more than 1.5 lb, same as possession.

Massachusetts
Possession: Any amount for personal use, probation.
Cultivation or sale: Any amount, up to 2 years/$5,000.

Minnesota
Possession: Up to 1.5 oz, up to $100; more than 1.5 oz, up to 3 years/$3,000.
Cultivation or sale: Any amount, up to 5 years/$30,000.

Mississippi
Possession: Up to 1 oz, not in vehicle, $100–$250; 1 g–oz in vehicle, up to 90 days/$1,000; 1 oz–2.2 lb, up to 2 years/$3,000; more than 2.2 lb, up to 20 years/$1 million.
Cultivation or sale: Up to 1 oz, up to 3 years/$3,000; 1 oz–2.2 lb, up to 20 years/$30,000; more than 2.2 lb, up to 30 years/$1 million.

Nebraska
Possession: Up to 1 oz, $100 and drug education; 1 oz–1 lb, up to 7 days/$500; more than 1 lb, up to 5 years/$10,000.
Cultivation or sale: Any amount, up to 5 years/$10,000.

New York
Possession: Up to 25 g, up to $100; 25 g–2 oz, up to 3 months/$500; 2–4 oz, up to 1 year/$1,000; 4–8 oz, up to 4 years; 1–10 lb, up to 7 years; over 10 lb, up to 15 years.
Cultivation: Up to 4 oz, up to 1 year/$1,000; 4–8 oz, up to 1 year/$10,000; 8 oz–1 lb, up to 4 years; 1–10 lb, up to 7 years; over 10 lb, up to 15 years.
Sale: Up to 25 g, up to 1 year/$1,000; 25 g–4 oz, up to 4 years; 4 oz–1 lb, up to 7 years; over 1 lb, up to 15 years.

Ohio
Possession: Up to 100 g, up to $100; 100–200 g, up to 30 days/$250; 200–600 g, 6 months–5 years/$2,500; more than 600 g, 1–10 years/$5,000:
Cultivation or sale: Up to 200 g, 6 months–5 years/$2,500; 200–600 g, 10 years/$5,000; more than 600 g, 2–15 years/$7,500.

Oregon
Possession: Up to 1 oz, up to $100; more than 1 oz, up to 10 years/$2,500.
Cultitivation or sale: Up to 20 years/$100,000.

West Virginia
Possession: Up to 15 g, conditional discharge; more than 15 g, 90 days–6 months/$1,000.
Cultivation and sale: 1–5 years/$15,000.

Note: One ounce (oz) is equivalent to approximately 28 grams.

Source: Updated from "Marijuana: Laws on sale, possession, and cultivation," July 11, 1989, *USA Today*, p. 6A.

6

SEXUALITY AND WELLNESS

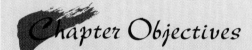

Chapter Objectives

By the end of this chapter, you should be able to:

1. Differentiate between sexuality and sex.

2. Describe the female and male reproductive systems and the roles of various structures that comprise the reproductive systems.

3. Cite threats to males' sexual health and ways in which men can maintain sexual wellness.

4. Cite threats to females' sexual health and ways in which women can maintain sexual wellness.

5. List the most prevalent sexually transmitted diseases, their causes, and means of prevention.

A YOUNG BOY ASKED his older brother where babies came from. The older brother told him that babies came from the stork. Seeking verification of this shocking revelation, the young boy asked his father where babies came from. The father said that babies came from the stork. Not wanting to be impolite but still not completely satisfied, the boy approached the wise old sage of the family, his grandfather, and asked him where babies came from. The grandfather, following the party line, said babies came from the stork. The next day in school the young boy related his conversations with his brother, father, and grandfather to the teacher and his classmates, concluding that there hadn't been normal sexual relations in his family for at least three generations.

Sex is something that many of us have difficulty discussing, and yet it is an important part of our lives and of our health and wellness. When we do finally get around to speaking of sex we too often speak nonsensically. How many times have you heard, "Sex is dirty. Save it for someone you love." Now, who would want to give a loved one something so dirty?

This chapter discusses sex and sexuality in the context of wellness. We pledge to be nonevasive and to have as our goal the enhancement of the quality of your life.

SEX AND SEXUALITY

We must first differentiate between sex and sexuality. Sex is something you do. Sexuality is something you are. Sex includes acts such as sexual intercourse, oral-genital sex, and masturbation. Sexuality, on the other hand, includes a comprehensive view of the many factors that comprise your sexual life. Human sexuality has at least four dimensions: biological, psychological, ethical, and cultural (see Figure 6.1).

- *Biological factors* include your physical appearance, your responses to sexual stimulation, your ability to reproduce or to control fertility, and your growth and development in general. Too often this dimension is thought to be the be-all and end-all of sexuality.

- *Psychological factors* include your attitudes about yourself and your body and how you regard others. Do you believe sex is dirty? Are you comfortable with and accepting of your body? Do you associate guilt or shame with your physical self and with sex?

- *Ethical factors* relate to how you treat yourself and others. This dimension of human sexuality involves such questions as what is right and what is good in terms of sexual matters. You may decide these issues by incorporating religious, humanistic, or pragmatic considerations.

- *Cultural factors* in sexuality are the sum of cultural influences that affect your thoughts and actions. These influences may be historical (for example, how societies come to view the roles of males and females over

Figure 6.1 ✦ Dimensions of Human Sexuality

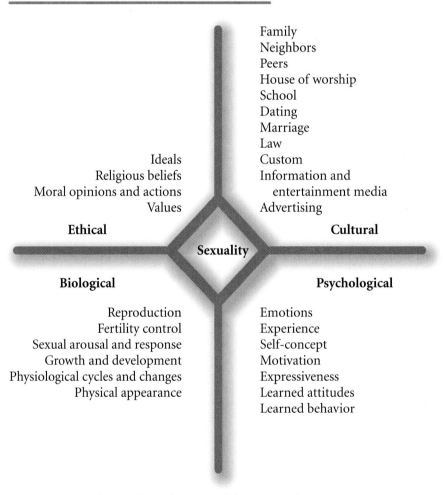

Source: From *Sexuality: Insights and Issues* (p. 5), by J. S. Greenberg, C. E. Bruess, & K. D. Mullen, 1993, Dubuque, IA: Brown and Benchmark.

many years) or contemporary (for example, the influences of television, popular music, advertisements, and interpersonal relationships).

It is through this perspective of human sexuality and all of its dimensions that we discuss sexual health and wellness. We begin with considerations of anatomy and physiology, but before this chapter ends, we discuss other dimensions of sexual well-being.

THE REPRODUCTIVE SYSTEMS

To achieve and maintain sexual health and wellness, you need to understand the anatomy and physiology of the male and female reproductive systems. Only with this awareness will you understand and appreciate the importance of the recommendations we present to maintain sexual health. If you understand why a certain recommendation is made, you will be more likely to remember it and to act on it.

The Male Reproductive System

Figure 6.2 depicts the male reproductive system and its external and internal structures. The external structures include the scrotum and the penis. The *scrotum* is a bag-ike structure containing the two *testes,* which produce *sperm* and the male sex hormone *testosterone* (see Figure 6.3). Each testis consists of several parts. The sperm is produced by

cells in the part of the testes called the *seminiferous tubules.* Each testis contains approximately 1,000 seminiferous tubules, and some 50,000 sperm, cells are produced each minute (150 million daily). Once produced, the sperm are carried through the *vas efferentia,* out of the testes to the *epididymis,* where the sperm are stored and nourished. Some of the sperm then proceed to the *ampulla,* by way of the *vas deferens,* and accumulate there until expelled at some later time. The vas deferens is encased in the *spermatic cord. Seminal vesicles* located nearby provide nutrients for the sperm's further maturation.

When *ejaculation* (forceful exit of *semen* during *orgasm)* is about to occur, the seminal vesicles empty into the ejaculatory duct, and the sperm pass through this duct into the *urethra.* As shown in Figures 6.2, the urethra passes through the *prostate,* which secretes a substance that helps increase sperm life. Next, the sperm pass through the urethra, which has been lubricated by the secretion of the *Cowper's gland.* This secretion neutralizes any acidity remaining in the urethra from urine. Any *preejaculatory fluid* that may be noticed is really secretion from the Cowper's gland, but it may also contain some sperm. The sperm next pass into the *penis,* which has become erect due to sexual stimulation, causing the arterioles leading to the *corpora cavernosa* to dilate. This dilation results in the corpora cavernosa becoming engorged with blood and thereby erect.

The head of the penis is called the *glans penis* and is covered by a foreskin called the *prepuce.* For hygienic, cultural, or religious reasons, the foreskin is

Figure 6.2 ✦ Structures of the Male Reproductive System

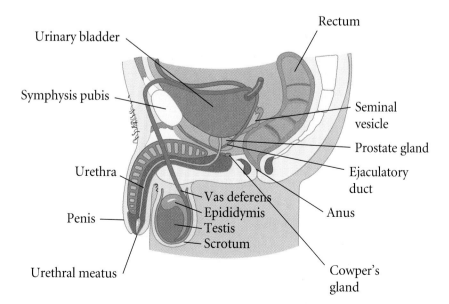

Figure 6.3 ✦ The Testis (plural: testes)

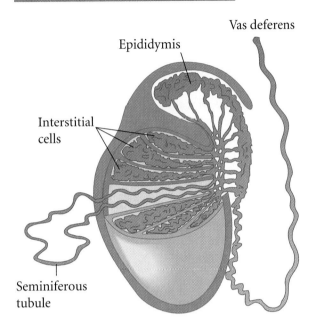

sometimes surgically removed. Removal of the foreskin—called *circumcision*—is more usual in the United States than it is in other countries.

The rationale for circumcision, other than cultural or religious reasons, is medical. Several glands are located in the foreskin that secrete an oily substance, which if not removed from under the foreskin, can combine with dead skin cells to form a cheesy substance called *smegma.* This can irritate the glans penis, causing discomfort and possibly infection. However, if a man washes daily and removes the smegma, there will be no irritation. The only verifiable health-related reason for circumcision pertains to recent studies indicating that circumcised male infants experience fewer urinary tract infections than noncircumcised ones. Still, these studies need to be verified before medical practitioners are justified in recommending circumcision as a routine procedure.

Ejaculation is the result of contractions of muscles in the glands and ducts of the male reproductive system. The ampulla and seminal vesicles contract, as does the *bulbocavernosa muscle,* all of which surround the *corpora spongiosa* of the penis. The semen, or ejaculate, consists of fluids from the seminal vesicles, prostate, and Cowper's gland, as well as sperm. Each ejaculate contains, on the average, 300 million sperm. Male hormone production in the male reproductive system is accomplished by the interstitial cells, which lie between the seminiferous tubules.

The Female Reproductive System

The female reproductive system includes structures on the outside of the body that can be readily seen. These are called the **external genitalia.** The structures

Figure 6.4 ✦ Female External Reproductive Organs

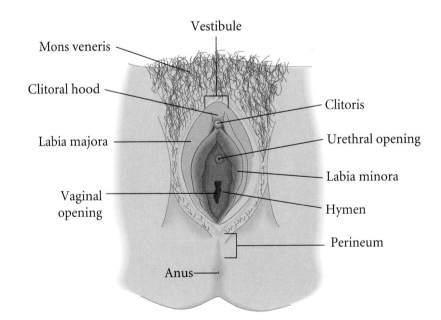

Figure 6.5 ✦ Organs of the Female Reproductive System

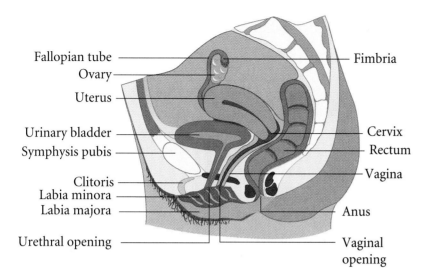

Fallopian tube — Fimbria
Ovary —
Uterus —
Urinary bladder — Cervix
Symphysis pubis — Rectum
— Vagina
Clitoris —
Labia minora —
Labia majora — Anus
Urethral opening — Vaginal opening

not easily observable are those located within the body, called the **internal genitalia.**

External Structures The external structures of the female reproductive system are known collectively as the *vulva* and consist of the mons veneris, labia majora, labia minora, vestibule, clitoris, and hymen. Figure 6.4 provides a view of the external female genitals.

The *mons veneris* or *mons pubis,* is a fleshy pad, usually covered with pubic hair, that extends back and divides to form the *labia majora,* the two large outer lips of the vulva. During sexual excitement, the labia majora become engorged with blood and pull back to open the vulva.

Just inside the labia majora lie two folds of tissue called the *labia minora.* Loaded with blood vessels and nerve receptors, the labia minora are very sensitive to stimulation. During sexual excitement, the blood vessels fill with blood, spreading the labia minora to reveal the shallow cavity called the *vestibule,* in which the vaginal opening, urethral (urinary) opening, and clitoris are located. The upper part of the labia minora forms a hood for the small, sensitive *clitoris.* Similar to the penis in the male, the clitoris contains a large number of nerve cells and has a corpora cavernosa (like the penis), but not a corpora spongiosa. During sexual excitement, the corpora cavernosa becomes engorged with blood and erect (like the penis).

The last external structure is the *hymen,* a thin membrane that separates the vestibule from the vagina. Although its function is uncertain, the hymen may protect the internal genitals from infec-

tion early in life. Most women find that the hymen stretches or breaks with relative ease when they masturbate, insert tampons, exercise, or experience their first sexual intercourse. However, a physician may have to remove the hymen surgically if the membrane is very thick.

Figure 6.4 also depicts a section of skin that extends from the bottom of the vulva to the anus. During childbirth, this piece of skin, called the *perineum,* is sometimes surgically cut to prevent tearing when the baby's head exits the vagina. This procedure is called an *episiotomy.*

Internal Structures Figure 6.5 depicts the relationship of the external and internal structures in the female reproductive system. The *vagina is* the tubular passageway that leads from the vaginal opening on the outside of the body to the uterus or "womb" on the inside. The vagina is an elastic organ whose walls contain muscular membranes that stretch during sexual arousal to accommodate the penis and that expand during childbirth to let the baby pass through. The walls of the vagina are also covered with tissues that secrete a lubricant that is the first physical sign of

External genitalia Those parts of the female genitals that can be clearly seen.

Internal genitalia Those parts of the genitalia that are within the body and are not directly observable.

Behavioral Change and Motivational Strategies

To help you eliminate or decrease barriers to achieving and maintaining your sexual health, we identify several of these barriers along with strategies for overcoming them.

Roadblock	Behavioral Change Strategy
You want to have regular medical checkups but you are afraid what the doctor might find. Fearing you might be told you have cancer, for instance, you decide not to have checkups.	The earlier a health condition (such as cancer) is identified, the less drastic will be the procedure required to remedy that condition. For example, if breast cancer is diagnosed early, a simple lumpectomy might be all that is needed, rather than a radical mastectomy for late-stage breast cancer. Furthermore, the earlier the diagnosis, the more likely the condition can be cured. Waiting too late might mean the health condition has progressed to the point where a cure is not possible and/or irrevocable damage has occurred. Use the behavioral change strategies of *social support* and *reminders*. Ask a close family member or a good friend to write on his or her calendar the date that you decide you want to have a medical checkup. Ask that person to remind you as the date approaches and to make sure you have actually scheduled the appointment. In addition, place your own reminders on your refrigerator or elsewhere. Then ask the family member or friend to accompany you to your checkup. This kind of social support and the use of reminders make it more likely you will actually get that medical checkup you need.
You want to perform regular breast self-exams or testicular self-exams but you never seem to remember. When you do remember, it is always at an inconvenient time and, although you vow to perform the self-exam when you can, you never seem to do so.	The behavioral change strategy known as *scheduling* would be useful in this instance. Scheduling a regular time for events results in those events actually being performed. Schedule yourself to perform breast self-exam or a testicular self-exam and write that schedule on your calendar. Since a breast self-exam needs to be done one week after the menstrual period, it is difficult to schedule it beforehand. However, if you get in the habit of making a notation in an appointment book or on a calendar right after menstruation begins, it is more likely that you will remember to do the exam at a convenient time. Schedule testicular self-exams for just after the first shower or bath taken each month. You can also use *reminders*. A good reminder would be to tape a copy the breast self-exam and/or testicular self-exam techniques on your bathroom mirror, wall, or on the inside door of the medicine chest. Tape it someplace where you will see it often and it will remind you to perform the self-exam regularly.

Roadblock	Behavioral Change Strategy
You periodically engage in sexual intercourse or other sexual activities and are concerned about contracting HIV or some other sexually transmitted disease. Consequently, you want to make sure to use "safer sex" techniques, but you're too embarrassed to discuss this with your partner.	You can use any of the *covert techniques* to help manage this behavior. For example, you could use *covert rehearsal* by imagining a discussion with your partner about using condoms and refraining from particularly high-risk behaviors. Or you could use *covert modeling* by imagining how an assertive friend might engage in the conversation in which you wish to engage, and then simply "replace" yourself for your friend in the image. Or you could use *covert reinforcement* by imagining the conversation and then rewarding yourself for being able to imagine this by taking a moment to recall a pleasant day you spent at a beach or in a park (or somewhere else).
List roadblocks interfering with your sexual health and well-being.	Now cite behavioral change strategies that can help you overcome the roadblocks you listed. If you need to, refer back to chapter 3 for behavioral change and motivational techniques.
1._____	1._____
2._____	2._____
3._____	3._____

female sexual arousal. The female's menstrual flow also leaves the body through the vagina.

Figure 6.6 offers a more detailed look at the female's internal reproductive organs. The *uterus* is a thick-walled muscular organ the size and shape of a pear. The mouth of the uterus, termed the *cervix*, extends into the vagina. The other end of the uterus is termed the fundus. It consists of three layers. The outer-most layer is the *perimetrium*, which is very elastic and allows the uterus to expand during pregnancy. The middle layer, the *myometrium*, is muscular (smooth muscle) and can contract to push the newborn out through the cervix and into the birth canal (vagina). The inner layer is the *endometrium*, which is abundant in blood vessels and is partly discharged during menstruation. It is in the uterus that the fertilized ovum (egg) is implanted and develops into *an embryo* (to 12 weeks) and then a *fetus* (after 12 weeks). Leading from the uterus back toward the ovaries are the *fallopian tubes,* also called *oviducts,* which are hollow and have muscular walls. The sperm usually fertilizes the ovum in one tube or the other. Once fertilized, the ovum passes down the fallopian tube toward the uterus. When a female is born, she already has a supply of about half a million immature eggs (ova) in each

of the two almond-shaped ovaries. Each egg is covered by a thin tissue called the follicle. When the female reaches puberty, the eggs begin to mature and their follicles burst open, releasing the eggs. Normally, only one egg is released each month. The ovum is caught by

Figure 6.6 ✦ An Anterior View of the Female Reproductive Organs

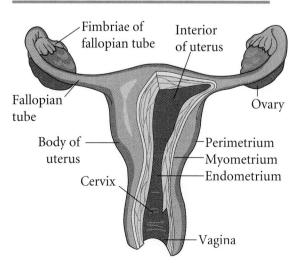

one of the *fimbria,* the fingerlike projections that jut out from the end of the fallopian tubes. The ovaries are also responsible for the production of the female hormones estrogen and progesterone.

SEXUAL DYSFUNCTIONS: THREATS TO WELLNESS

The inability to participate in typical sexual behaviors can pose a threat to sexual health and wellness. This condition is called sexual dysfunction. Although occasionally an individual may not be able to function sexually—for example, after drinking a lot of alcohol—these infrequent occurrences need not cause alarm. But if such occasions are the rule rather than the exception, there may be a problem requiring expert attention.

Sexual Problems in Males

The two most prevalent sexual problems in males are premature ejaculation and erectile dysfunction, although these are certainly not the only sexual problems that males experience.

Premature Ejaculation The inability to control timing of the ejaculate, resulting in a lack of sexual satisfaction for one's partner, is known as *premature ejaculation.* The difficulty in defining this condition lies in one's perception about what is "premature." For example, in their book *Human Sexual Inadequacy,* Masters and Johnson described it as premature if the male could not "control his ejaculatory process for a sufficient length of time during intravaginal containment to satisfy his partner in at least 50 percent of their coital connections". Another definition defines ejaculation as premature only if the man or his partner considers it premature. If they do not, regardless of the time before ejaculation, it is not premature. Premature ejaculation is estimated to affect approxi-

---

Impotence The inability of the male to maintain an erection long enough to have sexual intercourse.

Erectile dysfunction The correct term for describing difficulty in achieving and maintaining a penile erection; popularly known as "impotence."

Ejaculatory incompetence The inability of a man to ejaculate into the vagina during coitus.

---

mately 25 percent of college students—a not insignificant number.

Dealing with Premature Ejaculation Other than the rare cases caused by surgery, trauma, or disease, premature ejaculation is a function of the psyche; that is, the mind is not able to control the body's need to ejaculate. Several self-help techniques for overcoming rapid ejaculation have been proposed. Some men will drink an alcoholic beverage to decrease the rapidity of their sexual response. Others will allow themselves an orgasm rapidly, or a small orgasm, knowing that the next one will be longer in arriving. Waiting for sufficient vaginal lubrication may help prolong ejaculation. It seems that the glans penis may experience too much friction in the presence of insufficient lubrication of the vagina, causing increased sensitivity and rapid ejaculation. A condom reduces the direct stimulation to the glans penis and may help delay the ejaculatory response. Relaxing or switching positions so as to decrease muscle tension is another recommended control technique. Too much muscular tension encourages rapid ejaculation. There are also creams designed to decrease sensitivity that can be purchased and placed on the glans penis. Whether the benefit of controlling the ejaculate is worth the price of deadened sensations during coitus is a decision that only the sexual partners can make.

Fortunately, there is a proven, effective treatment for premature ejaculation. Developed by Masters and Johnson and described in detail in their book, *Human Sexual Inadequacy,* the "squeeze" technique is easily applied, effective, and well publicized so that sexual counselors and therapists are aware of it. The technique involves squeezing the glans penis by the man's partner when ejaculation is approaching. Repetition of this technique in several subsequent lovemaking sessions usually helps the man 'learn' to delay his ejaculation.

Erectile Dysfunction Men's difficulty in achieving and maintaining an erection is popularly known as **impotence.** The derivation of the term impotence is from Latin and means "without power." The word impotence is used to connote that a man has lost power—is no longer "manly"—when he cannot achieve or maintain an erection. Furthermore, he has lost power as a lover and has lost his reproductive capacity. The more professional, sensitive, and accurate term is **erectile dysfunction.** Men who have never had an erection sufficient for sexual intercourse are said to have *primary erectile dysfunction.* Men who have previously been able to maintain an erection long enough to have intercourse but subsequently developed an erection problem are said to have *secondary erectile dysfunction.* Secondary erectile dys-

Myth and Fact Sheet

Myth	Fact
1. Sexually transmitted diseases can be contracted by sitting on a toilet seat.	1. Organisms that cause sexually transmitted diseases need moisture to survive. These organisms die quickly once outside the body. Theoretically, if you sat on a moist toilet seat right after someone with an STD with open sores sat on that seat, it is possible you could contract that disease. However, the likelihood of that occurring is so small that this is not recognized as a way for STDs to be communicated. It is through sexual activities that these diseases are transmitted from one person to another.
2. HIV can be contracted through casual contact such as kissing, using the same eating utensils, or swimming in the same pool.	2. HIV is not transmitted through casual contact. It is transmitted by bodily fluids (blood, semen, vaginal fluids) passing from someone infected through a route of entry into the body (through puncture by a needle, through a cut on the body, or through sexual intercourse) of someone who is not infected. In addition, there is too little of the virus in saliva to make kissing a high-risk behavior for contracting HIV infection.
3. Conception can only occur if a man ejaculates in a woman's vagina.	3. Preejaculatory fluid emitted from the Cowper's gland may contain sperm. If this fluid is present on the tip of the penis prior to ejaculation, conception can occur.
4. Short of abstinence, there is not much you can do to prevent contracting HIV.	4. Using a condom during sexual intercourse and other sexual activities (preferably a condom containing the spermicide nonoxynol-9), refraining from intravenous drug use, and participating in a mutually monogamous relationship, will go a long way in preventing your contracting HIV infection.
5. As long as the behavior is not obvious and no physical contact is made, it is not sexual harassment.	5. Sexual harassment need not entail overt behaviors such as touching. Any behavior that creates a hostile work environment (such as posters of nude persons, the telling of crude sexual jokes, or repeated sexual innuendos) has been classified by the courts as constituting sexual harassment.

function is approximately 10 times more prevalent than primary erectile dysfunction.

Erectile dysfunction can be caused by a myriad of factors. It was previously believed that most erectile dysfunctions were caused by psychological factors, but more recent information suggests that 50 to 60 percent of such cases are at least partially the result of physiological factors. Among these factors are diabetes infections; the use of drugs or medications; alcoholism; spinal cord injury; injuries to the penis, testes, urethra, or prostate; and any conditions that interfere with the flow of blood to the erectile tissue of the penis. In addition, kidney disease, nerve damage (for example, from surgery), endocrine abnormalities, and neurological problems can also cause erectile dysfunction.

Among the nonorganic causes are fear of sexual performance—"Will I be an adequate sexual partner or show my ineptitude?" This fear can result in a self-fulfilling prophecy; that is, fear may make the man so anxious that he *is* unable to achieve and maintain an erection and his worst fears are realized. The result could be lowered self-esteem that contributes to the original fear. Thus a cycle of erectile dysfunction develops. In addition, guilt about sex or shame regarding one's involvement in sex can interfere with an erection.

Ejaculatory Incompetence For some men, the problem is not ejaculating too soon but, rather, not being able to ejaculate in the vagina at all. This condition is known as **ejaculatory incompetence,** sometimes referred to as *retarded ejaculation*. When a man has never ejaculated in the vagina and is incapable of doing so, he is classified as having *primary ejaculatory incompetence.* When he has previously been able to ejaculate in the vagina but can no longer do so, he is classified as having *secondary ejaculatory incompetence.* Men with these problems may still be able to maintain an erection and stay sexually aroused, but they can't ejaculate in the vagina. Nevertheless, they may be able to ejaculate by masturbating or through oral-genital stimulation. Treatment involves counseling to identify and respond to the causes of ejaculatory dysfunction.

Dyspareunia Painful sexual intercourse is called **dyspareunia.** During sexual intercourse, men may feel pain in the penis, testes, or some other internal part of their bodies. Infections of the penis, foreskin, testes, urethra, or the prostate can cause such pain, as can allergic reactions to a spermicidal cream or foam that may be used as a contraceptive. When intrauterine devices (IUDs) were more available, some men reported irritation of the glans penis from the string attached to the IUD which extended out of the uterus into the vagina.

There are still other causes of dyspareunia in men. A foreskin that is too tight can cause pain when an erection develops; smegma that has not been washed away from the glans penis can develop into an infection and irritate the glans; and Peyronie's disease, in which fibrous tissue and calcium deposits develop in the area around the cavernous bodies of the penis, may also create pain during sexual intercourse. Treatment involves identifying the cause and eliminating it through surgery or behavioral changes.

Sexual Problems in Females

The most common causes of sexual dysfunction in females are orgasmic dysfunction, sexual unresponsiveness, dyspareunia, and vaginismus.

Orgasmic Dysfunction Although they may enjoy sexual intercourse, some females are *anorgasmic;* that is, they cannot or can at best rarely achieve an orgasm. **Orgasmic dysfunction** may be caused by such psychological factors as anger, guilt, fear, embarrassment concerning one's body, or hostility. It may also be caused by factors external to the woman; for example, an inexperienced partner, inappropriate setting (such as the uncomfortable back seat of a car), or alcohol. Lack of orgasm in young women is usually caused by one of these external factors.

Other causes of orgasmic dysfunction are anatomical defects in the female reproductive system, hormonal deficiency or imbalance, disorders of the

nervous system, drugs, and alcohol. Note the similarity between the causes of female orgasmic dysfunction and the causes of male erectile dysfunction.

Therapy for orgasmic dysfunction that is psychological in nature usually involves both partners because communication between the partners is often at the core of the problem. A knowledgeable, understanding, and aware sexual partner is an important part of the therapy for orgasmic dysfunction.

Sexual Unresponsiveness This disorder used to be called *frigidity,* but therapists have dropped this value-laden term. **Sexual unresponsiveness** is defined as the inability to experience erotic pleasure from sexual contact. Some women with this problem are difficult to treat because they show evidence of personality disorders. Unhealthy socialization may contribute to the attitude that sex is sinful or that men are exploiters. Contrary to popular belief, however, rape does not seem to be a cause of this sexual dysfunction, although women who are raped may temporarily not want to engage in sexual relations.

Dyspareunia In females, **dyspareunia** (painful intercourse) can stem from physical or psychological causes. Painful intercourse might result from irritation of the vaginal barrel by the glans of the penis or insufficient lubrication of the vagina resulting from physical causes. Dyspareunia can also result from too-frequent intercourse or from insufficient vaginal lubrication due to insufficient sexual stimulation. Psychological reasons can also cause painful intercourse. For example, feelings of shame, guilt, or embarrassment can result in such tension that vaginal muscles will not widen enough when the penis is inserted, making intercourse painful (one such condition is *vaginismus,* described below). Because dyspareunia makes sexual intercourse unenjoyable, coitally active women should seek medical examination as soon as possible.

Vaginismus In **vaginismus,** the muscles in the vagina involuntarily tighten so that the penis either cannot enter or causes a good deal of pain when it does enter. This condition is primarily psychological in origin; therefore, the treatment is psychological in nature. Conditions found to be related to vaginismus include a sexual relationship with an impotent man, religious guilt, a traumatic sexual experience, or dyspareunia.

Inhibited Sexual Desire

In her book *Disorders of Sexual Desire,* sexual therapist Helen Singer Kaplan described **inhibited sexual** desire **(ISD)** as a lack of sexual appetite. It is characterized by a disinterest in sexual activity Both males and females experience ISD.

The causes of ISD are, for the most part, psychogenic. The majority of these cases are the result of such factors as poor self-esteem, a poor relationship, embarrassment regarding one's body, or a history of sexual abuse. ISD can also develop in response to another sexual dysfunction. For example, a man who has erectile dysfunction may develop a lack of interest in sex. When the thought of or opportunity for sex is presented, rather than becoming excited this man may only envision a threat to his self-image and, quite naturally, lack interest.

It should be emphasized that an occasional, temporary sexual dysfunction is not unusual, but a frequently recurring or permanent dysfunction is a threat to your sexual health and wellness. There are effective means of helping both males and females to overcome these problems. If you feel that you have a sexual problem, you should seek counseling. Perhaps the place to start is with your instructor or your own physician. If your physician determines that no physical problem exists, he or she can refer you to a reputable sexual or psychological counselor.

𝒮EXUALLY TRANSMITTED DISEASES

In addition to sexual dysfunctions, certain diseases can interfere with sexual activities. These used to be called venereal diseases (VD) named for Venus, the Roman goddess of love. Today they are known less euphemistically as sexually transmitted diseases (STDs). Although more than 20 organisms that are linked to STDs, we discuss only the most prevalent STDs. Find out how much you know about STDs by completing Lab Activity 6.1: Testing Your Knowledge of STDs.

Gonorrhea

Popularly known as the "clap," the "drip," and many equally descriptive names, **gonorrhea** is caused by the *Neisseria gonorrhoeae* bacterium. It is increasing in incidence—more than one million cases are reported in the United States per year, with the actual incidence estimated to be four times that amount—and is one of the most prevalent communicable diseases.

Gonorrhea is transmitted by intercourse and by oral-genital and anal-genital contact. Since the *Neisseria* gonorrhea needs the warmth and moisture

provided by the mucous membranes of the vagina, mouth, or anus, it is unlikely (though not impossible) that you could acquire gonorrhea from using someone else's towel or from sitting on a public toilet seat unless the bacterium has just been deposited there and the area is warm and moist. A male exposed to *Neisseria gonorrhoeae* bacteria through coitus has about a 20 percent chance of developing gonorrhea, whereas a female likewise exposed has about an 80 percent chance of contracting gonorrhea. The difference is due to the vaginal environment, which is conducive to the grow of the bacteria.

Effects of Gonorrhea Gonorrhea affects the urogenital tract in both sexes: the urethra in males and the urethra, vagina, and cervix in females. However, the symptoms are somewhat different in men and women. The early symptoms in men are a milky, bad-smelling discharge from the penis, and feelings of urgently having to urinate and a burning sensation when doing so. If untreated, the infection can cause swelling of the testicles and can damage the prostate gland, resulting ultimately in sterility. Additional complications may include kidney and bladder damage.

Whereas infected men are usually aware something is wrong with them, women may not notice the early signs of gonorrhea. One reason for this is that

---

Dyspareunia Painful sexual intercourse.

Orgasmic dysfunction Inability to achieve orgasm.

Sexual unresponsiveness The inability of a woman to experience erotic pleasure from sexual contact, popularly known as "frigidity."

Vaginismus The involuntary tightening of the muscles of the vagina so that the penis cannot enter or so that dyspareunia results.

Inhibited sexual desire (ISD) A lack of sexual appetite or a disinterest in sexual activity.

Sexually transmitted diseases (STDs) Bacterial, viral, and parasitic diseases that are transmitted through sexual contact, which usually affect the genital areas and may cause serious disease complications throughout the body.

Gonorrhea An STD that is caused by a bacterium. Although the disease can be treated with antibiotics, if left untreated it can lead to serious complications, including bladder and kidney disease and diseases of the pelvic and genital areas.

Improving Your Community

Promoting Healthy Sexuality

You can contribute to the sexual health of society while responding to your own sexual needs. Here are several ways in which you can accomplish that goal:

1. Refrain from manipulating or coercing someone into having sex with you. Psychological coercion may not be any less offensive than is physical coercion.

2. If coitally active, use a condom. In that way, you will be doing your part to prevent the spread of AIDS; even though abstinence would be even more effective.

3. Refrain from prejudiced behaviors toward people with a different sexual orientation than you. No one has the right to tell you to view homosexuality as moral if your religious beliefs dictate otherwise. But an opposing view does not give you the right to violate the basic human rights of gays.

4. Be understanding of friends and relatives who may experience sexual dysfunctions—whether temporary or more permanent. Let people know there is effective treatment for many sexual dysfunctions and help them to obtain such treatment.

5. Report sexual crimes immediately. You might consider a Peeping Tom a nuisance rather than a threat. However, "Tom" might escalate to a rapist some other day. All crimes—sexual and otherwise—are serious and need to be reported to the proper authorities. In doing so, you may save a neighbor from experiencing a similar or more serious crime in the future.

These are but a few ways you can exercise social responsibility as it relates to sexuality. What other ways can you think of to improve your society in the area of sexuality? ✦

---

the symptoms are similar to those in common vaginal infections: a slight burning sensation in the genital area and a mild discharge from the vagina. It is estimated that 80 percent of women who have gonorrhea are unaware of it until the disease has become more severe. If left untreated, gonorrhea invades the uterus, fallopian tubes, and ovaries. Pelvic infection may result, causing sterility or requiring surgical removal of infected pelvic organs. An additional concern in women is that gonorrhea can be passed from an infected mother to her infant as it passes through the vaginal canal during delivery, often resulting in blindness. To prevent this from occurring, the eyes of newborns are routinely treated with drops of silver nitrate.

Treatment of Gonorrhea Diagnosis of gonorrhea is not as simple as it is for some of the other STDs. It requires laboratory examination of a sample taken from the infected area with a cotton swab or growing the bacteria under laboratory conditions. The disease usually responds to penicillin treatment or, if the patient is allergic to penicillin, to tetracycline drugs. However, there is a growing concern about penicillin-resistant strains of gonorrhea, and researchers are attempting to development other drugs that will effectively eradicate the disease.

Those treated for gonorrhea are advised to return for a follow-up examination in about 10 days to be certain that the medication has been effective and that the infection has not reoccurred. During treatment, abstinence from sexual intercourse and other sexual activities that may transmit the bacteria is advised.

Syphilis

Known in the past as the "great pox" or the "great imposter" because people thought it resembled small pox, **syphilis** now is often referred to as just "the syph." Syphilis is caused by the *Treponema pallidum,* a corkscrewlike organism that resembles bacteria and which is part of a group of such organisms called spirochetes.

Because *Treponema pallidum* can survive only in the warmth and moisture provided by the mucous membranes of the human body, it quickly dies outside the body. For this reason, syphilis cannot usually be contracted from a toilet seat (unless the spirochete has recently been deposited there just prior to someone else with an open sore sitting on the seat, the chances of which are extremely remote). Syphilis is transmitted during sexual intercourse, oral-genital or anal-genital contact, or by kissing a person who has a syphilitic sore in the mouth. These activities provide the spirochete with a route of entrance to the body.

Effects of Syphilis The disease progresses through four stages. In Stage 1 (primary stage) a painless sore, called a **chancre** (pronounced 'shanker'), appears three to four weeks after the spirochete enters the body. The chancre looks like a pimple or wart and appears where the spirochete entered the body, often on the penis, the lips, or the vaginal wall. The chancre may go unnoticed in women or may be ignored in men, because it is painless and disappears in a few weeks without treatment.

Stage 2 (secondary stage) occurs about six weeks after contact. Symptoms may include a rash over the entire body, welts around the genitals, low-grade fever, headache, hair loss, and sore throat. These symptoms also disappear without treatment. However, if the symptoms are noticeable, most victims see a doctor at this time. Thus, it is uncommon for cases of syphilis in the United States to progress to the third stage.

Stage 3 (latency stage) begins about two years after contact (up to five years in some people). After one year, the victim cannot transmit the disease to anyone else. The only exception is that a pregnant woman can transmit the disease to her fetus through the placental wall. Latency may last 40 or more years. During this time, the organism infects and irreparably damages the heart, brain, and other organs. By Stage 4 (tertiary stage), the disease may lead to heart failure, blindness, other organ damage, and finally death.

Treatment of Syphilis Syphilis can be detected by means of a simple blood test. Because it is such a potentially dangerous disease and can be transmitted to unborn babies, most states require a blood test for syphilis before marriage and, in pregnant women, during the prenatal period. Syphilis generally responds well to penicillin or, in some cases, to other antibiotics. Because no immunity develops to the disease, prompt diagnosis and treatment after any possible exposure are essential.

When syphilis is passed from the mother to the fetus prior to birth, it is known as congenital syphilis. Until the 16th week of pregnancy, the fetus is protected from spirochetes by a membrane called Langhan's layer. However, after the 16th week, spirochetes can pass through the placental barrier and enter the fetus's bloodstream, causing a number of birth defects such as mental retardation or physical abnormalities.

Once syphilis is contracted, the individual should refrain from all sexual activity that can transmit the spirochete. Treatment should also consist of follow-up examinations to determine whether antibiotics have been effective in eliminating the spirochete. As with gonorrhea and the other STDs, since the disease-causing organism needs a route of entry into the body, the use of a condom can help prevent the spread of syphilis.

Genital Herpes

There are two types of *herpes simplex* viruses: type 1 causes cold sores in the mouth, and type 2 causes **genital herpes.** However, there is growing evidence that they are more related than previously thought. Genital herpes now rivals gonorrhea as one of the most prevalent sexually transmitted diseases in the United States.

Effects of Herpes Approximately 2 to 10 days after the virus enters the body, some symptoms such as sores and swollen glands (around the groin), flu-like symptoms (fever, muscle aches, and a sick feeling), and pain in the genital area during urination or intercourse may occur. Other symptoms may include fatigue, swelling of the legs, and watery eyes. The disease progresses through four stages:

1. **Prodrome stage.** An itching or tingling sensation (**prodrome**) develops near the site

---

Syphilis A serious STD caused by a spirochete; untreated syphilis has very serious complications and is eventually fatal. Treatment includes the use of antibiotics, but some strains of syphilis are resistant to treatment.

Chancre A painless sore on the penis, mouth, anus, or in the vagina where the spirochete that causes syphilis has entered the body.

Genital herpes An STD caused by the herpes simplex, type 2 virus. The disease is incurable. Carefully treated, it is not a serious disease, but its spread to the rest of the body can result in serious complications. It has been linked to the onset of cervical cancer.

Prodrome An itching or tingling sensation that develops near the site where the herpes simplex, type 2 virus enters the body.

where the virus invaded the body, with the skin turning red and becoming sensitive; prodrome is also an early symptom of a recurrent infection or out break.

2. **Blister stage.** A sore or cluster of sores appears; fever, swollen glands, and other symptoms may occur; after 2 to 10 days, the sores break open (on future outbreaks, fever and swollen glands usually do not occur).

3. **Healing stage.** Sores shrink; scabs form; pain, swollen glands, and fever subside (scabs fall off by the end of the second week).

4. **Inactive stage.** The virus retreats to nearby nerve cells; stress and poor health may cause the virus to reemerge.

Since the virus remains dormant in the nerve cells, reoccurrences can be experienced. However, these reoccurrences are not as frequent as most people believe. Although some people may experience future outbreaks several times monthly, others may encounter them only rarely. Approximately one third of those with the disease never have a reoccurrence, and another one third have outbreaks only rarely. Furthermore, reoccurrences of herpes are usually much less painful and much shorter than the initial outbreak.

Herpes has potentially more harmful effects on women than on men. Women who have herpes genitalis are eight times more likely to develop cervical cancer than noninfected women. In addition, a herpes-infected pregnant woman has a one-in-four chance of transmitting the infection to her infant during delivery, and the risks to the infant include death. Consequently, the recommended course of action for pregnant women with herpes is to obtain delivery by cesarean section (incision through the abdomen and uterus to remove the fetus rather than delivery through the vaginal canal).

Treatment of Herpes Herpes is treated with the drug Acyclovir, which can relieve some symptoms and suppress reoccurrences of the disease. To prevent passing the virus to others, it is recommended to refrain from sex from the onset of the prodrome until sores have completely healed and to use a condom during other times.

Chlamydia

Caused by a viruslike bacterium called *Chlamydia trachomatis,* **chlamydia** is the most prevalent sexually transmitted disease. Some estimate that 4 million new cases occur each year, with as many as 500,000 progressing to pelvic inflammatory disease. Others estimate that chlamydia is up to 10 times more prevalent than gonorrhea and may be present in as many as 4 percent of all pregnant women. Up to 10 percent of college students may also be infected with chlamydia.

Effects of Chlamydia In women, chlamydia can cause infections in the vagina and pelvic inflammatory disease, which can lead to infertility. Symptoms include vaginal discharge, itching and burning of the vulva, and some discomfort when urinating. However, as many as 70 percent of female chlamydia infections go undetected until more serious problems develop. As with other STDs, chlamydia can create problems during birth deliveries if the pregnant woman is infected. Conjunctivitis, an inflammation of the eye, can be contracted by the newborn during delivery, and blindness can result. These conditions can be prevented with ointments containing tetracycline or erythromycin applied to the newborn's eyes.

In men, chlamydia can cause inflammation of the urinary and reproductive tracts and, in extreme circumstances, sterility. Symptoms include a mild burning sensation when urinating, followed by a thin, watery, clear discharge. Left untreated, it can also lead to swelling of the testicles.

Treatment of Chlamydia Chlamydia can be easily detected with a simple culture test that can be performed by college health services. Once detected, it can be treated effectively with a week-long administration of the antibiotic drug tetracycline. As with other treatments consisting of antibiotics, it is important to finish the entire dosage of the tetracycline, otherwise the infection may reoccur and be more resistant to the drug than before.

Genital Warts

The result of a viral infection (human papillomavirus—HPV), **genital warts** occur on most areas of the genitals and anus. In females, the warts typically appear in the lower area of the vagina. In males, they appear on the glans, foreskin (if not circumcised), and shaft of the penis, and may appear in the anal area in some homosexual men. The incubation period for HPV is approximately three months after contact with an infected person. University health centers report that genital warts are quite prevalent among college students.

Effects of Genital Warts Researchers have found that several strains of HPV are associated with the development of cervical cancer. This revelation has led to a more urgent need for prevention of what was previously thought to be a relatively benign STD.

Some lesions are moist and some are dry. The moist lesions are the ones that respond well to treatment. Large warts should be biopsied for cancerous cell growth.

Diagnosis is made by the appearance of the warts. In the moist areas of the body they tend to be white, pink, or white to gray. In the dry areas, they are usually yellow and yellow-gray.

Treatment of Genital Warts The usual treatment is administration of the drug podophyllin, an irritant that causes the outer skin in the area containing the virus to slough off. Thus the drug does not kill the virus, it removes the infected tissue. Podophyllin is applied by the health practitioner to each lesion, allowed to dry, and is then washed off four hours later by the patient. Sometimes an antibiotic ointment is prescribed as well to treat infection at the site and to help keep the wart moist. The podophyllin is usually applied once a week for five or six weeks or for the time it takes to control the infection. However, genital warts often reoccur after the first bout, even if treated. These reoccurrences can be experienced for several months or years until immunity develops. In some cases, warts are removed by laser surgery, electrosurgery that uses electrical current, freezing with liquid hydrogen, or surgical incision.

Pelvic Inflammatory Disease

With the exception of AIDS (acquired immunodeficiency syndrome), pelvic inflammatory disease (PID) is the most dangerous and the most difficult to diagnose of all the STDs affecting women. That is because its symptoms may not be obvious until damage has already occurred. Left untreated, PID can result in infertility and even death.

Effects of Pelvic Inflammatory Disease Symptoms of PID include abdominal pain or tenderness, pain during intercourse, increased menstrual cramps, profuse bleeding during menstruation, irregular menstrual cycles, vaginal bleeding at times other than when menstruating, lower back pain, nausea, loss of appetite, vomiting, vaginal discharge, burning sensation during urination, chills, and fever. Unless PID is promptly diagnosed and treated, scar tissue forms inside the fallopian tubes. This scar tissue can result in

infertility by partially or totally blocking the tubes, thereby preventing the egg from entering the uterus or the sperm from fertilizing the egg. Scar tissue also increases the risk of a tubal pregnancy (in which the fertilized egg becomes implanted inside the fallopian tube rather than the uterus).

Treatment of Pelvic Inflammatory Disease Diagnosis of PID is based on medical and sexual history, a pelvic examination, and laboratory tests. Treatment is by administration of an antibiotic and is usually effective. However, any structural damage done to pelvic organs may be irreversible or, at the least, require more extensive medical treatment.

HIV Infection and AIDS

Acquired immunodeficiency syndrome (AIDS) is a condition caused by infection with the human immunodeficiency virus (HIV). It is called a syndrome because it consists of a number of conditions resulting from a decreased ability of the body's immunological system to ward off infections and other threats to health. Among the syndrome's manifestations are pneumonia, cancer, and other opportunistic infections (infections resulting from lowered resistance of a weakened immune system). HIV is transmitted through bodily fluids, predominantly blood, semen, and vaginal secretions. It can also be transmitted from an infected pregnant woman to her fetus. In order to infect someone, HIV must have a route of entry into the body. The most common ways HIV is transmitted are through sex and the use of intravenous drugs. Sexual intercourse, oral-genital sex, or anal intercourse in which bodily fluids are exchanged are particularly risky activities. Intravenous drug use, in which a needle is shared, may result in HIV being directly deposited into the bloodstream.

Chlamydia A common STD caused by a virus-like bacterium; can lead to sterility, inflammation in the reproductive and urinary tracts, and pelvic inflammatory disease. Treated with antibiotics.

Gential warts An STD of the genital and perineal areas of both men and women caused by a virus; linked to an increased incidence of cancer.

Acquired immunodeficiency syndrome (AIDS) An STD that weakens the human immune system, leading to serious opportunistic diseases; fatal in the long run.

Figure 6.7 ✦ AIDS Cases per 100,000 population—United States, July 1994–June 1995

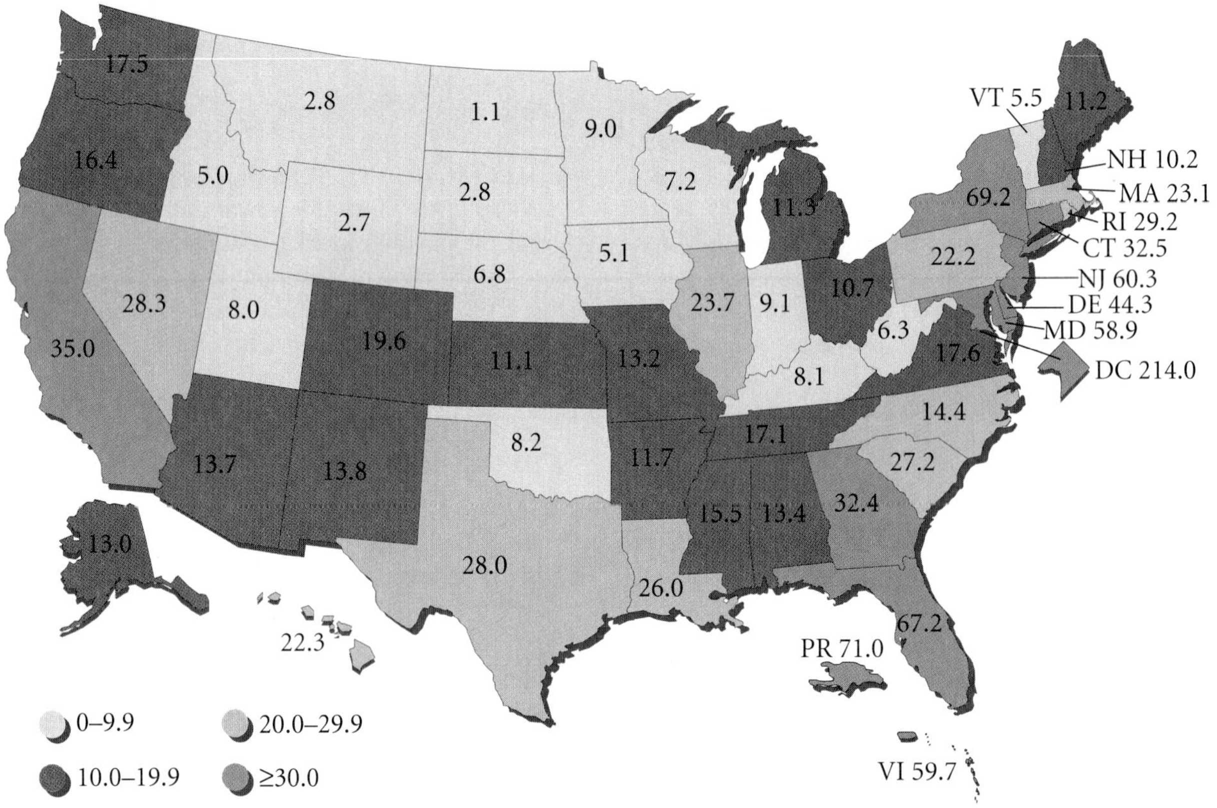

Source: "AIDS Map," *Morbidity and Mortality Weekly Report* 44:719, Centers for Disease Control and Prevention. September 29, 1995.

Prevalence of HIV Infection and AIDS The number of people infected with HIV and the number of people with AIDS keeps increasing. Although we realize that any figures we give you will soon be outdated, we present figures published by the World Health Organization (WHO) and the U.S. government to place the problem in perspective. As of the beginning of 1996, WHO estimates there were approximately 4.5 million cases of AIDS worldwide and an additional 18.5 million adults and 1.5 million children infected with HIV. In the United States, over half a million AIDS cases have been reported to the Centers for Disease Control and Prevention (CDC). That is larger than the population of the state of Wyoming or the city of Cleveland. Figure 6.7 depicts newly reported AIDS cases by state for a one-year period. Of course, many more of our fellow citizens are infected with the virus but have not yet developed AIDS.

Nearly 8,000 new cases of AIDS were diagnosed among U.S. individuals aged 13 and older in 1994. Of these newly diagnosed cases, 18 percent were women; with 77 percent of those cases African American and Hispanic women. Forty-one percent of the new AIDS cases among women were attributed to intravenous

drug use, 38 percent to heterosexual contact with an infected partner, and the remaining cases to transfusion with contaminated blood or of unknown origin.

Effects of HIV Infection Once in the body, HIV invades the cells of the immune system, resulting in its becoming less and less effective over time. Increasing incapacity results, with death being inevitable. Symptoms include loss of appetite, weight loss, fever, night sweats, skin rash, diarrhea, tiredness, lack of resistance to infection, and swollen lymph glands. Among the common conditions of full-blown AIDS, which usually develops some 8 to 10 years after HIV infection, are Kaposi's sarcoma (a form of cancer of the blood vessels that can be noticed by purple skin lesions), other cancers, pneumonia, and brain dementia.

Treatment of HIV Infection Rather than testing for the presence of the virus itself, HIV infection is diagnosed with a blood test (called ELISA—enzyme-linked immunosorbent assay) that identifies the presence of antibodies that develop in response to HIV. If the test is positive for these antibodies, another more sophisticated test (Western blot) is administered to confirm this result. However, it may take anywhere from three to eight months for enough of these antibodies to develop to be identifiable through the AIDS test. Consequently, someone may test negative even though he or she is infected. Further, this person may still transmit the virus to other people.

Although HIV infection is incurable and inevitably leads to death, there are some medications that appear to be effective in prolonging debilitating symptoms. The most well known of these drugs is AZT (azidothymidine). Recent studies have found a combination of AZT with other drugs is most effective in prolonging symptom-free living among people infected with HIV.

Prevention of HIV infection includes abstinence from high-risk sexual activities, the use of a condom with the spermicide nonoxynol-9 if sexually active, limiting the number of sexual partners, maintaining a monogamous relationship with someone who is HIV-free, and refraining from the use of intravenous drugs. For pregnant women who are HIV-infected, the administration of AZT can dramatically decrease the risk of their babies being born infected. Therefore, if they have participated in high-risk behaviors (or even if they have not), they might want to have an AIDS test to determine whether AZT is warranted.

The use of condoms is one of the most effective precautions sexually active people can take to prevent contracting HIV infection or other sexually transmitted diseases. Yet, there are various barriers preventing them from doing so. Lab Activity 6.2: How to Talk about Condoms with a Resistent, Defensive, or Manipulative Partner presents some of the objections to condom use a partner may present. After you are given a chance to respond to these objections, we offer suggestions for overcoming them. If you choose not to abstain from sex, condoms can save your life. Use them!

For More STD Information

1. CDC National AIDS Hotline (800) 342-AIDS

2. CDC National STD Hotline (800) 227-8922

3. SIDA Hotline (in Spanish) (800) 344-7432

4. National Institute for Drug Abuse (in Spanish) (800) 662-9832

5. CDC Hearing Impaired Hotline (800) 243-7889

6. AIDS-Related Community Services (800) 992-1442

7. National Herpes Hotline (919) 361-8488

𝓜AINTAINING SEXUAL HEALTH

Sexual dysfunction and the prevention of sexually transmitted diseases are but two concerns affecting sexual health and wellness. This section speaks to several others.

Men's Sexual Health and Wellness

There are several threats to the sexual health and wellness of men. Among these are cancer of the prostate and testicular cancer. Since these are discussed in detail in chapter 13, only a reminder of the importance of regular medical screening for these cancers and for monthly testicular self-examinations is offered here. The technique for performing this self-exam is described in chapter 13.

Other common conditions experienced by men are epididymitis and prostatitis. **Epididymitis** is an inflammation of the epididymis at the top of the testicle that causes swelling, pain, and tenderness in the scrotum (usually one side only). It is caused by bacteria (usually *Chlamydia trachomatis*) that enter through the urethra and travel through the vas deferens to the epididymis. Treatment is with antibiotics and is very effective, although in severe cases surgery may be necessary. **Prostatitis** is an inflammation of the prostate gland. Its symptoms include a thin discharge from the penis, pain in the lower abdomen and scrotum, and pain during ejaculation. In more severe cases there may be fever, chills, and pain when urinating. Prostatitis is treated with antibiotics.

In older men, enlargement of the prostate gland is not uncommon. Sometimes difficulty urinating accompanies this enlargement, and the pressure created on the bladder leads to a sensation of having to urinate frequently. Enlargement of the prostate also increases susceptibility to bladder and prostate infections. In severe cases, surgery may be necessary; although with the potential side effects of incontinence or erectile dysfunction (impotence), surgery is

Epididymitis Inflammation of the epididymis at the top of the testis causing swelling, pain, and tenderness in the scrotum.

Prostatitis Inflammation of the prostate gland resulting in a thin discharge from the penis, pain in the lower abdomen and scrotum, and pain during ejaculation.

only performed when other options are exhausted. Several different drugs are available to treat enlargement of the prostate in an attempt to avoid the need for surgery.

Women's Sexual Health and Wellness

Cancer of the breast, cervix, and uterus are all major illnesses affecting women's health and wellness. These are discussed in detail in chapter 13. Therefore, only a reminder of the need for regular medical checkups and breast self-examinations once each menstrual cycle is offered here.

One of the most prevalent conditions affecting women's sexual health and wellness is vaginal infection. Vaginal infections occur in two major forms: Trichomonas vaginitis and Monilial vaginitis. **Trichomonas vaginitis** is caused by a one-celled microorganism called *Trichomonas vaginalis* and results in frothy, greenish-white or yellowish-brown, foul-smelling discharge. This discharge is usually accompanied by a burning and itching sensation of the vagina and vulva. The most effective treatment is with a drug called Flagyl (metronidazole), which should also be administered to the woman's sexual partner.

Monilial vaginitis is a fungus or yeast infection caused by *Candida albicans,* a microorganism usually found in the vagina. This infection can be recognized by a thick, white, and cheesy discharge accompanied by itching. Treatment entails the use of vaginal creams or suppositories containing prescription medications such as Monistat (miconozole) or Lotrimin or Mycelex (clotrimazole). With this infection, treatment of the sexual partner is not necessary since Monilial vaginitis is not transmitted sexually.

The risk of contracting vaginal infections can be minimized by the following:

1. Wear cotton underwear, rather than nylon or other synthetic fiber or pantyhose. Cotton does not retain heat and moisture that allow bacteria to grow.

2. Avoid douching, which removes natural, protective microorganisms.

3. Wipe from front to back after going to the bathroom to avoid bringing bacteria from the rectum toward the vagina.

4. Regularly wash the genitals and anal region.

5. Avoid the use of feminine hygiene sprays, which can irritate the skin.

𝒮EX-ROLE STEREOTYPING AND SEXUAL HARASSMENT

Although not usually thought of in the same category as sexual dysfunctions, STDs, or infections of sexual organs, sex-role stereotyping and sexual harassment pose major threats to both men's and women's health and well-being.

Sex-Role Stereotyping

Before reading further, take a moment to complete Lab Activity 6.3: Abilities and Aptitudes Desirable for Men and Women. This will help you determine the degree to which you possess stereotypical thinking.

You may be surprised to learn that sex-role stereotyping can be bad for your health. Then again, if you have experienced it, you may not be surprised. Stereotyping begins as soon as a baby is born and a blue or pink ribbon is placed on his or her bassinet. From that point on, boys and girls are treated differently. There are numerous examples of this different treatment, but perhaps the most obvious and the one whose effects are quite dramatic is what occurs in school. Researchers tell us that teachers praise boys more often than they do girls, that they give boys more academic help than they give girls, and that they accept boys' comments to a greater extent than they accept girls' comments during classroom discussions.

The effect of these teacher behaviors is that boys are eight times more likely to call out answers, a sign of the self-confidence they develop. Conversely, girls lose self-esteem. A study conducted by the American Association of University Women found that 49 percent of elementary school girls said they felt proud of their schoolwork, whereas only 12 percent of high school girls said they felt such pride. A frightening statistic is that adolescent girls are four to five times as likely to attempt suicide than adolescent boys and,

---

Trichomonas vaginitis A vaginal infection caused by a one-celled microorganism called *Trichomonas vaginalis.* Symptoms include a frothy, greenish-white or yellowish-brown, foul-smelling discharge accompanied by a burning and itching sensation of the vagina and vulva.

Monilial vaginitis A vaginal fungus or yeast infection caused by *Candida albicans.* Symptoms include a thick, white, and cheesy discharge accompanied by itching.

A Thought-Provoking Riddle

A father and his son were involved in a car accident in which the father was killed, and the son was seriously injured. The father was pronounced dead at the scene of the accident and his body was taken to a local mortuary. The son was taken by ambulance to a local hospital and was immediately wheeled into an operating room. A surgeon was called. Upon seeing the patient, the attending surgeon exclaimed, "Oh, my God, it's my son." Can you explain this? (Keep in mind the father who was killed in the accident is not a stepfather, nor is the attending physician the boy's stepfather.) The answer appears below, upside down.

The surgeon was the boy's mother.

both during adolescence and adulthood, females have a higher rate of depression than do males.

Educators also argue that females are adversely affected by standardized tests and the consequences associated with them. For example, females score lower on the Scholastic Aptitude Test (SAT) than do males. In 1988, females scored 56 points lower: 13 points lower on the verbal section and 43 points lower on the math section. Since colleges use SAT scores to make admissions decisions, females have less chance of gaining admittance to the college of their choice than do males. And yet, when women and men compete for grades in college, women do at least as well as men. The perversity of this situation was demonstrated in 1971 when women began closing the gap with men. The result was that the SAT was revised, adding questions referring to science, business, and "practical affairs" (traditional strong points for males) and eliminating questions on human relations, the arts, and the humanities (traditional strong points for females).

In case male readers feel insulated from the effects of sex-role stereotyping, read on. The male role is stereotypically defined as one severely limited in its variety. Men must be strong, independent, active, competent, and analytical. It is quite stressful for men to live up to this stereotype. The result is that men who cannot admit their vulnerabilities, who cannot show their emotions, and who cannot be outwardly loving, develop heart disease in greater numbers and at an earlier age than do women, their "successful" suicide rates are higher, they have more problems with alcohol and other drugs, and they are more likely to be hospitalized for a psychiatric disorder.

The bottom line is that sex-role stereotyping is unhealthy for all of us. Recognizing this to be the case, it behooves us to refrain from contributing to this behavior and attitude. To do otherwise threatens the levels of health and wellness we can achieve.

Sexual Harassment

Typically, sexual harassment has meant sexual advances made by someone of power or authority who threatens firing, lack of promotion, or some other sanction if sexual activity is declined. A sexual advance that is politely made and that carries no threat of sanction is not sexual harassment, although some offended workers have interpreted such advances that way. The problem area in sexual harassment pertains to a sexual advance from someone of a higher status to someone of a lower status. The person of lower status may feel pressured to say yes even though no sanction has been made explicit.

However, sexual advances are not the only criteria for sexual harassment. If jokes and sexual innuendos permeate the workplace or school environment so that workers or students feel uncomfortable, unable to perform well, and suffer in their careers as a result, that in itself qualifies as sexual harassment. Furthermore, even if the institution is unaware that such harassment is occurring, the Supreme Court ruled in *Meritor Savings Bank v. Vinson* in 1986 that the company is still legally liable for the results of such harassment. It is for this latter reason that businesses and universities have instituted educational programs to notify supervisors that sexual harassment will not be tolerated in their organizations.

Both men and women can be victims of sexual harassment. However, women experience such harassment to a greater extent than men. When federal workers were studied by the Merit System Protection Board in 1980, it was found that nearly 25 percent of almost 2 million workers (42 percent females, 15 percent males) experienced some type of sexual harassment. Since 1981, complaints of sexual harassment to the Equal Employment Opportunity Commission have increased by 70 percent.

In 1988, the Merit System Protection Board again reported on a survey of sexual harassment among government workers. Although incidents of rape and assault declined from the 1980 results, touching, teasing, and joking remained high. The 1988 data disclosed that 42 percent of women surveyed experienced sexual harassment within the last two years. That is the same percent as reported sexual harassment seven years earlier—this despite attempts to educate federal workers and their supervisors so as to discourage sexual harassment. (The average federal worker has received one to two hours of training on sexual harassment.)

When the Merit System Protection Board revisited the issue of sexual harassment in 1995, 44 percent of the women and 19 percent of the men respondents reported they had been the targets of "uninvited, unwanted sexual attention" at work. It appears there has been no change in the amount of sexual harassment, at least as experienced at work.

More recent reports confirm the extent of sexual harassment. In fact, after the Clarence Thomas Supreme Court confirmation hearings at which Anita Hill accused Justice Thomas of sexual harassment, the Equal Employment Opportunity Commission reported formal complaints of sexual harassment against corporate employers jumped to 1,244 compared to 728 during the same period of time the previous year. Even junior and senior high school students report sexual harassment. In fact, a study conducted by the American Association of University Women of sexual harassment experienced by students in grades 8 through 11 found 81 percent of students (85 percent of girls and 76 percent of boys) had encountered sexual harassment.

The effects of sexual harassment are varied. Some people have been fined or had promotions withheld when they didn't make themselves sexually available. Others have felt guilty and wondered what they did to encourage the sexual advance. Many have felt helpless. In a study of sexually harassed women, 78 percent said they were affected emotionally or physically. Loss of self-esteem; feelings of fear and helplessness; headaches, backaches, and neck pains; gastrointestinal illness; and chronic depression have all been associated with sexual harassment.

Remedies have been developed for use by those who have been sexually harassed. Grievance procedures in many businesses or colleges have been established to deal with such complaints. Educational campaigns are being conducted at work and school sites. And women's groups have counseled the sexually harassed regarding their legal options.

Do you know your college or university's policies regarding sexual harassment? You can probably obtain a written copy of that policy by requesting one from your school's central administration office.

SUMMARY

Sex and Sexuality

Sex is what you do, sexuality is what you are. Sex includes acts such as sexual intercourse, oral-genital sex, and masturbation. Sexuality, on the other hand, includes a comprehensive view of the many factors that comprise your sexual life. Human sexuality has at least four dimensions: biological, psychological, ethical, and cultural. The biological factors include your physical appearance, your responses to sexual stimulation, your ability to reproduce or to control fertility, and your growth and development in general. The psychological factors include your attitudes about yourself and your body and how you regard others. The ethical factors relate to how you treat yourself and others. And the cultural factors are the sum of cultural influences that affect your thoughts and actions.

The Reproductive Systems

The external male genitalia consist of the scrotum and the penis. The internal male genitalia include the testes, urethra, prostate gland, seminal vesicles, and the Cowper's gland. The external female genitalia are known collectively as the vulva and consist of the mons veneris, labia majora, labia minora, vestibule, clitoris, and hymen. The internal female genitalia include the vagina, uterus, fallopian tubes, and ovaries.

Sexual Dysfunctions: Threats to Wellness

Sexual dysfunction is the chronic inability to participate in sexual activities. Among the sexual dysfunctions experienced by males are premature ejaculation, erectile dysfunction, ejaculatory incompetence, and dyspareunia. Among the sexual dysfunctions experienced by females are orgasmic dysfunction, sexual unresponsiveness, dyspareunia, and vaginismus. Both males and females can also experience inhibited sexual desire.

Sexually Transmitted Diseases

Some diseases are transmitted through sexual activity. These used to be called venereal diseases but are now referred to as sexually transmitted diseases or STDs. Among the most prevalent STDs are gonorrhea, syphilis, genital herpes, chlamydia, genital warts, pelvic inflammatory disease, and HIV infection and AIDS. Many of these diseases can be treated with antibiotics and/or other medications. Some STDs cannot be eradicated, such as herpes and HIV infection, although medications exist to diminish their effects. HIV, and eventually AIDS, are considered terminal, with an average life span of approximately 8 to 10 years after infection.

Sexually transmitted diseases can be prevented. The most effective means of prevention is abstinence from sexual activity. For those who choose not to abstain, the most effective means of prevention include the use of a condom with the spermicide nonoxynol-9, maintaining a monogamous relationship with a disease-free partner or limiting the number of sexual partners, and refraining from high-risk sexual behaviors (for example, anal sex).

Maintaining Sexual Health

Among the threats to the sexual health of males are epididymitis and prostatitis. Epididymitis is an inflammation of the epididymis at the top of the testes that causes swelling, pain, and tenderness in the scrotum. Prostatitis is an inflammation of the prostate gland with symptoms that include a thin discharge from the penis, pain in the lower abdomen and scrotum, and pain during ejaculation. Both of these conditions are treated with antibiotics.

Among the threats to the sexual health of females are cancer of the breast, cervix, and uterus. In addition, one of the most prevalent conditions affecting women's sexual heath is vaginal infection. Vaginal infections occur in two major forms: Trichomonas vaginitis (treated with Flagyl) and monilial vaginitis (treated with vaginal creams and suppositories in products such as Monistat, Lotrimin, or Mycelex).

Sex-Role Stereotyping and Sexual Harassment

Both sex-role stereotyping and sexual harassment pose threats to health and well-being. Among the ill effects of sex-role stereotyping experienced by females are lowered self-esteem, increased numbers of suicide attempts, and depression. Sex-role stereotyping can also affect males by contributing to increased heart attacks, higher rates of "successful" suicide attempts, more problems with alcohol and other drugs, and a greater likelihood of being hospitalized for a psychiatric disorder.

Sexual harassment is defined as more than just unwanted sexual advances made by someone of power who threatens firing, lack of promotion, or some other sanction if sex is declined. Although that certainly qualifies as sexual harassment, it also encompasses actions such as jokes and sexual innuendos that result in an uncomfortable work environment in which a worker cannot perform their duties well and whose careers suffer as a result. Studies indicate that almost half of women and almost one fifth of men have experienced sexual harassment at work. Many colleges and universities have developed guidelines that define sexual harassment on campus and describe remedies available to someone who is sexually harassed.

Lab Activity 6.1

Testing Your Knowledge of STDs

INSTRUCTIONS: Complete the following true-false test below to discover how much you know about sexually transmitted diseases.

	True	False
1. Syphilis can be acquired from contact with a contaminated toilet seat.	T	F
2. Syphilis and gonorrhea are the two most prevalent sexually transmitted diseases.	T	F
3. Gonorrhea is easily eradicated through the use of penicillin.	T	F
4. STDs cannot be transmitted from one partner to another unless one or both reach orgasm.	T	F
5. Some people have developed an immunity to STDs and need not take precautions.	T	F
6. Gonorrhea is easily detected in the female.	T	F
7. Syphilis can be transmitted by kissing an infected person.	T	F
8. STDs are uncommon, and there is generally no need for precautionary measures.	T	F
9. If one partner is infected with gonorrhea or syphilis, the other partner has only a slight chance of acquiring the disease during sexual contact.	T	F
10. Acquired immunodeficiency syndrome (AIDS) can be spread by mosquitoes.	T	F

✦ **Answers**

1. *False.* Highly unlikely and nearly impossible.

2. *False.* Chlamydia is more prevalent, with some estimates of over 10 million cases per year in the United States.

3. *False.* Some strains of gonorrhea are extremely resistant to penicillin and very difficult to eradicate with other antibiotics.

4. *False.* Reaching orgasm has nothing to do with contracting STDs.

5. *False.* No one can develop a natural immunity to STDs.

6. *False.* Gonorrhea in females is difficult to detect and may exist for months before any symptoms become noticeable.

7. *True.* A person with a chancre sore on the mouth could transmit syphilis to a partner through kissing.

8. *False.* STDs are quite common among all socioeconomic and age groups.

9. *False.* The probability of acquiring an STD from an infected partner is quite high.

10. *False.* It would take too many bites to transfer enough blood to cause infection.

◆ **Scoring**

9–10 correct: Excellent
7–8 correct: Good
5–6 correct: Poor
Fewer than 5 correct: Very poor

Read, or reread, the section about sexually transmitted diseases in this chapter carefully if you had less than seven correct answers.

Lab Activity 6.2

How to Talk about Condoms with a Resistant, Defensive, or Manipulative Partner

Abstinence is the only sure way to prevent the transmission of sexually transmitted diseases, including HIV infection and AIDS. However, for those who choose not to abstain from sex, the use of a condom can significantly decrease their risk of contracting an STD. Still, many people have difficulty convincing a resistant, defensive, or manipulative partner to use a condom. This lab is designed to help you respond to a partner's concerns in a way that results in a condom being used while maintaining a positive relationship with the partner.

INSTRUCTIONS: For each "partner" statement presented below, write in an assertive response that encourages the use of a condom. After you have completed writing in all of your responses, consult the responses suggested by the experts that appear at the end of this lab.

✦ **If your male partner says:**

1. "I *know* I'm clean (disease-free); I haven't had sex with anyone in X months."
   Your response: _____
   _____
   _____

2. "I am a virgin."
   Your response: _____
   _____
   _____

3. "I can't feel a thing when I wear a condom; it's like wearing a raincoat in the shower."
   Your response: _____
   _____
   _____

4. "I'll lose my erection by the time I stop and put it on."

Your response: _____

_____

_____

5. "It destroys the romantic atmosphere."

Your response: _____

_____

_____

6. "Condoms are unnatural, fake, a total turnoff."

Your response: _____

_____

_____

7. "I don't have a condom."

Your response: _____

_____

_____

8. "You carry a condom around with you? You were planning to seduce me?"

Your response: _____

_____

_____

◆ **If your female partner says:**

1. "I'm on the pill, you don't need a condom."

Your response: _____

_____

_____

2. "This is an insult! Do you think I'm some sort of disease-ridden slut?"

Your response: _____

_____

_____

Lab Activity 6.2 *(continued)*
How to Talk about Condoms with a Resistant, Defensive, or Manipulative Parnter

3. "None of my other boyfriends uses a condom. A *real* man isn't afraid."

   Your response: _____

   _____

   _____

4. "I love you! Would I give you an infection?"

   Your response: _____

   _____

   _____

5. "Just this once."

   Your response: _____

   _____

   _____

6. "I won't have sex with you if you're going to use a condom."

   Your response: _____

   _____

   _____

Experts suggest the following responses to the 'If Your Male Partner Says' statements:

1. "Thanks for telling me. As far as I know, I'm disease-free, too. But I'd still like to use a condom since either of us could have an infection and not know it."

2. "I am not. This way we'll both be protected."

3. "Even if you lose some sensation, you'll still have plenty left."

4. "I'll help you put it on—that'll help you keep your erection."

5. "It doesn't have to be that way."

6. "Please let's try to work this out—an infection isn't so great either. So let's give the condom a try. Or maybe we can look for alternatives."

7. "I do" or, "Then let's satisfy each other without intercourse."

8. "I always carry one with me because I care about myself. I have one with me tonight because I care about us both."

Experts suggest the following responses to the "If Your Female Partner Says" statements:

1. "I'd like to use it anyway. We'll both be protected from infections we may not know we have."

2. "I didn't say or imply that. I care for you, but in my opinion, it's best to use a condom."

3. "Please don't compare me to them. A real man cares about the woman he dates, himself, and about their relationship."

4. "Not intentionally. But many people don't know they're infected. That's why this is best for both of us right now."

5. "Once is all it takes."

6. "So let's put it off until we can agree." Or, "OK, then let's try some other things besides intercourse."

Lab Activity 6.3

Abilities and Aptitudes Desirable for Men and Women

INSTRUCTIONS: *For each trait listed below, indicate whether you feel it is more desirable in males (M), more desirable in females (F), or equally desirable in both sexes (B).*

1. Athletic ability
2. Social ability
3. Mechanical ability
4. Interpersonal understanding
5. Leadership
6. Art appreciation
7. Intellectual ability
8. Creative ability
9. Scientific understanding
10. Moral and spiritual understanding

11. Theoretical ability
12. Domestic ability
13. Economic ability
14. Affectional ability
15. Observational ability
16. Fashion sense
17. Common sense
18. Physical attractiveness
19. Achievement and mastery
20. Occupational ability

In one study, college students of both sexes were asked which abilities and aptitudes were desirable for males and females. They cited the odd-numbered items on this list and item 20 as desirable for males and the even-numbered items (except item 20) as desirable for females.

To determine what stereotypical thoughts you have regarding males and females, analyze your responses by answering the following questions:

1. How do your responses compare to the college students' responses mentioned above?

   _____

   _____

2. Why do you think you responded the way you did?

   _____

   _____

3. What have you learned about your views of sex roles, and what significance does this knowledge have in terms of your sexual health and well-being?

   _____

   _____

7

PRINCIPLES OF EXERCISE

Chapter Objectives

By the end of this chapter, you should be able to:

1. Identify the key components of a complete fitness program.

2. Apply the progressive resistance exercise (PRE) principle to your specific workout program.

3. Design formal warm-up and cool-down sessions for your exercise program.

4. Identify your target heart rate range, and determine whether your exercise program is intense enough to elevate and maintain your heart rate within that range.

5. Evaluate various exercise programs in terms of their effectiveness in developing aerobic fitness, muscular strength, muscular endurance, and flexibility, and in lowering body fat and improving lean body mass.

FOR THE PAST year, I have seen Maya in the university gymnasium almost every time I work out. It doesn't seem to matter what time I choose to exercise, she is also there exercising. Finally, I couldn't resist asking her about her exercise habits and was not surprised to learn that she trains seven times weekly for two to three hours each session in a combination of formal aerobic classes, weight training, jogging, and stationary cycling. Nor was I surprised to hear that she has recovered from a number of overuse injuries, is tired most of the time, and suffers from aching muscles and sore knees.

Although Maya is doing a lot of things correctly, it is obvious that she is overdoing the training and does not thoroughly understand the basic principles of exercise such as the PRE principle, cross training, altering light and heavy workouts, and other key concepts that protect the body from injury and ensure safe progression to higher levels of fitness.

You may know someone like Maya. The situation is a common one that can be avoided through the application of the exercise principles discussed in this chapter.

Once the decision to begin a fitness program has been made, you are ready to master the principles that will help you achieve a higher level of aerobic (cardiorespiratory) fitness; increase muscular strength, muscular endurance, and flexibility; and help you lose or maintain body weight and fat. It is important to keep in mind that participation in an exercise program or a sport is no guarantee that your fitness level will improve unless you apply the exercise principles discussed in this chapter to your routine.

THE IDEAL EXERCISE PROGRAM

The following principles can be applied to most exercise choices to develop the five key components of health-related fitness: (1) cardiorespiratory endurance, (2) body composition (fat, muscle, and bone), (3) flexibility, (4) muscular strength, and (5) muscular endurance. Programs that improve these components also provide the health benefits discussed in chapter 1. Since motor skill-related areas such as agility, explosive power, balance, coordination, and speed are important to competitive athletes but have very little to do with health-related fitness, these components are not addressed in this chapter.

Cardiorespiratory Function

Cardiorespiratory function, or aerobic fitness, is the most important health-related fitness component, and it should be the foundation of your complete program. It is necessary for you to choose at least one aerobic exercise activity that requires 20 to 30 minutes of uninterrupted exercise.

Walking (4 miles per hour or faster), jogging, running, cycling, lap swimming, aerobic dance, aerobic exercise classes, and conditioning classes are excellent aerobic choices. If you choose the sports approach to aerobic fitness, you may want to consider racquetball or squash (singles with a player of similar skill), tennis or handball (singles), soccer, rugby, lacrosse, or full-court basketball. These exercise and sports activities can help prevent heart disease and other disorders and can also contribute heavily to fat and weight loss or maintenance.

Body Composition

Aerobic exercise burns more calories than do other exercises. Activities such as walking, jogging, cycling, and lap swimming allow you to exercise for longer periods of time (20 to 60+ minutes) than do activities requiring a higher intensity such as sprinting and full-court basketball. The key to fat loss through exercise is volume, not intensity. The longer you can continue to exercise, the more calories you burn and the more your fat cells shrink. To reduce body fat, lower your weight, and improve appearance, you need only three ingredients: (1) a reduced caloric intake to put yourself into a negative daily calorie balance; (2) daily aerobic exercise to burn calories and tone the body; and (3) flexibility, strength, and endurance training to add muscle mass and eliminate skin sagging.

Flexibility, Muscular Strength, and Muscular Endurance

Improved flexibility may help reduce the incidence of both home and exercise-related injuries and allow you to perform various activities more efficiently and effectively.

Strength training will increase the strength and the size of your muscles. The additional muscle mass also elevates metabolic rate (calories burned at rest over a 24-hour period) and assists you in losing fat and maintaining body weight. By improving the ratio of muscle mass to body fat, you are also able to exercise longer and more intensely and efficiently.

Improved muscular endurance also enables you to exercise for longer periods of time and is critical to participants in sports requiring short, all-out efforts such as sprinting, football, field hockey, and soccer. Depending on the design of your weight-training

Preconditioning period A period of several weeks taken to prepare the body slowly for maximum effort testing or engagement in a vigorous activity or sport.

Progressive resistance exercise (PRE) The theory of gradually increasing the amount of resistance to be overcome and/or the number of repetitions each workout.

Stroke volume The amount of blood ejected per beat.

Cardiac output The volume of blood pumped by the heart per minute.

program (see chapter 6), you will develop muscular endurance and strength simultaneously.

FITNESS CONCEPTS

Study this section carefully until you can apply each concept discussed here to your specific exercise choice.

Begin with a Preconditioning Program

It requires a minimum of six to eight weeks to improve your aerobic fitness. Attempts to move quickly from one fitness level to another should be avoided in the early stages of your program. *Too much too soon* can produce muscle soreness, increase the chances of soft tissue injury (see chapter 14), and cause you to quit long before results are noticeable.

The first two to three weeks of your new program should be considered a **preconditioning period** during which you progress very slowly and enjoy each workout session. Although preconditioning will help reduce residual muscle soreness, you can expect some delayed soreness following an exercise session that involves unconditioned muscles. The time between the exercise session and the highest soreness level is somewhat dependent on your age—the older you are, the longer it takes to experience the soreness. Even with a preconditioning period, maximum-

effort fitness tests may result in severe muscle soreness the following day.

Apply the Progressive Resistance Exercise (PRE) Principle

The **PRE principle** is simple to understand and has fascinating implications when it is correctly applied. If you gradually overload one of the body's systems (muscular, circulatory, or respiratory), it will develop additional capacity. When you repeatedly perform more strenuous exercise, the body repairs itself through elaborate cellular changes to prepare for more challenging, difficult exercise demands.

Application of the PRE principle produces dramatic changes in the heart and also in the circulatory system. Regular exercise places stress on the heart, causing it to become larger and stronger and improving **stroke volume** (by pumping more blood each beat). A trained heart muscle with improved **cardiac output** pumps considerably more blood per beat and per minute, allowing the heart to slow down, beat fewer times per minute, and rest longer between beats. As the heart muscle adapts to the stress of exercise, the arteries that supply it also enlarge.

Although everyone starts at a different conditioning level, we can generalize about what happens to your body when you begin an exercise program. You start the program at a certain functioning, or conditioning, level (level A in Figure 7.1). During and immediately after your first workout, this condition-

Figure 7.1 ✦ Concept of Work Hypertrophy. (A) preexercising functioning level; (B) functioning level following exercise; (C) elevated functioning level following recovery; (A-2) elevated functioning level at the proper point to reconvene exercise; (A-3 and A-4) elevated functioning levels following additional workout and rest periods.

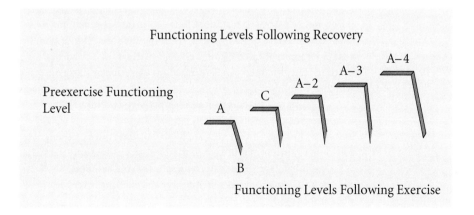

Myth and Fact Sheet

Myth	Fact
1. Aerobic development can be achieved in half the time by doubling the workout intensity.	1. Short, high-intensity workouts will improve anaerobic, not aerobic, fitness. There are no shortcuts to aerobic development.
2. More of a good thing results in added health benefits.	2. Health fitness levels for life can be achieved by following the concepts described in this text. Going too far beyond the FIT (frequency-intensity-time) limits increases the risk of injury. Those persons who exercise beyond the health fitness level are usually seeking conditioning for athletic competition rather than health.
3. You should stretch before you begin your exercise program.	3. It is important to avoid stretching cold muscles. Light jogging or walking that results in some sweating will prepare you for your stretching session.
4. The use of a rubber suit during exercise aids weight loss.	4. In hot, humid weather, a rubber suit traps heat, prevents cooling by evaporation, raises body temperature, increases fluid loss, and contributes to heat-related injuries and illnesses such as muscle cramps, heat exhaustion, and heat stroke. Since not even one extra calorie is burned from use of such clothing, additional weight and fat loss do not occur. In winter months, perspiration may be trapped and frozen to the skin, thus causing frostbite.
5. A hat should be used when exercising.	5. Although extremely popular in tennis, baseball, and some other activities, the value of a hat depends on the type you choose. Hats help keep sun off the face, reduce glare, and allow you to see better. A hat with an open top (visor) should be used in hot, humid weather since considerable heat loss and cooling occurs through the head. In cold weather, a full hat is recommended to prevent heat loss.
6. Since the main source of fuel for aerobic exercise is fat, this is the best choice for weight and fat loss.	6. A calorie is a calorie is a calorie is a calorie. To lose weight, your caloric intake must be less than expenditure, regardless of the type of fuel used. As the intensity of a workout increases from a resting state (when two thirds of energy used comes from stored fat) to low or moderate aerobic activity (when fat is still the main fuel) to more intense, anaerobic activity, the percentage of fat decreases as glycogen (stored glucose) provides much more fuel. After exercise ceases, regardless of the fuel used (fat or glucose), the internal calorie count is what matters. If you burned up more calories than you consumed on a particular day, you will lose weight.
	The main advantage of aerobic activity (walking, slow jogging, cycling, aerobic classes, lap swimming, etc.) for weight and body fat loss, is that you are likely to continue exercising for longer periods of time when the intensity is low and therefore will burn more total calories each workout. You also receive considerable health benefits that anaerobic exercise does not provide.

ing level temporarily declines to point B. You are now actually in worse shape, in terms of physical capacity to exercise, than you were before the workout. During the recovery phase, however, tissue will rebuild beyond your original level of conditioning to point C. You are now able to perform more work than you could before you began your exercise program with no more effort. You are also in better physical condition 24 hours later than you were before you completed your first workout. Repetition of this simple process will lead to continued improvement of conditioning levels, as indicated in Figure 7.1 by A–2, A–3, and A–4, providing you follow certain basic guidelines:

- Exercise must be sufficiently strenuous to cause an initial decrease in the conditioning level; the depth of the valley (A to B) and the corresponding increase (B to C) in Figure 7.1 is in proportion to the intensity and duration of your workout.
- Sufficient time must be allowed for recovery; improvement will not occur and conditioning will suffer if your second workout is performed before the recovery phase is complete (48 hours for strength training and 18 to 24 hours for aerobic and other workouts). Failure to follow this principle of recuperation can lead to overuse injuries and reduce the benefits of your workout.
- The next workout must occur within 24 to 48 hours; a greater time lapse will cause your conditioning level to decline.

If you apply this concept to any training program, improved conditioning is guaranteed. Even strength training (see chapter 9) uses this approach to acquire muscle mass and increase strength and endurance.

The resistance principle also applies to the skeletal system. Gradual stress to the bones stimulates the accumulation of calcium and other minerals. In the adult years, **osteoporosis** occurs. This process happens to astronauts freed from the stress of resisting gravity. It is also very common in postmenopausal women. When you walk, jog, run, or perform other aerobic exercise, the force of your feet hitting the ground sends an important signal to your body to maintain bone density. At this point, more of the calcium consumed in your diet reaches the orthopedic system. Other key factors that are also important in the prevention and treatment of osteoporosis are discussed in chapter 10.

Exercise Four Times a Week for 30 Minutes at Your Target Heart Rate (THR)

Although results can be attained without lengthy workouts, there are no shortcuts. Ten-second contractions, massage, mechanical devices, steam baths, three-minute slimnastic programs, and other such approaches vary from slightly effective to worthless.

To receive the health-related benefits of exercise, you must apply the FIT principle:

Frequency   three to four times weekly
Intensity   at or above your target heart rate
Time   20 to 30 minutes of continuous exercise

Frequency of exercise is the key to the success of your program. Exercising three to five times per week rather than one hard workout per week will greatly increase the chances of meeting your training objectives. Frequency is also strongly related to weight and fat loss, cardiovascular development, and disease prevention. One 30-minute session will not transform you into a lean, mean, muscle machine, but three to four sessions weekly for 6 to 12 months will do wonders. Regularity is also a critical factor in changing the way your body handles fats (cholesterol and triglycerides).

Intensity (work per unit of time) is the aspect of your training that determines whether you are receiving any cardiorespiratory (heart-lung) benefits. Researchers have developed simple formulas to determine how much your heart rate must increase during exercise and how long you need to keep it elevated (20 to 30 minutes) to improve cardiovascular fitness. In the early stages of your newly started program, you will need to work up to 20 to 30 minutes of continuous activity slowly, in four to six weeks, rather than attempt to maintain such a high intensity in early workout sessions. To calculate your THR, complete Lab Activity 7.1: Finding Your Target Heart Rate at the end of this chapter.

Time (the duration of your workout) is the final third of the complete cardiorespiratory exercise session. Exercise duration is affected by intensity. Obviously, you cannot sprint at near-maximum effort for 20 minutes. If aerobic conditioning is your goal, the session should maintain your target heart rate for 20 to 30 minutes. If the purpose of your program is cosmetic—to lose weight and fat and to im-

Osteoporosis An abnormal decalcification of bones causing loss of bone density.

prove your appearance—duration is the key. In general, the longer you exercise, the more calories you burn and the more fat you use as fuel. If weight loss is your primary objective, it is important to keep in mind that walking three miles burns only slightly fewer calories than running three miles. The longer you walk or run, the more calories you use. It may be good advice to slow down your walking, pedaling, running, rope jumping, and so on, and exercise longer. To exercise longer, it is important to stay near the lower portion of your THR range. Once you reach your THR, you are not only burning a high number of calories, you are improving the cardiovascular system as well.

Running or walking three miles on each of two successive days also burns more calories than one six-mile run. This is because of the extra 60 to 150 calories burned because of metabolic rate increases (calories burned while the body is at rest) following the exercise period. In other words, two short exercise sessions burn more calories than one long session, since metabolic rate will become, and remain, elevated for several hours after each session. This extra calorie usage after exercise ceases is called **afterburn**. If you walk or run too far in one day and are unable to exercise the next day, you will eliminate one afterburn period and forfeit 60 to 150 calories. Late afternoon, when metabolic rates begin to slow in most people, may be one of the best times to exercise. You then burn calories while exercising and activate a faster metabolic rate for two to four hours at a time in the day when metabolic rate normally slows down.

Apply the Principle of Specificity

The effect of training is unique to an activity or sport. Football or field hockey players who have just completed seasons, for example, will find that they are not capable of meeting the physical demands of wrestling or basketball. The scientific basis for this is that training occurs, in part, within the muscles themselves, and that training is specific to the energy system being used. Thus complete training transfer, regardless of the closeness of the activities, is not possible.

Training a particular muscle group is referred to as **neuromuscular specificity,** whereas training one of the energy systems is called **metabolic specificity**. If your main training objective is to improve aerobic fitness, you must include activities such as jogging, running, cycling, aerobic dance, and distance swimming. Although gains in cardiorespiratory fitness will occur from each of these activities, a specific

activity that closely simulates the movement of the sport for which you are training provides the most transfer. In other words, swimming is the preferred training method to improve distance swimming, running is the preferred training method for 10-K races, and so on.

Alternate Light and Heavy Workouts

The body responds best to training programs that alternate light and heavy workouts. This approach reduces the risk of injury, provides several emotionally relaxing workouts each week, and allows the body time to recover. In other words, it helps you receive maximum benefits from a fitness program. Consider: (1) never training extremely hard on consecutive days, (2) training hard no more than three times a week, (3) scheduling one extra-hard, all-out workout once a week, and (4) knowing your body and allowing it to direct you (if pain continues or worsens or if

Alternating light and heavy workouts reduces the risk of injury and gives the muscles time to recover. (Photo courtesy of the Aspen Hill Club.)

you get heavy-legged, stop regardless of whether it is a light- or heavy-workout day). The PRE principle is applied by increasing the volume and/or intensity on the heavy-workout days.

Warm Up Properly before Each Workout

A **warm-up** is almost universally used at the beginning of an exercise or activity session to improve performance and prevent injury. The theory behind the warm-up is that muscular contractions are dependent on temperature. Since increased muscle temperature improves work capacity and a warm-up increases muscle temperature, it is assumed that one is necessary. The amount of knee fluid is also increased with a warm-up; oxygen intake is improved; and the amount of oxygen needed for exercise is reduced. Nerve messages also travel faster at higher temperatures.

Suggestions that can be drawn from the findings of well-controlled studies on the warm-up include:

1. Warm-up for 10 to 15 minutes prior to the actual workout or exercise session. A longer period is needed in a cold environment to allow the body to reach the desired temperature prior to activity.

2. The main purpose of a warm-up is to elevate core temperature by one to two degrees before engaging in stretching exercises or explosive muscular movements; you will generally reach this point at the same time your warm-up routine causes sweating.

3. Only a few minutes should elapse from completion of the warm-up until the start of activity.

4. Warm-up will not cause early fatigue and hinder performance.

Warm-up methods fall into four categories:

1. **Formal** The skill or act that will be used in competition or in your workout, such as running before a 100-meter dash, jogging before a 3-mile run, or shooting a basketball and jumping before a basketball game.

2. **Informal** The general warm-up involving calisthenics or other activity unrelated to the workout routine to follow.

3. **Passive** Applying heat to various body parts.

4. **Overload** Simulating the activity for which the warm-up is being used by increasing the load or resistance, such as swinging two bats before hitting a baseball.

Each of these methods has been shown by some researchers to be helpful and by other researchers to be of little value. Formal warm-up appears superior to informal procedures. When body temperature is elevated and sweating occurs, your muscles are ready for a brief stretching or flexibility session.

How long you decide to engage in warm-up activities is also important. The temperature of your muscles will rise in about 5 minutes and continue to rise further for 25 to 30 minutes. If you stop exercising and become inactive, your muscle temperature will decline significantly, and you may need an additional warm-up period. The best advice is to use a 10- to 15-minute warm-up period that ends in an all-out effort and causes you to perspire. You should plan to complete your warm-up period about 5 minutes before an exercise session or competition begins. Find the magic combination for you and your activity and stay with it.

Warming up muscles improves performance and prevents injuries. (Photo cCourtesy of the American Heart Association.)

Afterburn The period of time following exercise when resting metabolism remains elevated.

Neuromuscular specificity Training a specific muscle group.

Metabolic specificity Training a specific energy system (citric acid cycle or glycolysis cycle).

Warm-up The preparation of the body for vigorous activity through stretching, calisthenics, running, and specific sport movements designed to raise core temperature.

Cool Down Properly at the End of Each Workout

The justification for a **cool-down** period following a vigorous workout is quite simple. Blood returns to the heart through a system of vessels called *veins*. The blood is pushed along by heart contractions, and the veins' milking action is assisted by muscle contractions during exercise. Veins contract, or squeeze, and move the blood forward against gravity while valves prevent the blood from backing up. If you stop exercising suddenly, this milking action will stop, and blood return will drop quickly and may cause blood pooling (blood remaining in the same area) in the legs, leading to shock or deep breathing, which may in turn lower carbon dioxide levels and produce muscle cramps.

It is at this point also that blood pressure can drop precipitously and cause trouble. The body compensates for the unexpected drop in pressure by secreting as much as 100 times the normal amount of **norepinephrine**. This high level of norepinephrine can cause cardiac problems for some individuals during the recovery phase of vigorous exercise such as a marathon or a triathlon.

Postexercise peril occurs in some individuals immediately after exercise, particularly among those who fail to use a cool-down period. The least desirable postexercise behavior is standing. Lying down flat is acceptable; the preferred activity, however, is walking or jogging (light exercise).

You should also cool down following a long aerobic exercise session. A general routine might consist of walking or jogging a quarter mile to a mile at a pace of three to four minutes per quarter mile, each quarter mile slower than the previous one. The ideal cool-down routine should take place in the same environment as the workout (except in extremely hot

or cold weather), last at least five minutes, and be followed by a brief stretching period.

Dress Appropriately for Ease of Movement and Heat Regulation

What you wear depends on your exercise program and the weather. The general rule is to have good shoes and to wear as little clothing as the weather permits.

Shoes To avoid injuries, good shoes are essential for most aerobic activities. The primary criteria are fit, comfort, and quality. Most activities require a specialized shoe, and although they often look identical, the construction styles affect individuals differently. Specialty stores are more likely to provide sound advice about the best shoe for your aerobic goals. Since fit is so important, wear the same style socks you use for exercising when you are selecting a shoe.

Clothes For indoor and warm-weather outdoor exercise, wear the least clothing possible. The cooling process requires air to pass over the skin and evaporate; clothing must allow this process to take place. Some individuals mistakenly think they will lose weight by wearing multiple layers of clothes to increase fluid loss. It is the total calories expended, however, not the total sweat count, that determines weight and fat loss.

When you are exercising outside during the winter, do not either overdress or underdress. Like summer clothing, winter attire must allow the skin to breathe. Windbreakers and other nylon garments are therefore not recommended. Combining a T-shirt with a wool sweater, a hat, and gloves is usually sufficient for protection in temperatures down to 32° F (0° C). In extremely cold conditions, however, frostbite is a real danger, particularly to exposed skin. The skin can be protected, but only to a degree, with creams and jellies. Men, for example, must protect the penis and testicles from frostbite; nylon shorts are of little value, and frostbite can occur without warning.

Take Special Precautions When Exercising Outdoors

Weather conditions are not your only concern when you exercise outside. *Pollution*, particularly lack of clear air, is a danger worth paying attention to. Although the benefits of exercise overshadow the dangers of unclear air, workouts during smog alerts and in high traffic areas should be avoided. *Motor vehicles* and even *bicycles* can present life-threatening

---

Cool-down The use of 3 to 10 minutes of very light exercise movements at the end of a vigorous workout designed to cool the body slowly to near-normal core temperature.

Norepinephrine An end product of some of the secretions of the adrenal gland; influences nervous system activity, constricts blood vessels, and increases blood pressure.

Postexercise peril Illness, dizziness, nausea, and sudden death following vigorous exercise, particularly when a cool-down period is not used.

Improving Your Community

Getting Others to Get the Message about Regular Exercise

Several alarming trends with serious implications for our nation's health have emerged in the last decade. These trends include a reduction in the number of required hours of physical education in public schools, chronic low-level fitness among children, adolescents, and young adults, and increased incidence of childhood and adult obesity. Furthermore, the number of Americans who exercise according to the Surgeon General's definition (three to four times weekly at the individual's target heart rate for a minimum of 20 minutes) are well below the *Year 2000 National Health Objectives.*

You can begin to alter some of these trends right now. The health behaviors of college students always become well known to the American public. A nation of physically active college students can positively influence other people to include regular exercise in their own lifestyles as well as to support exercise programs and opportunities in their schools and communities. One of the most important messages to get across to other people, however, is that exercise is not only for "the young and the beautiful." Exercise—like good nutrition and weight control—is for people of all ages. Here are some specific things you can do to convey this message:

1. Encourage family and friends to eliminate unhealthy behaviors such as sedentary living, dangerous weekend exercise sessions, and, of course, tobacco, alcohol, and other drug use. Help the people in your immediate circle to develop exercise regimens that are appropriate for them.

2. Become involved as a counselor or coach in college or local community-affiliated sports and recre-

ation programs. Such programs might involve day camps for elementary or middle school students or even extended week- or month-long sports and recreation programs. Some of these programs qualify as internships, many of them involve some sort of stipend or other form of payment, and all of them can be extremely valuable experiences in your own life.

3. Locate one or more faculty members or community health officers (such as doctors or physical therapists) who specialize in the care of older people. Discuss with these people how you could contribute your time and energy to the improvement of exercise opportunities for older people, especially for those currently confined to their homes or in nursing homes. There are many simple, healthful exercises that older people—even those who cannot leave a wheelchair—can perform that will help them to develop better muscle tone, feel better, and have higher energy levels.

4. Get physically involved in supporting physical education and exercise programs and opportunities in public schools, colleges, and universities. Inform yourself about the physical education elements in local school budgets and in your own college's budget, and lobby and rally voters and other students for support when necessary.

5. Encourage exercise and recreation programs in your own college community by participating in and otherwise supporting intramural sports, fitness, and recreation activities. Actively encourage other students to participate in these activities too. ✦

situations to runners and others who exercise outside. Cars and bicycles should be given the right-of-way no matter what you or the law indicates. It is also advisable to run or walk toward traffic and to use reflective gear at night. Do not be aggressive, since you are no match for a vehicle that weighs 3,000 pounds or more.

Dogs tend to have considerable bark and little bite, but the exceptions can produce disaster. Since

dogs are extremely territorial, it is wise to avoid crossing property lines. For the occasional dog that comes after you, the best action is to stop, face the dog, and assume a passive posture before slowly backing away. As you vacate the property, the animal generally becomes less aggressive. *Two-legged animals* are far more dangerous than any of the four-legged varieties. Women in particular must be alert to dangerous situations and take care to exercise with others, avoid outside exercise at night, ignore taunts, and remain alert at all times.

Choose Soft Surfaces Whenever Possible

Although exercise involves some risk of injury (see chapter 14), choice of surface can reduce the risk. Generally speaking, the harder the surface, the greater the injury potential. A surface that is too soft or uneven also increases the risk of certain types of exercise injuries. A soft, uneven surface, such as a beach, can cause ankle and knee injuries. Dirt and gravel paths and trails covered with wood chips are best for walking and running, but the isolated nature of most trails increases the chances of assault. Public park, vitae courses usually provide relatively safe, soft places to exercise. Exercising on concrete floors, sidewalks, hard tennis courts, and gymnasium floors should be avoided whenever possible. Daily activity on such surfaces is almost certain to produce injury.

Use Cross Training in the Aerobic Component of Your Program

Repetitive motion syndrome can produce both injury and loss of interest in exercise. Daily step classes or a 5-mile run, for example, both involve the same motion, movement, muscles, and joints over and over and are almost certain to result in injury over long periods of time. More and more individuals use **cross training** and avoid these dangers by varying their exercise choices weekly. Runners may choose to ride a stationary cycle or swim once or twice a week. Aerobic dance participants may alternate with cycling, walking, swimming, or racket sports. Such an approach provides a more complete workout and eliminates exercise boredom and burnout.

Use a Maintenance Approach after Reaching Your Desired Level of Fitness

It is possible to alter your exercise program to maintain the level of conditioning you have acquired. Considerable strength, for example, can be maintained by completing one or two hard

weight-training workouts weekly. Maintaining your cardiorespiratory endurance may require two to three workouts weekly. During times when you are unable to exercise daily, you may choose to alter your routine by increasing the intensity and duration of the workouts you complete.

Monitor Your Progress Carefully

Records can be a source of motivation in addition to aiding in the prevention of injury. Keeping records of resting heart rate, the number of miles walked or run, laps swum, weight lifted, and number of workouts completed can provide the needed incentive to continue an exercise program.

Record keeping also helps you apply the PRE principle to guarantee continued improvement. It is difficult to improve and work harder today when you are not aware of the intensity and duration of your previous workouts. See Lab Activity 7.2: Evaluating Your Exercise Program.

If an overuse injury occurs, a perusal of records can aid in determining its cause and help you in setting a course toward recovery. Unfortunately, records can also lead to compulsive behavior known as *negative addiction*. To the addicted, records are made to be broken, more is better, and the record rather than the fitness benefits becomes the goal. Such individuals experience frequent injury intermixed with emotional stress in attempting to maintain or break records.

The daily log in Table 7.1 can help you apply many of the exercise concepts discussed in this chapter. The log information should include the number of minutes spent in aerobic activity, distance covered, and rest intervals between repetitions, if applicable. Your log should also contain weather conditions, water temperature, heart rate, how you felt, particular problems that indicate the possibility of future injury, number and type of activities completed, and (for weight training) the weight and number of repetitions for each exercise. It is also important to periodically monitor your aerobic exercise choices. Complete Lab 7.2 to evaluate your workout routine.

MAKING THE RIGHT EXERCISE CHOICES

The ideal, complete exercise program should have four components: aerobics, muscular strength, muscular endurance, and flexibility. The aerobic compo-

---

Cross training The practice of alternating exercise choices throughout the week to avoid overuse injuries from repetitive movements.

Table 7.1 ✦ Daily Exercise Log

Date _____   Time of day _____

Distance covered or total exercise time _____

Weather conditions _____

Terrain (flat, hills, soft, hard, and so forth) _____

Intensity: Heart rate _____

          Repetitions _____

          Rest interval _____

          Distance covered _____   Pace _____

Duration: _____

Positive impressions of workout:

Unusual feelings or problems during workout:

Overall rating on a scale of 1 to 10 _____
(10 = Excellent, 1= Dreadful)

nent will provide the health-related benefits in addition to controlling and maintaining body weight and fat. A sound weight-training program will improve muscle tone, strength, and endurance; prevent the loss of lean muscle mass; add muscle mass; and help control body weight and fat by increasing metabolism. Stretching exercises will help maintain and improve your range of motion and prevent joint stiffness.

Aerobic Choices

It is important to select a program that is effective in developing the cardiorespiratory system and is compatible with your training objectives, amount of time available, and interests. Table 7.2 compares aerobic exercise choices based on the characteristics of the ideal program. Study this table carefully before making your selection. It is also a good idea to sample different approaches to help you find activities you enjoy for use in cross training later.

If you are interested in the sports approach to aerobic fitness, study Table 7.3 before making your selections. As you are now aware, the term **aerobic** means *with oxygen* and describes extended vigorous exercise that stimulates heart and lung activity enough to produce a training effect. This occurs

Table 7.2 ✦ Evaluation of Exercise Programs

Characteristics of the ideal program	Aerobic Exercise and Dance	Anaer-obics	Calis-thenics	Cycling	Rope Jumping	Running Programs	Sports[1]	Walking	Swimming (laps)	Weight Training
Easily adaptable to individual's exercise tolerance	P	Y	Y	Y	Y	Y	P	Y	Y	Y
Applies the progressive resistance principle	Y	Y	Y	Y	Y	Y	P	Y	Y	Y
Provides for self-evaluation	Y	Y	P	Y	Y	Y	P	Y	Y	Y
Practical for use throughout life	Y	N	N	Y	Y	Y	P	Y	Y	Y
Scientifically developed	Y	Y	P	Y	Y	Y	U	Y	Y	Y
Involves minimum time	Y	P	N	Y	Y	Y	N	Y	Y	Y
Involves little or no equipment	P	Y	Y	N	Y	Y	N	Y	Y	N
Performed easily at home	N	N	Y	Y	Y	Y	N	Y	Y	N
Widely publicized	Y	N	N	Y	Y	Y	Y	Y	Y	Y
Accepted and valued	Y	P	N	Y	Y	Y	P	Y	Y	Y
Challenging	Y	Y	N	Y	Y	Y	Y	Y	Y	Y
Firms body	Y	Y	Y	Y	Y	P	P	Y	Y	Y
Develops flexibility[2]	Y	N	Y	N	Y	Y	Y	N	P	N
Develops muscular endurance	Y	Y	Y	Y		Y	Y	Y	Y	Y
Develops cardio-vascular endurance: Prevents heart disease	Y	N	Y	Y	Y	Y	Y	P	Y	P
Develops strength	P	P	Y	P	P	Y	Y	P	P	Y
High caloric expenditure: Weight loss	Y	P	P	Y	Y	P	Y	Y	Y	N

Note: Y = yes, P = partially, N = no provision, U = unknown (referring to meeting ideal characteristics).

[1]The value of the sports approach depends on the activity and the level of competition.

[2]Flexibility can be improved only if the complete range of movement is performed in each exercise, applying static pressure at the extreme range of motion before returning to starting position.

Source: Adapted from *Improving Health and Fitness in the Athlete* (p. 180), by J. Unitas and G. B. Dintiman, 1979, Englewood Cliffs, NJ: Prentice-Hall.

Table 7.3 ✦ Ratings of Sports

Sport	Type	Cardiovascular	Caloric expenditure	Legs	Abdomen	Arms/ shoulder	Age range recommended
Archery	Anaerobic	L	L	L	L	L	Ages 10 and up
Backpacking	50% Aerobic	M-H	H	H	M	L	All ages
Badminton	40% Aerobic	M-H	H	H	L	M	Ages 7 and up
Baseball/softball	Anaerobic	L	L	M	L	L	All ages
Basketball	25% Aerobic	M	H	H	L	L	Ages 7 to 40
Bicycling (competitive)	Aerobic	H	H	H	L	M	All ages
Bowling	Anaerobic	L	L	L	L	L	All ages
Dance (aerobic)	Aerobic	M-H	M-H	M	M	M	All ages
Canoeing/rowing							
Recreational	Anaerobic	L	M	L	L	M	Ages 12 and up
Competitive	Aerobic	H	H	M	M	H	Ages 12 to 40
Fencing	Anaerobic	L-M	M	M	L	M	Ages 12 and up
Field hockey	40% Aerobic	M-H	M-H	H	L	M	Ages 7 and up
Golf (motor cart)	Anaerobic	L	L	L	L	L	All ages
Walking	Aerobic	L	M	M	L	L	All ages
Handball/racquetball/ squash (singles)	40% Aerobic	M-H	H	H	L	H	All ages
Hiking	Aerobic	L-M	M	H	L	L	All ages
Hunting	Aerobic	L-M	M	M	L	L	All ages
Ice/roller skating							
Speed	Anaerobic	L-M	M	H	L	L	Under 45
Figure	Aerobic	L-M	H	H	M	M	All ages
Lacrosse	40% Aerobic	M-H	H	H	M	M	Under 45
Orienteering	50% Aerobic	M-H	H	H	M	L	All ages
Rugby	60% Aerobic	H	H	H	L	H	Under 45
Skiing (cross-country)	Aerobic	H	H	H	H	H	All ages
Skin and scuba diving	Aerobic	M	M	M	M	L	All ages
Soccer	50% Aerobic	H	H	H	L	H	Under 45
Surfing	Anaerobic	L	M	H	M	L	Ages 7 and up
Tennis (singles)	40% Aerobic	M	M	H	L	L	All ages
Touch football	Anaerobic	L	L-M	H	L	L	Under 45
Volleyball	Anaerobic	L	L	M-H	L	M	All ages
Water skiing	Anaerobic	L-M	M	H	L	M	All ages
Weight training	Anaerobic	L	L	H	H	H	All ages
Wrestling	30% Aerobic	M	H	H	H	H	Under 45
Jogging	Aerobic	M-H	H	H	L	L	Ages 7 and up
Swimming	Aerobic	M	H	M	L	H	Ages 7 and up
Walking	Aerobic	L-M	M	H	L	L	All ages

H = high; M = medium; L = low

Behavioral Change
and Motivational Strategies

Many things can interfere with your application of sound exercise principles. Some of these barriers (roadblocks) and strategies for overcoming them are described here.

Roadblock	Behavioral Change Strategy
Exercise just isn't fun anymore, and you no longer look forward to your afternoon workout session. Even if you do get into the workout, there is no motivation to put forth much effort.	You may be experiencing some of the emotional and physical effects of overtraining or exercising too often. To renew your interest: 1. Change aerobic activities every other day as a cross-training technique. If you are jogging or using STEP daily, for example, substitute cycling, lap swimming, aerobic dance, or a sports activity two to three times weekly. 2. Change the time you exercise. Try early mornings, noon, or just before bedtime to see if time will improve your mood. 3. Apply the light-heavy concept discussed in this chapter and avoid two consecutive workouts of the same level of difficulty. 4. Add one or two fun workouts weekly, and exercise with a group of friends.
Muscle soreness the following morning is making your day unpleasant since sitting, standing, and moving around on the job is somewhat painful.	A number of factors may be causing the problem. You may be exercising untrained muscles; training much too hard; not consuming enough fluids before, during, and after your workout; or stretching improperly or not at all. Try some of these remedies for at least one week: 1. Hydrate 15 to 30 minutes before your workout by drinking three or four 8-ounce glasses of water. 2. Record the amount of water and other fluids you consume daily, making certain to drink at least eight glasses of water. 3. Alternate light- and heavy-workout days. 4. Warm up for a longer period of time than you normally do, then stretch carefully for at least 10 minutes. 5. At the end of your workout, cool down properly, and end with a mild 5-minute stretching session.
Although you have been exercising daily for a month, little weight and fat loss seems to be taking place.	To lose body fat and weight, you need to change your exercise emphasis and reduce your caloric intake. Don't give up. Be certain you: 1. Monitor both your exercise sessions and your food intake by keeping accurate records of total exercise volume and the daily calories consumed. 2. Increase the duration of your workout and exercise every day. If you are walking, try to walk continuously for at least one hour. Reduce the intensity of your workout and continue exercising longer each workout. 3. Schedule your workout about two hours before mealtime or two hours after your evening meal to help control hunger and the temptation to overeat or snack.
List other roadblocks that you are experiencing that seem to be reducing the effectiveness of your program and limiting your success. 1. _____ 2. _____ 3. _____	Now list behavioral change strategies that can help you overcome the roadblocks you listed. If you need to, refer to chapter 3 for behavioral change and motivational strategies. 1. _____ 2. _____ 3. _____

when your target heart rate is reached and maintained at that level for 20 minutes or more. Many sports are more **anaerobic** than aerobic and fail to improve heart-lung endurance or provide the health benefits you desire.

Anaerobic means *without oxygen* and describes short, all-out exercise efforts such as the 100-, 200-, or 400-meter dash and sports such as football and baseball. Anaerobic metabolism is the immediate energy source of all muscle work at the beginning of any type of exercise. This energy source, called adenosine triphosphate (ATP), is formed in the muscles primarily through the metabolism of carbohydrates. Every muscle needs ATP to perform its work. The process is anaerobic because ATP is metabolized without the need for oxygen. For short sprints and all-out efforts, the heart and lungs cannot deliver atmospheric oxygen to the muscles fast enough; anaerobic energy sources therefore must provide the fuel. The very instant that the amount of oxygen breathed in is not enough to supply active muscles, **oxygen debt** occurs and you begin to breathe heavily. After you stop exercising, oxygen debt is repaid and normal breathing returns. Unfortunately, anaerobic

Aerobics Activity performed in the presence of oxygen, using fat as the major source of fuel.

Anaerobics High-intensity activity, such as sprinting, that is performed in the absence of oxygen, using glucose as the major source of fuel.

Oxygen debt The difference between the exact amount of oxygen needed for an exercise task and the amount actually taken in.

activities cannot be sustained for long periods of time, burn fewer calories, and fail to provide some important health benefits. It is difficult to improve your aerobic fitness through mere participation in a sport, and we recommend that you supplement such participation with a minimum of two aerobic workouts weekly.

Aerobic exercises should produce some changes within 3 to 4 weeks. Complete Lab 7.3: Resting Heart Rate Reduction to monitor the changes in your resting heart rate over a period of 7 to 14 weeks.

Choosing Muscular Strength and Endurance Programs

Chapter 9 describes numerous choices for increasing your muscular strength and endurance effectively. Your choice of workout routine depends on your training objectives, which also help you decide between free weights and the other types of exercise equipment. Chapter 9 gives you enough details to help you make the correct decision.

Selecting an Appropriate Flexibility Training Program

Although a simple, static stretching routine is the wisest choice for effectively improving your flexibility, specific exercise choices depend on your objectives, including that of the particular activity for which you are training. The detailed information in chapter 9 will help you make the right decision. In less than ten minutes daily, you can maintain and even improve range of motion in your major joints.

SUMMARY

The Ideal Exercise Program

A complete exercise program should bring about improvement in five key health-related fitness areas: cardiorespiratory endurance, body composition, muscular strength, muscular endurance, and flexibility. Aerobic exercise is the most important component and should form the foundation of the ideal program. The principles of exercise must be applied specifically to your workout choice to guarantee continued improvement.

Fitness Concepts

A preconditioning period may be necessary before beginning a new exercise program, particularly for people who have previously been inactive. This three- to four-week period will prepare you for more vigorous workouts and allow you to reach and maintain your THR for 20 to 30 minutes safely.

The PRE principle can easily be adapted to aerobic, muscular strength and endurance, and flexibility training to ensure steady progress and improvement in these areas. To train for a specific sport or activity, you must apply the principle of specificity by using movements and exercises that closely simulate those performed in the sport. The use of a warm-up and cool-down period, the application of FIT to your aerobic workout, alternating light- and heavy-workout days, dressing appropriately for the weather, monitoring your progress with record-keeping, and cross training will improve the benefits of each workout, keep you emotionally and physically healthy, and eliminate boredom and overtraining.

Making the Right Exercise Choices

It is important to select aerobic activities you enjoy that are also effective and that meet your training objectives. The sports approach to aerobic fitness requires special care in selecting activities, such as soccer, rugby, field hockey, and racquetball (singles), that are primarily aerobic in nature. Anaerobic activity choices will provide very little in the way of health-related benefits. Two to three additional workouts weekly in an aerobic activity are also recommended.

REFERENCES

American Heart Association. (1992). Statement on exercise: Benefits and recommendations for physical activity programs for all Americans. *Circulation 86*, 340–344.

Berhhauer, E., et al. (1989). Exercise reduces depressed metabolic rate produced by severe caloric restriction. *Medicine and Science in Sports and Exercise 21*, 29–33.

Bouchard, C., et al. (Eds.). (1994). *Physical activity, fitness and health.* Champaign, IL: Human Kinetics.

CIBA Foundation. (1981). *Human muscle fatigue: Physiological mechanisms.* London: Pitman Medical.

Goldfine, H., et al. (1991, June). Exercising to health. *The Physician and Sportsmedicine 19*, 81–93.

Green, H., et al. (1991). Early muscular and metabolic adaptations to prolonged exercise training in humans. *Journal of Applied Physiology 70*(5), 2032–2038.

Greenberg, J., Dintiman, G., & Oakes, B. (1995). *Physical fitness and wellness.* Boston: Allyn & Bacon.

Hatfield, F. (Ed.). (1991) *Fitness: The complete guide.* Santa Barbara: International Sports Science Association.

International Federation of Sports Medicine. (March 1990). Physical exercise: An important factor for health. *The Physician and Sportsmedicine 18*, 155–156.

Parker, S., et al. (1989). Failure of target heart rate to accurately monitor intensity during aerobic dance. *Medicine and Science in Sports and Exercise 20*, S88.

Pollack, C. (1992, December). Does exercise intensity matter? *Physician and Sportsmedicine 20*, 123–126.

U.S. Department of Health and Human Services. (1990). Healthy people 2000: National health promotion and disease prevention objectives. Public Health Services Bulletin (PHS) 91–50212.

Lab Activity 7.1

Finding Your Target Heart Rate (THR)

INSTRUCTIONS: *The target heart rate (THR) is the range of heart rate that will produce training effects on the heart if it is maintained for a sufficient length of time (usually 20 to 30 minutes) at least three times per week. This is commonly known as aerobic exercise. The purpose of this lab is to determine your THR or exercise benefit zone (EBZ).*

✦ **Procedure**

1. Determine your resting heart rate (RHR). This is the lowest heart rate you experience anytime during your waking hours—day or evening. Check it several times during the day when you feel really relaxed. You are looking for the slowest heart rate. (Refer to step 1 of Lab Activity 7.2 for specific instructions on finding your RHR.)

2. Use the formula below to compute your 60 percent, 70 percent, and 85 percent target heart rates. This is the zone you should stay in during aerobic exercise.

60% THR	70% THR	85% THR
220	220	220
– _____	– _____ Subtract age	– _____
– _____	– _____ Subtract RHR	– _____
× .60	× .70	× .85
_____	_____	_____
+ RHR	+ RHR	+ RHR
_____	_____	_____
(60% THR)	(70% THR)	(85% THR)

Lab Activity 7.2

Evaluating Your Exercise Program

INSTRUCTIONS: *You can easily evaluate the effectiveness of your aerobic exercise program by taking your heart rate immediately after you complete the final seconds of your workout. Follow the steps below to determine whether you need to increase or decrease the intensity of your exercise session.*

✦ **Step 1** Find your resting heart rate by locating your radial pulse. To do this, place the index and middle fingers of your right hand in the wrist groove just below your thumb. Count the number of beats for 15 seconds and multiply by 4 to find the beats per minute. A faster approach is to obtain the number of beats in exactly 6 seconds before adding a 0 to determine the number of beats per minute. This may be a more accurate method of estimating the rate while you were exercising. In general, the lower the heart rate, the higher the aerobic fitness level. As you improve your cardiovascular fitness, your resting heart rate will decrease. The carotid pulse, located just under the jaw, can be used for those unable to feel a strong pulse at the wrist. Pressing too hard on the carotid pulse may slow heart rate and cause dizziness.

✦ **Step 2** Complete your normal workout. Just prior to entering the cool-down phase, after a minimum of 20 minutes of continuous activity, stop and take your radial or carotid pulse and record the number of beats per minute.

✦ **Step 3** Refer to Lab Activity 7.1 to see if this figure (number of beats per minute) falls within your THR range. If it is below the lower limit, you must run, walk, swim, or cycle faster or take shorter breaks between points in tennis, racquetball, handball, basketball, and so forth. If it is above the upper limit, you need to exercise at a slower pace and rest more.

Exercise activity _____

Exercise heart rate (number of beats per minute) _____

THR range _____ to _____

Recommended change _____

Lab Activity 7.3

Resting Heart Rate Reduction

INSTRUCTIONS: *The purpose of this lab is to plot your resting heart rate over a period of 7 to 14 weeks. If you are engaging in an aerobic exercise program three to four times weekly for 20 to 30 minutes each, working at your target heart rate, you should see a substantial reduction in the number of times your heart beats per minute. As your aerobic fitness level improves, your stroke volume increases and your heart becomes more efficient by ejecting more blood per beat. Follow the three steps below carefully.*

1. Your first lab is an easy one. Lie down for 15 minutes in a comfortable place. Be sure not to eat or drink for at least 3 hours before doing this lab. You have, of course, given up smoking. If not, do not smoke for at least 30 minutes prior to completing this lab.

2. After the rest period and while still lying down, take your pulse at the carotid artery (either side of the neck) or use the radial pulse (thumb side of the wrist). Since your thumb has its own pulse and will cause inaccurate readings, use only the fingers to find and count pulse. Count for an entire minute. The resulting number is your resting heart rate. Record it on the chart below.

3. This lab should be repeated at least once a week.

✦ Results

By connecting the dots on the heart rate reduction chart below, you should begin to see a decline in your resting heart rate within two weeks, indicating an increase in cardiovascular efficiency.

Heart Rate

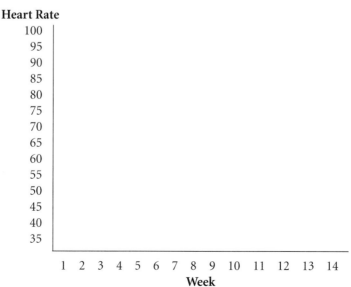

8

CARDIORESPIRATORY FITNESS

Chapter Objectives

By the end of this chapter, you should be able to:

1. Provide alternate names for cardiorespiratory endurance.

2. Express benefits to be derived from participating in a cardiorespiratory conditioning program.

3. Describe maximal oxygen uptake (VO_2) and show different ways of expressing it.

4. Assess your VO_2 and determine cardiorespiratory fitness.

5. Explain guidelines for safely beginning and progressing in an aerobic fitness program.

6. Develop your own cardiorespiratory conditioning program.

RECENTLY TWO WOMEN were shopping in a department store. Ms. Green, a professional, 40-year-old, single female, was purchasing exercise clothing and accidentally bumped into Mrs. Taylor, a 45-year-old, lower-income woman, who was purchasing clothing for her grandchildren. As the two women struck up a conversation, Ms. Green explained that she had just enrolled in the new Jane Fonda Step Aerobics class at the local health club. She asked Mrs. Taylor if she had considered joining the class because step aerobics is very popular and is a great form of exercise. Mrs. Taylor responded, "Well, you know, I'm so busy cleaning houses that I just don't have the time or the energy to join an exercise class!"

Unfortunately, the cardiorespiratory exercise boom has not reached all segments of the U.S. population for various reasons. Many obstacles, such as increased time demands, may make exercise seem impossible. As your time-management skills improve, however, finding time to exercise will not be as difficult as it may seem. Also, many people mistakenly believe, as Mrs. Taylor does, that participating in an exercise class will make them more fatigued. In reality, the opposite is true. Improved cardiorespiratory fitness often increases your energy level. Many other benefits are to be derived from participating in an aerobic conditioning program.

Cardiorespiratory endurance is referred to by many names, including aerobic power, **maximal oxygen consumption** (VO_2), physical fitness, and **aerobic metabolism**. **Cardiorespiratory endurance** is the ability of the heart, blood vessels, and the lungs to deliver oxygen to the exercising muscles in amounts sufficient to meet the demands of the workload. **Endurance** is the ability to perform prolonged bouts of work without experiencing fatigue or exhaustion. As your cardiorespiratory endurance level increases, so does your ability to engage in sustained physical activity. By the end of several months of cardiorespiratory activities, you will be able to exercise for long periods of time without experiencing prolonged fatigue.

As your body adapts to an aerobic conditioning program, you will also feel better and have a much higher energy level. A high level of cardiorespiratory fitness actually increases the daily energy level as well as your level of productivity. A high level of cardiorespiratory endurance is also beneficial in helping to delay several chronic diseases, such as heart disease and high blood pressure. Recent research has even shown that people with high levels of cardiorespiratory endurance are less susceptible to developing cancer. Since heart disease, high blood pressure, and cancer are among the leading causes of death in the United States, it is especially important to maintain a healthy cardiorespiratory system.

Table 8.1 lists the physiological benefits to be derived from participating in a cardiorespiratory endurance conditioning program. The list may seem overwhelming at first glance, but all these physiological changes can be reduced to one primary benefit— increased aerobic power. What effect do all these changes have on level of performance? First, all the changes that occur to the heart, blood, blood vessels, and lungs, which make up the **cardiorespiratory system**, are geared to increase the amount of blood that is delivered to the muscles. Also, these benefits make exercise feel easier at workloads below maximum. They increase your ability to perform at maximal exercise intensity. The changes that occur in the muscles, bones, and joints are all designed to increase your ability to extract oxygen from the bloodstream and use it to produce energy for exercise. Exercise duration is increased as well as exercise intensity. In short, the total amount of work that you are able to do increases as a result of cardiorespiratory adaptations from an aerobic conditioning program.

In the remainder of this chapter, we explore aerobic exercise choices and discuss the differences in VO_2 for various sports. We will also discuss guidelines for beginning and safely progressing in an aerobic conditioning program and conclude with some sample starter programs for aerobic activities. You will then have the opportunity to design your own aerobic exercise program.

Table 8.1 ✦ Physiological Benefits of Increased Cardiorespiratory Endurance after Participating in an Aerobic Training Program

Heart, blood vessels, and lungs	Muscles, bones, joints
Lower resting heart rate	Increased bone strength and density
Lower submaximal exercise heart rate	Increased thickness of cartilage, tendons, and ligaments
Increased maximal cardiac output	Increased oxygen consumed by muscles
Increased stroke volume	Increased number of mitochondria
Decreased recovery time	Increased size of mitochondria
Increased strength of heart muscle	Increased concentration of oxidative enzymes
Increased blood flow to muscles during exercise	Increased size of slow-twitch muscle fibers
Decreased resting blood pressure in hypertensives	Increased muscle glycogen stores
Increased number of capillaries in muscles	Increased ATP and phosphocreatine stores
Increased total blood volume	Increased ability to burn fat for energy
Increased hemoglobin (carries oxygen to muscles)	Decreased body fat percentage
Increased vital capacity (lung capacity)	Increased muscular endurance
Decreased blood lipids	Increased flexibility
Increased high-density lipoprotein (HDL) cholesterol	
Decreased low-density lipoprotein (LDL) cholesterol	
Decreased triglycerides (fats)	

OVERVIEW AND ANALYSIS OF AEROBIC EXERCISE CHOICES

Only aerobic activities will increase your level of cardiorespiratory endurance. Fortunately, numerous aerobic choices are available, including walking, jogging/running, swimming, bicycling, aerobic dancing and step aerobics, water aerobics, rope skipping, cross-country skiing, racket sports, and stepping.

Nearly all aerobic sports lead to the same benefits with respect to increased aerobic power, so it makes little difference whether you choose to walk, jog, or ride a bike. When you choose a conditioning program, however, it is important for you to realize that the larger the amount of muscle mass used in an activity, the greater will be your level of endurance, especially during the initial phase. For example, if you walk 45 minutes, you will probably not become fatigued as quickly as if you play tennis for 45 minutes. That is because the muscles that grip the tennis racket tire more quickly since you place a high energy demand on a very small muscle mass. Whereas your leg muscles, as used in walking, are a much larger group, they are more accustomed to this activity and will not fatigue as quickly. For this reason, you will find that your endurance is greater when you engage in activities such as swimming, walking, and jogging/running than is the case with activities that rely primarily on the arms. Remember that in the initial phase of a conditioning program, you can expect to tire sooner when small muscle groups are used.

Regardless of how exciting a new aerobic conditioning program may be, eventually boredom might creep in. Hence we recommend that you participate in a variety of aerobic activities in order to maintain cardiorespiratory fitness. The greater the diversity in your program, the greater the likelihood that you will maintain a lifetime of physical fitness. Also, whenever possible, exercise with a partner or with a group of people. The benefits of exercising with other people are discussed elsewhere in this book, but a major benefit is that exercising with a partner or a group increases the likelihood you will stay with your conditioning program.

MAXIMAL OXYGEN CONSUMPTION (VO_2)

Cardiorespiratory endurance is synonymous with VO_2, or maximal oxygen uptake. When a person is tested either in a laboratory or in the field, the highest level of oxygen uptake achieved is called the VO_2, which actually represents the volume of oxygen consumed by the muscles. The VO_2 is regarded as the single best indicator of cardiorespiratory endurance or aerobic fitness.

A high VO_2 indicates an increased ability of the heart to pump blood, of the lungs to fill with larger volumes of air, and of the muscle cells to use the oxygen and remove waste products that are produced during the process of aerobic metabolism. The two primary factors influencing maximal aerobic power are (1) the ability of the cardiorespiratory system to deliver oxygen to the muscles and (2) the ability of the muscles to extract oxygen from the blood.

Oxygen is used in the process of aerobic metabolism. When you exercise for prolonged periods of time, vast quantities of energy are needed by the muscles. Foodstuffs stored in the muscles, such as fats and **glycogen** (the stored form of carbohydrate in the muscles) are broken down continuously in order to provide **adenosine triphosphate (ATP)**, which is used by the muscles to provide energy for contractions. The greater the quantity of ATP available, the greater your work capacity is.

As long as adequate amounts of oxygen are deliv-

Maximal oxygen consumption (VO_2) The optimal capacity of the heart to pump blood, of the lungs to fill with larger volumes of air, and of the muscle cells to use the oxygen and remove waste products that are produced during the process of aerobic metabolism.

Aerobic metabolism The process of breaking down energy nutrients such as carbohydrates and fats in the presence of oxygen in order to yield energy in the form of ATP.

Cardiorespiratory endurance The ability of the heart, blood vessels, and lungs to deliver oxygen to the exercising muscles in amounts sufficient to meet the demands of the workload.

Endurance The ability to work a long time without experiencing fatigue or exhaustion.

Cardiorespiratory system Joint functioning of the respiratory system (the lungs and airway passages) and the circulatory system (the heart and blood vessels).

Glycogen The stored form of carbohydrate in the muscles and liver.

Adenosine triphosphate (ATP) The basic substrate used by the muscle to provide energy for muscle contractions.

Improving Your Community

Evaluating the Exercise Habits of Adults

Depending on the type of exercise habit survey you read, the number of adults in the United States who exercise ranges from a low of 15 to 20 percent to a high of 90 percent. The extremes occur because of the varied definitions of exercise. Unfortunately, many forms of exercise have very little health-related benefits and do not contribute to cardiorespiratory fitness.

As specified in the U.S. Department of Health and Human Services' health objectives for the nation, adults are considered part of the exercising population if their program meets these three criteria: (1) continuous activity for 20 to 30 minutes; (2) a level of intensity for this time period that elevates and maintains heart rate at or above their target heart rate, and (3) a program that they engage in three or four times each week. The ideal program would also include weekly sessions of strength and flexibility training.

Here are some suggestions for how you can help the students in your school and others in your community to evaluate their present exercise programs based on these criteria:

1. Call your local radio and TV stations and ask them to consider a small segment on a topic such as *"Is Your Exercise Program Worthwhile?"* Within two or three minutes, listeners and viewers merely respond to four simple questions: What, if any, form of exercise do you do? Is your exercise continuous; if so, for how long? Does your program increase your heart rate to the target level and keep it there for the entire workout? Anyone who answers "no" to either of the last two questions is not receiving the full health benefits of exercise.

2. Construct a brief survey using the above four questions that can be administered in less than 30 seconds. Ask your instructor to secure permission for you to collect data in other classes.

3. Form a class project and ask each student to complete 25 surveys at random around campus by asking fellow students these questions and recording the information. Analyze the data to obtain an indication of the exercise habits of your university.

4. Visit the weight room in your institution and determine whether participants also engage in aerobic exercise on a regular basis.

5. Discuss the benefits of a walking program with the sedentary individuals in your immediate family and circle of friends. Volunteer to walk with a friend or relative on a regular basis to help inspire someone to begin a cardiorespiratory fitness program. ✦

---

ered to the muscles, the process of breaking down glycogen proceeds aerobically (in the presence of oxygen). When you reach VO_2, however, you are no longer able to supply adequate amounts of oxygen to the muscles, and for a short period of time, glycogen is broken down anaerobically (in the absence of oxygen). You can only exercise for a brief period of time when energy is provided through **anaerobic metabolism**. Fat is the major energy source used for sustained physical activity, and it cannot be burned through anaerobic processes. Hence the higher your level of aerobic fitness, the more fat you can burn during an exercise session.

Oxygen uptake is influenced by factors such as age, sex, genetic background, and physical training. Typically, as you get older, your maximal level of aerobic power declines. After age 30, sedentary individuals experience a decrease in VO_2 of about 1 percent per year. The rate of decline is much slower among active individuals. Also, men tend to have a higher level of aerobic power than women of similar ages. This is primarily due to the larger body size of men and to a greater amount of lean muscle tissue.

Some people are born with a genetic predisposition to be elite endurance athletes. They inherit larger, stronger hearts, greater lung capacity, better blood supply in their muscles, larger quantities of red blood cells, and higher percentages of slow-twitch muscle fibers, which are found in greater percentages in the muscles used in aerobic exercise. These muscle fibers contain energy foodstuffs and enzymes that enhance aerobic metabolism and promote exercise of longer durations. As shown in Table 8.1, aerobic training also leads to many of these same changes. Thus even if you are not born an elite marathon runner, you can become a pretty good one by engaging in a prolonged aerobic conditioning program.

The VO_2, or aerobic power, of an individual is

Table 8.2 ✦ Cardiorespiratory Fitness Classification for Women and Men According to Maximal Oxygen Uptake in ml/kg per min and METS

			FITNESS CLASSIFICATION			
Sex	Age	(VO₂)	Fair	Average	Good	Excellent
Women	< 30	ml/kg/min	24–30	31–37	38–48	> 49
		METS	7–8	9–10	10–14	> 14
	30s	ml/kg/min	20–27	28–33	34–44	> 45
		METS	5–8	8–9	10–13	> 13
	40s	ml/kg/min	17–23	24–30	31–41	> 42
		METS	5–6	7–8	9–12	> 12
Men	< 30	ml/kg/min	25–33	34–42	43–52	> 53
		METS	7–9	9–12	12–15	> 15
	30s	ml/kg/min	23–30	31–38	39–48	> 49
		METS	6–8	8–11	11–14	> 14
	40s	ml/kg/min	20–26	27–35	36–44	> 45
		METS	5–7	8–10	10–12	> 13

expressed in volume (in liters) per unit of time (in minutes). Scores in the range of 3 to 4 l/min are common for the average healthy individual who exercises three to four times per week. Highly trained endurance athletes, however, may have a VO₂ ranging from 5 to 6 l/min. Usually, the greater the amount of muscle mass used in a sport, the higher the maximal oxygen uptake obtained through training. Thus people who engage in activities such as running, cross-country skiing, and cycling often have the highest measured VO₂.

There are several ways of expressing the maximal oxygen uptake. When expressed in units of l/min (**absolute** expression), it is often difficult to compare the actual fitness level of one individual to another. The reason is that the larger the body size, the higher the oxygen uptake, regardless of the level of fitness. Expressing VO₂ **relative** to a person's body weight allows individuals of different sizes to be compared. Hence, a smaller individual may have a lower VO₂ when it is expressed in units of l/min but when expressed in units of milliliters oxygen per kilogram of body weight per minute ($ml \times kg^{-1} \times min^{-1}$), the smaller person may actually have a much higher level of cardiorespiratory fitness.

Let's use an example to illustrate this point. Antony weighs 165 lb and has a maximal oxygen uptake of 4.2 l/min. Miranda weighs 130 lb and also has a maximal oxygen uptake of 4.2 l/min. Who is more fit? Antony's maximal oxygen uptake expressed in relative units is determined by:

$$\frac{4,200 \ (1,000 \ ml = 1l)}{75 \ kg \ (1 \ kg = 2.2 \ lb)} = 56 \ ml/kg \ of \ body \ weight$$

Miranda's oxygen uptake expressed in relative units is determined by:

$$\frac{4,200 \ (1,000 \ ml = 1l)}{59.1 \ kg \ (1 \ kg = 2.2 \ lb)} = 71.1 \ ml/kg \ of \ body \ weight$$

Were you surprised? What a big difference between their levels of fitness when you express the oxygen consumption relative to their body weights. Apparently, Miranda has a much higher level of fitness even though she has a much smaller body size than does Antony. Normally, active college-aged females have average maximal oxygen uptake values of 38 to 42 $ml/kg \times min^{-1}$, compared with a value of 44 to 50 $ml/kg \times min^{-1}$ for college-aged males.

Anaerobic metabolism The process of breaking down carbohydrates (glucose or glycogen) in the absence of oxygen in order to yield energy in the form of ATP.

Absolute VO₂ Expressing the volume of oxygen consumption in the units of liters of oxygen consumed per minute (l/min).

Relative VO₂ Expressing the volume of oxygen consumption in the units of milliliters of oxygen per kilogram of body weight per minute ($ml/kg \times min^{-1}$).

The most accurate method of measuring maximal oxygen uptake is through direct gas analysis in a laboratory setting. This procedure involves the use of computerized equipment such as a treadmill or a bicycle ergometer, and a mouthpiece, which is cumbersome to the individual. This procedure is quite sophisticated and the equipment is expensive. Thus, indirect methods of assessing the VO_2 in healthy individuals are often used.

Several field tests can be used to measure aerobic power indirectly. The most commonly used field tests include the 1-mile walking test, the 1.5-mile run, the 12-minute run test, the 3-mile walking test, the 12-minute swimming test, and the YMCA bicycle test. If you have been involved in a physical conditioning program, you may elect to complete the 1.5-mile run test. If you are just beginning your aerobic exercise program, however, you should assess your maximal oxygen uptake by completing Lab Activity 8.1: Assessing Your Level of Aerobic Fitness by the 3-Mile Walk Test at the end of this chapter.

The 3-mile walk test (see Lab 8.2) is an excellent means of assessing cardiorespiratory endurance with a low risk of injury for someone who is just beginning an exercise program. Use Table 8.2 to determine your fitness classification based on sex and age. If you are in the poor or fair fitness category, begin with the sample walking program presented later in this chapter. If you are in the good or excellent fitness category, begin with the sample jogging/running program also presented later in this chapter.

How to Safely Begin and Progress in an Aerobic Fitness Program

We recommend following seven guidelines in order to minimize risk of injury when you begin an aerobic fitness program.

1. **Total work concept** The total amount of work you do each week is important when you are attempting to increase cardiorespiratory fitness and change body composition. Total work is usually calculated in units of calories (kcal) per week. Total work is assessed by quantifying the frequency, intensity, and duration of your exercise sessions. For instance, if you burn 300 kcal per 30-minute exercise session, four times per week, your total energy expenditure is 1,200 kcal per week. The next week, however, you might exercise three times per week for 45 minutes at the same exercise intensity and burn 400 kcal per session. Your

total work would still be 1,200 kcal. Thus, if your schedule fluctuates constantly, you might still maintain your exercise schedule and meet your energy expenditure goals by manipulating exercise intensity, frequency, or duration. By the way, there are 3,500 kcal in one lb of fat.

2. **Shin splints** Exercisers who engage in hard-impact, high-intensity exercise for extended periods of time are at risk of developing shin splints. This condition is an inflammation of the muscle-tendon junction on the outer front side of the lower leg. Shin splints are believed to be caused by overuse, improper shoes, poor exercise technique, hard surfaces, and back defects. To avoid shin splints, use a variety of activities, especially water aerobics, and avoid chronic exercise on hard surfaces so that you will not overstress the lower extremities.

3. **Stitch-in-the-side phenomenon** Adequate breathing while running is essential for maintaining sufficient oxygen to exercising muscles. Diaphragmatic breathing (from the chest muscles) often results in the pain associated with the stitch-in-the-side phenomenon. The cause of this condition is unknown, but it is believed to be associated with an inability of the diaphragm muscle to use oxygen. If you use the abdominal muscles while breathing, the stitch-in-the-side phenomenon is less likely to occur. Expand your abdomen rather than your chest. Breathing should be rhythmic and closely associated with your stride. Most exercise physiologists recommend that you take a deep breath every two to four strides.

4. **Blisters** These can be very painful and are often debilitating. Friction develops at the point of contact between your foot and the running surface and initially causes hot spots. If this friction is not minimized, fluid will eventually develop between the layers of skin at the point of contact and swelling will occur, leading to a blister. To prevent blisters from developing, wear two pairs of cotton socks, especially when you are doing hard-impact exercises for long periods of time. Also, if you place a bandage at the point of contact before the exercise session, the skin is protected, and blisters are less likely to develop. If a blister ruptures, you should treat it as an open wound and keep it sterile.

5. **Muscle soreness Delayed-onset muscle soreness (DOMS)** often occurs within 12 to 24 hours

Myth and Fact Sheet

Myth	Fact
1. Smoking is not harmful as long as you exercise.	1. Smoking limits your level of performance because it increases the airway resistance and decreases the amount of oxygen available to muscles. It also increases your heart rate by as much as 12 to 20 beats per minute, so your exercise endurance is compromised. Even after training, smokers do not improve as much as nonsmokers.
2. You should exercise every day in order to increase your level of cardiorespiratory fitness.	2. When you begin an exercise program, you should *not* exercise every day, because you will increase the risk of getting injured. It is best to exercise on alternate days to allow adequate time for recovery. After you reach your maximal level of aerobic fitness, it is safe to exercise daily because your risk of injury will be lower after a long period of training.
3. You should wear a rubberized suit while exercising to increase the number of kcal you burn during a workout.	3. You should *never* wear any type of rubber exercise clothing because of the increased amount of heat that is trapped in the body. Rubberized clothes will not allow the sweat to evaporate from the surface of the body, and if sweat does not evaporate, your inner body temperature does not decrease. This leads to heat exhaustion and even heatstroke. Always wear loose-fitting, cotton clothing to aid the sweating mechanism.
4. Jogging or rope skipping will cause a woman's breasts to stretch or sag.	4. No researchers have found this to be true. Giving birth to children and getting older often contribute to stretching and sagging breasts, but not exercise. Some women complain of tenderness or soreness in the breasts, especially when they fail to wear a suitable bra. A well-fitted bra will often eliminate any such discomfort during exercise.

after a high-intensity exercise session. During the initial phases of an exercise program, DOMS is most likely to occur. Most physiologists believe the cause is related to minute tears in the muscle fibers and connective tissue. After one or two days, the pain eventually subsides. You may take aspirin or another painkiller, such as acetaminophen, to relieve the pain. Gentle stretching after the workout, mild-intensity exercise, and light massage may also help decrease the pain.

6. Heat illness symptoms Most heat problems arise because of inadequate fluid intake and/or improper heat dissipation. As you begin exercising, your body temperature increases greatly because of the increased rate of metabolism. Normally, the body temperature is regulated by sweating. As the sweat evaporates from your body, your body cools, and its inner temperature decreases. When you do not drink enough fluids before and during exercise, especially in hot, humid or hot, dry weather, however, the sweating mech-

anism becomes less effective and your inner-body temperature remains elevated. Also, when you do not wear proper exercise clothing, the sweating mechanism becomes ineffective, and the core temperature remains elevated.

As your core temperature rises, symptoms such as muscle cramps, excessive fatigue, nausea, dizziness, light-headedness, headaches, diminished coordination, and cotton mouth, or dry lips, may develop. You may have any combination of these symptoms when heat illness occurs. As **heat exhaustion** develops, your rate of sweating increases, and you develop cold, clammy skin. As

Delayed onset muscle soreness (DOMS) Muscle soreness that typically occurs 12 to 24 hours after a high-intensity exercise session.

Heat exhaustion (heat prostration) Collapse due to loss of fluid and salts caused by oversweating.

it intensifies, you may lose consciousness, and suddenly sweating will cease. If the skin becomes hot and dry and your pulse becomes rapid and strong, you may have suffered **heatstroke**.

If any of these symptoms occur while you are exercising, stop immediately, and begin removing layers of clothing. Also, drink as much fluid as you can tolerate, and elevate your feet. Begin cooling your body by using cold, wet towels; place ice on the body in more severe cases; and get out of the sun. Heat illness is extremely dangerous, and you should see a physician if it occurs.

7. **Rest, ice, compression, and elevation (RICE)** Avoidance of injury is crucial as you begin your conditioning program. RICE is the acronym for the recommended steps to follow in the immediate treatment of an injury. To avoid creating a more serious condition, we recommend isolating the injured extremity instead of trying to walk it off. Place ice on the injured part for 20 to 30 minutes repeatedly for one to three days, depending on the severity of the injury. This will help decrease pain and minimize swelling. Compressing the injury with an elastic bandage and elevating the injured part above the level of the heart and head also help reduce swelling.

Protect your body at all times by warming up before, and cooling down after, each exercise session. Also remember that pain is your body's mechanism for letting you know that something is wrong, so do not ignore it or try to *push through it*. Stop and investigate the problem in order to minimize the risk of developing a more serious situation.

$\mathcal{S}$AMPLE STARTER PROGRAMS

Sample Walking Program

In recent years, walking has become one of the most popular of all aerobic activities. One reason for its popularity is that it does not require any specialized skills and is both safe and painless when the guidelines we discuss in this chapter are followed. You can walk almost anywhere, at any time, and at little cost. Many people choose walking over activities like jogging because it puts less stress on the hips, knees, and ankles and results in a reduced risk of orthopedic injuries. Also, exercisers have found walking to be an excellent means of reducing body weight and lowering the percentage of body fat.

Many people feel that because they have been walking all their lives, they do not need instructions on how to begin a walking program. Any successful walking program depends, however, on understanding a few basic guidelines and principles. The basic principles of beginning an exercise program were covered earlier, so we will limit our discussion here to special considerations for the beginning and for the advanced walkers.

Duration   During the initial phase of a walking program, you should walk 10 to 15 minutes at a comfortable pace. After one or two weeks, you can advance to 30-minute sessions. Continue walking for 30 minutes per session for at least four weeks in order to decrease your risk of injury and to minimize fatigue. After approximately six weeks, you can increase the exercise period to 45 minutes. More advanced walkers typically progress to 60-minute walking sessions.

Intensity   The first step in regulating exercise intensity is to *forget* the familiar saying "no pain, no gain." Calculate your target heart rate (THR); begin your walking program at 50 to 60 percent of that rate. Once you advance to 30-minute walking sessions, you can increase your exercise intensity to 60 to 65 percent of your THR. As you advance to 45- to 60-minute exercise sessions, remember to stay within your THR.

It is best to use your THR as a measure of intensity rather than using a particular walking speed. That will give you the best measure of the cardiorespiratory benefits of your workout. During the initial phase of your walking program, check your exercise heart rate every 5 minutes. Use a 10-second pulse count while walking, multiplying the result by six to determine your heart rate per minute. At the end of your exercise session, if you have walked at a comfortable pace, your heart rate should drop below 100 beats per minute following a 10-minute cool-down period.

A great way of monitoring exercise intensity while walking without actually counting your pulse is to use the talk test. Any time you are walking with a partner, if your breathing rate is so fast that you cannot carry on a conversation with that person, you are probably

Heatstroke   Severe, sustained rise in fever due to the failure of the body-heat-regulating mechanism after a prolonged period of elevated temperature.

walking too fast. Beginning to feel winded is an instant indication that you should slow down the pace.

If you are walking alone, a simple test to monitor exercise intensity is to take one inward breath with every three strides and one outward breath with the following three strides. If you are inhaling and exhaling at every two strides, you are probably exercising above your THR and should slow down. Remember: Exercise intensity is inversely related to exercise duration. If your exercise heart rate is too high, you will tire more quickly and exercise for shorter periods of time, and you will also increase your risk of getting injured. Exercise should be fun and relaxing; it is not meant to cause pain.

Frequency At the beginning of your exercise program, you should walk every other day up to a maximum of three to four days per week. After the first six weeks you can increase your frequency to four to five days per week. Limit your exercise frequency to a maximum of five days per week in order to allow a few days for recovery, thereby minimizing your risk of injury.

Calorie Cost When you begin your walking program, choose some premeasured distance, whether on a track, a cross-country trail, or a treadmill. This will enable you to calculate the number of calories burned as an estimate of the total amount of work you have completed. Table 8.3 shows one method of determining the energy cost of walking in units of kcal per minute. To use this table, find horizontally the approximate speed you walk in miles per hour (or METs). One MET is equal to the resting metabolic rate. If your walking speed is 4 METs, the intensity is four times greater than that of the resting metabolic rate.

Next locate your approximate body weight on the vertical column. The figure at the intersection represents an estimate of the kcal used per minute. Multiply this figure by the number of minutes you exercise to get the total number of kcal used.

For example, Jennifer weighs 140 lb and walks at a speed of 3.5 mph for 45 minutes:

$$3.9 \ (\text{kcal/min}) \times 45 \ (\text{minutes}) = 176 \ \text{calories}$$

Her total caloric expenditure based on this table is approximately 176 kcal per exercise session.

An additional benefit of participating in activities that increase your level of cardiorespiratory fitness is that they also influence your body composition. Table 8.4 gives the number of days required to lose 5 to 25 lb by walking and lowering your daily caloric intake. This table demonstrates the combined benefits of exercise and caloric reduction in maintaining your body weight and lowering your body fat percentage. As you can see, the longer you exercise and the greater your caloric reduction, the quicker you lose weight. For instance, if Daniele walks 45 minutes a day and decreases her caloric intake by 400 kcal per day, it

Table 8.3 ✦ Energy Costs of Walking (kcal/min)

Body weight (lb)	MILES PER HOUR/METs						
	2.0/2.5	2.5/2.9	3.0/3.3	3.5/3.7	4.0/4.9	4.5/6.2	5.0/7.9
110	2.1	2.4	2.8	3.1	4.1	5.2	6.6
120	2.3	2.6	3.0	3.4	4.4	5.6	7.2
130	2.5	2.9	3.2	3.6	4.8	6.1	7.8
140	2.7	3.1	3.5	3.9	5.2	6.6	8.4
150	2.8	3.3	3.7	4.2	5.6	7.0	9.0
160	3.0	3.5	4.0	4.5	5.9	7.5	9.6
170	3.2	3.7	4.2	4.8	6.3	8.0	10.2
180	3.4	4.0	4.5	5.0	6.7	8.4	10.8
190	3.6	4.2	4.7	5.3	7.0	8.9	11.4
200	3.8	4.4	5.0	5.6	7.4	9.4	12.0
210	4.0	4.6	5.2	5.9	7.8	9.9	12.6
220	4.2	4.8	5.5	6.2	8.2	10.3	13.2

Source: From *Fitness Leader's Handbook* (p. 149), by B. D. Franks and E. T. Howley, 1989, Champaign, IL: Human Kinetics Publishers. Copyright 1989 by B. Don Franks, Edward T. Howley, and Susan Metros. Reprinted by permission.

Table 8.4 ✦ Days Required to Lose 5 to 25 Pounds by Walking* and Lowering Daily Caloric Intake

MINUTES OF WALKING	+	REDUCTION OF CALORIES PER DAY (IN KCAL)	DAYS TO LOSE 5 LB	DAYS TO LOSE 10 LB	DAYS TO LOSE 15 LB	DAYS TO LOSE 20 LB	DAYS TO LOSE 25 LB
30		400	27	54	81	108	135
30		600	20	40	60	80	100
30		800	16	32	48	64	80
30		1000	13	26	39	52	65
45		400	23	46	69	92	115
45		600	18	36	54	72	90
45		800	14	28	42	56	70
45		1000	12	24	36	48	60
60		400	21	42	63	84	105
60		600	16	32	48	64	80
60		800	13	26	39	52	65
60		1000	11	22	33	44	55

*Walking briskly (3.5–4.0 mph), calculated at 5.2 kcal/minute.
Source: From *Exercise Equivalents of Foods: A Practical Guide for the Overweight,* by F. Konishi, 1973, Carbondale, IL: Southern Illinois University Press.

should take her approximately 23 days to lose 5 lb. And if Karen walks 30 minutes per day and reduces her caloric intake by 400 kcal per day, it should take her approximately 27 days to lose five lb. Thus the longer you exercise, the quicker the results in terms of changes in body composition.

Rate of Progression Do not get discouraged if you don't see immediate progress, especially if you have not been exercising on a regular basis. During the initial phases of a walking program, first slowly increase the distance that you walk at a slow pace for a few weeks, and then increase the speed that you walk. This will give your body time to adjust to your new training program and reduce your chances of injury. It is best to increase your exercise time by no more than 10 percent a week. Most people will use from 90 to 150 calories per session during a 30-minute walk covering 1.5 miles. When you reach this level, you are ready to move on to a more advanced phase of walking.

Advanced walkers typically use 200 to 350 calories per session by manipulating their exercise intensity and duration. Once you reach an advanced level of walking, you may choose to begin a walk/jog/run program. Many people enjoy just walking, however, reaping many fitness benefits with little risk of injury.

As you begin your walking program, try to:

1. Maintain good postural alignment to avoid tension in the neck, back, and shoulders.

2. Hold your head high to help maintain good posture.

3. Use full, deep, abdominal breathing to enhance relaxation and monitor your walking pace.

4. Hold your arms in a relaxed position with the elbows flexed at a 90-degree angle.

5. Form a slightly clenched, relaxed fist with your hands.

6. Swing your arms naturally back and forth to add power to each stride.

7. Begin each stride with a slight forward lean of the body at the ankles.

8. As the foot contacts the surface, make contact on the outer edge of the heel.

9. On contacting the surface, roll the foot smoothly forward with most of the body weight distributed along the outer edge of the foot, transferring the weight to the ball of the foot and onto the toes as you push off.

10. Walk at a pace of 3 to 3.5 mph for a comfortable workout.

11. Walk at a pace of 3.75 mph for a vigorous workout.

12. Walk faster than 4 mph if you are an advanced walker.

13. Walk on dirt trails or grass for a more comfort-

able workout than if you walk on concrete sidewalks.

14. Be cautious when walking on uneven surfaces such as grass or dirt because of the increased risk of ankle sprains.

15. Walk in shoes with a comfortable fit, a cushioned sole, and good arch support.

16. Wear loose-fitting clothing to allow freedom of movement and dissipation of heat.

17. In cold weather, wear several layers of clothing to slow down the rate of heat loss.

18. In cold weather, wear a cap to avoid heat loss through the scalp.

19. Wear cotton socks to avoid getting blisters and to absorb perspiration.

20. Warm up before, and cool down after, each walking session.

To "kick off" your walking program, evaluate your current fitness level and learn about "pacing" by completing Lab Activity 8.3: The Straw Walk at the end of the chapter.

Sample Jogging/Running Program

Once you complete an advanced walking program, you may be ready for a jogging program. Some people find walking so enjoyable that it is their exercise of choice. If you are not excessively overweight and do not have any orthopedic problems, however, you may decide to increase your exercise intensity and begin jogging. If you have any congenital heart defects or metabolic and/or cardiorespiratory diseases, consult a physician before beginning a jogging program.

For purposes of changing body composition, increasing muscular endurance, and improving cardiorespiratory endurance, jogging is one of the most effective activities. The energy costs of running are greater than those of walking the same distance (see Table 8.5). Thus if you have reached a moderate to high level of fitness and want to increase your caloric expenditure but are unable to increase the amount of time you exercise, you should increase the exercise intensity by jogging instead of walking.

Complete the most advanced level of a walking program before you begin a jogging program. This will allow adequate time for the development of your cardiorespiratory system and the strengthening of your ligaments and tendons to reduce the risk of injury. There are many options in beginning a jogging program dependent on your initial level of fitness and prior exercise experience. Here are a few guidelines for jogging.

Duration In the initial phase of a jogging program, exercise 15 to 30 minutes. During the session, alternate brief periods of slow jogging (approximately 5 to 6 mph) with intervals of walking. Gradually increase the amount of time spent jogging and decrease walking time until you reach a level of fitness in which you

Table 8.5 ✦ Energy Costs of Jogging and Running (kcal/min)

Body weight (lb)	MILES PER HOUR/METS							
	3.0/5.6	4.0/7.1	5.0/8.7	6.0/10.2	7.0/11.7	8.0/13.3	9.0/14.8	10.0/16.3
110	4.7	5.9	7.2	8.5	9.8	11.1	12.3	13.6
120	5.1	6.4	7.9	9.3	10.6	12.1	13.4	14.8
130	5.5	7.0	8.6	10.1	11.5	13.1	14.6	16.1
140	5.9	7.5	9.2	10.8	12.4	14.1	15.7	17.3
150	6.4	8.1	9.9	11.6	13.3	15.1	16.8	18.5
160	6.8	8.6	10.5	12.4	14.2	16.1	17.9	19.8
170	7.2	9.1	11.2	13.1	15.1	17.1	19.1	21.0
180	7.6	9.7	11.8	13.9	15.9	18.1	20.2	22.2
190	8.1	10.2	12.5	14.7	16.8	19.1	21.3	23.5
200	8.5	10.8	13.2	15.4	17.1	20.1	22.4	24.7
210	8.9	11.3	13.8	16.2	18.6	21.1	23.5	25.9
220	9.3	11.8	14.5	17.0	19.5	22.2	24.7	27.2

Source: From *Fitness Leader's Handbook* (p. 150), by B. D. Franks and E. T. Howley, 1989, Champaign, IL: Human Kinetics Publishers. Copyright 1989 by B. Don Franks, Edward T. Howley, and Susan Metros. Reprinted by permission.

can jog continuously for 30 minutes within your THR. As you reach an advanced level of running, exercise sessions may last as long as 60 minutes. Most people jog two to three miles an exercise session during the first 10 weeks of a jogging/running program. When you can jog three miles comfortably within 27 to 30 minutes, you are probably ready to advance to a running program. More advanced runners can cover five miles per session within 35 to 40 minutes.

Intensity An important factor in a jogging/running program is to monitor your heart rate. During the initial phase of your program, stay in the 60 to 75 percent target heart rate zone. As you reach a higher level of fitness, you may increase exercise intensity to 70 to 85 percent. Remember, however, that as intensity increases, you tend to exercise less because of an earlier onset of fatigue. Keep the target heart rate in the moderate range in order to receive the double benefits of improving cardiorespiratory fitness and increasing the percentage of fat calories used. You will see changes in body fat percentage more quickly by exercising at a moderate intensity (60 to 75 percent THR zone).

Frequency The optimal frequency for jogging is every other day. If you want to exercise every day, use walking as a form of exercise on alternate days in order to decrease the amount of stress on your hips and the joints of the legs and feet. Even exercisers who participate in road races seldom exercise seven days per week. They recognize the need to allow a rest period between workouts. If you want to increase total work done on a weekly basis, it is better to increase exercise duration gradually and to maintain a moderate exercise intensity with a frequency of four to five times per week instead of jogging seven days per week.

Calorie Cost Table 8.5 shows one method of estimating the energy costs of jogging and running, expressed in units of kcal per minute. Let's consider the differences between walking and running for the same time periods.

If Joseph weighs 150 lb and jogs at 7 mph for 45 min, he will burn 13.3 kcal per min. To find his total energy expenditure:

$$13.3 \text{ (kcal/min)} \times 45 \text{ (min)} = 599 \text{ kcal}$$

If Mark weighs 150 lb and walks at 3 mph for 45 min, he will burn 6.4 kcal per min. To find his total energy expenditure:

$$6.4 \text{ (kcal/min)} \times 45 \text{ (min)} = 288 \text{ kcal}$$

Both of these young men, with similar body weights and exercise durations, but with different exercise intensities, have vastly different caloric expenditures.

Jogging is one of the most effective activities for increasing muscular endurance, changing body composition, and improving cardiorespiratory endurance. (Photo courtesy of the National Cancer Institute.)

Joseph burns more than twice as many calories as Mark does. And since Joseph is moving at a faster pace, he covers more distance and has a higher caloric expenditure.

Another explanation for the difference in their energy expenditures is that the caloric cost of walking one mile and running one mile are not the same. Walking at speeds slower than 3.5 mph requires approximately half the energy cost of running at speeds greater than 6 mph. That is because more energy is required to lift the body from the ground when you are running than is necessary when you are moving the body forward on a horizontal plane, as you do when you are walking. If a person walks at speeds of 5 mph, the energy cost of walking and running is similar. That is because your exercise heart rate will probably be nearly as high walking at 5 mph as it is when you are running at 6 mph. Thus the caloric cost is similar for walking at fast speeds and jogging at relatively slow speeds. Remember that walking at slow speeds burns half the calories as does jogging the same distance at faster speeds, but walking at fast speeds can burn the same number of calories as jogging.

Table 8.6 shows the estimated number of days required to lose 5 to 25 lb by jogging and lowering your daily caloric intake. To illustrate the difference between walking and jogging by using this chart, recall the example of Daniele who walked 45 minutes and reduced her caloric intake by 400 kcal per day. It took Daniele 23 days to lose 5 lb. Now let us assume that Joseph jogs for 45 minutes a day and reduces his caloric intake by 400 kcal per day. It will only take him 18 days to lose 5 lb because of the increased energy expenditure for jogging as compared to walking. Naturally, the greater your exercise duration, the higher the intensity, and the greater the reduction in caloric intake, the quicker you will see changes in your body composition.

Rate of Progression During the initial phase of a jogging program, you should combine walking and jogging. If you maintain a constant walking interval of 60 seconds, you can increase the jogging intervals until you are doing more jogging than walking. Always be careful to use exercise heart rate as your guide for determining the jogging/walking intervals. As your fitness level increases, you should be able to jog for longer periods of time while remaining within your target training zone. Most people use 350 to 750 kcal per session in a jogging/running program.

Concentrate on slow, steady progress. As long as you are constantly increasing the total amount of kcal used from your weekly workouts, remaining within your THR zone, and having no problems with injuries, you are probably working out at a suitable level.

After the first two months of a jogging program, you may notice that you do not seem to be improving as much as you expected. During this time, you might

Table 8.6 ✦ Days Required to Lose 5 to 25 Pounds by Jogging* and Lowering Daily Caloric Intake

MINUTES OF JOGGING +	REDUCTION OF CALORIES PER DAY (IN KCAL)	DAYS TO LOSE 5 LB	DAYS TO LOSE 10 LB	DAYS TO LOSE 15 LB	DAYS TO LOSE 20 LB	DAYS TO LOSE 25 LB
30	400	21	42	63	84	105
30	600	17	34	51	68	85
30	800	14	28	42	56	70
30	1000	12	24	36	48	60
45	400	18	36	54	72	90
45	600	14	28	42	56	70
45	800	12	24	36	48	60
45	1000	10	20	30	40	50
60	400	15	30	45	60	75
60	600	12	24	36	48	60
60	800	11	22	33	44	55
60	1000	9	18	27	36	45

*Jogging: Alternate jogging and walking, calculated at 10.0 kcal/min.

Source: From *Exercise Equivalents of Foods: A Practical Guide for the Overweight,* by F. Konishi, 1973, Carbondale, IL: Southern Illinois University.

easily become discouraged and bored with your training program. That is when you might consider changing the intensity and duration of your workouts or training for a short road race. Alternatively, you can change your exercise route so that the environment becomes more exciting. Try running with a partner or listening to music while you jog. By changing the environment and increasing the amount of visual or auditory stimulation during the workout, you will find that time seems to pass more quickly, and you become less focused internally on your body and more focused on external factors. This shift in your attention away from your body may enable you to exercise for longer periods of time without becoming bored.

Sample Swimming Program

Swimming is an excellent aerobic activity. Patients in cardiac rehabilitation programs and in physical therapy often use a pool as their primary means of aerobic conditioning because of the decreased stress on hips, knees, and ankles that exercising in water affords. In addition, the warmer water temperatures of a pool are therapeutic for arthritic patients. Furthermore, since body weight is supported, obese persons have fewer injuries while exercising in water. As a consequence, a growing number of people are choosing aquatic exercises as their primary mode of fitness. Since the cardiorespiratory benefits derived from water exercises are similar to those derived from jogging and cycling, consider including water exercises as a part of your training program.

Water aerobics are highly touted by exercise physiologists because they cause virtually no impact to the muscles and the skeletal system and are safe for people of all ages regardless of health status.

For years, water exercises were avoided because it was believed there was insufficient resistance in the pool to stimulate cardiorespiratory endurance. In reality, water is nearly 1,000 times more dense than air and thus creates greater resistance. This increased resistance provides a higher workload for the muscles. We now know that the resistance of the water is sufficient to challenge even the most elite athlete, and an increase in cardiorespiratory fitness can easily be experienced by participating in water exercises.

An added benefit is that this cushioned medium promotes a virtually injury-free environment. The density of water gives almost any object placed in it a certain buoyancy. Your body will weigh less in water because of this buoyancy, so less stress is placed on it when you exercise in water.

Obese people may especially enjoy exercising in water because it is much easier for them to dissipate heat. When you exercise, a great deal of heat is generated as a result of metabolism. This heat is often difficult for an obese person to release because of the thick layer of fatty tissue underneath the skin. Heat is

Water exercise places less stress on the body than many other exercises, and is a great way for people of all ages to improve their cardiorespiratory fitness. (Photo courtesy of the United States Water Fitness Association.)

much easier to dissipate in water than it is in air, so the obese find exercising in water much more comfortable. One advantage water aerobics provides over jogging is that jogging does nothing to work the upper body, but water greatly increases strength and endurance in the upper body as well as the lower body. Here are guidelines to follow when you begin a water exercise program.

Duration Start at a comfortable level. This will vary depending on your initial level of fitness. If you are a swimmer but have been inactive for a long time, you may need to spend a few weeks walking across the width of the pool in chest-deep water until you can complete two 10-minute intervals at your exercise heart rate. Gradually alternate walking and jogging across the pool until you can complete four 5-minute intervals of jogging at your target heart rate. As you progress, you can jog across the pool and swim back. Repeat this pattern until you jog/swim for about 20 to 30 minutes. As your level of fitness increases, spend more time swimming and less time jogging until you can swim continuously for 20 to 30 minutes. Advanced swimmers can swim 30 to 45 minutes each exercise session.

Intensity Research has shown that a person's maximal heart rate is approximately 10 beats lower in the water than it is on land. For example, if you are a woman, calculate your target heart rate for water activities, use the formula 210 (rather than 220) minus your age to determine your maximal heart rate. From there, follow the standard formula for calculating your target heart rate that appeared in chapter 7. During the initial phase of your swimming program, begin at a pace that keeps your heart rate at 50 percent of your target training zone. Gradually increase exercise duration and intensity as your level of fitness increases, but be careful to remain within your heart rate zone.

Frequency As with other forms of aerobic exercise, you should swim three to four days per week. If you have trouble tolerating chlorinated pools, you can alternate swimming with other forms of aerobic exercise. You can also wear swimming goggles to protect your eyes from irritation.

Calorie Cost It is difficult to estimate the energy costs associated with swimming because there are vast differences between individuals based on the efficiency of the stroke used. Table 8.7 shows the estimated caloric cost per mile of swimming the front crawl for men and women according to skill level. The values

are expressed in units of kcal per mile.

You may be surprised to find that the lower the skill level, the higher the energy expenditure for both men and women. That is because unskilled swimmers often fight the water and waste a lot of energy during each stroke. As the level of skill rises, the swimmer becomes more efficient and the caloric cost decreases. This might lead you to believe that poorly skilled swimmers will burn a lot more kcal per workout than highly skilled swimmers will. This is not true. Unskilled swimmers exercise for a shorter period of time because they tire earlier than skilled swimmers do and will probably spend more time resting than actually swimming. For this reason, poorly skilled swimmers should use a combination of water exercises with swimming to increase their caloric expenditure.

Table 8.8 shows the estimated number of days required to lose 5 to 25 lb by swimming and lowering daily caloric intake. When this table is compared to Table 8.6, which shows the same estimates for weight loss by jogging, you can see that swimming is very similar to jogging in terms of caloric expenditure. For instance, if Alexandra swims for 30 minutes and decreases her caloric intake 800 kcal per day, it should take her 14 days to lose 5 lb. If she jogs for 30 minutes and decreases her caloric intake 800 kcal per day, it should take her the same 14 days to lose 5 lb. But if she walks for 30 minutes at the same caloric reduction, it should take her 16 days to lose 5 lb. Undoubtedly, swimming is as beneficial as jogging in terms of changing body composition.

Rate of Progression Unless you are a very good swimmer, you may become exhausted after swimming only one or two laps. Since continuous exercise is essential for improving cardiorespiratory fitness,

Table 8.7 ✦ Caloric Cost Per Mile (kcal/mile) of Swimming the Front Crawl for Men and Women, by Skill Level

SKILL LEVEL	WOMEN	MEN
Competitive	180	280
Skilled	260	360
Average	300	440
Unskilled	360	560
Poor	440	720

Source: From *Fitness Leader's Handbook* (p. 155), by B. D. Franks and E. T. Howley, 1989, Champaign, IL: Human Kinetics Publishers. Copyright 1989 by B. Don Franks, Edward T. Howley, and Susan Metros. Reprinted by permission.

Table 8.8 ✦ Days Required to Lose 5 to 25 Pounds by Swimming* and Lowering Daily Caloric Intake

MINUTES OF SWIMMING	+	REDUCTION OF CALORIES PER DAY (IN KCAL)	DAYS TO LOSE 5 LB	DAYS TO LOSE 10 LB	DAYS TO LOSE 15 LB	DAYS TO LOSE 20 LB	DAYS TO LOSE 25 LB
30		400	23	46	69	92	115
30		600	18	36	52	72	90
30		800	14	28	42	56	70
30		1000	12	24	36	48	60
45		400	19	38	57	76	95
45		600	15	30	45	60	75
45		800	13	26	39	52	65
45		1000	11	22	33	44	55
60		400	16	32	48	64	80
60		600	14	28	42	56	70
60		800	11	22	33	44	55
60		1000	10	20	30	40	50

*Swimming at about 30 yards/min, calculated at 8.5 kcal/min.

Source: From *Exercise Equivalents of Foods: A Practical Guide for the Overweight,* by F. Konishi, 1973, Carbondale, IL: Southern Illinois University Press.

in this case begin with a walk/jog/swim program. As your level of aerobic conditioning increases and your swimming skills improve, you should be able to spend more time swimming and less time walking/jogging. It is not essential that you spend the entire workout actually swimming. You can easily achieve your exercise heart rate through other water exercises. As you begin your water aerobics program, follow these guidelines:

1. Always exercise in a supervised environment. It is possible to get muscle cramps in water. If you are exercising in chest-deep water, you could be in danger.

2. Exercise in water two to three inches above the waist. The depth of the water determines the amount of resistance experienced. When the water is too shallow, more stress is placed on the lower extremities. Conversely, when the water level is too high, buoyancy increases and less resistance results, making the exercises less effective.

3. Avoid excessive twisting in the water in order to minimize the risk of injury.

4. If the surface of the pool is rough, wear cotton socks to avoid scratching the soles of your feet.

5. Stand with your knees slightly bent, and avoid locking your joints.

6. Keep your arms in the water to generate more

resistance. This helps raise the heart rate into the target training zone.

7. Cup your hand during water activities to increase the amount of resistance.

8. Ankle weights may be used to increase the intensity of lower body workouts.

9. To improve your balance in the water, use a stride stance (one foot forward, the other behind) in the pool.

10. You may opt to use hand paddles, fins, pull buoys, and/or wrist weights to increase resistance.

11. When you are doing lower body exercises, keep your pelvis tilted upward to help support the lower back.

12. Include warm-up exercises before, and cooldown exercises after, your water workout.

Sample Bicycling Program

Bicycling, or cycling, has become an increasingly popular aerobic activity, especially for those who have joint problems or those who are overweight. For them, cycling is ideal because their weight is supported. Consequently they can often exercise for longer periods of time. Today, stationary bikes are as popular as 10-speed and mountain bikes are. Cycling has a high energy expenditure per minute and can result in tremendous increases in cardiorespiratory endurance and muscular strength and endurance.

Duration Each cycling session should last approximately 30 to 45 minutes. When you can cycle several miles within a 30-minute period, you have reached a high level of cardiorespiratory fitness.

Intensity As long as you are at the beginning of your cycling program, you may have to exercise below your THR in order to cycle 1 to 2 miles. After a few weeks of cycling this distance, however, you should be able to exercise at 60 percent of your heart rate zone. As you progress to cycling 3 to 5 miles, you may increase your exercise intensity to as high as 70 to 75 percent. Be careful to limit the intensity so that you can maintain your endurance. Once you reach a maximal level of fitness and can cycle 10 to 15 miles, you may increase your exercise intensity to 80 percent of your heart rate zone. A word of caution to those using stationary bikes: Periodically check your resistance setting because the work load tends to shift when you ride for long periods of time.

Frequency As with other forms of cardiorespiratory exercise, you should cycle three to five times per week. Bike on alternate days to allow adequate rest. During the first phase of a cycling program, bike a maximum of three days per week. Since cycling is not a familiar exercise to many people, they may experience more muscle soreness initially than they would with other activities such as walking.

Calorie Cost The type of bike you ride will affect the calories you expend. A person riding a 10-speed bike can cover the same distance as a person riding a mountain bike and probably burn fewer calories, depending on which gear the bike is in. Thus estimates of the calorie cost are approximations and may be less accurate than the estimates for activities such as walking and jogging.

Table 8.9 shows estimates for the calorie cost for cycling 10 to 60 minutes for distances of 1 to 15 miles on a flat surface. To use the table, find the time closest to the number of minutes you cycle on the horizontal line. Then find the approximate distance in miles you cover on the vertical column. The number at the intersection represents an approximate calorie cost.

For example, Anita weighs 185 lb and cycles 1.5 miles in 16 minutes. To find out her caloric expenditure:

$$185 \text{ (lb)} \times .032 \text{ (kcal/lb)} = 5.92 \times 16 \text{ min} = 95 \text{ kcal burned}$$

Table 8.10 shows the number of days required to lose 5 to 25 lb by cycling and lowering daily caloric intake. If we assume that Chris rode his bike for 60 minutes and reduced his caloric intake by 400 kcal per day, it would take him 19 days to lose 5 lb. By comparing this table to Table 8.6 you can see that the energy expenditure for cycling, even this slow cycling pace (7 mph), is superior to walking. Thus cycling is an excellent activity for both increasing cardiorespiratory endurance and changing body composition.

Progressive Cycling Program Begin a cycling program by riding 1 or 2 miles at a comfortable pace until your level of fitness increases to the point that you can train at the low end of your THR. Depending on your level of fitness, you may ride 1 to 2 miles per session for several weeks. Soon you should be able to ride approximately 3 to 5 miles. Continue at this level for several weeks. Gradually add mileage until you are able to cycle 10 to 15 miles each session. Depending on your rate of progression, you may be in a cycling program for six months or more before you can cycle continuously for 10 to 15 miles. Those who are very fit may need to ride faster than 13 to 15 miles per hour in order to reach their THR zone.

Rate of Progression As mentioned earlier, it is crucial to start at a comfortable pace in order to avoid injuries and extreme muscle soreness. It is better to increase the distance that you cycle instead of increasing your speed until you reach a high level of fitness. Following this advice will allow your body to adapt to this form of aerobic exercise. Do not be embarrassed to take

A regular bicycling program can result in tremendous increases in cardiorespiratory endurance. (Photo courtesy of the National Cancer Institute.)

Table 8.9 ✦ Determining Calorie Cost for Bicycling

DISTANCE (IN MILES)	TIME (IN MIN)										
	10	15	20	25	30	35	40	45	50	55	60
1.00	.032										
1.50	.042	.032									
2.00	.062	.039	.032								
3.00		.062	.042	.036	.032						
4.00			.062	.044	.039	.035	.032				
5.00			.097	.062	.045	.041	.037	.035	.032		
6.00				.088	.062	.047	.042	.039	.036	.034	.032
7.00					.081	.062	.049	.043	.040	.038	.036
8.00						.078	.062	.050	.044	.041	.039
9.00							.076	.062	.051	.045	.042
10.00							.097	.074	.062	.051	.045
11.00								.093	.073	.062	.052
12.00									.088	.072	.062
13.00										.084	.071
14.00											.081
15.00											.097

Source: From *Your Guide to Getting Fit*, 2nd ed., by I. Kusinitz and M. Fine, 1991, Mountain View, CA: Mayfield Publishing.

rest periods during the early phases of your cycling program, and if you ride a 10-speed bike, switch gears periodically to lessen the resistance and make the ride a little easier. The key to a successful cycling program is to increase your total work gradually. Follow these guidelines when beginning your cycling program:

1. Adhere to all traffic rules and wear appropriate safety gear when you are cycling outdoors.

2. Adjust the seat height so your knee has a slight bend when your foot is at the bottom of a pedal swing. This position gives you maximum power without creating stress on your spine.

3. Saddle soreness occurs because of either chafing caused by friction on the skin of the buttocks or increased pressure on the genital area and the buttocks that causes pain and numbness. To avoid or minimize saddle soreness, use corn starch or talcum powder. You may also consider purchasing a larger seat for the bicycle.

4. Wear cycling shorts padded by soft chamois sewn in the seat to increase the cushioning and reduce friction.

Sample Rope-Skipping Program

On days when you cannot do outdoor aerobic activities or when you want to try a different form of aerobic conditioning, rope skipping is an excellent alternative. One factor that deters many exercisers from using rope skipping as their primary form of exercise is the amount of skill involved in turning and jumping. Since exercise needs to be continuous in order for you to achieve maximal cardiorespiratory benefits, you need to become proficient in jumping and turning. With practice, however, even a novice can become a good rope skipper.

It is important to purchase a rope of the correct length. The rope should be long enough to reach from armpit to armpit while it is passing under both feet. When the rope is too short, you are forced to jump in a humped position, and poor posture while exercising at high intensities causes increased strain on the back muscles. In addition, buy a good pair of exercise shoes because of the stress to the balls of your feet.

Duration Most beginners use an interval program consisting of brief periods of jumping followed by periods of rest. Unless you are already involved in a

Table 8.10 ✦ Days Required to Lose 5 to 25 Pounds by Bicycling* and Lowering Daily Caloric Intake

MINUTES OF + BICYCLING	REDUCTION OF CALORIES PER DAY (IN KCAL)	DAYS TO LOSE 5 LB	DAYS TO LOSE 10 LB	DAYS TO LOSE 15 LB	DAYS TO LOSE 20 LB	DAYS TO LOSE 25 LB
30	400	25	50	75	100	125
30	600	19	38	57	76	95
30	800	17	34	51	68	85
30	1000	13	26	39	52	65
45	400	22	44	66	88	110
45	600	17	34	51	68	85
45	800	14	28	42	56	70
45	1000	12	24	36	48	60
60	400	19	38	57	76	95
60	600	15	30	45	60	75
60	800	13	26	39	52	65
60	1000	11	22	33	44	55

*Bicycling calculated at 6.5 kcal/min at approximately 7 mph.

Source: From *Exercise Equivalents of Foods: A Practical Guide for the Overweight,* by F. Konishi, 1973, Carbondale, IL: Southern Illinois University Press.

physical conditioning program, start with a beginning-level walking program to improve your level of fitness and strengthen your joints, tendons, and ligaments before you begin rope skipping. Since rope skipping can cause fatigue in the arms, stretch before and after each exercise session. Initially, the amount of time actually spent jumping may be small. As you continue exercising and your coordination improves, you will be able to increase the amount of time you spend jumping.

Intensity During the initial phase of a rope-skipping program, you may actually exercise at an intensity below your THR zone. Do not push too hard too soon. Rope skipping requires constant impact on the bones in the feet and can cause trauma to them. As your level of fitness increases, you will be able to exercise at 65 to 75 percent of your heart rate zone. Avoid very high exercise intensities while rope skipping because of the stress to your hips, knees, ankles, and feet.

Frequency As with other forms of aerobic exercise, rope skip no more than three days per week on alternate days. Because a lot of stress is placed on the lower parts of the body, you may choose to alternate rope skipping with other forms of exercise to reduce the risk of injury. Water exercises are an especially

good alternative because of the lack of stress on the joints.

Calorie Cost Table 8.11 shows the gross energy cost of rope skipping in units of kcal/min. By way of example, Natasha weighs 110 lb and skips slowly for 20

Table 8.11 ✦ Gross Energy Cost of Rope Skipping (kcal/min)

BODY WEIGHT (LBS)	SLOW SKIPPING	FAST SKIPPING
110	7.5	9.2
120	8.2	10.0
130	8.9	10.9
140	9.5	11.7
150	10.2	12.5
160	10.9	13.4
170	11.6	14.2
180	12.3	15.0
190	13.0	15.9
200	13.6	16.7
210	14.3	17.5
220	15.0	18.4

Source: From *Fitness Leader's Handbook* (p. 154), by B. D. Franks and E. T. Howley, 1989, Champaign, IL: Human Kinetics Publishers. Copyright 1989 by B. Don Franks, Edward T. Howley, and Susan Metros. Reprinted by permission.

Behavioral Change
and Motivational Strategies

Many things can interfere with your ability to improve your cardiorespiratory fitness. Here are some barriers (roadblocks) and strategies for overcoming them.

Roadblock	Behavioral Change Strategy
Your schedule fluctuates from week to week because you travel for your job. It is difficult to establish a regular time for exercise, and you find that your exercise frequency decreases during the weeks that you travel.	Several strategies included in chapter 3 apply to your situation. First, you need to consider *tailoring* a program to suit your needs. Since your schedule constantly changes, you should consider including a variety of cardiorespiratory activities in order to increase your fitness level. While you are traveling, you could use exercise equipment in the fitness center of your hotel. You could also jog, providing you are in a safe environment. Use the exposure to a new surrounding to increase your likelihood of exercising rather than as an excuse not to exercise. You could also manipulate your total work so that during the weeks when your exercise frequency decreases, you can extend the duration of exercise sessions and/or increase exercise intensity. Another principle from chapter 3 also applies here. Use *reminder systems* to help you remember the appropriate exercise intensity, frequency, and duration for the upcoming week based on your traveling schedule.
You are at the end of your second year of college and are horrified to find that you have gained 25 lb in two years! You have never been involved in an aerobic conditioning program and find it difficult to get started.	Begin by *contracting*. Once you establish exercise goals, develop a contract and have it witnessed by someone (see Figure 3.1 on page 42). Your chances of adhering to your exercise program will also be much greater initially if you use *social support*. Try to find an exercise partner who will motivate you to stick with the program. Finally, we recommend that you use *gradual programming*. Since you have not been a regular exerciser, it may be difficult to jump right into a program and maintain it. Do not get discouraged if you aren't 100 percent committed initially. You will find that, as the weeks pass and you begin to experience benefits from exercising, your level of motivation will increase and it will become easier to get off the couch and exercise.
Your friends have decided to join a health club. You were never good at sports and have gained 15 lb since graduation from college. Your level of fitness really is not great, but you don't want to be left out of the group.	Remember first that increasing your level of cardiorespiratory fitness can be fun. Select activities that you enjoy doing that require little skill. Many aerobic exercises require very little skill, so don't be discouraged if you are not ready for strenuous exercise at the club. You will find that, as your level of cardiorespiratory fitness increases, you will have greater stamina. Your coordination will also improve and you may find yourself trying sports that were beyond you when you first joined. Begin with a walk/jog program. Find a friend who has a fitness level similar to yours, and begin exercising together. By using these methods, you will feel more confident and not as self-conscious about exercising at the club.
List other roadblocks preventing you from participating in a cardiorespiratory endurance program or factors hindering your progress in your current program. 1. _____ 2. _____ 3. _____	Now cite behavioal change strategies that can help you overcome these roadblocks. 1. _____ 2. _____ 3. _____

minutes. Her estimated caloric expenditure is calculated as:

$$7.5 \text{ kcal/min} \times 20 \text{ min} = 150 \text{ kcal}$$

If Joyce also weighs 110 lb and skips at a fast pace for 20 minutes, her caloric expenditure would be:

$$9.2 \text{ kcal/min} \times 20 \text{ min} = 184 \text{ kcal}$$

Hence these two women, who have the same body weight, would have different energy expenditures based on the speed of turning the rope.

Rate of Progression Most beginners skip rope at 60 turns per minute. This is usually a comfortable pace that allows time for the beginner to develop coordination between turning and jumping. As you advance, you should be able to increase the number of turns to 70 to 100 per minute. Rope skipping can become boring, so as your skill level increases, you may use tactics such as jumping on one foot or changing the direction of the rope to introduce variety into your program. If you have trouble with coordination, try jumping while you listen to music.

SUMMARY

Many physiological benefits can be derived from participating in an aerobic fitness program, including a lower resting heart rate, a stronger heart, and a greater blood supply to exercising muscles. All these benefits will increase aerobic power and make exercise feel easier at work loads below maximum.

Overview and Analysis of Aerobic Exercise Choices

Only aerobic exercises will increase your cardiorespiratory endurance. There are many options for aerobic activities, of which a number are not dependent on your having a high skill level. During the initial phase of your program, participate in activities that rely on large muscle groups to increase your endurance and minimize your risk of injury.

Maximal Oxygen Consumption

Cardiorespiratory endurance is synonymous with maximal oxygen consumption. The maximal oxygen uptake is influenced primarily by (1) the ability of the cardiorespiratory system to deliver oxygen to the muscles and (2) the ability of the muscles to extract oxygen from the blood. When comparing the fitness level of individuals, it is best to express the maximal oxygen uptake in units of $ml/kg \times min^{-1}$. Although the maximal oxygen uptake is best measured by gas analysis, field tests are often used to decrease the expense while still providing an accurate indication of aerobic fitness.

How to Safely Begin and Progress in an Aerobic Fitness Program

It is important to manipulate the exercise intensity, duration, and frequency to both (1) maintain the targeted amount of total work and (2) adjust to the schedule. If you have a busy week planned, you can easily manipulate these factors and still maintain your caloric expenditure. Avoid shin splints by wearing good running shoes, exercising on soft surfaces, and using a variety of aerobic exercise choices. Use the abdominal breathing technique to reduce the pain associated with the stitch-in-the-side phenomenon. Wear two pairs of cotton socks and place a bandage on hot spots to reduce blisters. When muscle soreness occurs, use light massage, static stretching, and light-intensity exercise to decrease pain and stiffness. Always maintain your level of hydration, and wear adequate clothing to avoid heat illness. Use RICE as the immediate form of therapy for injuries.

Sample Starter Programs

Walking is one of the most popular aerobic activities because it does not require any specialized skills. When you start a walking program, begin walking 10 to 15 minutes per session at a comfortable pace at 50 to 60 percent of your THR three to four times per week. Gradually increase your rate of progression until you reach a distance of five miles. At this point you may consider beginning a jogging program. Complete the advanced walking program before beginning a jogging/running program. Gradually increase the amount of time spent jogging until you can jog continuously for 30 to 45 minutes. The average distance covered by more advanced runners is five miles per session within 35 to 40 minutes. During the initial phase, remain in the 65 to 75 percent target heart rate zone. The optimal frequency is three to four days per week. Overuse can quickly result in injuries. To prevent injury, increase your distance before you increase your speed.

Swimming and water aerobics have increased in popularity because of the high rate of musculoskeletal injuries associated with other aerobic activities. The resistance in water is sufficient to elicit increased cardiorespiratory endurance while providing a virtually injury-free environment. If you are not a strong swimmer, begin with a walking program, and spend more time doing water exercises. As both your level of fitness and your swimming ability increase, you may make your total workout program one of swimming. The exercise heart rate is lower in water, so be careful to adjust for that.

Cycling is a great aerobic activity because your body weight is supported. Begin cycling a distance of one or two miles, even if you are exercising below your THR zone. Increase your intensity and duration until you can cycle three to five miles at 70 to 75 percent intensity. The type of bike used will affect caloric expenditure; thus the caloric cost of cycling is difficult to estimate.

Rope skipping is too often avoided by aerobic exercisers because of the skill needed and of the high amount of impact involved. Begin with brief periods of jumping followed by periods of rest. Complete a beginning walking program first in order to increase your level of fitness and decrease your risk of injury. Begin at 65 to 75 percent of your target heart rate and exercise three days per week on alternate days. You may choose to participate concurrently in alternative aerobic activities, such as swimming, to experience a more rapid increase in cardiorespiratory fitness with little risk of injury.

ℛEFERENCES

American College of Sports Medicine. (1990). The recommended quantity and quality of exercise for developing and maintaining cardiorespiratory and muscular fitness in healthy adults. *Medicine and Science in Sports and Exercise 22,* 265–274.

American Heart Association. (1992). Statement on exercise: Benefits and recommendations for physical activity programs for all Americans. *Circulation 86,* 340–344.

Auble, T., et al. (1987, May). Aerobic requirements for moving hand weights through various ranges of motion while walking. *Physician and Sportsmedicine 15,* 109–113.

Blair, S. (1994). Physical activity, fitness and coronary heart disease, C. Bouchard, et al. in *Physical activity, fitness, and health.* Champaign, IL: Human Kinetics.

Greenberg, J., Dintiman, G., & Oakes, B. (1995). *Physical fitness and wellness.* Boston: Allyn & Bacon.

Poehlman, E., et al. (1992, December). Resting energy metabolism and cardiovascular disease risk in resistance-trained and aerobically trained males. *Metabolism 41,* 1351–1368.

Powers, S., & Howley, E. (1990). *Exercise physiology: Theory and application to fitness and performance.* Dubuque, IA: Wm. C. Brown.

Thomas, T., & Londeree, B. (1989, May). Energy cost during prolonged walking vs jogging exercise. *Physician and Sportsmedicine 17,* 93–102.

U.S. Department of Health and Human Services. (1990). Healthy people 2000: National health promotion and disease prevention objectives. Public Health Services Bulletin (PHS) 91–50212.

Williams, M. H. (1995). *Nutrition for fitness and sport,* 4th ed. Madison: Brown & Benchmark.

Lab Activity 8.1

Assessing Your Level of Aerobic Fitness by the 1-Mile Walking Test

INSTRUCTIONS: *This test is designed for older adults or for those who are just beginning an aerobic conditioning program. The time of the walk and the postexercise heart rate value are used to predict the subject's maximal oxygen consumption.*

✦ Step 1: Pretest Screening

1. If you are over age 35, seek the advice of your physician before taking this test.

2. Do not eat or drink anything except water for at least three hours before taking the test.

3. Avoid using any type of tobacco, including cigarettes and chewing tobacco, for at least three hours before taking this test.

4. Avoid heavy physical activity on the day of the test.

5. If you are on medication, report it to your instructor before you begin this test.

6. Wear loose-fitting clothes, such as shorts and a T-shirt, and running shoes.

✦ Step 2: Administration of the Test

1. Divide participants into two groups.

2. Each participant in the first group should choose a partner from the other group.

3. Those taking the test first complete a thorough warm-up session and slowly walk one lap around the track.

4. The partner maintains a scorecard that records time in minutes and seconds and keeps track of the number of laps walked.

5. The instructor explains the procedures (such as the fact that the faster the participants walk, the higher their level of cardiorespiratory fitness will be) and instructs the first group to begin.

6. The students are to walk the mile as fast as possible, and only walking is allowed.

7. As the walker completes each lap, the partner lets the walker know how many laps remain and encourages the partner to maintain a steady pace.

8. The instructor calls out the time in minutes and seconds periodically.

9. The partner writes the final time on the scorecard.

10. The partner immediately takes the walker's 10-second heart rate. Instruct the walker that the heart rate count should be completed within 15 seconds after the end of the mile walk. Any further time delay will result in an overestimation of the maximal oxygen consumption.

11. After all walkers in the first group have finished, the second group of walkers takes the test while the first group acts as partners.

✦ Step 3: Interpreting the Results

1. The tables following Step 4 contain the estimated maximal oxygen uptake ($ml/kg \times min^{-1}$) for women and men 20 to 39 years old based on the 1-mile walk test.

2. To use the tables, find the section that pertains to your age and sex. On the horizontal line across the top, find the amount of time (to the nearest minute) it took to walk a mile. In the vertical column, find the point of intersection for your walking time and your postexercise heart rate (listed in the far left column). The number where the postexercise heart rate and the 1-mile time intersect is your maximal oxygen consumption expressed in ml/kg 3 min^{-1}. For example, a 34-year-old woman who walked the mile in 17 minutes and had a postexercise heart rate of 170 would have an estimated oxygen consumption of 27.6 ml/kg 3 min^{-1}. According to Table 8.2 on page 80, she would be in the *fair/good* fitness category.

3. Review Table 8.2 to obtain an estimate of your maximal aerobic power based on your performance in this walk test.

✦ Step 4: Cardiorespiratory Endurance Record

Name _____   Date _____

Age _____ Sex _____   Body Weight _____ lbs

Walking Time _____   Fitness Category _____

Maximal VO$_2$ (ml/kg $\times$ min^{-1}) _____

Lab Activity 8.1 *(continued)*
Assessing Your Level of Aerobic Fitness by the 1-Mile Walk Test

Estimated Maximal Oxygen Uptake (ml/kg × min^{-1}) for Women, 20 to 39 Years Old

Heart rate	MIN/MILE										
	10	11	12	13	14	15	16	17	18	19	20
Women (20–29)											
120	62.1	58.9	55.6	52.3	49.1	45.8	42.5	39.3	36.0	32.7	29.5
130	60.6	57.3	54.0	50.8	47.5	44.2	41.0	37.7	34.4	31.2	27.9
140	59.0	55.7	52.5	49.2	45.9	42.7	39.4	36.1	32.9	29.6	26.3
150	57.4	54.2	50.9	47.6	44.4	41.1	37.8	34.6	31.3	28.0	24.8
160	55.9	52.6	49.3	46.1	42.8	39.5	36.3	33.0	29.7	26.5	23.2
170	54.3	51.0	47.8	44.5	41.2	38.0	34.7	31.4	28.2	24.9	21.6
180	52.7	49.5	46.2	42.9	39.7	36.4	33.1	29.9	26.6	23.3	20.1
190	51.2	47.9	44.6	41.4	38.1	34.8	31.6	28.3	25.0	21.8	18.5
200	49.6	46.3	43.1	39.8	36.5	33.3	30.0	26.7	23.5	20.2	16.9
Women (30–39)											
120	58.2	55.0	51.7	48.4	45.2	41.9	38.7	35.4	32.1	28.9	25.6
130	56.7	53.4	50.1	46.9	43.6	40.4	37.1	33.8	30.6	27.3	24.0
140	55.1	51.8	48.6	45.3	42.1	38.8	35.5	32.3	29.0	25.7	22.5
150	53.5	50.3	47.0	43.8	40.5	37.2	34.0	30.7	27.4	24.2	20.9
160	52.0	48.7	45.4	42.2	38.9	35.7	32.4	29.1	25.9	22.6	19.3
170	50.4	47.1	43.9	40.6	37.4	34.1	30.8	27.6	24.3	21.0	17.8
180	48.8	45.6	42.3	39.1	35.8	32.5	29.3	26.0	22.7	19.5	16.2
190	47.3	44.0	40.8	37.5	34.2	31.0	27.7	24.4	21.2	17.9	14.6

Calculations assume a body weight of 125 lb for women. For each 15 lb beyond 125 lb, subtract 1 ml from the estimated maximal oxygen uptake given in the table.

Source: From *Fitness Leader's Handbook* (pp. 90–91), by B. D. Franks and E. T. Howley, 1989. Champaign, IL: Human Kinetics Publishers. Copyright 1989 by B. Don Franks, Edward T. Howley, and Susan Metros. Reprinted by permission.

Estimated Maximal Oxygen Uptake (ml/kg × min^{-1}) for Men, 20 to 39 Years Old

Heart rate	Min/mile										
	10	11	12	13	14	15	16	17	18	19	20

Men (20–29)

Heart rate	10	11	12	13	14	15	16	17	18	19	20
120	65.0	61.7	58.4	55.2	51.9	48.6	45.4	42.1	38.9	35.6	32.3
130	63.4	60.1	56.9	53.6	50.3	47.1	43.8	40.6	37.3	34.0	30.8
140	61.8	58.6	55.3	52.0	48.8	45.5	42.2	39.0	35.7	32.5	29.2
150	60.3	57.0	53.7	50.5	47.2	43.9	40.7	37.4	34.2	30.9	27.6
160	58.7	55.4	52.2	48.9	45.6	42.4	39.1	35.9	32.6	29.3	26.1
170	57.1	53.9	50.6	47.3	44.1	40.8	37.6	34.3	31.0	27.8	24.5
180	55.6	52.3	49.0	45.8	42.5	39.3	36.0	32.7	29.5	26.2	22.9
190	54.0	50.7	47.5	44.2	41.0	37.7	34.4	31.2	27.9	24.6	21.4
200	52.4	49.2	45.9	42.7	39.4	36.1	32.9	29.6	26.3	23.1	19.8

Men (30–39)

Heart rate	10	11	12	13	14	15	16	17	18	19	20
120	61.1	57.8	54.6	51.3	48.0	44.8	41.5	38.2	35.0	31.7	28.4
130	59.5	56.3	53.0	49.7	46.5	43.2	39.9	36.7	33.4	30.1	26.9
140	58.0	54.7	51.4	48.2	44.9	41.6	38.4	35.1	31.8	28.6	25.3
150	56.4	53.1	49.9	46.6	43.3	40.1	36.8	33.5	30.3	27.0	23.8
160	54.8	51.6	48.3	45.0	41.8	38.5	35.2	32.0	28.7	25.5	22.2
170	53.3	50.0	46.7	43.5	40.2	36.9	33.7	30.4	27.1	23.9	20.6
180	51.7	48.4	45.2	41.9	38.6	35.4	32.1	28.8	25.6	22.3	19.1
190	50.1	46.9	43.6	40.3	37.1	33.8	30.5	27.3	24.0	20.8	17.5

Calculations assume a body weight of 170 lb for men. For each 15 lb beyond 170 lb, subtract 1 ml from the estimated maximal oxygen uptake given in the table.

Source: From *Fitness Leader's Handbook* (pp. 90–91), by B. D. Franks and E. T. Howley, 1989, Champaign, IL: Human Kinetics Publishers. Copyright 1989 by B. Don Franks, Edward T. Howley, and Susan Metros. Reprinted by permission.

Lab Activity 8.2

Assessing Your Level of Aerobic Fitness by the 3-Mile Walk Test

INSTRUCTIONS: *The objective of this walking test is to cover three miles in the fastest time possible without running. It can be performed on a track or on any distance that has been accurately measured. (If you are a jogger/runner, you may choose to substitute the 1.5-mile run test.)*

✦ Step 1: Pretest Screening

1. If you are over 35 years of age, seek the advice of your physician before taking this test.

2. Do not eat or drink anything except water for at least three hours before taking the test.

3. Avoid using any type of tobacco, including cigarettes and chewing tobacco, for at least three hours before taking the test.

4. Avoid heavy physical activity on the day of the test.

5. If you are on medication, report it to your instructor before you begin the test.

6. Wear loose-fitting clothes, such as shorts and a T-shirt, and running shoes.

✦ Step 2: Administration of the Test

1. Divide participants into two groups.

2. Each participant in the first group should choose a partner from the other group.

3. Those taking the test first complete a thorough warm-up session and slowly walk one lap around the track.

4. The partner maintains a scorecard that records time in minutes and seconds and keeps track of the number of laps walked.

5. The instructor explains the procedures again and instructs the first group to begin.

6. As the walker completes each lap, the partner lets the walker know how many laps remain and encourages the partner to maintain a steady pace.

7. The instructor calls out the time in minutes and seconds periodically.

8. The partner writes the final time on the scorecard.

9. After all walkers in the first group have finished, the second group takes the test while the first group acts as partners.

✦ Step 3: Interpreting the Results

1. The following table contains five fitness classifications based on age and sex.

2. To use the table, find on the horizontal line the approximate length of time it took for you to walk three miles in your age category. Then locate on the vertical column your fitness category, according to sex.

3. For example, if you are an 18-year-old male and it took 36 minutes and 12 seconds for you to walk three miles, you are in the *good* fitness category.

4. Review Table 8.2 on page 165 to obtain an estimate of your maximal aerobic power based on your performance in this test.

Three-Mile Walking Test (No Running) Time (Minutes)

Fitness category		AGE (YEARS)			
		13–19	20–29	30–39	40–49
1. Very poor	(men)	> 45:00*	> 46:00	> 49:00	> 52:00
	(women)	> 47:00	> 48:00	> 51:00	> 54:00
2. Poor	(men)	41:01–45:00	42:01–46:00	44:31–49:00	47:01–52:00
	(women)	43:01–47:00	44:01–48:00	46:31–51:00	49:01–54:00
3. Fair	(men)	37:31–41:00	38:31–42:00	40:01–44:30	42:01–47:00
	(women)	39:31–43:00	40:31–44:00	42:01–46:30	44:01–49:00
4. Good	(men)	33:00–37:30	34:00–38:30	35:00–40:00	36:30–42:00
	(women)	35:00–39:30	36:00–40:30	37:30–42:00	39:00–44:00
5. Excellent	(men)	< 33:00	< 34:00	< 35:00	< 36:30
	(women)	< 35:00	< 36:00	< 37:30	< 39:00

*< Means *less than*, > means *more than*.

Excerpts from "Tests" from *The Aerobics Program for Total Well Being,* by K. H. Cooper. Copyright 1982 by Kenneth H. Cooper. Used by permission of Bantam Books, a division of Bantam Doubleday Dell Publishing Group, Inc.

✦ Step 4: Cardiorespiratory Endurance Record

Name _____   Date _____

Age _____   Sex _____   Body Weight _____ lbs

Walking Time _____   Fitness Category _____

Maximal VO$_2$ (ml/kg × min^{-1}) _____

Lab Activity 8.3

The Straw Walk

INSTRUCTIONS: *The object is to walk quarter-mile laps at the fastest pace you can hold for a full 15 minutes. The more fit you become, the more laps you will be able to walk in 15 minutes. As you complete each lap, you will be handed a "straw." The trick is to keep moving in stride as your instructor hands you your straw. How many straws can you earn in 15 minutes of fast walking?*

✦ Specific Information about the Straw Walk

1. In just 15 minutes the straw walk helps you four different ways: (1) it tells you how fit you are, (2) it teaches you "pacing," (3) it tells you your walking speed, and (4) it provides you with great aerobic exercise.

2. To perform your best in the straw walk, it is helpful to save your breath and avoid talking, walk at your own pace, warm up slowly, pace yourself so you don't burn out, avoid eating a large meal just before the walk, and avoid slowing down for your straw hand-off.

3. Keep in mind that this is a walk, not a run. It is also not a test, but merely an exercise to help you determine your fitness level.

4. To begin the straw walk, assemble at the starting line and wait for the signal to begin walking fast. Each time you complete one lap, make certain you receive a straw. After 15 minutes a whistle will sound. Freeze in place and prepare to take your pulse. Count your heartbeats starting with the next whistle (second whistle) and ending 6 seconds later (third whistle). Record your heart rate and straw walk score below. As your instructor approaches, announce your score, hand over your straws and continue your cool-down walk.

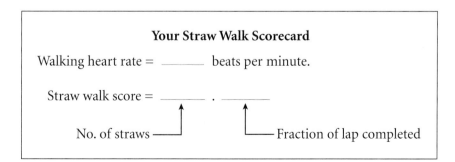

Your Straw Walk Scorecard

Walking heart rate = _____ beats per minute.

Straw walk score = _____ . _____

No. of straws ⬑   ⬏ Fraction of lap completed

Your straw walk score is the number of laps you completed plus your position on the course when the final whistle blows. For example, if you finish with 4 straws, at the 6th cone on the straw walk course, your straw walk score is 4.6 (4 and 6/10 laps). That means you averaged 4.6 mph for 15 full minutes.

5. To determine your fitness level, find your score on the fitness scale below. For example, if you score 4.8, you are in the top 10 percent (90th percentile) of American children.

Straw Walk Fitness Scale

	Straw Walk Score	Fitness Percentile		Straw Walk Score	Fitness Percentile
Excellent	5.4	99%	Fair	3.9	65%
	5.3	98%		3.8	60%
	5.2	97%		3.7	55%
	5.1	96%		3.6	50%
	5.0	95%		3.5	45%
Very Good	4.9	93%	Not So Good	3.4	40%
	4.8	90%		3.3	32%
	4.7	88%		3.2	24%
	4.6	85%		3.1	16%
	4.5	82%		3.0	10%
Good	4.4	80%			
	4.3	77%			
	4.2	75%			
	4.1	73%			
	4.0	70%			

✦ **How to Improve Your Straw Walk**

Study the high and low performance factors listed here. Which low performance factors in your life-style could you improve on?

Low Performance Factors	High Performance Factors
Pacing unevenly	Maintaining a steady pace
Talking while walking	Saving your "wind" for breathing
Walking with arms at your side	Swinging your arms to and fro
Walking with hunched-over posture	Walking tall
Being overweight	Trimming down
Watching too much TV	Being more physically avtive
Being too tense	Relaxing on the walk
Poor endurance training	Practicing longer walks
Using tobacco	Avoiding tobacco
Eating fatty/junk foods	Eating a balanced high-carbohydrate diet

Lab Activity 8.3 *(continued)*
The Straw Walk

6. Do a second straw walk. To improve your score in the straw walk, remember to relax at the start, pace yourself from the beginning, swing your arms, avoid conversation, stay on the inside lane, and give yourself an easy walking warm-up and cool-down.

Comparing Your Straw Walk Scores

First straw walk score = _____ . _____ Heart rate = _____ bpm

Second straw walk score = _____ . _____ Heart rate = _____ bpm

---

9

$\mathcal{M}$USCULAR $\mathcal{E}$NDURANCE, $\mathcal{M}$USCULAR $\mathcal{S}$TRENGTH, AND $\mathcal{F}$LEXIBILITY

$\mathcal{C}$hapter Objectives

By the end of this chapter, you should be able to:

1. Identify the factors that directly or indirectly affect muscular strength, muscular endurance, and flexibility.

2. Cite the advantages of acquiring and maintaining adequate muscular strength, muscular endurance, and flexibility throughout life.

3. Design a personalized strength, endurance, and flexibility program that applies sound training principles and meets your fitness objectives.

4. Complete a strength, endurance, and flexibility routine using the acceptable methods described in this chapter.

5. Design a sound girth control program to flatten your stomach.

$\mathcal{E}$STHER HAS BEEN interested in trying some form of strength training for years to firm her muscles and improve her appearance. She is also enthusiastic because she has heard something about this type of training benefiting weight and fat loss. Some of her friends who use the weight room at the gym seem to have improved their bodies and are looking good. Esther wants to get started too, but she has many questions. Esther is particularly concerned about becoming "muscle bound" and inflexible. She knows that inflexibility will interfere with her ability to enjoy recreational activities, competitive sports, and to perform daily tasks such as picking up an object, tying shoes, and even getting up out of a chair. What type of program should she choose? How often should she work out? Should she use heavy or light weights?

This chapter answers these and many more questions to help Esther and others begin sound strength, endurance, and flexibility training programs designed to meet their personal objectives.

MUSCULAR STRENGTH AND ENDURANCE

Although muscular strength and endurance are closely related, it is important to differentiate between the two. Muscular strength is the amount of force or weight a muscle or group of muscles can exert for one repetition. It is generally measured by a single maximal contraction. The amount of weight you can bench press overhead one time, for example, measures the strength of the triceps muscle. You can measure the strength of other muscle groups the same way with specific tests (see chapter 2). Muscular endurance is the capacity of a muscle group to complete an uninterrupted series of repetitions as often as possible with light weights. The total number of bench presses you can complete with half of your maximum weight on the barbell, for example, measures the endurance of the triceps and pectoralis muscles. Depending on the desired outcome, you can manipulate the training variables (choice of equipment and exercises, amount of resistance or weight, number of repetitions and sets, length of rest interval) to make your program strength- or endurance-oriented or a balance of both.

This chapter addresses the key factors involved in training for the development of strength and endurance, including importance, influencing factors, training principles and suggestions, specific exercises, equipment, girth control, and other related concerns to help design a program that meets your specific needs.

THE IMPORTANCE OF STRENGTH AND ENDURANCE

The improvement of muscular strength and endurance will affect almost every phase of your life. Some of the benefits, such as the loss of body fat and improved self-concept, have been overlooked in the past because of overemphasis on adding muscle mass and improving performance. A closer look at the true value of strength and endurance training makes it clear that a sound program can help to improve both physical and mental health. Begin by completing Lab Activity 9.1: Do You Need to Start a Strength-Training Program?

The Management of Body Weight and Fat

Although strength training is generally associated with muscle weight gain and not with body weight and fat loss, it is a critical part of a total weight-control program. Unfortunately, although metabolism slows with age, the amount of calories (kcal) we consume does not. As a result, body weight and fat increase and the amount of lean muscle mass decreases. From 25 to 50 years of age, **basal metabolism** slows by as much as 15 percent in some sedentary individuals. The typical 60-year-old, for example, burns about 350 fewer daily calories at rest than he or she burned at age 25. This is equivalent to 1 lb of fat (3,500 kcal = 1 lb of fat) every 10 days, 3 lb per month, 36 lb per year. As you can see, even small decreases in metabolism produce large increases in body weight and fat. A 5 percent slowing of metabolic rate, for example, can add 6 to 9 lb of body fat in just one year, depending on your weight and size at the time (see chapter 11 for more details on basal metabolism and weight loss).

This slowing of resting metabolism is a direct result of the loss of lean muscle mass through inactivity, something that happens to everyone who is, or becomes, inactive regardless of age. Although it requires energy (cal) to maintain muscle tissue at rest, fat or adipose tissue is almost metabolically inert and requires very few calories to maintain. A comparison of two individuals identical in weight, one with 10 lb more muscle than the other, clearly shows that the resting metabolism is significantly higher in the more muscled individual. According to some experts, resting metabolism increases by approximately 30 kcal daily for every pound of muscle weight added. In other words, you burn enough extra calories at rest to lose 2 to 3 lb a year for every pound of muscle mass you add.

Regular strength and endurance training and aerobic exercise can prevent much of this undesirable change in metabolic rate. In fact, a well-conceived weight-training program that emphasizes muscle-

Basal metabolism The energy expended (calories burned), measured by oxygen consumption, during a resting state over a 24-hour period.

weight gain will actually increase basal metabolism regardless of age. For both women and men, aerobic exercise followed by a half-hour strength-training session three to four times weekly, coupled with sound nutrition, is an ideal approach to weight control throughout life.

Improved Appearance, Body Image, and Self-Concept

Muscular strength and endurance training can improve your physical appearance. By reducing your caloric intake, losing body fat and weight, improving muscle tone, and adding muscle weight, you will look better.

When weight loss occurs too rapidly, particularly without exercise, skin gives the appearance of not fitting the body very well. Sagging skin on the back of the arms, for example, is often an indication of either too rapid, or too large an amount of, weight loss. With reduced caloric intake, fat cells shrink but the skin does not keep pace to provide a tight fit. One way to improve appearance and help your skin fit better during and after weight loss is to include strength training as part of your total program. As fat cells shrink in the back of your arms, for example, strength training can enlarge the tricep muscle tissue to help avoid sagging skin.

Keep in mind that these changes will not occur overnight. Depending on age and current physical state, it may take 12 months or more of regular aerobic exercise, strength and endurance training, and dietary management of calories to decrease total body fat significantly, add 5 to 10 pounds of muscle weight, tone the entire body, give skin sufficient time to rebound to a tight fit, and adjust to the new body. These changes will alter the way you both perceive yourself and feel others perceive you. Practically everyone who stays with a program experiences improved body image and self-concept that positively affects their personal and professional lives. Patience is necessary, however; proper nutrition and exercise, rather than diets, are meant to be lifetime activities.

Increased Bone-Mineral Content

Recent studies suggest that regular strength training aids in optimal bone development by improving bone-mineral content. The use of strength training in addition to weight-bearing exercise, such as walking, jogging, racket sports, and aerobic dance, may help women reach menopause with more bone-mineral mass, an important factor in the prevention, and delay, of osteoporosis (see chapter 10).

Increased Strength and Endurance for Work and Daily Activities

Each of the training programs discussed in this chapter will effectively increase both muscular strength and endurance in the relatively short period of 8 to 12 weeks. If you are, for example, in the process of moving or helping a friend to move, you will notice an improvement in your ability to lift furniture and other heavy objects without undue fatigue. Additional strength and endurance will also help you perform daily personal and work activities more efficiently and provide you with the extra strength needed to cope with unexpected emergencies in life.

Improved Performance in Sports and Recreational Activities

Children and adults often lack strength and endurance in the upper body (arms and shoulders) and in the abdominal area. Many studies also show that most women are weak in the arms and shoulders because they think strength training will cause a loss of femininity, a totally unfounded fear. It is important to recognize that individualized, safe weight-training programs can be designed for both sexes at all ages and that these programs will improve muscular strength and endurance in the upper body, stomach, lower back, and other areas with little or no health risks or change in femininity. Increased upper-body and abdominal strength and endurance also helps to improve physical appearance and self-concept. Such a program helps children and young adults to engage in a wide variety of sports such as tumbling, gymnastics, baseball, basketball, field hockey, touch football, and soccer. You will also notice a difference when you perform an aerobic exercise or participate in a dance class, conditioning class, or your favorite recreational activity. The additional strength and endurance will delay fatigue and make free movement easier.

Decreased Incidence of Sports and Work-Related Injuries

Improved strength in the musculature surrounding the joints helps prevent injuries to your muscles, tendons, and ligaments. With regular training, bones and connective tissue become stronger and more dense. These changes make you less vulnerable to muscle strain, sprains, contusions, and tears (see chapter 14 for more details). Even low back pain may be prevented by an improved balance of strength and flexibility in the abdominal and back extensor muscles.

Strength training is also an important part of recovery following certain injuries. Return to normal range of motion and strength following soft-tissue injuries occurs more rapidly and completely with rehabilitative strength training.

Muscle Structure

Cross sections of various parts of a muscle are shown in Figure 9.1. Each muscle contains bundles of tissue composed of cells referred to as **muscle fibers**. A muscle fiber is composed of contractile units called **myofibrils**.

The entire muscle, consisting of the bundles

Figure 9.1 ✦ The Structure of Muscle.   The whole muscle (a) is composed of separate bundles of individual muscle fibers (b). Each fiber is composed of numerous myofibrils (c), each of which contains thin protein filaments (d) arranged so they can slide by one another to cause muscle shortening or lengthening. Various layers of connective tissue surround the muscle fibers, bundles, and whole muscles, which eventually bind together to form the tendon.

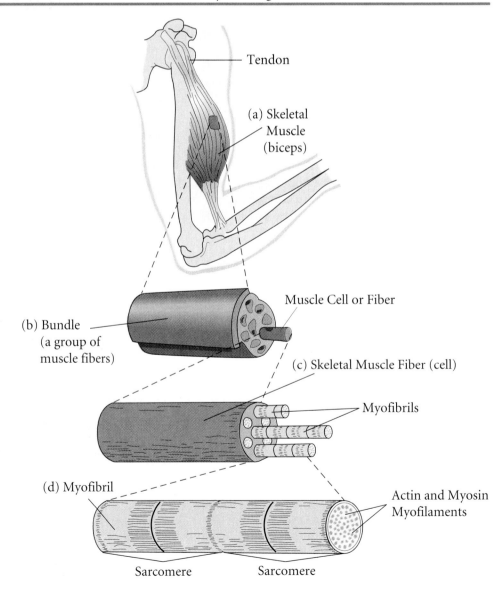

and the muscle fibers, is covered and bound together by layers of connective tissue that blend together to form the **tendon**. When you contract your bicep, for example, the muscle shortens with the force moving through the tendon to the bones to bend the elbow.

Types of Muscle Fiber

The three types of muscle fibers contained in each muscle in the body can be classified by two factors: the speed with which they contract and their main energy system (see Figure 9.2). **Slow-twitch, oxidative fiber** is used primarily in aerobic endurance activities such as jogging, marathon running, and cycling. These fibers contract slowly but are also slow to fatigue because of their tremendous vascular supply. **Fast-twitch, glycolytic fiber** is used primarily for explosive anaerobic movements such as sprinting, jumping, and throwing. These fibers contract explosively, tire rapidly, and are suitable for short-duration exercise. **Fast-twitch, oxidative, glycolytic fiber** has a speed of contraction that is faster than that of slow-twitch, oxidative fiber but slower than fast-twitch, glycolytic fiber, and fatigue occurs much more slowly than that of the fast-twitch, glycolytic fiber.

Figure 9.2 ✦ Muscle Fiber Types   SO is the slow-twitch, oxidative fiber; FOG is the fast-twitch, oxidative, glycolytic fiber; and FG is the fast-twitch glycolytic fiber.

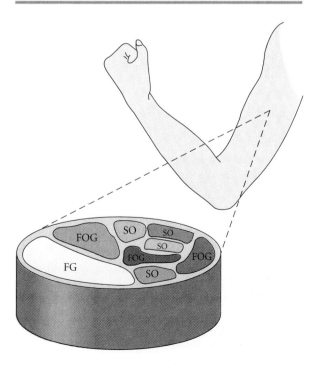

How Muscles Become Larger and Stronger

The capability of a muscle or muscle group to generate force for one maximum repetition depends on such factors as size, type, number of muscle fibers activated, and the ability of the nervous system to activate these fibers. Although your strength potential is limited by genetics and the number and size of fast-twitch fibers, everyone can improve strength with proper training. As training progresses, muscle cells will increase in size (particularly the fast-twitch fibers), the myofibrils in each cell may increase in number, and the connective tissue around your muscle fibers and bundles of muscle may also thicken. These three factors will significantly increase the size of a muscle in 8 to 10 weeks. Although women generally do not progress at the same rate as men do, significant increases in cell size also occur after engaging in a sound weight-training program.

You can improve your local muscular endurance by training both types of fast-twitch fiber by increasing the number of repetitions and by using lower weight. As training progresses, you will be capable of performing a greater number of repetitions for each exercise.

STRENGTH-TRAINING PRINCIPLES

The training principles discussed in this section will help you design a program to meet your specific

Muscle fibers Bundles of tissue composed of cells.

Myofibrils Thin protein filaments that interact and slide by one another during a muscular contraction.

Tendon A fibrous inelastic band which attaches some muscles to the bones they move when the muscles contract.

Slow-twitch, oxidative muscle fiber Red muscle fiber used in aerobic activity that contracts and tires slowly.

Fast-twitch, glycolytic muscle fiber White muscle fiber used in anaerobic activity that contracts rapidly and explosively but tires quickly because it has a poor blood supply.

Fast-twitch, oxidative, glycolytic fiber An intermediate fiber that can be used in both anaerobic and aerobic activity.

needs. First, consult Table 9.1 and choose a primary training objective. This table allows you to approximate the weight and number of sets and repetitions needed to fit your training objectives. The table is based on:

1. Heavy weight and low repetitions (three to six) develop considerably more strength and muscle mass than endurance. Your starting weight for each exercise should be about 80 percent of your 1-RM (maximum amount of weight you can lift one time). If your maximum lift on the bench press is 100 lb, your starting weight is 80 lb (100 × .80).

2. The closer you work to the 1-RM, the greater the strength gains. Unfortunately, the chance of injury increases with weight, so this approach is somewhat impractical.

3. Heavy weight, a moderate number of repetitions (six to eight), and multiple sets are more effective in adding muscle weight (mass).

4. Light weights and a high number of repetitions develop muscular endurance more than strength.

5. From a health standpoint, using the 6-RM as the starting weight and progressing to nine repetitions is ideal for general bodily development and the improvement of muscular strength and endurance.

6. Regardless of your training objective, the final repetition in each set should result in complete muscle failure or the inability to perform even one more repetition.

Types of Training

The three most commonly used strength and endurance training methods are isotonics, isokinetics, and isometrics, each with a number of variations and each requiring special equipment. During an isotonic contraction, such as the execution of an arm curl with free weights or universal or nautilus machines, the muscle shortens (**positive phase**) as the weight is brought toward the body and lengthens (**negative phase**) as it is returned to the starting position. Inertia helps move the weight during the positive phase, and the weight is slowly lowered under control

Table 9.1 ✦ Strength and Endurance Training Objectives and Variable Control

DESIRED PHYSICAL OUTCOMES	VARIABLE CONTROL
Strength	Heavy weight (3-RM or 80% of 1-RM), low repetitions (3 to 9), slow negative phase, multiple sets (3 to 5), moderate rest between each set and exercise (90 sec), use of maximum lift days.
Muscular endurance	Light weight (10-RM), high repetitions (10 to 15), slow negative phase, multiple sets (2 to 3), minimum rest between each set and exercise (2 min decreasing to 30 sec).
Strength and endurance/general body development/improved athletic performance	Moderate weight (6-RM), moderate repetitions (6 to 9), slow negative phase, multiple sets (2 to 3), moderate rest between each set and exercise (1 min).
Muscle mass or bulk	Heavy weight (3- to 5-RM), low repetitions, multiple sets (5 to 10), minimum rest between sets and exercises (1 min), use of a large number of different exercises for each muscle group and of periodization (2- to 3-week cycles that alter the resistance, repetitions, and sets from low through moderate to high).
Speed and explosive power	Moderate weight (5-RM), low repetitions (3 to 5), explosive contractions, slow negative phase, use of Olympic power lifts.
Rehabilitation from injury	Light weight and slow contractions performed without pain and to the full range of motion, 6 to 10 repetitions, 3 sets, and use of exercises that activate the supporting muscles of the joints (ankle, wrist, knee, and shoulder).

during the negative phase. During an **isokinetic** arm curl with special equipment, the muscle also shortens and lengthens during the positive and negative phases; however, maximal resistance is provided throughout the full range of movement in both phases. Without the benefit of inertia or gravity to allow a weight to drop, the routine would be considerably more difficult. In an isometric contraction, the exercised muscle contracts but its overall length remains unchanged.

You are performing isotonic contractions when you use Free Weights, Universal, Nautilus, Cam II, Polaris, and other similar equipment. New Life Cycle equipment has found a way to eliminate cheating and take full advantage of the negative phase of contraction. During the negative phase of each repetition, the weight automatically increases by 25 percent. It is also nearly impossible to drop the weight and cheat as you return to the starting position in the negative phase or to use inertia to help during the positive phase.

The Mini-Gym uses the isokinetic, or accommodating resistance, principle designed to overload the muscle group maximally through the entire range of motion. The harder you pull, the harder the Mini-Gym resists your pull. Since there is no negative phase, strength gains are not as rapid as they are with other equipment.

Hydra Fitness and Eagle Performance Systems combine the isotonic and isokinetic methods by automatically adjusting to the strength and speed of the individual.

Isometric exercises can be compared to weight-training movements in which the weight is so heavy that it cannot be moved. It involves a steady muscle contraction against immovable resistance for six to eight seconds. Strength gains appear to be specific to the angle and do not transfer into increased strength throughout the full range of motion.

Calisthenics is the oldest form of weight training. Using the body as resistance, it represents a safe, practical, and effective method of developing muscular strength and endurance. Since the resistance is low (body weight only) and since a high number of repetitions must be used to bring about fatigue, the program is more effective for developing muscular endurance than it is for developing strength. Calisthenics is also an ideal, safe strength and endurance training method for preadolescent children.

Professional athletes and experts prefer isotonic movements with free weights for the development of muscular strength and endurance, muscle mass, power, and speed. Special equipment that allows either isotonic or isokinetic movement is excellent for rehabilitation from injury, focusing on specific body areas, and improving general body development. This equipment is relatively safe and can be used without a spotter, or partner.

Amount of Resistance (Weight) to Use

The weight with which you can perform a specific number of repetitions is called the RM (repetitions maximum). The 9-RM, then, is the amount of weight that would bring you to almost complete muscle failure on the ninth repetition—you could not perform even one additional repetition. After you decide on the range of repetitions for your training objective, your starting weight is the RM for the lower repetition (for example, with a six to nine cycle, your starting weight is the 6-RM).

Number of Repetitions to Complete

The number of consecutive times you perform each exercise is called **repetitions**. A high number (10 to 20) with lighter weights favors the development of endurance, whereas a low number (3 to 5) with heavier weights tends to favor strength development.

Number of Sets to Complete

One group of repetitions for a particular exercise is a **set**. Depending on your training objectives and the method of progression you select, three to five sets are recommended. Sets should be performed consecutively for each exercise before moving on to another muscle group. To avoid excess muscle soreness and

---

Positive phase of muscular contraction The phase of a weight-training exercise when weight is lifted.

Negative phase of muscular contraction The phase of a weight-training exercise when weight is lowered or returned to the starting position.

Isokinetic contraction Muscular movement where the speed of the contraction is kept constant against a variable resistance.

Repetitions The number of times a specific exercise is completed.

Set A group of repetitions for a particular exercise.

Myth and Fact Sheet

Myth	Fact
1. Strength training will make me inflexible.	1. Strength training will actually improve your flexibility providing you go through the full range of motion on each exercise and stretch properly before and after each workout.
2. Strength training makes females unfeminine.	2. With only three to four strength training sessions weekly, it is impossible to acquire large, bulky muscles. A program using a moderate number of repetitions and weight will only improve your feminine appearance.
3. Strength training will turn my fat to muscle.	3. Fat (adipose) and muscle are separate tissue types. You cannot convert one to the other. When you burn more calories than you eat, fat cells shrink. Strength training causes muscle tissue to increase in size and helps your skin fit you better after weight loss.
4. Sit-ups are the best stomach flattening exercise.	4. Although exercises such as the "crunch" are helpful in flattening the stomach, they are not as effective as decreasing your caloric intake. Reduced calories will shrink the fat cells in your stomach area; the girth control program described in this chapter will improve the muscular strength and endurance of your abdominal muscles. Both programs must be used to obtain a flat stomach.
5. Lost flexibility is an inevitable part of aging.	5. Inactivity causes much more loss than aging does. Now that more of the graying population remains active, some previous findings are being reconsidered.
6. It is important to become as flexible as possible.	6. Joint laxity (looseness around a joint) and too much flexibility may decrease joint stability. Yoga-type exercises are often unsound and may lead to injuries associated with overstretching.
7. Stretching exercises are an excellent warm-up activity.	7. Stretching exercises are only one part of a sound routine to warm up the body. To prevent injury and muscle soreness, avoid stretching cold muscles. Begin with a general warm-up routine that involves large muscle groups. For example, walk or jog, for at least 5 minutes or until sweating is evident; then follow with 5 to 10 minutes of stretching to complete the warm-up phase of your workout.
8. Stretching is only needed before vigorous activity.	8. It is important to stretch before any workout. Stretching is also an excellent cool-down activity at the end of a workout, particularly after strength training.

stiffness, beginners should start with one set and gradually work up to three over a period of three to four weeks.

Amount of Rest between Sets

The time you take between each set is the **rest interval**. Muscle fibers will recover to within 50 percent of their capacity within 3 to 5 seconds and con-

tinue to near full recovery after about 2 minutes. In a program designed to increase strength only, the rest interval is less important and should approach 1 minute. For muscular endurance training, however, the rest interval should gradually decrease from 2 minutes to about 30 seconds over a six- to eight-week period. Unless you slowly decrease the rest interval between repetitions or increase the number of repetitions, you will not improve muscular endurance.

Amount of Rest between Workouts

For a total body workout, you will receive the best effect of training when you allow at least 48 hours of rest (alternate-day training) between each workout. With shorter rest periods, complete recovery is not taking place, and you are not receiving the full benefits of your workout. For split-body routines that emphasize the upper body one day and the lower body the next, it is possible to train for six consecutive days before taking a day of rest. If too much time (four or more days) passes before the next workout, acquired strength and endurance gains begin to diminish.

Speed for Completing Exercises

For most training objectives, you should return the weight to the starting position (negative phase) twice as slowly as you completed the positive phase. If it took you one second to bench press the weight overhead, it should take two seconds to lower the weight. It is important to raise the weight slowly enough to eliminate the help of inertia in the positive phase and lower the weight under control to receive the full benefit of the negative phase. If you merely drop the weight in the negative phase of each exercise, your muscles are not being exercised during one half of the workout and benefits are greatly reduced.

Applying the Principle of Specificity

To gain strength and endurance in a particular muscle, muscle group, or movement in a sport or activity, you must specifically train the muscle or muscles in a similar movement. To improve sprinting speed by increasing your strength and endurance, for example, the muscles involved in sprinting must be identified and isotonic exercises chosen that strengthen those muscles in a movement similar to the sprinting action.

Applying the Overload Principle

Strength gains occur either by muscle fibers producing a stronger contraction or by recruiting a higher proportion of the available fibers for the contraction. The overload principle improves strength both ways, providing the demands on the muscle are systematically and progressively increased over time and the muscles are taxed beyond their accustomed levels. In other words, during each workout your muscles must perform a higher volume of work than they did in the previous workout. This is achieved by increasing the amount of resistance (weight) on each exercise or the number of repetitions and/or sets.

Applying the Progressive Resistance Exercise (PRE) Principle

As training progresses and you grow stronger, you must continuously increase the amount of resistance (weight) if continued improvement is to occur. One way to apply the PRE principle is to choose your starting weight and the lower limit of repetitions for each exercise. If you are using three sets of six to nine repetitions, for example, you would perform six repetitions for each exercise on your first workout. On the second, third, and fourth workouts, you would complete seven, eight, and nine repetitions, respectively. Then you would add 5 lb of weight to each upper-body exercise and 10 lb to each lower-body exercise and return to three sets of six repetitions.

Numerous other methods of progression in weight training have been shown to be effective. The *rest-pause* method involves completion of a single repetition at near maximal weight (1-RM) before resting one to two minutes, completing a second repetition, resting again, and so on, until the muscle is fatigued and cannot perform one additional repetition. The *set system* involves use of multiple sets (3 to 10) of about five to six repetitions for each exercise.

The *burnout* method uses 75 percent of maximal weight for as many repetitions as possible. Without any rest interval, 10 lb are removed from the starting weight and another maximum RM set is performed. The procedure is repeated until the muscle does not respond (burnout). Each designated muscle group is put through the same demanding process.

Supersets involve the use of a set of exercises for one group of muscles followed immediately by a set for their antagonist. For example, one set of arm curls (biceps) is followed by a set of bench presses (triceps).

Each of the preceding methods has been effective in the development of muscular strength and endurance. Add variation to your program to avoid boredom and help overcome plateaus (periods when improvement is slow or nonexistent). It is good to alternate your program among these methods every three to four weeks.

Engaging in Body Building

Body builders are generally more concerned with flex appeal (size, shape, definition, and proportion) than they are with muscle strength. They use dumbbells, barbells, and resistance-designed machines to carve out and define individual muscles. Beauty of physique is much more important to them than feats of strength. Competitors perform posing routines and are judged on symmetry (body parts having been equally developed top and bottom, left and right), muscle definition, and poise. Female competitors complete their competition by engaging in a brief freestyle routine to music, a cross between sport and cabaret.

Maintaining Strength and Endurance Gains

You will see significant strength and endurance gains after about 8 weeks of consecutive training. Be patient, as it will take approximately 12 months to dramatically change the general appearance of your body and to add 12 to 14 lb of muscle mass.

Once you have acquired the level of muscular strength and endurance desired, one or two vigorous training sessions a week will maintain most of the improvement that has occurred.

LIFTING TECHNIQUES

Warm-up and Cool-down

To warm up properly, perform four to five minutes of walking or light jogging to raise body temperature, and follow it with a brief stretching period. The first of three sets can be used as a light set with a high number of repetitions (15 to 20) and low weight (20-RM). A four- to five-minute stretching period at the close of your workout will help prevent muscle soreness and aid in improving your range of motion.

Full Range of Motion

Each exercise should move through the full range of motion without locking out the joint. The arm curl, for example, should result in the weight being moved as close to the chest as possible on the positive phase, before returning to the starting position without locking the elbow joint. When lifting heavy arm or leg weights, injuries are much more likely to occur to a joint that is fully extended at both the beginning and ending phases of an exercise.

Proper Breathing

One recommended breathing procedure is to inhale as the weight is lowered and to exhale as the weight is raised or pushed away from the body. You should attempt to blow the weight away from the body. This procedure will improve your efficiency and reduce the risk of holding your breath and blacking out during demanding exertion. Until the correct breathing is mastered, practice the technique with light weights.

Sequence of Exercises

Exercises should be arranged to prevent fatigue from limiting your lifting ability. One approach is to exercise the large muscle groups before exercising the smaller muscles. It is difficult to exhaust large muscle groups when the smaller muscles that serve as connections between the resistance and the large muscle groups have been prematurely fatigued. It is also important for the abdominal muscles, used in most exercises to stabilize the rib cage, to remain relatively unfatigued until the latter phases of the workout. A typical sequence that applies the concept of large to small is: (1) hips and lower back; (2) legs (quadriceps, hamstrings, and calves); (3) torso (back, shoulders, chest); (4) arms (triceps, biceps, and forearms); (5) abdominals; and (6) neck.

Form and Technique

It is important to follow the specific form tips identified for each exercise in Figure 9.3 carefully. In addition, you can apply these general techniques to most exercises and equipment:

1. The basic stance can be achieved by placing the feet slightly wider than shoulder-width apart with the toes parallel. The stronger leg is sometimes placed back in a heel-toe alignment, depending on your preference.

2. Toes should be placed just under the bar in the starting phase of exercises in which the barbell is resting on the floor.

Figure 9.3 ✦ Barbell and Dumbbell Exercises

Bench press

Equipment: Barbell, bench rack, spotter

Movement: Using an overhand grip, slowly lower the bar to the chest, then press back to the starting position.

Hints: Bend knees at 90° and keep feet off the bench and the floor.

Muscle Groups: Pectoralis major, Anterior triceps, Deltoid

Incline bench press

Equipment: Incline bench, squat rack, spotter

Movement: Using an overhand grip, slowly raise and lower the bar to the chest (both feet flat on the floor).

Hints: Use a weight rack to support the weight above the bench. Avoid lifting the buttock or arching the back while lifting.

Muscle Groups: Anterior pectoralis major, Anterior deltoid, Tricep

Power cleans

Equipment: Barbell

Movement: Using an overhand grip, pull the bar explosively to the highest point of your chest. Rotate hands under the bar and bend your knees. Straighten up to standing position. Bend the arms, legs, and hips to return the bar to the thighs, then slowly bend the knees and hips to lower to the floor.

Hints: Grasp the bar at shoulder width. Start with knees bent so hips are knee level. Keep head up and back straight.

Muscle Groups: Trapezius, Erector spinae, Gluteus, Quadriceps

Deadlift

Equipment: Barbell

Movement: Using a mixed grip, bend knees so hips are close to knee level. Straighten knees and hips to standing position. Bend at knees and hips to return.

Hints: Keep the head up and back flat. Grasp bar at shoulder width.

Muscle Groups: Erector spinae, Gluteus, Quadriceps

Figure 9.3 ✦ Barbell and Dumbbell Exercises *(continued)*

Bent arm flys

Equipment: Dumbbells

Movement: Using an underhand grip, hold a dumb-bell in each hand above the shoulders with the elbows slightly bent.

Hints: Keep elbows slightly bent at all times.

Muscle Groups: Pectoralis major

Barbell rowing

Equipment: Barbell

Movement: Using an overhand grip, hold the barbell directly below your shoulders. With elbows leading, pull the barbell to chest and hold momentarily. Then slowly return to the starting position.

Hints: Grasp bar slightly wider than shoulder width. Refrain from swinging or jerking the weights upward to the chest region.

Muscle Groups: Latissimus dorsi, Rhomboid, Trapezius

One dumbbell rowing

Equipment: Dumbbells

Movement: Using an underhand grip, kneel with one hand and one knee on exercise mat. Pull weight on support side upward to chest.

Hints: Hold dumbbell briefly at chest before returning.

Muscle Groups: Latissimus dorsi

Shoulder shrug

Equipment: Barbell

Movement: Using an overhand grip, elevate both shoulders until they nearly touch the earlobes, then relax and return bar to the thighs.

Hints: Keep the extremities fully extended. Heavy weights (within limitations) will bring more rapid strength gains.

Muscle Groups: Trapezius

Figure 9.3 ✦ Barbell and Dumbbell Exercises *(continued)*

Military press

Equipment: Barbell

Movement: Using an overhand grip, slowly push bar overhead from chest until both arms are fully extended.

Hints: Keep neck and back erect, and knees extended and locked. Avoid jerky movements and leaning.

Muscle Groups: Deltoids, Triceps

Upright rowing

Equipment: Barbell

Movement: Using an overhand grip, raise bar to the chin, and then return to thighs.

Hints: Grasp bar 6 to 8 inches apart. Keep elbows higher than the hands. Maintain an erect, stationary position.

Muscle Groups: Trapezius

Bent-over lateral raise

Equipment: Dumbbells

Movement: Using an overhand grip, grasp dumbbell in each hand and draw arms to shoulder level. Slowly return to hanging position.

Hints: Keep knees and elbows slightly bent. Hold weights for 1–2 seconds before returning to hanging position.

Muscle Groups: Posterior deltoid, Latissimus dorsi, Rhomboids

Two-arm curl

Equipment: Barbell

Movement: Using underhand grip, raise bar from thighs to chest level, and return.

Hints: Keep body erect and motionless throughout.

Muscle Groups: Elbow flexors

Figure 9.3 ✦ Barbell and Dumbbell Exercises *(continued)*

Reverse curl

Equipment: Barbell

Movement: Using overhand grip, raise bar from thighs to chest level, and return.

Hints: Use less weight than in two-arm curl.

Muscle Groups: Upper arm flexors, Hand extensors, Finger extensors

Seated dumbbell curl

Equipment: Dumbbells

Movement: Using an underhand grip, curl one or both dumbbells to the shoulder, then slowly return the weight to the sides of the body.

Hints: Keep the back straight throughout the entire movement.

Muscle Groups: Elbow flexors

Close grip bench press

Equipment: Barbell, squat rack, spotter

Movement: Using an overhand grip, slowly lower the barbell to the chest and press back to the starting position.

Hints: Grasp center of bar (hands 2 to 4 inches apart). Bend knees at 90°; keep feet off the bench floor so as to avoid arching the back. Keep elbows in; extend arms fully.

Muscle Groups: Triceps, Anterior deltoid, Pectoralis major

Standing or seated tricep

Equipment: Dumbbell

Movement: With both hands grasped around the inner side of one dumbbell overhead, lower the weight behind your head, then return.

Hints: Keep the elbows close together throughout the maneuver.

Muscle Groups: Triceps, Deltoid

Figure 9.3 ✦ Barbell and Dumbbell Exercises *(continued)*

Barbell wrist curl

Equipment: Barbell

Movement: Using an underhand grip, let the bar hang down toward the floor and then curl toward you.

Hints: Grasp center of bar (hands 2 to 4 inches apart). Keep forearms in steady contact with the bench while moving the weight.

Muscle Groups: Wrist flexors

Reverse wrist curl

Equipment: Barbell

Movement: Using an overhand grip, and moving the wrists only, raise bar as high as possible, and return to the starting position.

Hints: Grasp barbell at shoulder width. Movement should only be at the wrist joint.

Muscle Groups: Forearm extensors

Front squat

Equipment: Barbell, squat rack, chair or bench, 2- to 3-inch board, spotters

Basic Movement: Using an overhand grip, flex legs to a 90° angle. Return to standing position.

Hints: Keep the heels up, and point the chin outward slightly. A chair or bench can be placed below the body (touch buttocks slightly to surface).

Muscle Groups: Quadriceps, Gluteals

Lunge with dumbbells

Equipment: Dumbbells

Movement: Overhand grip; alternate stepping forward with each leg, bending the knee of the lead leg, and lowering your body until thigh of the front leg is level to the floor. Barely touch the knee of rear leg before returning to the starting position.

Hints: Keep your head up and upper body erect throughout the exercise. Avoid bending front knee more than 90°.

Muscle Groups: Quadriceps, Gluteals

Figure 9.3 ✦ Barbell and Dumbbell Exercises *(continued)*

Heel raise

Equipment: Barbell, squat rack, spotters, 2- to 3-inch board

Movement: Using an overhand grip, the body is raised upward to maximum height of the toes.

Hints: Alter the position of the toes from straight ahead to pointed in and out. Keep the body erect.

Muscle Groups: Gastroenemius, Soleus

One dumbbell heel raise

Equipment: Dumbbell, 2- to 3-inch board

Movement: Using an overhand grip, shift entire body weight on the leg next to the dumbbell, and raise the foot off the floor behind. Raise the heel of the support foot upward as high as possible and hold momentarily.

Hints: A wall is useful for balance, but avoid using free hand for assistance.

Muscle Groups: Gastrocnemius, Soleus

3. The back should remain erect (unless it contains the muscle group being exercised) with the head up and the eyes looking straight ahead.

4. The bar is grasped with the hands or a shoulder-width apart using one of three grips:

   Overhand Grasp the bar until the thumb wraps around and meets the index finger. You may place the thumb next to the index finger without wrapping your hand around the bar if you prefer.

   Underhand Grasp the bar with the palms turned upward away from the body, and the fingers and thumb wrapped around the bar.

   Mixed Grip Combine the overhand and underhand grip, each hand assuming one of the grips.

5. Avoid leaning backward to assist a repetition.

6. Safety should be stressed at all times and should include workout partners to spot and protect you when you are using heavy free weights.

   • Avoid attempting to lift more weight than you can safely handle.

• Secure collars and engage pins before attempting a lift.

• Avoid holding your breath during the lift.

• Return the barbell to the floor, rack, or starting position in a controlled manner.

• Bend your knees when moving heavy weights from one place to another for storage.

Helpful hints for weight-training exercises are provided in Figure 9.3. These suggestions will help you prevent injury and improve the effectiveness of each exercise.

ℬARBELL AND DUMBBELL EXERCISES

Figure 9.3 shows specific exercises, describes the equipment needs, basic movement, and helpful hints, and identifies the muscle groups involved. This information will help you choose exercises that train the important muscle groups in your sport or activity. Table 9.2 includes some of the many barbell

Table 9.2 ◆ Basic and Alternate Weight-Training Programs: Programs for General Body Development

EXERCISES	REPETITIONS	STARTING WEIGHT (RM)	SPEED OF CONTRACTION
Basic program			
Two-arm curl	6–10	8	Moderate
Military press	6–10	8	Moderate
Sit-ups (bent-knee)	25–50	30	Rapid
Rowing (upright)	6–10	8	Moderate
Bench press	6–10	8	Moderate
Squat	6–10	8	Rapid
Heel raise	15–25	20	Rapid
Dead lift (bent-knee)	6–10	8	Rapid
Alternate I			
Reverse curl	6–10	8	Moderate
Triceps press	6–10	8	Moderate
Sit-ups (bent-knee)	25–50	30	Rapid
Shoulder shrug	6–10	8	Moderate
Squat jump	15–25	20	Rapid
Knee flexor	6–10	8	Rapid
Knee extensor	6–10	8	Rapid
Pull-overs (bent-arm)	6–10	8	Moderate
Alternate II			
Wrist curl	6–10	8	Moderate
Side bender	6–10	8	Moderate
Lateral raise	6–10	8	Moderate
Straddle lift	6–10	8	Rapid
Supine leg lift	6–10	8	Rapid
Hip flexor	6–10	8	Rapid
Leg abductor	6–10	8	Rapid
Forward raise	6–10	8	Moderate

and dumbbell exercises and their variations for a basic resistance program designed to improve your strength, local muscular endurance, and muscle size.

GIRTH CONTROL

Almost everyone wants a flat tummy. In fact, a flat stomach is strongly associated with fitness and wellness in our society. A large belly can make people appear much older than they really are. It also can be a sign of poor health—evidence of accumulating fat that may lead to hypertension, stroke, heart disease, adult-onset diabetes, and other ailments. Some fat around the midsection is not necessarily unhealthy.

Practically everyone acquires at least a small spare tire (fat on both sides of the hips) and some abdominal fat. Becoming obsessed with this somewhat natural change is a mistake. In fact, as you reach the third and fourth decades of life, maintaining the flat stomach you had in your teens may be impossible.

Some people attempt to solve the girth-control problem by using unnatural and worthless devices such as girdles, corsets, weighted belts, rubberized workout suits, and special exercise equipment that promises a flat stomach with just minutes of use daily. Although it is not an easy task, you can bring back some of the lost youth in your abdominal area by completing the program described in Lab Activity 9.2: Obtaining a Flat, Healthy Stomach, at the end of this chapter.

FLEXIBILITY

Of the five components of health-related fitness, flexibility is the aspect most neglected by the exercising population, by athletes, and by health care professionals and practitioners. Like Esther, whom we introduced at the beginning of the chapter, few individuals understand the importance of developing and maintaining acceptable levels of joint flexibility, yet the health, injury, and performance consequences of doing so are quite evident. In this section, we will provide answers to all of Esther's questions and examine the many aspects of joint flexibility, such as the factors affecting range of motion, the importance of a regular stretching routine, assessment techniques, sound training principles, and choice of specific stretching exercises to help evaluate range of motion and devise a program that meets your specific health and fitness needs.

FACTORS EFFECTING FLEXIBILITY

Since flexibility is specific to each joint, having good hip flexibility is no guarantee you will be flexible in the shoulders, back, neck, or ankles. Depending on your stretching routine and choice of exercises, you may become highly flexible in some joints and remain inflexible in others. A number of factors combine to determine the range of motion around each joint: heredity; gender; age; the elasticity of the muscles, ligaments, and tendons; previous injuries; lifestyle; adipose tissue (fat) in and around joints; and body type. Young children are more flexible than adults but seem to lose that flexibility more quickly than their more active counterparts of 20 years ago did. The tendency to become inflexible with age is closely associated with inactivity, which results in a loss of muscle elasticity, a tightening of tendons and ligaments, and an increase in fatty tissue in and around joints. Extra fat affects flexibility by increasing resistance to movement and creating premature contact between adjoining body surfaces. Sedentary living can lead to shortening of muscles and liga-

Muscle extensibility The ability of muscle tissue to stretch.
Vertebrae The 33 bones of the spinal column, some of which are normally fused together (sacral and the coccygeal vertebrae).

ments and can therefore restrict range of motion. Poor posture, long periods of sitting or standing, or immobilization of a limb can have a similar effect. Exercise that overdevelops one muscle group while neglecting opposing groups produces an imbalance that also restricts flexibility.

The formation of scar tissue following a muscle or connective-tissue injury (ligaments and tendons) can decrease flexibility. Arthritis and calcium deposits can damage joints by causing inflammation, chronic pain, and restriction of movement.

Fortunately, everyone is capable of increasing range of motion in particular joints. Regular stretching routines cause permanent lengthening of ligaments and tendons. Muscle tissue undergoes only temporary lengthening following a warm-up and stretching routine as **muscle extensibility** increases. Muscle temperature changes alone, attained through proper warm-up, can increase flexibility by 20 percent.

THE IMPORTANCE OF FLEXIBILITY

A regular stretching routine will help increase range of motion, improve performance in some activities, help prevent soft-tissue injuries, aid muscle relaxation, and help you cool down at the end of a workout. It is a valuable part of a complete exercise program, and it provides some benefits to everyone.

Increased Range of Motion and Improved Performance

Since we have established the fact that range of motion is joint-specific, a well-rounded flexibility program must devote attention to all the body's major joints: neck, shoulder, back, hip, knees, wrist, and ankles. You can increase your range of motion in each of these major joints in six to eight weeks by following one of the recommended stretching techniques discussed in this chapter.

In sports such as gymnastics, diving, skiing, swimming, and hurdling, and in other activities requiring a high level of flexibility, a stretching routine that focuses on the key joints can also help improve performance. Although little scientific evidence is available, the association between flexibility and sports performance is almost universally accepted.

Injury Prevention

Regular stretching routines may help reduce the incidence of injury during exercise for athletes and others. Continuous exercise such as jogging, running, cycling, and aerobics tightens and shortens muscles, and tight muscles are more vulnerable to injury from the explosive movements common in sports. A brief warm-up period followed by stretching will not only increase range of motion but will also provide some protection from common soft-tissue injuries such as strains, sprains, and tears. Striving to maintain a full, normal range of motion in each joint with adequate strength, endurance, and power throughout the range will reduce your chances of experiencing an exercise-induced injury.

Lower-Back Pain   Pain in the lower back occurs as frequently in our society as the common cold does. This 20th-century plague affects an estimated 8 to 10 million people in the United States who lose over 200 million work days each year. Informal surveys of middle and senior high school athletes indicate that as many as 40 percent have experienced back problems severe enough to result in missed practice time. Although back pain affects all age groups, the elderly are the most vulnerable. The older you are, the more likely you are to have problems with your lower back. No one seems to be immune.

A brief description of your spinal column will help you understand why the back is so vulnerable to injury (see Figure 9.4). The human body has 33 vertebrae that extend from the base of the skull to the tailbone. The **vertebrae** form a double *S*, reverse curve to ensure proper balance and weight-bearing. If the vertebrae were placed directly on top of one another, the back would be only five percent as strong as it is and one step would produce enough trauma and brain jolt to cause concussion. Shock absorbers, known as *disks*, are located between each vertebra. These capsules of gelatinous matter contain approximately 90 percent water in young people but only 70 percent in older

Figure 9.4 ✦ The Vertebral Column and Muscle Support

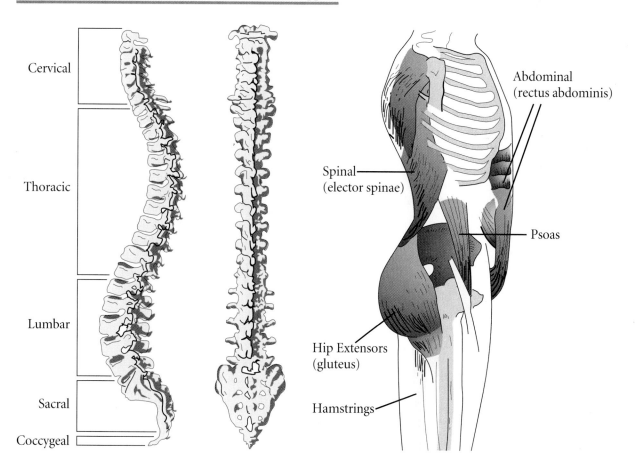

The vertebrae that make up the spinal column are designed for support, strength, and flexibility.

Adequate strength and flexibility in the muscle groups of both the back and abdomen are essential for supporting the back and maintaining posture.

Behavioral Change and Motivational Strategies

Many things may interfere with your strength and flexibility training progress. Some of these barriers (road-blocks) and strategies for overcoming them to keep you moving toward your training goals are described here.

Roadblock	Behavioral Change Strategy

You are aware of your need to engage in strength and flexibility training but just cannot seem to stay interested enough to avoid skipping workouts.

The first month of any exercise program is the most difficult. Muscle soreness, discomfort, and a body that looks the same as when you started can discourage you at this stage. Try some of these techniques to overcome this critical period:

1. Set a realistic goal for each exercise, such as only a 10-lb gain in the amount of weight you can move for three weeks.
2. Take a tape measure and record the size of your upper arm, upper leg, and abdominal area.
3. Avoid remeasuring yourself until you have added 10 lb to most of the exercises in your program. You can be assured that you will meet this goal at your own pace and that, when you do, you will have acquired additional muscle mass.
4. Arrive at the exercise site early with plenty of time to enjoy your workout.
5. After you walk or jog a few minutes, take 5 to 10 minutes to relax, wind down, and enjoy stretching the major joints.
6. Make a mental note of how far beyond your toes you can reach, how difficult it is to reach behind your back and touch both hands, or how far forward you are able to move when stretching your calf muscle. Having these mental notes will help make you aware of improvement in future workouts.
7. Force yourself to stretch carefully prior to every workout until it becomes a habit and you discover the benefits of stretching.

After three to four months of training, you seem to have leveled off or reached a plateau. Improvement is occurring so slowly that you are becoming discouraged and feel you have already improved as much as possible.

What you are experiencing happens to everyone. Initial gains in strength and endurance are always much greater than those you achieve months later. Consider some behavioral changes to help overcome this leveling:

1. Incorporate one fun day into your weekly schedule, preferably on the day you are most likely to skip. Use lighter weights, rest longer between sets and exercises, and enjoy yourself.
2. Find a partner or group of people at about your level to work out with, and encourage one another to put a strong effort in your remaining two workouts weekly.
3. Incorporate a *maximum lift day* into your workout routine once every four weeks to demonstrate how you are progressing in each exercise. Use this session to reestablish your 1-RM and record the results.

Roadblock	Behavioral Change Strategy
At the end of a workout your calves feel tight and are sometimes sore.	A feeling of tightness or even some mild soreness should only occur after your first three or four workouts. If it continues, examine every phase of your program. Are you properly warmed up prior to beginning your stretching session? Are you using static or PNF stretching exercises rather than ballistic movements (described later in the chapter)? Are you stretching for three to five minutes at the end of your workout? Are you performing the correct exercises? Are you stretching both the calf muscle and the heel cord? You should find the answer to the problem in one or more of these questions.
List other roadblocks you are experiencing that seem to be reducing the effectiveness of your strength and flexibility training program.	Now list the behavioral change strategies that can help you overcome these roadblocks.
1. _____	1. _____
2. _____	2. _____
3. _____	3. _____

individuals. With loss of water comes a loss of compressibility and increased vulnerability to injury often referred to as *slipped, ruptured,* or *herniated* disk. Ruptured disk material may bulge through the rear portion of the outer ring and put pressure on nerves, thereby producing pain in the lower back that can radiate down into the leg and toes (**sciatica**).

Not all sufferers of lower-back pain have bone or disk disorders. In fact, the problem for most individuals involves muscles, tendons, or ligaments. No single cause can be isolated that triggers an episode of back pain. Some of the more common factors include physical injury, hard sneezing or coughing, improper lifting or bending, standing or sitting for long hours, sitting slumped in overstuffed chairs or automobile seats, tension, anxiety, and depression, obesity, and disease (for example, arthritis and tumors). Some individuals merely have a genetically weak back involving one or more of the approximately 140 muscles that provide support to the back and control its movements. Typically, a muscle, ligament, or tendon strain or sprain causes nearby muscles to spasm to help support the back. It is estimated that 7 out of 10 problems are due to the improper alignment of the spinal column and pelvic girdle caused by inflexible and weak muscles.

Prevention and treatment require similar action and may involve changing the way you stand, bend,

lift objects, sit, rest, sleep, and exercise. Figure 9.5 summarizes the key factors for taking care of your back and for recovering from low back pain. Study this figure carefully and complete the recommended lower-back exercises at least once a day.

For most victims of lower-back pain, treatment involves one to three days of bedrest on a firm mattress supported by plywood, moderate application of heat and cold, and gentle massage until muscle spasms are eliminated or significantly reduced. Once this occurs, use a series of daily exercises, such as those shown in Figure 9.5, that are designed to strengthen the four key muscle groups supporting your back and important abdominal muscles. Three other components are needed to complete your rehabilitation and prevention program: exercising more, decreasing your stomach fat by reducing your caloric intake, and continuing to do lower-back exercises daily in addition to 30 minutes of aerobic activity three to four days a week after recovery. Only rarely is surgery needed to correct lower-back problems.

Sciatica Pain along the course of the great sciatic nerve (hip, thigh, leg, foot).

Figure 9.5   ✦   Your Back and How to Care For It

Whatever the cause of low back pain, part of its treatment is the correction of faulty posture. But good posture is not simply a matter of "standing tall." It refers to correct use of the body at all times. In fact, for the body to function in the best of health it must be so used that no strain is put upon muscles, joints, bones, and ligaments. To prevent low back pain, avoiding strain must become a way of life, practiced while lying, sitting, standing, walking, working, and exercising. When body position is correct, internal organs have enough room to function normally and blood circulates more freely.

With the help of this guide, you can begin to correct the positions and movements which bring on or aggravate backache. Particular attention should be paid to the positions recommended for resting, since it is possible to strain the muscles of the back and neck even while lying in bed. By learning to live with good posture, under all circumstances, you will gradually develop the proper carriage and stronger muscles needed to protect and support your hard-working back.

How to Stay on Your Feet without Tiring Your Back

To prevent strain and pain in everyday activities, it is restful to change from one task to another before fatigue sets in. Housewives can lie down between chores; others should check body position frequently, drawing in the abdomen, flattening the back, bending the knees slightly.

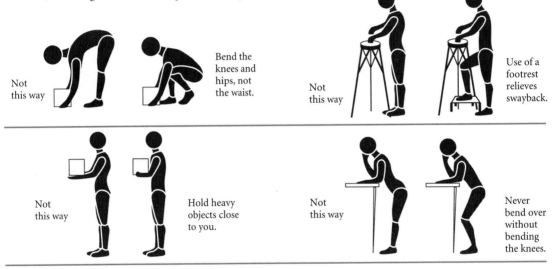

Check Your Carriage Here

In correct, fully erect posture, a line dropped from the ear will go through the tip of the shoulder, middle of hip, back of kneecaps, and front of anklebone.

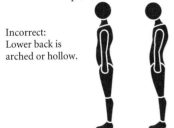

To Find the Correct Standing Position

Stand one foot away from wall. Now sit against wall, bending knees slightly. Tighten abdominal and buttock muscles. This will tilt the pelvis back and flatten the lower spine. Holding this position, inch up the wall to standing position, by straightening the legs. Now walk around the room, maintaining the same posture. Place back against wall again to see if you have held it.

Figure 9.5 ✦ Your Back and How to Care For It *(continued)*

How to Sit Correctly

A back's best friend is a straight, hard chair. If you can't get the chair you prefer, learn to sit properly on whatever chair you get. *To correct sitting position from forward slump:* Throw head well back, then bend it forward to pull in the chin. This will straighten the back. Now tighten abdominal muscles to raise the chest. Check position frequently.

Relieve strain by sitting well forward, flatten back by tightening abdominal muscles, and cross knees.

Use of footrest relieves swayback. Aim is to have knees higher than hips.

Correct way to sit while driving, close to pedals. Use seat belt or hard backrest, available commercially.

TV slump leads to "dowager's hump," strains neck and shoulders.

If chair is too high, swayback is increased.

Keep neck and back in as straight a line as possible with the spine. Bend forward from the hips.

Driver's seat too far from pedals emphasizes curve in lower back.

Strained reading position. Forward thrusting strains muscles of neck and head.

How to Put Your Back to Bed

For proper bed posture, a firm mattress is essential. Bedboards, sold commercially, or devised at home, may be used with soft mattresses. Bedboards, preferably, should be made of $^3/_4$-inch plywood. Faulty sleeping positions intensify swayback and result not only in backache but in numbness, tingling, and pain in arms and legs.

Incorrect:
Lying flat on back makes swayback worse.

Correct:
Lying on side with knees bent effectively flattens the back. Flat pillow may be used to support neck, especially when shoulders are broad.

Incorrect:
Use of high pillow strains neck, arms, shoulders.

Correct:
Sleeping on back is restful and correct when knees are properly supported.

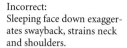  

Incorrect:
Sleeping face down exaggerates swayback, strains neck and shoulders.

Correct:
Raise the foot of the mattress eight inches to discourage sleeping on the abdomen.

Incorrect:
Bending one hip and knee does not relieve swayback.

Proper arrangement of pillows for resting or reading in bed.

When Doing Nothing, Do It Right

Rest is the first rule for the tired, painful back. The following positions relieve pain by taking all pressure and weight off the back and legs. Note pillows under knees to relieve strain on spine.

For complete relief and relaxing effect, these positions should be maintained from 5 to 25 minutes.

A straight-back chair used behind a pillow makes a serviceable backrest.

Figure 9.5 ✦ Your Back and How to Care For It *(continued)*

Exercise — without Getting Out of Bed

Exercises to be performed while lying in bed are aimed not so much at strengthening muscles as at teaching correct positioning. But muscles used correctly become stronger and in time are able to support the body with the least amount of effort.

Do all exercises in this position. Legs should not be straightened.    Bring knee to chest. Lower slowly but do not straighten leg. Relax.

Exercise — without Attracting Attention

Use these inconspicuous exercises whenever you have a spare moment during the day, both to relax tension and improve the tone of important muscle groups.

1. Rotate shoulders forward and backward.
2. Turn head slowly side to side.
3. Watch an imaginary plane take off, just below the right shoulder. Stretch neck, follow it slowly as it moves up, around and down, disappearing below the other shoulder. Repeat, starting on left side.
4. Slowly, slowly, touch left ear to right shoulder. Raise both shoulders to touch ears, drop them as far as possible.
5. At any pause in the day—waiting for an elevator to arrive, for a specific traffic light to change—pull in abdominal muscles, tighten, hold for the count of eight without breathing. Relax slowly. Increase the count gradually after the first week. Practice breathing normally with abdomen flat and contracted. Do this sitting, standing, and walking.

Bring both knees slowly up to chest. Tighten muscles of abdomen, press back flat against the floor. Hold knees to chest 20 seconds. Then lower slowly. Relax. Repeat 5 times. This exercise gently stretches the shortened muscles of the lower back, while strengthening abdominal muscles. Clasp knees, bring them up to chest at the same time coming to a sitting position. Rock back and forth.

Rules to Live By — From Now On

1. Never bend from the waist only; bend the hips and knees.
2. Never lift a heavy object higher than your waist.
3. Always turn and face the object you wish to lift.
4. Avoid carrying unbalanced loads; hold heavy objects close to your body.
5. Never carry anything heavier than you can manage with ease.
6. Never lift or move heavy furniture. Wait for someone to do it who knows the principles of leverage.
7. Avoid sudden movements, sudden "overloading" of muscles. Learn to move deliberately, swinging the legs from the hips.
8. Learn to keep the head in line with the spine when standing, sitting, lying in bed.
9. Put soft chairs and deep couches on your "don't sit" list. During prolonged sitting, cross your legs to rest your back.
10. Your doctor is the only one who can determine when low back pain is due to faulty posture. He is the best judge of when you may do general exercises for physical fitness. When you do, omit any exercise which arches or overstrains the lower back: backward or forward bends, touching the toes with the knees straight.
11. Wear shoes with moderate heels, all about the same height. Avoid changing from high to low heels.
12. Put a footrail under the desk and a footrest under the crib.
13. Diaper a baby sitting next to him or her on the bed.
14. Don't stoop and stretch to hang the wash; raise the clothesbasket and lower the washline.
15. Beg or buy a rocking chair. Rocking rests the back by changing the muscle groups used.
16. Train yourself vigorously to use your abdominal muscles to flatten your lower abdomen. In time, this muscle contraction will become habitual, making you the envied possessor of a youthful body profile!
17. Don't strain to open windows or doors.
18. For good posture, concentrate on strengthening "nature's corset"– the abdominal and buttock muscles. The pelvic roll exercise is especially recommended to correct the postural relation between the pelvis and the spine.

Aid the Cool-Down Phase

As we discussed in chapter 7, the final three to eight minutes of a workout should be a period of slowly diminishing intensity through the use of a slow jog or walk followed by a brief stretching period. By stretching at the end of your workout as the final phase of the cool-down, you are helping fatigued muscles return to their normal resting length and to a more relaxed state.

THE ASSESSMENT OF FLEXIBILITY

Since range of motion is joint-specific, no single test provides an accurate assessment of overall flexibility. Instead, each joint must be evaluated. This explains why so few physical fitness batteries employ a flexibility test. Only recently have test developers begun to include flexibility as part of health-related, physical fitness test batteries. Unfortunately, modern tests generally include only the **sit-and-reach test** that measures only lower-back and hamstring (the large muscle group located on the back of the upper leg) flexibility. Although this test is quite valuable and accurate, primarily because it involves some of the muscle groups associated with lower-back pain, a more thorough test is also needed.

Take a moment to obtain a quick evaluation of your overall flexibility level, using a less objective approach, by completing the seven subjective tests described in Lab Activity 9.3: Determining Your Total Body Flexibility at the end of the chapter. If you check "yes" in any test, your flexibility is considered *good* in that joint. Strive to improve your flexibility in the areas where you checked "no." Repeat this series of tests after you have followed a stretching routine for six to eight weeks. You will discover how easy it is to increase your range of motion substantially.

FLEXIBILITY-TRAINING PRINCIPLES

Who Should Stretch

Some individuals need to stretch more than others. Lean body types with a high range of motion may need very little stretching, whereas stocky, more powerfully built athletes with limited motion need 5 to 10 minutes of flexibility exercise before making any radical moves, such as bending over to touch the toes or explosive jumping or sprinting. Almost every healthy individual of any age or level of fitness can benefit from a regular stretching routine. Routines can be gentle, easy, relaxing, and safe or extremely vigorous. Daily stretching will help maintain flexibility throughout life and help prevent joint stiffness.

When to Stretch

Stretching exercises are used as part of a warm-up routine to prepare the body for vigorous activity, during the cool-down phase of a workout to help muscles return to a normal relaxed state, merely to improve range of motion in key joints, and to aid in rehabilitation after injury.

Warm-up and Cool-down Flexibility (stretching) exercises are often too closely associated with warm-up. Consequently, most individuals make the mistake of stretching cold muscles before beginning a workout rather than first warming the body up with some large-muscle activity such as walking or jogging for five to eight minutes or until perspiration is evident. At this point, body temperature has been elevated two to four degrees, and muscles can be safely stretched. Keep in mind that you warm up to stretch, you do not stretch to warm up.

Table 9.3 provides a suggested order for stretching for those who engage in jogging, walking, cycling, swimming, racket and team sports, and strength training. Most organized aerobics classes follow a similar routine that involves a slow, gentle warm-up to cause sweating, followed by careful stretching, vigorous aerobics, and a cool-down period. Joggers and runners may choose to cover the first half mile or so at a very slow pace, then do stretching exercises before completing the run, as opposed to the more common routine of stretching cold muscles prior to the jog or run. Ideally, the majority of a stretching routine should follow the jog, run, cycle, swim, strength-training, or aerobics session and take place at the end of a workout during the cool-down phase. Stretching at the end of your workout when muscle-tissue temperature is high may effectively improve

---

Sit-and-reach test A test designed to measure the flexibility of the lower-back and hamstring muscles.

Table 9.3 ✦ Suggested Order for a Typical Exercise Session

PROGRAM	WORKOUT ORDER	EXPLANATION
3-Mile jog (or run, cycle, or swim)		
Slow jog (1/2 mile)	1	This will elevate body temperature, produce some sweating, and warm the muscles around the joints for stretching.
Stretch (5 min)	2	Muscles can now be safely stretched.
Fast jog (2 miles)	3	The pace can now be increased to elevate the heart rate above the target level for the aerobic portion of the workout.
Cool-down jog (slow 1/2 mile)	4	This final portion of the run can be used to help the body slowly return to the preexercise state.
Cool-down stretch (6 to 10 min)	5	This concentrated, slow, stretching session will help prevent muscle soreness and improve range of motion.
Racket sports (or team sports or strength training)		
Slow, deliberate strokes and movement	1	Movements specific to the sport are used to elevate body temperature and produce sweating.
Stretch (5 min)	2	Muscles can now be safely stretched using sport-specific flexibility exercises.
Actual play or workout	3	Muscles are now prepared for vigorous, explosive movement.
Cool-down (5 min)	4	The final portion of the workout should involve a return to slow, deliberate stroking or movements of the sport.
Cool-down stretch (6 to 10 min)	5	Concentrated, slow, stretching session.

range of motion and reduce the incidence of muscle soreness the following day.

Stretching to Improve Range of Motion   If your main purpose is to improve body flexibility, you can safely stretch any time you desire—early in the morning, at work, after sitting or standing for long periods of time, when you feel stiff, after an exercise session, or while you are engaged in passive activities such as watching television or listening to music. Remember, you must first elevate body temperature and produce some sweating by engaging in large-muscle group activity before you stretch.

Ballistic stretching Flexibility exercises employing bouncing and jerking movements at the extreme range of motion or point of discomfort.

Static stretching Flexibility exercises in which a position is held steady for a designated period of time at the extreme range of motion.

Proprioceptive neuromuscular facilitation (PNF) stretching A two-person stretching technique involving the application of steady pressure by a partner at the extreme range of motion for a particular exercise and steady resistance to the pressure.

Rehabilitation from Injury   When you are recovering from soft-tissue injuries, focus attention on the reduction of pain and swelling, a return to normal strength, and achieving a full, unrestricted range of motion. Unless regular stretching begins as soon as pain and swelling have been eliminated, some loss of flexibility in the injured joint is almost certain.

What Stretching Technique to Use

You can choose one of several different techniques that have been shown to increase joint flexibility effectively (see Figure 9.6). Each method has advantages and disadvantages.

Ballistic Stretching This technique employs bouncing or bobbing at the extreme range of motion or point of discomfort. When stretching the hamstring muscle group, for example, individuals bounce vigorously three or four times as they reach for their toes in an attempt to aid the stretch forcefully. This method has several disadvantages. A muscle that is stretched too far and too fast in this way may actually contract and create an opposing force, causing soft-tissue injury. An injury may also occur if the force generated by the jerking motions becomes greater than the extensibility of the tissues. **Ballistic stretching** is also likely to result in muscle soreness the following day.

Static Stretching After moving slowly into the stretch, steady pressure is applied at the point of discomfort in a particular joint for 10 to 30 seconds without bouncing or jerking. Each exercise can be performed two or three times. **Static stretching** is superior to ballistic stretching since it is safe and injury-free, is not likely to result in muscle soreness, and is as effective as the other techniques.

Proprioceptive Neuromuscular Facilitation (PNF) Stretching This popular two-person technique is based on a contract-and-relax principle. **PNF stretching** requires a partner to apply steady pressure to a body area at the extreme range of motion until slight discomfort is felt. When stretching the hamstring muscle group, for example, lie on your back with one leg raised to 90 degrees or to a comfortable stretch. Have your partner apply steady pressure in an attempt to raise your leg overhead further (see Figure 9.6). As pressure is applied, begin to push against your partner's resistance by contracting the muscle being stretched. This isometric hamstring contraction produces no leg movement since your partner will resist whatever force you apply during the push phase. After a 10-second push, relax your hamstring muscles while your partner again applies pressure for 5 seconds to increase the stretch even further. Repeat this two or three times.

The PNF method, then, involves four phases: (1) an initial, easy stretch of the muscle, (2) an isometric contraction with resistance provided by a partner, (3) relaxation for 5 seconds, and (4) a final passive stretch for 5 seconds. For variety, your partner may allow your leg to move slightly downward during the push phase. PNF stretching relaxes the muscle group being stretched, which produces greater muscle length and improves flexibility. Obvious disadvantages include some discomfort, a longer workout time, and the inability to stretch without a partner.

Figure 9.6 ✦ A Comparison of Three Stretching Techniques

Ballistic Stretching

Static Stretching

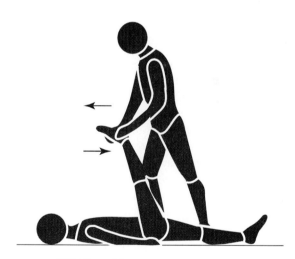

PNF Stretching

How Much Intensity to Use

Proper stretching should take the form of slow, relaxed, controlled, and relatively pain-free movement. It is important to disregard the "no pain, no gain" mentality when you stretch since improvement occurs without undue pain. Joint pressure should produce only mild discomfort. Too much pain and

Improving Your Community

Helping Others Recognize the Importance of Strength and Flexibility Training

One critical area of neglect by both the exercising and sedentary population is strength and flexibility training. Although more than 50 percent of adults avoid all forms of exercise, numerous others focus entirely on aerobic training because of the many health-related benefits of long-term involvement. As a result, loss of lean muscle mass, strength, and flexibility occurs more rapidly as we age. By age 50, most individuals possess considerably less lean muscle mass and have lost both strength and range of motion. Loss of lean muscle mass is a key factor in the slowing of metabolism with aging—a major contributor to overfatness and obesity in the elderly. Because of loss of flexibility, many adults will eventually be unable to perform without discomfort daily functions that they now take for granted, such as tying their shoes, combing their hair, getting in and out of vehicles, and bending over to pick up objects.

The good news is that both strength and flexibility can be maintained throughout life with minimum effort. You can help relay this message to college students, who need to form the habit of including these two areas in their workout routines, and to your parents, grandparents, and the elderly. Consider doing one or more of the following as a project in your health or physical education class, after clearing with your instructor:

1. Review the numerous benefits of strength and flexibility training discussed in this chapter before developing an easy, safe program the elderly can perform in the home without any special equipment in less than 25 minutes. Include both a maintenance program and a program to improve both fitness components.

2. Prepare a similar program for college students and present your findings in class.

3. Ask permission for you and some colleagues to visit a retirement home in your area to deliver a 30-minute presentation and demonstration of a practical strength and flexibility program for the elderly.

4. Prepare minimum strength and flexibility standards by gender and body weight and ask your instructor if you can administer the test to your class. Use this data to generate a discussion on the importance of these two fitness components. ✦

discomfort is a sign you are overloading soft tissue and are at risk of injury. After experiencing mild discomfort with each stretch, relax the muscles being stretched before the next repetition. You will learn to judge each exercise by the *stretch-and-feel method,* easing off the push if pain becomes intense or increases as the phase progresses.

How Long to Stretch

Depending on the stretching technique you choose, the length of your workout will be determined by the number of repetitions (ballistic stretching) and/or the length of time each repetition is held in the stretched position (static and PNF stretching). The amount of time the position is held should progress from 10 seconds at first to 30 seconds after two to three months of regular stretching. A 30- to 60-second stretch appears to only slightly increase the benefits and may be impractical.

If your main purpose for stretching is to prepare your body for vigorous exercise and to maintain the existing range of motion in the major joints, 6 to 9 minutes is sufficient time. For athletes and other individuals striving to increase their range of motion, 10 to 30 minutes of careful stretching may be necessary. Several different stretching exercises may be performed for each joint.

How Flexible to Become

Just how much flexibility a person needs depends on the person. The gymnast, ballet dancer, and hurdler must be more flexible than those who merely want to maintain a high enough level to reap the health benefits, perform daily activities, and engage in regular exercise.

According to the Virginia Commonwealth University Sportsmedicine Center, orthopedic surgeons are treating more injury cases associated with excessive stretching and attempts to acquire high levels of flexibility than injuries associated with failure to stretch. This may be partially due to a renewed interest in stretching and the popularity of various forms of yoga and aerobics that tend to overemphasize flexibility or use questionable stretching exercises.

How Often to Stretch

Those who are just beginning a flexibility-training program should do their routine three to four times a week. After several months, two or three workouts a week will maintain the flexibility you have acquired. As we pointed out previously, stretching should also be a part of the regular warm-up routine prior to participation in aerobics, sports, or other forms of exercise.

FLEXIBILITY EXERCISES

It is important to choose at least one stretching exercise for each of the major muscle groups and to apply exercises equally to both sides of the body. Although there are hundreds of different stretches in use, many are unsafe and should be avoided. This section identifies the proper way to stretch and some of the more commonly used exercises that have been shown to be potentially harmful, with safe alternatives.

Establishing Your Routine

It is important to focus on a stretching routine that will increase the range of motion in particular joints of your choice. Stretching routines are also available that are designed for a specific sport or activity. After you warm up properly and are perspiring, complete each exercise gradually and slowly, beginning with a 10-second hold and adding 2 to 3 seconds to your hold time each workout until you can comfortably maintain the position at your extreme range of motion for 30 seconds. You can begin with the neck and progress downward to the shoulders and chest, trunk and lower back, groin and hips, abdomen, and upper and lower legs.

Exercises to Avoid

As we pointed out previously, stretching can be harmful when the routine is too vigorous or too long or when bouncing at the extreme range of motion is used. The wrong choice of exercises also imposes serious risk of injury to joints. In fact, many popular stretching exercises used in the past are considered potentially harmful. Unfortunately, most people acquire their stretching knowledge by watching others. This informal, copycat approach has created a series of popular but dangerous exercises capable of damaging the knee, neck, spinal column, ankle, and lower back. Figure 9.7 identifies nine of the most popular "hit list" of stretching exercises that should be avoided and offers safe substitutes that will effectively stretch the same muscle group.

Figure 9.7 ✦ Dangerous Popular Stretching Exercises and Suggested Replacements

Old method	New method

Neck roll (circling)

Danger: Drawing the head backward could damage the disks in the neck area, and may even precipitate arthritis.

Forward neck roll

Description: Bend forward at the waist with the hands on the knees. Gently roll the head.

Figure 9.7 ✦ Dangerous Popular Stretching Exercises and Suggested Replacements *(continued)*

OLD METHOD	NEW METHOD

Quadricep stretch

Danger: If the ankle is pulled too hard, muscle, ligament, and cartilage damage may occur.

Opposite leg pull

Description: Grasp one ankle with your opposite hand. Instead of pulling, attempt to straighten the right leg.

Hurdler's stretch

Danger: Hip, knee, and ankle are subjected to abnormal stress.

Everted hurdler's stretch

Description: Bend the right leg at the knee and slide the foot next to the left knee. Pull yourself forward slowly by using a towel, or by grasping the toe.

Deep knee bend (or any exercise that bends the knee beyond a right angle)

Danger: Excessive stress is placed on ligament, tendon, and cartilage tissue.

Single knee lunge

Description: Place one leg in front of your body and extend the other behind. Bend forward at the trunk as you bend the lead leg to right angles.

Yoga plow

Danger: This exercise could overstretch muscles and ligaments, injure spinal disks, or cause fainting.

Extended one-leg stretch

Description: Lead leg extended and slightly bent at the knee. With your foot on the floor, draw the knee of the other leg toward your chest. Bend forward at the trunk as far as possible.

Figure 9.7 ✦ Dangerous Popular Stretching Exercises and Suggested Replacements *(continued)*

OLD METHOD	NEW METHOD

Straight-leg sit-up

Danger: Produces back strain and sciatic nerve elongation. It also moves the hip flexor muscles and does not flatten the abdomen.

Bent-knee sit-up

Description: Cross both hands on your chest, with the knees slightly bent. Raise the upper body slightly to about 25° on each repetition.

Double leg raise

Danger: Stretches the sciatic nerve beyond its normal limits, and places too much stress on ligaments, muscles, and disks.

Knee-to-chest stretch

Description: Clasp both hands behind the neck. Draw the knee toward the chest, and hold that position of maximum stretch for 15–30 seconds.

Prone arch

Danger: Hyper-extension of the lower back places extreme pressure on spinal disks.

Stomach push-up

Description: Lie flat on your stomach, rest on your elbows. Push slowly to raise the upper body as the lower torso remains pressured against the surface.

Back bends

Danger: Spinal disks can easily be damaged.

No alternate exercise has been approved.

SUMMARY

The Importance of Strength and Endurance

Strength and endurance training provides health-related benefits for people of all ages. Such training burns calories, adds muscle mass, prevents the slowing of metabolism with age, and is an important aspect of controlling body weight and body fat throughout life. Over a period of 6 to 12 months of this training, your general physical appearance, body image, and self-concept will improve. Strength training also aids in the development of the skeletal system and in improving bone-mineral content. The added strength and endurance acquired also increase energy and productivity on the job and in recreational activities and reduce the incidence of sports- and work-related injuries. Finally, strength and endurance training plays a major role in the rehabilitation of soft-tissue injuries such as muscle strains, tears, contusions, and surgery.

Factors Affecting Muscular Strength and Endurance

A muscle is composed of fibers and myofibrils bound together by layers of connective tissue. There are three general types of fiber tissue: slow-twitch, oxidative (aerobic); fast-twitch, glycolytic (anaerobic); and fast-twitch, oxidative, glycolytic (aerobic and anaerobic). Strength training predominantly affects the fast-twitch fibers, while endurance training affects the slow-twitch fibers. Your strength and endurance potential is governed by genetics and the number, size, and distribution of your fast- and slow-twitch fibers. Everyone can increase muscle size, strength, and endurance with training.

Strength-Training Principles

Three basic training methods are commonly used to develop strength and endurance: isotonics, isokinetics, and isometrics. On completion of an isotonic or isokinetic contraction, the muscle shortens during the positive phase as weight is brought toward the body and lengthens in the negative phase as the weight is returned to the starting position. No muscle shortening occurs when force is applied to an immovable object (isometric contraction). Isotonic and isokinetic workouts are more beneficial to sports performance than isometric workouts are.

Training variables can be altered to meet specific objectives. By manipulating the number of sets, repetitions, rest intervals, and speed of contraction, programs can be altered to focus on strength, muscular endurance, general body development, muscle mass, speed and explosive power, or rehabilitation from injury.

Lifting Techniques

Sound lifting techniques with free weights or special equipment require careful warm-up and cool-down periods with stretching, the full range of motion on each repetition, proper breathing, use of a partner or spotter, and careful attention to ideal form in each exercise.

Barbell and Dumbbell Exercises

A variety of exercises can be chosen that focus on the major muscle groups of the body. One sound approach is first to identify the key muscles involved in the activity or those you want to train, then to select specific weight-training exercises that activate these muscles, preferably in a similar movement.

Girth Control

To obtain a flat stomach, it is necessary to restrict your daily calories enough to cause fat cells in the abdominal area to shrink in size and to engage in a series of high-repetition abdominal exercises daily. You cannot change fatty tissue to muscle tissue, and muscle tissue will not change to fatty tissue when exercise ceases. Abdominal exercises alone will only improve the strength and endurance of your stomach muscles; little or no change will take place in the size of the stomach unless calories are also restricted. The combination of these two methods can significantly reduce the size of your stomach and improve your abdominal strength and endurance.

Factors Affecting Flexibility

A number of factors combine to place some limitation on the degree of flexibility you attain. After age, gender, heredity, and injury, your choice of lifestyle has the greatest influence on the range of motion in your joints. By engaging in a regular aerobic exercise program, stretching before and after your workout, and maintaining normal body weight and fat, you can remain relatively flexible throughout your life.

The Importance of Flexibility

Regular involvement in stretching exercises two to three times a week will increase joint flexibility, help improve performance in sports, aid in the prevention of soft-tissue injuries, help you prevent and recover from lower-back problems, and assist your muscles in returning to a relaxed status following a workout. Stretching can provide some benefit to almost everyone and make daily chores at home and at work easier and safer.

The Assessment of Flexibility

To properly evaluate your body's flexibility, one test should be used for each of the major joints. Although the sit-and-reach test is one of the most common and accurate, it only measures hamstring and lower-back flexibility. Tests are also needed to measure the range of motion in the neck, elbow, wrist, groin, trunk, hip, and shoulder.

Flexibility-Training Principles

Two to three sessions a week in addition to the stretching routine you normally perform before an aerobic workout will improve your flexibility. About 5 minutes of stretching should take place before every workout but only after body temperature has been elevated, as indicated by the presence of perspiration following some large-muscle activity such as jogging. It is important to avoid stretching cold muscles. A more concentrated 10-minute session should be used during the cool-down phase of a workout.

All three of the most common methods of stretching (ballistic, static, and PNF) have been shown to be equally effective in improving joint range of motion. Ballistic and PNF methods are more likely to result in injury and muscle soreness than static stretching is.

Stretching should produce only mild discomfort. Pain is an indication of risk of injury from overextending soft tissue. Stretching for too long a period of time in an attempt to obtain an extremely high degree of flexibility may also result in injury. Extreme flexibility is unimportant for most individuals and yoga-style contortions should be avoided.

Effective stretching involves a warm-up period, stretching before and after exercise, stretching slowly and gently, holding the stretch for 10 to 30 seconds, and relaxing the body parts other than the muscle group you are stretching.

Flexibility Exercises

A sound program requires at least one exercise for each major joint and emphasis on both sides of the body. Exercises can be chosen that focus on the particular joints you identify as inflexible or important to your personal life, job, sport, or activity. Although not everyone who uses so-called banned stretching exercises will suffer an injury, it is wise to avoid those known to have the potential to damage a joint.

REFERENCES

Alter, J. (1988). *Science of stretching.* Champaign, IL: Human Kinetics.

American Academy of Pediatrics. (1983, March). Weight training and weight lifting: Information for the pediatrician. *Physician and Sportsmedicine 11,* 157–161.

Baechle, T. (Ed.). (1994). *Essentials of strength training and conditioning.* Champaign, IL: Human Kinetics.

Bartels, R. (1992, March). Weight training. How to lift and eat for strength and power. *Physician and Sportsmedicine 20,* 223–234.

Beaulieu, J. E. (1981). Developing a stretching program. *Physician and Sportsmedicine 9*(11), 59–69.

Bouchard, C., et al. (Eds.). (1994) *Physical activity, fitness and health.* Champaign, IL: Human Kinetics.

Clark, N. (1991, September). How to gain weight healthfully. *Physician and Sportsmedicine 19,* 53–54.

Croce, P. (1982). *Stretching for athletics.* Champaign, IL: Leisure Press.

Dintiman, G. B., & Ward, B. (1988). *Sportspeed: The number one speed improvement book for all athletes.* Champaign, IL: Human Kinetics.

Fleck, S. (1988). Cardiovascular adaptations to resistance training. *Medicine and Science in Sports and Exercise 20,* S146–S151.

Fleck, S., & Kraemer, W. (1988). *Designing resistance training programs.* Champaign, IL: Life Enhancement Publications.

Goldberg, A. (1989). Aerobic and resistive exercise modify risk factors for coronary heart disease. *Medicine and Science in Sports and Exercise 21,* 669–674.

National Strength and Conditioning Association. (1989). Strength training for female athletes: A position paper: Part I. *National Strength and Conditioning Association Journal* 11, 29–36, 43–55.

National Strength and Conditioning Association. (1989). Strength training for female athletes: A position paper: Part II. *National Strength and Conditioning Association Journal* 11, 29–36.

National Strength and Conditioning Association. (1989). Breathing during weight training. *National Strength and Conditioning Association Journal* 9, 17–24.

Poehlman, E., et al. (1992, December). Resting energy metabolism and cardiovascular disease risk in resistance-trained and aerobically trained males. *Metabolism 41,* 1351–1368.

Tesch, P. (1988). Skeletal muscle adaptations consequent to long-term heavy resistance exercise. *Medicine and Science in Sports and Exercise 20,* S132–S134.

Wescott, W. (1982). *Strength fitness.* Boston: Allyn & Bacon.

Lab Activity 9.1

Do You Need to Start a Strength-Training Program?

INSTRUCTIONS: *Answer each question below before reading the interpretation section to find out how badly you are in need of a strength-training program.*

		Yes	No
1.	Have you been on a diet within the past 6 to 12 months?	_____	_____
2.	Have you ever lost, then regained, 8 to 10 lb in the same year?	_____	_____
3.	Do you have difficulty controlling your body weight?	_____	_____
4.	Do you have excess, sagging skin on the back of your upper arms, your thighs, backs of your legs, stomach, or other body part?	_____	_____
5.	Are you interested in changing your appearance by adding muscle and reducing the size of fat deposits?	_____	_____
6.	Would a firmer, more muscular body help your body image, how you feel about yourself, and how you think others feel about you?	_____	_____
9.	Would additional strength or muscular endurance improve your performance in any sports or recreational activities?	_____	_____
8.	Would additional strength or local muscular endurance help you perform better on the job and at home?	_____	_____
9.	Are there any specific muscle groups in your body that you would prefer to strengthen?	_____	_____
10.	Have you sustained a soft-tissue injury within the past 12 months, such as an ankle sprain, a pulled muscle, or a contusion?	_____	_____

✦ Interpretation

If you answered "yes" to two or more of the questions, a strength and endurance program may be needed.

Questions 1–3 are concerned with body weight and fat. Strength and endurance training can help your skin fit better, help you focus on your body, help you shrink fat cells, and add muscle mass.

Questions 4–6 are concerned with body image and your interest in improving your appearance through strength and endurance training.

Questions 7–9 are concerned with the need for additional strength and endurance to aid performance on the job, at home, and in recreational activities.

Question 10 is concerned with the prevention of job-, home-, and sports-related injuries.

Lab Activity 9.2

Obtaining a Flat, Healthy Stomach

INSTRUCTIONS: *Take a moment to measure and record the size of your waist. Now apply the pinch test or use skinfold calipers one inch to the right of your belly button and on the left side of your hip to locate the excess fat. If you can pinch more than an inch in these areas, consider following the program described in this lab activity.*

A girth-control program is designed to flatten your stomach and improve the strength and endurance of your abdominal muscles. It is based on two sound principles:

1. Consume fewer calories than you burn, and remain in a negative calorie balance daily for a few months. Keep in mind that fat or adipose tissue and muscle tissue are different tissue types; one cannot be transformed to the other no matter what you do. Reducing caloric intake to produce a fat loss of one to two pounds weekly (see chapter 11) will shrink the size of your fat cells in the abdominal area. It is important to engage in an aerobic exercise program three to four times weekly to help burn extra calories and to allow consumption of sufficient nutrients and calories to spare protein, thus reducing the amount of lean muscle-tissue loss that occurs when you diet without exercise.

2. Supplement your dietary management with aerobic exercise (see chapter 7) and the six abdominal exercises described in this lab activity. For each exercise, work toward 100 repetitions daily. Begin with the maximum number you can perform in one set and add 2 to 5 repetitions each day until you reach 100. Complete these exercises daily, and expect to train for three to four months before you notice significant results. Remember that these abdominal exercises only strengthen muscles that lie beneath the fat. Unless you reduce calories to shrink the fat cells, you will merely have firm abdominal muscles beneath the fat with little reduction in the size of your stomach.

   A. **Sit-ups** Lie flat on your back with knees slightly bent and both hands resting on your chest. Pull your chin to your chest and sit up slowly to approximately 60 degrees.

   B. **Crunches** Lie flat on your back with knees bent and pulled toward the chest. Raise your head and shoulders off the floor as you thrust your upper body toward your knees, then return to the starting position.

   C. **Twisting crunches** Lie flat on your back with hands behind your head. Touch elbow to opposite knee while the other leg straightens; keep feet flexed.

D. **Alternate knee kicks** Lie flat on your back with hands under the buttocks. Bend one knee with the other leg straight and raised 6 inches off the floor. Straighten the bent knee, and bend the other leg as in walking or marching.

E. **Side raise** Lie on your side with arm extended and head on bicep muscle. Hold both legs 6 inches off the floor with feet together. Raise top leg up, and return to leg-together position.

F. **Back scissors** Lie on your stomach with hands at sides and palms down for support. Start with legs apart and feet off the floor; bring feet together, then move them apart.

Lab Activity 9.3

Determining Your Total Body Flexibility

INSTRUCTIONS: *You can test aspects of your flexibility subjectively alone or with a partner. The only equipment needed is a straight-backed chair and a ruler. Score each test by checking Yes or No, depending on whether you can meet the standard cited.*

	Yes	No

1. **Neck**   Normal neck flexibility will allow you to use your chin to sandwich your flattened hand against your chest.   ____ ____

2. **Elbow and wrist**   You should be able to hold your arms out straight with palms up and little fingers higher than your thumbs.   Right arm/wrist ____ ____
   Left arm/wrist ____ ____

3. **Groin**   While standing on one leg, raise the other leg to the side as high as possible. You should be able to achieve a 90-degree angle between the two legs.   Right leg ____ ____
   Left leg ____ ____

   While you are sitting on the floor, put the soles of your feet together and draw your heels as close to your body as possible. Try to touch your knees to the floor or to press your upright fists to the floor using your knees.   ____ ____

4. **Trunk**   While sitting in a straight chair with your feet wrapped around the front legs, twist your body 90 degrees without allowing your hips to move.   Right twist ____ ____
   Left twist ____ ____

5. **Hip**   While standing, hold a yardstick or broom handle with your hands shoulder-width apart. Without losing your grasp, bend down and step over the stick (with both feet, one at a time) and then back again.   ____ ____

6. **Shoulder**   In a standing position, attempt to clasp your hands behind your back by reaching over the shoulder with one arm and upward from behind with the other. Repeat, reversing the arm positions.   Right arm top ____ ____
   Left arm top ____ ____

10

NUTRITION: *You Are What You Eat*

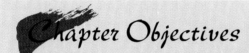

Chapter Objectives

By the end of this chapter, you should be able to:

1. Discuss the functions of the six categories of nutrients in the diet.

2. Compare carbohydrates, fats, and proteins in terms of how each provides energy to the body.

3. Describe a sound nutritional plan based on the RDA, *Dietary Guidelines for Americans,* and the nutrition pyramid.

4. Demonstrate the ability to read a food label.

5. Discuss the role of nutrition in the prevention of disease.

6. Describe the special nutritional needs of the active individual.

7. Dispel common nutritional myths.

$\mathcal{D}$URING RITA'S FRESHMAN year, cafeteria food became unappealing. She had gained nine pounds, had low energy, and was aware she was eating too much fat. She also was sick a number of times and wondered whether any of these illnesses were related to her poor eating habits. Rita had to admit, she just didn't know enough about proper nutrition. Even if she discontinued the university meal plan, she would not know what to do.

This chapter focuses on Rita's concerns and presents an overview of sound nutrition to help her (and others like her) make appropriate choices in the cafeteria or prepare her own nutritional program. We discuss the basic food components, the energy nutrients (carbohydrates, fats, and proteins), the nonenergy nutrients (vitamins, minerals, and water), food density, dietary guidelines for good health and high energy, food labeling, nutrition-disease relationships, and special needs of the active person.

BASIC FOOD COMPONENTS

Six categories of nutrients—carbohydrates, fats, and proteins (the energy nutrients), and vitamins, minerals, and water (the nonenergy nutrients)—satisfy the basic body needs:

- Energy for muscle contraction
- Conduction of nerve impulses
- Growth
- Formation of new tissue and tissue repair
- Chemical regulation of metabolic functions
- Reproduction

The body's use of these nutrients for conversion into tissue, production of energy for muscle contraction, and maintenance of chemical machinery is called **metabolism**.

THE ENERGY NUTRIENTS: CARBOHYDRATES, FATS, AND PROTEINS

Carbohydrates and fat provide the body with its two main sources of energy. All food has energy potential, measured in calories. Since one calorie is too small a unit to be convenient, nutritionists use a large, or **kilocalorie** (kcal), as a measure. One kilocalorie is equal to 1,000 small calories. One kilocalorie is the amount of heat required to raise the temperature of one kilogram (about one quart) of water one degree Celsius. The energy in one peanut, for example, can add one degree of heat to two gallons of water. Only carbohydrates, fats, and protein contain calories; vitamins, minerals, and water do not.

Just how much energy do these nutrients provide? Carbohydrates and protein contain 4 cal per gram (g), fat contains 9 kcal per g, and alcohol contains 7 kcal per g (1 g equals 1/5 of a level teaspoon, 100 g equal 1/2 cup, 1 milligram [mg] equals .001 g).

Basal metabolism is the number of calories expended by a resting person over a 24-hour period to meet the energy requirements of the cellular and tissue processes in a resting state. Basal metabolism depends on age, gender, height, weight, and activity patterns (work and play).

Carbohydrates

Carbohydrates are organic components of various elements that provide a continuous supply of energy in the form of glucose (sugar) to trillions of body cells. **Simple carbohydrates (monosaccharides** and **disaccharides)** come in concentrated forms—as in refined sugar, which is made from cane or beet sugar, molasses, and honey—and natural forms—as in the sugars in some fruits, vegetables, and grains. **Complex carbohydrates (polysaccharides)** are chains of sugar molecules found in fruits, vegetables, and grains. Carbohydrates are broken down into six simple carbon-sugar molecules to permit absorption into the bloodstream. After food is eaten, the blood-sugar level is elevated, and there is an increase in the amount of glucose transported to the cells. Excess sugar is converted to glycogen and stored for future use in the liver and muscles. Once maximum storage capacity is reached, excess sugars are converted to body fat and stored in **adipose** (fat) cells.

Simple carbohydrates (sugars) are consumed in four forms: sucrose, glucose, fructose, and lactose. Annual cane and beet sugar intake in the United States exceeds 100 lb per person; 20 to 25 lb of syrups (glucose and fructose) are also consumed, bringing the total to over 125 lb of sugar intake per person per year. Consumed in these large quantities, sugar contributes to dental cavities, excessive weight, and body fat, and indirectly to such degenerative diseases as diabetes and heart disease. As you can see from Table

---

Metabolism The sum of energy expended in carrying on the normal body processes: converting nutrients into tissue, muscle contraction, and maintenance of the body's chemical machinery.

Kilocalorie A large calorie, equal to 1,000 small calories; one kilocalorie is the amount of heat required to raise the temperature of one kilogram (about one quart) of water one degree Celsius.

Simple carbohydrates (monosaccharides and **disaccharides)** Sugars; chains of sugar molecules (one or two) found in concentrated sugar and the sugar that occurs naturally in food.

Complex carbohydrates (polysaccharides) Starch and fiber; chains of sugar molecules (three or more) found in fruits, vegetables, and grains.

Adipose tissue Fatty tissue.

Nutrition density A quality of foods that are high in nutrients and low in calories.

Dietary fiber The indigestible portion of food after it is exposed to the body's enzymes.

10.1, it is not unusual for a person to consume the equivalent of 50 teaspoons of sugar per day.

Sugar intake should be managed from infancy. Infants seem to be born with a preference for sweet foods, and it is not until early adulthood that the desire for sugar slowly decreases. You can reduce your own sugar intake by reading the labels for sweeteners and sugars in products you are considering (the terms *sucrose, glucose, dextrose, fructose, corn syrup, corn sweetener, natural sweetener,* and *invert sugar* all mean that the product contains sugar); substituting water and unsweetened fruit juices for sodas and punches; buying fruit canned in its own unsweetened juice; cutting back on desserts; purchasing cereals low in sugar; reducing the amount of sugar called for in recipes; and avoiding sweet snacks. If you never again consumed concentrated sugars, it would have absolutely no effect on sound nutrition.

Complex carbohydrates are your major source of

(Photo courtesy of the American Heart Association.)

vitamins (except vitamin B12) and minerals, an important long-term energy source, and the only source of fiber. Complex carbohydrates burn efficiently, leave no toxic waste in the body, and do not tax the liver or raise blood-fat levels. Fruits, vegetables, and grains also have high **nutrition density**, providing a high percentage of our needed daily nutrients in a low number of calories. In the past 75 years, our intake of complex carbohydrates has declined by about 30 percent as sugar intake increased by a similar amount. Unlike sugars, complex carbohydrates are the body's chief source of fuel. Sugar, on the other hand, provides empty calories and very little long-term energy.

Complex carbohydrates should make up at least 48 percent of your total daily calories. Simple carbohydrates should comprise only 10 percent of total calories.

Dietary Fiber The indigestible portion of complex carbohydrates is a nonnutritive substance that cannot be broken down by the enzymes in the human body. Six of the seven types of **dietary fiber** are carbohydrate. Only lignin, found in fruit and vegetable skins and the woody portions of plants, is a noncarbohydrate.

Table 10.2 provides an overview of key information on fiber, including water-soluble and -insoluble varieties, recommended daily intake, nutritional advantages of adequate amounts, dangers of excess intake, and the food sources for both types. Complete Lab Activity 10.1: Estimating Your Daily Fiber Intake at the end of the chapter to discover whether your diet contains enough fiber.

Blood-Glucose Control Blood-glucose levels are carefully regulated by the pancreas. When blood-sugar levels are too high, the pancreas releases a hor-

Table 10.1 ✦ Sugar Content of Common Foods and Drinks

Food	Size	Approximate Content in Teaspoons
Beverages	12 oz	
Sodas		5–9
Sweet cider		4¼
Jams and jellies, candies	1 tbsp	4–6
Milk chocolate	1½ oz	2½
Fudge	1 oz	4½
Hard candy	4 oz	20
Marshmallow	1	1½
Fruits and canned juices		
Dried raisins, prunes, apricots, dates	3–5	4
Fruit juice	8 oz	2½–3½
Breads		
White	1 slice	¼
Hamburger/hot dog bun	1	3
Dairy products		
Ice cream cone	Single dip	3
Sherbet	One scoop	9
Desserts		
Pie (fruit, custard, cream)	1 slice	4–13
Pudding	½ cup	3–5

Table 10.2 ✦ All About Fiber

Water-insoluble (dietary fiber)	Cellulose, forming the cell walls of many plants, is the most abundant insoluble fiber. Cellulose and lignin (from the woody portion of plants, parts of fruit and vegetable skins, and whole grains) cannot be broken down, digested, or made to provide calories for the body.
Water-soluble	The fiber types that either dissolve or swell when placed in water. Dried beans and peas (8 grams per ½ cup), oat bran, tofu, and the flesh of fruits and vegetables are excellent sources of water-soluble fiber.
Daily needs of dietary fiber	25–35 grams. It is important to increase your daily intake slowly, if you are unaccustomed to adequate fiber, to avoid frequent bowel movements and diarrhea. Add several grams daily over a period of a few weeks to give your system a chance to adjust.
Nutritional advantages of consuming adequate fiber	*Insoluble* fiber increases transit time (digestion and elimination of food) and decreases the amount of time the bacteria in the food has to act on intestinal walls. It helps prevent colon and rectal cancer and *diverticulosis* (outpouchings in the wall of the large intestine), provides bulk to the stools, helps eliminate constipation, helps maintain normal bowel movement, and helps to control and maintain normal body weight and fat. *Water-soluble* fiber is associated with lower cardiovascular disease, lower blood cholesterol, lower blood pressure, and possible help in the prevention of diabetes and obesity.
Dangers of excess fiber	Excess dietary fiber binds to some trace minerals and causes excretion prior to the absorption of these minerals. Excessive fiber intake causes poor absorption of nutrients, interferes with the absorption of some drugs, reduces the ability to digest and absorb food by speeding up digestive time, and causes irritation of the intestinal wall. The high phosphorus content of high-fiber foods may create special problems for some individuals, such as those with kidney problems.
Food sources	Foods rich in insoluble (dietary) fiber include apples, bananas, brown rice, cabbage, cauliflower, green beans and peas, legumes, nuts and seeds, pears, peaches, plums, tomatoes, wheat bran, and whole grain breads and cereals.
	Foods rich in soluble fiber include apples, bananas, barley, black-eyed peas, broccoli, carrots, citrus fruits, corn, green peas, legumes, oat bran, oatmeal, potatoes, prunes, seeds, and zucchini.
	Many hot and cold cereals (unprocessed bran, 100 percent bran, shredded wheat, oatmeal) contain 2 to 5 g of fiber per serving. Legumes provide about 8 g per portion (½ cup of garbanzo beans, kidney beans, or baked beans). Fruits provide about 2 g per serving (one small apple, banana, orange; two small plums, a medium peach, ½ cup strawberries, ten large cherries). Vegetables also provide about 2 g per serving (broccoli, brussels sprouts, two stalks of celery, small corn cob, lettuce, green beans, small potato, tomato), and 1 g of fiber is provided by ten peanuts, ¼ cup walnuts, 2½ teaspoons of peanut butter, and a pickle. Additional foods with fiber are breads (whole wheat, whole grain), crackers, and flours (wheat germ, wild rice, cornmeal, buckwheat, millet, rice, raisins, and popcorn). Cooking does not significantly reduce the fiber content of foods.

Source: From *Exploring Health: Expanding the Boundaries of Wellness,* by J. Greenberg and G. B. Dintiman, 1992, Englewood Cliffs, NJ: Prentice-Hall.

mone called **insulin**, which promotes the movement of glucose into certain cells, dropping blood-sugar levels. When levels are too low, the pancreas secretes a hormone called **glucagon**, which stimulates the changing of stored liver glycogen into glucose and the conversion of noncarbohydrates into glucose to raise the blood-sugar level (see Figure 10.1). The pancreas of individuals suffering from **Type I** (insulin depen-

Figure 10.1 ✦ Controlling Blood Glucose Levels

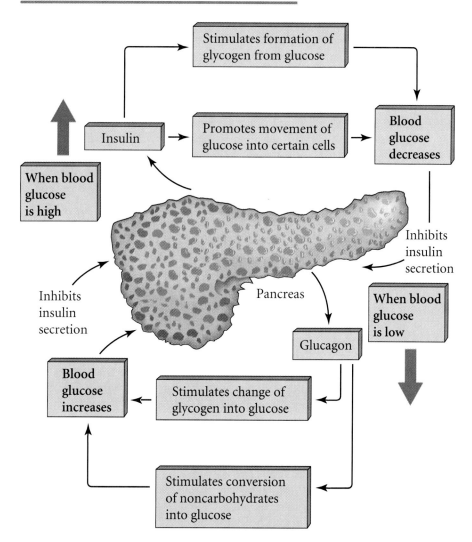

Source: From David C. Nieman, et al., *Nutrition,* Revised First Edition, Copyright © 1992 Wm. C. Brown Communications, Inc., Dubuque, IA. All rights reserved. Reprinted by permission.

dent) **diabetes mellitus** fails to produce insulin, so it must be injected to control blood-glucose levels. The pancreas of most individuals suffering from adult-onset, **Type II** (noninsulin dependent) **diabetes mellitus** produces insulin; glucose uptake at the cellular level, however, does not occur normally and blood-sugar levels remain high. For most individuals, the pancreas does its job and, in conjunction with proper diet, maintains blood glucose at normal levels regardless of what we eat and how much we exercise.

Alcohol   For light drinkers (no more than 1/2 oz of alcohol daily for women, 1 oz for men; one or two 12-oz beers, small glasses of wine, or average cocktails) who are well nourished and in good health, the occa-

Insulin A natural hormone produced in the pancreas gland that aids in the digestion of sugars and other carbohydrates; it is secreted when blood sugar is too high.

Glucagon A natural hormone secreted by the pancreas that stimulates the metabolism of sugar; it is secreted when blood sugar is too low, a condition that causes the release of liver glycogen and its transformation into glucose.

Diabetes mellitus A disease caused by insufficient production of insulin by the endocrine portion of the pancreas; **Type I** (insulin dependent) or **Type II** (noninsulin dependent).

sional use of alcohol will have little effect on nutrition except for the additional 250–300 kcal. Any amount of alcohol, however, affects metabolism. With larger amounts, your nutritional status becomes compromised and several problems occur, such as protein deficiency; failure of intestinal cells to absorb thiamin, folate, and vitamin B12; excretion of increased quantities of magnesium, calcium, potassium and zinc by the kidneys; the dislodging of B6 to create a deficiency that lowers the production of red blood cells; reduced capacity of the liver to activate vitamin D; and numerous other changes. Although proper nutrition is important for those who consume alcohol, it does not prevent changes in the excretion absorption, and utilization of numerous nutrients.

Fats

Fat is a critical nutrient that provides a tremendous source of energy to the human body. Fat also stores and transports vitamins A, D, E, and K; carries linoleic acid (an essential fatty acid); increases the flavor

---

Saturated fat Fat that contains glycerol and saturated fatty acids; found in high quantities in animal products (such as meat, milk, butter, and cheese) and in low quantities in vegetable products; high intake is associated with elevated blood-cholesterol levels.

Polyunsaturated fat Fat containing two or more double bonds between carbons; found heavily in vegetable oils, nuts (such as almonds, pecans, walnuts, and filberts), fish, and margarines.

Monounsaturated fat Fat containing one double bond between carbons, found in foods such as avocados, cashews, and peanut and olive oils.

Cholesterol One of the sterols, or fatlike chemical substances, manufactured in the body and consumed from foods of animal origins only; high intake is associated with elevated blood-cholesterol levels and heart disease.

Nonessential nutrient A nutrient the body can manufacture in sufficient quantities without any in your diet.

Visible fat Fat content of food that can be seen, such as the fat in butter and oils.

Invisible fat Hidden fat in food that cannot be seen such as the fat in dairy products, egg yolks, and meat.

---

and palatability of foods; provides sustained relief from hunger; and helps to keep protein from being used as energy. The fatty tissue in our bodies supports organs, cushions them from injury, and aids in the prevention of heat loss. Fat is in most body tissue, with bone marrow containing 96 percent, liver 2.5 percent, and blood 0.5 percent. Unfortunately, too much body fat and high blood-fat levels can shorten life and increase vulnerability to numerous chronic and degenerative diseases, such as cardiorespiratory disease and cancer.

The fat in food is classified as **saturated, polyunsaturated**, and **monounsaturated**. **Cholesterol** is used in the synthesis of sex hormones, vitamin D, and bile salts. It is also associated with artery clogging and heart disease (see chapter 12). Cholesterol is a **nonessential nutrient**. Blood levels depend on the cholesterol consumed in your diet and that produced by the liver (see Table 10.3). The intake of saturated fat stimulates the liver to produce more cholesterol.

The average person in the United States consumes over 55 lb of **visible fat** and over 130 lb of **invisible fat** each year. Dietary fat contributes approximately 36 to 38 percent of the total calories, although the recent favorable pattern of fat intake shows that more fat is being consumed from plants and less from animal sources. Since saturated fat intake stimulates the production of cholesterol, it is important to reduce cholesterol intake to less than 300 milligrams daily and total saturated fat to less than 10 percent of daily calories. Both dietary saturated fat and cholesterol contribute to elevated blood-cholesterol levels.

The five kinds of foods containing the highest percentage of kilocalories from fat are hamburgers and meat loaf (63 percent); hot dogs, ham, and luncheon meats (58 percent); whole milk (54 percent); doughnuts, cakes, and cookies (54 percent); and beefsteak and roasts (50 percent). Another major source of saturated fat in our diet is the food eaten in fast-food restaurants. Most hamburgers, hot dogs, and chicken and fish sandwiches served by major fast-food chains contain more than 50 percent fat and are very high in calories. Even McDonald's McLean Deluxe Sandwich (taken off the menu due to poor sales) contained 320 calories and 10 g of fat (90 kcal) for a total of 28 percent fat. Other popular sandwiches and their percentage of calories from fat include: McDonald's Filet-O-Fish (440 calories, 53 percent fat), Burger King's Broiler Chicken Sandwich (379 calories, 42 percent fat), Burger King's Double Whopper with Cheese (935 calories, 59 percent fat), Wendy's Grilled Chicken Sandwich (340 calories, 34

Table 10.3 ✦ Comparison of Saturated Fat, Total Fat, and Cholesterol in Selected Foods[1]

The following foods within each grouping are ranked from low- to high-saturated fat.[2] The foods chosen for this chart are meant to be representative of their type. You will want to select most often the low-saturated fat and cholesterol foods from the upper portion of each group.

	GRAMS OF SATURATED FAT	GRAMS OF TOTAL FAT	MILLIGRAMS OF CHOLESTEROL	TOTAL CALORIES
Beef (3½ oz)				
Top round	1.7	5.0	90	199
Sirloin	2.6	6.8	89	191
Chuck, arm pot roast	2.8	7.6	101	210
Ground lean	7.2	18.5	87	272
Salami, about 4 slices	8.4	20.1	60	254
Pork (3½ oz)				
Ham steak, extra lean	1.4	4.2	45	122
Fresh tenderloin	1.7	4.8	93	166
Fresh leg, rump half	3.7	10.7	96	221
Lamb (3½ oz)				
Leg	2.8	7.7	89	191
Loin chop	3.5	9.7	95	216
Arm chop	5.0	14.1	121	279
Poultry (3½ oz)				
Turkey, fryer-roasters				
Light meat without skin	0.4	1.2	86	140
Light meat with skin	1.3	4.6	95	164
Chicken, broilers				
Light meat without skin	1.3	4.5	85	173
Dark meat without skin	2.7	9.7	93	205
Light meat with skin	3.0	10.9	84	222
Dark meat with skin	4.4	15.8	91	253
Ground turkey	3.8	13.8	88	228
Fish (3½ oz)				
Haddock	0.2	0.9	74	112
Halibut	0.4	2.9	41	148
Tuna	1.6	6.3	48	164
Salmon	1.9	11.0	87	216
Shellfish (3½ oz)				
Lobster	0.1	0.6	72	98
Clams	0.2	2.0	67	148
Shrimp	0.3	1.1	195	90
Oysters	1.3	5.0	109	137
Clams, breaded and fried	2.7	11.2	61	202

[1]If you want to check whether you are eating 30 percent of your total calories from fat (or 10 percent of your total daily calories from saturated fat), use this table to add up the grams of fat (or saturated fat) you eat each day. Your total fat intake in grams should not exceed one-half of your body weight. A 120-lb individual should consume less than 60 grams of fat daily; only 20 of these should be saturated fat.

[2]All values for meat, poultry, and fish are for products prepared by broiling, braising, roasting, or moist-heat cooking methods rather than frying, unless otherwise indicated.

Table 10.3 ✦ Comparison of Saturated Fat, Total Fat, and Cholesterol in Selected Foods *(continued)*

	GRAMS OF SATURATED FAT	GRAMS OF TOTAL FAT	MILLIGRAMS OF CHOLESTEROL	TOTAL CALORIES
Milk (8 oz)				
Nonfat	0.3	0.4	4	86
Buttermilk	1.3	2.2	9	98
Low-fat, 1%	1.6	2.6	10	102
Low-fat, 2%	2.9	4.7	18	121
Whole	5.1	8.2	33	150
Yogurt (4 oz)				
Plain nonfat yogurt	0.1	0.2	2	63
Plain yogurt	2.4	3.7	14	70
Soft cheeses (4 oz)				
Cottage cheese, low-fat	0.7	1.2	5	82
Cottage cheese, creamed	3.2	5.1	17	117
Ricotta, part-skim	5.5	8.9	34	171
Ricotta, whole milk	9.3	14.5	57	216
Hard cheeses (1 oz)				
Mozzarella, part skim	2.9	4.5	16	72
Mozzarella	3.7	6.1	22	80
Swiss	5.0	7.8	26	107
American processed	5.6	8.9	27	106
Cheddar	6.0	9.4	30	114
Frozen desserts (1 cup)				
Orange sherbert	2.4	3.8	14	270
Vanilla ice milk	3.5	5.6	18	184
Vanilla ice cream	8.9	14.3	59	269
Eggs (1 large)				
Egg white	0	trace	0	16
Egg yolk	1.6	5.1	213	59
Fats and oils (1 tbsp)				
Canola oil	1.0	14.0	0	124
Safflower oil	1.2	13.6	0	120
Peanut butter	1.5	7.9	0	94
Corn oil	1.7	13.6	0	120
Olive oil	1.8	13.5	0	119
Margarine, soft tub	2.1	11.4	0	101
Margarine, stick	2.1	11.4	0	101
Butter	7.1	10.8	31	101
Nuts and seeds (1 oz)				
Almonds	1.4	14.8	0	167
Pecans	1.5	19.2	0	190
Sunflower seeds	1.5	14.1	0	162
English walnuts	1.6	17.6	0	182
Pistachios	1.7	13.7	0	164
Peanuts	1.9	13.8	0	159

Table 10.3 ✦ Comparison of Saturated Fat, Total Fat, and Cholesterol in Selected Foods *(continued)*

	GRAMS OF SATURATED FAT	GRAMS OF TOTAL FAT	MILLIGRAMS OF CHOLESTEROL	TOTAL CALORIES
Breads (1 whole item)				
Corn tortilla	0.1	1.0	0	65
English muffin	0.3	1.0	0	140
Bagel	0.3	2.0	0	200
Whole-wheat bread	0.4	1.0	0	70
Hamburger bun	0.5	2.0	trace	115
Croissant	3.5	12.0	13	235
Sweets and snacks				
Air-popped popcorn, 1 cup	trace	0	trace	30
Angel food cake, $1/12$ cake	trace	trace	0	125
Vanilla wafers, 5	0.9	3.3	12	94
Fig bars, 4	1.0	4.0	27	210
Potato chips, 1 oz	2.6	10.1	0	147
Pound cake, $1/17$ cake	3.0	5.0	64	110
Chocolate chip cookies, 4	3.9	11.0	18	185

Source: Adapted from *Facts about Blood Cholesterol* (pp. 12–16), October 1990, Bethesda MD: National Heart, Lung, and Blood Institute, U.S. Department of Health and Human Services, Public Health Service, National Institutes of Health, NIH Publication No. 90–2696.

percent fat), Wendy's Big Classic (570 calories, 52 percent fat), Kentucky Fried Chicken's Lite 'n Crispy Drumsticks (242 calories, 52 percent fat), and Kentucky Fried Chicken's Chicken Sandwich (482 calories, 50 percent fat).

The search for a fat substitute, or artificial fat, that provides the same taste and texture with about one fourth the calories and none of the disadvantages of dietary fat continues. After spending more than $200 million, Proctor and Gamble introduced *olestra*

To maintain sound nutrition, choose lower fat foods whenever possible. (Photo courtesy of the American Heart Association.)

as a fat substitute in several products in the United States. Olestra is a synthetic compound of sugar and vegetable oil that tends to scoop up the fat-soluble vitamins A, D, E, and K, as well as nutrients such as carotenoids found in fruits and vegetables, potentially causing deficiencies. Its use has also been shown to cause gastrointestinal problems such as cramps and severe diarrhea in some individuals. Taste tests on potato chips, ice cream, and other products with artificial fats have been encouraging. It is apparent that the public wants the best of both worlds (the taste of fat without the calories) and is ready to purchase FDA-approved products with artificial fat, providing the risks are minimal. In November 1995, an FDA panel of experts concluded that olestra chips were not harmful. It is anticipated that numerous products in the future will contain this artificial fat. The debate will continue, however, on whether the benefits of reduced calories, saturated fat, and total fat outweigh the absorption and side-effect problems.

Protein

Protein, from the Greek word *proteios*, or *primary*, is critical to all living things. In the human body, it is used to repair, rebuild, and replace cells; aid in growth; balance fluid, salt, and acid-base; and provide needed energy when carbohydrates and fats are insufficient or unavailable. Protein is produced in the body through building blocks called **amino acids.** Some of these amino acids are produced in the body; others are derived only from food sources. **Nonessential amino acids** can be manufactured by the body if not obtained from the diet. **Essential amino acids**, 8 to 10 of which must be present in the body in the proper amount and proportion to the nonessential acids for normal protein metabolism to proceed, cannot be manufactured by the body and must be acquired through diet. All 22 amino acids must be present simultaneously (within several hours) in order for the body to synthesize them into proteins that will be used for optimal maintenance of body growth and function.

Humans obtain protein from both animal and plant foods. In general, animal protein is superior to plant protein because it contains all the essential amino acids in the proper proportions. If one essential amino acid is missing or present in the incorrect proportion, protein construction may be blocked.

Eggs are the complete protein by which all other protein is judged. Milk, cheese, other dairy products, meat, fish, and poultry compare favorably with eggs as excellent sources of protein. Although eggs contain about 213 milligrams (mg) of cholesterol and 5 g of fat (60 percent), they are a low-calorie (75-kcal) source of protein, vitamin A, riboflavin, vitamin B12, iron, zinc, phosphorus, calcium, potassium, and other nutrients. It is still advisable to consume no more than two to three eggs per week, never more than one per day, to eliminate or substitute other food products in recipes calling for eggs as an ingredient, and to purchase small eggs rather than medium, large, or extra large. The American Heart Association guideline of no more than 300 mg of cholesterol per day is difficult to follow if you start the day with an egg rather than with cold or hot cereal.

Protein containing all essential amino acids is termed a **complete**, or a high-quality, **protein**; protein from most vegetable sources is low in some amino acids and will not support growth and development when used as the only source of protein. This sort of protein is called **incomplete**, or low-quality, **protein**. Terms such as **low** and **high biological value** are also used to describe the quality of protein.

Approximately 54 g of protein are recommended daily for college-aged males and 46 to 48 g for females. To determine your specific protein needs multiply your body weight in kilograms (kg) by 0.8 g. A 132-lb woman, for example, weighs 60 kg (132 divided by 2.2) and needs 48 g ($60 \times 0.8 = 48$) of protein daily. Larger individuals, pregnant and lactating women, adolescents, and those who are ill may need slightly more protein. Physically active individuals generally do not require additional protein unless the weather is hot and profuse sweating that produces additional nitrogen loss occurs. Those living in extremely hot climates may also need slightly more protein. Approximately 12 to 15 percent of the total daily calories in the U.S. diet should come from protein.

It is not difficult for most people to obtain their recommended daily intakes (RDIs) of protein. Meat contains about 7 g per oz; milk has 8 g per glass; and protein is plentiful in eggs and dairy products and present in small quantities in vegetables and grains. Two glasses of milk; 1 oz of cheese; and 3 oz of beef, chicken, or fish provide all the protein the average person needs in one day.

Vegetarian Diets   Believing that vegetables are healthier than meats, that it is morally wrong to consume meat, or that meat is contaminated with growth-enhancing drugs, more and more people in the United States are resorting to some form of vegetarianism.

There are three basic kinds of vegetarians: the **vegan**, the **lactovegetarian**, and the **ovolactovegetarian**. All vegetarians must plan their diets carefully since it is more difficult for them to consume adequate protein, iron, and vitamin B12 than it is for people who are not vegetarians. Since dairy products and eggs are excellent protein sources, lacto- and ovolactovegetarians have much less difficulty than vegans do. Vegans must use complementary protein combinations of vegetables and grains to include proper amounts of protein in their diets. Traditional complementary protein diets include combinations of soy beans or tofu with rice (China and Indochina); peas with wheat (the Middle East); beans with corn (Central and South America); and rice with beans, black-eyed peas, or tofu (United States and the Caribbean). Other protein combinations readily available to U.S. vegans include peanut butter and whole-grain bread, brown bread and baked beans, and black bean and rice soup. These combinations of complete proteins are excellent substitutes for meat, egg, and dairy proteins.

Because fruits, vegetables, and grains contain no cholesterol, little saturated fat, and high fiber, vegans tend to escape heart disease for 10 years longer than meat eaters do. Vegetarians may also be able to avoid certain kinds of digestive system cancers; however, vegans are especially prone to dangerous deficiencies in iron, calcium, and vitamin B12 (available only in animal products). In order to combat serious nutrient shortages, vegans should follow certain daily dietary recommendations and include in their diets:

- Two cups of legumes daily for proper levels of calcium and iron.

- One cup of dark greens daily to meet iron requirements (for women).

- At least one gram of fat daily for proper absorption of vitamins.

- A supplement of fortified plant foods (like soy or nut milks or a multiple vitamin and mineral) to obtain vitamin B12.

The Energy Systems Practically all energy your muscles use is formed by the chemical reactions of two unique pathways of energy formation: the **glycolysis** and the **citric acid cycle**.

The majority of energy formed by glycolysis is derived from glucose, and since it is anaerobic, it can be produced quickly. The glucose used to fuel glycolysis comes from blood glucose, glycogen (stored form of glucose), glycerol (small fraction of stored fat molecules), and several amino acids. Most college-aged people have approximately 1,400 kcal of stored glycogen in the muscles and 300 to 400 stored in the liver (liver glycogen can be used to supply glucose to muscles). Short, intense anaerobic exercises such as sprinting, weight training, pull-ups, diving, and push-ups, are fueled by the glycolysis energy cycle.

The citric acid cycle uses three different types of fuel: glucose fragments produced by glycolysis, fatty acids, and certain amino acids. Fatty acids drawn from the body's fat stores are by far the largest supplier of energy in this aerobic cycle. Only in the aerobic cycle where oxygen is present can fat be burned as

Amino acids The basic component of most proteins.

Nonessential amino acids Amino acids that can be manufactured by the body if they cannot be acquired from food sources.

Essential amino acids Amino acids that cannot be manufactured by the body and therefore must be acquired from food sources.

Complete protein Food source containing all essential amino acids in the correct proportions.

Incomplete protein Food source that does not contain all essential amino acids or contains several in incorrect proportions.

Low biological value A protein source such as corn and wheat that does not contain all eight essential amino acids or contains some in low proportions.

High biological value A protein source such as meat that contains all eight essential amino acids in the correct proportions.

Vegan A strict vegetarian who consumes only fruits, vegetables, and grains.

Lactovegetarian An individual who eats fruits, vegetables, grains, and dairy products and avoids meat products.

Ovolactovegetarian An individual who eats fruits, vegetables, grains, dairy products, and eggs but avoids meat products.

Glycolysis energy cycle The anaerobic energy pathway fueled primarily by glucose.

Citric acid energy cycle The aerobic energy pathway fueled primarily by fat, small quantities of glucose fragments, and certain amino acids.

fuel. Activities such as walking, jogging, running, lap swimming, aerobic dance, cycling, basketball, and soccer are fueled by fat in the citric acid cycle. These aerobic activities are ideal for weight and fat loss. Fat cannot be burned in the anaerobic cycle since oxygen is not present.

Nonenergy Nutrients: Vitamins, Minerals, and Water

Vitamins

Vitamins are essential in helping chemical reactions take place in the body and are required in very small amounts. Water-soluble vitamins (vitamin C and the B-complex vitamins) need to be consumed in the proper amounts over a five- to eight-day period since they are easily dissolved in water, not stored for long periods of time, and eliminated in the urine (see Table 10.4 and Table 10.5). Fat-soluble vitamins (vitamins A, D, E, and K) are stored in large amounts in fatty tissues and the liver and are absorbed through the intestinal tract as needed.

Regardless of the claims, vitamin C does not cure or prevent the common cold. Large supplements of other vitamins and minerals are being examined for their disease-fighting potential and their ability to assist in medical treatment. It is important to realize three important things about taking supplements: (1) The best way to obtain adequate vitamins and minerals is from food, not from supplements. Food has the added benefit of containing fiber and water. (2) The vast majority of people in the United States get all the vitamins and minerals they need from their diets and do not need supplements. (3) Vitamin and mineral toxicity problems are found predominantly in those who take supplements.

Minerals

Minerals are present in all living cells. They serve as key components of various hormones, enzymes, and other substances that aid in regulating chemical reactions within cells. Mineral elements play a part in the body's metabolic processes, and deficiencies can result in serious disorders. *Macrominerals*, such as sodium, potassium, calcium, phosphorus, magnesium, sulfur, and chlorides, are needed by the body in large amounts. *Trace minerals* are needed in small amounts. A minimum of 14 trace minerals must be ingested for

optimum health. Iron, iodine, copper, fluoride, and zinc are the ones most important for body function. The body is composed of about 31 minerals, 24 of which are considered essential for sustaining life (see Table 10.6 and Table 10.7).

Iron is one of the body's most essential minerals. Approximately 85 percent of our daily iron intake is used to produce new hemoglobin (the pigment of the red blood cells that transports oxygen); the remaining 15 percent is used for the production of new tissue or held in storage. Iron needs also vary according to age and gender. Table 10.8 summarizes these variables. Iron deficiency results in loss of strength and endurance, rapid fatigue during exercise, shortening of the attention span, loss of visual perception, impaired learning, and numerous other physical disorders. Although the importance of sufficient dietary iron is common knowledge, many women may not get enough iron in their diets. In the United States, iron intake has been reduced by the removal of iron-containing soils from the food supply and the diminished use of iron cooking utensils. Whereas animals can ingest iron from muddy water and soil, humans must rely solely on food.

Iron deficiency anemia, a major health problem in the United States, is common in older infants, children, women of childbearing age, pregnant women, and low-income people. People must also be aware, however, that too much iron can be dangerous. Iron toxicity is rare, but a condition called *iron overload* occurs when the body is overwhelmed with too much iron given by vein (by blood transfusion) or when too much iron is absorbed because of hereditary defects, heavy supplementation, and alcohol abuse (which increases absorption). Iron overload can cause tissue and liver damage. Rapid ingestion of large amounts of iron can also cause sudden death. Iron overdose is the second most common cause of accidental poisoning in small children. High blood-iron levels may also be related to heart disease in men.

Iron is more easily absorbed from meat, fish, and poultry (heme iron) than it is from vegetables (non-heme iron). Twice the volume of vegetable iron is absorbed when vegetables and meats are consumed during the same meal.

Supplementation Some people take large doses of vitamins and minerals in the belief that these are necessary to correct dietary deficiencies or to prevent or cure a variety of ills. More commonly, the multiple vitamin/mineral pill is taken as an *insurance policy* against improper nutrition. Unfortunately, consuming too many vitamins and minerals, especially fat-

Table 10.4 ✦ Summary of Information on Fat-Soluble Vitamins

NAME	RDA FOR ADULTS*	SOURCES	STABILITY	COMMENTS
Vitamin A (retinol; α-, β-, γ-carotene)	M: 1000 RE F: 800 RE	Liver, kidney, milk fat, fortified margarine, egg yolk, yellow and dark green leafy vegetables, apricots, cantaloupe, peaches.	Stable to light, heat, and usual cooking methods. Destroyed by oxidation, drying, very high temperature, ultraviolet light.	Essential for normal growth, development, and maintenance of epithelial tissue. Essential to the integrity of night vision. Helps provide for normal bone development and influences normal tooth formation. Toxic in large quantities.
Vitamin D (calciferol)	M: 5 μg F: 5 μg	Vitamin D milk, irradiated foods, some in milk fat, liver, egg yolk, salmon, tuna fish, sardines. Sunlight converts 7-dehydrocholesterol to cholecalciferol.	Stable to heat and oxidation.	Really a prohormone. Essential for normal growth and development; important for formation of normal bones and teeth. Influences absorption and metabolism of phosphorus and calcium. Toxic in large quantities.
Vitamin E (tocopherols and tocotrienols)	M: 10 α-TE F: 8 α-TE	Wheat germ, vegetable oils, green leafy vegetables, milk fat, egg yolk, nuts.	Stable to heat and acids. Destroyed by rancid fats, alkali, oxygen, lead, iron salts, and ultraviolet irradiation.	A strong antioxidant. May help prevent oxidation of unsaturated fatty acids and vitamin A in intestinal tract and body tissues. Protects red blood cells from hemolysis. Role in reproduction (in animals). Role in epithelial tissue maintenance and prostaglandin synthesis.
Vitamin K (phylloquinone and menaquinone)	M: 80 μg F: 65 μg	Liver, soybean oil, other vegetable oils, green leafy vegetables, wheat bran. Synthesized in intestinal tract.	Resistant to heat, oxygen, and moisture. Destroyed by alkali and ultraviolet light.	Aids in production of prothrombin, a compound required for normal clotting of blood. Toxic in large amounts.

*M = male; F = female; RE = retinol equivalents; α-TE = alphatocopherol equivalents.
Source: From *Food Nutrition and Diet Therapy* (p. 105), by K. L. Mahan and M. Arlin, 1992, Philadelphia: W. B. Saunders. Used by permission.

Table 10.5 ✦ Summary of Information on Water-Soluble Vitamins

NAME	RDA FOR ADULTS*	SOURCES	STABILITY	COMMENTS
Thiamin	M: 1.5 mg F: 1.1 mg	Pork, liver, organ meats, legumes, whole-grain and enriched cereals and breads, wheat germ, potatoes. Synthesized in intestinal tract.	Unstable in presence of heat, alkali, or oxygen. Heat stable in acid solution.	As part of cocarboxylase, aids in removal of CO_2 from alpha-keto acids during oxidation of carbohydrates. Essential for growth, normal appetite, digestion, and healthy nerves.
Riboflavin	M: 1.7 mg F: 1.3 mg	Milk and dairy foods, organ meats, green leafy vegetables, enriched cereals and breads, eggs.	Stable to heat, oxygen, and acid. Unstable to light (especially ultraviolet) or alkali.	Essential for growth. Plays enzymatic role in tissue respiration and acts as a transporter of hydrogen ions. Coenzyme forms FMN and FAD.
Niacin (nicotinic acid and nicotinamide)	M: 19 mg NE F: 15 mg NE	Fish, liver, meat, poultry, many grains, eggs, peanuts, milk, legumes, enriched grains. Synthesized by intestinal bacteria.	Stable to heat, light oxidation, acid, and alkali.	As part of enzyme system, aids in transfer of hydrogen and acts in metabolism of carbohydrates and amino acids. Involved in glycolysis, fat synthesis, and tissue respiration.
Vitamin B_6 (pyridoxine, pyridoxal, and pyridoxamine)	M: 2.0 mg F: 1.6 mg	Pork, glandular meats, cereal bran and germ, milk, egg yolk, oatmeal, and legumes. Synthesized by intestinal bacteria.	Stable to heat, light, and oxidation.	As a coenzyme, aids in the synthesis and breakdown of amino acids and in the synthesis of unsaturated fatty acids from essential fatty acids. Essential for conversion of tryptophan to niacin. Essential for normal growth.
Folate	M: 200 µg F: 180 µg	Green leafy vegetables, organ meats (liver), lean beef, wheat, eggs, fish, dry beans, lentils, cowpeas, asparagus, broccoli, collards, yeast. Synthesized in intestinal tract.	Stable to sunlight when in solution; unstable to heat in acid media.	Appears essential for biosynthesis of nucleic acids. Essential for normal maturation of red blood cells. Functions as a coenzyme: tetrahydrofolic acid.
Vitamin B_{12}	2 µg	Liver, kidney, milk and dairy foods, meat, eggs. Vegans require supplement.	Slowly destroyed by acid, alkali, light, and oxidation.	Involved in the metabolism of single-carbon fragments. Essential for biosynthesis of nucleic acids and nucleoproteins. Role in metabolism of nervous tissue. Involved with folate metabolism. Related to growth.
Pantothenic acid	Level not yet determined but 4–7 mg believed safe and adequate.	Present in all plant and animal foods. Eggs, kidney, liver, salmon, and yeast are best sources. Possibly synthesized by intestinal bacteria.	Unstable to acid, alkali, heat, and certain salts.	As part of coenzyme A, functions in the synthesis and breakdown of many vital body compounds. Essential in the intermediary metabolism of carbohydrate, fat, and protein.
Biotin	Not known but 30–100 µg believed safe and adequate.	Liver, mushrooms, peanuts, yeast, milk, meat, egg yolk, most vegetables, banana, grapefruit, tomato, watermelon, and strawberries. Synthesized in intestinal tract.	Stable.	Essential component of enzymes. Involved in synthesis and breakdown of fatty acids and amino acids through aiding the addition and removal of CO_2 to or from active compounds, and the removal of NH_2 from amino acids.
Vitamin C (ascorbic acid)	60 mg	Acerola (West Indian cherry-like fruit), citrus fruit, tomato, melon, peppers, greens, raw cabbage, guava, strawberries, pineapple, potato.	Unstable to heat, alkali, and oxidation, except in acids. Destroyed by storage.	Maintains intracellular cement substance with preservation of capillary integrity. Cosubstrate in hydroxylations requiring molecular oxygen. Important in immune responses, wound healing, and allergic reactions. Increases absorption of nonheme iron.

*M = male; F = female; NE = niacin equivalents

Source: From *Food Nutrition and Diet Therapy* (p. 105–106), by K. L. Mahan and M. Arlin, 1992 Philadelphia: W. B. Saunders. Used by permission.

Table 10.6 ✦ Macronutrients Essential at Levels of 100 mg/day or More

MINERAL	LOCATION IN BODY AND SOME BIOLOGIC FUNCTIONS	RDA OR ESADDI* FOR ADULTS	FOOD SOURCES	COMMENTS ON LIKELIHOOD OF A DEFICIENCY
Calcium	99% in bones and teeth. Ionic calcium in body fluids essential for ion transport across cell membranes. Calcium is also bound to protein, citrate, or inorganic acids.	800 mg 1200 mg for women 19–24 yr	Milk and milk products, sardines, clams, oysters, kale, turnip greens, mustard greens, tofu.	Dietary surveys indicate that many diets do not meet recommended dietary allowances for calcium. Since bone serves as a homeostatic mechanism to maintain calcium level in blood, many essential functions are maintained, regardless of diet. Long-term dietary deficiency is probably one of the factors responsible for development of osteoporosis in later life.
Phosphorus	About 80% in inorganic portion of bones and teeth. Phosphorus is a component of every cell and of highly important metabolites, including DNA, RNA, ATP (high energy compound), and phospholipids. Important to pH regulation.	800 mg 1200 mg for women 19–24 yr	Cheese, egg yolk, milk, meat, fish, poultry, whole-grain cereals, legumes, nuts.	Dietary inadequacy not likely to occur if protein and calcium intake are adequate.
Magnesium	About 50% in bone. Remaining 50% is almost entirely inside body cells with only about 1% in extracellular fluid. Ionic Mg functions as an activator of many enzymes and thus influences almost all processes.	350 mg for male, 280 mg for female	Whole-grain cereals, tofu, nuts, meat, milk, green vegetables, legumes, chocolate.	Dietary inadequacy considered unlikely, but conditioned deficiency is often seen in clinical medicine, associated with surgery, alcoholism, malabsorption, loss of body fluids, certain hormonal and renal diseases.
Sodium	30 to 45% in bone. Major cation of extracellular fluid and only a small amount is inside cell. Regulates body fluid osmolarity, pH, and body fluid volume.	500–3000 mg	Common table salt, seafoods, animal foods, milk, eggs. Abundant in most foods except fruit.	Dietary inadequacy probably never occurs, although low blood sodium requires treatment in certain clinical disorders. Sodium restriction necessary practice in certain cardiovascular disorders.
Chloride	Major anion of extracellular fluid, functioning in combination with sodium. Serves as a buffer, enzyme activator; component of gastric hydrochloric acid. Mostly present in extracellular fluid; less than 15% inside cells.	750–3000 mg	Common table salt, seafoods, milk, meat, eggs.	In most cases dietary intake has little significance except in the presence of vomiting, diarrhea, or profuse sweating, when a deficiency may develop.
Potassium	Major cation of intracellular fluid, with only small amounts in extracellular fluid. Functions in regulating pH and osmolarity, and cell membrane transfer. Ion is necessary for carbohydrate and protein metabolism.	2000 mg	Fruits, milk, meat, cereals, vegetables, legumes.	Dietary inadequacy unlikely, but conditioned deficiency may be found in kidney disease, diabetic acidosis, excessive vomiting, diarrhea, or sweating. Potassium excess may be a problem in renal failure and severe acidosis.
Sulfur	Most dietary sulfur is present in sulfur-containing amino acids needed for synthesis of essential metabolites. Functions in oxidation-reduction reactions. Also functions in thiamin and biotin, and as inorganic sulfur.	Need for sulfur is satisfied by essential sulfur-containing amino acids.	Protein foods such as meat, fish, poultry, eggs, milk, cheese, legumes, nuts.	Dietary intake is chiefly from sulfur-containing amino acids and adequacy is related to protein intake.

*RDA = recommended dietary allowance; ESADDI = estimated safe and adequate daily dietary intake.
Source: From *Food Nutrition and Diet Therapy* (p. 137), by K. L. Mahan and M. Arlin, 1992 Philadelphia: W. B. Saunders. Used by permission.

Table 10.7 ✦ Micronutrients Essential at Levels of a Few mg/day

MINERAL	LOCATION IN BODY AND SOME BIOLOGIC FUNCTIONS	RDA OR ESADDI* FOR ADULTS	FOOD SOURCES	COMMENTS ON LIKELIHOOD OF A DEFICIENCY
Iron	About 70% is in hemoglobin; about 26% stored in liver, spleen and bone. Iron is a component of hemoglobin and myoglobin, important in oxygen transfer; also present in serum transferrin and certain enzymes. Almost none in ionic form.	10 mg for male, 15 mg for female	Liver, meat, egg yolk, legumes, whole or enriched grains, dark green vegetables, dark molasses, shrimp, oysters.	Iron-deficiency anemia occurs in women in reproductive years and in infants and preschool children. May be associated in some cases with unusual blood loss, parasites, and malabsorption. Anemia is last effect of deficient state.
Zinc	Present in most tissues, with higher amounts in liver, voluntary muscle, and bone. Constituent of many enzymes and insulin; of importance in nucleic acid metabolism.	15 mg for male, 12 mg for female	Oysters, shellfish, herring, liver, legumes, milk, wheat bran.	Extent of dietary inadequacy in this country not known. Conditioned deficiency may be seen in systemic childhood illnesses and in patients who are nutritionally depleted or have been subjected to severe stress, such as surgery.
Copper	Found in all body tissues; larger amounts in liver, brain, heart, and kidney. Constituent of enzymes and of ceruloplasmin and erythrocuprein in blood. May be integral part of DNA or RNA molecule.	1.5–3 mg	Liver, shellfish, whole grains, cherries, legumes, kidney, poultry, oysters, chocolate, nuts.	No evidence that specific deficiencies of copper occur in the human. Menkes' disease is genetic disorder resulting in copper deficiency.
Iodine	Constituent of thyroxine and related compounds synthesized by thyroid gland. Thyroxine functions in control of reactions involving cellular energy.	150 μg	Iodized table salt, seafoods, water and vegetables in nongoitrous regions.	Iodization of table salt is recommended especially in areas where food is low in iodine.
Manganese	Highest concentration is in bone; also relatively high concentrations in pituitary, liver, pancreas, and gastrointestinal tissue. Constituent of essential enzyme systems; rich in mitochondria of liver cells.	2.5–5.0 mg	Beet greens, blueberries, whole grains, nuts, legumes, fruit, tea.	Unlikely that deficiency occurs in humans.
Fluoride	Present in bone and teeth. In optimal amounts in water and diet, reduces dental caries and may minimize bone loss.	1.5–4.0 mg	Drinking water (1 ppm), tea, coffee, rice, soybeans, spinach, gelatin, onions, lettuce.	In areas where fluoride content of water is low, fluoridation of water (1 ppm) has been found beneficial in reducing incidence of dental caries.
Molybdenum	Constituent of an essential enzyme xanthine oxidase and of flavoproteins.	75–250 μg	Legumes, cereal grains, dark green leafy vegetables, organs.	No information.
Cobalt	Constituent of cyanocobalamin (vitamin B_{12}), occurring bound to protein in foods of animal origin. Essential to normal function of all cells, particularly cells of bone marrow, nervous system, and gastrointestinal system.	2.0 μg of vitamin B_{12}	Liver, kidney, oysters, clams, poultry, milk.	Primary dietary inadequacy is rare except when no animal products are consumed. Deficiency may be found in such conditions as lack of gastric intrinsic factor, gastrectomy, and malabsorption syndromes.
Selenium	Associated with fat metabolism, vitamin E, and antioxidant functions.	70 μg—male 55 μg—female	Grains, onions, meats, milk, vegetables variable—depends on selenium content of soil.	Keshan disease is a selenium-deficient state. Deficiency has occurred in patients receiving long-term TPN without selenium.
Chromium	Associated with glucose metabolism.	0.05–0.2 mg	Corn oil, clams, whole-grain cereals, meats, drinking water variable.	Deficiency found in severe malnutrition, may be factor in diabetes in the elderly and cardiovascular disease.
Tin Nickel Vanadium Silicon	} Now known to be essential but no RDA or ESADDI established.			

*RDA = recommended dietary allowance; ESADDI = estimated safe and adequate daily dietary intake.
Source: From *Food Nutrition and Diet Therapy* (p. 137–138), by K. L. Mahan and M. Arlin, 1992, Philadelphia: W. B. Saunders. Used by permission.

Table 10.8 ✦ Recommended Dietary Allowances
for Iron

	AGE (YEARS)	RDA (MG)
Infants	0.0–0.5	6
	0.5–1.0	10
Children	1–3	10
	4–6	10
	7–10	10
Males	11–14	12
	15–18	12
	19–24	10
	25–50	10
	51+	10
Females	11–14	15
	15–18	15
	19–24	15
	25–50	15
	51+	10
	Pregnant	30
	Lactating	
	1st 6 mo	15
	2nd 6 mo	15

Source: From *Recommended Dietary Allowances,* 10th ed. Copyright 1989 by the National Academy of Sciences. Courtesy of the National Academy Press, Washington, DC. Reprinted with permission.

soluble vitamins, which the body stores for long periods, can be toxic. The **megavitamin** approach may result in **hypervitaminosis**. The body also has an adequate reserve storage system for key vitamins and minerals (see Table 10.9) to prevent health problems. This reserve capacity helps prevent deficiencies when you fail to eat right for a few days or weeks, but it should not be relied on for long periods of time.

With very few exceptions, individuals who experience toxicity problems from overdose of a specific vitamin or mineral are involved in heavy supplementation. It is extremely difficult to produce toxic reactions from food intake alone. See Table 10.10 to help decide whether you should consider use of supplementation.

Water

The most critical food component is water. Water is necessary for energy production, temperature control, and elimination. Although water is present in all foods, experts recommend a minimum of 6 to 8

glasses of it daily, exclusive of other fluids, and 12 to 15 glasses when you are trying to lose weight. For a more detailed discussion of daily water needs, see the section entitled "Special Needs of the Active Individual" later in this chapter.

FOOD DENSITY

You can easily determine whether a food item or meal is nutritionally dense by examining the calorie and nutrient content. A high-density food or meal is one that provides more nutrients than calories, or in other words, is low in calories and high in the percentage of key vitamins and minerals you need daily. A good cold cereal with skim milk, for example, provides about 190 calories and 20 to 30 percent of practically all vitamins, minerals, carbohydrates, and protein for the day. Since the cold-cereal breakfast contains only 190 calories and about 8 percent of a 120-lb woman's daily energy needs, the meal is said to be nutritionally dense. Fruits, vegetables, and grains are examples of foods that are dense for a given nutrient or group of nutrients. Potato or corn chips and cake are examples of low-density foods that supply a high percentage of your daily calories and a low percentage of key nutrients.

Cold or hot cereal is an excellent way to start the day. Read the labels and choose cereals that contain no sugar, fat, or sodium and at least two grams of protein and three grams of fiber.

DIETARY GUIDELINES FOR GOOD HEALTH

Describing a practical plan for healthy eating is not as easy as it may sound. Complicated tables and elaborate analysis are impractical for most people. Although some record keeping is needed, a good system should allow some quick, daily spot checking without time-consuming analysis. A basic understanding of RDAs, the nutrition pyramid, and the dietary recommendations for people in the United States provides such a method.

Megavitamin intake Consuming 10 to 100 times the RDA for a particular vitamin.

Hypervitaminosis The toxic side effects that result from the consumption of excess vitamins.

Table 10.9 ✦ Extent of Body Reserves of Nutrients and Nutrient/Health Consequences of Depletion

NUTRIENT	APPROX. TIME TO DEPLETE	POTENTIAL HEALTH IMPLICATIONS
Amino acids	3–4 hours	Although you awake each morning with your amino acids depleted, no health consequences occur.
Calcium	2500 days	The majority of the body's calcium storage is in the skeletal system; drawing on this storage supply for long periods of time will adversely affect the bones.
Carbo-hydrates	12–15 hours	Short-term depletion causes no problems since the body can switch to protein and fat for energy. Long-term use of protein for energy can cause serious health problems.
Fat	25–50 days	Adipose tissue provides approximately 100,000–150,000 kcal of energy and is the body's greatest reserve source of fuel.
Iron	125 days (women) 750 days (men)	Women possess a smaller reserve capacity due to monthly loss of iron in blood during menstruation.
Sodium	2–3 days	After prolonged sweating without food intake, muscle cramps, heat exhaustion and heatstroke may occur.
Vitamin C	60–120 days	Most excess intake of this water-soluble vitamin is excreted in urine.
Vitamin A	90–360 days	Excess intake of this fat-soluble vitamin is stored in the fat cells.
Water	4–5 days	Death.

Recommended Dietary Allowances (RDAs)

Every five years, the Food and Nutritional Board of the National Academy of Sciences' National Research Council reviews the recommended dietary allowances (RDAs) of certain essential nutrients that supply the body with the known nutritional needs for maintaining health in people in the United States. The margin of safety is substantial, and it is estimated that two thirds of the recommended amounts is adequate for most healthy people. Failing to meet the

Table 10.10 ✦ Situations in Which Vitamin and Mineral Supplements May Be Beneficial

SITUATION	SUPPLEMENT TYPE
Oral contraceptive use	Folic acid, vitamin B_6
Pregnancy	Iron, folic acid
Diagnosed deficiency disease (for example, anemias)	As indicated
Vegan diets	B_{12}, vitamin D, zinc, iron
Osteoporosis	Calcium, vitamin D, fluoride
Chronic dieting	Multivitamin and mineral
Use of drugs that interfere with the micronutrients (for example, antihypertensives and antibiotics)	As indicated by type of drug
Diseases that produce malabsorption (for example, cystic fibrosis, celiac disease)	Multivitamin and mineral or as indicated
Inadequate diets due to food allergies, alcoholism, or a narrow selection of food types	Multivitamin and mineral or as indicated by type of deficiency signs

Source: From *The Science of Human Nutrition,* by J. E. Brown. Copyright 1990 by Harcourt Brace & Company. Reproduced by permission of the publisher.

Myth and Fact Sheet

Myth	Fact
1. A candy bar or cola before exercise gives you extra energy.	1. If you eat large amounts of sugar at one time, such as an entire candy bar, the blood releases too much insulin, starting a series of complex chemical reactions. As a result, too much glucose is removed from the blood and stored in the fat cells and liver. This process can leave you with less energy than you would have had without eating the candy bar or drinking an entire can of cola. Sugar also draws fluid from other body parts into the gastrointestinal tract and may contribute to dehydration, distention of the stomach, cramps, nausea, and diarrhea. To avoid these problems, dilute concentrated fruit juices with twice the recommended water, add an equal volume of water to commercial drinks, and eat only small quantities of sugar. Sugar is absorbed faster than the muscles can use it, thus, frequent small amounts are preferable to single doses. Your blood-glucose level will reach a peak about half an hour after consumption, and then rapidly decline. Eating large quantities of sugar causes more rapid decline and greater shortage of glucose for energy.
2. Honey provides quick energy for exercise.	2. For years, honey has been used before, during, and after exercise for quick energy and rapid recovery. Since 40 percent of the sugar in honey is fructose, which is rapidly converted to glycogen, it has been stated that honey will quickly restore glycogen reserves. Unfortunately, there is no evidence to support this theory. There are no quick-energy foods, and honey has the same limitations and advantages of any sugar.
3. Starchy foods are fattening and should be avoided.	3. Starch is the main energy source of complex carbohydrates. Their reputation as fattening is due to the fact that they are normally eaten with fat, such as butter on bread and sour cream on potatoes.
4. Gelatin improves physical fitness.	4. Plain, dry gelatin added to water is almost pure protein. The dessert-type gelatin contains about 4 g of protein and 34 g of carbohydrate. Athletes consider gelatin a good source of protein and a precursor for the formation of phosphocreatine, which helps provide anaerobic energy. The theory advanced is that gelatin may help form phosphocreatine in the muscle. Findings of recent researchers indicate no beneficial effect on performance or on fitness.
5. Wheat germ oil (vitamin E) improves fitness.	5. Recent research suggests that vitamin E may help prevent early heart disease. There is no evidence to support any claims for improved fitness levels.
6. Alcohol keeps you warm and improves performance.	6. The initial increase in warmth comes from dilation of blood vessels near the skin. Actually, after you consume alcoholic drinks, heat loss increases, and you are more susceptible to chilling.
7. Milk cuts your wind and brings on early fatigue.	7. Drinking milk or putting it on cereal does not result in early fatigue or loss of fitness. Skim milk with no fat is still a sound, high-density, nutritional choice.
8. Exercise, particularly swimming, should be avoided following a meal.	8. People have avoided exercise after eating for years, believing that it hindered digestion, brought on stomach cramps, and contributed to drowning. Exercise does slow acid secretion and the movement of food from the stomach during activity and for about an hour later. After this time, there is actually increased digestive action. In the final analysis, over a 12- to 18-hour period, exercise has little effect on the speed of digestion. Performance could be hindered, although that is unlikely, because of the discomfort of overeating or a feeling of lethargy. Stomach cramps while you are swimming are highly unlikely, even if you swim immediately after eating. It may be wise to wait about 45 minutes if you are a beginning swimmer and are tense about the water.

Table 10.11 ♦ Recommended Dietary Allowances [1]

Category	Age (years) or Condition	Weight [2] (kg)	Weight [2] (lb)	Height [2] (cm)	Height [2] (in)	Protein (g)	Fat-Soluble Vitamins A (μg RE) [3]	D (μg) [4]	E (mg α-TE) [5]	K (μg)	Water-Soluble Vitamins C (mg)	Thiamin (mg)	Riboflavin (mg)	Niacin (mg NE) [6]	B6 (mg)	Folate (μg)	B12 (μg)	Minerals Calcium (mg)	Phosphorus (mg)	Magnesium (mg)	Iron (mg)	Zinc (mg)	Iodine (μg)	Selenium (μg)
Infants	0.0–0.5	6	13	60	24	13	375	7.5	3	5	30	0.3	0.4	5	0.3	25	0.3	400	300	40	6	5	40	10
	0.5–1.0	9	20	71	28	14	375	10	4	10	35	0.4	0.5	6	0.6	35	0.5	600	500	60	10	5	50	15
Children	1–3	13	29	90	35	16	400	10	6	15	40	0.7	0.8	9	1.0	50	0.7	800	800	80	10	10	70	20
	4–6	20	44	112	44	24	500	10	7	20	45	0.9	1.1	12	1.1	75	1.0	800	800	120	10	10	90	20
	7–10	28	62	132	52	28	700	10	7	30	45	1.0	1.2	13	1.4	100	1.4	800	800	170	10	10	120	30
Males	11–14	45	99	157	62	45	1000	10	10	45	50	1.3	1.5	17	1.7	150	2.0	1200	1200	270	12	15	150	40
	15–18	66	145	176	69	59	1000	10	10	65	60	1.5	1.8	20	2.0	200	2.0	1200	1200	400	12	15	150	50
	19–24	72	160	177	70	58	1000	10	10	70	60	1.5	1.7	19	2.0	200	2.0	1200	1200	350	10	15	150	70
	25–50	79	174	176	70	63	1000	5	10	80	60	1.5	1.7	19	2.0	200	2.0	800	800	350	10	15	150	70
	51+	77	170	173	68	63	1000	5	10	80	60	1.2	1.4	15	2.0	200	2.0	800	800	350	10	15	150	70
Females	11–14	46	101	157	62	46	800	10	8	45	50	1.1	1.3	15	1.4	150	2.0	1200	1200	280	15	12	150	45
	15–18	55	120	163	64	44	800	10	8	55	60	1.1	1.3	15	1.5	180	2.0	1200	1200	300	15	12	150	50
	19–24	58	128	164	65	46	800	10	8	60	60	1.1	1.3	15	1.6	180	2.0	1200	1200	280	15	12	150	55
	25–50	63	138	163	64	50	800	5	8	65	60	1.1	1.3	15	1.6	180	2.0	800	800	280	15	12	150	55
	51+	65	143	160	63	50	800	5	8	65	60	1.0	1.2	13	1.6	180	2.0	800	800	280	10	12	150	55
Pregnant						60	800	10	10	65	70	1.5	1.6	17	2.2	400	2.2	1200	1200	320	30	15	175	65
Lactating	1st 6 Months					65	1300	10	12	65	95	1.6	1.8	20	2.1	280	2.6	1200	1200	355	15	19	200	75
	2nd 6 Months					62	1200	10	11	65	90	1.6	1.7	20	2.1	260	2.6	1200	1200	340	15	16	200	75

[1] The allowances, expressed as average daily intakes over time, are intended to provide for individual variations among most normal persons as they live in the United States under usual environmental stresses. Diets should be based on a variety of common foods in order to provide other nutrients for which human requirements have been less well defined. See the RDA publication for detailed discussion of allowances and of nutrients not tabulated.

[2] Weights and heights of Reference Adults are actual medians for the U.S. population of the designated age, as reported by NHANES II. The use of these figures does not imply that the height-to-weight ratios are ideal.

[3] Retinol equivalents. 1 retinol equivalent = 1 μg retinol or 6 μg β-carotene.

[4] As cholecalciferol, 10 μg cholecalciferol = 400 IU of vitamin D.

[5] α-Tocopherol equivalents. 1 mg d-α tocopherol = 1 α-TE.

[6] 1 NE (niacin equivalent) is equal to 1 mg of niacin or 60 mg of dietary tryptophan.

Source: From *Recommended Dietary Allowances*, 10th ed. Copyright 1989 by the National Academy of Sciences. Courtesy of the National Academy Press, Washington, DC. Reprinted with permission.

Figure 10.2 ✦ USDA's Food Guide Pyramid. A guide to daily food choices, food groups, and number of servings to consume of each.

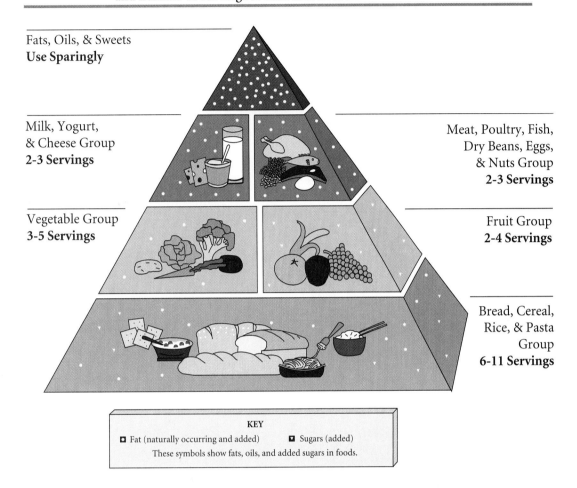

Fats, Oils, & Sweets
Use Sparingly

Milk, Yogurt,
& Cheese Group
2-3 Servings

Meat, Poultry, Fish,
Dry Beans, Eggs,
& Nuts Group
2-3 Servings

Vegetable Group
3-5 Servings

Fruit Group
2-4 Servings

Bread, Cereal,
Rice, & Pasta
Group
6-11 Servings

KEY
▢ Fat (naturally occurring and added)   ◼ Sugars (added)
These symbols show fats, oils, and added sugars in foods.

allowances for one day does not mean you have a deficient diet; the RDAs, however, should average out over a five- to eight-day period. Separate RDAs are provided for infants, children, males, females, and pregnant and lactating women.

The most recent RDAs are shown in Table 10.11. Unless computer software and/or elaborate record keeping is used, the RDA does not provide a practical means of evaluating your daily nutrition. A much easier approach involves the use of the nutrition pyramid and general dietary recommendations.

The Nutrition Pyramid

After decades of use, the basic four food group plan was discarded in favor of the **nutrition pyramid** shown in Figure 10.2. The pyramid contains five food groups and emphasizes complex carbohydrates (fruits, vegetables, and grains). The small space at the top of the pyramid, not a sixth food group, singles out fats, oils, and sweets as items that should be used sparingly or not at all. Neither the meat nor the dairy industry are happy with their tiny spaces on the pyramid, although the number of servings represent the daily needs of most people in the United States. Variety, moderation, and balance, the three key elements of sound nutrition, are met by consuming the recommended number of servings from the five food groups over a five- to seven-day period. Recommended serving sizes are relatively small. A sandwich with two pieces of bread, for example, provides two servings of grains; one egg, two to three ounces of meat, or a small piece of fresh fruit is one serving. Those

Nutrition pyramid New dietary guidelines emphasizing fruits, vegetables, and grains and deemphasizing meats, dairy products, sweets, fats, and oils.

Improving Your Community

Working for Better Nutrition

There can be no doubt that health, wellness, and nutrition are closely related. Nevertheless, surveys of American eating habits reveal some alarming trends. Fast-food restaurants and fast cooking of high-fat, high-salt, and high-calorie foods dominate our lives. Childhood and adult obesity are on the rise. Osteoporosis, cardiovascular disease, and cancer remain major health problems whose development, control, and even prevention have been linked to dietary habits. Generally, we continue to consume too much saturated fat, cholesterol, salt, sugar, alcohol, coffee, tea, soft drinks, and calories, and too little water, fruits, vegetables, and grains.

There are a number of things you can start doing now to help yourself and others adopt healthier nutritional habits.

1. First, and perhaps toughest of all, adopt healthier eating habits for yourself and set an example of friends, family, and acquaintances. As a college student, it's easy for you to eat "on the run" and not really think about what you're eating. Make a conscious effort every day to cut down on fast foods and high-calorie, high-fat, and high-salt snacks by brown bagging healthy breakfasts, lunches, and snacks that feature whole-grain breads, fruit juices with no added sugar, and fresh fruits and vegetables.

2. Get involved with student groups that work for the availability of healthier food choices for students and a reduction in the number of unhealthy snacks in food vending machines. Ask about such groups at your student council or fraternity or sorority council offices.

3. After securing permission from the university administration, devise a brief survey form for distribution to students in dormitories and cafeterias. You may be able to use results of the survey to convince food service managers and university administrators of the need for certain changes in nutritional offerings in the cafeteria. Here is a sample survey:

Food Survey

This is a survey to find out how many of the students who use this cafeteria would like to see more vegetarian food choices.

Are you a vegetarian?

_____Yes   _____No

If so, what kind of vegetarian are you?

_____ Vegan (I eat vegetables only; no meat, eggs, milk, or other dairy products).
_____ Lactovegetarian (I eat vegetables and all dairy products; no meat or eggs).
_____ Ovolactovegetarian (I eat vegetables, all dairy products, and eggs; no meat).
_____ Semi-vegetarian (I eat all foods except red meat).

If you're *not* a vegetarian, would you nevertheless like to see more vegetarian food choices in your cafeteria?

_____Yes   _____No

General Question I: If more vegetarian food choices were available in this cafeteria, would you include them more often in your diet?

_____Yes   _____No

General Question II: Do you have any suggestions for changing or improving the nutritional choices available in this cafeteria?

Thank you for your cooperation.

4. Create a series of "Nutrition Tips" you can write or have printed on single sheets of 8 1/2-by-11-inch paper or on larger sheets of colored construction paper. Designate a day of each week as "Nutrition Awareness Day" and post your Nutrition Tips on bulletin boards in your house, dormitory, or cafeteria.

5. Working with classmates or other interested friends, develop a brief 15-to-30-minute presentation on sound basic nutrition. Be sure to make use of pictures, charts, slides, overhead transparencies and even recorded music. Now take the program out into the community, perhaps to local elementary, middle, and secondary schools. Call local PTAs and school administrators to discuss appropriate formats and dates for your presentation. ✦

who follow the nutritional pyramid will consume less total fat, saturated fat, cholesterol, sugar, salt, and calories and more fruits, vegetables, grains, and dietary fiber.

Dietary Guidelines

The U.S. Department of Agriculture and the U.S. Department of Health and Human Services have listed seven dietary guidelines that have implications for good health:

1. Eat a variety of foods.
2. Maintain ideal weight.
3. Avoid too much fat, especially saturated fat, and cholesterol.
4. Eat foods with adequate starch and fiber.
5. Avoid too much sugar.
6. Avoid too much sodium.
7. If you drink alcohol, do so in moderation.

An awareness of these guidelines is also helpful for daily nutritious eating.

Table 10.12 compares the current U.S. dietary intake of food and drink with the proposed dietary goals or recommendations. In most areas, our current dietary intake in percent of daily calories fails to

Table 10.12   ✦   Summary of Dietary Recommendations to the American Public

NUTRIENT	CURRENT DIETARY INTAKE	PROPOSED DIETARY GOALS
Carbohydrate	50% of daily calories	58% of daily calories
Simple	24%	10%
Refined and processed sugars	18%	5% or less
Naturally occurring sugars (in fruits, vegetables, and grains)	6%	6–8%
		5%
Complex Fruits, vegetables, and grains	26%	48%
Protein	13% of daily calories	12%
Total Fat	36–38%	30%
Saturated	14–18%	10%
Monounsaturated	14–18%	10%
Polyunsaturated	7%	10%
Cholesterol	500–1000 mg	less than 300 mg
Salt[1]	6–18 g	less than 5 g(1100–3300 mg)
Dietary fiber	11 g	25–35 g
Fluid		
Water	2–3 glasses[2]	6–8 glasses, 10–12 if on any type of diet
Alcohol	—	Less than 10% of daily calories, 1/2–1 oz alcohol; no more than 1 (women) to 2 (men) drinks daily
Carbonated Drinks	—	No more than l–2 daily
Coffee or Tea	—	No more than l–2 daily

[1]Salt substitutes that contain potassium chloride may not be wise choices. Some evidence indicates that it is the chloride in salt (sodium chloride), not the sodium, that is associated with high blood pressure in some individuals. Salt substitutes containing potassium also contain chloride.

[2]Results of a four-year survey of students at Virginia Commonwealth University, 1986–1990.

Source: Adapted from *Exploring Health: Expanding the Boundaries of Wellness* (p. 176), by J. Greenberg and G. B. Dintiman, 1992. Englewood Cliffs, NJ: Prentice-Hall.

Diets that include five servings of fruits and vegetables seem to be protective against heart disease and cancer. In addititon, they replace unhealthy foods, such as foods high in fats. (Photo courtesy of the American Cancer Institute.)

meet the proposed goals. There is too much total fat in our total daily calories (36 to 38 percent instead of 30 percent), saturated fat (14 to 18 percent instead of 10 percent), and sugar (24 percent instead of 10 percent) and too little total carbohydrates (50 percent instead of 58 percent) and complex carbohydrates (26 percent instead of 48 percent). In addition, we consume too much cholesterol (500 to 1,000 mg instead of less than 300 mg), salt (6 to 19 g instead of 5 g), and alcohol; too many carbonated drinks; too much coffee and tea; too many total calories; and not

Recommended daily intakes (RDIs) The levels of intake of essential nutrients considered adequate to meet the known nutritional needs of healthy persons in the United States.

enough water. It is obvious that our eating habits are much more influenced by taste than they are by concern for our own health. To compare your nutritional practices to the standards in Table 10.12 complete Lab Activity 10.2: Do You Meet the U.S. Government Dietary Recommendations? at the end of the chapter.

FOOD LABELING

The Food and Drug Administration (FDA) is responsible for food labeling, excluding meat, poultry, and alcoholic beverages, in the United States, while the Federal Trade Commission (FTC) regulates the advertising of food products and takes action, through the FDA, against unsubstantiated food claims. Although fresh fruits, vegetables, and meats were not subject to labeling requirements in the past, most of them now contain labels. Foods with a *standard of identity*—those that filed a specific recipe with the FDA—were also once exempt from listing ingredients unless special items, such as extra spices and flavors, were added. Catsup, ice cream, mustard, and mayonnaise all fell into this category. Before 1994, over 60 percent of all food and beverages sold in the United States contained a nutrition label; about half of these were voluntarily provided by manufacturers.

The new law that went into effect in May 1994 requires the majority of food products to be labeled and to follow strict guidelines (see Figure 10.3). New food labels, previously called the U.S. RDAs, are now called **recommended daily intakes (RDIs)**. With the new labels, the daily recommended values (DRVs) have been determined by the FDA for parts of the diet not covered by the 1989 RDA labels, such as carbohydrates, fats, and dietary fiber.

General changes resulting from the new law are as follows:

- Practically all products must contain a label.

- Specific listings on the label concerning health claims must be accurate and must keep pace with changing health concerns in the United States.

- Names of nutrient allowances have been changed to percent of *daily value* (DV). RDIs and DRVs are used as reference values to show how the nutrients contribute toward a sound diet.

- A *dictionary of terms* with consistent and uni-

Figure 10.3 ✦ The Nutrition Label

Serving Size

Is your serving the same size as the one on the label? If you eat double the serving size listed, you need to double the nutrient and calorie values. If you eat one-half the serving size shown here, cut the nutrient and calorie values in half.

Calories

Are you overweight? Cut back a little on calories! Look here to see how a serving of the food adds to your daily total. A 5'4", 138-lb. active woman needs about 2,200 calories each day. A 5'10", 174-lb. active man needs about 2,900. How about you?

Total Carbohydrate

When you cut down on fat, you can eat more carbohydrates. Carbohydrates are in foods like bread, potatoes, fruits and vegetables. Choose these often! They give you more nutrients than **sugars** like soda pop and candy.

Dietary Fiber

Grandmother called it "roughage," but her advice to eat more is still up-to-date! That goes for both soluble and insoluble kinds of dietary fiber. Fruits, vegetables, whole-grain foods, beans and peas are all good sources and can help reduce the risk of heart disease and cancer.

Protein

Most Americans get more protein than they need. Where there is animal protein, there is also fat and cholesterol. Eat small servings of lean meat, fish and poultry. Use skim or low-fat milk, yogurt, and cheese. Try vegetable proteins like beans, grains and cereals.

Vitamins & Minerals

Your goal here is 100% of each for the day. Don't count on one food to do it all. Let a combination of foods add up to a winning score.

Nutrition Facts

Serving Size 1/2 cup (114g)
Servings Per Container 4

Amount Per Serving

Calories 90	Calories from Fat 30

	% Daily value*
Total Fat 3g	**5%**
Saturated Fat 0g	**0%**
Cholesterol 0mg	**0%**
Sodium 300mg	**13%**
Total Carbohydrate 13g	**4%**
Dietary Fiber 3g	**12%**
Sugars 3g	
Protein 3g	

Vitamin A 80%	Vitamin C 60%
Calcium 4%	Iron 4%

* Percent Daily Values are based on a 2,000 calorie diet. Your daily values may be higher or lower depending on your calorie needs:

	Calories	2,000	2,500
Total Fat	Less than	65g	80g
Sat Fat	Less than	20g	25g
Cholesterol	Less than	300mg	300mg
Sodium	Less than	2,400mg	2,400mg
Total Carbohydrate		300g	375g
Fiber		25g	30g

Calories per gram:
Fat 9 • Carbohydrate 4 • Protein 4

More nutrients may be listed on some labels.

Total Fat

Aim low: Most people need to cut back on fat! Too much fat may contribute to heart disease and cancer. Try to limit your **calories from fat.** For a healthy heart, choose foods with a big difference between the total number of calories and the number of calories from fat.

Saturated Fat

A new kind of fat? No – saturated fat is part of the total fat in food. It is listed separately because it's the key player in raising blood cholesterol and your risk of heart disease. Eat less!

Cholesterol

Too much cholesterol – a second cousin to fat – can lead to heart disease. Challenge yourself to eat less than 300 mg each day.

Sodium

You call it "salt," the label calls it "sodium." Either way, it may add up to high blood pressure in some people. So, keep your sodium intake low – 2,400 to 3,000 mg or less each day.*

*The AHA recommends no more than 3,000 mg sodium per day for healthy adults

Daily Value

Feel like you're drowning in numbers ? Let the Daily Value be your guide. Daily Values are listed for people who eat 2,000 or 2,500 calories each day. If you eat more, your personal daily value may be higher than what's listed on the label. If you eat less, your personal daily value may be lower.

For fat, saturated fat, cholesterol and sodium choose foods with a low % **Daily Value**. For total carbohydrate, dietary fiber, vitamins and minerals, your daily value goal is to reach 100% of each.

g = grams (About 28 g = 1 ounce)
mg = milligrams (1,000 mg = 1 g)

Key Words: *Fat Free:* Less than 0.6 g of fat per serving; *Low Fat:* 3 g of fat or less per serving; *Lean:* Less than 10 g of fat, 4 g of saturated fat and 96 mg of cholesterol per serving; *Light (Lite):* 1/2 less calories or no more than 1/2 the fat of the higher-calorie, higher-fat version; or no more than 1/2 the sodium of the higher-sodium version; *Cholesterol Free:* Less than 2 mg of cholesterol and 2 g or less of saturated fat per serving. **To Make Health Claims About...The Food Must be...**Heart Disease and Fats: Low in fat, saturated fat and cholesterol; Blood Pressure and Sodium: Low in sodium; Heart Disease and Fruits, Vegetables, and Grain Products: A fruit, vegetable, or grain product low in fat, saturated fat and cholesterol, that contains at least 0.6 g soluble fiber, without fortification, per serving.

Source: Food and Drug Administration, American Heart Association, 1993.

form definitions has been developed for terms such as *free, low, high, source of, light, reduced, less, more, fat free, low fat, no cholesterol,* and *high fiber.*

- Definitions must be specific for fatty acid and cholesterol content.

Specific changes now require that labels include:

- Cholesterol content.
- Saturated fat content.
- Total dietary fiber.
- Total calories from fat, saturated fat, complex carbohydrates, and sugars.
- Polyunsaturated and monounsaturated fats and water-soluble and -insoluble fibers are required if a health claim is made for the product.

- Thiamin, niacin, riboflavin, and other nutrients are optional in listings since the concern about deficiencies is no longer valid.

Nutrition labeling reform was long overdue to eliminate misleading and false advertising by manufacturers who seemed to change their lines only when the majority of people in the United States became aware of a specific nutritional practice. Public knowledge of the hazards of dietary cholesterol and sodium prompted such changes. Unfortunately, manufacturers produce and advertise as low-cholesterol products, foods that actually contain saturated fat, which is known to elevate blood cholesterol levels. That practice and numerous other attempts at deception should be eliminated by the new labeling regulations. False claims, such as "95 percent fat free" and "2 percent fat," which referred to the weight of the fat content and not the percent of total calories from fat, will also be eliminated.

Reform is of little value, however, unless people develop the habit of reading food labels before making selections. The dietary guidelines discussed here will help focus on the key aspects for making quick decisions about products. For many products, it is only necessary to look for a reasonable portion size; the number of calories; and zero grams of fat, cholesterol, salt, sodium, and sugar. Since it is difficult to avoid these health-related ingredients, which also occur naturally in some foods, it is wise to purchase processed foods (any food item that is packaged) with these ingredients absent or in very low quantities.

NUTRITION-DISEASE RELATIONSHIPS

Scientific evidence associating diet with numerous diseases has increased in the past decade. Although cause-and-effect relationships are still rather uncommon, dietary risk factors have been identified for a number of diseases and disorders (see Table 10.13), and the consumption of various nutrients has been associated with the prevention of some diseases.

High-fat diets have been linked to cardiorespiratory disease and cancer; high sodium and alcohol intake to a small percentage of the hypertense popu-

Table 10.13 ✦ Nutrition Risk Factors Associated with the Development of Diseases and Disorders

DISEASE OR DISORDER	NUTRITION RISK FACTORS
Heart disease and atherosclerosis ("hardening of the arteries")	Diets high in animal fat and cholesterol; obesity
Cancer*	Diets high in fat and low in vitamin A, beta-carotene, dietary fiber, and certain types of vegetables
Diabetes (in adults)	Obesity
Cirrhosis of the liver	Excessive alcohol consumption, malnutrition
Infertility	Underweight, obesity, zinc deficiency (in men)
Health problems of pregnant women and newborns	Maternal underweight, obesity, malnutrition, and excessive use of vitamin and mineral supplements or alcohol
Growth retardation in children	Diets low in calories, protein, iron, zinc
Tooth decay	Frequent consumption of sweets, diets low in fluoride
Iron-deficiency anemia	Diets low in iron
Constipation	Diets low in fiber and fluids
Obesity	Excessive calorie intake
Underweight	Deficient calorie intake
Hypertension	Diets high in sodium, excessive alcohol consumption, obesity
Osteoporosis	Diets low in calcium and vitamin D

*The development of most types of cancer, notably excluding leukemia, have been associated with nutrition risk factors.

Source: From *The Science of Human Nutrition,* by J. E. Brown. Copyright 1990 by Harcourt Brace & Company. Reproduced by permission of the publisher.

lation; and high-calorie intake and obesity to high blood pressure, diabetes, cardiorespiratory disease, and cancer. On the other hand, diets high in complex carbohydrates (fruits, vegetables, and grains) that contain vitamin A, beta-carotene, dietary fiber, and cruciferous vegetables have been tied to the prevention of cancer (colon, stomach, and so forth), diverticulitis, and constipation; and low-fat diets with the prevention of cardiorespiratory disease and certain types of cancer.

The prevention of osteoporosis is associated with adequate intake of calcium, vitamin D, and fluoride; weight-bearing exercise; a reduction in bone toxins produced from cigarettes and alcohol, and hormone therapy. The idea is to reach menopause with as much bone mass as possible by practicing a drug-free lifestyle, sound nutrition, and regular aerobic exercise. Although hormone-replacement therapy is effective in treating osteoporosis and providing protection from heart disease, many women choose to avoid or abandon such therapy due to the side effects (weight gain, depression, menstrual bleeding and cramps, a slightly higher risk of breast cancer). Fortunately, a new nonhormonal drug, Fosamax, has been shown not only to slow the process by which bone mineral is lost but also to increase the replenishment phase, resulting in a net gain of bone mass. Evidence suggests that the use of Fosamax increases bone mass by an average of 10 percent and significantly cuts the number and severity of bone fractures in postmenopausal women. To date, the only side effects reported in a small number of patients is a slight abdominal pain, which eventually disappeared.

Consumers must resist the temptation to consume large amounts of any nutrient identified as having the potential for disease prevention until supportive evidence is found. In early 1996, National Cancer Institute researchers shut down a $42 million vitamin study of 18,000 smokers almost two years early, because too many of those being given high doses of beta-carotene supplements were dying. The government declared that beta-carotene supplements do not protect Americans against cancer or heart disease and might increase a smoker's risk of deadly tumors. Another study of 22,000 doctors receiving mega-doses (10 times the average recommended daily intake) of beta-carotene for 12 years found no evidence of harm nor any benefit from beta-carotene supplementation.

Evidence suggests that supplementation in many areas does not adequately replace the complex mix of chemicals and the high-fiber low-fat benefits in food such as fruits, vegetables, and grains. The fact that phytochemicals and antioxidants found in food may help prevent disease does not necessarily mean that heavy intake through supplementation will produce similar effects. Once again, it is important for you to stress moderation, variation, and balance in all aspects of your diet.

SPECIAL NEEDS OF THE ACTIVE INDIVIDUAL

Active individuals who follow the nutritional plan already presented in this chapter have a few special nutritional needs. There are five other areas of concern for those who exercise three to seven times weekly:

1. Eating enough calories for energy and body repair in order to benefit fully from the conditioning program.
2. Eating a sufficient amount of carbohydrates and fats to spare the body from using protein as fuel.
3. Drinking sufficient fluids to prevent dehydration, heat-related illness, and early fatigue.
4. Replacing electrolytes (potassium, sodium, and chloride) lost in perspiration.
5. Considering the use of iron supplements (for women).

Eating Enough Calories

If you are neither losing nor gaining weight, you are taking in the correct number of calories daily to maintain your present weight and fat level. Weigh yourself

Developing wellness means adopting a healthy lifestyle that includes, among other variables, physical activity and eating well. (Photo courtesy The Aspen Hill Club.)

Table 10.14 ✦ Approximate Number of Calories Needed Daily Per Pound of Body Weight

AGE RANGES	7–10	11–14	15–22	23–35	36–50	51–75
Males						
Very active	21–22	23–24	25–27	23–24	21–22	19–20
Moderately active	16–17	18–19	20–23	18–29	16–17	11–15
Sedentary	11–12	13–14	15–18	13–14	11–12	10–11
Females						
Very active	21–22	22–23	20–21	20–21	18–19	17–18
Moderately active	16–17	18–19	16–18	16–17	14–15	12–13
Sedentary	11–12	13–14	11–12	11–12	9–10	8–9

Sedentary—No physical activity beyond attending classes and desk work.

Moderately active—Involved in a regular exercise program at least three times weekly.

Very active—Involved in a regular aerobic exercise program four to six times weekly, expending more than 2,500 calories per week during physical activity.

at exactly the same time of day and under the same conditions, preferably in the morning on rising. If no weight gain or loss is occurring, there is no real need for complicated record keeping of caloric intake and expenditure, unless you wish to lose or gain weight.

You can estimate the number of calories you need from Table 10.14. Multiply your body weight times the calories recommended per pound for your activity level. This is only an estimate of your needs. Your body has an infallible computer that accurately registers your caloric intake daily; the output is body-weight changes. Complete Lab Activity 10.3 Estimating Caloric Expenditures for a more accurate indication of your energy expenditure.

Your source of calories is also an important factor in providing sufficient energy for exercise. The percentage of calories from carbohydrates, fats, and protein, shown in Table 10.12, is sufficient for most exercising individuals. Increasing your complex carbohydrate (fruits, vegetables, and grains) intake from 48 percent to 60 percent of total calories will increase your energy level. Total fat intake should be decreased by 10 to 12 percent.

Protein Sparing

Eating sufficient fruits, vegetables, and grains is extremely critical for the exercising individual. When the body does not have adequate carbohydrates available for energy, it will convert dietary protein and lean protein mass (muscle) to glucose to supply the nervous system. When this occurs, loss of lean muscle tissue takes place throughout the body, including major organs such as the heart. Failing to spare protein for long periods of time may jeopardize health. A high percentage of complex carbohydrates in your diet will spare protein, provide a high level of energy, and protect your health.

Carbohydrate Loading or Supercompensation

The body has an adequate supply of energy available in the form of glucose and glycogen for performing regular exercise or competing in a sport. Glucose (sugar in the blood available for energy) and glycogen (the chief storage form of carbohydrate) are available in the blood, muscles, and liver and provide sufficient energy for most anaerobic workouts.

Individuals who compete in marathons, triathlons, and other endurance contests lasting several hours need additional energy and can benefit from a technique called **carbohydrate loading**, or **supercompensation**. New evidence indicates that the depletion stage may be unnecessary. By merely increasing carbohydrate intake three to four days before an important exercise activity or competition, liver and muscle glycogen stores will more than double. Such an increase provides approximately 3,060 calories of energy—enough for practically any endurance event. Two large, high-carbohydrate meals (300 g, 1,200 kcal per meal) are recommended daily for three or four days.

Replacing Fluids (Water)

Water needs depend on the individual and on factors such as body weight, activity patterns, sweat loss, loss through expired air and urine, and the amount

Figure 10.4 ✦ Water Intake and Loss

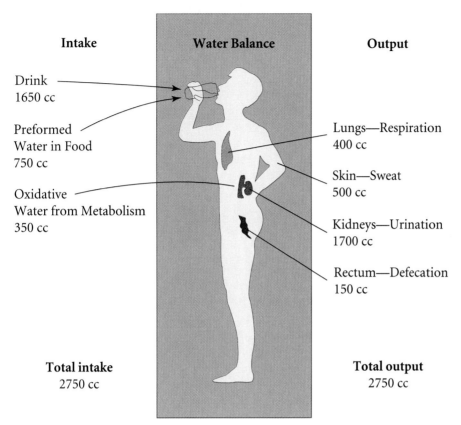

Intake

Drink
1650 cc

Preformed
Water in Food
750 cc

Oxidative
Water from Metabolism
350 cc

Total intake
2750 cc

Water Balance

Output

Lungs—Respiration
400 cc

Skin—Sweat
500 cc

Kidneys—Urination
1700 cc

Rectum—Defecation
150 cc

Total output
2750 cc

Source: David C. Nieman et al., *Nutrition,* Revised First Edition, Copyright © 1992 Wm. C. Brown Communications, Inc. All rights reserved. Reprinted by permission.

of liquid consumed through other foods and drinks (see Figure 10.4).

The active individual needs a minimum of 8 to 10 glasses (2 quarts or more) of water daily—much more in hot, humid weather. It is not unusual to lose 1 to 2 liters of water per hour when exercising in extremely hot, humid weather. Drinking too much water generally poses no problem; water is rarely toxic, and the kidneys merely excrete it efficiently. The kidneys are also capable of conserving water when the body is deprived by excreting more highly concentrated urine. If the color of your urine is darker than a manila folder, you need to consume additional water (not fluid from other drinks). In our own surveys of undergraduate students at Virginia Commonwealth University, we have found that the college-aged generation is becoming a waterless society, as soft drinks, coffee, tea, cocoa, beer, wine coolers, and juices dominate palates. The average daily intake of water, as shown in a June 1990 survey we conducted, was slightly less than two glasses. These findings were almost identical to the results of a similar survey we conducted in 1980. More soda, coffee, tea, and

beer were consumed than water. It bears stating again that the body needs plain water for heat regulation and proper functioning of systems.

If you exercise in hot, humid weather, thirst sensations will underestimate your needs. By the time you are thirsty, a water deficit has been created that

Carbohydrate loading (supercompensation) An attempt to reduce carbohydrate intake to near zero for two to three days (depletion stage) before resorting to a high-carbohydrate diet for three to four days (loading phase). The object is to raise glycogen stores in skeletal muscles and the liver and increase energy levels on the day of competition.

Electrolytes Chemical compounds (water, sodium, potassium, and chloride) in solution in the human body that are capable of producing electric current; important in the prevention of cramps, heat exhaustion, and heatstroke.

Behavioral Change and Motivational Strategies

People in the 1990s are more educated about nutrition than previous generations have been. Unfortunately, knowledge about proper nutrition does not readily translate into sound eating behavior. Busy schedules, lack of money, fad diet and nutrition information, easy access to fast-food restaurants, youthful feelings of inde-structibility, culture and religion, and many other factors help explain why, in spite of this knowledge, the typ-ical diet of people in the United States is too high in saturated fat, cholesterol, total fat, calories, sodium, and sugar and too low in complex carbohydrates (fruits, vegetables, and grains) and water. These problems are very much related to present and future health, behavior, mood, and energy level. With only minimum effort, some of these problems can be corrected.

Roadblock	Behavioral Change Strategy
Some people just do not seem to like water and therefore consume less than three of the recommend-ed six to eight glasses daily. Most liquid consumed is coffee, tea, or high-calorie (150 kcal per 12-oz serving) soft drinks, juices, milk, beer, and other alcoholic drinks. Avoiding water allows more room for calories and salt, sugar, and fat.	You can change your liquid consumption patterns slowly and reacquire your taste for water. For a seven-day period, try: 1. Placing your favorite glass in the bathroom and drinking one full glass of water immediately on rising in the morning and just before bed-time. You are now already drinking more water than most people do. 2. Not passing a water fountain, even if you are not thirsty. Take at least five swallows (about three oz). 3. Placing a cold pitcher of water in the front of your refrigerator so it is the first thing you see. 4. Drinking at least one glass of water with each meal.
So much of what we eat is processed food, which is typically high in sodium. There seems to be no way of avoiding the problem.	Although high sodium intake may not be as much of a health hazard as originally suspected, it is a good idea to cut back. About one-third of the salt you consume comes from processed food, one-third from table salt, and the rest occurs naturally in food. There are a number of things you can do: 1. Restrict your visits to fast-food restaurants to no more than once a month. 2. Avoid or use very little table salt, substituting herbs and spices such as lemon and orange. Use a salt substitute that does not contain sodium potassium. Plan on three or four weeks to become adjusted to not adding table salt to your food. 3. Read food labels and purchase products with no or low salt. 4. Avoid luncheon meats, smoked meats, hot dogs, sausage, and high-salt cheeses.
Although you are aware of the association between high total fat, high saturated fat, high-cholesterol diets, and heart disease, it is just too difficult to avoid high fat in the diet.	It does seem that way, particularly if you eat on the run and do not have time to plan meals. There are some specific things you can do that are certain to reduce the percent of calories you consume from fat daily: 1. Take the time to glance at the label of every product you purchase. If it does not say it has zero grams of fat, do not buy it. 2. If you eat ice cream, purchase one of the brands that uses artificial fat; the taste is excellent and the product is nearly fat- and cholesterol-free. 3. Pack a lunch every day consisting of fruit, vegetables, and a low-calorie sandwich. This will keep you from skipping a meal or running to a fast-food restaurant during the day.

Roadblock	Behavioral Change Strategy
	4. Reduce your intake of invisible fat by reducing your consumption of chocolate, eggs, red meat, poultry skin, and dairy products. 5. Cut the skin off the raw poultry before cooking, avoid frying, and choose cooking methods that do not require the use of oils. 6. Use paper towels to soak up the fat when you cook hamburger and other meats.
List some roadblocks that interfere with your following sound nutritional practices. 1. _____ 2. _____ 3. _____	Now, cite behavior-change strategies that can help you overcome the roadblocks you just listed. If you need to, refer back to chapter 3 for behavior change and motivational strategies. 1. _____ 2. _____ 3. _____

cannot be undone for several hours. Forced drinking (hydrating), even when no thirst sensation exists, will minimize water deficit, keep body temperature one or two degrees lower in hot weather, result in more efficient performance, and delay fatigue. The most beneficial approach is to force down an extra 16 to 32 ounces of water less than 15 minutes before you begin to exercise. Earlier consumption may fill the bladder and make you uncomfortable during the activity.

Water will not interfere with your performance; drink it freely before, during, and after your workout. It is the single most important substance in preventing heat-related illnesses and in restoring the body to normal following exercise in hot, humid weather. For the quickest absorption of fluid, drink plain water chilled to about 40° F. (Water plays an important role in preventing heat exhaustion, muscle cramps, and heatstroke—see chapter 14.)

Maintaining Electrolyte Balance

Electrolytes lost through sweat and water vapor from the lungs must be replaced. It is the proper balance of each electrolyte that prevents dehydration, cramping, heat exhaustion, and heatstroke. Too much salt without adequate water, for example, actually draws fluid from the cells, precipitates nausea, and increases urination and potassium loss. A salt supplement is therefore rarely needed, in spite of the weather or intensity and duration of exercise. The salt that occurs naturally in food, salt in processed food, and that used from the salt shaker will provide sufficient sodium even for active individuals.

Potassium is critical to maintaining regular heartbeat, and it also plays a role in carbohydrate and protein metabolism. Profuse sweating over several days can deplete potassium stores by as much as 3 mg per day. The average diet provides only 1.5 to 2.5 mg daily. If you sweat profusely and exercise almost daily, you may need five to eight servings of potassium-rich foods each day. Excellent sources of potassium include orange juice, skim milk, bananas, dried fruits, and potatoes. A potassium supplement is not recommended since too much potassium is just as dangerous as too little.

Ionic chloride is part of hydrochloric acid and serves to maintain the strong acidity of the stomach. Loss of too much chloride upsets the acid-base balance of the body. Adding chlorine to public water provides this valuable element and makes water safe for human consumption.

Water alone will not restore electrolyte balance. One alternative is to use commercially prepared, concentrated electrolyte drinks, providing you alter their contents. Some of these drinks contain too much sugar and should be diluted with twice the normal amount of water to increase absorption time and prevent a rapid drop in blood-glucose level shortly after consumption.

While it is useful before and after exercise, the addition of electrolytes to water is of minimal value during a workout. Research suggests that electrolyte replacement is also secondary in importance to water replacement during rehydration after exercise. Fruit juices have the same pitfalls as commercial electrolyte drinks, and the concentrated varieties should be diluted with at least twice the amount of water suggested on the container.

Replacing Iron

Iron deficiency can lead to loss of strength and endurance, early fatigue during exercise, shortening of attention span, loss of visual perception, and im-

paired learning. Check the results of Lab Activity 10.2: Do You Meet the U.S. Government Dietary Recommendations? to see if you are consuming enough iron. Adolescent girls are more apt to be iron-deficient than women are at any other age. During menstruation, female athletes of all ages should discuss the need for an iron supplement with their physicians.

SUMMARY

Basic Food Components

Six categories of nutrients satisfy the basic body needs: the energy nutrients (carbohydrates, fats, and proteins) and the nonenergy nutrients (vitamins, minerals, and water).

Carbohydrates and fats provide the main sources of energy (kcal) to perform work. Simple carbohydrates found in concentrated sugar provide empty calories to the diet and very little nutrition in terms of key vitamins and minerals. Complex carbohydrates (fruits, vegetables, and grains) are our only source of fiber and a major supplier of long-term energy. Complex carbohydrates are nutritionally dense foods, providing low calories and a high percentage of our daily needs in vitamins and minerals. Both water-insoluble (dietary) and water-soluble fibers provide important health benefits.

Dietary fat is a critical nutrient and a source of high energy for the human body. Fat is classified as saturated, polyunsaturated, or monounsaturated. Cholesterol, a type of fat, is found in animal sources and also manufactured by the human liver.

Protein can be obtained from both animal and plant foods. In the human body, protein is used for the repair, rebuilding, and replacement of cells; growth; fluid, salt, acid-base balance; and energy in the absence of sufficient dietary carbohydrate and fat. Protein from meat, eggs, and dairy products is termed *complete* since it contains all the essential amino acids in the correct proportion. The correct combinations of various vegetables and grains also make up complete protein sources. With proper planning, vegetarians can easily obtain sufficient protein in their diets without consuming meat, eggs, or dairy products.

Vitamins help chemical reactions take place in the body and are needed in only small amounts. A

balanced diet provides the necessary vitamins and minerals needed daily for most people.

Minerals are present in all living cells and serve as components of hormones, enzymes, and other substances aiding chemical reactions in cells. Macro-minerals are needed in large amounts, whereas 14 trace minerals are required in small quantities for optimum health. Your daily mineral needs can also be obtained through a balanced diet.

Although it has no nutritional value, water is necessary for all energy production, temperature control, and elimination. A minimum of six to eight glasses of water should be consumed daily, exclusive of all other beverages.

Food Density

A food is said to be nutritionally dense if it contains a low percentage of the daily caloric needs and a high percentage of key nutrients such as protein, vitamins, and minerals. Complex carbohydrates are the most nutritionally dense foods; foods high in fat are the least dense.

Dietary Guidelines for Good Health

You can be assured of sound nutrition by planning your diet around the nutrition pyramid. The recommended servings from each of five key food groups and the limited use of the sixth group (fats, oils, and sweets) will provide you with excellent nutrition. The pyramid offers a less complicated approach to sound nutrition for the layperson than RDA tables and complicated calculations do.

Dietary recommendations have also been made in terms of percentage of total calories to guide your intake of carbohydrates, protein, fat, and alcohol.

Specific guidelines in grams or milligrams are also available for fiber, salt, and cholesterol.

Nutrition and Disease

The evidence associating nutritional practices with various diseases and disorders and linking sound nutrition to the prevention of some of these diseases continues to mount. Diets that are high in complex carbohydrates and low in fat, cholesterol, sodium, and calories offer the greatest advantage.

Special Needs of the Active Individual

Physically active individuals who follow the nutritional guidelines presented in this chapter have only a few special needs. Sufficient calories must be consumed to support activity levels and to prevent weight and muscle loss; adequate carbohydrates and fat must be consumed to prevent the loss of lean muscle mass; water intake should increase dramatically; electrolyte balance must be maintained; and care must be taken to obtain sufficient dietary iron.

𝑅EFERENCES

Cataldo, C. B., & Nyenhuis, J. R. (1989). *Nutrition and diet therapy: Principles and practice,* 2nd ed. St. Paul: West Publishing.

Dupuy, N. A., & Mermel, V. L. (1995). *Focus on nutrition.* St. Louis: Mosby.

International Center for Sports Nutrition and the United States Olympic Committee. (1990). *Vegetarianism—Implications for athletes.* International Center for Sports Nutrition.

Katch, F. I., & McArdle, M. T. (1992). *Introduction to nutrition, exercise and health* 4th ed. (1993). Philadelphia-London: Lea & Febiger.

Mahan, L. K., & Arlin, M. T. (1992). *Krause's food, nutrition and dietary therapy,* 8th ed. Philadelphia: W. B. Saunders.

Sizer, F., & Whitney, E. (1994). *Nutrition: Concepts and controversies,* 6th ed. (1993, January). St. Paul: West Publishing.

Testing the food guide pyramid. (1993, January). *Eating Well.*

Toussaint-Samat, M. (1993). *History of food.* Cambridge, MA: Blackwell Publishers.

U.S. Department of Agriculture, Agricultural Research Service, Dietary Guidelines Advisory Committee. (1995) *Report of the Dietary Guidelines Advisory Committee on the dietary guidelines for Americans.*

Whitney, E. N., Hamilton, E. M. N., & Rolfes, S. R. (1990). *Understanding nutrition, 5th ed.* St. Paul: West Publishing.

Williams, M. H. (1995). *Nutrition for fitness and sport,* 4th ed. Madison, WI: Brown & Benchmark

Lab Activity 10.1

Estimating Your Daily Fiber Intake

INSTRUCTIONS: *Record all the fiber-containing foods you eat for a period of three days in the chart below. Remember that you must only keep records of the amount and portion size of all fruits, vegetables, and grains eaten.*

   To help you estimate the grams of fiber in each food item consumed, turn to Table 10.2. Now record the number of grams of dietary fiber you consume in each food daily in the last column. Divide the total grams by three to determine your average daily intake.

✦   **Record of Daily Fiber Intake**

DAY	FOOD ITEM	SIZE OR AMOUNT	GRAMS OF FIBER
1	Fruits:		
	Vegetables:		
	Grains:		
2	Fruits:		
	Vegetables:		
	Grains:		
3	Fruits:		
	Vegetables:		
	Grains:		

Total grams of dietary fiber in three days _____

Average grams per day _____

Recommended daily intake = 35 g

Additional daily fiber needed _____

- Are you consuming at least 25 g of dietary fiber daily?   _____ Yes   _____ No

- If you responded "no," on the reverse side of this sheet list three or four ways you can alter your meal and snacking to increase fiber intake.

Lab Activity 10.2

Do You Meet the U.S. Government Dietary Recommendations?

INSTRUCTIONS: *The first step toward developing healthful eating habits is to identify your current behavior. This requires careful recording of everything you eat and drink for a three- to four-day period. Estimate the portion size and secure the calories, fiber, salt, cholesterol, and fat content from the tables in this chapter and in Appendix B. Reproduce copies to complete your three- to four-day log.*

✦ **Food and Drink Diary of** _____ **Date** _____

TIME	FOOD/DRINK QUANTITY	ESTIMATED				
		CALORIES	FIBER	SALT	CHOL.	FAT
Breakfast						
Between meal						
Lunch						
Between meal						
Dinner						
Evening						

1. Record the percentage of your daily calories that come from the following:

   Simple carbohydrates _____

   Complex carbohydrates _____

   Protein _____

   Saturated fat _____

   Polyunsaturated fat _____

   Monounsaturated fat _____

2. Are you consuming too much salt? Cholesterol?

3. Are you consuming enough water?

4. Summarize the strengths and weaknesses of your diet in terms of food and fluid intake. What steps can you take toward a more healthful diet?

Lab Activity 10.3

Estimating Caloric Expenditure

INSTRUCTIONS: *The energy needs of the body depend on three factors: (1) body size, (2) age, and (3) the type and amount of your daily physical activity. Your basic metabolic rate (BMR) and caloric expenditure in normal daily activities combine to represent your required energy needs. Locate your height on Scale 1 in Table A and then your weight on Scale 2. Using a straight edge, connect the appropriate points on Scale 1 and Scale 2. The intersection of this line with Scale 3 is your body surface area.*

TABLE A: BODY SURFACE AREA

Scale 1 Height	Scale 3 Surface area	Scale 2 Weight
in. cm	m^1	lb kg
8"	2.9	160
6'6" 200	2.8	340 150
4"	2.7	320 140
4" 190	2.6	300
2"	2.5	280 130
6'0"	2.4	260 120
10" 180	2.3	240 110
8"	2.2	220
5'6" 170	2.1	100
4" 165	2.0	200 95
4" 160	1.9	190 90
2" 155	1.8	180 85
5'0" 150	1.7	170 80
10" 145	1.6	160 75
8" 140	1.5	150 70
4'6" 135	1.4	140 65
4" 130	1.3	130 60
2"	1.2	120 55
4'0" 125		110 50
120	1.1	100 45
10" 120		95 90 40
10" 115	1.0	85 80 35
8" 110		75
3'6" 105	0.9	70 65 30
4" 100	0.8	60 55 25 50

TABLE B: BASAL METABOLIC RATE ACCORDING TO AGE AND SEX

Age	BMR (kcal/m¹/hr) Men	Women	Age	BMR (kcal/m¹/hr) Men	Women
10	47.7	44.9	28	37.8	35.0
11	46.5	43.5	29	37.7	35.0
12	45.3	42.0	30	37.6	35.0
13	44.5	40.5	31	37.4	35.0
14	43.8	39.2	32	37.2	35.0
15	42.9	38.3	33	37.1	34.9
16	42.0	37.2	34	37.0	34.9
17	41.5	36.4	35	36.9	34.9
18	40.8	35.8	36	36.8	34.8
19	40.5	35.4	37	36.7	34.7
20	39.9	35.3	38	36.7	34.6
21	39.5	35.2	39	36.6	34.5
22	39.2	35.2	40–44	36.4	34.1
23	39.0	35.2	45–49	36.2	33.8
24	38.7	35.1	50–54	35.8	33.1
25	38.4	35.1	55–59	35.1	32.8
26	38.2	35.0	50–64	34.5	32.0
27	38.0	35.0	65–69	33.5	31.6
			70–74	32.7	31.1
			75+	31.8	

✦ Activity Levels

To your BMR you must add the calorie cost for your daily activities. It would be impractical to try to calculate your daily energy needs exactly every day, but you can arrive at a close estimate. Select the figure, from the following list, that best describes your activitry level.

40%	Sedentary activities—limited to walking and sitting
50%	Semisedentary activities—standing, walking, and recreational activities
60%	Laborer or limited physical exercise
70%	Heavy worker—regular participation in sports and other physical activities
80%	Engaged in intercollegiate sports or in a vigorous daily physical fitness program

Lab Activity 10.3 *(continued)*
Estimating Caloric Expenditure

◆ **Calculating Total Energy Expenditure**

Step 1	Determine body surface area from Table A		_____
Step 2	BMR factor (from Table B)	×	_____
Step 3	BMR/hour at rest (Step x Step 2)	=	_____
Step 4	Number of hours in a day	× 24 hours	_____
Step 5	BMR/day at rest (Step 3 × Step 4)	=	_____
Step 6	Activity level (enter .40, .50, .60, .70, or .80)	×	_____
Step 7	Activity calories (Step 5 x Step 6)	=	_____
Step 8	BMR/day at rest (enter number from Step 5)	+	_____
Total energy expenditure (total kcal/24 hours)		=	_____

11

Exploring Weight Control: A Sensible and Healthy Approach

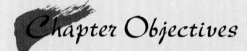

Chapter Objectives

By the end of this chapter, you should be able to:

1. Identify the major causes of obesity and overfatness in the United States.
2. Evaluate and determine your ideal weight and percentage of body fat.
3. Define overweight, overfat, and obesity.
4. Describe a sound, long-term weight-loss program.
5. Discuss the role of exercise in weight and fat management.
6. Differentiate between anorexia nervosa and bulimia.
7. Identify the key behaviors linked to weight and fat loss, and describe how to use several behavior-modification techniques to achieve your desired weight.

SUSAN HAS ALWAYS been preoccupied with her weight. As far back as she can remember, she was too fat. For years she considered it purely a genetic problem. After all, her father is obese and her mother is stocky. She thinks perhaps the cards are stacked against her. As an adult, she has tried every diet described in *Good Housekeeping, Redbook,* or that appeared on the best-seller list. Perhaps there is nothing she can do about it. According to the literature, diets don't work and she hates to exercise. Why diet for a lifetime when you need to lose only 8 to 10 pounds?

Is there any hope for women and men like Susan? This chapter provides the answers to these and other questions about weight control.

During the late 19th century in the United States, human muscle power provided 33 percent of the energy needed to run the farms, homes, and factories. Today, muscular effort contributes only 0.05 percent of the energy. Most people in the United States work in office-bound, service-oriented jobs and use business machines, pens, and pencils to accomplish their tasks. The jobs we do and the types of energy needed for those jobs have changed over the past 100 years. The human body has remained the same, however, as we have become victims of a technology-oriented lifestyle. As a result, more and more Americans of all ages are *overweight,* 20% above their range on height-weight tables; *overfat,* more than 20% (men) or 25% (women) body fat; or *obese,* more than 25% (men) or 30% (women) body fat.

In 1995 it was revealed that the incidence of overfatness and obesity among those aged 6 to 17 doubled in the past 25 years; from 5 percent to 11 percent. A similar increase occurred among adults. A February 1996 Harris Poll of randomly selected adults indicated that 74 percent weighed above their recommended weight on the new Metropolitan Life tables. Data on overfatness and obesity using the percentage of body fat rather than weight charts reveal similar findings. The increased number of overfat children will result in a significantly higher number of overfat adults in the future. With each passing decade, the typical adult in the United States also accumulates additional pounds of excess fat and loses some lean muscle tissue until, by middle age, over 50 percent are overfat or obese.

At all ages we are growing several pounds heavier each decade. Although our average height is also increasing, the majority of this weight gain is fat, not muscle. This trend must be brought under control since obesity is associated with a number of disorders, including atherosclerosis, hypertension, diabetes, heart/lung difficulties, early heart attack, and numerous other chronic and degenerative diseases and disorders. The death rate for obese men between the ages of 15 and 69 is 50 percent higher than that of normal-weight persons and 30 percent higher than those classified as merely overweight. For every 10 percent a person is above normal weight, it is esti-mated that life span is decreased by one year. Unfortunately, the quality of life also declines dramatically in obese individuals.

This chapter examines the critical aspects of weight control: causes of obesity, assessment, safe weight-loss methods, the role of exercise in weight and fat management, underweight and eating disorders, and the role of behavior-modification techniques in helping young people to manage body weight and fat during late teenage and early adulthood.

CAUSES OF OBESITY

Inactivity and overeating are the two most common causes of obesity and overfatness. Physical activity can do much to offset weight gain and regulate the tendency to put on unwanted pounds. Weight gain of genetically obese mice, for example, is drastically reduced by treadmill exercise. In humans, extremely high caloric intake can also be offset by a vigorous exercise program and result in little or no weight gain.

Social, genetic, and psychological factors may also result in overeating and obesity. It has been found that in only a small percentage of cases are glandular or other physiological disorders related to weight problems, although many obese people blame these factors. Sedentary living and excessive eating are the two greatest perpetuators of obesity; both can be controlled.

Set Point Theory

The human body regulates its own functions with tremendous precision. Body weight is one of these functions. Each individual appears to have an ideal biological weight (the **set point**), and the body will

Set point A theory postulating that each individual has an ideal weight (the set point) and that the body will attempt to maintain this weight against pressure to change it.

A regular exercise program, such as walking, can be a person's greatest defense against weight gain (Photo courtesy of Cable News Network.)

defend it against pressure to change. Those who do succeed in losing or gaining weight generally return to their set point weight in a few months or years. Within 24 hours of beginning a very low calorie diet, for example, metabolic rate (amount of calories burned at rest) slows by 5 to 20 percent as a means of conserving energy, making it more difficult to lose weight. The body is convinced it is starving, and calorie conservation is a way of hanging on to the energy for a longer period of time. In addition, once excess fat cells become depleted, they signal the central nervous system to alter feeding behavior by increasing caloric intake so that the set point can be maintained. In other words, some experts theorize that an internal thermostat regulates body fat and weight and triggers an increase in food intake when fat and weight are lowered too much. Overcoming the set point is difficult. Willpower and other factors that aid in tolerating the discomfort of hunger are poor matches for a computerlike system that never quits.

Research suggests that one of the ways to take weight off and keep it off may be to lower the thermostat. *Yo-yo dieting* (the cycle of losing and regaining weight and fat) may have the opposite effect and actually result in a higher setting on the thermostat with the body then defending an even higher weight. This may explain why people who complete several cycles of losing and regaining 10 pounds find it nearly twice as hard to lose weight and twice as easy to gain weight on their next attempt. With each yo-yo cycle, the individual also acquires extra body fat and loses some muscle mass. Regular, aerobic exercise four to five times weekly, combined with a sound nutritional plan, appears to lower the thermostat over time and allows loss of weight and maintenance of that lower weight.

Early Eating Patterns

Most experts agree that the eating habits formed in infancy and childhood carry over into the adult years. Rats who are exposed to unlimited milk, for example, continue to eat much more and exercise less after they are weaned than rats who receive only limited milk. In other words, rats who are overfed prior to weaning, become sedentary adult rats who overeat, become fat, and suffer from early cardiorespiratory disease. By contrast, rats who eat less prior to weaning, continue to eat less, exercise more, live longer, and experience less cardiorespiratory disease. The response in humans is similar. Children who are inactive and overeat are also more likely to continue these behaviors later in life and become overfat adults.

Environmental forces appear to influence eating patterns more than physiological forces such as hunger. Negative eating behavior may begin in infancy. Some experts feel that bottle feeding, for example, may predispose infants to obesity. Approximately three times more bottle-fed than breast-fed babies are overfat. Bottle feeding fails to provide the solace of breast feeding and tends to produce anxiety, which may provoke overeating. Breast-fed babies also learn to stop feeding when the richest portion of the milk gives way to more watery milk. The bottle does not provide such a natural mechanism, so bottle-fed babies require more calories to satisfy their hunger.

Perhaps a more important problem is feeding babies solid foods too early, which may contribute to the production of excess fat cells. Experts recommend that parents start feeding their infants solid foods at the age of 5 months rather than earlier, except for cases of very large or fast-developing babies. This is no easy task for sleep-deprived mothers who long for the day the baby sleeps through the night without waking for a feeding.

There is little danger that a growing child will be obese if the child itself decides when to stop eating at a meal. Forcing children to clean the plate is a mistake and is the same as forcing a child to overeat. Making sweets plentiful, using them as rewards, and placing emphasis on the fat baby also compound the problem by shortening life span, encouraging premature heart disease, forming undesirable eating habits that will be continued throughout life, and condemning the child to a life of restricted eating because of the high number of fat cells formed in early life. A lean child with a great deal of energy and vitality is healthier and more likely to be healthy later in life.

There is no stage in life when excess fat is desirable; however, the earlier in life a child is obese, the greater the chance is that the child will eventually be

Overweight children are likely to grow into overweight adults. (Photo courtesy of Cable News Network.)

of normal weight. The later in life a child is obese, the less likely it is that he or she will ever return to normal weight. It is estimated that an obese adolescent, for example, has approximately a 1 in 16 chance of returning to normal weight as an adult. The fatter you are at any age, the less likely you will ever return to normal weight. It is therefore advisable to start children off right and avoid overstuffing. If their mechanism for pushing up from the table when they are full is destroyed, they are certain to need plenty of real push-ups in the adult years to control weight.

Fat Cells

Our fat cells are formed early in life and increase in both size and number until the end of adolescence. Calorie restriction will decrease only the size of fat cells, not the number. With a large number of fat cells formed, a return to an overfat condition is quite easy. This partially explains why adults who were fat babies often have difficulty keeping their weight down. These extra adipose cells also affect metabolism and result in the need for fewer calories to maintain normal weight than are needed by someone who generally remains at normal weight. Unlike muscle, fat requires little energy to maintain, and additional fat weight will not increase metabolic rate.

The number of fat cells in the human body grows rapidly during three stages of development: (1) the last trimester of pregnancy (in the unborn child), (2) the first year of life, and (3) the adolescent growth spurt. Fat is acquired by increasing the size of existing adipose cells (**hypertrophy**) and by new fat-cell formation prior to adulthood (**hyperplasia**). It is doubtful that new fat cells are formed after age 21 (approximately) unless someone becomes extremely obese.

There is a wide variation in the number of fat cells in different people. A nonobese person has approximately 25 to 30 billion fat cells, while an extremely obese person may have as many as 260 billion. A formerly obese adult may never be cured because weight loss does not reduce the number of existing cells, it only reduces their size.

Hypertrophy The enlargement of existing fat cells.

Hyperplasia New fat-cell formation.

Genetics

It is now quite clear that the genes we inherit influence our body weight and the amount and disposition of fat. Children of overfat or obese parents, particularly the biological mother, are much more likely to develop weight problems. Studies of twins also support the influence of genetics on overfatness and obesity. Heredity may be tied to weight and fat problems in a number of ways, such as a predisposition to sweet, high-fat foods, impaired hormonal functions (insulin and cortisol), a lower basal metabolic rate, differences in calories used during the metabolism of food, inability of nutrients to suppress the appetite control center, differences in the inefficiency to store fat and burn calories during light exercise, and a tendency to develop more fat cells. Ongoing research dealing with the presence of a so-called fat gene, drugs to permanently control hunger, and numerous other studies may offer encouraging breakthroughs for individuals in the future.

It is important to keep in mind, however, that environment is still critical. Genetics may merely predispose you or provide you with the tendency to become fat—a problem that regular exercise and proper nutrition can help overcome.

Environmental Factors

Sound exercise and eating and drinking habits can overcome the genetic tendency to be either thin or fat. One of the clearer causes of obesity and overfatness in children is watching television. People on television programs eat about eight times per hour, and commercials generally advertise high-calorie, high-fat foods. Television watchers pick up on these cues and tend to eat more often and more high-fat, high-calorie foods. In addition, television is a passive activity; almost any other activity will burn more calories. While it is a good idea to restrict the number of television-watching hours for all children and teenagers, it is absolutely necessary to do so for the overfat child.

Other environmental influences, such as eating and exercise habits of parents, food availability, and nutritional knowledge, may not be as important as was once believed. Experts feel that genetic influences account for about 70 percent of the differences in body mass index (BMI) that are found later in life and that childhood environment has less influence than was once thought. This does not mean that environment has no influence on obesity. Nongenetic factors are important determinants of body fat. These

Improving Your Community

Helping "Fat America" Slim Down

Overfatness and obesity represent a major health problem in the United States. The number of obese and overfat adults and children has now reached epidemic proportions, translating into tremendous health costs to manage the numerous related disorders and diseases. Medical experts are alarmed not only at the physical, but also the emotional impact of "Fat America." Society continues to discriminate heavily against the obese of all ages in the workplace, in the home, in schools and universities, and in leisure pursuits. To date, little has been done on national or local levels to reverse these powerful trends in our affluent society. Their causes are complicated and confusing, and a simple solution is unlikely. However, you can start right now to help increase your own and other people's awareness of this serious problem and, perhaps, begin to defeat its effects.

1. First, inventory your own health status in terms of body weight and fat. Are you overfat? If so, identify and implement immediately five changes you can make in your diet to reduce your caloric intake. Also, identify and implement five exercise activities you can do every day (such as riding a bike or walking to school, swimming, sit-ups, etc.). Record your progress over three to six months. If you are not overfat, help an overfat friend inventory her or his body weight and fat and implement a similar weight-loss program.

2. Prepare a six-month program to help yourself or a friend gain 10 to 12 pounds of muscle weight. As in the program described in the previous step, be sure to include both nutritional and exercise aspects in your muscle-weight gain program.

3. Snacking is a part of most college students' lives. Nutritious snacking on high-density foods need not contribute to overeating. In fact, the right snack choices can actually help to control appetite and reduce the occurrence of snacking on high-calorie, low-density foods. What snack food choices do your college or university food service and vending machines offer? Develop a simple program to increase other students' awareness that it's OK to snack but that there are healthy snack food choices.

4. Although they are always potentially unhealthy and dangerous, fad diets that promise rapid weight loss will probably always appeal to the impatient American public. Identify and analyze several diet fads in your college or local community. Compare the diet to the key components of a safe, sound diet listed in Lab Activity 11.1: Evaluating Your Favorite Fad Diet at the end of the chapter. What are the main factors that lead you to believe the fad diet is unhealthy? Submit your findings for publication in a student or community newsletter.

5. Working by yourself or with several of your classmates, develop a survey of elementary school children in your community to determine how many of these children are or may be in danger of becoming overfat or obese. Start by collecting data on height and weight and progress to information about dietary and exercise habits. Your survey could be directed to the children's teachers or to the children themselves, but be sure to work in conjunction with school administrators and teachers. Include as many children in the survey as you can. Use the results to make specific suggestions for weight control among these children to teachers, administrators, and PTA members. ✦

factors are reversible and capable of overcoming some of the genetic factors that make us fat.

Metabolic Factors

Even small changes in metabolic rate translate into large increases in body fat and weight. A 10 percent decline in metabolism, for example, could result in an annual weight gain of about 15 lb for the average individual. Aerobic exercise increases metabolic rate both during and after the exercise session. The afterburn continues from 20 minutes to several hours, depending on the duration and intensity of the workout.

Although coffee, tea, cocoa, colas, and other caffeine-containing food and drink, do increase metabolic rate, these products should be used sparingly. In midafternoon, metabolism tends to slow, making this an excellent time for aerobic exercise to boost metabolic rate. As we age, metabolism also slows until, at age 50, metabolic rate may have decreased by as much as 15 to 25 percent in a sedentary individual. In those who have remained active through a combination of aerobic exercise and strength training, metabolic rate slows only slightly. Loss of muscle mass is one of the leading causes of reduced metabolic rate with aging.

Body composition

Many people have an ideal image of their bodies that they would someday like to achieve. For some, such an image may be unrealistic. Regardless of your motivation to change, several methods derived from research or actuarial tables may help you set realistic goals for a better-looking body.

A simple method of estimating proper body weight is to use the Metropolitan Life Insurance height-weight standards shown in Table 11.1. Charts of so-called ideal weight for men and women are based on data associating average weights by height and age with long life. Prior to 1980, figures indicated that those who weighed less than their recommended weight on the charts lived up to 20 percent longer than other people. The charts, which became the national guide for determining overweight and obesity for the general public, worked on the theory that "the greater the weight, the greater the risk of death." The validity of such data is now being questioned since it is evident that less-than-average weights may involve health risks even greater than those associated with overweight and that the U.S. preoccupation with *thinness* may not be much of a health advantage.

Authorities do not dispute that people who are much heavier than average (more than 20 percent above ideal weight on the charts) obtain health benefits from weight reduction. Even small amounts of weight loss, for example, may aid the diabetic patient. For those in normal health who are at average or near average weight, there is less health benefit to losing weight. The key factor that determines what is too much or too little is body fat, not total body weight. There are two additional limitations with height-

Table 11.1 ✦ Metropolitan Life Insurance Height-Weight Table

MEN						WOMEN					
HEIGHT		FRAME				HEIGHT		FRAME			
Feet	*Inches*	*Small*	*Medium*	*Large*		*Feet*	*Inches*	*Small*	*Medium*	*Large*	
5	2	128–134	131–141	138–150		4	10	102–111	109–121	118–131	
5	3	130–136	133–143	140–153		4	11	103–113	111–123	120–134	
5	4	132–138	135–145	142–156		5	0	104–115	113–126	122–137	
5	5	134–140	137–148	144–160		5	1	106–118	115–129	125–140	
5	6	136–142	139–151	146–164		5	2	108–121	118–132	128–143	
5	7	138–145	142–154	149–168		5	3	111–124	121–135	131–147	
5	8	140–148	145–157	152–172		5	4	114–127	124–138	134–151	
5	9	142–151	148–160	155–176		5	5	117–130	127–141	137–155	
5	10	144–154	151–163	158–180		5	6	120–133	130–144	140–159	
5	11	146–157	154–166	161–184		5	7	123–136	133–147	143–163	
6	0	149–160	157–170	164–188		5	8	126–139	136–150	146–167	
6	1	152–164	160–174	168–192		5	9	129–142	139–153	149–170	
6	2	155–168	164–178	172–197		5	10	132–145	142–156	152–173	
6	3	158–172	167–182	176–202		5	11	135–148	145–159	155–176	
6	4	162–176	171–187	181–207		6	0	138–151	148–162	158–179	

Weights at ages 25 to 29 based on lowest mortality. Weights in pounds according to frame (in indoor clothing weighing 5 lb for men or 3 lb for women; shoes with 1-inch heels). For frame size standards, see Table 11.2.

Source: Basic data from *1979 Build Study,* Society of Actuaries and Association of Life Insurance Medical Directors of America, 1980. Copyright © 1983 Metropolitan Life Insurance Company. All rights reserved. Reproduced by permission.

Table 11.2 ✦ Approximating Frame Size

MEN		WOMEN	
Height in 1" heels	*Elbow breadth*	*Height in l" heels*	*Elbow breadth*
5'2"–5'3"	2½"–2⅞"	4'10"–4'11"	2¼"–2½"
5'4"–5'7"	2⅝"–2⅞"	5'0"–5'3"	2¼"–2½"
5'8"–5'11"	2¾"–3"	5'4"–5'7"	2⅜"–2⅝"
6'0"–6'3"	2¾"–3⅛"	5'8"–5'11"	2⅜"–2⅝"
6'4"	2⅞"–3¼"	6'0"	2½"–2¾"

Extend your arm and bend the forearm upward to a 90-degree angle. Keep fingers straight and turn the inside of your wrist toward your body. If you have a caliper, use it to measure the space between the two prominent bones on *either* side of your elbow. Without a caliper, place thumb and index finger of your other hand on these two bones. Measure the space between your fingers against a ruler or tape measure. Compare it with these tables that list elbow measurements for *medium-framed* men and women. Measurements lower than those listed indicate you have a small frame. Higher measurements indicate a large frame.

Source: From *1979 Build Study,* Society of Actuaries and Association of Life Insurance Medical Directors of America, 1980. Copyright 1983 Metropolitan Life Insurance Company. All rights reserved. Reproduced by permission.

weight charts: Non-Caucasians are underrepresented, and age is not considered. Desirable weights are too high for young people, too low for the elderly, and correct for those in their 40s.

Determining Ideal Body Weight from Height-Weight Charts

Check your ideal weight on Table 11.1. Frame size can be determined by wrapping your thumb and middle finger around your opposite wrist. If the thumb and finger do not meet, you have a large frame. If they just meet or barely overlap, you have a medium frame, and if they overlap, you have a small frame. For a much more accurate indicator of frame size, follow the directions in Table 11.2 to obtain the exact width of your elbow.

Table 11.1 identifies the range for your desirable body weight. See how your actual weight compares. If you fall 10 percent below or above the range for your height, you are roughly classified as underweight or overweight; 20 percent above classifies you as obese. Keep in mind that this table provides only a rough guide to desirable weight, and it is not uncommon for an individual to fall considerably above a weight range and still possess normal or even below-normal body fat. This is particularly common in muscular men and women. Conversely, it is entirely possible to fall within the desired range and still possess excess body fat.

Determining Percentage of Body Fat

A more important consideration in goal setting for a better-looking and healthier body involves not body weight but the amount of adipose tissue you possess. Weight control is simply another name for fat control, and measurement of body fat is essential in setting goals for your body.

The average percentage of body fat is approximately 22 to 25 percent for females and 15 to 18 percent for males. Individuals are considered obese if they possess more than 25 percent (men) or 30 percent (women) body fat (see Table 11.3).

Since about half of all body fat lies just beneath the skin, it is possible to pinch certain body parts, measure the thickness of two layers of skin and the connected fat, and estimate the total percentage of fat on the body.

You can measure the thickness of four skinfold sites with a caliper. Considerable practice is needed, however, before accurate measurements can be taken. Take a moment to complete Lab Activity 11.1: Determining Your Percentage of Body Fat at the end of this chapter to develop your skills and determine your estimated percentage of body fat.

There are other methods of estimating percentage of body fat. **Electrical impedance** is a quick method. Electrodes are attached to the wrist and ankle of the reclining subject. In less than two minutes, a printout provides your percentage of body fat, total amount of fat weight, ideal percent of fat, and ideal body weight. It is necessary to follow certain

Electrical impedance A quick, moderately accurate means of determining an individual's percentage of body fat that uses electrodes attached to wrists and ankles.

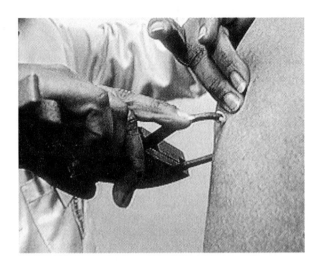

Measurement of body fat using skinfold calipers. (Photo courtesy of Cable News Network.)

nutritional and exercise rules for 24 hours before the test. **Hydrostatic weighing** is probably the most accurate method of estimating body fat. In the test the subject sits on a scale in a tank of water, exhales as completely as possible, and is submerged for approximately 10 seconds while weight is recorded. The proportions of lean body mass and fat mass are determined from calculations that involve weight underwater, weight out of water, and known densities of lean and fatty tissues.

𝒮AFE WEIGHT-LOSS PROCEDURES

Hunger and Appetite

Hunger is generally considered physiological, an inborn instinct, whereas **appetite** is a psychological, or a learned, response. This helps to explain why it is so common to have an appetite and eat when you are not hungry; conversely, some very thin people or those with eating disorders may experience hunger without appetite. Hunger is an active experience, whereas appetite is passive.

The feeling of fullness or satisfaction that prompts us to stop eating is called *satiety,* one of the key regulators of eating behavior. Some experts think that eating behavior is always in operation except when the satiety signal turns it off. Just how that happens is unknown, although many theories have been advanced. The **glucostatic theory** of hunger regulation suggests that blood-glucose levels and the exhaustion of liver glycogen may account for the starting and stopping of eating. The liver stores about

75 grams (g) of glycogen or 300-plus energy units (calories). When liver glycogen levels fall significantly, feelings of hunger may occur. The **lipostatic theory** suggests that hunger is regulated in some way by the number of fat-storing enzymes on the surfaces of fat cells. The messenger that the cells send to the brain in this theory has not been identified. The **purinegic theory** is relatively new and untested and proposes that the circulating levels of purines—molecules found in DNA and RNA—govern hunger. Exactly where and how the brain receives these messages is also unknown. The **hypothalamus gland** appears to be important in regulating eating. Damage to this area can produce eating disorders and severe weight loss or gain.

Eating behavior appears to occur in response to numerous signals. The possibility also exists that an inherited, internal regulatory defect is at least partially responsible for obesity, rather than its being a purely learned behavior or genetically caused.

It is obvious that there is much to be learned about the causes of obesity. There are many other theories. A summary of research currently in progress to discover the answers to these and other questions appears in Figure 11.1. An understanding of the

---

Hydrostatic weighing An accurate method of measuring body fat by submerging an individual in water.

Hunger A physiological response of the body involving unpleasant sensations that indicate a need for food.

Appetite The desire to eat; pleasant sensations aroused by the thoughts of the taste and enjoyment of food.

Glucostatic theory A theory about hunger regulation suggesting that blood-glucose levels determine whether one is hungry or satiated through the exhaustion of liver glycogen.

Lipostatic theory A theory about hunger control suggesting that the size of fat stores signals us to eat.

Purinegic theory A theory about hunger suggesting that the circulating levels of purines—molecules found in DNA and RNA—govern hunger.

Hypothalamus gland A portion of the brain that regulates body temperature and other functions; thought to be important in the regulation of food intake.

Figure 11.1 ✦ Hunger and Appetite: Some of the Factors Suspected of Controlling Food Intake

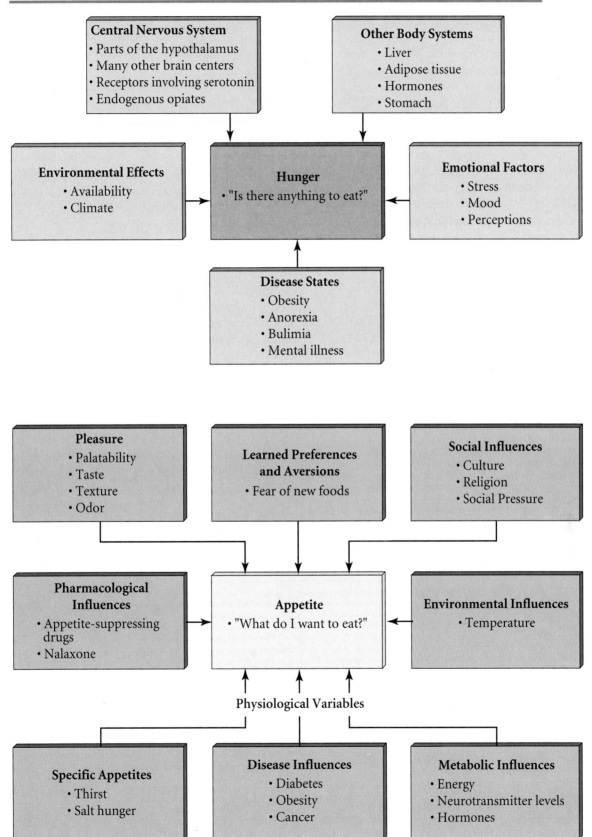

Source: Adapted from "Hunger and Appetite: Old Concepts/New Distinctions," T. W. Castonguay et al., April 1983, *Nutrition Reviews* 41. Copyright by ILSI-Nutrition Foundation. Used with permission.

difference between hunger and appetite and the factors suspected of controlling food intake will help you control your body weight and fat.

Controlling Appetite From the limited information available, it is known that two basic approaches to controlling appetite are somewhat effective: (1) keeping the stomach full of low-calorie food and drink and (2) raising the body's blood-sugar level. Increasing your fluid intake (particularly your water consumption) and consuming complex carbohydrates such as raw fruits and vegetables both between meals and at mealtimes will keep the stomach relatively full. New raw-grain products are also available that are equally effective. Small amounts of candy, such as one or two chocolate squares, 20 to 30 minutes before a meal, or when you have the urge to snack, is another technique you can use. Slow eaters (those taking 20 minutes or more) also experience this elevated blood-sugar level and are less likely to overeat.

Exactly how to control appetite remains somewhat of a puzzle. Modern researchers continue to examine areas such as appetite centers in the brain, feedback from centers outside the brain such as the liver and intestines, hormone actions, and the ratio of daily dietary protein to carbohydrate to unlock some of the mystery.

Calorie Counting

If you are overfat according to the guidelines in this chapter, you may want to consider an exercise and diet regimen to lose body fat and weight. When you set goals for body-fat loss, you can expect to lose about 0.5 millimeters (mm) of body fat per week with an appropriate combination of diet and exercise. For example, if you are now classified as *above average fat*, it is realistic to expect to reach the *average fat* category after a 10-week program.

As a first step in losing body fat, turn to Lab Activity 11.3: Determining Your Caloric Needs at the end of the chapter to determine how many calories you need to maintain your present weight. These figures will help you decide how much to increase your daily energy expenditure and reduce your daily caloric intake to meet your weight- and fat-loss goals. You can then reduce your caloric intake and increase your exercise expenditure to produce a slow, safe weight and fat loss.

How Exercise Helps

A pleasant occurrence often accompanying weight losses of over 5 to 10 lb is enhanced self-concept and increased energy levels. Remember that the weight you choose as a target is one that, once reached, must be maintained for the rest of your life. It is not just weight loss per se, but the acceptance of a healthy lifestyle that is most likely to keep your *thin self* going in the future. Regular vigorous exercise is an essential part of this healthy, holistic lifestyle.

If you expect to lose body fat and weight and then maintain this lower level, you need both to restrict your caloric intake and to engage in regular exercise. By remaining physically active, you will be able to consume more calories daily. The alternative is to remain mildly hungry most of your life. There are numerous other reasons why both diet and exercise should be

Table 11.3 ✦ Activity Rating Chart (Calories Burned per Hour)

	110 LB		120 LB		130 LB		140 LB		150 LB	
ACTIVITY	M	F	M	F	M	F	M	F	M	F
Sleeping, reclining	–	45	–	50	–	54	–	58	68	62
Very light: sitting, standing, driving	–	65	–	72	–	77	–	83	102	88
Light: walking on level, shopping, golf, table tennis, carpentry, light housekeeping	–	130	–	143	–	153	–	166	197	177
Moderate: walking, weeding, cycling, skiing, tennis, dancing	–	205	–	226	–	242	–	262	292	279
Heavy: walking uphill, shoveling, basketball, swimming, climbing, football, jogging, running	–	400	–	440	–	472	–	512	571	544

Courtesy of Safeway, Inc., 1994.

– – Data unavailable

included in a weight-loss or weight-management program.

Exercise Depresses Appetite   The amount of body weight and fat lost during an exercise program is greater than what can be attributed to the number of calories expended. This suggests that exercise acts on the body to further increase energy expenditure through changes in metabolism or to decrease energy intake through changes in appetite. It is also a well-established principle that physical activity decreases appetite. Physical inactivity and high body fat and decreases in appetite and regular aerobic exercise are all strongly associated. The food intake of elementary school-aged children has also been shown to decrease by scheduling the recess period before, rather than after, lunch.

Exercise Maximizes Fat Loss and Minimizes Loss of Lean Muscle Tissue   There is a difference between weight loss in terms of pounds and fat loss in terms of adipose tissue. A diet without exercise can result in about 70 to 80 percent fatty-tissue loss and 20 to 30 percent lean-muscle loss. With the combination of exercise and diet, fatty-tissue loss can be increased to 95 percent and lean-muscle loss kept to 5 percent or less of total weight loss.

Exercise Burns a High Number of Calories and Increases Metabolic Rate   Exercise burns kcal both during an exercise session and for 20 minutes to several hours after exercise ceases (afterburn). A 3-mile run or walk will expend 250 to 300 cal depending on the individual. For the next 20 minutes (for the walk-er) to several hours (for the jogger or runner), an additional 25 to 40 kcal per hour will be burned due to an increase in metabolic rate. The total caloric benefit of a 3-mile run then may be as high as 500 kcal. Four to five such workouts weekly would produce a body weight/fat loss of about 3 lb monthly, or 36 lb per year.

Strength-training programs involving weights add muscle mass and increase metabolism permanently. Keep in mind that fat is a dormant tissue and requires very few kcal to maintain. Muscle tissue, on the other hand, requires considerable kcal to maintain. It is estimated that for every pound of muscle you add, metabolic rate increases 30 to 40 cal per 24-hour period. If you add 5 lb of muscle over a six-month period, your metabolic rate may increase as much as 200 kcal daily. This translates into about 6,000 kcal monthly and nearly 2 lb of fat (3,500 kcal = 1 lb of fat). This is obviously a very significant change.

The best system of controlling body weight is changing your eating habits and beginning an exercise program you enjoy and are likely to continue throughout life. If you change your behavior in these two areas, you will go through life at your ideal body weight and fat. Body weight is carefully regulated by complex forces, but the formula for weight loss is simple. If you eat more calories than you burn through activity, a positive caloric balance exists and produces weight gain. If you burn up more calories than you eat, a negative caloric balance exists and weight and fat loss will occur.

Table 11.3 shows the number of calories used per hour in various activities. It does not reflect the addi-

160 LB		170 LB		180 LB		190 LB		200 LB		210 LB		220 LB		230 LB	
M	F	M	F	M	F	M	F	M	F	M	F	M	F	M	F
72	66	77	70	81	75	86	78	90	83	95	–	99	–	104	–
110	95	116	100	123	107	129	112	137	118	143	–	150	–	158	–
212	190	223	200	238	213	250	224	264	237	276	–	290	–	305	–
314	300	331	316	353	336	370	353	391	373	409	–	430	–	452	–
613	584	647	616	689	656	722	688	764	728	798	–	840	–	882	–

tional effects of afterburn or the changes in metabolic rate that occur from muscle-weight gain. Walking, bicycling, swimming, dancing, jogging, and other aerobic activities are all effective means of exercise for weight loss. Some types of physical activity and sports are relaxing and enjoyable. Other activities are superior in weight loss and aerobic benefits.

When you choose a particular exercise program, consider that:

1. You are more likely to continue exercising in activities you enjoy.

2. Activities that expend a moderately high number of calories per minute (aerobic) and allow you to continue exercise for 30 to 90 minutes are the best choices.

3. Lifelong physical-recreational sports that provide heart-lung benefits are superior.

4. The choice you make should allow you to start at your present fitness level and progress to higher levels later.

Exercise Brings Needed Calcium to the Bones As a result of normal aging and weight loss, bones lose calcium and other minerals and become brittle. It takes adequate calcium in your diet (see chapter 10) plus weight-bearing exercise (walking, jogging, running, aerobic dance) to increase the amount of calcium that reaches the bones and thereby helps prevent osteoporosis.

Exercise Changes the Way Your Body Handles Fats
Exercise helps lower and maintain serum cholesterol (LDL) and triglycerides. HDL (high-density lipoprotein, the good cholesterol) increases, and the ratio of HDL to total cholesterol improves. High HDL counts and a high ratio of HDL to total cholesterol (1:4 or higher) have been associated with a lower incidence of heart attacks.

𝒮PECIAL DIETS

There are numerous reasons why the average diet lasts only 5 to 7 days: boredom, monotony, lack of energy, fatigue, depression, complicated or expensive meal planning and purchasing, and failure to lose weight and fat fast enough. These problems are less likely to occur for individuals on a sound diet. Unfortunately, diet choices are often restricted to magazine, book, or television publicity that promises some *secret* easy method of shedding pounds and fat. These and practically all other diets simply do not

work, are potentially dangerous, and should be avoided. Safe, effective, and long-term management of body weight and fat involves a lifelong plan of proper nutrition and regular exercise. Quick weight-loss approaches provide only a temporary fix, with over 90 percent of those who try any of them regaining the lost weight within 6 to 12 months. In the meantime, the body may have been exposed to numerous health hazards. Analyze your favorite diet by completing Lab Activity 11.1 Evaluating Your Favorite Fad Diet at the end of this chapter.

Snacking

Between-meal and late-evening snacking is a leading cause of overfatness. It is not uncommon to consume over 1,000 calories between 8 P.M. and midnight—nearly one third of a pound of fat. Yet it is unrealistic to expect people to avoid snacking altogether. In fact, planned snacking on the right foods can help you control hunger and eat less. Snacks likely to be low in calories are those that are thin and watery (for example, tomato juice), crisp but not greasy (celery, carrots, radishes, cucumbers, broccoli, cauliflower, apples, berries, and other fresh fruits and vegetables and raw grains), and bulky (salad greens). Prepare a tray of these nutritious, low-calorie snacks and place it in the front of your refrigerator. Most snackers are compulsive and consume the first thing they see.

Characteristics of the Ideal Diet Plan

This 10-point plan is nothing more than sound nutrition and exercise advice, and it should be followed throughout life. Although you can always find a diet book on the best-seller list, the fact remains that most diets fail, and most individuals who lose weight return to their overweight or overfat condition within a very short time. A lifetime plan for proper eating and exercise offers you the best chance for success and safety.

1. Consume a minimum of 1,200 calories daily.

2. Drink a minimum of 10 glasses of water daily when you diet.

3. Eat sufficient protein daily. Consult the recommended dietary allowance (RDA) table in chapter 10 to determine your exact needs.

4. Eat at least 50 to 100 g (200 to 400 kcal) of carbohydrate and 10 g of fat (90 cal) daily to spare protein. Unless your carbohydrate and fat intake are sufficient to meet your daily

needs, some dietary protein and lean protein mass (muscle) will be converted to glucose to nourish the nervous system. Failing to spare protein for months at a time is not recommended. Fat is also very important for satiety.

5. Never skip a meal, even if you are not hungry. Choose a variety of foods from the nutrition pyramid in chapter 10.

6. Gear your program to a weight loss of between one and two pounds weekly and stay with it until you reach your goal.

7. Premeasure each food portion, keep records of your food and drink intake, identify problem areas, and take steps to change.

8. Avoid laxatives, stimulants, and diuretics, and use a multiple vitamin and mineral daily.

9. Combine dieting with exercise in one aerobic and one strength training activity or aerobic program you enjoy; exercise a minimum of three times weekly, for at least 30 minutes each time.

10. Plan to stay with your new eating and exercise routine for a minimum of 12 months.

𝒰NDERWEIGHT CONDITIONS AND EATING DISORDERS

The problems of gaining weight are just as complex as those associated with weight loss. Hunger, appetite, and satiety irregularities; psychological factors; or metabolic problems can cause dangerous underweight. For some individuals who need additional weight and muscle for sports and others who merely want to be and appear stronger, gaining a pound is just as difficult as losing a pound is for others.

Gaining Weight

A drug-free muscle-weight-gain program requires considerable dedication to both diet and exercise. Sound approaches strive to add no more than a half-pound of muscle per week, or two pounds per month. This is about as quick as the body can add lean muscle tissue. Faster approaches involving too many calories are almost certain to add adipose tissue.

A sound strength-training program, such as weight training, is an absolute must for muscle-weight gain (see chapter 9). It may be necessary to train for several hours six times weekly, alternating muscle groups each day.

The nutritional support for a sound weight-gain program involves an increase in food (about 400 to 500 additional calories daily) that provides high calories in as small volume as possible to keep you from getting uncomfortably full, a slight increase in total protein intake (14 to 15 percent of daily calories), and a slight reduction in total fat intake (18 to 20 percent of daily calories). Extra calories should come from complex carbohydrates (65 to 70 percent of daily calories) to provide long-term energy and for **protein sparing**. Most individuals who have difficulty gaining weight do not eat enough calories to support their vigorous workout schedule. Using protein or amino acid tablets is not a good idea, as they are hazardous and a waste of money. In the majority of cases, individuals consume more protein than they need already; adding more in the form of supplements is unnecessary.

Eating Disorders

The current overemphasis on flat stomachs, lean thighs, firm buttocks, and slimness is at least partially responsible for aggravating two serious eating disorders that can lead to death: **anorexia nervosa** and **bulimia**. Both disorders are known only in developed nations and are most common in higher economic groups.

Anorexia The number of cases of anorexia nervosa is increasing and now occurs in almost 1 of every 100 people, 19 out of 20 of whom are young women. The disease is four to five times more common in identical than in fraternal twins, suggesting an inherited predisposition to the disease. Unfortunately, our culture encourages anorexia nervosa.

A typical case involves a young woman from a middle-class family who values appearance more than self-worth and self-actualization. Typically, family ties

---

Protein sparing Consuming sufficient amounts of dietary carbohydrate and fat on a daily basis to prevent the conversion of dietary and lean muscle protein to glucose.

Anorexia nervosa An eating disorder that involves lack or loss of appetite to the point of self-starvation and dangerous weight loss.

Bulimia An eating disorder found most often in women, involving excessive and insatiable appetite and eating binges followed by self-induced vomiting or the use of laxatives to expel the unwanted food.

Myth and Fact Sheet

Myth	Fact
1. Overweight and obese people are always big eaters.	1. In both children and adults, studies show that the major cause of heaviness is inactivity followed by overeating. The major problem for the majority of over-fat people in the United States is inactivity. A regular exercise program is still the best health insurance policy and the best approach to weight and fat loss.
2. The major part of excess weight and fat is water.	2. This is not true. Do not restrict your water intake in any way. Water is essential to the proper function of every body system. Fluid retention is common while dieting since water remains in the spaces freed by the disappearance of fat. This fluid generally remains for two to three weeks and often obscures actual weight loss. Drink water freely at all times, particularly when you are restricting your calories. The majority (about 80 percent) of excess weight is fat, not water.
3. Beer helps me relax and avoid food calories.	3. Alcohol in any form is high in calories (7 cal per g, 150 cal per beer, mixed drink, or 4-oz glass of wine). Since alcohol is a depressant, it encourages relaxation, and relaxation improves appetite. In addition, high-calorie snack foods and alcohol seem to go together.
4. Candy and other sweets help me curb my appetite.	4. Very small amounts, such as one or two squares of a chocolate bar, one or two pieces of hard candy, or three or four ounces of soda, raise blood-sugar levels and give you the impression you are not hungry. In larger amounts, however, high blood-sugar levels rapidly fall, leaving you with little energy and hungry enough to eat several more high-calorie candy bars.
5. There's nothing wrong with resorting to quick weight-loss diets.	5. You should lose weight at the rate of no more than one to two pounds weekly. Very low calorie diets that produce rapid weight loss have a number of pitfalls: (1) They are dangerous; possibly life-threatening. (2) Rapid weight loss is usually followed by rapid weight gain. (3) Your percentage of body fat increases each time you lose and reacquire the weight. (4) Sufficient carbohydrate is often not consumed to spare protein, resulting in lean-tissue loss even from the heart muscle itself. Sufficient cardiac tissue loss might cause serious rhythm problems.
6. Cellulite can be eliminated with special foods and exercise.	6. From a medical point of view, there is no such thing as cellulite as a particular form of fat. Fat is merely fat, although the size and appearance of fat cells vary in different body parts and in different people. The lumpy, dimplelike deposits called cellulite tend to be most visible in women and often appear on the thighs, backs of legs, and buttocks. These deposits are merely large fat cells that show through the somewhat thinner skin of women. Thicker-skinned males tend not to develop this appearance unless they become extremely fat. Prevention is easier than treatment and focuses on proper nutrition, maintaining normal weight and fat, and avoiding rapid weight-loss attempts or yo-yo dieting.
7. It is better to remain fat than to lose weight and end up with wrinkled skin.	7. This is partially correct. It is better to stay somewhat fat than to lose, then regain, body weight rapidly. If you lose weight and fat slowly through a combination of diet and exercise and lose only 10 to 15 lb, skin wrinkling is unlikely. It is also helpful to include weight training as part of your exercise routine. As your fat cells shrink, the added muscle mass will help your skin fit you better in some areas, such as the back of the arm. If you have more than 15 lb to lose, work with your physician on a 6- to 12-month program.

Myth	Fact
8. Sit-ups will remove fat from the stomach.	8. It requires reduced calories, regular exercise, and abdominal exercises to flatten your stomach. With calorie restriction, the fat cells in the stomach will shrink, and your stomach will get smaller. Your sit-up routine (see chapter 9) will strengthen the underlying muscle tissue. Both adipose and muscle tissue need changing; you cannot convert fatty tissue to muscle tissue, nor will muscle tissue change to fat when you become sedentary.
9. Laxatives help you lose weight.	9. The use of laxatives causes gastrointestinal trouble and can result in dehydration and undernourishment. It is better to be fat than to endanger your health. It is impossible to defecate away unwanted pounds safely.
10. Weight-reducing pills are a safe approach to depressing the appetite.	10. The use of drugs and drug combinations to depress appetite is dangerous and sometimes fatal. Drug usage is an attempt to cause weight loss by increasing metabolic rate, curbing the appetite, or causing fluid loss. Amphetamines and diuretics are the two most commonly used diet pills. Amphetamines toy with the thyroid gland, cause nervousness, speed up metabolism, and require increasingly stronger dosages as tolerance develops; diuretics result in rapid fluid loss. Both are dangerous, ineffective approaches to weight loss.
11. Reducing aids such as vibrators, body wraps, rubber suits, steam baths, and massage effectively remove fat from the body.	11. Each of these popular gimmick approaches to weight loss results in little calorie burning and is totally ineffective. To lose weight and fat, you must engage in exercise that burns a high number of calories, such as aerobics. You then enter a negative calorie balance and lose weight and fat.

are strong and the patient is efficient, eager to please her parents, and somewhat of a perfectionist. An absentee or distant father is also common. The characteristic behavior of anorexia is obsessive and compulsive, resembling addiction. Patients may become obsessed with the idea that they are, or will become, fat. They may fear the transition from girlhood to womanhood resulting in a more curvaceous figure, and become determined to stave it off by controlling their weight. This starvation approach is then carried to the extreme of undernourishment until total adolescent body weight is dangerously low. Even at that extreme, patients may still feel fat and continue to starve themselves, sometimes literally to death.

Young female anorexics generally develop **amenorrhea**. Females must reacquire 17 to 22 percent body fat before the menstrual cycle resumes. Young male anorexics lose their sex drive and become impotent. Thyroid hormone secretions, adrenal secretions, growth hormones, and blood pressure-regulating hormones reach abnormal levels. The heart pumps less efficiently as cardiac muscle weakens; the chambers diminish in size, and blood pressure falls. Heart

rhythm disturbances and sudden stopping of the heart may occur due to lean-tissue loss and mineral deficiencies, producing sudden death in some patients. Other health problems include anemia, gastrointestinal problems, atrophy of the digestive tract, abnormal function of the pancreas, blood-lipid changes, dry skin, decreased core temperature, and disturbed sleep.

Early treatment is essential to avoid permanent damage. Without treatment, about 10 percent of the patients die of starvation. Forced feeding may temporarily improve health, but the condition can reappear unless proper psychological and medical therapy is initiated and is then successful. Treatment is directed at restoring adequate nutrition, avoiding medical complications, and altering the psychological and environmental patterns that have supported or permitted the emergence of anorexia. About 5 per-

Amenorrhea Loss of at least three consecutive menstrual cycles when they are expected to occur.

Behavioral Change and Motivational Strategies

Some of the more critical eating behaviors associated with weight gain that have high potential for behavioral change include: drinking high-calorie drinks instead of water, consuming too much sugar, consuming too many foods high in saturated fat, binge eating, between-meal snacking, overeating at lunch and dinner, skipping breakfast or lunch, and failing to plan snacks. Exercise behaviors rated important and having the potential to be changed include: weekend leisure inactivity, long hours spent watching television, and no regular exercise program.

It is important to remember that you are in complete control of your own eating and exercise behavior. You have the power to alter behavior that is contributing to overfatness. The following table includes some of the most common behavioral principles of weight loss. It should help you prepare specific motivational strategies to eliminate roadblocks.

Behavioral Principles of Weight Loss

1. Stimulus Control
   A. Shopping
      1. Shop for food after eating
      2. Shop from a list
      3. Avoid ready-to-eat foods
      4. Don't carry more cash than needed for shopping list
   B. Plans
      1. Plan to limit food intake
      2. Substitute exercise for snacking
      3. Eat meals and snacks at scheduled times
      4. Don't accept food offered by others
   C. Activities
      1. Store food out of sight
      2. Eat all food in the same place
      3. Remove food from inappropriate storage areas
      4. Keep serving dishes off the table
      5. Use smaller dishes and utensils
      6. Avoid being the food server
      7. Leave the table immediately after eating
      8. Don't save leftovers
   D. Holidays and Parties
      1. Drink fewer alcoholic beverages
      2. Plan eating habits before parties
      3. Eat a low-calorie snack before parties
      4. Practice polite ways to decline food
      5. Don't get discouraged by an occasional setback
2. Eating Behavior
   1. Put fork down between mouthfuls
   2. Chew thoroughly before swallowing
   3. Prepare foods one portion at a time
   4. Leave some food on the plate
   5. Pause in the middle of the meal
   6. Do nothing else while eating (read, watch television)

3. Reward
   1. Solicit help from family and friends
   2. Help family and friends provide this help in the form of praise and material rewards
   3. Utilize self-monitoring records as basis for rewards
   4. Plan specific rewards for specific behaviors (behavioral contracts)
4. Self-monitoring
   Keep diet diary that includes:
   1. Time and place of eating
   2. Type and amount of food
   3. Who is present/How you feel
5. Nutrition Education
   1. Use diet diary to identify problem areas
   2. Make small changes that you can continue
   3. Learn nutritional values of foods
   4. Decrease fat intake; increase complex carbohydrates
6. Physical Activity
   A. Routine Activity
      1. Increase routine activity
      2. Increase use of stairs
      3. Keep a record of distance walked each day
   B. Exercise
      1. Begin a very mild exercise program
      2. Keep a record of daily exercise
      3. Increase the exercise very gradually
7. Cognitive Restructuring
   1. Avoid setting unreasonable goals
   2. Think about progress, not shortcomings
   3. Avoid imperatives like "always" and "never"
   4. Counter negative thoughts with rational restatements
   5. Set weight goals

Source: From *American Journal of Clinical Nutrition* 41 (p. 823), 1985. Copyright 1985, by American Society for Clinical Nutrition Inc. Reprinted with permission.

Roadblock	Behavioral Change Strategy
Snacking before bedtime is a major problem. You just seem to get hungry after 9:00 P.M. and often devour everything in sight.	You have identified one of the major eating habits contributing to weight and fat gain. To reduce the number of calories consumed between your evening meal and bedtime, try: 1. Going to bed by 10:00 P.M. or earlier; the longer you stay up, the more likely you are to eat and drink. 2. Preparing a tray of fruits and vegetables for snacking and placing it in the front of your refrigerator for easy access. 3. Taking a 2- or 3-mile walk several hours after your evening meal. 4. Drinking two or three glasses of water two hours after your evening meal.
You find that you are able to control snacking during the day but overeat at mealtime until you are stuffed and uncomfortable.	Try some of the following suggestions to reduce your intake at mealtime: 1. Eat one or two chocolate squares or drink three or four ounces of fruit juice about 30 minutes before mealtime to raise your blood-sugar level. 2. Drink two 8-oz glasses of water at mealtime before you eat anything. 3. Measure food quantities, and prepare only the amount you want to eat. 4. Eat a small amount of dessert first, followed by your salad. 5. Take small portions and eat slowly, taking at least 30 minutes to complete the meal. 6. Never skip breakfast or lunch and never let yourself get too hungry; this is the main cause of overeating at the evening meal. 7. Take a walk or exercise an hour before mealtime.
You just cannot seem to find the time to exercise, and by the time the work day is over, you are too exhausted even to consider it.	Lack of time is the number one excuse of the sedentary individual. In most cases, even extremely busy people, can work a 30-minute exercise session into the schedule. Evaluate each of the following to determine which suggestion may work for you: 1. Walk two or three miles each noon during your lunch break just before you eat. 2. Exercise moderately about two hours after your evening meal just before bedtime. 3. Consider getting up one hour earlier for a 30-minute exercise session followed by a shower. 4. Look into programs that aid muscle toning that you can perform at your desk and in your automobile.
Circle the behaviors in the table that you feel contribute to your weight problem or to a potential weight problem in the future.	Now prepare a list of some of the things you might try in order to eliminate the barriers and alter your behavior. Refer to the specific strategies discussed in this chapter, and if you need to, refer back to chapter 3 for behavioral change and motivational strategies. 1. _____ 2. _____ 3. _____

This woman developed anorexia nervosa in college because controlling her weight made her feel more in control of her life. (Photo courtesy of Cable News Network.)

cent of those in treatment eventually reach 25 percent of their desired weight, and 50 to 75 percent resume normal menstrual cycles. After treatment ends, about 66 percent fail to eat normally and 7 percent die (of which 1 percent commit suicide).

Bulimia   More common than anorexia nervosa, bulimia occurs in males as well as females, and afflicts an estimated 10 to 20 percent of all college students. Only 5 percent of these students meet the criteria for anorexia nervosa, and less than 1 percent are actively anorexic. The typical profile of bulimia victims is similar to those suffering from anorexia nervosa, although they tend to be slightly older and healthier, malnourished but closer to normal weight. The bulimic binge is generally not a response to hunger, and the food is not consumed for nutritional value. As the binge-vomit cycle is repeated, medical problems grow. Fluid and electrolyte imbalance may lead to abnormal heart rhythm and kidney damage. Infections of the bladder and kidneys may cause kidney failure. Vomiting results in irritation and infection of the pharynx, esophagus, and salivary glands; erosion of the teeth; and dental caries. In some cases, the esophagus or the stomach may rupture.

Bulimic patients are more cooperative and somewhat easier to treat than anorexic patients since they seem to recognize that the behavior is abnormal. Most treatment programs attempt to help people gain control over their binge eating and encourage a minimum of 1,500 calories daily. Lithium and other drugs have been shown to reduce the incidence of bulimic episodes by 75 to 100 percent. Most patients can also be helped by antidepressant medication.

$\mathcal{S}$UMMARY

Causes of Obesity

Overfatness and obesity are caused by a number of factors, with both genetics and environment playing key roles. Although it is a disadvantage to inherit the tendency to become fat, environment can overcome this predisposition. Inactivity and overeating are still the two major behaviors associated with weight and fat gain.

The body appears to defend its biological weight, referred to as the set point, by resisting attempts to lose weight. Lowering the set point requires regular aerobic exercise and reduced caloric intake for 6 to 12 months or until it is evident that the body is now defending the lower weight and fat levels.

Overeating in infancy, bottle feeding instead of breast feeding, and early consumption of solid foods prior to the age of 5 months may contribute to the development of excess fat cells and overeating later in life.

Fat cells increase in number only until growth ceases, at which time one becomes fat only through the enlargement of existing adipose cells. Adults who become obese may develop some new fat cells.

Small changes in metabolism result in large increases or decreases in weight over a period of 6 to 12 months. Only a small percentage of individuals with weight problems suffer from an underactive thyroid gland. If this condition is suspected, it is wise to see a physician.

Body Composition

There are several ways to determine ideal body weight and percentage of body fat. Height-weight tables should only be used as a guide to ideal weight since they provide no indication of percentage of body fat, the key factor in determining health risks.

By measuring the thickness of two layers of skin

and the underlying fat, you can secure an estimate of total body fat and identify ideal body weight. A number of different skinfold sites can be used. Electrical impedance and underwater weighing can also be used; however, special equipment is needed.

Safe Weight-Loss Procedures

Hunger is a physiological, inborn instinct designed to control food intake, whereas appetite is a psychological, learned response. Although numerous theories have been advanced to explain how food intake is controlled, the exact signals that cue us to consume food have not been positively identified.

Calories count, and the body handles the matter with computerlike precision, storing one pound of fat for every 3,500 excess calories consumed.

Exercise is essential to the control of body weight and fat. Regular aerobic exercise depresses appetite, minimizes fat loss, maximizes the loss of lean-muscle tissue, burns a high number of calories, brings needed calcium to the bones, and changes the way the body handles dietary fat.

Special Diets

The majority of special diets fail. In many cases, this occurs within five to seven days. Approximately 90 percent of those who succeed in losing weight will regain the weight within one year.

Dieting is extremely dangerous and can prove fatal if certain nutritional guidelines are not followed. The best approach is to develop sound exercise and eating habits that you can follow throughout life.

Underweight and Eating Disorders

Weight gain is just as difficult as weight loss. A complete program of muscle-weight gain requires sound nutritional support and an organized weight-training program that involves up to six 2-hour workouts weekly.

The number of cases of anorexia nervosa and bulimia continues to increase in the United States. As long as U.S. society places such high value on thinness, this trend will continue. Both disorders are extremely difficult to treat and can produce numerous health consequences and even death.

ℛEFERENCES

American Dietetic Association. (1989). Position on optimal weight as a health promotion strategy. *Journal of the American Dietetic Association 80*; 1814–1817.

American Dietetic Association. (1990). Position on very-low-calorie weight loss diets. *Journal of the American Dietetic Association 90*; 722–724.

Bray, G. (1990). Obesity. In *Present knowledge in nutrition*, 6th ed. (pp. 23–38). Washington, DC: International Life Sciences Institute Nutrition Foundation.

Brownell, K. D., Rodin, J., & Wilmore, J. H. (1992). *Eating, body weight and performance in athletes: Disorders of modern society.* Philadelphia: Lea & Febiger.

Calloway, W., et al. (1992). A quartet of approaches to obesity. *Patient Care 26*(14); 157, 165.

Castanaguay, T. W., & Stern, J. S. (1990). Hunger and appetite. In *Present knowledge in nutrition*, 6th ed. Washington, DC: International Life Sciences Institute Nutrition Foundation.

Dietz, W. H., & Gortmaker, S. L. (1985). Do we fatten our children at the television set? Obesity and television viewing in children and adolescents. *Pediatrics 75*; 805–810.

Forbes, G. B. (1992). Exercise and lean body weight: The influence of body weight. *Nutrition Reviews 51*; 296.

Forbes, G. B. (1993). Diet and exercise in obese subjects: Self-reported versus controlled measurements. *Nutrition Reviews 51*; 296.

Rand, C. (1992). Breakfast eating and weight loss success. *American Journal of Clinical Nutrition 55*; 645.

Lab Activity 11.1

Evaluating Your Favorite Fad DIet

INSTRUCTIONS: Although most individuals are aware that fad diets are an unwise choice for safe, permanent weight and fat loss free from the risk of illness, millions of Americans continue to try practically any new, highly publicized diet that enters the market. Quick weight-loss programs possessing some so-called secret easy method of rapidly shedding pounds and fat are often too much to resist. Unfortunately, an unsound diet is dangerous and can result in permanent health consequences and even death. If you are tempted to try a diet, first follow these steps to evaluate how safe and healthy it is.

1. Before you even consider using a gimmick diet, consult your physician about your personal health concerns and ask your dietician to evaluate the entire program.

2. Compare the fad diet to the critical 10-point program for safety listed in this lab. Study the fad diet carefully and place a "yes" or "no" in the column to the right of each of the 10 criteria for a sound, safe diet.

3. If you placed a "no" in the right-hand column, even in one area, the diet is suspect and possibly unsafe if used for longer than a few days. If you placed a "no" in the right-hand column in two or more areas, don't even consider its use, even for a day.

Ten-Point Weight-Loss Program for a Sound, Safe Diet

Name _____ Date _____ Weight _____ % Body Fat _____

Weight/Fat-Loss Objective _____ Time Period _____
(1–2 lb weekly only

Week (circle)   1   2   3   4   5   6   7   8   9   10

M	T	W	TH	F	S	SU	Daily requirements	Yes/No
❏	❏	❏	❏	❏	❏	❏	**1.** 12+ 8-oz glasses of water.	
❏	❏	❏	❏	❏	❏	❏	**2.** One multiple vitamin/mineral.	
❏	❏	❏	❏	❏	❏	❏	**3.** A minimum of 8 calories per pound of your ideal weight (ideal weight $\times$ 8 =).	
❏	❏	❏	❏	❏	❏	❏	**4.** Three meals daily (no skipping).	
❏	❏	❏	❏	❏	❏	❏	**5.** Sufficient fat intake for satiety and essential fatty acids.	
❏	❏	❏	❏	❏	❏	❏	**6.** Servings from the five food groups: bread, cereal, grains, pasta—6–11; vegetables—3–5; fruits—2–4; milk, yogurt, cheese—2–3; meat, fish, poultry, dry beans, eggs, nuts—2–3.	
❏	❏	❏	❏	❏	❏	❏	**7.** Sufficient carbohydrates (simple and complex) to spare protein and prevent ketosis: 50–120 g (200–480 calories), depending on body weight.	
❏	❏	❏	❏	❏	❏	❏	**8.** 25–35 g of dietary fiber.	
❏	❏	❏	❏	❏	❏	❏	**9.** 30 min of aerobic exercise daily; 3 weight training workouts weekly.	
❏	❏	❏	❏	❏	❏	❏	**10.** Record keeping of food/fluid intake.	

*Weigh yourself no more than once weekly at the same time, under the same conditions. Pinch fatty areas the first 14 days; no weighing.

Lab Activity 11.2

Determining Your Percentage of Body Fat

INSTRUCTIONS: *One way to determine your percentage of body fat is to measure the thickness of four skinfolds. The procedure for measuring skinfold thickness is to grasp a fold of skin and subcutaneous (just under the skin) fat firmly with the thumb and forefinger, pulling it away and up from the underlying muscle tissue. Attach the jaws of the calipers one centimeter below the thumb and forefinger. All measurements should be taken on the right side of the body with the subject standing. Working with a partner, practice taking each other's measurements in the four areas described below.*

Triceps With the arm resting comfortably at the side, take a vertical fold parallel to the long axis of the arm midway between the tip of the shoulder and the tip of the elbow.

Biceps With the arm in the same position, take a vertical fold halfway between the elbow and top of the shoulder on the front of the upper arm.

Subscapula Just below the scapula (shoulder blade), take a diagonal fold across the back.

Suprailiac Just above the hip bone, take a diagonal fold following the natural line of the iliac crest.

Record the information below to complete your evaluation (for example, John is a 20-year-old who weighs 185 pounds. His four skinfold measurements were 16, 12, 37, and 15; follow his evaluation to help you understand the procedure):

1. Total of the four skinfold measures in millimeters
   (16 + 12 + 37 + 15 = 80 millimeters).   80 mm

2. Percentage of body fat based on this total from the table shown in this
   lab. Moving down in the first vertical column to 80 and over to the 17-
   to-29 age group for males in column two, we find that John has
   about 24.8 percent fat.   24.8%

3. According to current standards John's ideal fat percentage is 14.9
   percent or less.   14.9%

4. Percentage of fat to lose to reach the ideal percentage. John
   possesses about 10 percent too much fat (24.8 − 14.9 = 10) and therefore
   needs to lose 10 percent of his body weight.   10%

5. Total pounds of fat loss needed to reach ideal weight (10 percent
   times 185 or 18.5 pounds of fat).   18.5

6. Ideal weight with 14.9 percent fat (high end of recommended ideal body
   fat for college men) is 167 (185 − 18 = 167).   167

Fat as a Percentage of Body Weight Based on the Sum of Four Skinfolds, Age, and Sex

SKINFOLDS (MM)	PERCENT OF FAT, MALES (AGE IN YEARS)				PERCENT OF FAT, FEMALES (AGE IN YEARS)			
	17–29	30–39	40–49	50+	16–29	30–39	40–49	50+
15	4.8	—	—	—	10.5	—	—	—
20	8.1	12.2	12.2	12.6	14.1	17.0	19.8	21.4
25	10.5	14.2	15.0	15.6	16.8	19.4	22.2	24.0
30	12.9	16.2	17.7	18.6	19.5	21.8	24.5	26.6
35	14.7	17.7	19.6	20.8	21.5	23.7	26.4	28.5
40	16.4	19.2	21.4	22.9	23.4	25.5	28.2	30.3
45	17.7	20.4	23.0	24.7	25.0	26.9	29.6	31.9
50	19.0	21.5	24.6	26.5	26.5	28.2	31.0	33.4
55	20.1	22.5	25.9	27.9	27.8	29.4	32.1	34.6
60	21.2	23.5	27.1	29.2	29.1	30.6	33.2	35.7
65	22.2	24.3	28.2	30.4	30.2	31.6	34.1	36.7
70	23.1	25.1	29.3	31.6	31.2	32.5	35.0	37.7
75	24.0	25.9	30.3	32.7	32.2	33.4	35.9	38.7
80	24.8	26.6	31.2	33.8	33.1	34.3	36.7	39.6
85	25.5	27.2	32.1	34.8	34.0	35.1	37.5	40.4
90	26.2	27.8	33.0	35.8	34.8	35.8	38.3	41.2
95	26.9	28.4	33.7	36.6	35.6	36.5	39.0	41.9
100	27.6	29.0	34.4	37.4	36.4	37.2	39.7	42.6
105	28.2	29.6	35.1	38.2	37.1	37.9	40.4	43.3
110	28.8	30.1	35.8	39.0	37.8	38.6	41.0	43.9
115	29.4	30.6	36.4	39.7	38.4	39.1	41.5	44.5
120	30.0	31.1	37.0	40.4	39.0	39.6	42.0	45.1
125	30.5	31.5	37.6	41.1	39.6	40.1	42.5	45.7
130	31.0	31.9	38.2	41.8	40.2	40.6	43.0	46.2
135	31.5	32.3	38.7	42.4	40.8	41.1	43.5	46.7
140	32.0	32.7	39.2	43.0	41.3	41.6	44.0	47.2
145	32.5	33.1	39.7	43.6	41.8	42.1	44.5	47.7
150	32.9	33.5	40.2	44.1	42.3	42.6	45.0	48.2
155	33.3	33.9	40.7	44.6	42.8	43.1	45.4	48.7
160	33.7	34.3	41.2	45.1	43.3	43.6	45.8	49.2
165	34.1	34.6	41.6	45.6	43.7	44.0	46.2	49.6
170	34.5	34.8	42.0	46.1	44.1	44.4	46.6	50.0
175	34.9	—	—	—	—	44.8	47.0	50.4
180	35.3	—	—	—	—	45.2	47.4	50.8
185	35.6	—	—	—	—	45.6	47.8	51.2
190	35.9	—	—	—	—	45.9	48.2	51.6
195	—	—	—	—	—	46.2	48.5	52.0
200	—	—	—	—	—	46.5	48.8	52.4
205	—	—	—	—	—	—	49.1	52.7
210	—	—	—	—	—	—	49.4	53.0

In two thirds of the instances the error was within ± 3.5% of the body weight as fat for the women and ± 5% for the men.

Source: "Body Fat Assessed from Total Body Density and Its Estimation from Skinfold Thickness," by J. V. G. A. Dumin and J. Womersley, 1974, *British Journal of Nutrition* 32, p. 95. Reprinted with the permission of Cambridge University Press.

Lab Activity 11.3

Determining Your Caloric Needs

INSTRUCTIONS: *Complete each of the following steps carefully to identify how many calories you need daily to attain and maintain your ideal weight as determined in Lab Activity 11.2: Determining Your Percentage of Body Fat.*

1. Rate your level of physical activity from the following list by honestly estimating your activity level.

ACTIVITY PATTERN	CALORIES NEEDED PER LB
Very inactive (sedentary, never exercise)	13
Slightly inactive (occasional physical activity)	14
Moderately active (fairly active on the job; engage in aerobic exercise twice weekly)	15
Relatively active (almost always on the go; engage in aerobic exercise three to four times a week)	16
Frequent strenuous activity (daily aerobic exercise for one hour or more)	17

2. Multiply your rating (calories per pound) times your actual weight. A sedentary female who is 18 to 21 years old and weighs 130 pounds, for example, would need 1,690 calories per day ($130 \times 13 = 1,690$). In theory, if she is consistently eating more than 1,690 calories daily, she is gaining weight.

3. Multiply your physical activity rating times your ideal weight from Lab Activity 11.2. This figure is the number of calories needed per day to maintain your ideal weight. The ideal weight in the example in Lab Activity 11.2 is 167 pounds. Since John is sedentary, he needs only 13 calories per pound and 2,171 calories daily to maintain this weight ($167 \times 13 = 2,171$).

Once you find your ideal weight, you can eventually reach that weight by consuming only the number of calories necessary to maintain that weight. This is a common, sound approach to weight and fat loss and is used in some clinics in the United States. Weight loss that occurs slowly and safely is much more likely to be maintained in the future.

12

PREVENTING HEART DISEASE

Chapter Objectives

By the end of this chapter, you should be able to:

1. Cite the prevalence and describe the causes of heart disease.
2. Describe how to prevent or postpone the development of heart disease.
3. Discuss the role of physical fitness in preventing heart disease and cancer.

THERE IS A person we know that we will call Frank. When Frank WAS young he assumed he was invulnerable. He knew intellectually that he would someday die; sooner or later everyone does. But that was not a reality Frank had internalized. In fact, he acted as though he was impervious to the effects of his health decisions. He smoked cigarettes; rarely exercised; took on too much work, thereby "stressing himself out"; and did not eat well by often choosing fatty meals at fast-food restaurants.

Frank eventually paid the price for his health-related choices. By the time he reached his 50th year, he had a cough diagnosed as lung cancer, and had blocked arteries that threatened a heart attack. Contributing to his heart condition was the amount of stress to which he subjected himself, the cigarettes he smoked, and his lack of regular exercise. Frank's early years may have been carefree but his later adult life was fraught with discomfort and fear. He realized he would not live as long as he might have. Unfortunately, Frank's situation, extreme though it may sound, is not all that unusual.

Too many people have experienced the death of a loved one from heart disease. If you have not experienced any heart disease yourself, you almost certainly know others who have—parents, grandparents, relatives, friends. This is not surprising since heart disease and cancer account for 57 percent of all deaths that occur in the United States each year. When you add stroke, which is also a developmental disease associated with an unhealthy lifestyle, and you have accounted for almost two-thirds of the deaths that occur in this country every year.

In this chapter, we will define heart disease and discuss its causes. More importantly, we describe how to prevent its occurrence or at least how to delay its arrival. Much of that latter discussion pertains to lifestyle decisions that include physical fitness and wellness considerations.

How the heart functions

One of the authors of this book recently moved into a new house—one that was just built—and has experienced a most frustrating situation. Every few weeks the faucets have to be dismantled to clean out the debris. The builder says this is to be expected in a new house, that it is the lead and material from inside the pipes that accumulates and clogs the faucets. The fact remains that every few weeks the screen in the faucets gets clogged and has to be taken out and cleaned.

The situation with the faucets is analogous to that of the body's fluid system, which includes the heart,

---

Coronary heart disease (CHD) A condition in which the heart is supplied with insufficient blood due to clogging of coronary arteries.

Occluded Clogged arteries that no longer allow the normal amount of blood to pass through them.

Plaque A collection of blood fats and other substances that combine to clog blood vessels.

Atherosclerosis A condition in which plaque has formed and blocks the passage of blood through a blood vessel.

Angina pectoris Chest pain caused by restricted blood flow to the heart.

Lipoproteins Fatty particles that can collect on the walls of the blood vessels.

Triglyceride The fatty substance in lipoproteins.

---

the blood, and the blood vessels. As the faucets carry water to where it is needed, so do the blood vessels carry blood to where it is needed. As the pumping station somewhere in town pumps the water, so does the heart pump the blood. And as pipes can become clogged with debris, so can your blood vessels.

The heart's main function is to pump blood containing oxygen and nutrients to parts of the body. It also receives blood filled with waste products (such as carbon dioxide) that are to be eliminated from the body. The heart pumps this blood through the circulatory system and into and from the lungs via blood vessels. If these blood vessels become obstructed or if they rupture thereby interfering with the passage of oxygenated blood, the part of the body deprived of blood can die. And if it is the heart's blood supply that is blocked, it too can die. That is what happens when a heart attack occurs. The arteries supplying the heart are called the coronary arteries, any problem with them is referred to as either **coronary heart disease (CHD)** or coronary artery disease.

Coronary heart disease (CHD)

Some people are born with heart disease. They may have a heart chamber missing or malformed, a valve between the chambers of the heart not opening or closing adequately, or a weak heart that is unable to pump with enough power to expel sufficient amounts of blood throughout the body. Others may have blood vessels that do not work normally because they are malformed. And still others may have heart disease because they have had rheumatic fever (which affects the heart valves), or they may experience an irregular heartbeat known as an *arrythmia*.

The most prevalent form of heart disease, however, is CHD. The coronary arteries can become **occluded** when blood fats and other substances collect on their inside walls, thereby narrowing the opening through which blood can flow (see Figure 12.1). This collection of blood fats and other substances can also break loose and travel through the arteries until they get caught and block the flow of blood at that point. That is called a *thrombosis*. The clogging material is called **plaque,** and the condition is known as **atherosclerosis**. Plaque consists of fatty substances, cholesterol, cellular waste products, calcium, and the clotting material *fibrin*. If blood flow is restricted, individuals can become fatigued easily and may feel **angina pectoris** when they are active. If the coronary arteries are so narrowed or blocked that lit-

Figure 12.1 ✦ Coronary Artery Blockage

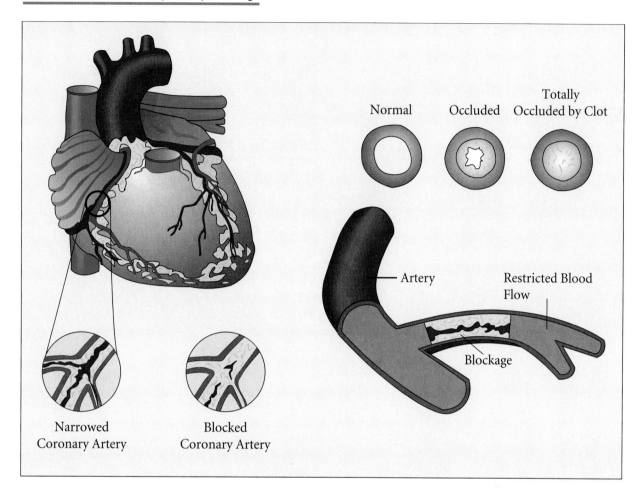

tle, if any, blood can pass through, the part of the heart deprived of oxygenated blood can die. And if that part is important or involves a large enough section of the heart, the person to whom this happens can die.

FAT AND CHOLESTEROL

Lipoproteins consist of **triglycerides**, a blood protein (to make the fat soluble in the portion of the blood that is water), and cholesterol. Although some people are suspicious of the role of triglycerides in causing CHD, researchers have found no clear-cut association between the two. The real culprit in CHD is the cholesterol found in the foods we eat and that are manufactured by the liver. When we eat foods high in saturated fats, the liver is stimulated to manufacture cholesterol. Add that to the cholesterol in the foods of animal origin that we eat, and the amount in our blood can be excessive. The recommended daily consumption of cholesterol is 300 milligrams. Yet the average person in the United States consumes 1½ to 3 times that amount. The recommended amount of saturated fat to be consumed daily is 10 percent of

Eating foods high in fat exposes you to the danger of contracting coronary heart disease.

Behavioral Change
and Motivational Strategies

To assist you in eliminating or decreasing barriers to achieving and maintaining a healthy heart, we list several of these barriers below, along with strategies for overcoming them.

Roadblock	Behavioral Change Strategy
You may enjoy eating foods high in saturated fats. Many of us grew up on french fried potatoes and hot dogs or hamburgers. They taste good, are easy to prepare, and are relatively inexpensive. Unfortunately, they also put us at risk for both CHD and certain cancers.	Use *reminder* systems to encourage buying and eating more healthful foods. Put notes on your refrigerator and pantry to remind you to refrain from eating certain foods when you are looking for a snack. And place a picture of a clogged artery at the top of your shopping list to remind you not to buy unhealthful foods. You can also use *covert modeling*. Find a friend who eats well, who looks good, and whose behavior you would like to follow. Then observe what this friend eats. After obtaining a good picture of how this friend selects and prepares foods, model your behavior on him or her. Eat and prepare similar foods—at least those that you enjoy eating and that are also low in fat and other unhealthy food ingredients.
You don't seem to be able to find the time nor the interest to exercise regularly, although you know you should.	Use *reminders* on your bathroom mirror, your refrigerator, and any other places that will serve as a stimulus to exercise. Keep a *log* of the amount and type of exercise in which you engage daily. Use *gradual programming* by developing an exercise plan that is both realistic and incorporates room for incremental improvements. You can also join an exercise or health club, thereby using *chaining*. That is, you would have started the first link in the chain of regular exercise.
You may find exercise uncomfortable. Your muscles may ache, your clothes and body may get sweaty, and you may not enjoy the activity itself. With this attitude, you cannot be expected to maintain an exercise program even if you are motivated to begin one. After all, most people don't want to feel uncomfortable and will choose not to be so.	Use *goal-setting strategies* to establish realistic and achievable fitness goals. If you are experiencing aches and pains, you are overtraining or exercising inappropriately. The maxim "no pain, no gain" has long been discarded by fitness experts. You should feel good after a workout. You can also use *selective awareness* described in chapter 14. Focus on the benefits of the exercise: how it will burn up calories, make you look and feel better, help you be healthier, and make your clothes fit better. If you focus on the benefits rather than on the temporary discomforts, you will be more likely to maintain your exercise program.
You recognize that you are an intense person. You always seem to be rushed, you express hostility too often and too easily, you tend to be too competitive when you should be more cooperative, and you usually do two or more things at the same time, thereby not focusing well enough on the task at hand. In other words, you are the stereotype of the Type A behavior pattern and want to change so that you exhibit more Type B behavior.	Use *reinforcement* to encourage Type B behavior and to discourage Type A behavior. For example, when you find yourself doing more than one thing at a time, decide which one to focus on and delay the other activities. When you are successful doing this, reward yourself by taking a few minutes to think of a day you can recall that was terrific! Recall all the events of that day—the sights, sounds, smells—and relive it as best you can. Or if you find that you are rushing through an activity or task for which you have ample time, punish yourself by taking time away from the activity so you delay its completion. Or if you act angrily or in a hostile manner to someone, punish yourself by purchasing that person a "gift of apology." After a while, your budget may require that you adjust your responses to people.

Roadblock	Behavioral Change Strategy
What other roadblocks are interfering with your ability to be heart healthy?	Cite behavioral change strategies that can help you overcome the roadblocks you just listed. If you need to, refer back to chapter 3 for behavioral change and motivational strategies.
1. _____	1. _____
2. _____	2. _____
3. _____	3. _____

total calories. Yet the average person in the United States consumes over three times that amount. No wonder heart disease is the leading cause of death in the United States.

LOW-DENSITY AND HIGH-DENSITY LIPOPROTEINS (LDLS AND HDLS)

There are several different kinds of lipoproteins, of which **low-density lipoproteins (LDLs)** and **high-density lipoproteins (HDLs)** have the most significance for CHD. LDLs are produced in the liver and released into the bloodstream where they carry cholesterol to cells throughout the body. Cholesterol helps form cell membranes and the covering that protects nerve fibers; aids in the formation of vitamin D and the sex hormones androgen, estrogen, and progesterone; and helps produce bile salts that aid digestion of fats. When LDLs carry more cholesterol than the body requires, however, it can build up on the artery walls.

HDLs are also produced by the liver and released into the bloodstream. Although they also carry cholesterol, HDLs pick up unused cholesterol and return it to the liver where it is used to produce bile salts. In addition, it is thought that HDLs possibly provide a protective layer of grease to help prevent a buildup of substances on artery walls.

When LDL is elevated and HDL is too sparse, there is a likelihood that arteries will be clogged and CHD will be promoted. It is recommended that HDL (the *good* cholesterol) levels exceed 35 for adult men and 45 for adult women and that LDL (the *bad* cholesterol) levels remain less than 165. A total cholesterol/HDL ratio of 5:1 (20 percent of total cholesterol being of the HDL variety) begins to provide some protection from CHD. Physical activity can increase

HDL levels in the bloodstream. That is one reason it is recommended as a way of preventing CHD.

To determine whether the composition of your blood is healthful, complete Lab Activity 12.1: Is Your Blood in Tune? at the end of this chapter.

OTHER RISK FACTORS FOR HEART DISEASE

You already know that the foods we eat and the cholesterol our bodies produce are two reasons that blood vessels can become clogged. There are also other causes of clogged coronary arteries and for the development of heart disease.

Hypertension

Systolic blood pressure in excess of 140 mm Hg or diastolic blood pressure in excess of 90 mm Hg is known as **hypertension. Systolic blood pressure**

Low-density lipoproteins (LDLs) Fatty particles in the blood that carry cholesterol to cells throughout the body.

High-density lipoproteins (HDLs) Fatty particles in the blood that pick up unused cholesterol and transport it for processing and elimination from the body.

Hypertension High blood pressure; usually greater than 140 systolic blood pressure and/or greater than 90 diastolic blood pressure.

Systolic blood pressure The force of the blood against the arterial blood-vessel walls when the left ventricle contracts and blood is pumped out of the heart.

The average American eats too much fat and cholesterol, substances that contribute to both heart disease and cancer. (Photo courtesy of the National Cancer Institute.)

refers to the force of the blood against the arterial blood vessel walls when the left ventricle contracts and blood is pumped out of the heart. **Diastolic blood pressure** represents the force of the blood against the arterial walls when the heart is relaxed. High blood pressure forces the heart to work harder than normal and places the arteries under strain. Eventually, hypertension contributes to heart attacks, strokes, and atherosclerosis. In 90 percent of high blood-pressure *essential hypertension* cases, the causes are unknown. In the remaining 10 percent, it is

caused by kidney abnormality, tumor of the adrenal gland, or a congenital defect of the aorta (the main artery leading out of the heart). Regular physical activity and a more healthful diet are often recommended for people whose blood pressure is too high. In some cases, medication is needed to reduce blood pressure to healthier levels.

Obesity or Overweight

Excess weight places added strain on the heart and increases blood pressure and blood cholesterol. For these reasons, people who have gained more than 20 pounds since they were 18 years old have been found to have doubled their risk of experiencing a heart attack. In addition, obesity is linked to diabetes, and is usually associated with lack of physical activity, thereby further increasing the risk of heart attack.

Stress

Excessive stress also increases a person's chances of contracting heart disease. That is because stress results in an increase in cholesterol in the blood, an increase in heart rate, higher blood pressure, and other effects detrimental to normal heart functioning. Stress results in the release of hormones called *catecholamines*, which prepare the body to respond

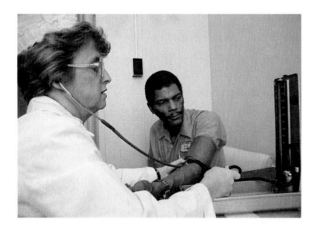

One of the benefits of participating in regular physical activity is maintaining normal blood pressure and/or helping to control hypertension.

Myth and Fact Sheet

Myth	Fact
1. If CHD runs in your family, there is not much you can do to prevent getting it.	1. CHD is related to a number of factors of which heredity is but one. Other risk factors include smoking, lack of exercise, high blood cholesterol, obesity, and high blood pressure. You can do much to eliminate or diminish the effects of these risk factors.
2. All cholesterol is bad.	2. Cholesterol that accumulates on the walls of the arteries, LDL, is bad for you. HDL, however, helps to carry blood fats out of the body and is therefore helpful.
3. You can recognize whether your blood pressure is high but there is little you can do to lower it.	3. High blood pressure occurs without any noticeable symptoms, but with a more healthful diet and regular physical activity, blood pressure can be lowered, even without medication.
4. In order to exercise to the point at which I am doing something good for my heart, I need to work out so intensely that I feel exhausted and my muscles hurt.	4. Consider this: The American Heart Association states that brisk walking is an excellent exercise and that low-intensity exercises performed daily can have long-term health benefits and lower your risk of contracting heart disease.
5. Heart disease is a problem for older people, so I don't have to worry about it until I am much older.	5. Heart disease is a degenerative disease. That is, it takes a long time to develop since degeneration occurs relatively slowly. Autopsies of young accident victims have revealed the beginning of blockage in coronary arteries. You need to prevent heart disease starting today. When you get older, too much damage may already have occurred.

physically to the fight-or-flight response. The heart beats faster, blood pressure increases, and blood glucose and cholesterol levels increase. If stress occurs often, these detrimental effects become chronic and can lead to CHD.

Researchers have even found a coronary-prone personality type. As we discussed in chapter 4, this Type A behavior pattern is characterized by being focused on time (hurried and time pressured), competitive, aggressive, hostile, and multiphasic (doing two or more things at a time). The opposite, Type B behavior pattern, seems to protect people from developing CHD. More recent research indicates that hostility is the major ingredient in the Type A behavior pattern. That is, people who are easily angered and who are often hostile are the most susceptible to CHD. Stress also too frequently interferes with people engag-

ing in regular exercise. They become so concerned with managing the source of the stress—whether that be their classes, jobs, or home lives—that they allow too little time, if any, for physical activity.

Sedentary Lifestyle

We have just discussed the effect of stress on physical activity. In addition, a sedentary lifestyle does not allow for the production of sufficient HDL, strength-

Diastolic blood pressure The force of the blood against the arterial walls when the heart is relaxed.

ening of the heart muscle, or control of mild hypertension. To make matters worse, inactivity is associated with overweight and obesity, two other risk factors for CHD. And, inactivity deprives you of an outlet for the release of built-up stress by-products.

Smoking Tobacco

Research has linked smoking with various diseases such as cancer, emphysema, and heart disease. When a person smokes, the blood vessels constrict thereby causing increased blood pressure. In addition, the heart speeds up in response to nicotine, a central nervous system stimulant. Furthermore, cigarettes contain substances that can damage the inside walls of the arteries. Once they have been damaged, it is easier for cholesterol and other substances to adhere to, and accumulate in, the arteries. All of this, coupled with carbon dioxide from cigarette smoke replacing oxygen in the bloodstream, means the heart is overworking and heart disease is more likely.

Family History

Not all risk factors are amenable to change. Heredity, for example, is not. Some people are born with a predisposition to heart disease. However, that predisposition only means there is the potential to develop CHD. Your lifestyle will influence whether you do and when you do. Some people prefer to use a family history of heart disease as an excuse for behaving in ways that are unhealthy for the heart. That is unfortunate because they might be able to delay or even prevent CHD if they change their behavior.

To determine your risk of acquiring CHD, complete Lab Activity 12.2: Risk Factor Analysis: The Game of HEALTH at the end of this chapter.

𝓗OW TO PREVENT CORONARY HEART DISEASE

It is possible to manage many of the risk factors for CHD. Hypertension can be controlled by some combination of diet, exercise, or medication. Overweight or obesity can be controlled by diet and exercise. Stress can be managed by a change in lifestyle and engaging regularly in some form of relaxation. Sedentary lifestyles can be remedied by participation in an exercise program. Smoking can be stopped by joining a smoking cessation program or quitting cold turkey. And periodic medical screenings can be useful to an-

alyze blood lipids and evaluate the functioning of the heart. The good news is that you have a great deal of influence over whether you develop CHD. If you are serious about preventing CHD, you can do so.

The Role of Physical Activity

Physical activity is one of the most important components of a CHD prevention program. That is because it is either directly or indirectly related to so many of the risk factors. Physical activity exercises the heart muscle, encourages the production of HDL, and aids in the control and prevention of mild hypertension. It enhances cardiorespiratory endurance and increases stroke volume of the heart (the amount of blood pumped out of the heart with each contraction). It also is an excellent stress-management technique since it uses the stress by-products that prepare the body to respond physically to a stressor. And

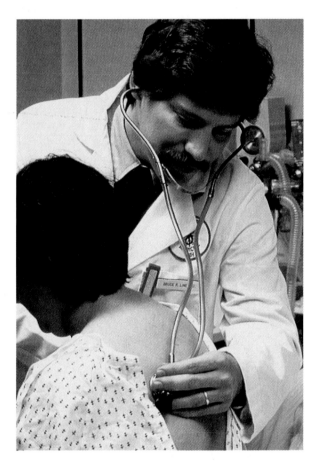

If you have been relatively inavtive and now want to begin an exercise program, you should have a medical examination to rule out any conditions that would restrict the types of physical activities in which you engage.

physical activity can help you maintain desirable weight and the proper amount of lean body mass.

These effects are somewhat direct and obvious, but there are less direct and less obvious CHD-related benefits of physical activity as well. Engaging in regular exercise will tone your body, provide you with confidence in your ability to perform physically, and make you feel better about yourself. In short, it will improve your self-esteem. The result will be less stress, fewer catecholamines produced, and therefore less potential damage to your heart.

Physical activity also encourages smoking cessation. Smoking is incompatible with aerobic activity since carbon monoxide replaces oxygen in the bloodstream. Furthermore, doing one good thing for your health, such as becoming physically fit, encourages other healthy lifestyle adjustments.

It is for these and other reasons that an effective CHD prevention program includes a physical activity component. As prestigious an organization as the American Heart Association (AHA) recognizes the importance of physical activity in preventing CHD. In 1992, the Committee on Exercise and Cardiac Rehabilitation of the Council on Clinical Cardiology of the AHA published a position paper entitled "Statement on Exercise: Benefits and Recommenda-tions for Physical Activity Programs for All Americans." That AHA statement serves as a good summary of the role physical activity can play in preventing and treating CHD. In it the AHA states that:

> Exercise helps control blood lipid abnormalities, diabetes, and obesity.... Inactivity is a risk factor for the development of coronary artery disease.... There is also evidence that physical activity probably alleviates symptoms of mild and moderate depression and provides an alternative to alcoholism and drug abuse.

The AHA goes on to suggest specific activities that are most beneficial:

> Activities such as walking, hiking, stair-climbing, aerobic exercise, calisthenics, jogging, running, bicycling, rowing, and swimming and sports such as tennis, racquetball, soccer, basketball, and touch football are especially beneficial when performed regularly. Brisk walking is also an excellent choice.... The evidence also supports the notion that even low-intensity activities performed daily can have some long-term health benefits and lower the risk of cardiovascular disease. Such activities include walking for pleasure, gardening, yard work, house work, dancing, and prescribed home exercise.

SUMMARY

How the Heart Functions

The heart's main purpose is to pump blood containing oxygen and nutrients to parts of the body. In addition, the heart receives blood containing waste products (such as carbon dioxide) for elimination. It is through the circulatory system and its blood vessels that the heart pumps and receives blood.

Coronary Heart Disease

If the blood vessels to the heart become obstructed or if they rupture, thereby interfering with the passage of oxygenated blood, the part of the body deprived of blood may die. If it is the arteries supplying the heart (coronary arteries) that become obstructed, a part of the heart may die. This is what happens when a heart attack occurs.

Coronary arteries can become occluded by blood fats and other substances that accumulate on their inside walls. When this collection of substances breaks loose and travels to another part of the body, it is called a thrombosis. The clogging material itself is called plaque, and the blockage of the coronary arteries is known as atherosclerosis.

Fat and Cholesterol

When foods are eaten that are high in saturated fats, the liver is stimulated to manufacture cholesterol. Cholesterol, along with the blood protein triglycerides, form lipoproteins. It is the cholesterol from foods, added to the cholesterol the body normally produces, that can become excessive and result in occlusion of the coronary arteries.

Low-Density and High-Density Lipoproteins

Low-density lipoproteins (LDLs) are produced in the liver and released into the bloodstream where they carry cholesterol cells throughout the body. When LDLs carry more cholesterol than the body requires, the cholesterol can build up on the artery walls.

High-density lipoproteins (HDLs) are also produced by the liver and released into the bloodstream. However, they help prevent buildup on the artery walls by picking up unused cholesterol and returning it to the liver.

A total cholesterol/HDL ratio 5:1 begins to provide some protection from coronary heart disease. One way to increase HDL levels is by engaging in physical activity.

Other Risk Factors

Hypertension, obesity and overweight, stress, a sedentary lifestyle, smoking tobacco, and a family history of heart disease are other risk factors for CHD. Systolic blood pressure above 140 mm Hg or diastolic blood pressure above 90 mm Hg is termed hypertension. High blood pressure forces the heart to work harder and can lead to strokes, atherosclerosis, and heart attack.

People who have gained over 20 pounds since they were 18 years old have doubled their risk of hav-ing a heart attack. People who experience a great deal of stress and people who live sedentary lifestyles also subject themselves to a greater risk of heart disease. Furthermore, smoking tobacco results in blood vessels constricting (thereby increasing blood pressure), rapid heartbeat, and damage to the interior walls of the arteries.

One factor that is irreversible is a history of heart disease in the individual's family. However, lifestyle will affect how soon heart disease will manifest itself and the degree to which it will interfere and/or cut short one's life.

How to Prevent Coronary Heart Disease

To prevent heart disease, you need to modify CHD risk factors. For example, adjusting the diet, employing stress management techniques, refraining from smoking tobacco products, exercising regularly, and obtaining periodic medical screenings can go a long way in preventing or postponing the development of CHD.

Since physical activity is related to so many of the CHD risk factors, it is one of the most important components of a CHD prevention program. Physical activity exercises the heart muscle, encourages the production of HDLs, helps control hypertension, is effective in managing stress, is incompatible with smoking tobacco, and contributes to the maintenance of recommended fat and weight guidelines.

ℛEFERENCES

American Heart Association. (1992). *Statement on exercise: Benefits and recommendations for physical activity programs for all Americans.* Dallas: American Heart Association.

Friedman, M. & Rosenman, R. H. (1974). *Type A Behavior and Your Heart.* Greenwich, CT: Fawcett.

Lab Activity 12.1

Is Your Blood in Tune?

INSTRUCTIONS: *The composition of your blood is very important when it comes to preventing CHD. You can easily have your physician check your blood fat levels. Sometimes this is done with a simple finger prick, but to be as accurate as possible, it should be done by having blood drawn from a vein after you have fasted for about 12 hours. Record the results of that assessment below:*

_____ Total cholesterol below 200: No further evaluation necessary, recheck in 5 years.

_____ Total cholesterol is more than 200: Recheck in 1 to 8 weeks.

_____ Total cholesterol is 200 to 239 (borderline high cholesterol): Evaluate risk factors to see what lifestyle changes you can make (diet, exercise, and so forth). If your physician says you are not in the high-risk category for CHD, active treatment is not necessary.

_____ Total cholesterol is above 240 (high cholesterol): Analyze and measure HDL, LDL, and triglycerides.

Once the above is completed, answer the following questions:

Yes	No	
_____	_____	1. Is your total cholesterol no more than $4.5 \times$ HDL cholesterol?
_____	_____	2. Is your cholesterol/HDL ratio at least $5:1$?
_____	_____	3. Is your HDL reading above 35?
_____	_____	4. Is your LDL cholesterol less than 160?

If the answers to these questions are "Yes," your lipid profile is good. Regardless of how your lipid profile turned out, list the important changes you can make to lower your total cholesterol and increase your HDL cholesterol over the next 12 months.

Lab Activity 12.2

Are You Type A or Type B?

INSTRUCTIONS: *Opposing behavior patterns are presented in the left- and right-hand columns with a horizontal line between. Place a vertical mark across the line where you feel you belong between these two extremes. For example, most of us are neither the most competitive nor the least competitive person we know; we fall somewhere in between. Your task is to make a vertical line where you feel you belong between the two extremes.*

1. Never late _____ Casual about appointments

2. Not competitive _____ Very competitive

3. Anticipate what others are saying _____ A good listener, hear others out

4. Always rushed _____ Never feel rushed, even under pressure

5. Take things one at a time _____ Try to do many things at once; think about what to do next

6. Emphatic speech (may pound desk) _____ Slow, deliberate talker

7. Want a good job to be recognized by others _____ Only care about satisfying self, no matter what others think

8. Do things quickly (eating, talking, etc.) _____ Do things slowly

9. Sit on feelings _____ Express feelings

10. Easygoing _____ Hard driving

11. Many interests _____ Few interests except work

12. Satisfied with job _____ Ambitious

13. Can wait _____ Impatient when waiting patiently

14. Go "all out" _____ Casual

✦ Scoring

Using a ruler, one point is scored for each 1/16 inch you fall from the non-Type A behavior end of the line to the point marked. Points are summed up for all 14 questions. Items 2, 5, 10, 12, and 13 are measured from the left of the line to your mark; items 1, 3, 4, 6, 7, 8, 9, 11, and 14 are measured from the right of the line to your mark. Now add your points for all 14 questions.

Type A average score: 178.21

Type B average score: 211.51

Source: From "A Short Rating Scale as a Potential Measure of Pattern A Behavior," by R. W. Bortner, 1969, *Journal of Chronic Diseases* 22. Copyright 1969, by Pergamon Press, Ltd. Reprinted with permission.

Lab Activity 12.3

Risk Factor Analysis: The Game of HEALTH

INSTRUCTIONS: *Carefully complete the following form to determine your risk of heart attack. Tabulate points, and compare your score with those below to identify your risk. Keep in mind that a high score does not mean you will develop heart disease; it is merely a guide to make you aware of your potential risk. Because no two people are alike, an exact prediction is impossible without a carefully individualized evaluation.*

	1	**2**	**3**	**4**	**6**
Heredity	No known history of heart disease	One relative with heart disease over 60 years	Two relatives with heart disease over 60 years	One relative with heart disease under 60 years	Two relatives with heart disease under 60 years

	1	**2**	**3**	**5**	**6**
Exercise	Intensive exercise, work, and recreation	Moderate exercise, work, and recreation	Sedentary work and intensive recreational exercise	Sedentary work and moderate recreational exercise	Sedentary work and light recreational exercise

	1	**2**	**3**	**4**	**6**
Age	10–20	21–30	31–40	41–50	51–65

	0	**1**	**2**	**4**	**6**
Lb.	More than 5 lbs below standard weight	± 5 lb standard weight	6–20 lb overweight	21–35 lb overweight	36–50 lb overweight

	0	**1**	**2**	**4**	**6**
Tobacco	Nonuser	Cigar or pipe	10 cigarettes or fewer per day	20 cigarettes or more per day	30 cigarettes or more per day

	1	**2**	**3**	**4**	**6**
Habits of eating food	0% No animal or solid fats	10% Very little animal or solid fats	20% Little animal or solid fats	30% Much animal or solid fats	40% Very much animal or solid fats

◆ **Your risk of heart attack**

4–9	Very remote
10–15	Below average
16–20	Average
21–25	Moderate
26–30	Dangerous
31–36	Urgently dangerous—reduce score!

Other conditions, such as stress, high blood pressure, and increased cholesterol, detract from heart health and should be evaluated by your physician.

13

$\mathcal{P}$REVENTING $\mathcal{C}$ANCER

$\mathcal{C}$hapter Objectives

By the end of this chapter, you should be able to:

1. Cite the prevalence of cancer.

2. Discuss the causes of cancer.

3. Describe how to prevent cancer.

4. Detail how to perform breast and testicular self-examinations.

5. Describe the roles of nutrition, reduced exposure to the sun, and exercise in preventing cancer.

$\mathcal{M}$ANY PEOPLE DECIDE to live with cancer, rather than to die from it. They do not let the fact that they have cancer limit the quality or importance of their lives. Rabbi Hirschel Jaffe is an example. In 1978, shortly after crossing the finish line of the New York marathon, Rabbi Jaffe began the fight of his life, the fight against cancer. When Hirschel Jaffe found he had recovered from leukemia, he decided to share his good fortune by counseling cancer patients. But that was not all that he did. He then wrote *Gates of Healing* (a book distributed to hospital patients everywhere), wrote a highly acclaimed book called *Why Me? Why Anyone?* and developed a videotape entitled "Hanging on to Hope." As though that were not enough, in 1980 Hirschel Jaffe visited U. S. hostages in Iran to give them comfort and support, and in 1992 he led a unity march in Newburgh, New York to protest the appearance of the Ku Klux Klan in his town. Over 3,000 people attended that march. In 1988, Rabbi Jaffe received the American Cancer Society's Award of Courage from then President Ronald Reagan. Those who know Rabbi Hirschel Jaffe call him "the running Rabbi" for his marathon participation and his tireless efforts on behalf of others. Sometimes cancer can lead to a positive outcome.

WHAT IS CANCER?

What we call **cancer** is not a single disease but rather a group of more than 100 diseases involving abnormal cell growth. In normal body cells, the rate of cell division is under precise control. Cancer cells, in contrast, grow wildly, divide rapidly, and assume irregular shapes; tumors develop and invade nearby normal tissue. These abnormal cells eventually spread to distant body areas via the blood and lymphatic system; this process of spreading is referred to as **metastasis** (see Figure 13.1). At the time of diagnosis, the spread of cancer to other body parts has already occurred in 6 of 10 patients. For those individuals, eradicating the deadly cells is much more difficult.

Cancer is capable of destroying the body in a number of ways, eventually resulting in death. Cancer cells actively divide and crowd out normal specialized cells; they rob vital nutrients from and "starve" normal cells. Eventually, normal tissues, organs, and body systems cannot perform their vital functions and death occurs. Malignant tumors may obstruct blood vessels, the digestive and urinary tracts, or other body parts, eliminating the normal function of an entire system or organ. Tumors may also decrease or eliminate the intake or absorption of nutrients, causing the body literally to waste away, or they may decrease the capacity of the lungs to oxygenate blood. In addition, the body's immune system is weakened and death

Figure 13.1 ✦ Metastasis: A Process in Which Cancerous Cells Entering a Blood Vessel Spread to Distant Body Areas

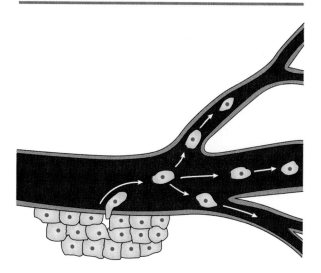

may occur from the inability to fight invading pathogens. Patients are considered cured if there is no evidence of cancer for five years; others may survive in **remission,** an asymptomatic state in which the spread of cancerous cells is assumed to be temporarily stopped.

The various forms of cancer are named according to the type of tissue involved. **Carcinomas** begin

Table 13.1 ✦ Estimated Cancer Incidence in the United States, by Site and Sex

MALES		FEMALES	
New Cases	*Type*	*New Cases*	*Type*
244,000	Prostate	182,000	Breast
96,000	Lung	73,900	Lung
70,700	Colon and rectum	67,500	Colon and rectum
37,300	Bladder	48,600	Uterus
18,800	Lymphoma	26,600	Ovary
18,700	Oral	24,700	Lymphoma
17,100	Melanoma of skin	15,400	Melanoma of skin
14,700	Kidney	13,200	Bladder
16,700	Leukemia	13,000	Pancreas
14,000	Stomach	11,700	Kidney
11,000	Pancreas	11,000	Leukemia
9,000	Larynx	9,350	Oral

Source: From *Cancer Facts & Figures—1995* (p. 11), by American Cancer Society, New York. Used with permission. Copyright by American Cancer Society, Inc.

Table 13.2 ✦ Estimated Cancer Deaths in the United States, by Site and Sex

MALES		FEMALES	
Deaths	Type	Deaths	Type
95,400	Lung	62,000	Lung
40,400	Prostate	46,000	Breast
27,200	Colon and rectum	28,100	Colon and rectum
13,200	Pancreas	14,500	Ovary
12,820	Lymphoma	13,800	Pancreas
11,100	Leukemia	11,330	Lymphoma
8,800	Stomach	10,700	Leukemia
8,200	Esophagus	9,300	Liver
7,700	Liver	6,500	Brain
7,500	Bladder	6,000	Uterus
7,300	Brain	5,900	Stomach
7,100	Kidney	5,000	Multiple myeloma

Source: From *Cancer Facts & Figures—1995.* (p. 11) by American Cancer Society, New York. Used with permission. Copyright by American Cancer Society, Inc.

in the epithelial cells, which form the lining of the lungs, digestive organs, reproductive organs, skin, mouth, and other body cavities. Carcinomas tend to spread through the circulatory or lymphatic system, forming solid tumors. With early detection, treatment can be successful. A second major type of cancer arises in the mesodermal or middle layers of tissue that form the bones, muscles, and connective tissue. **Sarcomas,** as these are known, tend to spread through the blood stream, forming solid tumors. Although less common, they are more difficult to treat and control. **Lymphomas** develop in the infection-fighting regions of the body and metastasize through the lymph system, forming solid tumors. Hodgkin's disease, an example of one type of lymphoma, is now being successfully treated. *Leukemia* is a cancer of the blood-forming parts of the body, such as the bone marrow and spleen. These nonsolid tumors are characterized by an abnormally high number of white blood cells. Treatment advances have greatly extended life in many patients. Sites for cancer and incidence by sex are shown in Tables 13.1 and 13.2.

CAUSES OF CANCER

Researchers theorize that cancer is produced from a basic change in the nucleic acid chain located in the nucleus of the cell. DNA (deoxyribonucleic acid) may control the rate of cell division. RNA (ribonu-

cleic acid) appears to assist DNA with this control. It is believed that factors inside or outside the cell may act on the DNA or RNA through a physical or chemical disturbance and result in abnormal, erratic cell division.

The World Health Organization estimates that up to 85 percent of all cancer cases are the result of

Cancer Not a single disease, but a group of 100 diseases that are characterized by abnormal cell growth.

Metastasis The spread of cancer cells through the circulatory and lymphatic systems to other parts of the body, causing cancer in new areas of the body.

Remission A situation in which cancer remains asymptomatic, when it ceases to grow or to spread, or when it disappears.

Carcinomas Cancers that begin in the epithelial cells (the linings) of the lungs, digestive organs, reproductive organs, mouth, and other body cavities.

Sarcomas Cancers that arise in the mesodermal or middle layers of the tissues that form the bones, muscles, and connective tissues.

Lymphomas Cancers that begin in the infection-fighting regions of the body—principally the lymphatic system.

exposure to environmental factors. Of the 1,400 chemicals, drugs, and pollutants suspected of causing cancer, 22 have been declared carcinogenic to humans. Uncovering cancer-causing substances is no easy task and is complicated by three problems: the 20- to 35-year "latent" period between exposure and symptoms of the disease occurring, the amount of exposure that produces cancer, and the controversy over whether animal test results can be applied to humans. Regardless of these obstacles, it is evident that the environment has become a major target of cancer researchers.

Occupational Agents

Certain physical and chemical environmental agents tend to contribute to cancer information. In 1775, coal soot was identified as a contributor to cancer of the scrotum. One hundred years later, during the Industrial Revolution, a type of lubricating oil constantly sprinkled on men working beside cotton-spinning machines was also linked to this type of cancer. The air in mines contains a fine radioactive dust which can cause lung cancer in miners. During the 1920s, bone cancer was observed in factory workers who painted numbers on the hands of watch faces with a radium compound to make them glow in the dark. By twirling the end of a fine brush in their mouths to acquire a "tip" before dipping the brush into the compound, the workers absorbed minute quantities of radium, which eventually worked into the bones. Researchers and epidemiologists continue searching for carcinogens in today's workplace.

Environmental Pollution

Many experts believe that some cancers are a product of our environment. Many blame high levels of hydrocarbons leaked into the air from automobiles and other vehicles for certain types of cancer. Asbestos and radiation exposure, asphalt road and street surfaces, chemicals in some water supplies, food additives or preservatives (such as nitrites), and

> **Melanoma** Skin cancers, often related to overexposure to the sun, that may spread to other parts of the body.
>
> **Oncogenes** Genes found in tumor cells whose activation is associated with the transformation of norm cells into cancer cells.

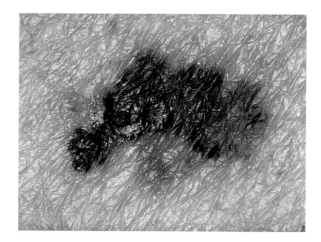

Skin cancer is the result of exposure to the sun, but can be prevented by using a sunscreen and protective clothing when out in the sun.

insecticides are examples of contaminants that appear to have the potential to cause some types of cancer. Scientists are concerned about a cumulative or multiplying effect from these environmental agents. Even if so-called safe levels are maintained, there may be an effect from continuous daily exposure. There is evidence that some cancers develop after years of exposure to certain agents.

Chronic Irritation or Tissue Damage

Repeated low-grade tissue damage may lead to cancer. Gallstones on the lining of the gallbladder, some tissue injuries, a few chronic infections to certain organs, chronically infected scars (such as burn scars), repeated ulcerations, and bladder infections have been linked to cancer.

Viruses

Some malignancies in animals may be caused by viral agents, and considerable research is under way to identify viruses related to cancer in human beings. Studies have linked acute leukemia, sarcoma, and melanoma to viral agents. At one time, it was believed that breast cancer might be caused by a virus, but the majority of scientists today reject this view. The virus that causes herpes has been linked to cancer of the cervix.

Radiation

Excessive exposure to ionized radiation increases cancer risks and may be linked to leukemia and other forms of cancer, including thyroid and bone cancer. Sources of ionized radiation include X-rays, the sun, radon, and radium. Most medical and dental X-rays and radium rays now deliver the lowest possible doses and offer good protection to patients. The sun is the major factor in the development of **melanoma** (a malignant skin tumor) as well as of 600,000 new cases of nonmelanoma skin cancer each year. Excessive *radon* in homes is suspected of increasing the risk of lung cancer, particularly among cigarette smokers. X-rays and radium can also cause cancer. No evidence is available to link cosmic rays from outer space with cancer.

Individual Susceptibility

The known and suspected causes of cancer discussed in this section account for only some of the cases of cancer that develop. Also, most people who are exposed even to recognized carcinogens do not develop cancer. It therefore appears that there exists within the living organism a quality of individual susceptibility. That susceptibility seems to be related

To prevent skin cancer or sunburn, use a sunscreen when out-of-doors on a sunny day.

to personality factors. A "cancer personality" has been identified and characterized as depressed, rigid, self-condemning, and unable to develop meaningful relationships with others. Scientists theorize that some people with this personality pattern are unable to release their pent-up feelings and so turn them inward, thereby disrupting their hormonal levels or other aspects of metabolism. This theory is becoming an important focus of research.

Hereditary and Congenital Factors

Hereditary factors appear to be related to some cancers. For example, retinoblastoma, a malignant eye tumor occurring in infants and young children, has been found to be hereditary. More common, however, is a predisposition, or tendency, of members of a family to acquire a particular form of cancer. In some types of cancers, such as cancer of the breast, uterus, stomach, intestine, and colon, immediate family members face a greatly increased risk. However, it should be noted that a predisposition does not mean that a person will definitely develop the disease. It does mean that people in such families should be alert to signs of possible conditions, have regular checkups, and develop healthy eating and exercise patterns. To determine the history of cancer in your family, complete Lab Activity 13.1: Your Family Tree of Life and Death at the end of this chapter.

Congenital causes, or cancer occurring during the development of the embryo during the prenatal period, involve a few special groups of tumors affecting infants, children, and young adults. Congenital tumors (most are benign) account for only a small fraction of tumors and cancer.

New findings in genetics have identified the importance of **oncogenes;** the genes found in tumor cells whose activation is associated with the transformation of normal cells into cancer cells. An analysis of the products of these oncogenes may predict which tumors are likely to recur after surgery.

Precancerous Conditions

Some precancerous conditions—but not all—tend to develop into cancer, with the cause of cancer being the same as the cause for the precancerous condition. Benign tumors, a mass or overgrowth of cells in the mouth, lip, tongue, or cheek, or a patch of cells on the skin (small scab, scaly patch, brown to black warts) fall into the category of precancerous conditions. Moles are not precancerous, and the average person has about twenty-two to twenty-three of them. A mole that is constantly irritated is much more likely to become malignant. Benign tumors should be removed as soon as possible, regardless of how low the probability of developing cancer is.

Tobacco Use

There is a strong link between tobacco use and lung cancer, cancer of the lip and mouth, and cancer of the pharynx, larynx, esophagus, pancreas, and bladder. Smoking accounts for approximately 30 percent of all cancer deaths. The incidence of lung cancer is related to the number of cigarettes smoked, the degree of inhalation, and the number of years one has smoked. The American Cancer Society estimates that cigarette smoking is responsible for 90 percent of lung cancer cases among men and 79 percent among women—more than 87 percent overall. The gap between male and female levels of lung cancer has been narrowing, due to the increased number of women who have been smoking for 10 years or more. Use of smokeless tobacco also increases the risk of cancer of the mouth, larynx, throat, and esophagus.

Other Cancer Risk Factors

Estrogen Estrogen treatment to control meno-pausal symptoms can increase the risk of contracting uterine cancer. However, including progesterone in estrogen replacement therapy helps minimize this risk. Estrogen replacement therapy helps prevent osteo-porosis in women—a far more prevalent condition in older women than is uterine cancer. Continued research is being conducted to clarify the relationship between estrogen replacement therapy and the subsequent development of breast cancer. Studies to date have been contradictory. Consultation with a physician will help each woman to assess personal risks and benefits of estrogen treatment.

Alcohol Excessive alcohol consumption in any form is another cancer risk factor. Oral cancer and cancers of the larynx, throat, esophagus, and liver occur more frequently among heavy drinkers of alcohol, especially among those who smoke cigarettes or chew tobacco.

Carcinogens Agents (toxins, chemicals, and so forth) that can cause cancer.

Abstaining from any type of tobacco products greatly reduces the risk of cancer. (Photo courtesy of the American Heart Association.)

Nutrition The foods we eat are related to our risk of contracting cancer. Diets high in fatty foods may be a factor in the development of breast, colon, and prostate cancers. Eating salt-cured and smoked foods frequently places you at risk of cancer of the esophagus and stomach. And, individuals 40 percent and more overweight have an increased risk of colon, breast, prostate, gallbladder, ovary, and uterine cancers. On the other hand, diets consisting of recommended servings of fruits and vegetables are associated with a decreased risk of lung, prostate, bladder, esophagus, colorectal, and stomach cancers; and ingestion of high-fiber foods appears related to a decreased risk of colon cancer.

To determine your risk of contracting cancer, complete Lab Activity 13.2: Determining Your Risk of Acquiring Cancer at the end of this chapter.

Cancer Prevention

Although not all cancers can be prevented, more than two thirds probably can be. If people gave up smoking, ate diets consisting of less fat and more vegetables and fruits, limited the amount of alcohol they ingested, and protected themselves from exposure to the sun, the decrease in the incidence of cancer would be significant. Here are some things you can do to decrease your chances of contracting cancer, or if you do contract it, to detect it early:

- Abstain from using tobacco in any form, including the smokeless variety.
- Eliminate or reduce your consumption of alcohol; drink only in moderation.

- Avoid contact with known **carcinogens** whenever possible.

- Decrease your exposure to the sun; avoid sunbathing for long periods of time; and use a sunscreen with the appropriate sun protection factor (SPF) for your skin type any time you plan to be in the sun.

- Follow a dietary plan that increases your consumption of vitamins A and C, cruciferous vegetables (for example, cauliflower and broccoli), and fiber. Reduce your consumption of artificial sweeteners, heat-charred food, nitrite-cured or smoked foods, fats, and calories.

- Maintain recommended body weight and fat.

- Obtain cancer screenings as recommended (see Table 13.3 to identify early signs of cancer.

Table 13.3 ✦ Summary of American Cancer Society Recommendations for the Early Detection of Cancer (for People without Symptoms)

TEST OR PROCEDURE	SEX	AGE	FREQUENCY
Sigmoidoscopy, preferably flexible	M&F	50 and over	Every 3–5 years
Fecal occult blood test	M&F	50 and over	Every year
Digital rectal[1] examination	M&F	40 and over	Every year
Prostate exam*	M	50 and over	Every year
Pap test	F	All women who are, or who have been, sexually active, or have reached age 18, should have an annual Pap test and pelvic examination. After a woman has had three or more consecutive satisfactory normal annual examinations, the Pap test may be performed less frequently at the discretion of her physician.	
Pelvic examination	F	18–39	Every 1–3 years with Pap test
		40 and over	Every year
Endometrial tissue sample	F	At menopause, if at high risk[2]	At menopause and thereafter at the discretion of the physician
Breast self-examination	F	18 and over	Every month
Breast clinical examination	F	18–39 40 and over	Every 3 years Every year
Mammography[3]	F	40–49 50 and over	Every 1–2 years Every year
Health counseling Cancer checkup[4]	M&F M&F	18–39 40 and over	Every 3 years Every year

[1]Annual digital rectal examination and prostate-specific antigen should be performed on men 50 years and older. If either is abnormal, further evaluation should be considered.

[2]History of infertility, obesity, failure to ovulate, abnormal uterine bleeding, or unopposed estrogen therapy.

[3]Screening mammography should begin by age 40.

[4]To include examination for cancer of the thyroid, testicles, ovaries, lymph nodes, oral region, and skin.

Copyright by American Cancer Society, Inc. Reprinted with permission.

Figure 13.2 ✦ Breast Self-Examination

Master the following technique and examine your breasts during a bath or shower once per month. Regular examination will soon get you used to the normal feel of your breast. Keep a record of your examination dates and the results. Indicate the type and location of any nodule, changes in the contour of each breast, swelling, dimpling of skin, changes in the nipple, or any discharge. Consult your physician immediately if you notice any of these symptoms.

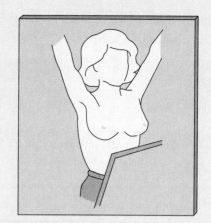

In the shower. Examine your breasts during your bath or shower since hands glide more easily over wet skin. Hold your fingers flat and move them gently over every part of each breast. Use the right hand to examine the left breast and the left hand for the right breast. Check for any lump, hard knot, or thickening.

Before a mirror. Inspect your breasts with arms at your sides. Next, raise your arms high overhead. Look for any changes in the contour of each breast: a swelling, dimpling of skin, or changes in the nipple.

Then rest your palms on your hips and press down firmly to flex your chest muscles. Left and right breast will not exactly match—few women's breasts do. Again look for changes and irregularities. Regular inspection shows what is normal for you and will give you confidence in your examination.

Lying down. To examine your right breast, put a pillow or folded towel under your right shoulder. Place your right hand behind your head: This distributes tissue more evenly on the chest. With the left hand, fingers flat, press gently in small circular motions around an imaginary clock face. Begin at the outermost top of your right breast for 12 o'clock, then move to 1 o'clock, and so on, around the circle back to 12. (A ridge of firm tissue in the lower curve of each breast is normal).

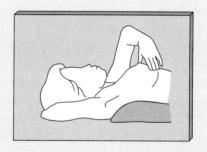

Then move one inch inward toward the nipple and keep circling to examine every part of your breast, including the nipple. This requires at least three more circles. Now slowly repeat the procedure on your left breast with a pillow under your left shoulder and your left hand behind your head. Notice how your breast structure feels.

Finally, squeeze the nipple of each breast gently between thumb and index finger. Report any discharge, clear or bloody, to your doctor immediately.

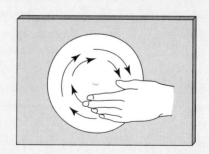

324

Figure 13.3 ✦ Testicular Self-Examination

Follow the instructions in the diagram carefully and examine your testes immediately after your next hot bath or shower. Heat causes the testicles to descend and the scrotal skin to relax, making it easier to find unusual lumps.

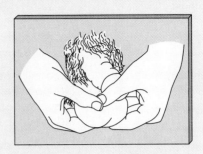

Examine each testicle by placing the index and middle fingers of both hands on the underside of the testicle and the thumbs on the top. Gently roll the testicle between your thumb and fingers, feeling for small lumps.

Changes or anything abnormal will appear at the front or side of your testicle. Did you find any unusual lumps? Are there any unusual signs of any kind? Are there any markings or lumps at any site?

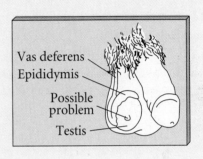

Vas deferens
Epididymis
Possible problem
Testis

Keep in mind that not all lumps are a sign of testicular cancer. Unusual lumps at any location, however, should be checked by a physician. Early detection greatly increases your chances of a complete cure. Repeat the examination every month and record your findings.

• Learn how to do breast (females) and testicular (males) self-examinations and do them regularly. Refer to Figures 13.2 and 13.3 for the proper way to perform these self-exams.

• Check for changes in your skin that might indicate skin cancer.

• Report any family history of cancer to your doctor and have that history noted on your medical records.

Table 13.4 summarizes the things you can do to prevent developing cancer.

Physical Activity and Cancer Prevention

Physical activity has been found to help prevent the onset of cancer. The exact reason for this is unclear, although several theories have been proposed. For example, some researchers attribute the decreased incidence of cancer among people who are physically active to their being leaner. Excess fat is associated with cancer of the colon, prostate, endometrium, and breast. Whether physical activity has a direct effect on cancer or an indirect effect by reducing body fat is unknown.

The National Cancer Institute also reports that men who exert the energy equivalent of walking 10 or more miles per week have half the risk of developing colon cancer of less active men. One theory explaining this finding is that exercise increases the rate of transit of food through the digestive tract. If there are carcinogens in the fecal stream, the faster they proceed through the system, the less chance there is that they will attach themselves to mucosa lining the tract and develop into cancer.

There is also evidence that women who exercise regularly are less prone to develop cancer of the breast or of the reproductive system. One theory relates a lower rate of these cancers and exercise to the amount of body fat. Fat is needed to make estrogen. This theory hypothesizes that excess fat increases the risk of these cancers because it leads to too much estrogen being produced.

These findings pertain to moderate amounts of exercise. That does not mean that very intense exercise is also protective of cancer. In fact, some researchers believe that very intense exercise is actually detrimental because it suppresses the immune system, resulting in the body being less able to ward off carcinogens. The discovery by researchers that prostate cancer is more common among male athletes lends credence to this theory.

Table 13.4 ✦ How to Prevent Cancer

Here are some things you can do to minimize your risk of developing cancer.

Do not smoke	Cigarette smoking is responsible for 90 percent of lung cancer cases among men and 79 percent among women—about 87 percent overall. Smoking accounts for about 30 percent of all cancer deaths. Those who smoke two or more packs of cigarettes a day have lung cancer mortality rates 12 to 25 times greater than nonsmokers.
Limit exposure to sunlight	Almost all of the more than 800,000 cases of nonmelanoma skin cancer diagnosed each year in the United States are considered to be sun-related. Recent epidemiologic evidence shows that sun exposure is a major factor in the development of melanoma and that the incidence increases for those living near the equator.
Limit ingestion of alcohol	Oral cancer and cancers of the larynx, throat, esophagus, and liver occur more frequently among heavy drinkers of alcohol, especially when accompanied by smoking cogarettes or chewing tobacco.
Avoid smokeless tobacco	Use of chewing tobacco or snuff increases risk of cancer of the mouth, larynx, throat, and esophagus and is a highly addictive habit.
Consult with physician regarding estrogen treatment	Estrogen treatment to control menopausal sysmptoms can increase risk of endometrial cancer. However, including progesterone in estrogen replacement therapy helps to minimize this risk. Consultation with a physician will help each woman to assess personal risks and benefits. Continued research is needed in the area of estrogen use and breast cancer.
Limit exposure to radiation	Excessive exposure to ionizing radiation can increase cancer risk. Most medical and dental X-rays are adjusted to deliver the lowest dose possible without sacrificing image quality. Excessive radiation exposure in homes may increase risk of lung cancer, especially in cigarette smokers. If levels are found to be too high, remedial actions should be taken.
Limit exposure to occupational hazards	Exposure to several different industrial agents (nickel, chromate, asbestos, vinyl chloride, and so forth) increases risk of various cancers. Risk from asbestos is greatly increased when combined with cigarette smoking.
Eat well	Individuals 40 percent or more overweight have an increased risk of colon, breast, prostate, gallbladder, ovary, and uterus cancers. A varied diet eaten in moderation offers the best hope for lowering the risk of cancer. Studies show that daily consumption of vegetables and fresh fruits is associated with a decreased risk of lung, prostate, bladder, esophagus, colorectal, and stomach cancers. High-fiber diets are a healthful substitute for fatty foods and may reduce the risk of colon cancer. A diet high in fat may be a factor in the development of certain cancers, particularly breast, colon, and prostate. In areas of the world where salt-cured and smoked foods are eaten frequently, there is a higher incidence of cancer of the esophagus and stomach. Modern methods of food processing and preserving appear to avoid the cancer-causing by-products associated with older methods of food treatment.

Source: From *Cancer Facts & Figures—1995* (p. 19) by American Cancer Society, New York. Copyright by American Cancer Society, Inc. Used with permission.

Early Detection and Diagnosis of Cancer

Many cancers are highly curable if they are detected early. For example, both breast and testicular cancer detected in their earliest stages are well over 90 percent curable. The later the cancer is detected, the less positive is the prognosis. That is why it is so important to detect cancer as early as possible. Obtaining regular medical checkups is one way of assuring that cancers are found in their earliest stages. Medical screenings recommended are listed in Table 13.4. Another method of early detection is by performing regular self-examinations. Two of the most frequently recommended self-examinations are of

Myth and Fact Sheet

Myth	Fact
1. Cancer is contagious.	1. There is no evidence that you can contract cancer from someone else. Cancer results from coming in contact with a cancer-causing agent, and this agent cannot be passed from one person to another. Cancer-causing agents include certain toxins in the air, certain chemicals, viruses, and radiation from the sun.
2. Fluoridation of the water causes cancer.	2. Fluoridation of the water supply has been one of the most significant developments in the prevention of dental disease. It in no way causes cancer. If fluoride were detrimental to the health of people, scientists would long ago have discovered that, politicians and government regulators would have banned the use of fluoride, and citizen's watch groups would have insisted on this action.
3. Lumps found during a breast self-examination are more than likely cancerous.	3. The great majority of lumps identified during breast self-exams are benign. However, since early detection is the key to successfully treating cancer, all lumps should be checked out by a physician as soon as possible. To wait is to gamble with your health and with your life.
4. Everything causes cancer.	4. This is just not true. Although cancer can result from toxins, carcinogens in cigarette smoke, chemicals, and viruses, saying that everything causes cancer is just an excuse for ignoring specific causes.
5. Cancer affects all groups of people to the same extent.	5. More African-American men and women than white men and women die of cancer. And white men and women contract skin cancer to a much greater extent than do African-American men and women.

the breast for women and of the testicles for men (shown in Figures 13.2 and 13.3).

TREATMENT OF CANCER

The three main forms of treatment for cancer are radiation, surgery, and chemotherapy. The choice of treatments (or treatments) depends on the type of cancer and the extent to which it has spread. For example, surgery is most successful at treating cancers that have not spread beyond the original site, whereas chemotherapy and radiation are used to treat cancers that have spread into different areas of the body.

Radiation Therapy

Radiation treatment involves using X-rays, radium and betatron. Cancer cells are more vulnerable than healthy cells to X-rays and radium. The ideal dosage would destroy cancer cells, with minimal damage to normal cells. Often, however, the dose required to destroy cancer cells permanently damages surround-

ing normal cells. Some kinds of cancer can be entirely destroyed using radiation.

Surgery

Surgery is also employed in the treatment of cancer for removal of tumors. Three out of four women with breast cancer can now be saved through surgery, depending on the stage of the disease. *Radical mastectomy* (removal of the entire breast and surrounding muscles) is no longer considered necessary in the early stages of the disease. A modified mastectomy (removal of the affected part of the breast and surrounding lymph nodes) or *lumpectomy* (removal of the tumor and the surrounding tissue only) followed by radiation is just as effective as radical surgery. Regardless of the location and size of the tumor, there is no difference in survival rates.

Chemotherapy

Chemotherapy is a treatment that uses chemicals (drugs) to seek out and attack cancer cells. More than

Behavioral Change and Motivational Strategies

There are many things that might interfere with your behaving in ways to prevent cancer. Here are some barriers (roadblocks) and strategies for overcoming them.

Roadblock	Behavioral Change Strategy
Friends or relatives may smoke cigarettes. That means that you may be tempted to do so yourself. Even though we like to think we act independently, other people's behaviors influence us, particularly if we like and respect those people. Furthermore, you do not even have to smoke to be subjected to the harmful effects of tobacco products. Breathing secondhand, or sidestream, smoke, can affect your susceptibility to CHD and cancer.	Two behavioral change strategies appropriate here are *contracting* and *social support*. Find a friend or relative who would like to give up smoking. This will not be difficult. Smokers often try to quit; the problem is that they are usually unsuccessful. Draw up a contract for each of you to smoke less gradually over a period of weeks *(gradual programming)*. Use the contract format described in chapter 3. If you do not presently smoke, make your contract for not starting to smoke and the other person's contract specific to gradually reducing the number of cigarettes smoked per week. Each of you then sign the other's contract as a witness. The support you can provide each other, and the pressure of a contract that will periodically be evaluated, can be just the motivation needed to counteract the influence of other smoking friends and relatives.
You are afraid to perform self-examinations or have regular medical checkups because you fear that a cancer will be uncovered. In addition, you are fearful of the discomfort or embarrassment that might accompany medical screenings.	Use a technique called *self-talk* to convince yourself that it is in your best interest to overcome your fear. Self-talk requires you to make statements to yourself that make you less anxious about the behavior you wish to perform. In this case, you can say the following to yourself: It will be better to find any cancer earlier rather than later. It is highly unlikely that I have cancer. An ounce of prevention is worth a pound of cure. I will probably not have cancer and will then feel a hundred times better for knowing that I am healthy.
You want to limit your ingestion of alcohol, but all of your friends drink and you don't think you can hang with them unless you join them in drinking as well. They might think you no longer fit in if you don't drink and won't want anything to do with you as a result.	Make a *contract* with your friends to be the designated driver when you go out with them so they will be more likely to appreciate your not drinking. Or use *social support*. Ask another friend who also might not want to drink to join you in abstaining. Or *substitute* a soft drink for the alcoholic drink you would usually hold in your hand. You could also use *self-talk* and tell yourself that by abstaining you are decreasing your chances of developing certain cancers.
List roadblocks interfering with your working at preventing cancer.	Now cite behavioral change strategies that can help you overcome the roadblocks you just listed. If you need to, refer back to chapter 3 for behavioral change and motivational strategies.
1. _____	1. _____
2. _____	2. _____
3. _____	3. _____

25 drugs have been identified that will poison cancer cells and stop or slow their growth; all of them damage normal cells and cannot be used indefinitely. In addition, most of the drugs have serious side effects.

The control of hormones in the body has been used with varying degrees of success in treating breast cancer and prostate cancer.

It is clear that chemicals can alter the genetic

Improving Your Community

Preventing Cancer

You can contribute to the prevention of cancer in your community while responding to your own cancer prevention needs. Below are several ways in which you can accomplish that goal:

1. Insist that laws prohibiting smoking in public places are enforced. That may mean tactfully confronting someone who is smoking where smoking is disallowed. It may also mean speaking with owners of businesses (for example, restaurants) that allow smoking too close to those wishing not to inhale secondhand smoke.

2. Organize a "Smoke-Free Day" on campus during which smokers are encouraged to go one day without smoking. If you plan for this day with an educational campaign—posters placed in residence halls and dining facilities, interviews of health professionals on the campus radio station, speakers provided in health classes—you can expect some students will use this day as an excuse to stop smoking altogether.

3. Develop a speakers' bureau of experts on tobacco and smoking cessation and make speakers available to local schools. High school and middle school students often look up to college students, and they may be influential with a stop smoking/never start presentation.

4. Lobby local legislators to require the proper authorities to enforce tobacco-related laws. Letter-writing campaigns, personal interviews, and mailings regarding the problem are all examples of the techniques you can use. You might seek strict enforcement of the laws prohibiting the sale of tobacco products or reduced availability of cigarette vending machines located near hangouts for minors.

5. Obtain pictures or slides of skin cancer from the local cancer society or the health department and develop a display that can be posted in heavily traveled areas on campus (for example, the student union, dining halls, dormitories). You might even make this a part of a health fair you organize.

6. Do research on the cancer-causing agents commonly found in offices (for example, associated with photocopying machines) and write a pamphlet that you distribute to businesses in the community.

These are but a few ways you can be socially responsible as it pertains to helping to prevent cancer in the communities in which you work, attend school, and live. What other ways can you think of to exercise your civic responsibility and help decrease the incidence of cancer among your neighbors, coworkers, and fellow students? ✦

message of cancer cells and change them into cells that can no longer grow. Although this principle of transforming cancer to benign cells, called *differentiation therapy,* is still in the experimental stages, it shows great promise.

Bone Marrow Transplants

Leukemia is sometimes treated with *bone marrow transplants.* Unless a compatible donor is found, the "warrior cells" (T lymphocytes) attack the leukemia patient, producing a fatal condition called g*raft versus host* disease. For the procedure to succeed, marrow must come from an identical twin or a brother or sister with closely matched blood. Less than 30 percent of leukemia patients have such a donor.

Researchers are evaluating a new technique in which a portion of the patient's own marrow is removed before treatment, saved, and later restored by transplantation. This procedure eliminates the problem of locating a suitable donor and allows the patient to tolerate larger doses of anticancer drugs or radiation therapy.

SUMMARY

What Is Cancer?

Cancer is not a single disease but rather a group of several hundred diseases. Cancer involves abnormal cells that grow wildly, divide rapidly, and assume irregular shapes. Tumors develop and invade nearby tissue, and these cells may spread to distant parts of the body in a process referred to as metastasis. Once metastasis occurs, a cure is more problematic. Patients may be considered cured if there is no evidence of cancer in five years, whereas others may survive in an asymptomatic state in which the spread of cancerous cells is assumed to be temporarily stopped (referred to as remission).

There are different forms of cancer, named according to the type of tissue involved. Carcinomas begin in the epithelial cells that form the lining of various organs of the body. Sarcomas arise in the mesodermal or middle layers of tissue that form the bones, muscles, and connective tissue. Lymphomas develop in the infection-fighting regions of the body.

Causes of Cancer

Cancer can be caused by occupational agents; environmental pollution; chronic irritation or tissue damage; viruses; radiation; individual characteristics and/or personality; hereditary and congenital factors; precancerous conditions; tobacco use; estrogen treatment; excessive alcohol consumption; and diets high in fatty foods, salt-cured foods, and smoked foods and low in fruits and vegetables.

Cancer Prevention

Cancer can be prevented by changes in lifestyle behaviors. These behaviors include abstaining from the use of tobacco products, if ingesting alcohol doing so only in moderation, avoiding contact with known carcinogens, and decreasing exposure to the sun. In addition, following a diet that increases consumption of vitamins A and C, cruciferous vegetables, and fiber; and decreases consumption of artificial sweeteners, heat-charred food, nitrite-cured or smoked foods, fats, and calories will help prevent cancer.

Physical activity has been found to prevent the onset of cancer. The reason for this is unclear but may relate to using calories and decreasing body fat, speeding the transport of food through the digestive tract, and/or decreasing estrogen production.

Furthermore, learning to conduct breast and testicular self-examinations, checking for changes in the skin, and obtaining regular medical screenings at recommended intervals can help detect a cancer in its early stages, thereby making treatment more effective and less severe and discomforting.

Treatment of Cancer

Treatment decisions depend on the type of cancer and the extent to which it has spread. Some cancers can be treated with radiation, some with surgery, others with chemotherapy, some with bone marrow transplants, and some with a combination of methods. The earlier the cancer is detected, the more successful and less disturbing is the treatment.

REFERENCES

American Heart Association. *Statement on Exercise: Benefits and Recommendations for Physical Activity Programs for All Americans.* Dallas, TX: American Heart Association, 1992.

Friedman, Meyer, and Rosenman, Ray H. *Type A Behavior and Your Heart.* Greenwich, CT: Fawcett, 1974.

Lab Activity 13.1

Your Family Tree of Life and Death

INSTRUCTIONS: Some types of cancers seem to run in families. When this is the case, family members are advised to pay particular attention to behaviors that put them at risk (for example, decreasing exposure to the sun) and assuring they have medical screenings on a regular basis. To determine the degree to which cancer is prevalent in your family background, complete the family tree of life and death below. For each family member listed, write in the date that person was born and, if deceased, the date that person died, the cause of death, and the age at death. After the tree is completed, share it with your physician and seek his or her advice regarding your risk of cancer and any adaptations that you should make in your lifestyle. Be assured that even though you may have a history of cancer in your family, that does not mean you will inevitably acquire the disease. All it means is that you may be more susceptible. With appropriate risk-reducing behaviors, you can significantly decrease your risk and/or eliminate it.

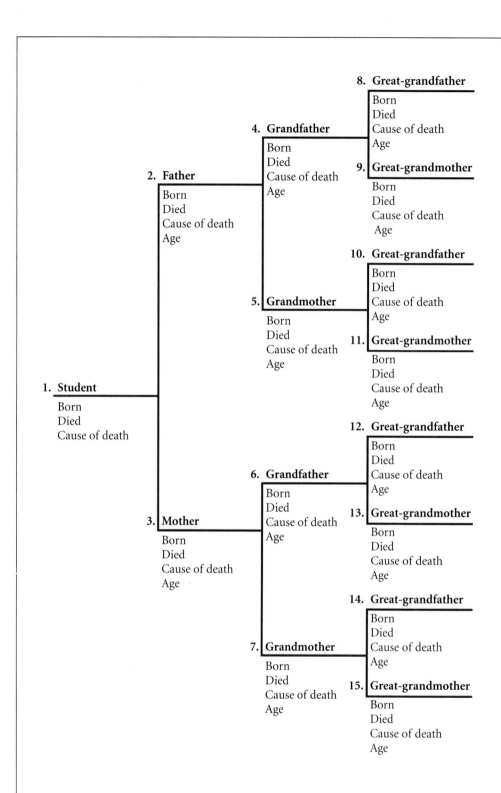

8. Great-grandfather
Born
Died
Cause of death
Age

9. Great-grandmother
Born
Died
Cause of death
Age

10. Great-grandfather
Born
Died
Cause of death
Age

11. Great-grandmother
Born
Died
Cause of death
Age

12. Great-grandfather
Born
Died
Cause of death
Age

13. Great-grandmother
Born
Died
Cause of death
Age

14. Great-grandfather
Born
Died
Cause of death
Age

15. Great-grandmother
Born
Died
Cause of death
Age

4. Grandfather
Born
Died
Cause of death
Age

5. Grandmother
Born
Died
Cause of death
Age

6. Grandfather
Born
Died
Cause of death
Age

7. Grandmother
Born
Died
Cause of death
Age

2. Father
Born
Died
Cause of death
Age

3. Mother
Born
Died
Cause of death
Age

1. Student
Born
Died
Cause of death

Lab Activity 13.2

Determining Your Risk of Acquiring Cancer

INSTRUCTIONS: *Select the response that best describes you for each question and record the point value in the space provided. Total your points for each section separately.*

Lung Cancer	**Lung**

1. Sex
    a. Male (2)
    b. Female (1)
	1. _____

2. Age
    a. 39 or less (1)
    b. 40–49 (2)
    c. 50–59 (5)
    d. 60+ (7)
	2. _____

3. Smoker (8) Nonsmoker (1)	3. _____

4. Type of smoking
    a. Current cigarettes or little cigars (10)
    b. Pipe and/or cigar but not cigarettes (3)
    c. Ex-cigarette smoker (2)
    d. Nonsmoker (1)
	4. _____

5. Number of cigarettes smoked per day
    a. 0 (1)
    b. Less than 1/2 pack per day (5)
    c. 1/2–1 pack (9)
    d. 1–2 packs (15)
    e. More than 2 packs (20)
	5. _____

6. Type of cigarettes
    a. High tar/nicotine (10)[a]
    b. Medium tar/nicotine (9)
    c. Low tar/nicotine (7)
    d. Nonsmoker (1)
	6. _____

[a] High T/N = More than 20 mg tar and 1.3 mg nicotine
Medium T/N = 16–19 mg tar and 1.1–1.2 mg nicotine
Low T/N = 15 mg or less tar and 1.0 mg or less nicotine

7. Duration of smoking   7. _____
   a. Never smoked (1)
   b. Ex-smoker (3)
   c. Up to 15 years (5)
   d. 15–25 years (10)
   e. More than 25 years (20)

8. Type of industrial work   8. _____
   a. Mining (3)
   b. Asbestos (7)
   c. Uranium and radioactive products (5)

                                            Lung Total _____

Colon/Rectal Cancer   **Colon/Rectal**

   1. Age   1. _____
      a. 39 or less (10)
      b. 40–59 (20)
      c. 60 and over (50)

   2. Has anyone in your immediate family ever had: 2. _____
      a. Colon cancer (20)
      b. One or more polyps of the colon (10)
      c. Neither (1)

   3. Have you ever had: 3. _____
      a. Colon cancer (100)
      b. One or more polyps of the colon (40)
      c. Ulcerative colitis (20)
      d. Cancer of the breast or uterus (10)
      e. None (1)

   4. Bleeding from the rectum (other than obvious
        hemorrhoids or piles)   4. _____
      a. Yes (75)
      b. No (1)

                                    Colon/Rectal Total _____

Skin Cancer   **Skin**

   1. Frequent work or play in the sun   1. _____
      a. Yes (10)
      b. No (1)

   2. Work in mines, around coal tars, or around radioactivity   2. _____
      a. Yes (10)
      b. No (1)

   3. Complexion—fair or light skin.   3. _____
      a. Yes (10)
      b. No (1)

                                            Skin Total _____

Lab Activity 13.2 *(continued)*
Determining Your Risk of Acquiring Cancer

Women Only—Breast Cancer	Breast
1. Age Group	**1.** _____
a. 20–34 (10)	
b. 35–49 (40)	
c. 50 and over (90)	
2. Race/ethnicity	**2.** _____
a. Oriental (5)	
b. African American (20)	
c. White (25)	
d. Mexican American (10)	
3. Family history	**3.** _____
a. Mother, sister, aunt, or grandmother with breast cancer (30)	
b. None (10)	
4. Your history	**4.** _____
a. Previous lumps or cysts (25)	
b. No breast disease (10)	
c. Previous breast cancer (100)	
5. Maternity	**5.** _____
a. First pregnancy before 25 (10)	
b. First pregnancy after 25 (15)	
c. No pregnancies (20)	
	Breast Total _____

Women Only—Cervical Cancer[b]	Cervical
1. Age group	**1.** _____
a. Less than 25 (10)	
b. 25–39 (20)	
c. 40–54 (30)	
d. 55 and over (30)	
2. Race/ethnicity	**2.** _____
a. Oriental (10)	
b. Puerto Rican (20)	
c. African American (20)	
d. White (10)	
e. Mexican American (20)	
3. Number of pregnancies	**3.** _____
a. 0 (10)	
b. 1 to 3 (20)	
c. 4 and over (30)	
4. Viral infections	**4.** _____
a. Herpes and other viral infections or ulcer formations on the vagina (10)	
b. Never (1)	

[b]Lower portion of uterus. These questions do not apply to women who have had total hysterectomies.

5. Age at first intercourse   **5.** _____

    a. Before 15 (40)

    b. 15–19 (30)

    c. 20– 24 (20)

    d. 25 and over (10)

    e. Never (5)

6. Bleeding between periods or after intercourse   **6.** _____

    a. Yes (40)

    b. No (1)

                                           Cervical Total _____

Women Only—Endometrial Cancer[c]   **Endometrial**

    1. Age group   **1.** _____

        a. 39 or less (5)

        b. 40–49 (20)

        c. 50 and over (60)

    2. Race/ethnicity   **2.** _____

        a. Oriental (10)

        b. African American (10)

        c. White (20)

        d. Mexican American (10)

    3. Births   **3.** _____

        a. None (15)

        b. 1 to 4 (7)

        c. 5 or more (5)

    4. Weight   **4.** _____

        a. 50 or more pounds overweight (50)

        b. 20–49 pounds overweight (15)

        c. Underweight for height (10)

        d. Normal (10)

    5. Diabetes   **5.** _____

        a. Yes (3)

        b. No (1)

    6. Estrogen hormone intake   **6.** _____

        a. Yes, regularly (15)

        b. Yes, occasionally (12)

        c. None (10)

    7. Abnormal uterine bleeding   **7.** _____

        a. Yes (40)

        b. No (1)

    8. Hypertension   **8.** _____

        a. Yes (3)

        b. No (1)

                                           Endometrial Total _____

[c]Body of uterus. These questions do not apply to women who have had total hysterectomies.

Lab Activity 13.3 *(continued)*
Determining Your Risk of Acquiring Cancer

◆ **Analysis of Results**

Lung

1. Men have a higher risk of lung cancer than women when type, amount, and duration of smoking are the same. Since more women are smoking cigarettes for a longer duration than previously, their incidence of *lung and upper respiratory tract (mouth, tongue and larynx) cancer* is increasing.
2. The occurrence of lung and *upper respiratory tract* cancer increases with age.
3. Cigarette smokers have up to 20 times or even greater risk than nonsmokers. However, the rates of ex-smokers who have not smoked for 10 years approach those of nonsmokers.
4. Pipe and cigar smokers are at a higher risk for lung cancer than nonsmokers. Cigarette smokers are at a much higher risk than nonsmokers or pipe and cigar smokers. *All forms of tobacco, including chewing, markedly increase the user's risk of developing cancer of the mouth.*
5. Male smokers of less than one-half pack per day have 5 times higher lung cancer rates than nonsmokers. Male smokers of one to two packs per day have 15 times higher lung cancer rates than nonsmokers. Smokers of more than two packs per day are 20 times more likely to develop lung cancer than nonsmokers.
6. Smokers of low-tar/nicotine cigarettes have slightly lower lung cancer rates.
7. The frequency of lung and *upper respiratory tract* cancer increases with the duration of smoking.
8. Exposures to materials used in these industries have been demonstrated to be associated with lung cancer. Smokers who work in these industries may have greatly increased risks. Exposures to materials in other industries may also carry a higher risk.

If your lung total is:

24 or less	You have a low risk for lung cancer.
24–49	You may be a light smoker and would have a good chance of kicking the habit.
50–74	As a moderate smoker, your risks of lung and upper respiratory tract cancer are increased. If you stop smoking now, these risks will decrease.
75–over	As a heavy cigarette smoker, your chances of getting lung and upper respiratory tract cancer are greatly increased. Your best bet is to stop smoking now—for the health of it. See your doctor if you have a nagging cough, hoarseness, persistent pain or sore in the mouth or throat.

Colon/Rectal

1. Colon cancer occurs more frequently after the age of 50.
2. Colon cancer is more common in families with a previous history of this disease.
3. Polyps and bowel diseases are associated with colon cancer.
4. Rectal bleeding may be a sign of colorectal cancer.

If your colon total is:

29 or less	You are at a low risk for colon-rectal cancer.
30–69	This is a moderate-risk category. Testing by your physician may be indicated.
70–over	This is a high-risk category. You should see your physician for the following tests: digital rectal exam, guaiac slide test, and proctosocopic exam.

Skin
1. Excessive ultraviolet causes cancer of the skin. Protect yourself with a sun-screen medication.
2. These materials can cause cancer of the skin.
3. Light complexions need more protection than others.

If your skin total is:

Numerical risks for skin cancer are difficult to state. For instance, a person with a dark complexion can work longer in the sun and be less likely to develop cancer than a light-complected person. Furthermore, a person wearing a long-sleeve shirt and wide-brimmed hat may work in the sun and be less at risk than a person who wears a bathing suit for only a short period. The risk goes up greatly with age.

The key here is if you answer "yes" to any question, you need to protect your skin from the sun or any other toxic material. Changes in moles, warts, or skin sores are very important and need to be seen by your doctor.

Breast
If your breast total is:

Under 100	Low-risk women should practice monthly breast self-examination and have their breasts examined by a doctor as part of a cancer-related checkup.
100–199	Moderate-risk women should practice monthly breast self-examinations and have their breasts examined by a doctor as part of a cancer-related checkup. Periodic breast X-rays should be included as your doctor may advise.
200 or higher	High-risk women should practice monthly breast self-examinations and have the above examinations more often. See your doctor for the recommended (frequency of breast physical examinations or X-ray) examinations related to you.

Cervical
1. The highest occurrence is in the 40 and over age group. The numbers represent the relative rates of cancer for different age groups. A 45-year-old woman has a risk three times higher than a 20-year-old.
2. Puerto Ricans, African Americans, and Mexican Americans have higher rates of cervical cancer.
3. Women who have delivered more children have a higher occurrence.
4. Viral infections of the cervix and vagina are associated with cervical cancer.
5. Women with earlier intercourse and with more sexual partners are at a higher risk.
6. Irregular bleeding may be a sign of uterine cancer.

If your cervical total is:

40–69	This is a low-risk group. Ask your doctor for a Pap test. You will be advised how often you should be tested after your first test.
70–99	In this moderate-risk group, more frequent Pap tests may be required.
100 or more	You are in a high-risk group and should have a Pap test (and pelvic exam) as advised by your doctor.

Lab Activity 13.2 *(continued)*
Determining Your Risk of Acquiring Cancer

Endometrial

1. Endometrial cancer is seen in older age groups. The numbers by the age groups represent relative rates of endometrial cancer at different ages. A 50-year-old woman has a risk 12 times higher than a 35-year-old woman.
2. Caucasians have a higher occurrence.
3. The fewer children one has delivered the greater the risk of endometrial cancer.
4. Women who are overweight are at greater risk.
5. Cancer of the endometrium is associated with diabetes.
6. Cancer of the endometrium may be associated with prolonged continuous estrogen hormone intake. This occurs in only a small number of women. You should consult your physician before starting or stopping any estrogen medication.
7. Women who do not have cyclic, regular menstrual periods are at greater risk.
8. Cancer of the endometrium is associated with high blood pressure.

If your endometrial total is:

45–59	You are at very low risk for developing endometrial cancer.
60–99	Your risks are slightly higher. Report any abnormal bleeding immediately to your doctor. Tissue sampling at menopause is recommended.
100 and over	Your risks are much greater. See your doctor for tests as appropriate.

Source: From *Cancer Facts & Figures—1993.* (p. 12) by American Cancer Society, New York. Copyright by American Cancer Society, Inc. Used with permission.

Lab Activity 13.3

Are You and Your Family Following the Cancer Diagnostic Test Guidelines?

INSTRUCTIONS: *The earlier cancer is diagnosed the more effective is the treatment and the less severe is the medical intervention. With this in mind, the American Cancer Society publishes recommended guidelines for the types of diagnostic tests people who have no symptoms of cancer should obtain, and how often these tests should be conducted. To determine whether you and your family's behaviors are consistent with these guidelines, circle the answers to the questions below for yourself. Then ask your family members to do the same.*

	True	**False**
1. If you are between 18 and 39 years of age, do you have a checkup for cancer of the thyroid, mouth, skin, and lymph nodes every three years?	_____	_____
2. If you are age 40 or older, do you have a checkup for cancer of the thyroid, mouth, skin, and lymph nodes every year?	_____	_____
3. If you are age 50 or older, do you have a stool slide test every year?	_____	_____
4. If you are age 50 or older, do you have a sigmoidoscopy, preferably flexible, every three to five years?	_____	_____

✦ For Females

1. If you are between 18 and 39 years of age, do you have a checkup for ovarian cancer every three years?	_____	_____
2. If you are between 18 and 39 years of age, do you have a checkup by a health care professional for breast cancer every three years?	_____	_____
3. If you are between 18 and 39 years of age, do you have a pelvic examination every one to three years?	_____	_____
4. Do you have a Pap test every year?	_____	_____

	True	False

5. Do you do a breast self-examination every menstrual cycle? _____ _____

6. If you are age 40 or over, do you have a checkup for ovarian cancer by a health care provider every year? _____ _____

7. If you are age 40 or over, do you have a checkup by a health care professional for breast cancer every year? _____ _____

8. If you are age 40, have you had a mammogram at that age? _____ _____

9. If you are between ages 40 and 49, do you have a mammogram every one to two years? _____ _____

10. If you are age 50 or older, do you have a mammogram every year? _____ _____

11. If you have reached menopause, and are at risk for contracting uterine cancer, have you had your endometrial tissue examined? _____ _____

✦ For Males

1. If you are between 18 and 39 years of age, do you have a checkup for testicular cancer every three years? _____ _____

2. If you are age 50 or older, do you have a digital rectal examination every year? _____ _____

3. If you are age 50 or older, do you have a prostate-specific antigen blood test every year? _____ _____

✦ Interpretation

If you answered "False" to any of these questions, you are not completely adhering to the American Cancer Society's recommended guidelines for cancer diagnostic tests for people without symptoms. The more False answers, the more at risk you and/or your family are for a late-stage cancer being discovered as opposed to an early diagnosis. Reconsider your cancer screening behavior and use the behavioral change strategies in this and other chapters to help maintain your health and wellness.

Exploring Exercise Injuries and Preventing Injury, Illness, and Disease

Chapter Objectives

By the end of this chapter, you should be able to:

1. Design a 10-point injury prevention plan for someone who is about to begin a new exercise program.

2. Describe the body's response to soft-tissue injury and the three stages of healing.

3. Discuss the correct use of cold, heat, and massage in the emergency treatment of exercise injuries.

4. Demonstrate the correct technique of RICE therapy in the treatment of an ankle sprain and other soft-tissue injuries.

5. Describe the proper use of common over-the-counter and prescription drugs for the treatment of soft-tissue injuries.

6. Describe the proper emergency treatment for at least 25 common exercise injuries.

7. Describe how disease-causing agents, or pathogens, cause disease in the human body.

8. Discuss how nonspecific and specific forms of immunity defend the body against attack.

9. Describe the available treatment and preventive measures for infectious diseases.

$\mathcal{M}$OST OF LEE'S friends exercise regularly. Some jog, cycle, and swim; others engage in aerobic exercise classes, or play sports such as tennis, racquetball, basketball, soccer, and touch football. At some time or other, it seems as if every one of them has experienced an injury. Sprained ankles, torn Achilles tendons, sore knees and backs, inflamed shoulders and elbows are just a few of the complaints Lee hears. Lee feels good most of the time although his weight is creeping upward, and he is generally tired by late afternoon. If it were not for the risk of injury, Lee would join his friends in an aerobic activity he enjoys.

Lee is also concerned about contracting infectious diseases. Four colds and a bout of influenza last year, and a father with type A hepatitis, frighten Lee and may be making him somewhat afraid of his environment. Lee doesn't understand how viral, bacterial, and other infections occur; let alone what he can do to prevent them. He isn't sure if regular exercise will reduce or add to his worries.

This chapter presents a program designed to keep Lee as injury and disease-free as possible while he receives the full benefits of an exercise program of his choice. Although there are no guarantees, the information in this chapter can significantly reduce Lee's risk of injury and illness.

Entering into a fitness program involves a slight risk of injury or illness during the first month or so. Later a key benefit of improved conditioning is the reduction in the incidence and severity of serious exercise-, job-, and home-related injuries. The danger of injury increases considerably, however, when you fail to follow simple rules of training. For the *weekend athlete*, exercise can even be fatal. This chapter is designed to help you avoid common hazards and to make exercise a safe, enjoyable experience. It includes 10 steps for injury prevention for your body; discusses how tissue responds to injury; describes the proper use of cold, heat, and massage; provides basic treatment

procedures for common injuries and illnesses; and desribes several common infectious diseases and where they come from.

PROTECTING YOUR BODY FROM INJURY AND ILLNESS

Common sense and the application of some basic conditioning concepts can eliminate the majority of risks in most exercise programs. The 10-point injury prevention program that follows is designed to help minimize your risk of injury and initiate a sound, safe fitness program.

Analyze Your Medical History before You Begin

If you are over 40 years of age, have been inactive for more than two to three years regardless of age, or are in a high-risk group (obese, hypertense, diabetic, or have high blood lipids), a thorough physical examination is recommended. A qualified fitness instructor can also check your heart rate and blood pressure during exercise on a stationary bicycle to secure valuable information about how you will respond to a program. Although the chances of a serious problem are slight for young people, even they are better safe than sorry.

Improve Your General Conditioning Level

It is important to be extra careful in the first month of a new exercise program when you are particularly vulnerable to muscle, joint, **ligament**, tendon, **cartilage**, and other **soft-tissue** injuries. Injuries of all types are also more likely to occur when you are generally fatigued since blood supply to muscles is reduced, muscle fibers are somewhat devitalized and easily torn, and joint stability and muscle groups are weakened. A state of general fatigue is common during the early stages of an exercise program. Strengthening the injury-prone areas such as the ankle, wrist, knee, shoulders, lower back, and neck (see chapter 9) before beginning a new program will help reduce the incidence of fatigue-related injuries.

Warm Up Properly before Each Workout

At the beginning of every exercise session, it is important to raise your body temperature one to two degrees to prepare muscles, ligaments, and tendons

Ligament Fibrous bands or folds that support organs, hold bones together, or attach some muscles to the bones they act upon.

Cartilage Fibrous connective tissue between the surfaces of movable and immovable joints.

Soft tissue Tissue other than bone.

for vigorous movement. A fast walk, a slow jog, or a mild form of exercise specific to your workout activity for 4 to 5 minutes to elevate core temperature, followed by several minutes of stretching, will help prevent common muscle pulls, strains, sprains, and lower-back discomfort and reduce muscle soreness that may occur 8 to 24 hours later (chapter 9).

Cool Down at the End of Each Exercise Session

The cool-down is a key phase of the fitness workout that should be enjoyed rather than avoided. Experienced joggers or runners, for example, complete the final half to one mile at a slow, easy pace rather than with a kick or sprint. The final three to five minutes of any workout should also include several minutes of stretching as the body cools and slowly returns to a near resting state (see chapter 7). The cool-down will reduce the incidence of injury during this fatigued state of your workout and decrease muscle soreness the next day.

Progress Slowly

It is wise to add only small increments to your workout each exercise session. Too much, too soon is a common cause of muscular injuries. Plan your program over a three- to six-month period to maximize enjoyment and minimize pain and the risk of injury.

Table 14.1 classifies runners, a group who typically tend to add extra mileage too soon, according to mileage and pace and identifies the injuries common to each group. Within each category, injuries are often the result of excessive mileage, intensive work-

outs, and a rapid increase in distance over a short time. Compounding the problem is running surface (a soft, level surface is preferred); running up and down curbs, which increases shock to the legs, feet, and back; sloping or banked roads, which force the foot on the higher part of the slope to twist inward excessively; overstressing tendons and ligaments; or running uphill (strains the Achilles tendon and lower-back muscles) and downhill (force to the heel is increased). Complete Lab Activity 14.1: Evaluating Your Potential for Foot and Leg Injuries at the end of this chapter.

Your workout should also avoid increasing your heart rate to more than 60 percent of your maximum the first two to four weeks. After this acclimation period, you can train at higher heart rates more safely.

Alternate Light- and Heavy-Workout Days

Many people make the mistake of trying to exercise hard every day. The body then does not have adequate time to repair or rebuild, and the full benefit of your workout may not be realized. In addition, injuries, boredom, and peaking out early are much more likely to occur. The chance of an exercise-related injury can be reduced by alternating light- and heavy-workout days each week, and your workout routine or type of exercise at least once weekly.

Avoid the Weekend Athlete Approach to Fitness

One sure way to guarantee numerous injuries and illnesses is to exercise vigorously only on weekends.

Table 14.1 ✦ Classification of Runners and Potential Injuries

CLASSIFICATION	MILEAGE	POTENTIAL INJURIES
Jogger or novice runner	3–20 miles per week at 9–12 minutes per mile	Shin splints, chondromalacia (runner's knee), soreness, hamstring strains, and low-back pain
Sports runner	20–40 miles per week, participant in fun runs and races of 3–6 miles	Achilles tendonitis, stress fractures
Long distance runner	40–70 miles per week at 7–8 minutes per mile; may compete in 10,000 meters (6.2 miles) or marathons (26.2 miles)	More serious injuries to thigh, calf, and back; sciatica and tendon pulls
Elite marathoner	70–200 miles per week at 5–7 minutes per mile	Stress fractures, acute muscle strain in the back, sciatica

Source: From *Clinical Symposia,* By D. M. Brody, 1980. Copyright by Ciba-Geigy Corp. Reprinted with permission.

The older weekend athlete is particularly susceptible to heart attack, and individuals of all ages increase their chances of soft-tissue injuries to muscles, tendons, and ligaments.

In the early spring of each year and during the first major snowfall, approximately 25 to 50 men die of heart attacks. The early spring victims are generally middle-aged men who recently purchased a pair of $200 running shoes and decided to get in shape in just one workout. The 5-mile run usually attempted is often the first time this person has exercised in the past year. Or the snow shoveling after the first major snowfall is the first exposure to exercise since the previous winter. For these individuals, who may have underlying disease, the result is often fatal. These deaths can probably be prevented by a few months of walking as a means of preconditioning.

Death occasionally occurs following unaccustomed exertion in cold weather even though an autopsy reveals no signs of a heart attack. While this condition is rare, it is a possibility when men and women try to do it all in one weekend workout. Cold air constricts the blood vessels of the skin and increases blood pressure slightly. Vigorous exercise also increases blood pressure, heart rate, and the oxygen needs of the heart dramatically. Without proper warm-up and with the presence of hidden signs of heart disease, a heart attack may occur.

If the weekend is the only time you can exercise, avoid long bouts in hot or cold weather and strenuous exercise (jogging, running, racquetball, handball, tennis, basketball, soccer, rugby, and so on) unless you take frequent breaks. Consider supplementing your weekend routine with one other workout during the week. After one month, try increasing to two workouts during the week in addition to one on weekends. If you choose an aerobic activity and progress slowly for several months, you can minimize the risk of serious illness or injury. With a total of three workouts weekly, you have the foundation for a good conditioning program.

Pay Close Attention to Your Body's Signals

Pain and other distress signals during exercise should not be ignored. Although some breathing discomfort and breathlessness is common and minor pain may be present in joints or muscles, severe, persistent, and particularly sharp pain is a warning sign to stop exercising. Also, stop exercising immediately if you notice any abnormal heart action (pulse irregularity, fluttering, palpitations in the chest or throat, rapid heartbeats); pain or pressure in the middle of the chest, teeth, jaw, neck, or arm; dizziness; lightheadedness; cold sweat; or confusion.

Table 14.2 ✦ Disqualifying Conditions for Sports Participation

CONDITION	COLLISION[1]	CONTACT[2]	NONCONTACT[3]	OTHERS[4]
General health				
Acute infections	×	×	×	×
Respiratory, genitourinary, infectious mononucleosis, hepatitis, active rheumatic fever, active tuberculosis				
Obvious physical immaturity in comparison with other competitors	×	×		
Hemorrhagic disease	×	×	×	
Hemophilia, purpura, and other serious bleeding tendencies				
Diabetes, inadequately controlled	×	×	×	×
Diabetes, controlled[5]				
Jaundice	×	×	×	×
Eyes				
Absence or loss of function of one eye	×	×		
Respiratory				
Tuberculosis (active or symptomatic)	×	×	×	×
Severe pulmonary insufficiency	×	×	×	×

Table 14.2 ✦ Disqualifying Conditions for Sports Participation *(continued)*

CONDITION	COLLISION[1]	CONTACT[2]	NONCONTACT[3]	OTHERS[4]
Cardiovascular				
Mitral stenosis, aortic stenosis, aortic insufficiency, coarctation of aorta, cyanotic heart disease, recent carditis of any etiology	×	×	×	×
Hypertension on organic basis	×	×	×	×
Previous heart surgery for congenital or acquired heart disease[6]				
Liver, enlarged	×	×		
Skin				
Boils, impetigo, and herpes simplex gladiatorum	×	×		
Spleen, enlarged	×	×		
Hernia				
Inguinal or femoral hernia	×	×	×	
Musculoskeletal				
Symptomatic abnormalities or inflammations	×	×	×	×
Functional inadequacy of the musculoskeletal system, congenital or acquired, incompatible with the contact or skill demands of the sport	×	×	×	
Neurological				
History of symptoms of previous serious head trauma or repeated concussions	×			
Controlled convulsive disorder[7]				
Convulsive disorder not moderately well controlled by medication	×			
Previous surgery on head	×	×		
Renal				
Absence of one kidney	×	×		
Renal disease	×	×	×	×
Genitalia				
Absence of one testicle[8]				
Undescended testicle[8]				

[1]Football, rugby, hockey, lacrosse, and so forth.

[2]Baseball, soccer, basketball, wrestling, and so forth.

[3]Cross country, track, tennis, crew, swimming, and so forth.

[4]Bowling, golf, archery, field events, and so forth.

[5]No exclusions.

[6]Each individual should be judged on an individual basis in conjunction with his or her cardiologist and surgeon.

[7]Each patient should be judged on an individual basis. All things being equal, it is probably better to encourage a young boy or girl to participate in a noncontact sport rather than a contact sport. However, if a patient has a desire to play a contact sport and this is deemed a major ameliorating factor in his or her adjustment to school, associates, and the seizure disorder, serious consideration should be given to letting him or her participate if the seizures are moderately well controlled or the patient is under good medical management.

[8]The Committee approves the concept of contact sports participation for youths with only one testicle or with an undescended testicle(s), except in specific instances such as an inguinal canal undescended testicle(s), following appropriate medical evaluation to rule out unusual injury risk. However, the athlete, parents, and school authorities should be fully informed that participation in contact sports with only one testicle carries a slight injury risk to the remaining healthy testicle. Fertility may be adversely affected following an injury. But the chances of an injury to a descended testicle are rare, and the injury risk can be further substantially minimized with an athletic supporter and protective device.

Source: From *Modern Principles of Athletic Training* (pp. 51–52), by Daniel D. Arnheim, 1989, St. Louis: Times Mirror/Mosby College Publishing.

After each workout, let your body analyze the severity of your exercise session. The workout was probably too light if you did not sweat; and it was too heavy if you were still breathless 10 minutes after you stopped exercising, your pulse rate was above 120 beats per minute 5 minutes after stopping, prolonged fatigue remained for more than 24 hours, nausea or vomiting occurred, or sleep was interrupted. To remedy these symptoms in the future, exercise less vigorously and lengthen your cool-down period. For some individuals, the lower back is highly susceptible to injury during the early stages of a newly started exercise routine. Complete Lab 14-3 to determine if you have muscle "tightness" that may put you at risk for back problems.

Exercise may also be inadvisable for some individuals afflicted with certain medical conditions. Study Table 14.2 to identify the adjustments that should be made when you are ill, injured, or suffering from a medical condition that requires modifications. When you are obviously ill or not up to par, avoid exercise, rest a few days, and return to a lower level or an easier workout.

Master the Proper Form in Your Activity

For all activities, correct form improves efficiency and reduces the risk of injury. Proper running form, for example, is important to most fitness programs. Joggers should avoid running on the toes, which produces soreness in the calf muscles. The heel should strike the ground first before rolling the weight along the bottom of the foot to the toes for the push-off. A number of other running form problems often produce mild muscle or joint strain.

Participants in racquet sports are also susceptible

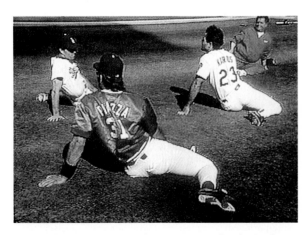

Under the management of Tommy Lasorda, the Dodgers are required to stretch before each practice and each game. The team has considerably reduced its injury rate. (Photo courtesy of Cable News Network.)

Mastering the proper form improves efficiency and reduces the risk of injury. Tennis players are especially susceptible to elbow, shoulder, wrist, and lower-back problems. (Photo courtesy of the United States Handball Association.)

to numerous form-related injuries (elbow, shoulder, and wrist inflammation and lower-back problems) from faulty stroke mechanics such as elbow-led ground strokes, bent-elbow hits, muscles not firming at impact, and so on. A few professional lessons in your sport can help to reduce the risk of these types of injuries.

Dress Properly for the Weather

Weather extremes can also cause health problems during exercise. Consider the suggestions in Table 14.3 to reduce the risk of overheating on hot, humid days or overexposure on cold days. It is also helpful to become familiar with the early symptoms and emergency treatment for heat- and cold-related injuries such as heat exhaustion, heat stroke, **hypothermia,** and **frostbite** (see Table 14.4).

If you are a runner, plan your jogging course to avoid being too far out on either a hot or cold day should symptoms of heat exhaustion or overexpo-

Table 14.3 ✦ Preventive Techniques on Hot and Cold Days

HOT, HUMID WEATHER	COLD WEATHER
1. Listen to weather reports and avoid vigorous exercise if the temperature is above 90° and the humidity is above 70 percent. Make hot days your light workout.	1. Listen to weather reports noting temperature and wind-chill factor. Unless the equivalent temperature is in the "little danger" area, avoid outside exercise.
2. Avoid adding to normal salt intake. Do not use salt tablets. Increase consumption of fruits and vegetables.	2. Eat well during cold months: the body needs more calories in cold weather.
3. Avoid lengthy warm-up periods.	3. Warm up carefully until sweating is evident.
4. Wear light-colored, porous, loose clothing to promote evaporation. Remove special equipment, such as football gear, every hour for 15 minutes.	4. Use two or three layers of clothing rather than one heavy warm-up suit.
5. Avoid wearing a hat (except for an open visor with brim) since considerable heat loss occurs through the head.	5. Protect the head (warm hat), ears, fingers, toes, nose, and genitals. A hat should cover the ears and face. Fur-lined supporters for men can also prevent frostbite to sensitive parts.
6. Never use rubberized suits that hold the sweat in and increase fluid and salt/potassium loss.	6. Never use rubberized, air-tight suits that keep the sweat in. When the body cools, the sweat starts to freeze.
7. Wet clothing increases salt and sweat loss. Replace whenever possible.	7. Keep clothing dry, changing wet items as soon as possible.
8. Slowly increase the length of your workout by 5 to 10 minutes daily for nine days to acclimate to the heat.	8. Slowly increase the length of your workout by 5 to 10 minutes daily for nine days to acclimate to the cold.
9. Drink cold water (40°F) before (10–20 ounces 15 minutes prior to exercise), during, and after exercise. Hydrate before the workout with two or three glasses of water.	9. Drink cold water freely before, during, and after exercise

sure to cold occur. If you run against the wind in cold weather on the way out, on the way back, when you are likely to be sweating much more, you will be running with the wind. Running into a head wind with wet clothes will draw heat away from your body.

Both weather extremes can be dangerous. Heatstroke (when core temperature may rise to 105 or 106°) symptoms are difficult to reverse unless immediate, rapid cooling takes place. On the other hand, a one-degree drop in core temperature will produce pain. Should body temperature drop to 94°, shivering ceases and rigidity sets in; at 75° death usually occurs from heart failure.

Properly fitted shoes, appropriate equipment, avoidance of gimmicky exercise devices, and acceptable equipment for contact sports are also important for injury prevention and need special attention. A good-quality shoe is your best protection against injury to the feet, ankles, knees, hips, and lower back.

𝒯ISSUE RESPONSE TO INJURY

The actual healing process is unique to each individual and to different types of tissue. Age, nutrition, and the proper use of treatment techniques also affect the way tissue responds to the injury and the healing process. An understanding of how soft tissue responds (heals) to **acute** and **chronic** injuries will help you understand emergency treatment tech-

Hypothermia Subnormal body temperature.

Frostbite Destruction of tissue by freezing.

Acute Disease or pain characterized by sudden onset and a short, severe course.

Chronic Disease or pain of slow onset and long duration.

Table 14.4 ✦ Prevention and Emergency Treatment of Common Exercise Injuries

INJURY	GENERAL COMMENTS	PREVENTION AND TREATMENT	NEED FOR A PHYSICIAN
Extremities			
Ankle	Most injuries involve inversion sprains (outer edge of foot turns inward). Ankles are not strong enough for most sports, and are poorly supported by muscles and ligaments that often stretch and tear from high-speed direction changes, cutting, and contact.	Improved support-muscle strength offers some protection, along with preventive taping (inversion sprains only). RICE therapy is the preferred treatment. Use crutches for two or three days if pain is severe.	If swelling or pain remains for three days; If ligament or tendon damage is present; If pain prevents walking; If symptoms of fracture exist.
Bruise (charley horse)	A charley horse is nothing more than a thigh contusion from a direct blow to a relaxed thigh muscle (the tissue is compressed against the bone). Bruises to other areas occur in a similar way.	Prevention involves use of proper equipment in contact sports. RICE therapy is the preferred emergency and home treatment. Replace ice with heat on the third or fourth day.	If pain and discoloration do not disappear with rest, treatment, and mild exercise. If numbness, weakness, or tingling occurs, or there are signs of vascular compromise, immediate referral is necessary.
Elbow (tennis and pitcher's)	The movement causing the condition is a forceful extension of the forearm and a twisting motion (serve in tennis, curve in baseball). The more you play and the older you are, the more likely you are to be afflicted. Pain is present over the outer (lateral epicondyle) or inner (medial epicondyle) elbow and radiates down the arm. Pain is produced by tears, inflammation, and scar tissue at the attachment of the extensor muscles to the bony prominence of the elbow.	Prevention centers around use of warm-up, correction of poor stroke mechanics, avoiding use of wet tennis balls and heavy, inflexible racquets, and reducing the frequency of curveball pitches (should be greatly restricted in Little League baseball with growing youngsters).	If condition remains more than two or three weeks; If pain makes exercise impossible; If severe swelling is present. If night pain occurs
Fractures	A fracture should be suspected in most injuries where pain and swelling exist over a bone.	Apply ice packs, protect and rest the injured part for 72 hours. In severe cases, splint the bone where the victim lies and transport to emergency room.	If limb is cold, blue, or numb; If pelvis or thigh are involved; If limb is crooked or deformed; If shock symptoms are present; If rapid, severe swelling occurs.
Hamstring strains	The large muscle group in the back of the upper leg is commonly strained during vigorous exercise. Pain is severe and prohibits further activity. In a few days, discoloration may appear.	Prevention includes proper stretching before exercise, proper diet, improved flexibility, and care in running around wet areas. For treatment use RICE therapy.	If severe discoloration occurs; If pain and discomfort remain after 10 to 15 days of treatment. If numbness, weakness, or tingling occurs, or there are signs of vascular compromise, immediate referral is necessary.

INJURY	GENERAL COMMENTS	PREVENTION AND TREATMENT	NEED FOR A PHYSICIAN
Knee	The knee is a vulnerable joint that depends on ligaments, cartilage, and muscles for support. *Chondromalacia* of the patella, or roughing of the undersurface of the kneecap, is the most common injury; kneecap pain and grating symptoms are evident. A tear of the cartilage is the second most common injury. Pain is evident along the inner or outer part of the knee joint along with swelling. *Ligament* tears are less common but occur from a blow to the leg. Swelling and knee instability result.	Prevention involves flexibility and strength. Exercises should stretch and strengthen the hamstrings, quadriceps, and Achilles tendon. Chondromalacia is treated through use of arch supports, or by bulking up the inner part of the heel of the shoe. Aspirin, Ibuprofin, or Naprozen and quadriceps exercises also help. Serious knee injury (cartilage and ligament damage) requires an examination by an orthopedic surgeon. Use of the arthroscope to examine and insert small tools through puncture wounds offers effective treatment and rapid recovery.	If swelling and pain persist more than three to five days; If ligament or cartilage damage is suspected; If chondromalacia is suspected.
Shin splints	A shin splint is merely an inflammation of the anterior and posterior tendons of the large bone in the lower leg. It is an overuse syndrome developing in poorly conditioned individuals in the beginning of their training program. Hard surfaces add to the problem.	Avoid hard surfaces, too much mileage, doing too much too soon, using improperly fitted shoes, and running on banked tracks or road shoulders. RICE therapy is recommended for two to four days, followed by taping and heat therapy, and stretching exercises.	If condition remains more than two to three weeks; If condition reoccurs after reconvening your exercise routine. If signs or symptoms of a stress fracture occurs
Tendonitis	The location of the pain and swelling of the tendon varies in different sports. With considerable running, the Achilles tendon is affected. In sports involving repeated movement of the upper arms (swimming, baseball), it is the shoulder tendon. When a snapping or rotation of the elbow is involved (tennis/ handball), it is the elbow tendon.	For both prevention and treatment, stretch the involved tendon daily and exercise lightly until pain disappears. RICE therapy is helpful in the early stages for three to four days. See *Elbow* in this table. Pain may disappear during a workout, only to return and grow worse later.	If pain and inflammation continue after two to three weeks of treatment.
Varicose veins	Varicose veins are nothing more than abnormally lengthened, dilated veins. Surrounding muscles support deep veins, whereas superficial veins get little support. In some individuals, vein valves that prevent blood from backing up become defective, enlarged, and lose their elasticity. The condition is uncommon in young people.	Prevention and treatment for those with symptoms or a family history include bed rest and leg elevation, avoiding long periods of standing, use of elastic bandages and support stockings, surgery for severe cases, and removal of intra-abdominal pressure (obesity, tumor, or tight girdles).	If pain is severe enough to make walking difficult; If cosmetic problem is bothersome. If swelling in the calf or foot is present.

Table 14.4 ✦ Prevention and Emergency Treatment of Common Exercise Injuries *(continued)*

INJURY	GENERAL COMMENTS	PREVENTION AND TREATMENT	NEED FOR A PHYSICIAN
Feet and Hands			
Athlete's foot	Athlete's foot is caused by a fungus and is accompanied by a bacterial infection. Itching, redness, and a rash on the soles, toes, or between the toes is common.	Prevention and treatment are similar; wash between the toes with soap and water, dry thoroughly, use medication containing Tinactin twice daily, and place fungistatic foot powder in shoes and sneakers.	If treatment does not relieve symptoms in two to three weeks.
Blisters	Blisters are produced by friction causing the top skin layer to separate from the second layer. Blisters can become severely inflamed or infected unless properly treated. A porous inner sole can be purchased that almost completely eliminates getting blisters on the feet.	Use clean socks, comfortably fitting shoes, and Vaseline to reduce friction. Avoid breaking open blisters (skin acts as a sterile bandage). If the blister breaks, trim off all loose skin and apply antibiotic salve. Avoid use of tincture of benzoin, and of powder that increases friction, since this is more likely to cause blisters than prevent them.	If inflammation and soreness develop; If redness occurs in the involved limb; If pain or sensitivity occurs under the arms or in the groin area. If blood blister is present.
Bunions	Bunions are merely growths on the head of the first or fifth toe that produce inflammation (swelling, redness, and pain).	Bunions can be prevented by using properly fitted shoes.	If symptoms of infection occur.
Corns	Hard corns may result from poorly fitted shoes. Inflammation and thickening of soft tissue (top of toes) occur. Soft corns are often caused by excessive foot perspiration and narrow shoes. The corn forms between the fourth and fifth toe in most cases.	Prevention and treatment involves use of properly fitted shoes, soaking feet daily in warm water to soften the area, and protecting the area with a small felt or sponge rubber doughnut. Trim and file corns to reduce pressure.	If a change of shoes and treatment does not improve the condition.
Heel bruise	The most common cause of heel pain is plantar fasciitis—inflammation of the broad band of fibrous tissue that runs from the base of the toes back to the heel and inserts on the inner aspect of the heel. Mild tears and severe bruises are also common.	Prevention involves proper stretching and use of a plastic heel cup. Aspirin, Ibuprofin, or Naprozen should be used to reduce inflammation (two tablets, four times daily or as directed); rest is indicated for five to seven days.	If pain persists for more than five to seven days after rest and treatment.
Ingrown toenails	The edge of the toenail grows into the soft tissue, producing inflammation and infection.	Prevention and treatment involves proper nail trimming, soaking the toe in hot water two to three times daily, and inserting a small piece of cotton under the nail edge to lift it from the soft tissue.	If infection occurs.

Table 14.4 ✦ Prevention and Emergency Treatment of Common Exercise Injuries *(continued)*

INJURY	GENERAL COMMENTS	PREVENTION AND TREATMENT	NEED FOR A PHYSICIAN
Stress fracture	A stress fracture is a small crack in a bone's surface, generally a foot, leg, or hand. Unexplained pain may exist over one of the small bones in the hand or foot. X-rays will not reveal small cracks until the bone heals and a callus (scar tissue) forms.	Prevention involves not running too many miles, not increasing mileage too fast, running on soft surfaces, and taking care to progress slowly in your fitness program. Treatment requires rest and proper equipment (especially footwear).	If unexplained pain exists in the lower back, hip, ankle, wrist, hands, or feet. If night pain occurs. If pain increases with activity.

Head and Neck

INJURY	GENERAL COMMENTS	PREVENTION AND TREATMENT	NEED FOR A PHYSICIAN
Cauliflower ear	A deformed painful outer ear is common in wrestling, rugby, and football from friction, hard blows, and wrenching in a headlock position. With poor circulation to the ear, fluid is absorbed slowly, and the ear remains swollen, sensitive, and discolored.	Use protective ear guards, apply Vaseline to reduce friction, and apply ice as soon as a sore spot develops. Once a deformed ear develops, only a plastic surgeon can return the ear to normal appearance.	If symptoms of infection develop; If cosmetic surgery is desired. If swelling is present.
Concussion	Any injury to the head producing dizziness or temporary unconsciousness should be considered serious.	Apply ice to the area. Observe the patient for 72 hours for alertness, unequal pupil size (although about one person in four has unequal pupil size all the time), and vomiting. Pressure inside skull may develop in 72 hours.	If unconsciousness occurred; If bleeding occurs from ears, eyes, or mouth; If there is unequal pupil size, lethargy, fever, vomiting, convulsions, speech difficulty, stiff neck, or limb weakness.
Dental injuries	Common in basketball and contact sports from elbow contact.	Chipped tooth—avoid hot and cold drinks. Swelling due to abscess—apply ice pack. Excessive bleeding of socket—place gauze over socket and bite down. Toothache—aspirin and ice packs.	If tooth is chipped, abscess is present, or bleeding of socket or toothache is present. If tooth is bleeding or knocked out (place in proper solution and see dentist immediately).
Eye (object in eye, contusion from a ball or elbow)	Eye injuries are more common in racket sports and handball from ball contact, and in contact sports from elbow contact. In racket sports, the ball may ricochet off the top of the racket into the eye, or the victim may turn to see where his or her partner is hitting the ball in doubles play.	Protective eye guards should be used in racquetball and handball. Never turn your head in doubles play. Avoid rubbing—you could scratch the cornea. Close both eyes to allow tears to wash away a foreign body. Grasp the lashes of the upper lid and draw out and down over the lower lid. If it feels like an object is in the eye but none can be seen, cornea scrape probably occurred, and will heal in 24 to 48 hours. To remove object, moisten corner of handkerchief and touch object lightly.	If object is on the eye itself; If object remains after washing; If object could have penetrated the globe of the eye; If blood is visible in eye; If vision is impaired; If pain is present after 48 hours. If pain is present after object has been removed.

Table 14.4 ✦ Prevention and Emergency Treatment of Common Exercise Injuries *(continued)*

INJURY	GENERAL COMMENTS	PREVENTION AND TREATMENT	NEED FOR A PHYSICIAN
Nasal fracture	The blow may come from the side or front. The side hit causes more deformity. Hemorrhage is profuse (mucous lining is cut), and swelling is immediate.	Prevention involves use of a face guard in football. Bleeding should be controlled immediately (see *Nosebleed*).	If bleeding continues; If deformity and considerable swelling are present.
Extremities			
Neck	Neck injuries are more common in contact sports and require immediate and careful attention. Assume a vertebrae is involved, and avoid movement of any kind until a physician or rescue squad arrives.	Neck flexibility exercises should be part of your warm-up routine. Neck-strengthening exercises are a necessity for contact sport participants.	If any injury to the neck occurs.
Nosebleed	Nosebleed may occur even from mild contact to the nose.	Do not lie down when bleeding starts. Squeeze the nose between the thumb and forefinger just below the hard portion for 5 to 10 minutes while seated with the head tilted forward. Avoid blowing the nose or placing cold compresses on the bridge of the nose.	If bleeding occurs frequently and is associated with a cold; If victim has a history of high blood pressure; If emergency treatment fails to stop the bleeding.
Torso			
Back	The first 7 vertebrae control the head, neck, and upper back. The next 12 provide attachments for the ribs. The 5 lumbar vertebrae of the lower back support the weight of the upper half of the body. It is this area that plagues millions of Americans.	Avoid exercise motions that arch the back. Back pain may be caused by muscular and ligamentous sprains, mechanical instability, arthritis, and ruptured disks. Most problems will improve with rest, ice, pain medication, and an exercise program.	If pain, weakness, or numbness in legs is present; If pain remains after rest and ice therapy; If aching sensation occurs in buttocks, or further down the leg.
Chest pain	Chest pain provides a heart attack scare to everyone over age 30. Actually, pain could be in the chest wall (muscle, rib, ligament, or rib cartilage), the lungs or outside covering, or the pleura, diaphragm, skin, or other organs in the upper part of the diaphragm. Sharp pain that lasts a few seconds, pain at the end of a deep breath, or one that worsens with a deep breath, pain upon pressing a finger on the spot of discomfort, and painful burning when the stomach is empty are all symptoms that are probably not associated with a heart attack.	Any of the symptoms to the right require immediate hospitalization and physician care.	If any of the following symptoms are present: mild to intense pain with a feeling of pressure or squeezing on the chest; pain beneath the breastbone; accompanying pain in the jaw or down the inner side of either arm; accompanying nausea, sweating, dizziness, or shortness of breath; or pulse irregularity.

Table 14.4 ✦ Prevention and Emergency Treatment of Common Exercise Injuries *(continued)*

INJURY	GENERAL COMMENTS	PREVENTION AND TREATMENT	NEED FOR A PHYSICIAN
Groin strain	The groin muscles (area between the thigh and abdominal region) are easily torn from running, jumping, and twisting. It is a difficult injury to prevent and cure. Pain, weakness, and internal bleeding may occur.	Prevention involves proper stretching prior to exercise. RICE therapy is suggested for treatment.	If symptoms remain after several days of rest and mild exercise.
Hernia	The protrusion of viscera (body organs) through a portion of the abdominal wall is referred to as a hernia. Hernias associated with exercise and sports generally occur in the groin area.	Prevention involves attention to proper form in weight lifting and weight training, and care in lifting heavy objects.	If a protrusion is located that protrudes further with coughing.
Hip pointer	A hard blow to the iliac crest or hip produces what is commonly called a hip pointer. The injury is severely handicapping and produces both pain and spasm.	Prevention involves the use of protective hip pads in contact sports. RICE therapy is suggested for treatment.	If symptoms of a fracture are present.
Jock itch	Jock itch is acquired by contact and is associated with bacteria, fungi, molds, and ringworm.	Prevention and treatment involve practicing proper hygiene (showering in warm water, use of antiseptic soap, powder, and proper drying); drinking enough water; regularly changing underwear, supporter, and shorts; disinfecting locker benches, mats, and other equipment; and avoiding long periods of sitting in warm, moist areas.	If condition persists for more than 10 days.
Wind knocked out	With a hard blow to the right place, such as a relaxed midsection, breathing is temporarily hampered. Although you will have trouble convincing the victim, breathing will return. The blow has only increased abdominal pressure, produced pain, and interfered with the diaphragmatic cycle reflex due to nerve paralysis or muscle spasm.	The victim should be told to try to breath slowly through the nose (no easy task for someone who is gasping, dizzy, and 100 percent convinced death is only seconds away). Clothing is loosened at the neck and waist, and ice is applied to the abdomen.	If breathing is still not normal in one or two minutes; If breathing stops (start CPR); If pain persists in the midsection.
Shoulder			
Tendonitis	Tendonitis is common in tennis and baseball. Soreness results on the front of the shoulder when elevating the arm from the side.	Ice and aspirin are used. Prevention and treatment involve flexibility and weight-training exercises. Flexibility movements concentrate on back stretching, while weight-training choices are lateral lifts, military, and bench presses.	If soreness remains for 7 to 10 days.

Table 14.4 ✦ Prevention and Emergency Treatment of Common Exercise Injuries *(continued)*

INJURY	GENERAL COMMENTS	PREVENTION AND TREATMENT	NEED FOR A PHYSICIAN
Thorax			
Rib fracture and bruises	Fractures may occur from direct contact or, uncommonly, from muscular contraction. A direct blow may displace the bone and produce jagged edges that cut the tissue of the lungs, producing bleeding or lung collapse.	The type of contact helps reveal rib fracture. Pain when breathing and palpitation are also signs. RICE therapy should be initiated immediately.	If pain is present when breathing after a direct blow to the thorax; If fracture is suspected. If shortness of breath or difficulty breathing.
Miscellaneous Injuries and Illnesses			
Abrasions	Superficial skin layers are scraped off. Injury imposes no serious problem if cleaned properly.	Clean with soap and warm water. Use a bandage if the wound oozes blood. Remove loose skin flaps with sterile scissors if dirty; allow to remain if clean. Check to see if subject has been immunized for tetanus within the last 10 years.	If all dirt and foreign matter cannot be removed; If infection develops.
Common cold	Handshaking with an infected person or breathing in particles after a sneeze are two ways of transmitting a cold virus. Contributing factors may be low resistance, improper nutrition, tension, bacteria entering the respiratory tract, and remaining indoors in winter months, which increases the likelihood of close contact with a contagious person.	A cold will typically last about seven days. There is no known protection or cure. Antihistamines, decongestants, and cold tablets are of little value. Aspirin (for those over 16 years of age) or acetaminophen (for those under 16), combined with rest and plenty of fluids are sound advice. Exercise only lightly and include one or two days of rest. No exercise if patient has a fever or muscle soreness.	If fever or sore throat lasts more than a week; If pain is present in one or both ears.
Fainting and dizziness	Lack of blood flow to the brain commonly occurs with increasing age and may result in temporary loss of vision or light-headedness.	Place the victim in a lying position with the feet elevated. If it is not possible to lie down, an alternative position is a sitting posture with the head lowered between the legs.	If loss of consciousness occurs; If dizziness occurs frequently. If dizziness or fainting occur with exercise.
Frostbite	Frostbite, a destruction of tissue by freezing, is more likely to occur on small parts of the nose, cheeks, ears, fingers, and toes.	Thaw rapidly in a warm-water bath. Avoid rubbing areas with snow. Water should be comfortable to a normal, unfrozen hand (not over 104°F). When a flush reaches the fingers, remove the frostbitten part from the water immediately. For an ear or nose, use cloths soaked in warm water.	Always see a doctor.

Table 14.4 ✦ Prevention and Emergency Treatment of Common Exercise Injuries *(continued)*

INJURY	GENERAL COMMENTS	PREVENTION AND TREATMENT	NEED FOR A PHYSICIAN
Heat exhaustion/ heat stroke	The body loses heat to the environment and maintains normal temperature by: *Evaporation*—sweat evaporates into the atmosphere. *Radiation*—With body temperature higher than air temperature, heat loss occurs. *Convection*—As body heat loss occurs, air is warmed. This warmed air rises and cooler air moves in to take its place, cooling the body. *Conduction*—Heat moves from deeper body organs to skin through blood vessels. The skin acts as a radiation surface for heat loss to the air.	Symptoms of heat exhaustion include nausea, chills, cramps, and rapid pulse. Treatment requires immediate cooling with ice packs to the head, torso, and joints, and maintaining proper water and electrolyte balance.	If rapid improvement is not evident; If multiple cramps occur; If core temperature does not immediately return to normal. If lethargy or confusion is present. If skin is warm and dry.
Hypothermia	With extremely cold temperatures and high wind chill, core body temperature may drop below normal levels.	Prevention involves following the steps outlined in the section "Dressing Properly for the Weather" earlier in the chapter. Treatment calls for warming with blankets, heating pads, replacing wet clothing, and administering warm drinks.	If core temperature drops below 94°. If lethargy or confusion is present.
Infected wounds	Bacterial infection in the bloodstream (septicemia).	Keep area clean, changing the bandage and soaking and cleaning in warm water twice daily. Up to 10 to 12 days may be needed for normal healing.	If fever is above 100°; If thick pus and swelling occur the second day.
Minor cuts	Minor cuts can develop into serious problems if mistreated or neglected. Avoid use of antiseptics that may destroy tissue and actually retard healing.	Clean the wound with soap and water or hydrogen peroxide, removing all dirt and foreign matter. Use a butterfly bandage or steri-strip to bring the edges of the wound tightly together without trapping the fat or rolling the skin beneath.	If cut occurs to face or trunk; If deep cut involves tendons, nerves, vessels, or ligaments; If blood is pumping from a wound; If tingling or limb weakness occurs; If cut cannot be pulled together without trapping the fat; If direct pressure fails to stop the bleeding.

Table 14.4 ✦ Prevention and Emergency Treatment of Common Exercise Injuries *(continued)*

Injury	General comments	Prevention and treatment	Need for a physician
Muscle soreness	You may experience two different types of soreness: general soreness that appears immediately after your exercise session and disappears in 3 to 4 hours, or localized soreness appearing 8 to 24 hours after exercise.	You can help prevent soreness by warming up properly, avoiding bouncing-type stretching or flexibility exercises, and progressing slowly in your program. Doing too much too soon is a common cause. You can expect to have some soreness after your first few workouts, especially if you have been inactive. Don't stop exercising, it will only reoccur later.	If muscle soreness persists after the second week.
Muscle cramps	Muscular cramps commonly occur in three areas: back of lower leg (calf), back of upper leg (hamstring group), and front of upper leg (quadriceps group). Cramps may be related to fatigue, tightness of the muscles, or fluid, salt, and potassium imbalance.	Stretch before you exercise and drink water freely. If cramp occurs, stretch area carefully.	If multiple cramps occur; If symptoms of heat exhaustion are present.

Prepared by Eugene L. Kastleberg, Dept. of Orthopaedic Surgery, Medical College of Virginia, Virginia Commonwealth University.

niques and reinforce the correct use of heat, cold, and massage as treatment modalities.

Musculoskeletal injuries incurred through sports or exercise fall into three phases: acute, repair and regeneration, and remodeling.

Acute Phase

The acute phase of inflammation (the first three or four days after an injury) occurs as the body initially reacts to an injury with redness, heat, swelling, pain, and loss of function or movement. During this peri-od, pressure on nerve endings or **ischemia** may produce considerable pain. Some tissue death also takes place from the initial trauma or the lack of oxygen following the trauma. Acute inflammation is actually a protective mechanism designed to keep the problem local and remove some of the injurious agents so healing and repair can begin. Almost immediately after the injury occurs, blood flow to that area is decreased for a period from several seconds to as long as 10 minutes, and coagulation begins to seal the broken blood vessels. Numerous other vascular and cellular events occur to prepare the site for the next phase.

Ischemia A condition of localized diminished blood supply.

Cryotherapy The therapeutic application of cold in any form.

Vasodilation Increase or opening of the blood vessels.

Collagen The connective tissue portion of the true skin and of other organs.

Thermotherapy The application of heat.

Repair and Regeneration Phase

For a period of 48 to 72 hours after the injury to about six weeks, healing begins when cellular debris, erythrocytes, and the fibrin clot are being removed. Although some scar tissue will form following soft-tissue injuries, a desirable goal is to treat the injury properly to produce as little of such tissue as possible, since scar tissue is less viable than normal tissue. Primary healing occurs with little scar tissue formation in injuries where the edges are held closely together. When a gaping lesion and large tissue loss are present, considerable scar tissue forms during the

Always wear appropriate protective equipment. Eye guards should be worn while playing handball, racquetball, and squash in order to prevent serious eye injuries. (Photo courtesy of the United States Handball Association.)

healing process to replace lost tissue and bridge the gap.

Remodeling Phase

In this phase, which overlaps the repair and regeneration phase, scar tissue continues to increase and become stronger for three to six weeks following an injury. The actual strength of scar tissue increases for three months to a year. The complete remodeling of ligamentous tissue generally requires a year.

GENERAL TREATMENT MODALITIES

Cryotherapy

The application of cold (cryotherapy) to the skin for 20 minutes or less at a minimum temperature of 50° F causes the constriction of vessels and reduces the flow of blood to the injured area. When cold is applied for longer than 20 minutes, an intermittent period of **vasodilation** occurs for 4 to 6 minutes. This prevents tissue damage from too much exposure to cold. At this point, cold is no longer effective. It also reduces muscle spasm, swelling, and pain; slows metabolic rate; and increases **collagen** inelasticity and joint stiffness. Cold is somewhat more penetrating than heat, and the effects last longer.

Cold applications should be used immediately after an injury and continued for several days until swelling subsides. Cold can be applied intermittently for 20 minutes every 1-1/2 waking hours in combination with compression, elevation, and rest (see RICE later in this chapter). The longer the cold is applied, the deeper the cooling. *Ice massage* can be used on a small body area by freezing water in a plastic-foam cup to form a cylinder of ice. After removing one or two inches of the plastic foam at the top of the cup, the cup portion can be used as a handle, and the ice can be rubbed over the skin in overlapping circles for 5 to 10 minutes to produce cold, burning, aching, and numbness in the area. *Ice packs* can be made by placing flaked or crushed ice in a wet towel or self-sealing plastic bag. Unless ice massage is being used, ice should not come in direct contact with the skin.

Thermotherapy

In general, proper **thermotherapy** to an injured area raises skin temperature and increases the amount of blood flow to the area. Heat can also be used to relieve joint stiffness, pain, muscle spasm, and inflammation, and to increase the extensibility of collagen tissues. Temperatures should not exceed 116° and a treatment session should never exceed 30 minutes. Additional cautions in the use of heat include:

1. Never apply heat immediately after an injury.
2. Never use heat when there is loss of sensation or decreased arterial circulation.

3. Never apply heat directly to the eyes, genitals, or the abdomen of a pregnant woman.

4. Never fall asleep while applying heat or apply heat over Ben Gay® or other topical heat ointments.

Heat can be safely applied through the use of moist heat and commercial packs as well as whirlpool and paraffin baths. You can use moist heat at home by soaking a towel in hot water and allowing it to drain for several seconds before applying to an injured area, which is already covered by four to six layers of toweling. The moist towel should not directly contact the skin.

Electrotherapy

The use of **electrotherapy** as a form of heat should be performed only by a physician, physical therapist, or licensed athletic trainer.

Massage

The use of massage to manipulate soft tissue is a helpful adjunct to heat and cold. Stroking, kneading, friction, percussion, and rapid shaking are some of the more common techniques used to increase heat, improve blood flow to the injured area, remove metabolites such as lactic acid, overcome edema, improve circulation and the venous return of blood to the heart, and aid relaxation.

PREVENTION AND EMERGENCY TREATMENT OF COMMON EXERCISE INJURIES AND ILLNESSES

Additional common injuries, illnesses, and problems associated with exercise are discussed in Table 14.4 which serves as a guide for diagnosis, prevention, emergency treatment, and determination of the need for a physician. If in doubt, consult a physician immediately or transport the injured person to a hospital emergency room.

RICE

Emergency home treatment for most muscle, ligament, and tendon strains, sprains, suspected fractures, bruises, and joint inflammations involve four simple actions known as the RICE approach.

Rest To prevent additional damage to injured tissue, stop exercising and immobilize the injured

area immediately. If the lower extremities are affected, use crutches to move about.

Ice To decrease blood flow to the injured area and decrease swelling, apply ice (crushed in a towel or ice pack) directly to the skin immediately for 15 to 20 minutes. Use cold applications intermittently for 1 to 72 hours.

Compression To limit swelling and decrease the likelihood of hemorrhage and hematoma formation, wrap a towel or bandage firmly around the ice and injured area. An elastic wrap soaked in water and frozen in a refrigerator can be used to apply both compression and cold.

Elevation To help drain excess fluid through gravity, improve the venous return of blood to the heart, and reduce internal bleeding and swelling, raise the injured limb above heart level.

Home treatment should begin as soon as possible. The procedure should be: (1) Evaluate the injured area. (2) Apply ice for 20 minutes. (3) Compress the ice firmly against the injury. (4) Replace the ice pack with a compress wrap and pad. (5) Rest the injured area. (6) Reapply ice in 1 to 1-1/2 hours. (7) Remove the elastic wrap and elevate the area before you go to bed. (8) Begin ice therapy immediately on rising in the morning. On the fourth or fifth day, discontinue cold treatments, and begin to apply moist heat or dry heat or use a whirlpool twice daily for 15 to 20 minutes. Depending on the severity of the injury and amount of swelling and pain, mild exercise can resume in four or five days. Another acronym to remind you of the proper procedure in treating minor injuries is PRICE; the "P" is a reminder to see a physician.

Considerable misinformation is available concerning proper home emergency treatment. Unfortunately, incorrect treatment can worsen the injury or actually produce serious side effects that may require surgery later.

Shock

Many injuries, such as fractures, concussions, profuse bleeding, heart attack, back and neck damage, and severe joint trauma, can produce shock. Shock is one of the body's strongest natural reactions to disease and injury. It slows blood flow, which acts as a natural tourniquet, reduces pain, and decreases the body's agony in serious injury. All three types of shock can kill: *traumatic* (injury or loss of blood), *septic* (infection-induced), and *cardiogenic* (from a heart attack). Shock is much easier to prevent than it is to treat. You should assume that shock is present with the above injuries and illnesses, splint broken

Table 14.5 ✦ Your Home Pharmacy

MEDICAL CONCERN	MEDICATION
Allergy	**Antihistamines***
Cold and coughs	Cold tablets and cough drops
Constipation	**Milk of magnesia**
Diarrhea	Antidiarrheal, paregoric
Eye irritations	Eye drops
Exercise injury problems (inflammation)	See your physician; **aspirin**, NSAID medication
Exercise injury problems (pain)	**Acetaminophen, aspirin** and use of heat and cold
Pain and fever (children)	Children's aspirin, acetaminophen, liquid acetaminophen, aspirin, rectal suppositories
Fungus	**Antifungal preparations**
Sunburn (preventive)	**Sunblock**
Sprains	**Elastic bandages**
Stomach, upset	Antacid (nonabsorbable)
Wounds (general)	**Adhesive tape, bandages, sodium bicarbonate (soaking agent)**
Wounds (antiseptics)	**Ethyl alcohol (60–90%)**, isopropyl alcohol
Wounds (protectant)	Topical antibiotics

*Items in bold print are basic requirements; other preparations are also useful and should be considered.

bones, handle the victim with care, stop the bleeding, and keep the victim warm at all times.

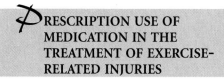

PRESCRIPTION USE OF MEDICATION IN THE TREATMENT OF EXERCISE-RELATED INJURIES

Numerous prescription and nonprescription (over-the-counter) drugs are available to combat infection, treat fungi, control pain and bleeding, and reduce inflammation. It is wise, however, to consult your physician before using any medication. It is also important to update your home medicine cabinet to make certain you are stocking the basics for common illnesses and injuries. Take a moment to analyze your home pharmacy by completing Lab Activity 14.2: Evaluating Your Home Medicine Cabinet at the end of this chapter. Then compare your findings to the recommended home pharmacy in Table 14.5.

Infection can often be prevented by including at least one antiseptic and one wound protectant in your home medicine kit. Your physician may also prescribe an antibiotic—either a topical dressing or a systemic medication.

Pain may be controlled through the skin by applying a topical anesthesia to inhibit pain sensations through quick evaporation and cooling or by counterirritating the skin so you are no longer aware of the pain. Liniments, analgesic balms, heat, and cold are examples of **counterirritants**. Some central ner-

Electrotherapy The use of electricity (infrared radiation therapy, shortwave and microwave diathermics, and ultrasound therapy) in the treatment of disease or injury.

Counterirritants Medication, heat, cold, electricity, and so forth, used to eliminate pain and inflammation.

vous system drugs such as acetaminophen (Tylenol®) and aspirin reduce pain by acting on the nerves that carry the pain impulse to the brain.

Inflammation to soft tissue can be reduced through the use of one of several drugs. Aspirin is effective for conditions such as tendonitis, bursitis, chondromalacia, and tendosynovitis. Some enzymes can help treat swollen joints, reduce inflammation, edema, pain, swelling, and redness. NSAIDs (non-steroid-anti-inflammatory drugs) are also quite effective in eliminating inflammation. A physician's prescription and guidance is needed, however, since side effects may occur and dangers exist with long-term use.

NUTRITION AND HEALING

Individuals who do not eat correctly and have poor nutritional status do not heal as rapidly as normal. Although the recommended daily allowances (RDAs) (see chapter 10) for protein and for some vitamins and minerals increase during periods of recovery from illness and injury, a sufficient safety margin exists in the RDA to promote normal healing and recovery, providing you are consuming adequate fluids and calories.

PROTECTING YOUR BODY FROM INFECTIOUS DISEASES

All living creatures have suffered from infectious and noninfectious diseases since the beginning of recorded history. Infectious diseases such as plague, smallpox, tuberculosis, and polio were once common throughout the world. Now these diseases occur mainly in developing countries. However, infectious diseases such as AIDS and other sexually transmitted diseases (STDs) have come forward to wreak havoc on Americans, the industrialized nations, and other peoples throughout the world. In addition, although Americans enjoy a relatively high level of hygiene and standard of living, they nevertheless experience a very high level of pain and death from noninfectious diseases such as cardiovascular disease, stroke, and cancer. With the exception of AIDS, most of the infectious diseases Americans experience are not life threatening, due to advanced medical diagnosis and treatment. However, cardiovascular disease (including stroke) and cancer are the leading causes of death in the United States today.

In this section, we will discuss several other infectious diseases that are common in the United States. Your instructor may wish you to read chapter 6 on (infectious) STDs in conjunction with this section. Chapters 12 and 13 cover noninfectious cardiovascular disease and cancer.

Infectious diseases are transmitted from an infected object, animal, or person to an uninfected individual through agents that include bacteria, viruses, fungi, and animal parasites. Some infectious diseases are spread from one *host* to another and are said to be *communicable,* or *contagious.* Some of these communicable infectious diseases, such as rubella (German measles) and influenza (the "flu"), are highly contagious, while others—certain types of pneumonia, for example—are much less contagious. *Non-communicable* or *noncontagious* infectious diseases are acquired from the environment but do not spread from one host to another even though they are caused by infectious agents. Tetanus, for example, is an acute bacterial infection transmitted to a body wound by spores in soil.

Relatively long-lasting vaccines and treatments have been developed for a number of communicable and noncommunicable infectious diseases. Most children, for instance, are vaccinated for diseases such as polio and rubella. Other infectious diseases require repeated vaccinations, or have no vaccines and only limited treatments. For example, a person can contract the "common" cold several times in a year. Similarly, the flu can be contracted many times in one's life despite the availability of yearly flu vaccinations.

We will examine how infectious diseases are spread, some of the mechanisms the body uses to defend against infection, and how infectious diseases can be controlled and prevented.

Agents of Infection

By practicing a healthy lifestyle, avoiding substances like tobacco, drugs, and alcohol that can compromise your health, and by maintaining good general health, you will reduce your chances of being attacked by disease-causing agents, which are called **pathogens.** However, when your immune system is weakened or when you make contact with a virulent pathogen, even if your immune system is healthy, the risk of disease is increased. Knowing about the pathogens that can cause infectious diseases and where they come from will help you better understand your body and your health. Figure 14.1 depicts the various pathogens that cause disease in humans.

Figure 14.1 ✦ Examples of Various Pathogens That Cause Diseases in Humans. Most pathogens are microorganisms that can only be seen with a microscope. However, some parasitic worms can grow to lengths of several meters.

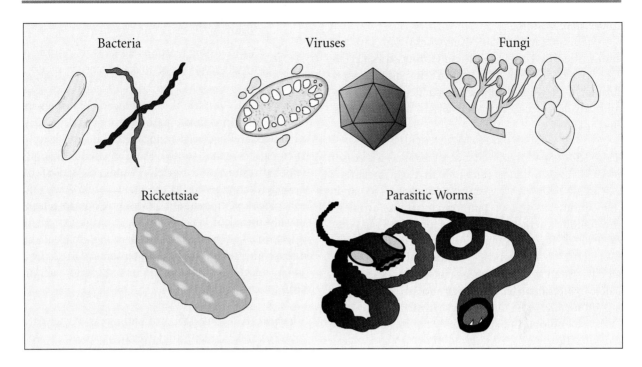

Bacteria Both harmful and helpful, bacteria are microscopic single-celled organisms, plantlike in some characteristics, that can be classified by shape. *Cocci* are spherical, *bacilli* are cylindrical, and *spirilla* and *spirochetes* are spiral. Some bacteria reproduce by dividing into two cells. The time between divisions is referred to as the *generation time* and is the key to how quickly a disease spreads through the body. Still other bacteria reproduce by creating spores that are inactive and highly resistant to dryness and heat. Under favorable conditions, these bacteria become active, as is the case with **botulism** (serious food poisoning) and **tetanus** (an infectious disease causing spasm of muscle groups). Many harmful bacteria grow on surfaces or between cells and do not actually invade the cell.

Most kinds of bacteria originating within the body are not harmful and are actually vital to our existence, like the bacterium *Escherichia coli*, which lives in our intestines. Still other bacteria help to ward off foreign infectious organisms. When our own endogenous bacteria get out of hand, problems, such as acne, pyorrhea, urinary tract infections, and other conditions, may result.

Staphylococcal Infections Staphylococci are bacteria that can be present on the skin without causing seri-

ous infection ("staph" infection). But once infection begins, the bacteria multiply and produce various toxins and enzymes that allow the infection to spread to the bloodstream, causing *bacteremia,* or bacteria in the blood. In the central portion of the lesion, the tissue dies and is used to nourish the bacteria. Thus, an abscess is formed, leading to breakage at the point of least resistance (skin), or to internal drainage of abscess contents in deep-tissue infections. You may have seen a dog suffering from an abscess acquired in a fight with a cat. Or you may have had a group of staph-infected hair follicles (pimples) appear on your

Pathogens Any disease-causing agents, such as bacteria, viruses, or toxins.

Bacteria Microscopic, single-celled organisms; plantlike in some characteristics. Some bacteria cause disease; others are beneficial. They are often classified by shape.

Botulism A serious food-poisoning disease caused by the botulism bacteria.

Tetanus A serious blood-poisoning disease caused by the tetanus bacteria.

cheeks and chin just in time to embarrass you for a Saturday night date. The pus pockets forming in response to the infections should be drained, flushed with an antibiotic, and allowed to continue draining to promote healing.

Staph organisms are everywhere and can be transmitted by contact with contaminated material (for instance, blankets) or in the air (sneeze droplets). Newborn babies are particularly at risk and can develop an infection if skin breaks due to diaper chafing.

Toxic Shock Syndrome   First recognized as a disease in 1978, it was not until June 1980 that an association was made between toxic shock syndrome (TSS) and the continuous use of tampons by young women throughout their menstrual periods. TSS victims experience flu-like symptoms in the early stages: fever (102° F or higher), vomiting, diarrhea, sore throat, and in some cases headache and muscle ache. These symptoms later disappear and are replaced by a sunburnlike rash and shock involving a rapid decrease in blood pressure, kidney failure, and heart irregularities.

TSS is more common in menstruating women, although nonmenstrual TSS does occur. The cause appears to be a *Staphylococcus,* which spreads through the body. Blood-soaked tampons in the vagina provide a fertile haven for these bacteria. After the initial infection, the bacteria produce a strong toxin that causes the serious symptoms of TSS. Nonmenstrual TSS also appears to be caused by *Staphylococcus aureus,* which grows in wounds, surgical incisions, or other body openings.[1]

A woman has about 15 chances in 100,000 (less than 0.5 percent) of contracting TSS. This low incidence has prompted the Centers for Disease Control in Atlanta to state that it seems "unwarranted to recommend the use of tampons be discontinued." Many women, however, feel that any risk is too high. To reduce the chances of contracting TSS, the following suggestions are offered:

- Select your tampon very carefully. Avoid superabsorbent tampons, and use the traditional cottonlike materials until further evidence is available. Sea sponges, which some women use as tampons, may be contaminated with ocean pollutants and are suspected in several cases of TSS.

- Avoid changing the tampon too often. Repeated insertion and removal may irritate the vagina and provide additional entry points for TSS bacteria.

- Switch to maxipads at bedtime and minipads as the flow tapers; avoid continuous use of tampons throughout menstruation.

- If you use maxipads, avoid those with super-absorbent fibers.

- Avoid using tampons to absorb nonmenstrual secretions or to disguise vaginal odor.

Streptococcal Infections   *Streptococci* cause sore throats, ear infections, nasopharyngitis, tonsillitis, impetigo, and bacterial endocarditis and can lead to rheumatic fever and tooth decay. Infection in wounds (skin abrasions or surgical wounds) is caused by Group A streptococci, as are many sore throats and ear infections. Impetigo is a Group A skin infection, usually prevalent among children, and is extremely infectious. Gymnasts and wrestlers can contract the disease after exercising on contaminated mats. Like staph infections, strep infections respond well to antibiotic treatment.

Viruses   A second group of pathogens, **viruses** are minute parasitic agents that live and reproduce inside other living cells. They consist of a core of genetic material surrounded by a protective protein membrane and have no metabolic activity of their own. They do, however, control the metabolism of the cell in which they live and direct it to produce many hundreds of new viruses. The cell eventually becomes engorged with new viruses and breaks apart, spewing its contents in all directions. Each new virus can then enter another cell and repeat the cycle. Viruses cause such diseases as yellow fever, measles, mumps, rabies, poliomyelitis, smallpox, warts, fever blisters, chicken pox, and the common cold.[2]

Unfortunately, viruses are unaffected by antibiotics, and drugs neither combat nor cure a viral infection. The body itself, however, produces a protective substance known as **interferon.** Interferons are proteins released from body cells that are infected with a virus. Interferons can help protect the body against certain other types of viruses. Interferons interact with cell membranes to block viral invasion. Not all viruses trigger the production of interferons, but certain synthetic chemicals and bacteria have been found to stimulate interferon production.

Fungi   A group of many-celled organisms—**fungi,** yeasts and molds—must live on other plants or animals because they contain no chlorophyll and cannot manufacture their own food. Fungi generally form filaments called *hyphae* and are blown to new locations in great numbers through the release of spores or seedlike cells. In humans, fungi usually affect the external body parts such as the skin, scalp, or nails. Dermatomycoses is an example of a fungus responsible for skin infections. Common ringworm is spread from animals or from other humans. Athlete's foot fungus is spread from person to person in showers, locker rooms, and so forth. Some generalized fungal infections, usually from the soil or vegetation, attack the lungs and the meninges of the brain.

Fungi require an environment of high humidity and warmth and are therefore more common in tropical climates. Fungal infections are rarely serious and can be controlled by topical application of fungicides. Proper personal hygiene (regular bathing, clean clothes, drying properly, and avoiding the use of other people's shoes, socks, and clothes) prevents fungal infections. Since practically all antibiotics are extracted from soil fungi, they are of little help in fighting fungal diseases and may actually destroy harmless bacteria in the body that help restrain the growth of these diseases. The trend toward overuse of antibiotic therapy may be contributing to the increase in fungal diseases.

Rickettsia   Once considered to be a kind of virus, **rickettsia** is now believed to be a small form of bacteria. Rickettsia need an insect acting as a **vector** (carrier in order for disease to be transmitted to humans). There are two common types of rickettsial disease: *typhus,* carried by the tick or flea, and *Rocky Mountain spotted fever,* carried by the tick. Symptoms for both diseases include fever, rash, general weakness, and eventually coma. Both are potentially life threatening. Rickettsia produce toxins within small blood vessels that block the flow of blood and cause tissues to die. It is important to realize that you don't actually have to be bitten by a tick or flea to be infected with rickettsia. Infection may also result if an insect vector deposits excrement on any small or large skin wound.

Animal Parasites: Protozoa and Parasitic Worms
Animal parasites, including the single-celled **protozoa** and the multicelled **parasitic worms,** live on or inside another living organism (host). Many animal parasites live part of their lives on one animal and part on another, with both hosts essential to the life cycle of the parasite. Generally, the development of a fertilized egg to the larva stage occurs in the first host, with the adult form living on the second. Typically, offspring are produced in one animal and growth occurs in another. To ensure survival, large quantities of eggs are produced (the beef tapeworm lays more than 1 million eggs per day). Parasitic worms vary

from 1 inch to 60 feet long and are not a major health problem in the United States. Pinworms, flukes, and tapeworms are examples of common parasitic worms found in humans.

Some major diseases, most common in tropical areas with poor sanitation, are caused by protozoan parasites. The *Plasmodium* protozoan parasite causes malaria. African sleeping sickness, transmitted by the tsetse fly, and amebic dysentery are other protozoan diseases common outside the United States. Trichomoniasis, caused by *Trichomonas,* is a common vaginal infection in women in the United States. Drugs are effective in the treatment of protozoan diseases.

Defenses against Infectious Diseases

Now that you know something about pathogens, let's examine exactly how these agents are able to take hold in the body and how the body defends itself against them.

Setting the Stage for Infection   Generally speaking, infection occurs when a microorganism (1) successfully penetrates the host's defense barriers and (2) multiplies. When microorganisms have destroyed tissue or used large quantities of host nutrients in sustaining their growth and causing infection to such an extent that a person senses noticeable discomfort,

---

Viruses Minute parasitic agents that live and reproduce inside living cells; viruses cause many diseases, including the common cold and serious, often fatal, illnesses.

Interferon A protein released by body cells infected with a virus that works with body membranes to prevent and fight viral infection.

Fungi Plantlike organisms that obtain nutrition by growing on the tissue of other organisms. Fungi cause some diseases in humans.

Rickettsia Now believed to be a very small form of bacteria, rickettsia cause the diseases of typhus and Rocky Mountain spotted fever in humans.

Vector An organism or some other object that carries a disease-causing agent from one organism to another.

Protozoa Single-celled animals that live in or on other organisms, sometimes causing disease.

Parasitic worms Multicelled animals that live in or on other organisms, sometimes causing disease.

fever, and malaise, we use the term, **disease** to characterize the symptoms. As normal, healthy humans we all carry infections around with us continually. For instance, more than 90 percent of throat cultures taken at random contain streptococcal bacteria. Such low-level infections, however, are not sufficiently debilitating to cause discomfort

Six factors set the stage for debilitating infectious diseases in humans: (1) A pathogen (live virus or bacteria) must be present, and the pathogen must be able to (2) live in, (3) multiply in, and (4) escape from a place where it has settled ("a reservoir"). Then the pathogen must (5) contract and enter an appropriate host (in this case, a human), and (6) the host must receive the pathogen. Table 14.6 describes these six factors, along with explanations of what they are and how they operate. If all of these six factors are met, a pathogen may be able to cause disease.

Nonspecific Defenses: Defense Mechanisms Your body's nonspecific defenses, which help prevent infection from spreading when microorganic pathogens enter include the skin; the respiratory tract (mucous membranes of the nose, throat, and lungs); the gastrointestinal tract (oral cavity, esophagus, stomach, and alimentary tract); the urogenital tract (bladder, ureters, penis, vagina); the eyes; and the ear canals. These defenses represent a first line of defense against disease.

After the pathogen penetrates the body's external defenses, it encounters a second line of defense. Various enzymes and other compounds in blood can kill an infectious organism by causing it to break open,

---

Disease The destructive processes found during an illness that lead to noticeable symptoms of pain and discomfort.

Immunity The ability of the human body, or another organism's body, to recognize and defend itself against specific infectious agents.

Antigen A specific outside agent that, upon entering the body, promotes antibody formation.

Antibodies Specific protein complexes that are produced by a body to defend against, destroy, or neutralize antigens.

Lymphocytes White blood cells formed in the bone marrow that produce antibodies to battle specific disease-causing agents.

Toxin A poison formed by antigens; toxins stimulate an immune response in the body, causing antibodies to the toxin to be formed.

---

destroying its cell wall, or preventing it from multiplying. Special white blood cells, called *phagocytes,* engulf and digest bacteria. Larger phagocytic cells, called *macrophages,* are contained in the body's tissues, and these also fight off bacteria so that the offending organism may never be able to establish itself.

If the invader does become established, the body then resorts to a third line of defense in which tissue fluids and antibacterial proteins accumulate. Recall from the discussion of viruses that, in the case of a viral (rather than bacterial) infection, *interferons* are released from body cells that are infected with the virus. Interferons work in two ways: they can keep viruses from multiplying in infected body cells, or they can keep viruses from entering healthy body cells. The body's fight to repel the disease becomes evident through inflammation of the infected area and accompanying discomfort. Fever is also a sign that the body is fighting infection.

Once the third line of defense is penetrated, the infection may spread through the body tissues and perhaps into the bloodstream. If this happens, the infection becomes serious. If the infection remains localized, an abscess may form as more and more tissue in the infected area is destroyed. An *abscess* is a cavity filled with fluid, white cells battling the disease microbe, and *pus* (dead white cells). The body returns to normal only when enough of the infectious organisms are killed or rendered inactive so that the disease and its symptoms disappear.

Specific Defenses: The Immune Mechanism Many specific kinds of infectious agents require the body's *specific defenses.* Specific defenses make up the body's immune mechanism. **Immunity** refers to the body's ability to recognize and defend itself against specific infectious agents. When the body recognizes a specific harmful outside agent, called an **antigen,** the body produces specific proteins, called **antibodies,** to battle this agent. This process is called the *immune response.* Antibodies are produced by **lymphocytes**—white blood cells formed in the bone marrow. *B lymphocytes,* or *B cells,* play the primary role in manufacturing antibodies. Antibodies are found primarily in the blood but are also present in mucous membranes in the respiratory, urogenital, and gastrointestinal tracts. They are very important in preventing both initial infection and the subsequent spread of infectious agents. Another kind of lymphocyte, *T-lymphocytes* or *T-cells* (also called T-suppressor or T-helper cells) circulate in the bloodstream, either suppressing or helping the general immune responses to other lymphocytes.

Let's look at an example of how the specific immune response works. A practical example of an

Table 14.6 ✦ Six Factors Necessary to Produce Infectious Disease in Humans

FACTOR	INTERPRETATION	EXAMPLES	COMMENTS
A causative agent	A living organism (pathogen) must exist that is capable of invading the body and causing disease.	Viruses, bacteria	Viruses and bacteria that cause disease are in the environment at all times.
A reservoir	The pathogen must have a place to live and multiply until it is passed on to a host, such as a human being.	Humans: infected human or someone who is a carrier and is not affected; or an animal, insect, or bird.	Animal diseases that are transmitted to humans are generally not transmitted from human to human.
A means of escape	The pathogen must have a means of excape from the reservoir.	Through the respiratory tract (nose, throat, lungs, bronchial tree via coughing, sneezing, or breathing); the digestive tract (feces, saliva, vomitus, contaminated items); open sores, wounds, and lesions.	Each disease has a period when the pathogen is most likely to escape (infectious period) and infect another human. Quarantine during this period reduces the risk of spreading the disease.
A means of transmission	The pathogen must have a means of contacting a host.	Body to body (kissing, touching, sexual contact); animals and insects; inanimate objects (clothing, eating utensils, tissues, toilet articles).	Pathogens that can survive outside a host pose the greatest threat to humans.
A means of entry	The pathogen must have a way to enter the host.	Respiratory tract (breathed in), digestive tract (swallowed), breaks in the skin (cuts, abrasions), or mucous membranes (lining of the mouth, nose, eyes, vagina, anus).	Hand-to-mucuous membrane contact is a common way the pathogen enters the human body.
A host that is suceptible to the pathogen	The host must receive the pathogen.	Strong body defenses or immunity can fight off the pathogen before the disease occurs.	The period between entry of the pathogen and the disease's first symptoms is called the incubation period. It is easier to eradicate the disease during this period than during subsequent stages of the disease.

antigenic stimulus is **toxin,** produced during a bacterial infection. Your immune system recognizes the toxin (antigen) as foreign, and antibodies produced in response to the toxin (by plasma cells), either in the past or during the present infection, combine chemically with the toxin. The resulting aggregation of toxin and antibodies is engulfed by immune cells, metabolized, and excreted. Thus the primary role antibodies is to combine with a specific antigens and aid in the clearance of antigen, from your body. Once you have been exposed to an antigen, you retain the ability to respond to it for a period of months or years.

Primary and Secondary Immune Response The first time you are infected with a virus—influenza, for example—you react immunologically to antigens produced by the virus. A virus is usually inhaled in mucus droplets from an infected person (for exam-

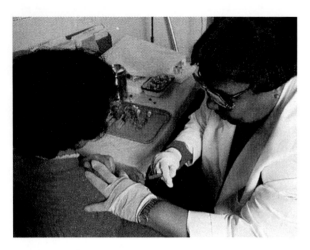

Vaccination against measles and other diseases is a valuable part of maintaining public health.

ple, after a sneeze); it is absorbed in the mucous layer of the respiratory tract, penetrates susceptible cells in the nose, bronchi, or lungs, and multiplies. While infection is continuing, macrophages in the infected area are engulfing virus particles. Macrophages then present some form of the virus protein to a B lymphocyte that is predetermined to produce an antibody to that antigen. The B lymphocyte then produces an antigen (IgM) to influenza virus.

Up to this point, the virus has had one to two days to incubate in the respiratory tract. During this time you may have chills, aching muscles, and fever. Fever may continue for several days. As soon as enough virus is present to be detected by your immune cells, you begin your defense against the infection. Within 24 hours after immune cell recognition of the viral antigen, you may produce some specific IgM. Within seven days after antigen recognition, you have a high level of IgM in your blood, and some IgG, another antibody, is being produced. Within two weeks after antigen recognition, you have a high level of IgG in your blood; it is this IgG that

Vaccination The injection or ingestion of a vaccine in order to stimulate an immune response to a specific antigen.

Vaccine A pharmaceutical preparation made from specific antigens that, when injected or ingested by an individual, stimulates the production of antibodies against that antigen, causing either a partial or complete immune response to that antigen.

can protect you from subsequent influenza virus infections. This is your primary immune response.

When infected a year later with similar influenza, you have an antibody present in your blood that can react with the virus (and macrophages) to aid in ridding your body of the virus. At this time, some of your plasma cells, which were previously committed to making the specific antibody to influenza A virus, recognize the antigen of this year's virus (A group). These committed cells are now ready to commence production of IgG directly, and do so immediately. The second dose of natural influenza virus antigen acts like a vaccination that stimulates your immune cells to produce an influenza-specific antibody. This is your secondary immune response.

Treatment of Infectious Diseases

Vaccination   The term **vaccination** is derived from the word *vaccinia,* or cowpox. Edward Jenner performed the first vaccination against smallpox in 1798. He noted that milkmaids rarely contracted smallpox and wondered why this was so. He found that milkmaids did contract a related disease from cows (cowpox), but that the illness was not serious and left no disfiguring marks. He prepared an inoculum from the pustule of a milkmaid with cowpox, inoculated susceptible humans, and found that these vaccinated individuals did not contract smallpox even when exposed to virulent smallpox virus.

Since Jenner's time, medical professionals have prepared vaccines against many different infectious agents. A **vaccine** is a preparation of an antigen or antigens from an infectious agent that, when injected into a normal, susceptible body, initiates an immune response against a subsequent infection by the organism. A vaccine may consist of live organisms that retain their antigenic properties and can replicate in the body but will not cause severe illness; killed organisms that retain antigenic properties but will not replicate in the body and will not cause severe illness; or pure antigens.

Many successful vaccine preparations have been developed over the years, particularly to combat virus infections. Some of these are polio, rubella, measles, mumps, adenovirus, smallpox, and influenza. Table 14.7 indicates the principal used to prevent human viral diseases.

The vaccines most commonly used to protect against bacterial infections are diphtheria, pertussis, and tetanus toxoid (the latter to protect against infection by *Clostridium tetani,* the causative agent of lock jaw). Although there are thousands of strains of bac-

Table 14.7 ✦ Principal Vaccines Used in Prevention of Human Virus Diseases

DISEASE	SOURCE OF VACCINE	CONDITION OF VIRUS	ROUTE OF ADMINISTRATION
Recommended Immunization for General Public (in U.S. and Other Developed Countries)			
Poliomyelitis	Tissue culture (human diplod cell line, monkey kidney)	Live	Oral
Measles[1]	Tissue culture (chick embryo)	Live	Subcutaneous[2]
Mumps[1]	Tissue culture (chick embryo)	Live	Subcutaneous
Rubella[1, 3]	Tissue culture (duck embryo, rabbit, or dog kidney)	Live	Subcutaneous
Immunization Recommended Only under Certain Conditions (Epidemics, Exposure, Travel, Military)			
Smallpox	Lymph from calf or sheep (glycerolated, lyophilized); choorioallantois, tissue cultures (lyohilized)	Active	Intradermal: multiple pressure, multiple puncture, or (with specially prepared vaccine) by jet injection
Yellow Fever	Tissue cultures and eggs (17D strain)	Live	Subcutaneous or intradermal
Influenza	Chick embryo allantoic fluid (formalized or UV-irradiated, concentrated by various processes)	Inactive	Subcutaneous
	Highly purified or subunit forms recommemded where available	Inactive	Subcutaneous
Rabies	Duck embryo treated with phenol or ultraviolet light	Inactive	Subcutaneous
Adenovirus[4]	Monkey kidney tissue cultures (formalinized)	Inactive	Intramuscular
	Human diploid cell cultures	Live	Oral, by entericcoated capsule
Japanese B encephalitis	Mouse brain (formalinized), tissue culture	Inactive	Subcutaneous
Venezuelan equine encephalomyelitis[5]	Guinea pig hear cell culture	Live	Subcutaneous
Eastern equine encephalomyelitis[4]	Chick embryo cell culture	Inactive	Subcutaneous
Western equine encephalomyelitis[4]	Chick embryo cell culture	Inactive	Subcutaneous
Russian spring-summer encephalitis[4]	Mouse brain (formalinized)	Inactive	Subcutaneous

[1]Available also as combined vaccines.

[2]With less attentuated strains, gamma globulin is given in another limb at the time of vaccination.

[3]Neither monovalent rubella vaccine nor combination vaccines incorporating rubella should be administered to a post-pubertal, susceptible female unless she is not pregnant and understands that it is imperative not to become pregnant for at least three months after vaccination. (The time immediately postpartum has been suggested as a safe period for vaccination.)

[4]Not available in the United States except for the Armed Forces or for investigative purposes.

[5]Available for use in domestic animals (from the U.S. Department of Agriculture) and for investigative purposes.

Source: From *Review of Medical Microbiology,* (p. 323), by E. Jarvetz, J. L. Melnick, & E. A. Adelberg, 1979, Los Altos, CA: Lange Medical Publication. Used by permission.

teria, only a few bacterial vaccines have been developed because most bacterial infections are readily controlled through the use of antibiotics. In contrast, most viral infections cannot be controlled by drugs; therefore, immunization by vaccination is of more benefit.

Active and Passive Immunity When your body is capable of producing its own antibodies to fight off specific disease-causing organisms, you possess what is called **active immunity.** Active immunity can develop naturally in your body or it can be acquired "artificially" from a vaccination. Once you have active immunity against certain infectious diseases, you seldom need to worry about being infected by them.

Sometimes, however, your active immunity might be threatened by unusual health circumstances, or it might be reduced by sickness or by chemotherapy for cancer (see chapter 13). During times when your body's immune mechanism is especially weak, it may need an extra boost in the form of antibodies taken from another person or animal. The result of this extra boost is called **passive immunity.** Produced from *gamma globulins* taken from donors' blood, passive immunity antibodies tend to be short-lived, but they will get your immune mechanism through difficult periods. Mother's milk is a good source of passive immunity for newborns, which is one of the most important reasons why breast-feeding is preferable to bottle feeding.

Antibiotics Chemicals had been used to combat infectious disease for hundreds of years before Paul Ehrlich made chemotherapy a science. In 1903, he developed Salvarson, a drug containing arsenic, which is effective against the causative agent of syphilis. In 1929, Sir Alexander Fleming discovered that a compound (later shown to be penicillin) produced by a fungus could inhibit the growth of certain

bacteria. In 1940, Chain and Florey reported that penicillin could be used to treat humans with bacterial infections. Meanwhile, Domagk, in 1935, discovered sulfonamides and their inhibitory action on bacterial multiplication. Once these compounds had been discovered, advances in antimicrobial chemotherapy were rapid. **Antibiotic** (*anti*—against; *bios*—life) was originally a term used to mean natural products of microorganisms, but it now includes synthetic compounds (for example, synthetic penicillin, ampicillin) as well.

Antibiotics can successfully control several major bacterial diseases, such as strep and staph infections, bacterial pneumonia, and many of the sexually transmitted diseases. However, these drugs cannot treat viruses. Although antibiotics have made a vital contribution, some problems are associated with their use, including allergic reactions and the development of strains resistant to the drugs.

In 1980, infectious diseases ranked as America's fifth leading killer, resulting in about 41 deaths per 100,000 and was the third leading cause of death. Although AIDS caused the largest jump in death among males aged 25 to 44, mortality rose 22 percent when HIV-related deaths were eliminated. Deaths from septicemia (bacteria in the blood), for example, rose 83 percent, respiratory tract infections increased 20 percent, and invasive strep bacterial infections rose from 4 to 14 percent in three years. New, lethal food-borne bacterial infections have also sprung up that are resistant to current antibiotics. Experts are alarmed about the spread of new antibiotic-resistant strains of bacteria and the increased resistance of bacterial infections to current antibiotic therapy. According to the American Medical Association, the current situation is serious. There is an urgent need to develop new antibiotics to improve the treatment of infections that are becoming resistant to traditional medications as well as to handle the wave of new bacterial infections being identified in the 1990s.

Common Infectious Disease

The Common Cold Contrary to popular belief, you cannot "catch" a cold from a draft, wet feet, a chill, or going out without a hat in inclement weather. The infection can, however, be transmitted by direct contact, such as handshakes or kissing, through mucus droplets coughed or sneezed into the air, and through contact with soiled tissues used by an infected person. The common cold is an infection of the membrane lining the upper respiratory tract, including the nose, the sinuses, and the throat. There is currently no known means of preventing, curing,

Active immunity When a body can produce antibodies against a specific antigen, causing a long-term immune response to that antigen and its associated disease.

Passive immunity The injection or ingestion of pharmaceutically produced antibodies against a specific antigen in order to boost the immune system and provide short-term immunity to a disease.

Antibiotic A pharmaceutical, such as penicillin, which will destroy bacteria and other microbes that cause disease.

Myth and Fact Sheet

Myth	Fact
1. When an injury occurs to most body parts, heat should be applied.	1. Injuries to soft tissue should be treated with RICE therapy, which requires ice, not heat. Heat should be avoided for two to three days until swelling begins to subside. Early use of heat in any form increases swelling, delays healing, and can result in serious tissue changes that may require surgery to correct.
2. Ice should be applied directly to the skin for one hour.	2. The maximum amount of time ice should be applied is 20 minutes. Longer periods can actually bring about tissue damage. And it should not come in contact with the skin unless an ice massage is being used.
3. Individuals who have the wind knocked out of them are in danger of dying.	3. The temporary inability to breathe following a blow to a relaxed midsection will slowly subside until breathing is restored. Meanwhile, you will gasp for breath, possibly suffer dizziness, nausea, weakness, or even collapse. A hard blow to the solar plexus increases intra-abdominal pressure, causes pain, and interferes with the diaphragmatic cycle reflex due to nerve paralysis or muscle spasm. Breathing is only temporarily affected by a blow that momentarily paralyzes the nerve control of the diaphragm. Loosen clothing at the neck and waist; apply ice to the abdomen; and breathe slowly through the nose.
4. A popping or snapping sound in the knee is a sign of serious trouble.	4. The sound generally comes from a tendon flipping over bony fulcrums and may be quite natural in some athletes who just never really noticed the sound before. Joint mice or the presence of some loose cartilage or other tissue may also produce a clicking sound as the knee flexes and extends. Bone, tendon, ligament, or cartilage damage may not be indicated unless other symptoms are present such as inflammation, swelling, fluid, and knee locking.
5. Avoid getting chilled or you will "catch" a cold.	5. The common cold is transmitted by a virus through direct contact (handshake or contact with soiled objects of an infected person followed by touching a mucous membrane, kissing, or mucus droplets sneezed or coughed into the air). Becoming chilled will not increase your chances of acquiring the common cold.
6. Acquiring mumps as an adult will produce sterility.	6. Once the virus replicates and enters the blood, it can localize in the reproductive organs and develop swelling in about 20 percent of males around the age of puberty. The condition passes, however, and generally does not cause sterility.

or shortening a cold, but the symptoms can be treated with aspirin (for headache, fever, and body aches); a humidifier; saltwater gargle or lozenges (for sore throat); limited use of nasal decongestants; and fluids, such as juice, tea, or soup. Antibiotics are ineffective in treating a cold virus, and the value of taking massive doses of vitamin C to prevent or cure a cold is debatable.

Colds are more prevalent during the winter months, when people spend more time indoors. Preventive measures include, avoiding carriers (particularly during the first 24 hours of symptoms, when the virus is most contagious), avoiding handshakes, avoiding contact with the mucus membranes, and practicing proper hygiene (washing hands and face frequently).

Improving Your Community

Preventing Infectious and Noninfectious Diseases

It is well known that, among other factors, our own behavior affects the level of risk we face in contracting both infectious and noninfectious diseases. Consequently, there is much you can do to reduce your own risk as well as that of family, friends, and other people.

1. By maintaining a high level of general health, you will help to set an example for other people. Your lifestyle should include a solid schedule of aerobic activity, sound nutrition, a complete absence of illicit drugs and tobacco, avoidance of alcohol, and regular medical and dental care.

2. How many unhealthy behaviors—smoking, careless use of alcohol, lack of regular exercise—can you identify among your family and friends? Make a list of the infectious and noninfectious diseases associated with each person who engages in unhealthy behaviors. Don't use scare tactics or pushiness, but let the person know that you care and that his or her behavior could be dangerous to that individual's health in terms of disease.

3. Do you have a friend or relative who has a noninfectious disease, such as diabetes, hypercholesteremia, or backache? If you would feel comfortable doing so, go to that person and discuss the disease with him or her. Learn as much as you can bout the disease and how this person copes with it. This will not only increase your understanding of and compassion for people with that disease, but it will also enable you to offer help and information to other people who have or are in some way affected by this disease.

4. Become informed about the cause, prevention, and treatment of backache. This will help you reduce your own risk of developing a problem later in life and also increase your sensitivity to the needs of friends and family members who suffer from this problem.

5. Develop a proposal for "Reducing Your Risk" disease awareness day on your campus. Focus on health behaviors that can reduce or prevent the risk of serious diseases. Discuss your proposal with personnel at the student health office at your college or university in order to develop a strategy for advertising and implementing your program. The program can be as simple as a series of posters or as elaborate as a series of speeches or brief seminars by faculty or student health service representatives. ✦

Influenza The viral infection of the respiratory tract known as **influenza (flu)** is caused by three types of viruses (A, B, and C), and each has several strains that tend to change slightly from year to year. Type A occurs in epidemic cycles every 10 to 12 years and is the most serious. Type B produces a milder virus but can also reach epidemic proportions. Epidemics of Type C virus do not occur. Because so many different strains of flu exist, a vaccine must be repeated annually and may not offer protection unless the specific type of flu virus is identified. The elderly and the chronically ill whose resistance is lower may benefit from vaccination against Type A virus.

Treatment involves bed rest until body temperature is back to normal, along with symptomatic treatment similar to that for the common cold. If complications develop, such as earache, sinus pain, persistent cough, or sore throat, a physician should be consulted.

Measles A highly contagious disease, **measles** is caused by the measles virus. The airborne virus enters the upper respiratory tract, where it replicates and is spread via blood, mucus, or secretions throughout the respiratory tract. A red rash appears in the mouth and on the skin. The rash is caused by serum seepage from the blood and dead or dying cells forming discrete spots on the skin.

Measles is a serious disease and, under certain circumstances, can lead to inflammation of the brain, or **encephalitis.** It is a common disease: More than 80 percent of individuals over age 20 have an antibody to the virus. A measles vaccine is now available for children and adults; infants are usually protected by the maternal antibody until 6 months of age and should be vaccinated at 15 months.

Approximately 5 percent of young adults are susceptible to measles. Some of these individuals were never vaccinated and others received a vaccine that did not offer lifetime protection. Individuals who were born after 1956 should be protected by live vaccine. Revaccination should also be considered for those who received the live vaccine before age 1 and those who received the killed measles vaccine during the years 1963 to 1967. Those who are allergic to eggs or the antibiotic neomycin, pregnant women, and those with impaired immune responses should not be vaccinated.

Mumps   The mumps virus exists in only one form. After inhalation of the virus, infection may proceed in the outer layer of cells of the respiratory tract or through the oral cavity into the parotid glands, located in the tissue in the floor of your mouth to either side of the tongue. Once the virus replicates and enters the blood, it can localize in salivary glands, reproductive organs (testes and ovaries), pancreas, thyroid, and brain.

The incubation period is 12 to 35 days, and the disease is characterized by swelling of the parotid glands, fever, and general malaise. In adults, the reproductive glands can be affected: Twenty percent of males around the age of puberty develop a swelling of the testes, but this does *not* generally lead to sterility. You may have heard that if only one side of your face swells during mumps infection, you could contract mumps again. This is not true. Once you have had mumps virus infection in one or both parotid glands, with or without swelling of the reproductive glands, you are protected against a future mumps infection.

Rubella   Generally a disease of childhood, rubella is often referred to as "German measles" because it was closely studied in Germany in the 19th century. The rubella virus infects the outer layer of cells of the upper respiratory tract but may replicate in the cervical lymph nodes. The virus appears in the blood about a week after infection and persists for an additional two weeks. A characteristic skin rash develops when the antibody appears in the blood. Once you have contracted the rubella virus, you are generally immune. However, reinfection may occur in some cases, due to inadequate levels of antibody

Rubella infection may have serious effects if contracted during early pregnancy. Infection during the first 10 weeks of pregnancy can lead to birth defects in the fetus.

Children are generally given the combined measles, mumps, and rubella vaccine at 15 months. Adults may be immunized at any time, although the majority of adults are already immune, even if they have no history of the disease. If a woman is pregnant and there are unimmunized children in the household, those children should be vaccinated, as they are the most likely rubella carriers. Table 14.8 indicates the recommended schedule for immunization of infants and children against a number of viral diseases.

Mononucleosis   Infectious mononucleosis can be transmitted in the saliva during kissing or in a manner similar to the common cold. The highest rate of occurrence is in the 15-to-19 age range, followed by the 20-to-24 age range. Symptoms appear from two weeks to two months after exposure: fever, sore throat, enlargement of the spleen and other lymph glands, headache, and fatigue. Serious complications occur in only a small percentage of cases, but the disease is debilitating and requires several weeks to months for full recovery.

Treatment is similar to that for a common cold; the course of the disease is not altered. Bed rest may be required in the early stages. There is currently no known prevention, although a vaccine is under development.

Hepatitis   Hepatitis is essentially an inflammation of the liver that is caused by a number of different viruses, although two well-known viruses are the culprits in most cases. There are two basic types of

---

Influenza (flu)   A viral infection of the upper respiratory tract causing severe coldlike symptoms. There are several strains of flu and various vaccines manufactured to combat them. Influenza can lead to pneumonia or death in weak or aged people.

Measles   A highly infectious disease caused by the measles virus.

Encephalitis   An inflammation of the brain. Encephalitis is sometimes a complicatation of measles.

Infectious mononucleosis   A viral infection like the common cold, but lasting much longer; occasionally there are serious complications.

Table 14.8 ✦ Recommended Schedule for Active Immunization of Normal Infants and Children

RECOMMENDED AGE	IMMUNIZATION(S)	COMMENTS
2 months	DTP[1], OPV[2]	Can be initiated as early as 2 weeks of age in areas of high endemicity or during epidemics.
4 months	DTP, OPV	2-month interval desired for OPV to avoid interference from previous dose.
6 months	DTP (OPV)	OPV is optional (may be given in areas with increased risk of poliovirus exposure).
15 months	Measles, Mumps, Rubella (MMR)[3]	MMR preferred to individual vaccines; tuberculin testing may be done.
18 months	DTP,[4,5] OPV[5]	
24 months	HBPV[6]	
4–6 years[7]	DTP, OPV	At or before school entry.
14–16 years	Td[8]	Repeat every 10 years throughout life.

[1]DTP—Diphtheria and tetanus toxoids with pertussis vaccine.
[2]OPV—Oral, poliovirus vaccine contains attenuated poliovirus types 1,2, and 3.
[3]MMR—Live measles, mumps, and rubella viruses in a combined vaccine.
[4]Should be given 6 to 12 months after the third dose.
[5]May be given simultaneously with MMR at 15 months of age.
[6]Haemophilus B polysaccharide vaccine.
[7]Up to the seventh birthday.
[8]Td—Adult tetanus toxoic (full dose) and diphtheria toxoid (reduced dose) in combination.

hepatitis. **Infectious hepatitis** or **type A hepatitis,** is caused by fecal contamination of food or the environment and is easily preventable by proper hygiene. Type A hepatitis is more common and usually much less severe than **serum hepatitis,** or **hepatitis type B,** which accounts for only 10 percent of all hepatitis cases. Hepatitis B is transmitted through the blood, semen, and saliva—but not the fecal matter—of infected people. Sexual transmission is common for hepatitis B, especially among homosexual men, as is transmission by the sharing of used hypodermic needles among intravenous drug users. Occasionally, hepatitis B is also transmitted by tattooing, ear piercing, and breast-feeding by an infected nursing mother.

Common symptoms for both types of hepatitis include fever (possibly mild or absent in hepatitis B), general weakness and fatigue, loss of appetite, nausea, abdominal discomfort in the upper-right quadrant, and sometimes **jaundice** (yellowing of the skin and eyes).

Onset of the disease is usually sudden for hepatitis A and gradual for hepatitis B. Recovery can be very low for both types of hepatitis, and some cases require as much as several months. Unlike hepatitis A, hepatitis B can remain in the bloodstream for many years following general recovery from its symptoms. Hepatitis B also greatly increases the risk of developing liver cancer and cirrhosis of the liver. The disease is fatal to approximately 1 percent of those afflicted.

It is possible to receive temporary protection or immunity against hepatitis through an injection of gamma globulin. A new vaccine has been developed for hepatitis B. It is costly but recommended for high-risk groups, including homosexual males, intravenous drug users, patients of kidney dialysis, hemophiliacs, morticians, and some health care workers.

Herpes Simplex, Type 1   As discussed in chapter 6, herpes simplex is a virus that occurs in two types: Herpes, type 1, causes cold sores and fever blisters; herpes, type 2, is a sexually transmitted disease.

Although cold sores may disappear rapidly, the type 1 herpes virus remains in a dormant state until triggered to reappear at a lesion site. You may have had a cold sore on your lip and recall that it hurt and looked unsightly, and you were quite relieved when it was gone. The bad news is that it isn't really gone. The virus is still with you in a latent or dormant form, just waiting for the proper stimulus (sunburn, nervous tension, hormone imbalance) to reappear as a lesion. Infection recurs in spite of high levels of antibody and good cell-mediated immunity because the virus leads a relatively sheltered existence in a part of your nervous system where antibody and immune cells can't reach it. Your immune system can only act against the virus after your skin has been traumatized.

Lyme Disease Earlier, we discussed vectors which are animals or insects that transmit a disease-producing organism from a host to a noninfected animal or human. One vector-borne bacterial infection that has held popular attention for the last few years is **Lyme disease,** which was identified in Lyme, Connecticut, in 1975. In 1982, Willy Burgdorfer of the National Institutes of Health laboratory in Montana discovered the actual agent of infection, a type of bacteria previously unknown *(Borrflia burgdorferi).* The insect vector for this bacteria is the deer tick *Ixodes dammini* which feeds on small wild mammals in addition to deer. Humans and domestic animals bitten by the poppy seed-sized deer tick can be infected with Lyme disease.

Although symptoms of Lyme disease vary, in about 50 percent of the cases a "bull's-eye" rash develops within a few days where the bite occurred. Other symptoms may include flu-like symptoms, fever, chills, dizziness, and fatigue. If left untreated, bouts of severe headache, stiffness in the neck and joints, arthritic pain, and even cardiac and neurological problems may occur. Eventually, these problems can become much worse, to the point where people who are already ill or at risk in some other way may die.

Lyme disease can be treated with antibiotics but the best treatment for the disease is prevention. Are you planning a camping trip or hike through the woods? Don't change your plans because of Lyme disease! Wear tightly woven, light-colored long trousers (with the legs tucked into your socks) and a long sleeve shirt. Check your clothing often for ticks. Be sure to check places on your body where ticks can easily hide, such as your scalp and in the genital area. If you must wear light clothing, shorts, and a short-sleeve shirt, use insect repellent at least on your legs, socks, and footwear. If you do find a tick firmly stuck in your skin, don't panic. Using tweezers, grasp the

The deer tick (Ixodes dammini), *a vector of Lyme disease, is about the size of a pinhead.*

tick firmly as close to its head as possible and slowly pull it out. Make sure you have removed the entire tick. If you develop any of the symptoms discussed above after a few days, seek medical help.

Infectious Lung Diseases

Fungus Infections The air contains many spores (fungi) or moldlike substances that enter the lungs without producing disease. Unfortunately, some fungi produce TB-like symptoms. *Histoplasmosis* is caused by tiny spores that float in dusty air and flourish in warm, moist dark places, such as old chicken houses, pigeon lofts, barns, and under trees where birds roost. The inhaled spores may enter the air sacs and multiply in the lymph nodes. The infection may

Infectious hepatitis (type A hepatitis) A common disease characterized by an inflammation of the liver, caused by a virus. Contracted usually through fecal contamination of food; usually not a severe disease.

Serum hepatitis (type B hepatitis) A serious disease characterized by an inflammation of the liver, caused by a virus. Transmitted through the blood, semen, and saliva of infected people; it is much less common than infectious hepatitis.

Jaundice A yellowing of the skin and the whites of the eyes, caused by an inflammation of the liver.

Lyme disease A disease caused by a vector-borne bacteria; it resembles arthritis. Effectively treated with antibiotics; transmitted by deer ticks.

Behavioral Change and Motivational Strategies

Many things might interfere with the use of some practices known to prevent exercise-related injuries and illnesses. Here are some of these barriers (roadblocks) and strategies for overcoming them.

Roadblock	Behavioral Change Strategy
Although you are aware of the value of a proper warm-up before exercise, you just never seem to do it. It seems so natural to change into your workout clothing and immediately start the 3-mile jog or the tennis match. Yet you have noticed a tightness in the calf muscles after exercise for a week or so now.	Most people are impatient and want to get right into exercise, without wasting time. It is a mind-set that is difficult to overcome. One approach may be to avoid viewing the warm-up as a separate component of your program. Continue what you are doing but divide the run into three continuous segments: (1) Begin jogging immediately but very slowly for the first mile, progressing from a 1/4-mile walk to a slow jog. (2) Stop and stretch for at least 5 minutes, emphasizing calf and Achilles tendon exercises (see chapter 7). (3) Complete the remaining two miles of your run. Other forms of exercise can also be planned that permit considerably less effort in the initial 5 to 10 minutes to build in a warm-up period.
You are totally exhausted at the end of your workout and feel nauseated, uncomfortable, and have some muscle soreness.	Many individuals develop the habit of saving the most vigorous part of their workout routine for the final 5 to 10 minutes, before stopping and standing around to talk or sitting down to relax. Failure to use a cool-down period produces the roadblock symptoms. You can avoid this problem by adding one more segment to the 3-mile run. Segment three should involve the most vigorous portion of the workout for about 1.5 miles or 10 to 20 minutes, followed by a fourth segment involving a 1/2-mile slow jog or walk and a brief stretching period to taper off at the end of your workout.
As a college student, you are generally in a hurry and sometimes don't take the time to wash your hands, or you wash them very quickly without soap.	Environmental microbiologists have discovered that kitchen sponges, dishrags, countertops, door handles, hospitals, doctor's offices, and just about anything you touch is covered with microbes, often left by others who did not bother to wash their hands. The alarming spread of new antibiotic-resistant strains of bacteria make hand washing for a minimum of 30 seconds critical to keep you healthy. Slow down and take the time to wash your hands carefully after each visit to the bathroom, periodically during the day, after visiting a hospital, doctor's office, a sick friend, or working around the kitchen or bathroom areas. Without becoming obsessed, try to identify key times during the day when washing your hands makes a lot of sense.
List roadblocks interfering with your approach to exercise injury prevention, and the prevention of infectious diseases.	Now, cite the behavioral change strategies that can help you overcome the roadblocks you listed. If you need to, refer back to chapter 3 for behavioral change and motivational strategies.

1. _____   1. _____

2. _____   2. _____

3. _____   3. _____

4. _____   4. _____

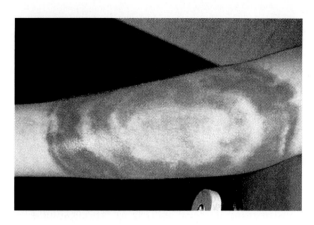

If you are bitten by a deer tick, you might develop, after 2 to 30 days, the "bull's-eye" rash that is a characteristic symptom of Lyme disease.

remain in the lungs where it can be effectively treated, or it may spread throughout the body producing a fatal reaction. *Coccidioidomycosis* (valley fever) is caused by inhaling dust contaminated by spores. Most people exhibit no symptoms; others develop a fever one to three weeks after the spores invade the lungs and body, followed by a measlelike rash, sores on the shins, and joint pain. Within several months symptoms disappear.

Skin tests, blood tests, chest X-rays, and tests of body fluids can detect fungus infections. Modern drugs generally offer effective treatment.

Pneumonia Acute lung inflammations, called pneumonia, are caused by bacteria, viruses, fungi, aspiration of food or fluid, inhalation of poisonous gases, and other factors. Common symptoms include fever, coughing, shortness of breath, chest pains, blood in the phlegm, and a bluish tinge in the skin. *Double pneumonia* involves an inflammation in both lungs. *Bronchial pneumonia* refers to an inflammation in the bronchi or air tubes and the lungs.

Pneumonia An acute inflammation of the lungs; pneumonia can be caused by a variety of agents, such as bacteria, viruses, fungi, or inorganic chemicals.

Tuberculosis (TB) A highly contagious disease most commonly affecting the lungs. Serious complications can lead to death if the disease is untreated.

Walking pneumonia is a mild form of pneumonia that does not require hospitalization or confinement.

Bacterial pneumonia is a major killer among older Americans, directly causing over 50,000 deaths and contributing to 200,000 other deaths each year. The severe pneumonia (infection with group A streptococcus bacteria) that killed Muppets' creator Jim Henson is a rare complication from a common bacteria. This bacteria causes a variety of infections and most are mild, such as sore throat and impetigo. A vaccine that is 60 to 75 percent effective is available that protects against the 23 types of bacterium *Streptococcus pneumoniae*, which accounts for about 90 percent of all cases of bacterial pneumonia. Unfortunately, less than 15 percent of the high-risk population have been vaccinated. Some experts feel that all healthy Americans over the age of 50 should receive the vaccine.

Tuberculosis Commonly known as **TB, tuberculosis** is a highly contagious disease that produces symptoms similar to those of other lung disease or of no particular disease at all. Anyone experiencing chronic cough, fatigue, weakness, unexplained weight loss, loss of appetite, or spitting of blood should see a physician immediately. Most individuals who develop TB have had the germs in their bodies for a long time. They may have had contact with a TB patient years ago, breathed in the germs, and fought them off with the body's defenses. Instead of killing the germs, the body may have walled them up in tiny hard capsules (the "tubercles" of tuberculosis). Years later, when resistance is low and when the immune system is not functioning properly, the germs break out of the capsules, spread, and do their damage. It is estimated that 15 million Americans have TB germs in their body: They are infected and prime candidates for coming down with TB. Although a simple tuberculin test would reveal the presence of the germ, most people do not know they are infected.

Treatment to prevent TB involves medication for approximately one year to kill the walled-up germs that may break free years from now. Treatment to cure TB involves a tuberculin test, chest X-ray, laboratory tests, and outpatient treatment with regular medication. Thanks to new drugs, patients can usually continue with their present job and family activities and avoid long hospital stays and surgery. Combinations of several drugs are usually administered for about nine months.

SUMMARY

Protecting Your Body from Injury and Illness

Many exercise-related injuries are preventable. You can significantly reduce your risk of injury and illness by using a preconditioning period before beginning your exercise program, warming up and cooling down properly, analyzing your medical history, progressing slowly in the early stages of your program, monitoring body signals, dressing properly for the activity, and mastering proper form.

Tissue Response to Injury

The healing process is unique to each individual. Factors such as age, nutrition, treatment, and type and severity of the injury play major roles. In the acute stage immediately following an injury, the body attempts to keep things localized to prevent further damage and aid the healing process that will occur over the next five to six weeks. Complete regeneration and repair, however, may require up to one year.

General Treatment Modalities

The immediate and continued use of cold applications over the first several days after a soft-tissue injury should be followed by heat therapy during the repair and remodeling stage of healing. Numerous techniques to apply heat and cold can be safely used.

Prevention and Emergency Treatment of Common Exercise Injuries and Illnesses

Proper home emergency treatment for a soft-tissue injury to an extremity requires the use of RICE. Certain symptoms suggest the need for immediate care by a physician. If you are in doubt, take the injured person to an emergency room or physician as soon as possible.

Some injuries involving fractures, concussions, bleeding, heart attack, and severe joint trauma can produce shock. Since shock is considerably easier to prevent than it is to treat, precautions should be taken with all patients when dealing with these types of injuries.

Prescription Use of Medication in the Treatment of Exercise-Related Injuries

The home medicine cabinet should contain the basic items necessary for the emergency treatment of common exercise injuries. Over-the-counter medication to treat inflammation, fungi, pain, fever, wounds, and basic problems such as allergy, colds, constipation, diarrhea, and eye irritations should be readily available.

Nutrition and Healing

Sound nutrition is important during recovery from both injury and illness. Nutritional needs increase somewhat during the recovery period, and it is important to continue to eat well, avoid skipping meals, drink plenty of water and other fluids, and consider the use of a multiple vitamin and mineral supplement.

Infectious Diseases

Infectious diseases are transmitted from an infected object, animal, or person to an uninfected individual through agents that include bacteria, viruses, fungi, rickettsia, and animal parasites. Infectious diseases are spread from one host to another, wheras non-infectious diseases, even though they are caused by infectious agents, are acquired from the environment rather than from a host.

Agents of Infection

Bacteria are single-celled organisms, plantlike in nature, that can produce infection. Viruses are even smaller than bacteria and have an amazing ability to survive and reproduce. Certain factors must exist for an infectious disease to occur in humans: a pathogen (live virus or bacteria) must be present; the pathogen must be able to live, multiply in, and escape from a reservoir; the pathogen must then contact and enter a host (human); and the host must receive the pathogen.

Defenses against Infectious Diseases

The body's nonspecific defense mechanisms generally fight off potentially harmful microbes before serious infections occur. In order to ward off severe infections, the body's immune system manufactures specific antibodies in response to specific, potentially harmful outside agents (antigens).

Treatment of Infectious Diseases

Vaccination can prevent several infectious diseases of childhood, including polio, measles, mumps, rubella, and diphtheria. Active immunity to specific antigens is achieved naturally or through vaccinations, and vaccination while extra antibodies when the immune system is weakened can provide valuable short-term passive immunity. Antibiotic therapy has no effect on viral infections: it does control many secondary bacterial infections that penetrate the body's defense mechanisms.

Common Infectious Diseases

There is still neither a prevention nor a cure for the common cold, and despite available vaccinations, influenza outbreaks are a common recurring epidemic. Measles, mumps, and rubella (German measles) are examples of infectious diseases that were fairly common until the development of reliable long-lasting vaccines. There is no known prevention for infectious mononucleosis, which is spread in a manner similar to the common cold. Hepatitis is essentially an inflammation of the liver that is caused by a number of different viruses, although two well-known viruses are the culprits in most cases. Infectious, or type A, hepatitis is more common and usually much less severe than serum, or type B, hepatitis.

Infectious Lung Disease

Most people who were healthy just prior to infection can be treated effectively for infectious lung diseases such as fungus infections, pneumonia, and tuberculosis.

References

American College of Sports Medicine. (1991). *Guidelines for exercise testing and prescription*, 4th ed. (p.7). Philadelphia: Lea & Febiger.

American Running and Fitness Association, Taylor, P. M., & Taylor, D. K. (Eds.), (1988). *Conquering athletic injuries*. Champaign, IL: Leisure Press.

Arnheim, D. D., & Prentice, W. E. (1993). *Principles of athletic training*, 8th ed. St. Louis: Mosby.

Burkett, L. (1970). Causative factors in hamstring strains. *Medicine and Science in Sports and Exercise 2*, 39–42.

Dintiman, G. B., & Ward, R. (1988). *Train America: Achieving peak performance and fitness for sports competition*. Dubuque, IA: Kendal Hunt.

Fahey, T. D. (Ed.). (1986). *Athletic training: Principles and practice*. Mountain View, CA: Mayfield.

Greenberg, J., Dintiman, G., & Oakes, B. (1995). *Physical fitness and wellness*. Boston: Allyn & Bacon.

Klein, K., & Allman, F. (1970). *The knee in sports*. Baltimore: Williams & Watkins.

Powers, S. K., & Howley, E. T. (1990). *Exercise physiology*. Dubuque, IA: Brown.

Staron, R., et. al. (1989). Effects of heavy resistance weight training on muscle fiber size and composition in females. *Medicine and Science in Sports and Exercise 21*; S71.

Stone, M. (1988). Implications for connective tissue and bone alterations resulting from resistance exercise training. *Medicine and Science in Sports and Exercise 20*; S162–S168.

Lab Activity 14.1

Evaluating Your Potential for Foot and Leg Injuries

INSTRUCTIONS: *Injuries to the feet and legs are common in most sports and activities. If you continue the same activity long enough, overuse injuries are almost certain. There are also certain aspects in the makeup of the lower extremities that may require some adjustment to prevent injury. To evaluate your potential for lower extremity injury, examine yourself carefully in the following areas:*

1. **Length of both legs below the ankle:** Stand erect, ankles together, and ask a helper to measure the distance from the floor to a spot marked with a magic marker at the bony protrusion of your ankle.

2. **Length of both legs above the ankle:** Sit in a chair with your feet on the floor, heels together, and toes pointed. If a carpenter's level placed on both knees is uneven, your problem is above the ankle.

3. **Morton's toe:** Stand erect without shoes or socks and determine whether your second toe is larger than your great toe.

4. **Excessive pronation:** Examine your running or athletic shoes for excessive wear on the outside back of the shoe heel.

✦ **Results**

1. Does the length of your legs differ by more than 1/16 of an inch?

2. Is the problem below the ankle or from the ankle to the knee?

3. Is your second metatarsal longer than your great toe?

4. Are your shoes wearing evenly?

5. Are you experiencing pain in the lower back, hip, knee, ankle, or feet during or following exercise?

If you answered "yes" to any of the questions, consult your orthopedic physician for advice on how to prevent a future injury.

Lab Activity 14.2

Evaluating Your Home Medicine Cabinet

INSTRUCTIONS: *It is very important to analyze your home medicine cabinet at least once a year and discard outdated prescriptions and other medicine. Replace used items, discard unnecessary items, place dangerous medicine out of the reach of children, and purchase newly needed products. Since you are beginning a new exercise program, some new items may be needed to prepare you for the treatment of common injuries. Complete the three steps below to evaluate and update your home medicine cabinet.*

1. Prepare a list of all items in your home medicine cabinet and complete the form below.

ITEM	DATE	PURPOSE	EFFECTIVENESS

2. List all unneeded and outdated items that can be discarded.

3. Study Table 14.5 on page 361 to make certain your cabinet contains the bare necessities for treatment of common exercise injuries and ailments. List the items you are missing and may want to consider purchasing.

Name _____

Date _____

Lab Activity 14.3

Healthy Back Tests

INSTRUCTIONS: *Complete each of the Healthy Back Tests and the Backache Risk Assessment to help determine whether you are at risk for back problems.*

These tests are among the ones used by physicians and therapists to make differential diagnoses of back problems. You and your partner can use them to determine whether you have muscle tightness that may make you at risk for back problems. Discontinue any of these tests if they produce pain or numbness, or tingling sensations in the back, hips, or legs. Experiencing any of these sensations may be an indication that you have a low back problem that requires diagnosis by your physician. Partners should use *great caution* in applying force. Be gentle and listen to your partner's feedback.

	Pass	Fail

✦ Test 1—Back to Wall   ❏   ❏

Stand with your back against a wall, with head, heels, shoulders, and calves of legs touching the wall as shown in the diagram. Try to flatten your neck and the hollow of your back by pressing your buttocks down against the wall. Your partner should just be able to place a hand in the space between the wall and the small of your back. If this space is greater than the thickness of his/her hand, you probably have lordosis with shortened lumbar and hip flexor muscles.

✦ Test 2—Straight Leg-Lift   ❏   ❏

Lie on your back with hands behind your neck. The partner on your left should stabilize your left leg by placing his/her right hand on the knee. With the left hand, your partner should grasp the right ankle and raise your right leg as near to a right angle as possible. In this position (as shown in the diagram), your lower back should be in contact with the floor. Your left leg should remain straight and on the floor throughout the test. If your right leg bends at the knee, short hamstring muscles are indicated. If your back arches and/or your left leg does not remain flat on the floor, short lumbar muscles or hip flexor muscles (or both) are indicated. Repeat the test on the opposite side. (Both sides must pass in order to pass the test.)

385

	Pass	Fail

✦ Test 3—Thomas Test ❏ ❏

Lie on your back on a table or bench with your right leg extended beyond the edge of the table (approximately one third of the thigh off of the table). Bring your left knee to your chest and pull the thigh down tightly with your hands. Your lower back should remain flat against the table as shown in the digram. Your right thigh should remain on the table. If your right thigh lifts off the table while the left knee is hugged to the chest, a tight hip flexor (iliopsoas) on that side is indicated. Repeat on the opposite side. (Both sides must pass in order to pass the test.)

✦ Test 4—Ely's Test ❏ ❏

Lie prone; flex right knee. Partner *gently* pushes right heel toward the buttocks, stopping when resistance is felt or when partner expresses discomfort. Pelvis should remain on floor with no flexion at hip. Knee should bend freely 135 degrees, or heel should touch buttocks if there is no tightness in the quadriceps muscles. Repeat on the other side. (You must pass on both sides to pass the test.

✦ Test 5—Ober's Test ❏ ❏

Lie on your left side with your leg flexed 90 degrees at the hip and 90 degrees at the knee. Partner places right hip in neutral position (no flexion) and right knee in 90-degree flexion; partner then allows the weight of the leg to lower it toward the floor. If there is no tightness in the iliotibial band (fascia and muscles on lateral side of leg), the knee touches the floor without pain and the test is passed. Repeat on the other side. (Both sides must pass in order to pass the test.)

Lab Activity 14.3 *(continued)*
Healthy Back Tests

	Pass	Fail

✦ Test 6–Press-Up (Straight Arm)

Lie on your stomach and place your hands at shoulder width just opposite your head. Straighten your arms by pressing upward while keeping your pubis in contact with the floor.

✦ Test 7—Knee Roll

Lie supine with both knees and hips flexed 90 degrees, arms extended to the sides at shoulder level. Keep the knees and hips in that position and lower them to the floor on the right and then on the left. If you can accomplish this and still keep your shoulders in contact with the floor, you have adequate rotation in the spine, especially at the lumbar and thoracic junction. (You must pass both sides in order to pass the test.)

✦ Healthy Back Test Rating

	Number of tests passed
Excellent	7
Very good	6
Good	5
Fair	4
Poor	1–3

✦ Backache Risk Assessment

Check "yes" if the statement applies to you; check "no" if it does not apply. Total the number of "yes" answers.

	Yes	No
1. I often have a backache at the end of the day.	_____	_____
2. I usually don't think of my back when I lift and carry things.	_____	_____
3. I often move heavy loads without getting help.	_____	_____
4. I'm not sure I use good body mechanics when I work.	_____	_____
5. I frequently push and pull things.	_____	_____
6. I do a lot of bending over.	_____	_____
7. I do a lot of reaching in work or exercise and sports.	_____	_____
8. I do a lot of twisting in work or exercise and sports.	_____	_____
9. I do a lot of lifting and carrying.	_____	_____
10. I don't do strength exercises for my back and abdomen regularly.	_____	_____
11. I don't do stretching exercises for my trunk, hips, and legs regularly.	_____	_____
12. I sit for long periods without a break.	_____	_____
13. I spend a lot of time leaning over my work.	_____	_____
14. I do exercises that are considered "questionable."	_____	_____
Total	_____	

✦ Back Risk Rating

	Number of Yes Answers
Extremely high risk	10–14
High risk	7–9
Moderate risk	4–6
Some risk	1–3
Low risk	0

15

Designing a Program Uniquely for You: A Lifetime of Wellness

Chapter Objectives

By the end of this chapter, you should be able to:

1. Identify your wellness goals.

2. Select activities to meet your wellness goals.

3. Design an exercise program that is appropriate for you now and that can be continued and/or adapted for many years to come.

4. List criteria for evaluating an exercise club and selecting exercise equipment to purchase.

5. Describe how you can keep healthy and well as you age.

When Mandy was an infant she crawled around her playpen and on the carpet endlessly. A full day of that type of exercise tired her out and she had no problem sleeping through the night. When she started school, Mandy participated in physical education and soon learned sports skills she used to become physically fit and healthy. She became enamored with soccer, in particular, and joined a recreational soccer league that played on the weekends. By the time she enrolled in college, Mandy was interested in weight training and aerobic dance classes. She used the college's exercise room to lift weights and signed up for an aerobic dance class to meet the physical education course requirement before graduation.

Mandy is now in her 60s and no longer interested in aerobic dance, is not in condition to play soccer, and cannot lift the amount of weight she could when younger. Yet, Mandy still exercises regularly. She walks daily and joins her contemporaries in the pool for aqua aerobics four days a week. She found that the local Y has a weight room with a staff person qualified to advise her on the type of weight training best for someone of her age and in her condition, so she even weight trains three days a week. In a very real sense, Mandy is still enrolled in physical education, only this time with a different type of instructor.

Today there are some excellent physical education instructors who understand the nature of physical fitness and how it relates to health and wellness. There has been this kind of instructor for many years. Unfortunately, there are many inadequate physical education instructors who force individuals to run long distances even though they are not in shape to do so or who only teach how to play softball, basketball, or football. These inadequate instructors teach individuals to hate running, as it tires them out for the rest of the day and creates aches and pains where they do not even know they have body parts. The team sports, on the other hand, may be great fun, but once the class is over, it is nearly impossible to get 22 people together to play football, 18 people to play softball, or even 10 people to play basketball. Of course, there are coed softball leagues, and pickup basketball games at the local YMCA or community center, and some people still meet on the weekends to play touch football. And yet, most of us would prefer physical activities that require less organization. That may be why we join health clubs and weight train. Or why we take up jogging and swimming. Or why we play tennis or golf. These lifetime sports activities can be done alone or at most require only one other person. And our bodies can withstand the activity even into our later years.

Today, more and more physical education courses of study include instruction on tennis, golf, weight training, and badminton, while not neglecting more aerobically intensive physical activities such as basketball, soccer, football, and jogging.

As with physical education and physical fitness, health and wellness activities, taught by health educators, can be important adjuncts to a lifetime of quality living. Not only can the knowledge and skills learned in these courses contribute to how long you live, they also can result in living better; that is, without infirmity and with the ability to function independently as you age. After all, living to a ripe old age but being confined to a bed or a house, unable to walk upstairs or even dress yourself, is no fun. If you eat well, exercise regularly, refrain from smoking or excessive use of alcohol, and obtain periodic health screenings and medical examinations, you increase your chances of living well, rather than merely living long.

In this concluding chapter of this book, we provide you with the information you need to continue your wellness program for the rest of your life. We do this by helping you determine your goals and by then showing you how to achieve them. We even help you evaluate fitness and health clubs and iden-

tify what you should look for when purchasing exercise equipment.

Identifying Your Wellness Goals

Why do you want to engage in wellness activities? Some people just want to be healthy. Others want to look good, to have energy, to develop strength, or to compete for the sake of competing. It stands to reason that if you do not know why you participate in these activities, you cannot select activities that will help you meet your goals. For example, to determine your fitness goal complete Lab Activity 15.1: Why I Want to Be Physically Fit at the end of this chapter.

Health Promotion and Disease Prevention

One of your wellness goals is probably to maintain good health. We have already discussed the fact that this requires more than just exercise. For example, you know that in order to remain healthy, you need to eat nutritionally, to use stress-management techniques to prevent illness and disease, and to refrain from using chemical substances that can harm you (such as tobacco and illicit drugs). When you do all this, you can prevent, or at least postpone, the onset of cardiovascular diseases (such as coronary heart disease and stroke) as well as precursors of these diseases (such as high blood pressure). You can also decrease your risk of contracting cancer or other life-threatening diseases. But beyond merely preventing illness and disease, you can also enhance your well-being by engaging in a variety of lifestyle behaviors. First we will focus on exercise behaviors. Next, we consider other lifestyle behaviors you should include when designing a wellness program for yourself. We will return to this at the conclusion of this chapter.

Fitness Activities to Help You Achieve Your Wellness Goals

There is a seemingly endless array of physical activities in which you can participate. Now that you have completed Lab Activity 15.1: Why I Want to Be Physically Fit and have a better idea of why you

Walking is an activity that does not require either equipment or other people. This, coupled with its effectiveness in developing cardiovascular endurance and in maintaining desirable weight, makes walking an excellent lifetime wellness activity. (Photo courtesy of the Aspen Hill Club)

want to exercise, it will be easier for you to choose one of these activities. We will describe several of the more popular and effective exercise options in this section. If we missed your favorite activity, we apologize but be comforted by knowing a trip to the library will probably disclose all you ever wanted to know about it.

Walking

Walking is an excellent way to keep fit without putting undue stress on your connective tissue and bones. Studies have shown that adults who walk for exercise 2½ to 4 hours a week tend to have less than half the prevalence of elevated serum cholesterol as those who do not walk or exercise regularly. Walking can develop cardiorespiratory endurance (especially if the speed of the walking is brisk) and is effective as

> **Jogging** Running at a 9-minute-per-mile pace or slower.
> **Running** Running faster than 9 minutes per mile.

a calorie burner. What is more, walking is an activity in which all ages can participate. Finally, walking can have psychological benefits as well: It can help to reduce anxiety and depression.

The President's Council on Physical Fitness and Sports offers some tips to help you develop an efficient walking style:

- Hold your head erect and keep your back straight and abdomen flat. Your toes should point straight ahead and your arms should swing loosely at your sides.
- Land on the heel of your foot and roll forward to drive off the ball of your foot. Walking only on the balls of your feet or flat-footed may cause fatigue and soreness.
- Take long, easy strides, but do not strain for distance. When walking up or down hills or at a very rapid pace, lean forward slightly.
- Breathe deeply (with your mouth open, if that is more comfortable).

To help you to begin a walking program, follow the regimen in Table 15.1.

Jogging and Running

If walking is too slow for you, try **jogging** or **running**. With either, you can get a comparable workout

Table 15.1 ✦ A Walking Program

Week One

Walk briskly for 5 minutes. (Do not walk so briskly that you become breathless.)

Walk slowly for 3 minutes.

Walk briskly for 5 minutes.

Repeat for a total of about 30 minutes of walking.

Week Two

Same as week one. If you can pick up the pace a little without becoming breathless, do so.

Week Three

Same as week one but increase brisk walking to 8 minutes at a time. Increase time for a total of about 40 minutes of walking.

Week Four

Same as week three. If you can pick up the pace a little without becoming breathless, do so.

After four weeks, increase brisk walking for as long as it is comfortable.

in a shorter period of time. Unfortunately, jogging puts stress on your body, subjecting you to a greater chance of injury than walking does. Foot, ankle, knee, and back problems can develop. Yet with the proper precautions (good shoes and not doing more than you are in condition to do), jogging injuries can be minimized.

Having the right running shoes is important if you choose to jog. There are many shoes from which to choose. We will discuss how to purchase shoes in which to run or jog later in this chapter. Personnel in stores selling running shoes can help you select a shoe that is right for you, but *you* need to be the final judge. If the shoe feels comfortable and provides enough support, that is probably the right shoe for you.

The President's Council on Physical Fitness and Sports points out that running for fitness is different from running for speed and power. When you run for fitness, you should maintain a comfortable, economical running style:

- Run in an upright position, avoiding excessive forward lean. Keep your back as straight as you comfortably can and keep your head up. Do not look down at your feet.

- Carry your arms slightly away from your body, with your elbows bent so your forearms are roughly parallel to the ground. Occasionally shake and relax your arms to prevent tightness in your shoulders.

- Land on the heel of your foot and rock forward to drive off the ball of your foot. If this proves difficult, try a more flat-footed style. Running only on the balls of your feet will tire you quickly and make your legs sore.

- Keep your stride relatively short. Do not force your pace by reaching for extra distance.

- Breathe deeply with your mouth open.

One concern about either walking or running is safety. Recognizing the need to advise runners how to exercise to limit vulnerability, the Road Runners Club of America offers these tips in their booklet entitled *Women Running: Run Smart. Run Safe.*

Stay Alert

- Do not wear headphones. If you wear them, you will not hear an approaching car or an approaching attacker.

- Run against traffic so that you can observe approaching vehicles.

- Practice identifying characteristics of strangers and memorizing license tags.

- Tune into your environment, not out of it.

Avoid Isolation

- Run in familiar areas.

- Run with a partner or dog.

- Write down or leave word about the direction of your run. Tell friends and family of your favorite running routes.

- Befriend neighbors and local businesses.

Use Your Intuition

- Trust your intuition about an area or a person, avoiding any place or person you are unsure of.

- Use discretion in acknowledging verbal harassment by strangers. Look directly at others and be observant, but keep your distance and keep moving.

- Call police immediately if something happens to you or someone else or if you notice anyone out of the ordinary.

Be Prepared

- Carry identification or write your name, phone number, and blood type on the inside of your running shoe.

- Do not wear jewelry.

- Carry a noisemaker.

- Be prepared to scream and break the silence.

- Wear reflective material.

- Know the location of telephones.

- Vary your route.

Jogging or running costs relatively little (good running shoes are the only major expense), can be done almost anywhere (indoors or outdoors), and is an excellent aerobic exercise.

Rope Jumping

When one of the authors was 13, he fell head over heels in love with 12-year-old blonde-haired, adorable, vivacious Jill, heart-poundingly, palm-perspiringly, any-spare-time-spent-with-her love. The problem was that Steven was also in love with Jill. In the competition to win Jill's heart, Steven and yours

Rope skipping is an excellent cardiovascular exercise, and can be done just about anywhere at any time. (Photo courtesy of the Aspen Hill Club.)

truly learned how to jump rope that summer. While their friends played basketball and softball, they jumped rope with Jill. They were frantic not to be seen by their friends in this sissy activity. If their other friends had seen them, they would have died.

Well, no longer crippled by that thought, we have learned that the gender you were born with need not stop you from participating in any enjoyable activity, and that rope jumping is an excellent way of developing cardiorespiratory endurance, strength, agility, coordination, and a sense of wellness. Here are some pointers for rope jumping:

1. Determine the best length for your rope by standing on the center of the rope. The handles should reach from armpit to armpit.

2. When you are jumping, keep your arms close to your body with your elbows almost touching your sides. Have your forearms out at right angles, and turn the rope by making small circles with your hands and wrists. Keep your feet, ankles, and knees together.

3. Relax. Do not tense up. Enjoy yourself.

4. Keep your body erect, with your head and eyes up.

5. Start slowly.

6. Land on the balls of your feet, bending your knees slightly.

7. Maintain a steady rhythm.

8. Jump just one or two inches from the floor.

9. Try jumping to music and maintaining the rhythm of the music.

10. When you get good, improvise. Create new stunts. Have fun.

See Table 15.2 for recommended rope-jumping stunts. Why not get a jump rope and try them out?

Swimming

Swimming is both popular and a very good physical fitness activity. What's more, it enhances physical fitness while diminishing the chances of injury. That is because it limits the amount of weight your body must bear. When you are submerged up to the neck in water, you experience an apparent loss of 90 percent of your weight. If you weigh 130 pounds, when you are in water up to your neck, your feet and legs have to support a weight of only 13 pounds. Therefore, you are less apt to injure your legs and feet.

Many people who use swimming for conditioning do lap swimming, that is, they swim back and forth. When you are lap swimming, you should periodically check your heart rate to determine whether you are at your target. But lap swimming is not appropriate for everyone. Backyard pools usually are not large enough. Most residential pools are no longer than 36 feet (ft) by 17 ft, with approximately 600 square ft of water surface, starting at 3 to 8.5 ft in depth. In a swimming pool of this size, a workout must be adjusted considerably from that usually practiced in the typical school, college, or athletic club pool. Otherwise swimming in the backyard pool becomes largely diving in, gliding across, and climbing out. For the typical person, it means only inactive bathing. But swimming pools, regardless of size, have a high potential as exercise facilities. This potential can be realized as individuals learn how to exercise in limited water areas.

The President's Council on Physical Fitness and Sports recommends an exercise program for limited water areas in its booklet *Aqua Dynamics*. The program involves standing water drills (for example, alternate toe touching, side straddle hopping, toe

Table 15.2 ✦ Basic Single Short Rope Skills

1. **Basic Jump**
   1. Jump on both feet.
   2. Land on balls of feet.
   3. Jump once for each revolution of rope.

   Tips: Keep feet, ankles and knees together.
   Cue: JUMP - JUMP - JUMP

2. **Side Swing**
   1. Swing rope to left side.
   2. Repeat to the right side.
   3. Swing rope alternately from side to side.

   Tips: Hold one rope handle in each hand.
   Keep hands together, keep feet together.
   Cue: LEFT - RIGHT - LEFT - RIGHT

3. **Double Side Swing and Jump**
   1. Swing rope to left side.
   2. Swing rope to right side.
   3. Jump over rope.

   Tips: Keep hands together on side swings,
   keep feet together.
   Cue: LEFT - RIGHT - JUMP

4. **Single Side Swing and Jump**
   1. Swing rope to left side.
   2. Jump over rope.
   3. Swing rope to right side.
   4. Jump over rope.

   Tips: Hold one rope handle in each hand.
   Keep hands together on side swings,
   keep feet together.
   Cue: LEFT - JUMP - RIGHT - JUMP

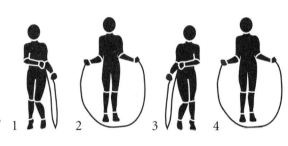

5. **One-Handed Side Swing (Twirl)**
   1. Hold both handles in left hand.
   2. Twirl rope on left side.
   3. Repeat to right side.

   Tips: Keep rope parallel to side of body.
   Practice on both sides.
   Cue: SWING - SWING

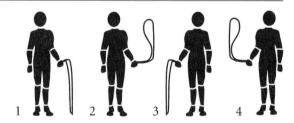

6. **Skier**
   1. Jump left.
   2. Jump right.

   Tips: Feet move laterally 4–6" to each side,
   keep feet together.
   Cue: LEFT - RIGHT

Source: From *Jump Rope for Heart Curriculum Guide,* 1991. Copyright American Heart Association. Reproduced with permission.

Table 15.2 ✦ Basic Single Short Rope Skills *(continued)*

7. Bell
1. Jump forward.
2. Jump backward.

Tips: Feet move 4–6" forward and
         backward as a bell clapper, keep feet together.
Cue: FORWARD - BACK

8. Side Straddle
1. Jump to straddle position.
2. Return to basic jump.

Tips: Spread feet shoulder width apart as
         rope passes under.
Cue: APART - TOGETHER

9. Scissors (Forward Straddle)
1. Jump to stride position with left foot forward.
2. Jump and reverse position of feet.

Tips: Feet should be 8–12" apart.
Cue: LEFT - RIGHT

10. Straddle Cross
1. Jump to straddle position.
2. Jump to crossed legs.

Tips: Feet shoulder width apart. Alternate
         leg in front with each cross.
Cue: APART - CROSS

11. Wounded Duck
1. Jump, toes and knees together, heels spread.
2. Jump, heels together, toes and knees spread.

Tips: Alternate toes together and
         heels together.
Cue: TOES - HEELS

12. Criss Cross
1. Cross arms until elbows touch and jump.
2. Open rope and perform basic jump.

Tips: Handles in extended position. Keep
         hands down low on the cross.
Cue: CROSS - OPEN

13. Full Turn (one complete circle with rope in front)
1. Turn body to left with left side swing.
2. Facing rope, continue to turn body left a full turn,
     lifting the rope up.
3. Jump rope forward.

Tips: Follow rope, keep rope in front of body. May
         also turn to right.
Cue: SWING - TURN - LIFT - JUMP

Table 15.2 ✦ Basic Single Short Rope Skills *(continued)*

14. Heel to Heel
1. Jump and touch left heel to floor in front.
2. Jump and touch right heel to floor in front.

Tips: Heel touches are forward.
Cue: HEEL - HEEL - HEEL

1   2

15. Toe to Toe
1. Hop on left foot, touch right toe to floor in back.
2. Hop on right foot, touch left toe to floor in back.

Tips: Keep body over weighted foot.
Cue: TOE - TOE - TOE

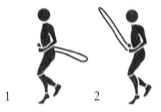

1   2

16. Heel-Toe
1. Hop on left foot, touch right heel forward.
2. Hop on left foot again, touch right toe backward.
3. Repeat on opposite side.

Tips: Heel-toe as in a polka.
Cue: HEEL - TOE - HEEL - TOE

1   2   3   4

17. Kick Swing
1. Hop on left foot, swing right leg forward.
2. Hop on right foot, swing left leg forward.

Tips: Repeat directions sideward and backward.
Cue: KICK - KICK - KICK

1   2

18. Toe Touch
1. Hop on left foot, touch right toe to right.
2. Hop on right foot, touch left toe to left.

Tips: Keep feet close to floor.
Cue: RIGHT - LEFT

1   2

19. Double Toe Touch
1. Hop on right foot, touch left toe to left about 6".
2. Hop on right foot again, touch left toe to left about 12".
3. Repeat with right toe 6" and 12".

Tips: Keep feet close to floor. Bring foot in to avoid rope between toe touches.
Cue: LEFT - LEFT - RIGHT - RIGHT

1   2

20. Forward 180 (half turn to backward jumping position)
1. Side swing left, half turn body to left.
2. Jump over backward turning rope.

Tips: Turn body to follow rope. May be performed to left or right.
Cue: JUMP - TURN - JUMP BACKWARDS

1   2

bounding, and jogging in place); poolside standing drills (such as stretching the arms out, pressing the back flat against the wall, and raising the knees to the chest); gutter-holding drills (such as knees to chest, hop twisting, front and back flutter kicking, and side flutter kicking); bobbing; and treading water. If you have your own pool and feel it is too small for lap swimming, you might write to the President's Council on Physical Fitness and Sports, Washington, DC 20201, for the *Aqua Dynamics* booklet. Another good source is Jane Katz's article, "The W.E.T. Workout," which was published in the June 1986 issue of *Shape* magazine, or you can contact your nearest health club, YMCA, or JCC to see if they have water aerobics classes.

Tennis

As with all fitness activities, duration and intensity will determine how much your tennis game contributes to your physical fitness and wellness. A doubles match generally results in less of a workout than does a singles match. In fact, a doubles match will use up to 330 calories (cal) per hour, whereas a singles match will use up to 390 cal per hour.

The contribution of tennis to wellness, however,

Tennis can contribute to overall fitness, muscular strength, and flexibility. (Photo courtesy of Wendy Parks/National Foundation of Wheelchair Tennis.)

is another matter. As we have stated so often in this book, even if your physical health is improved, if the other components of your health suffer, you have not improved your health. Playing tennis may improve the efficiency of your heart, but if your attitude and behavior on the court loses you friends, results in your not enjoying yourself, or frustrates you, you would be better off not playing at all. In spite of exercising, you are making yourself *less well.* Two solutions make the most sense to us: Either approach tennis with a different attitude, or select a less competitive exercise to engage in regularly.

When stroking the ball, if you roll over the shot too much (too much topspin), you can contribute to tennis elbow. Using too much wrist in the shot will lead you to roll over; instead you should stroke through the ball with your wrist locked. If tennis elbow does develop, you can switch to a lighter racket, which will aggravate the elbow less. Applying ice after playing will also help.

A warm-up that includes stretching is a must. Tennis involves dynamic, quick movements with a great deal of stretching to reach the ball. Therefore, if you are not flexible enough, you may be prone to muscle and connective-tissue injury, such as muscle pulls or sprained ligaments.

Racquetball, Handball, and Squash

Indoor racquet sports can be excellent ways to develop and maintain fitness. That is because they contribute to cardiorespiratory endurance, muscular strength and endurance of the legs, flexibility, agility, balance and coordination, and weight control. They are also usually fun. Yet there is danger involved in these sports. Every year, over 3,000 eye injuries result from them. That need not be the case if players wear appropriate eye protectors. Eye protectors should be made of polycarbonate and offer a complete shield (do not use the kind with narrow bands with openings between them).

Another risk involved in these sports can be found in the environment in which they are played. Exercising in a hot room can be hazardous unless you take certain precautions. You should drink plenty of water before starting to play and intermittently take breaks to replenish the water you lose through perspiration. You should not play longer than you are in condition to play; to overdo it in a hot room can be risky. Know when to stop.

Last, you must be in good physical condition before engaging in these sports. Since they are highly competitive, they are usually played in a hot environment, and they involve dynamic (stop and go) and stretching movements. If you are not in good physical condition, you may injure yourself. If you *are* in good condition, these sports are excellent activities to help you remain fit.

Aerobic Dance

One of the best fitness activities is dance, especially if you're serious about your training. Look at the bodies of dancers. They are remarkably muscular, incredibly supple, and ready to meet the demands strenuous exercise places on their hearts and circulatory and respiratory systems. Dance is one good way to develop and maintain physical fitness.

The traditional dance programs were tap, ballet, and modern dance. In recent years a different form of dance has swept the country and become a significant part of the fitness movement. It combines calisthenics and a variety of dance movements, all done to music, and is called aerobic dance. The term, coined by Jacki Sorenson in 1979, involves choreographed routines that include walking, jumping, hopping, bouncing, kicking, and various arm movements designed to develop cardiorespiratory endurance, flexibility, and muscular strength and endurance. Dancing to music is an enjoyable activity for many people who would not otherwise seek to exercise. And since aerobic dance is often done in groups, the social contact makes it even more enjoyable.

To maximize the fitness benefits of aerobic dance, you should maintain the dancing for approximately 35 to 45 minutes and work out three or four times a week. In addition, you should check periodically to see if you are maintaining your target heart rate (THR). Since many communities offer aerobic dance classes (some may be called Dancercize or Jazzercise) through YM/YWCAs, Jewish Community Centers, colleges, local schools, and even on morning television programs, maintaining a regular dance regimen should not be difficult. The only equipment you will need is a good pair of aerobic dance shoes with good shock absorbency, stability, and outer sole flexibility and clothes to work out in. One caution: Do not dance on a concrete floor, since the constant pounding could result in shin splints. A wooden floor is ideal.

Low-Impact Aerobics

Several factors associated with aerobic dance have led some experts to question the way it is usually conducted. A study by the American Aerobics Association found 80 percent of its teachers and stu-

dents were getting injured during workouts, and another questionnaire administered to aerobic instructors found 55 percent reported significant injuries. Among the causes of these injuries are bad floors (too hard), bad shoes (too little shock absorbency and stability), and bad routines offered by poorly trained instructors. With the popularity of aerobics, it is not surprising what is done in its name. Even a *pet aerobics* routine has been developed for the pudgy dog or cat. It is therefore no surprise that many aerobics instructors are poorly trained and teach routines that are inappropriate and injury producing, using surfaces that cause high-impact injuries.

To respond to these concerns, several things have happened. One is the certification of aerobics instructors. Organizations, such as the American College of Sports Medicine (ACSM), the Aerobics and Fitness Association of America, National Dance-Exercise Instructor's Training Association, Ken Cooper's Aerobics Way, and the Aerobic Center, have all instituted certification programs for aerobics instructors. Unfortunately, the requirements for certification by these organizations vary greatly. Some form of certification, however, is probably better than none.

Another attempt at limiting the injuries from aerobics is the development of *low-impact* aerobic routines. Low-impact aerobics features one foot on the ground at all times and the use of light weights. The idea is to cut down on the stress to the body caused by jumping and bouncing while deriving the muscle toning and cardiorespiratory benefits of high-impact aerobics. These routines have become more and more popular as the risk of injury from high-impact aerobics has become better known. Something called *chair aerobics* has even been developed. It involves routines done while the participant is seated in a chair. Low-impact aerobics are not totally risk-free. Injuries to the upper body caused by the circling and swinging movements with weights are not infrequent. Many of these injuries can be treated at home, however, and are not serious. With any form of physical activity, there is always the chance of injury. The benefits to the cardiorespiratory system and the rest of the body—benefits that we have described in this book—are often worth the slight chance of injury.

A recent aerobic dance development is *step aerobics,* which involves stepping up and down on a small platform (step) to the rhythm of music and the directions of an instructor. The workout can vary from mild to extremely intense, depending on the speed, the movements, and the duration of the exercise. Double step aerobic routines have been developed that involve the use of two platforms. Step aerobic classes are usually offered at the same places aerobic dance classes are conducted. If you are interested in double step aerobics, you can read an article about it in the May 1993 issue of *American Health* magazine (page 92).

Bicycling

To begin a bicycle exercise program, you obviously need a bicycle. A good 10-speed bike will cost approximately $300. You can get an adequate 10-speed or a mountain bike (a sturdier bike) for less, however, if you shop around or buy one secondhand. You will also need a helmet to protect your head from injury should you fall. Gloves with padded palms can also make your ride more comfortable. In addition, think about adding pant clips and/or clothes designed specifically for biking.

Of course, you can exercise with any bike—it need not have 10 speeds or be a mountain bike—if you choose. A good bike, however, will allow you to take trips that add to the enjoyment of biking in addition to enhancing overall health and wellness.

When you are biking, follow this advice:

- Keep your elbows slightly bent.
- Lower your upper body for a streamlined position.
- Do not grip the handlebars too tightly.
- Wear bright clothing so motorists can easily see you.
- Obey all traffic laws.
- Always lean into the turn.
- Learn and use hand signals that indicate which way you are turning.
- Leave the radio at home so you can focus on the road and hear cars and other potential hazards.
- Keep your bike in good working order, well oiled with grease and dirt removed from around the chain and gears.

Some people bike for terrific exercise and yet go nowhere. They use a stationary bike. Many health clubs have computerized stationary bikes that can be set for various kinds of riding (for example, hilly or high speed) and for various distances. Still other people remove a wheel from their bicycle, raise the frame, and bike indoors during the winter months. There is equipment you can buy called a wind trainer that does this for you.

When you ride a stationary bike, you need to pay

Figure 15.1 ✦ Seat Adjustment When Riding a Stationary Bike

Correct seat height is depicted in the middle drawing. The seat on the left is too high, and the one on the right is too low. Maintain a slight bend in the lower leg when vertical.

attention to adjusting the seat and handlebars so that they are just right. To work your leg muscles properly, your knee should be slightly bent when the pedal is in the fully down position (see Figure 15.1). Too great a bend or too little a one will result in inefficient use of the leg muscles. The handlebars should be adjusted so you are relaxed and leaning slightly forward (see Figure 15.2).

Select the Right Activity

Even though you find an exercise that is enjoyable and helps you meet your fitness goals, that does not mean you will stay with it. It just means you are *more likely* to maintain your exercise program. It also does not necessarily mean you will even begin the program. One way to exercise even when you are not in the mood or when you doubt its benefits is to employ self-talk. This is when you identify your negative thoughts

Figure 15.2 ✦ Handlebar Adjustment When Riding a Stationary Bike

Correct handlebar adjustment is depicted in the middle drawing.

There are so many different ways to maintain fitness, health, and wellness that you should be able to find something to do that is fun. Even if it is as strange as kayaking in a swimming pool or running with swim fins on your feet. (Photos courtesy of the Aspen Hill Club)

and convert them to positive ones. Lab Activity 15.2: Developing a New Mind-Set about Exercise at the end of this chapter shows you how to use self-talk.

Furthermore, some sports will better match your personality than others. To identify which sports those are, complete Lab Activity 15.3, Which Sports Match Your Personality? at the end of this chapter.

BEING A FITNESS CONSUMER

To remain fit your whole life, you need to know how to be an effective fitness consumer. You need to know how to select a health/fitness club and how to buy the right equipment.

Selecting an Exercise Club

Joining a health/fitness club is an excellent strategy for beginning and/or maintaining your exercise program. The club will encourage your participation in several ways. First, once you shell out the membership fee, you will want to get your money's worth. Second, after working out a few times, you will probably meet other people at the club whom you would like to get to know better. That social contact is reinforcing, and the subtle peer pressure to be there—"Hey, Betty, where were you last Wednesday?"—may be just enough to get you to the club when you do not feel like working out.

Since a health/fitness club can be expensive, inconvenient to get to, or both, you should select the

When choosing fitness activities, do not limit yourself by choosing only typical ones. (Photo courtesy of the Aspen Hill Club.)

one you join carefully. It should meet your needs, be safe, and be supportive of your exercise goals. Table 15.3 provides you with a way to evaluate a club and decide whether it is right for you.

Purchasing Exercise Equipment

Some fitness activities require little, if any, equipment. Just a pair of running shoes, shorts, a top, and socks is usually enough for jogging. On the other hand, you cannot play tennis without a tennis racquet nor bike without a bicycle. In this section, we make brief comments to help you make sensible decisions when you purchase exercise equipment.

Athletic Shoes The major criteria to use when selecting athletic shoes are comfort and support. Here are a few suggestions that will help you purchase the right shoe (and the left one, too, for that matter):

Choosing an exercise club can be a troublesome decision if you do not know what to look for. This club offers rowing machines, stationary bikes of several kinds, a running track along its periphery, and even a basketball court. (Photo courtesy of the Aspen Hill Club)

Table 15.3 ✦ Is This the Club for Me?

To decide whether a particular fitness facility is the one you want to join, check as many of the following as apply.

A. The Staff

_____ Do professional staff members have the appropriate educational background and/or certification from a nationally recognized professional organization?

_____ Are all staff members certified in cardiopulmonary resuscitation (CPR)?

_____ Does the specialty staff have the appropriate credentials?

_____ Are adequate staff available in the exercise and activity areas?

_____ Are staff members friendly and helpful?

_____ Are all staff in uniform and wearing some type of identification?

_____ Does the staff provide each new member of the facility with an orientation and instruction to using the areas and equipment in the facility?

_____ Does the staff provide an avenue for ongoing communication between members and themselves?

B. Facility and Equipment

_____ Does the facility have the necessary types and quantity of equipment to enable you to achieve your personal program goals?

_____ Does the facility have the necessary activity areas to enable you to achieve your personal program goals?

_____ Does the facility have sufficient equipment so that enough is available at the time of day you'll be using it?

_____ Are all activity areas regularly cleaned and maintained?

_____ Is all equipment regularly cleaned and maintained?

_____ Are all unsafe conditions and equipment malfunctions remedied promptly?

_____ Is the equipment arranged within an activity area in such a way that maximizes its safety and effectiveness?

_____ Are the surrounding outdoor areas that lead to the facility well illuminated?

_____ Does the facility have adequate parking?

_____ Are childcare facilities available if you need them?

C. Programming

_____ Does the facility offer structured exercise activity programs?

_____ Are the structured exercise programs based on sound principles of exercise prescription and exercise physiology?

_____ Does the facility offer personalized exercise programs tailored specifically to your needs and interests?

_____ Does the facility offer structured exercise programs which address the specific fitness component(s) in which you are interested?

_____ If you have a special medical condition does the facility offer programs which address those needs?

_____ Does the facility offer exercise and recreational programs at convenient times?

_____ Does the facility offer either unstructured or structured recreational programming in an activity in which you are interested?

Table 15.3 ✦ Is This the Club for Me? *(continued)*

_____ Does the facility offer programs for specific age groups, such as children and the elderly?

_____ Does the facility offer instruction in an activity you would like to learn?

_____ Does the facility offer specifically focused health promotion programs?

_____ Does the facility provide the option of evaluating your fitness level before you begin an exercise program?

D. Safety Issues

_____ Does the facility refer at-risk individuals to appropriate medical personnel for clearance?

_____ Does the facility have users complete a risk/benefit disclosure form when they initially join the facility?

_____ Does the facility offer ongoing monitoring of all facility users?

_____ Does the facility have a written emergency plan which is available for review?

_____ Does the facility have a first aid kit that is properly stocked and available at all times?

_____ Are all areas in the facility free from physical hazards?

_____ Are all activity areas in the facility free from environmental hazards?

_____ Is the equipment maintained, suitable for use, and well cared for?

_____ Is the staff CPR certified and is at least one first aid certified individual on duty at all times?

E. General Business Practices

_____ Does the facility's management provide a grace period in which users can cancel their memberships and receive a full refund on their payments?

_____ Does the facility provide a trial membership or guest pass that allows the prospective user to utilize the facility prior to joining?

_____ Does the facility provide written literature on its facilities, services, programs, and pricing which you can take with you after visiting the club?

_____ Does the facility allow you time to make the decision to purchase a membership?

_____ Does the facility's management provide a written set of rules and policies which governs the club's dealings with users?

_____ Does the facility management survey its members periodically to determine their interests and needs?

_____ Does the facility provide a feedback system by which members can express their concerns or needs as they apply to the club?

_____ Does the facility have a system of communication that informs its users of any changes in services, policies, etc., on a periodic basis?

_____ Is the facility a member of a nationally recognized trade organization related to their business?

After completing this checklist, only you can decide if the club is right for you. No club is perfect. Can you live with the club's deficits? Are its benefits worth putting up with its shortcomings?

Source: From *ACSM's Health/Fitness Facilities Consumer Selection Guide,* 1992, Indianapolis: American College of Sports Medicine. Reprinted with permission.

Improving Your Community

Choosing Medical Services and Health Insurance

The United States is experiencing a health care crisis. Rising health care costs threaten not only the economic but also the physical well-being of all Americans. New technology, malpractice lawsuits, the spread of AIDS among people who simply cannot afford to pay for health care, and social and economic factors continue to drive the cost of health care upward. This means that in order for most families to maintain even a minimum level of professional health care, they will have to divert an increasingly larger proportion of income to health care from necessities such as food, transportation, housing, and savings, as well as from luxuries and leisure items and activities.

The American people and federal and state governments are fast approaching a time when some very painful and far-reaching decisions will have to be made about health care in this country. Some of these decisions may involve the creation, for example, of some form of "nationalized" health care. Many people are upset with this particular idea because they believe it would ultimately limit the individual's choices and possibly reduce the overall quality of medical treatment. Other people claim that a highly unfair, two-tiered health "system" is emerging in the United States, with younger, wealthier, and healthier people enjoying substantially better health care than older, less wealthy, and less healthy people.

We urge you to educate yourself about the causes and some of the possible solutions to the current health care crisis. Some of your self-education will probably involve moral and political decisions on your part. The information you gather and think about should also provide you with a solid basis for getting involved in some of the decisions that federal and state governments and health care organizations will have to make about health care in this country.

In the meantime, there are some things you can do for yourself and for the other people in your life to keep the cost of health care down:

1. Take charge of your own medical care and encourage family and friends to do so as well. Consult the interns at a local hospital to identify physicians and dentists who emphasize *preventive* health care. Medical and dental care that focuses on prevention rather than treatment after the fact will be much less expensive in the long run and provide a healthier life.

2. Review the health insurance policies of several insurance companies or organizations and see if reduced premiums are offered for a healthy lifestyle that includes the limited use of alcohol, absence of smoking, regular exercise, and the maintenance of normal body weight and fat. Do you or people you know already have policies that do not offer reduced premiums for a healthy lifestyle? If so, why not?

3. Visit your student health care office and discuss the possibility of including self-care sessions at the annual university health fair or health awareness day.

4. Get directly involved in the health care systems of your community by volunteering to work a few hours each week with a local ambulance service or a free clinic. ✦

- Recognize whether you **pronate** or **supinate.** Buy a shoe made specifically for either pronators or supinators.

- Shop for shoes late in the day. Your feet tend to swell at that time. No sense buying a shoe that fits snugly in the morning when you usually, or even occasionally, exercise in the afternoon.

- Try shoes on with the kind of socks you usually wear when you are exercising.

- Buy shoes with uppers made of leather or nylon that breathe.

- Look for brands of shoes that come in different widths if you have an exceptionally narrow or wide foot.

- Get a shoe with a last (the form on which the shoe is made) made for your size foot. That means most women ought to buy shoes made for women because women's and men's lasts differ.

- Shop at a store with experienced salespeople. Discuss your particular concerns with them. For example, if you want a shoe with shock absorption, one that is extra wide, or one that will hold up, the salesperson should be able to recommend a shoe that has the characteristics you are looking for. If you want a shoe for tennis or basketball or some other sport, an experienced salesperson should be able to help with that also.

- When trying the shoes on, perform some of the moves you will use when exercising in them. Jump or twist or bend or stretch. Make sure the shoe is comfortable during these movements.

- Once you decide which shoe you want to buy, check the price at different stores or from several athletic shoe distributors. You can do this by telephone quite easily. Also, check the back of sports magazines for distributors who discount the price of shoes.

Orthotics   Some people have problems with their feet that need correcting when they are exercising. They may have leg imbalances (one leg longer than the other), or they may pronate or supinate. Orthotic devices can be placed in athletic shoes to correct these problems and allow people to exercise in comfort. They also diminish the risk of injury. Orthotics come in rigid or soft forms. The rigid orthotic, made of plastic, is usually recommended, but a podiatrist or orthopedic physician may have reason to advise a soft one. Ready-made inserts are available in drugstores and sporting goods shops and may be all that is needed in some cases. Since each foot is different from every other foot, however, if you have a problem, it is wise to consult an expert.

Bicycles   There are many different kinds of bikes: city bikes, all-terrain mountain bikes, touring bikes, racing bikes, and so forth. An experienced salesperson can guide you to the right type of bike depending on the use you wish to make of it. When you buy a bike (usually somewhere between $300 and $1,200) factor in the cost of a helmet, a water bottle, a repair kit for flat tires, shorts, shoes, and gloves. That means approximately another $300. Purchase the bike at a store that offers good service and is staffed by professionals who *really* know bikes. When you think you are interested in a particular bike, test ride it. Also, test ride others for comparison. Try all the gears. Do they shift easily? Do the brakes work well? How does

it corner? Purchasing the right bike is important to the enjoyment you will experience biking, and consequently, to whether you will maintain your exercise program.

Home Exercise Equipment   Some people prefer to exercise alone. If you can afford to purchase home exercise equipment, you might consider buying a stationary bike (maybe one with a built-in computer), a recumbent bicycle (a stationary bike that is low to the floor so your legs are straight out instead of hanging down), a climber (imitating stair climbing), a rower, a cross-country ski machine, a treadmill, and/or weights. Since this equipment can be quite expensive, you should be careful to buy exercise equipment that will help you meet your fitness goals safely.

The following should be considered when you are deciding what equipment to purchase.

- **What are your fitness goals?** If you are trying to develop cardiorespiratory endurance, you would be better advised to buy a treadmill or stationary bike than weights.

- **Who is going to use the equipment?** If more than one person will exercise with this equipment, it needs to be easily adjustable.

- **How much space do you have?** You might have room for a stationary bike but not if you are going to add a rower. In this case, you will need to decide which piece of equipment you most want.

- **How much can you spend?** In a perfect world, money would not be of concern, but this is not a perfect world so you will need to decide the best way to spend your limited resources.

Try out the equipment before buying it. Is the seat comfortable? Is the climbing motion smooth? Is the machine sturdy? Is it fun to do? Do you get the type of workout you want?

KEEPING FIT AS YOU AGE

The Andean village of Vilcabamba in Ecuador and the Abkhazian Republic in what was formerly the

Pronate Rolling the foot inward when it is pushing off.
Supinate Rocking the foot to the outside when it is pushing off.

Myth and Fact Sheet

Myth	Fact
1. Jogging is a better physical fitness activity than is walking.	1. Walking is as good an activity to develop physical fitness as any other. You just have to walk for a longer time to get comparable benefits.
2. Jogging leads to all sorts of injuries.	2. You can limit injuries from jogging if you take certain precautions. Wear the appropriate athletic shoes and do not overdo your workout.
3. Rope jumping is for wimps.	3. You can get a great workout while having fun if you know several rope-jumping stunts.
4. Most health/fitness clubs are the same as all others.	4. Health/fitness clubs differ in a number of significant ways. Some clubs do not have enough equipment or enough variety of equipment. Others do not have adequately trained staff, do not offer a safe environment in which to exercise, or cost too much.
5. Elderly people do not need to exercise.	5. Everyone can benefit from regular exercise. Not only can exercise help elderly people maintain their physical fitness, it can also enhance their social, mental, emotional, and spiritual health, thereby helping to maintain their overall wellness.
6. It's none of my business that some people do not have health insurance.	6. When uninsured people obtain medical care at no fee, the insured are really paying; either through taxes which go toward Medicaid or through increased costs added to medical bills by hospitals and health care providers.

U.S.S.R. share an unusual reputation. They are places where people supposedly live longer and remain more vigorous in old age than is the case in most places. What factors contribute to the unusual longevity of people in these communities, where men and women who are well beyond 100 years of age are common? In the United States, the average life expectancy is in the 70s (depending on such factors as gender, ethnicity, education, and socioeconomic status), and there are only slightly more than 3 centenarians per 100,000 persons.

Clearly, genetic factors play a major role. This is true in the communities just cited. Many of the elderly had parents who also lived to be quite old. And yet when researchers studied these communities intensely, they found other factors related to longevity. Elders are held in high esteem. They receive encouragement to work and be productive community members. Their efforts are appreciated and valued. These 100-year-old individuals eat low-calorie diets, about 1,800 calories a day compared with the 3300-calorie diet of the average American. These communities are located in remote and mountainous regions and tend to be agricultural. That means that daily living requires sig-

nificant climbing and descending steep slopes and vigorous physical activity.

Exercise for the Elderly

Americans are generally less physically active than the centenarians just described. Therefore, we need to plan regular exercise. If we do, we will not only live longer, we will also live better. We will be less ill, less dependent on other people, more pain-free, and more psychologically healthy.

Planning exercise for elderly people requires some special considerations:

- Skeletal structures are more prone to fracture (especially in older women).
- Connective tissue is more dense and ligaments and tendons less elastic. Range of motion may be significantly limited.
- Muscle mass is somewhat diminished and reaction and reflex times slower.

For these reasons, careful assessment should be made before prescribing exercise for an elderly indi-

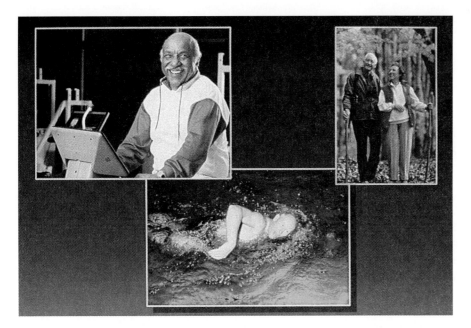

There are many ways to maintain a lifetime commitment to health and wellness.
(Photo courtesy the American Heart Association.)

vidual. Wrenching and twisting movements should be avoided; so should sudden starting and stopping or changing direction. Slow, rhythmic stretching activities are best. And frequent rests should be built into the program.

Walking is an excellent activity for older people, especially in groups where they can socialize. Supervised swimming or exercises in the water are other good activities since they decrease weight bearing and tend to be fun. Also, do not forget dancing, which can enhance fitness goals when it is done rigorously. See Table 15.4 for one possible program for elders.

Benefits of Exercise for Elders

Exercising will increase longevity and provide older people with a more fulfilling life. It can also enhance wellness when exercising with other people (social health), when exercising out of doors and appreciating the surroundings (spiritual health), when exercising with family members and learning to control emotions that interfere with performing the activity (emotional health), and when reading and learning about the particular exercise and its benefits (mental health). In addition, exercise can postpone the inevitable changes associated with aging. Table 15.5

Table 15.4 ✦ Good Physical Activities for the Elderly

ACTIVITY	HOW OFTEN	DURATION
Walking	3 times per week	3/4 hour
Swimming	3 times per week	1/2 hour
Dancing	2 times per week	Sets of 20 minutes with intervals of rest
Stretching/Calisthenics	Every day	10–15 minutes
Golf	2 or 3 times per week	As long as necessary to complete 9 or 18 holes
Horseshoe pitching	According to desire	1/2 hour
Shuffleboard	According to desire	1 hour
Bocce	According to desire	1 hour
Croquet	According to desire	1 hour

Behavioral Change
and Motivational Strategies

Many things might interfere with your ability to maintain a lifetime of physical fitness, health, and wellness. Here are some barriers (roadblocks) and strategies for overcoming them.

Roadblock	Behavioral Change Strategy
There will be occasions when you will decide not to work out. Either you will be too busy, too tired, or too interested in doing something else. It is interesting to note that the most effective behavioral change programs allow for periodic deviation from the goal. That is understandable when you consider a dieter who diets for two months but has an ice cream sundae one weekend. Those who recognize that a deviation is just that, that it need not mean the diet is ruined, are more likely to continue dieting. Those who believe once they go off their diet, they have failed, are likely to cease dieting after eating the sundae. It is similar with exercise. It is okay not to exercise when you are supposed to, as long as this does not happen frequently. If it happens often, you need to make an adjustment in your exercise program.	Make a list of the benefits and disadvantages of the exercise(s) that make up your routine. List as many benefits and disadvantages as you can, big ones and little ones. Now go over the list and decide: 1. Are the benefits worth the potential disadvantages? 2. Are there other physical activities that can give you similar benefits with fewer disadvantages? Or less significant disadvantages? 3. Are there ways you can decrease the barriers to engaging in a fitness program? For example, can you exercise closer to home (using chaining to your advantage)? Or exercise with a friend (social support)? 4. What changes do you need to make to maintain an exercise regimen?
You have participated in competitive athletics all your life and have maintained a high level of fitness by doing so. Now you are getting older and the competition is potentially harmful. You are getting bumped around too much and getting injured. In addition, winning is not as important to you as it was when you were younger. Now maintaining fitness, health, and wellness are your exercise goals.	You need to find noncompetitive physical activities that can help you achieve your new fitness goals. Ask friends who are noncompetitive what they do for exercise. Use their help (social support). You can also use covert techniques. Imagine yourself participating in noncompetitive activities and reward yourself by thinking of a relaxing image or pleasant thought (covert rehearsal). If that is too much unlike you, imagine someone you know who is not competitive engaging in a noncompetitive physical activity and then substitute yourself for that person (covert modeling).
You dislike exercising but you know it is good for you. You need to find ways to continue your fitness program. You are afraid you will give it up before too long.	You can use self-monitoring by keeping a record of the times you engage in exercise activities. Then boast to friends in a nice way about sticking with your program. You can also make a contract with yourself that if you exercise at least three times a week for at least 20 or 30 minutes each time, you will reward yourself. Think up really rewarding rewards. Rewards that are realistic and feasible as well as worth striving for will be most effective. You may also want to question your choice of exercise activity. Exercise should be fun or else you are likely to discontinue it before too long. What other activities can you substitute for what you have been doing that would be more fun but still help you achieve your fitness goals?

Roadblock	Behavioral Change Strategy
List roadblocks that interfere with your maintaining a lifetime of physical fitness, health, and wellness.	Cite behavioral change strategies that can help you overcome the roadblocks you just listed. If you need to, refer back to chapter 3 for behavioral change and motivational strategies.
1. _____	1. _____
2. _____	2. _____
3. _____	3. _____

shows which physical activities relate to which of these aging changes.

HEALTH ACTIVITIES TO HELP YOU ACHIEVE YOUR WELLNESS GOALS

As with physical fitness activities, health activities are important to achieve and maintain high-level wellness. This section presents some of the health activities we recommend for inclusion in a wellness program.

Table 15.5 ✦ Aging Effects and Physical Activities That May Postpone or Reduce Them

EFFECTS	PHYSICAL ACTIVITIES
1. Reduced cardiac output	Aerobic activities, jogging, swimming, cycling
2. Lowered pulmonary ventilation	Exercises that stretch rib cage joints, aerobic activities of moderate-to-high intensity
3. Elevated blood pressure	Aerobic activities, jogging, swimming, cycling
4. Decrease in muscular strength	Weight training (resistance training)
5. Decrease in muscular endurance	Aerobic dance, calisthenics
6. Decrease in flexibility	Stretching, bending
7. Increase in percentage of stored body fat	Jogging, running, swimming, cycling
8. Loss of skin elasticity	Weight training (to maintain muscle tone and fill skin out)

Health Screenings and Medical Exams

The best strategy for treating illness and disease is to diagnose it early so treatment is minimal, both in terms of the medical intervention required and the cost associated with that intervention. Cholesterol screening, hypertension screening, dental check-ups, Pap smears, vision and hearing screenings, and health risk appraisals are appropriate for all ages and should be obtained periodically. The need for and the recommended frequency of other screenings and/or medical exams depends on your age. For example, mammographies that screen for breast cancer should be obtained at least by age 50, with some experts recommending starting at age 40. Tests for glaucoma should occur yearly after age 40. Other screenings that should be conducted periodically are a test for blood in the stool; a total blood work-up to identify levels of triglycerides, high-density and low-density lipoproteins, and blood glucose; examination of the prostate gland in men and of the breasts in women; a stress test; a test for polyps in the colon; and other exams depending on your health and medical condition. We recommend you consult with your physician regarding the appropriateness and timing of screenings and medical exams for you.

Choosing Health Insurance

It is tragic that in this country over 40 million people (many of whom are children) do not have health insurance. These uninsured often delay seeking medical care, and when they do, they often receive inferior services. What is often overlooked, is that the insured population pays for the care of the uninsured. This is so because hospitals and medical personnel add a sufficient amount of money to cover the cost of unreimbursed care provided the poor to the medical bills of the insured. Furthermore, through Medicaid, tax dollars paid by people who can afford to pay taxes go toward the medical care of poor Americans.

Selecting health insurance is an important decision since both costs and coverage can vary greatly. There are two basic choices: fee-for-service and managed care plans. Fee-for-service plans require you to pay for a portion of your care depending on how often you seek care. You pay when you receive service. Managed care plans—sometimes called prepayment plans—require a fee before any service is provided. Subsequently, when service is needed, no payment (or a very small payment) is required. In the fee-for-service plans you usually can choose which doctor you see. In managed care plans—such as health maintenance organizations—you usually can only see health care providers who are part of the plan. Uf you see physicians who are not part of the plan, you pay a substantially higher fee. Check with your employer regarding the advantages and disadvantages of each form of health insurance as they apply to your specific needs.

Lifestyle Behaviors

It has been suggested that approximately 50 percent of illness and disease is a result of lifestyle behaviors. Cigarette smoking is a major part of this, but other behaviors contribute to illness and disease as well; for example, being sedentary, eating unhealthy diets, engaging in unhealthy sexual practices or in an unhealthy way, ignoring the need for relaxation and stress relief, and ingesting too much alcohol or misusing other drugs. Refer back to Lab Activity 1.2: Assessing Your Health Risk to determine which of these behaviors need you attention.

Conclusion: Some Last Words on Wellness

- To be well, pay attention to your body. If you do, you will know when it is doing fine and when it needs special care.

- Pay attention to your mind. When you choose an activity to include in your wellness program, choose one that is enjoyable, one you look forward to doing. Not only will this improve the chances of your continuing the activity, it will also increase your wellness by making you feel good.

- Pay attention to your spirit too. Gain spiritual health from your wellness selections. Feel closer to nature or to a supreme being. Feel connected to your past and your future. To do so is to move toward high-level wellness.

- Be aware of the effects of your lifestyle choices on your mental and social health. Do your choices add to your knowledge? To your learning? Do they improve your relationships or help you establish new ones?

- Remember that improving one component of your health to the neglect of the others is not being well. Wellness is coordinating and integrating activities with the physical, mental, social, emotional, and spiritual parts of your life.

We can think of no better image to leave you with than that of the Special Olympics—athletic competition for the mentally and physically challenged. These athletes try their best, train long and hard, and feel good about participating and competing. What better example of wellness is there? The learning (mental health) that must precede the competition, the good feelings developed between athletes and their coaches and competitors (social health), the satisfaction derived from trying one's best (emotional health), and the sense of oneness and closeness developed in competition (spiritual health), not to mention the physical fitness level needed to participate in the first place (physical health), provide evidence of the wellness of these competitors. They may not be totally healthy, but they certainly are *well*.

We wish for all of you the same degree of wellness, and we hope this book helps you achieve it.

Summary

Identifying Your Wellness Goals

There are many reasons people engage in wellness activities. Some do so for their health, others to look good, or to have energy, and still others to develop strength or because they enjoy competition. In order to select activities to meet your wellness goals, you need to identify why you want to achieve high-level wellness.

Fitness Activities to Help You Achieve Your Goals

There are many physical activities that can contribute to the development of physical fitness; among these activities are walking, jogging, running, rope jumping, swimming, tennis, racquetball, handball, squash, aerobic dance, low-impact aerobics, and bicycling. Some of these help develop cardiorespiratory endurance; others, muscular strength or muscular endurance; and still others, other components of physical fitness. In choosing an activity in which to engage regularly, make sure it matches your personality. You may be sociable, spontaneous, disciplined, aggressive, competitive, able to concentrate well, a risk-taker, or a combination of two or more of these traits. Since people's personalities differ, their choices of exercise will differ.

Being a Fitness Consumer

When you are deciding whether a health/fitness club is right for you, determine whether the facility and the equipment are such that they can be used to achieve your fitness goals. The staff should be well trained and the equipment abundant enough so you will not have to wait too long to use it. Safety procedures should be in place so your chances of being injured are minimized. And the club should be easily accessible to you (with adequate parking, not too far from where you live or work, and with a membership fee within your budget).

Purchasing athletic equipment should be done thoughtfully so you do not waste your money. When buying athletic shoes, choose shoes that are comfortable and consistent with any foot problems you may have (for example, if you pronate or supinate). If orthotics are needed because of a foot abnormality, a podiatrist should be consulted, although, in some cases, ready-made shoe inserts are all that is needed.

There are many different kinds of home exercise equipment you can purchase. These include stationary bikes, climbers, rowers, cross-country ski machines, treadmills, and weights. In deciding what home exercise equipment to purchase, you should determine your fitness goals, who is going to use the equipment, the space you have available to house the equipment, and how much you have to spend.

Keeping Fit as You Age

Exercise can help you live longer and live better. It also staves off some of the effects of aging. For example, it can help with problems such as reduced cardiac output, lowered pulmonary ventilation, elevated blood pressure, a decrease in muscular strength and endurance, a decrease in flexibility, an increase in body fat, and a loss of skin elasticity. Furthermore, exercise is an excellent way for elders to enhance their overall wellness.

Health Activities to Help You Achieve Your Wellness Goals

As with physical fitness activities, health activities are important to achieve and maintain high-level wellness. Since the best strategy for treating illness and disease is to diagnose it early so treatment is minimal, both in terms of medical intervention and cost, various screenings are recommended. These include hypertension screening, dental checkups, Pap smears, vision and hearing screenings, and health risk appraisals, mammographies, tests for glaucoma, and others. Consult with your physician regarding the appropriateness and timing of screenings and medical exams for you.

Selecting health insurance is an important decision since both costs and coverage can vary greatly. There are two basic choices: fee-for-service and managed care plans. Fee-for-service plans require you to pay each time you receive care. Managed care plans—sometimes called prepayment plans—require a fee before any service is provided. Subsequently, when service is needed, no payment (or a very small payment) is required. Since health insurance is most often provided through places of work, check with your employer regarding the advantages and disadvantages of each form of health insurance as it applies to your specific needs.

Approximately 50 percent of illness and disease is a result of lifestyle behaviors; for example, being sedentary, eating unhealthy diets, engaging in unhealthy sexual practices or in an unhealthy way, ignoring the need for relaxation and stress relief, and ingesting too much alcohol or misusing other drugs.

REFERENCES

Katz, J. (1986, June). "The W.E.T. Workout." *Shape*, pp. 82–88.

President's Council on Physical Fitness and Sports. *Aqua Dynamics*. Washington, DC.

Road Runners Club of America. *Women running: Run smart. Run safe: Safety tips for women runners*. Alexandria, VA: RRCA.

Winters, C. (1993, May). "For Step Aerobic Addicts, a Challenging New Workout: Doing the Two-Step." *American Health*, p. 92.

Lab Activity 15.1

Why I Want to Be Physically Fit

INSTRUCTIONS: *There are many reasons why people engage in physical activity in an effort to become physically fit. If you know why you exercise, you will be able to choose activities that help you achieve your goals. To determine the reason(s) why you exercise, rank order the statements below.*

✦ **I Exercise Because**

_____ I want to lose or maintain my weight.

_____ I want to look good.

_____ I want to have a healthy heart and lungs.

_____ I want to be strong.

_____ I want to make new friends or socialize with my present friends.

_____ I want to channel my aggression positively.

_____ I like competition.

_____ I like to be out in natural surroundings.

_____ I want to develop enough energy not to be tired during the day.

_____ I want to be flexible.

_____ I want to have fun.

✦ **Interpretation of Results**

Consult Table 7.2 on page 150 to match the reasons you exercise with the benefits of the various physical activities. For example, if you exercise to lose weight, consider activities such as aerobic dance, basketball, or bicycling. If you exercise to make friends, play softball or volleyball. If you exercise to look good, weight train.

Matching your fitness goals with activities that can help you achieve those goals is the best way of assuring you will maintain your exercise program. Conversely, if you exercise regularly but do not achieve your goals because you have chosen the wrong physical activities, you will probably not continue with your program.

Mix and match activities so you achieve more than one of your goals. That way you will further increase the probability that you will become a lifetime participant in physical fitness activities.

Lab Activity 15.2

Developing a New Mind-Set about Exercise

INSTRUCTIONS: *When people try to develop a new habit, they are often plagued by thoughts of failure. During the early stages of your new exercise program, you can become your own worst enemy. Examine the list of excuses. Do any of these look familiar to you? Take a minute to prepare your own list of self-defeating thoughts about exercise. Prepare a list of positive thoughts, too.*

Learn to use these lists wisely. When self-defeating thoughts enter your mind, counteract them immediately with positive ones. Write your list of positive thoughts on a card, and carry it in your wallet or purse so you can refer to it when you are about to avoid a scheduled exercise session. List both long-term benefits (such as more energy, weight loss, and prevention of disease) and more immediate benefits (such as using up calories and feeling good).

Negative Thoughts about Exercise

1. I'm too busy to exercise today. I'm working too hard anyway and need a break.

2. I'm too tired to exercise today, and if I do work out, I won't have enough energy to do other things I must do.

3. I missed my workout today. I might as well forget all this fitness stuff. I do not have the self-control to keep at it.

4. None of my friends are fit or trim and they don't worry about it. I am not going to worry either.

5. I am already over the hill. I should just let myself go and enjoy life more.

Positive Thoughts about Exercise

1. I can find time to exercise today. I just have to think about my routine and plan carefully.

2. I may feel tired today, but I will do a light exercise routine instead of the heavy one I usually do. If I keep working out on a regular basis, I will build my stamina so I will not feel so tired during the day.

3. Just because I missed one exercise session does not mean that I should give up. I'm not going to let this small setback ruin everything I've accomplished.

4. What my friends do about exercising has nothing to do with my exercise habits. I'll make additional friends who do exercise.

5. I can get in shape and stay there. All I have to do is stick to my schedule. Knowing I can control my behavior is something I can enjoy every day.

Negative Thoughts about Exercise

1. _____

2. _____

3. _____

4. _____

Positive Thoughts about Exercise

1. _____

2. _____

3. _____

4. _____

Source: From *Exploring Health: Expanding the Boundaries of Wellness* (p. 225), by J. S. Greenberg & G. B. Dintiman 1992, Englewood Cliffs, NJ: Prentice Hall.

Lab Activity 15.3

Which Sports Match Your Personality?

INSTRUCTIONS: *Fitness experts tell us that if you match your personality with your choice of exercise, the chances are you will stay with your program. Here is a way to do that. Read the description of each psychosocial personality variable, and then rate yourself on the scorecard that follows.*

Sociability: Do you prefer doing things on your own or with other people? Do you make friends easily? Do you enjoy parties?

Spontaneity: Do you make spur-of-the-moment decisions, or do you plan in great detail? Can you change direction easily, or do you get locked in once you make up your mind?

Discipline: Do you have trouble sticking with things you find unpleasant or trying, or do you persist regardless of the obstacles? Do you need a lot of support, or do you just push on alone?

Aggressiveness: Do you try to control situations by being forceful? Do you like pitting yourself against obstacles, or do you shy away when you must assert yourself physically or emotionally?

Competitiveness: Are you bothered by situations that produce winners and losers? Does your adrenaline flow when you're challenged, or do you back off?

Mental Focus: Do you find it easy to concentrate, or do you have a short attention span? Can you be single-minded? How good are you at clearing your mind of distractions?

Risk-Taking: Are you generally adventurous, physically and emotionally, or do you prefer to stick to what you know?

Scorecard Fill in the appropriate circles and connect them with a line.	Very High ⟷ Very Low				
Sociability	O	O	O	O	O
Spontaneity	O	O	O	O	O
Discipline	O	O	O	O	O
Aggressiveness	O	O	O	O	O
Competitiveness	O	O	O	O	O
Mental Focus	O	O	O	O	O
Risk-taking	O	O	O	O	O

Walking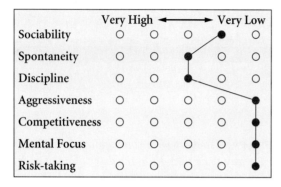

Running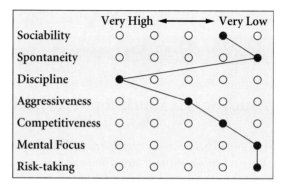

Cycling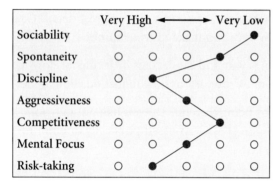

Weight Training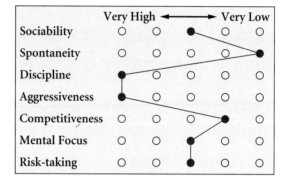

✦ **Understanding Your Score**

To see how well your profile matches your sport or exercise activity, look at the four sample profiles in this lab activity. If you have the typical personality of a runner, walker, cyclist, or bodybuilder, your profile should look similar to one of these profiles. If your athletic preference lies elsewhere, turn to the "Your Personality/Your Sport" chart on the next page to see where your activities rank on each characteristic. Then compare these rankings with how you scored yourself.

Compared with running, for example, walking is more spontaneous and less aggressive. (It is also safer, in terms of physical stress.) Racquet sports are high in sociability, spontaneity, competitiveness, and focus but low in discipline. Swimming is fairly high in discipline and low in sociability, spontaneity, and aggressiveness.

If you've been having trouble sticking to a fitness program, these charts may help explain why. If you're still looking for a sport, use your findings as a guide.

Source: From "Your Brand of Sweat," by J. Gavin, March 1989, *Psychology Today,* pp. 50–57. Copyright 1989 by Sussex Publishers, Inc. Reprinted with permission from *Psychology Today* magazine.

Your Personality/Your Sport

← Higher   Lower →

A chart ranking sports along seven personality dimensions, arranged from Higher (left) to Lower (right).

Dimension	Sports (Higher → Lower)
SOCIABILITY	Golf, Tennis, Martial Arts, Downhill Skiing, Aerobics, Dance, Weight Training, Cross-country Skiing, Walking, Running, Cycling, Yoga, Swimming
SPONTANEITY	Tennis, Weight Training, Downhill Skiing, Martial Arts, Dance, Cross-country Skiing, Walking, Aerobics, Cycling, Swimming, Yoga, Running, Golf
DISCIPLINE	Downhill Skiing, Golf, Tennis, Weight Training, Cross-country Skiing, Cycling, Walking, Aerobics, Dance, Martial Arts, Yoga, Running, Swimming
AGGRESSIVENESS	Martial Arts, Tennis, Weight Training, Downhill Skiing, Dance, Cycling, Running, Cross-country Skiing, Aerobics, Walking, Golf, Yoga, Swimming
COMPETITIVENESS	Martial Arts, Tennis, Downhill Skiing, Dance, Golf, Cycling, Running, Cross-country Skiing, Aerobics, Swimming, Walking, Yoga
MENTAL FOCUS	Golf, Tennis, Downhill Skiing, Yoga, Martial Arts, Weight Training, Cycling, Cross-country Skiing, Swimming, Aerobics, Walking, Running
RISK-TAKING	Downhill Skiing, Martial Arts, Tennis, Golf, Cycling, Weight Training, Dance, Cross-country Skiing, Aerobics, Swimming, Yoga, Running, Walking

419

Appendix A

Caloric Expenditure per Minute for Various Activities

BODY WEIGHT

	90	99	108	117	125	134	143	152	161	170	178	187	196	205	213	222	231	240	249	257	266	275
Archery	3.1	3.4	3.7	4.0	4.5	4.6	4.9	5.2	5.5	5.8	6.1	6.4	6.7	7.0	7.3	7.6	7.9	8.2	8.5	8.5	9.1	9.4
Badminton (recreation)	3.4	3.8	4.1	4.4	4.8	5.1	5.4	5.6	6.1	6.4	6.8	7.1	7.4	7.8	8.1	8.3	8.8	9.1	9.4	9.8	10.1	10.4
Badminton (competition)	5.9	6.4	7.0	7.6	8.1	8.7	9.3	9.9	10.4	11.0	11.6	12.1	12.7	13.3	13.9	14.4	15.0	15.6	16.1	16.7	17.3	17.9
Baseball (player)	2.8	3.1	3.4	3.6	3.9	4.2	4.5	4.7	5.0	5.3	5.5	5.8	6.1	6.4	6.6	6.9	7.2	7.5	7.7	8.0	8.3	8.6
Baseball (pitcher)	3.5	3.9	4.3	4.6	5.0	5.3	5.7	6.0	6.4	6.7	7.1	7.4	7.8	8.1	8.5	8.8	9.2	9.5	9.9	10.2	10.6	10.9
Basketball (half-court)	2.5	3.3	3.5	3.8	4.1	4.4	4.7	4.9	5.3	5.6	5.9	6.2	6.4	6.7	7.0	7.3	7.5	7.6	8.2	8.5	8.8	9.0
Basketball (moderate)	4.2	4.6	5.0	5.5	5.9	6.3	6.7	7.1	7.5	7.9	8.3	8.8	9.2	9.6	10.0	10.4	10.8	11.2	11.6	12.1	12.5	12.9
Basketball (competition)	5.9	6.5	7.1	7.7	8.2	8.8	9.4	10.0	10.6	11.1	11.7	12.3	12.9	13.5	14.0	14.6	15.0	15.2	16.3	16.9	17.5	18.1
Bicycling (level) 5.5 mph	3.0	3.3	3.6	3.9	4.2	4.5	4.8	5.1	5.4	5.6	5.9	6.2	6.5	6.8	7.1	7.4	7.7	8.0	8.3	8.6	8.9	9.2
Bicycling (level) 13 mph	6.4	7.1	7.7	8.3	8.9	9.6	10.2	10.8	11.4	12.1	12.7	13.4	14.0	14.6	15.2	15.9	16.5	17.1	17.8	18.4	19.0	19.6
Bowling (nonstop)	4.0	4.4	4.8	5.2	5.6	5.9	6.3	6.7	7.1	7.5	7.9	8.3	8.7	9.1	9.5	9.8	10.2	10.6	11.0	11.4	11.8	12.2
Boxing (sparring)	3.0	3.3	3.6	3.9	4.2	4.5	4.8	5.1	5.4	5.6	5.9	6.2	6.5	6.8	7.1	7.4	7.7	8.0	8.3	8.6	8.9	9.2
Calisthenics	3.0	3.3	3.6	3.9	4.2	4.5	4.8	5.1	5.4	5.6	5.9	6.2	6.5	6.8	7.1	7.4	7.7	8.0	8.3	8.6	8.9	9.2
Canoeing, 2.5 mph	1.8	1.9	2.0	2.2	2.3	2.5	2.7	3.0	3.2	3.4	3.6	3.7	3.9	4.1	4.2	4.4	4.6	4.8	5.0	5.1	5.3	5.5
Canoeing, 4.0 mph	4.2	4.6	5.0	5.5	5.9	6.3	6.7	7.1	7.5	7.9	8.3	8.7	9.2	9.4	10.0	10.5	10.8	11.2	11.6	12.0	12.4	12.9
Dance, modern (moderate)	2.5	2.8	3.0	3.2	3.5	3.7	4.0	4.2	4.5	4.7	5.0	5.2	5.4	5.7	5.9	6.2	6.4	6.7	6.9	7.2	7.4	7.6
Dance, modern (vigorous)	3.4	3.7	4.1	4.4	4.7	5.1	5.4	5.7	6.1	6.4	6.7	7.1	7.4	7.7	8.1	8.4	8.7	9.1	9.4	9.7	10.1	10.4
Dance, fox-trot	2.7	2.9	3.2	3.4	3.7	4.0	4.2	4.5	4.7	5.0	5.3	5.5	5.8	6.0	6.3	6.6	6.8	7.1	7.3	7.6	7.9	8.1
Dance, rumba	4.2	4.6	5.0	5.4	5.8	6.2	6.6	7.0	7.4	7.8	8.2	8.6	9.0	9.4	9.8	10.2	10.6	11.0	11.5	11.9	12.3	12.6
Dance, square	4.1	4.5	4.9	5.3	5.7	6.1	6.5	6.9	7.3	7.8	8.1	8.5	8.9	9.3	9.7	10.1	10.5	10.9	11.3	11.7	12.1	12.4
Dance, waltz	3.1	3.4	3.7	4.0	4.3	4.6	4.9	5.2	5.5	5.8	6.1	6.4	6.7	7.0	7.3	7.6	7.9	8.2	8.5	8.8	9.1	9.4
Fencing (moderate)	3.0	3.3	3.6	3.9	4.2	4.5	4.8	5.1	5.4	5.6	6.0	6.2	6.5	6.8	7.1	7.4	7.7	8.0	8.3	8.6	8.9	9.2
Fencing (vigorous)	6.2	6.8	7.4	8.0	8.6	9.2	9.8	10.4	11.0	11.6	12.2	12.8	13.4	14.0	14.6	15.2	15.8	16.4	17.0	17.6	18.2	18.8
Football (moderate)	3.0	3.3	3.6	4.0	4.2	4.5	4.8	5.1	5.4	5.7	6.0	6.2	6.5	6.8	7.1	7.4	7.7	8.0	8.3	8.6	8.9	9.2
Football (vigorous)	5.0	5.5	6.0	6.4	6.9	7.4	7.9	8.4	8.9	9.4	9.8	10.3	10.8	11.3	11.8	12.3	12.8	13.2	13.7	14.2	14.7	15.2
Golf, twosome	3.3	3.6	3.9	4.2	4.5	4.8	5.2	5.5	5.8	6.1	6.4	6.7	7.1	7.4	7.7	8.0	8.3	8.6	9.0	9.3	9.6	10.0
Golf, foursome	2.4	2.7	2.9	3.2	3.4	3.6	3.9	4.1	4.3	4.6	4.8	5.1	5.3	5.5	5.8	6.0	6.2	6.5	6.7	7.0	7.2	7.4
Handball	5.9	6.4	7.0	7.6	8.1	8.7	9.3	9.9	10.4	11.0	11.6	12.1	12.7	13.3	13.9	14.4	15.0	15.6	16.1	16.7	17.3	17.9
Hiking, 40-lb pack, 3.0 mph	4.1	4.5	4.9	5.3	5.7	6.1	6.5	6.9	7.3	7.7	8.1	8.5	8.9	9.3	9.7	10.1	10.5	10.9	11.3	11.7	12.1	12.5
Horseback riding (walk)	2.0	2.3	2.4	2.6	2.8	3.0	3.1	3.3	3.5	3.7	3.9	4.1	4.3	4.5	4.7	4.9	5.1	5.3	5.5	5.7	5.8	6.0
Horseback riding (trot)	4.1	4.4	4.8	5.2	5.6	6.0	6.4	6.8	7.2	7.6	8.0	8.4	8.8	9.2	9.6	10.0	10.4	10.8	11.2	11.6	12.0	12.4
Horseshoe pitching	2.1	2.3	2.5	2.7	3.0	3.3	3.4	3.6	3.8	4.0	4.2	4.4	4.6	4.8	5.0	5.2	5.4	5.6	5.8	6.0	6.3	6.5
Judo, Karate	7.7	8.5	9.2	10.0	10.7	11.5	12.2	13.0	13.7	14.5	15.2	16.0	16.7	17.5	18.2	19.0	19.7	20.5	21.2	22.0	22.7	23.5

BODY WEIGHT

	90	99	108	117	125	134	143	152	161	170	178	187	196	205	213	222	231	240	249	257	266	275
Mountain climbing	6.0	6.5	7.2	7.8	8.4	9.0	9.6	10.1	10.7	11.3	11.9	12.5	13.1	13.7	14.3	14.8	15.4	16.0	16.6	17.2	17.8	18.4
Paddleball, racquetball	5.9	6.4	7.0	7.6	8.1	8.7	9.3	9.9	10.4	11.0	11.6	12.1	12.7	13.3	13.9	14.4	15.0	15.6	16.1	16.7	17.3	17.9
Pool, billiards	1.1	1.2	1.3	1.4	1.5	1.6	1.7	1.8	1.9	2.0	2.1	2.2	2.4	2.5	2.6	2.7	2.8	2.9	3.0	3.1	3.2	3.3
Push-ups	4.3	4.7	5.1	5.6	6.0	6.4	6.8	7.2	7.7	8.1	8.5	8.9	9.4	9.8	10.2	10.6	11.0	11.5	11.9	12.3	12.7	13.2
Racquetball	6.0	6.6	7.2	7.8	8.3	8.9	9.5	10.1	11.7	11.3	11.9	12.5	13.1	13.7	14.2	14.8	15.4	16.0	16.6	17.2	17.8	18.4
Rowing (recreation)	3.0	3.3	3.6	3.9	4.2	4.5	4.8	5.1	5.4	5.6	6.0	6.2	6.5	6.8	7.1	7.5	7.7	8.0	8.3	8.6	8.9	9.2
Rowing (machine)	8.2	9.0	9.8	10.6	11.4	12.2	13.0	13.8	14.6	15.4	16.2	17.0	17.8	18.6	19.4	20.2	21.0	21.8	22.6	23.4	24.2	25.0
Running, 11-min mile, 5.5 mph	6.4	7.1	7.7	8.3	9.0	9.6	10.2	10.8	11.5	12.1	12.7	13.4	14.0	14.6	15.2	15.9	16.5	17.1	17.8	18.4	19.0	19.6
Running, 8.5-min mile, 7 mph	8.4	9.2	10.0	10.8	11.7	12.5	13.3	14.1	14.9	15.7	16.6	17.4	18.2	19.0	19.8	20.7	21.5	22.3	23.1	23.9	24.8	25.6
Running, 7-min mile, 9 mph	9.3	10.2	11.1	12.9	13.1	13.9	14.8	15.7	16.6	17.5	18.9	19.3	20.2	21.1	22.1	23.0	23.9	24.8	25.7	26.6	27.5	28.4
Running, 5-min mile, 12 mph	11.8	13.0	14.1	15.3	16.4	17.6	18.7	19.9	21.0	22.2	23.3	24.5	25.6	26.8	27.9	29.1	30.2	31.4	32.5	33.7	34.9	36.0
Sailing	1.8	2.0	2.1	2.3	2.4	2.7	2.8	3.0	3.2	3.4	3.6	3.8	3.9	4.1	4.3	4.4	4.6	4.8	5.0	5.1	5.3	5.5
Sit-ups	4.3	4.7	5.1	5.6	6.0	6.4	6.8	7.2	7.7	8.1	8.5	8.9	9.4	9.8	10.2	10.6	11.0	11.5	11.9	12.3	12.7	13.2
Sprinting	13.8	15.2	16.6	17.9	19.2	20.5	21.9	23.3	24.7	26.1	27.3	28.7	30.0	31.4	32.7	34.0	35.4	36.8	39.2	39.4	40.3	42.2
Skating (moderate)	3.4	3.8	4.1	4.4	4.8	5.1	5.4	5.8	6.1	6.4	6.8	7.1	7.4	7.8	8.1	8.3	8.8	9.1	9.4	9.8	10.1	10.4
Skating (vigorous)	6.2	6.8	7.4	8.0	8.6	9.2	9.8	9.9	11.0	11.6	12.2	12.8	13.4	14.0	14.6	15.2	15.8	16.4	17.0	17.6	18.2	18.8
Skiing (downhill)	5.8	6.4	6.9	7.5	8.1	8.6	9.2	9.8	10.3	10.9	11.4	12.0	12.6	13.1	13.7	14.3	14.8	15.4	16.0	16.5	17.1	17.7
Skiing (level, 5 mph)	7.0	7.7	8.4	9.1	9.8	10.5	11.1	11.8	12.5	13.2	13.9	14.6	15.2	15.9	16.6	17.3	18.0	18.7	19.4	20.0	20.7	21.4
Skiing (racing downhill)	9.9	10.9	11.9	12.9	13.7	14.7	15.7	16.7	17.7	18.7	19.6	20.6	21.6	22.6	23.4	24.4	25.4	26.4	27.4	28.3	29.3	30.2
Snowshoeing (2.3 mph)	3.7	4.1	4.5	4.8	5.2	5.5	5.9	6.3	6.7	7.0	7.4	7.8	8.1	8.5	8.8	9.2	9.6	9.9	10.3	10.6	11.0	11.4
Snowshoeing (2.5 mph)	5.4	5.9	6.5	7.0	7.5	8.0	8.6	9.1	9.7	10.2	10.7	11.2	11.8	12.3	12.8	13.3	13.9	14.4	14.9	15.4	16.0	16.5
Soccer	5.4	5.9	6.4	6.9	7.5	8.0	8.5	9.0	9.6	10.1	10.6	11.1	11.6	12.2	12.7	13.2	13.4	14.3	14.8	15.3	15.8	16.9
Squash	6.2	6.8	7.5	8.1	8.7	9.3	9.9	10.5	11.1	11.7	12.3	12.9	13.5	14.2	14.8	15.4	16.0	16.6	17.2	17.8	18.4	19.0
Stationary running, 140 counts/min	14.6	16.1	17.5	18.9	20.4	21.8	23.2	24.6	26.1	27.5	28.9	30.4	31.8	33.2	34.6	36.1	37.5	38.9	40.4	41.8	43.2	44.6
Swimming, pleasure 25 yds/min	3.6	4.0	4.3	4.7	5.0	5.4.	5.7	6.1	6.4	6.8	7.1	7.5	7.8	8.2	8.5	8.9	9.2	9.6	10.0	10.3	10.6	11.0
Swimming, back, 20 yd/min	2.3	2.6	2.8	3.0	3.2	3.5	3.7	3.9	4.1	4.2	4.6	4.8	5.0	5.3	5.5	5.7	6.0	6.2	6.4	6.6	6.9	7.1
Swimming, back, 30 yd/min	3.2	3.5	3.8	4.1	4.4	4.7	5.1	5.4	5.7	6.0	6.3	6.6	6.9	7.2	7.4	7.9	8.2	8.5	8.8	9.1	9.4	9.7
Swimming, back, 40 yd/min	5.0	5.5	5.8	6.5	7.0	7.5	7.9	8.5	8.9	9.4	9.9	10.4	10.9	11.4	11.9	12.3	12.8	13.3	13.8	14.3	14.8	15.3
Swimming, breast, 20 yd/min	2.9	3.2	3.4	3.8	4.0	4.3	4.6	4.9	5.1	5.4	5.7	6.0	6.3	6.5	6.8	7.1	7.4	7.7	7.9	8.2	8.5	8.8
Swimming, breast, 30 yd/min	4.3	4.8	5.2	5.7	6.0	6.4	6.9	7.3	7.7	8.1	8.6	9.0	9.4	9.9	10.3	10.8	11.1	11.5	11.9	12.4	13.0	13.3
Swimming, breast, 40 yd/min	5.8	6.3	6.9	7.5	8.0	8.6	9.2	9.7	10.3	10.8	11.4	12.0	12.5	13.1	13.7	14.2	14.8	15.4	15.9	16.5	17.0	17.6

BODY WEIGHT

	90	99	108	117	125	134	143	152	161	170	178	187	196	205	213	222	231	240	249	257	266	275
Swimming, butterfly, 50 yd/min	7.0	7.7	8.4	9.1	9.8	10.5	11.1	11.9	12.5	13.2	13.9	14.6	15.2	15.9	16.6	17.3	18.0	18.7	19.4	20.0	20.7	21.4
Swimming, crawl, 20 yd/min	2.9	3.2	3.4	3.8	4.0	4.3	4.6	4.9	5.1	5.4	5.7	5.8	6.3	6.5	6.8	7.1	7.3	7.7	7.9	8.2	8.5	8.8
Swimming, crawl, 45 yd/min	5.2	5.8	6.3	6.8	7.3	7.8	8.3	8.8	9.3	9.8	10.4	10.9	11.4	11.9	12.4	12.9	13.4	13.9	14.4	15.0	15.5	16.0
Swimming, crawl, 50 yd/min	6.4	7.0	7.6	8.3	8.9	9.5	10.1	10.7	11.4	12.0	12.6	13.2	13.9	14.5	15.1	15.7	16.3	17.0	17.4	17.9	18.8	19.5
Table tennis	2.3	2.6	2.8	3.0	3.2	3.5	3.7	3.9	4.1	4.2	4.6	4.8	5.0	5.3	5.5	5.7	6.0	6.2	6.4	6.6	6.9	7.1
Tennis (recreation)	4.2	4.6	5.0	5.4	5.8	6.2	6.6	7.0	7.4	7.8	8.2	8.6	9.0	9.4	9.8	10.2	10.6	11.0	11.5	11.9	12.3	12.6
Tennis (competition)	5.9	6.4	7.0	7.6	8.1	8.7	9.3	9.9	10.4	11.0	11.6	12.1	12.7	13.3	13.9	14.4	15.0	15.6	16.1	16.7	17.3	17.9
Timed calisthenics	8.8	9.6	10.5	11.4	12.2	13.1	13.9	14.8	15.6	16.5	17.4	18.2	19.1	19.9	20.8	21.5	22.5	23.9	24.2	25.1	25.9	26.8
Volleyball (moderate)	3.4	3.8	4.0	4.4	4.8	5.1	5.4	5.8	6.1	6.4	6.8	7.1	7.4	7.8	8.1	8.3	8.8	9.1	9.4	9.8	10.1	10.4
Volleyball (vigorous)	5.9	6.4	7.0	7.6	8.1	8.7	9.3	9.9	10.4	11.0	11.6	12.1	12.7	13.3	13.9	14.4	15.0	15.6	16.1	16.7	17.3	17.9
Walking (2.0 mph)	2.1	2.3	2.5	2.7	2.9	3.1	3.3	3.5	3.7	4.0	4.2	4.4	4.6	4.8	5.0	5.2	5.4	5.6	5.8	6.0	6.2	6.4
Walking (4.5 mph)	4.0	4.4	4.7	5.1	5.5	5.9	6.3	6.7	7.1	7.5	7.8	8.2	8.6	9.0	9.4	9.8	10.1	10.6	10.9	11.3	11.7	12.0
Walking 110–120 steps/min	3.1	3.4	3.7	4.0	4.3	4.7	5.0	5.3	5.6	5.9	6.2	6.5	6.8	7.1	7.4	7.7	8.0	8.3	8.6	8.9	9.2	9.5
Waterskiing	4.7	5.1	5.6	6.1	6.5	7.0	7.4	7.9	8.3	8.8	9.3	9.7	10.2	10.6	11.1	11.5	12.0	12.5	12.9	13.4	13.8	14.3
Weight training	4.7	5.1	5.7	6.2	6.7	7.0	7.5	7.9	8.4	8.9	9.4	9.9	10.3	10.8	11.1	11.7	12.2	12.6	13.1	13.5	14.0	14.4
Wrestling	7.7	8.5	9.2	10.0	10.7	11.5	12.2	13.0	13.7	14.5	15.2	16.0	16.7	17.5	18.2	19.0	19.7	20.5	21.2	22.0	22.7	23.5

Source: From Physiological Measurements of Metabolic Functions in Man, by Consolazio, C., Johnson, R., & Pecora, L., 1963, New York: McGraw-Hill.

Nutritional Information for Selected Foods

Food item	Serving size	Grams	Calories	Protein (g)	Carbohydrate (g)	Fat (g)	Cholesterol (mg)	Sodium (mg)
Beverages								
Alcoholic								
Beer								
Regular	12 fl oz	360	150	1	13	0	0	18
Light	12 fl oz	355	95	1	5	0	0	11
Gin, rum, vodka, whiskey								
80-proof	1½ fl oz	42	95	0	Tr	0	0	Tr
86-proof	1½ fl oz	42	105	0	Tr	0	0	Tr
90-proof	1½ fl oz	42	110	0	Tr	0	0	Tr
Wines								
Dessert	3½ fl oz	103	140	Tr	8	0	0	9
Table								
Red	3½ fl oz	102	75	Tr	3	0	0	5
White	3½ fl oz	102	80	Tr	3	0	0	5
Carbonated								
Club soda	12 fl oz	355	0	0	0	0	0	78
Cola type								
Regular	12 fl oz	369	160	0	41	0	0	18
Diet, artificially sweetened	12 fl oz	355	Tr	0	Tr	0	0	32[a]
Ginger ale	12 fl oz	366	125	0	32	0	0	29
Grape	12 fl oz	372	180	0	46	0	0	48
Lemon-lime	12 fl oz	372	155	0	39	0	0	33
Orange	12 fl oz	372	180	0	46	0	0	52
Pepper type	12 fl oz	369	160	0	41	0	0	37
Root beer	12 fl oz	370	165	0	42	0	0	48
Fruit drinks, noncarbonated								
Canned								
Fruit punch drink	6 fl oz	190	85	Tr	22	0	0	15
Grape drink	6 fl oz	187	100	Tr	26	0	0	11
Pineapple-grapefruit juice drink	6 fl oz	187	90	Tr	23	Tr	0	24
Frozen lemonade concentrate, diluted with 4⅓ parts water by volume	6 fl oz	185	80	Tr	21	Tr	0	1

Tr = trace amount.

[a]Blend of aspartame and saccharin; if only saccharin is used, sodium is 75 mg; if only aspartame is used, sodium is 23 mg.

Source: Information summarized from *Nutritive Value of Foods,* Revised 1981, Superintendent of Documents, Washington DC: U.S. Government Printing Office.

FOOD ITEM	SERVING SIZE	GRAMS	CALORIES	PROTEIN (G)	CARBOHYDRATE (G)	FAT (G)	CHOLESTEROL (MG)	SODIUM (MG)
Dairy products								
Butter. See **Fats and Oils**								
Cheese								
Cheddar								
Cut pieces	1 oz	28	115	7	Tr	9	30	176
	1 in	17	70	4	Tr	6	18	105
Shredded	1 cup	113	455	28	1	37	119	701
Creamed (cottage cheese, 4% fat):								
Large curd	1 cup	225	235	28	6	10	34	911
Small curd	1 cup	210	215	26	6	9	31	850
With fruit	1 cup	226	280	22	30	8	25	915
Lowfat (2%)	1 cup	226	205	31	8	4	19	918
Cream	1 oz	28	100	2	1	10	31	84
Feta	1 oz	28	75	4	1	6	25	316
Mozzarella, made with								
Whole milk	1 oz	28	80	6	1	6	22	106
Part skim milk (low moisture)	1 oz	28	80	8	1	5	15	150
Muenster	1 oz	28	105	7	Tr	9	27	178
Parmesan, grated	1 oz	28	130	12	1	9	22	528
Provolone	1 oz	28	100	7	1	8	20	248
Swiss	1 oz	28	105	8	1	8	26	74
Pasteurized process cheese								
American	1 oz	28	105	6	Tr	9	27	406
Swiss	1 oz	28	95	7	1	7	24	388
Pasteurized process cheese food, American	1 oz	28	95	6	2	7	18	337
Pasteurized process cheese spread, American	1 oz	28	80	5	2	6	16	381
Cream, sweet								
Half-and-half (cream and milk)	1 cup	242	315	7	10	28	89	98
	1 tbsp	15	20	Tr	1	2	6	6
Light, coffee or table	1 cup	240	470	6	9	46	159	95
	1 tbsp	15	30	Tr	1	3	10	6
Cream, sour	1 cup	230	495	7	10	48	102	123
	1 tbsp	12	25	Tr	1	3	5	6
Ice cream. See **Milk desserts, frozen**								
Milk								
Whole (3.3% fat)	1 cup	244	150	8	11	8	33	370
Low-fat (2% fat)	1 cup	244	120	8	12	5	18	377
Low-fat (1% fat)	1 cup	244	100	8	12	3	10	381
Nonfat (skim)	1 cup	245	85	8	12	Tr	4	406

Food item	Serving size	Grams	Calories	Protein (g)	Carbohydrate (g)	Fat (g)	Cholesterol (mg)	Sodium (mg)
Dairy products *(continued)*								
Chocolate milk (commercial)								
Regular	1 cup	250	210	8	26	8	31	149
Low-fat (2% fat)	1 cup	250	180	8	26	5	17	151
Low-fat (1% fat)	1 cup	250	160	8	26	3	7	152
Milk beverages								
Cocoa and chocolate-flavored beverages								
Prepared (8 oz whole milk plus ¾ oz powder)	1 serving	265	225	9	30	9	33	176
Eggnog (commercial)	1 cup	254	340	10	34	19	149	138
Malted milk, chocolate	¾ oz	21	85		18	1	1	49
Prepared (8 oz whole milk plus ¾ oz powder)	1 serving	265	235	9	29	9	34	168
Shakes, thick								
Chocolate	10-oz container	283	335	9	60	8	30	314
Vanilla	10-oz container	283	315	11	50	9	33	270
Milk desserts, frozen								
Ice cream, vanilla Regular (about 11% fat)	1 cup	133	270	5	32	14	59	116
Yogurt								
Made with low-fat milk								
Fruit-flavored[b]	8-oz container	227	230	10	43	2	10	133
Plain	8-oz container	227	145	12	16	4	14	159
Made with nonfat milk	8-oz container	227	125	13	17	Tr	4	174
Made with whole milk	8-oz container	227	140	8	11	7	29	105
Eggs								
Eggs, large (24 oz per dozen):								
Cooked								
Fried in margarine	1 egg	46	90	6	1	7	211	162
Hard-cooked, shell removed	1 egg	50	75	6	1	5	213	62
Poached	1 egg	50	75	6	1	5	212	140
Scrambled (milk added) in margarine	1 egg	61	100	7	1	7	215	171

[b]Carbohydrate content varies widely because of amount of sugar added and amount of added flavoring. Consult the label if more precise values for carbohydrate and calories are needed.

FOOD ITEM	SERVING SIZE	GRAMS	CALORIES	PROTEIN (G)	CARBOHYDRATE (G)	FAT (G)	CHOLESTEROL (MG)	SODIUM (MG)
Fats and oils								
Butter (4 sticks per lb)								
Stick	½ cup	113	810	1	Tr	92	247	933[c]
Tablespoon (⅛ stick)	1 tbsp	14	100	Tr	Tr	11	31	116[c]
Pat (1-in square, ⅓ in high; 90 per lb)	1 pat	5	35	Tr	Tr	4	11	41[c]
Margarine								
Regular (about 80% fat)								
Stick	½ cup	113	810	1	1	91	0	1066[d]
Tablespoon (⅛ stick)	1 tbsp	14	100	Tr	Tr	11	0	132
Pat (1-in square, ⅓ in high; 90 per lb)	1 pat	5	35	Tr	Tr	4	0	47[d]
Oils, salad or cooking								
Corn	1 tbsp	14	125	0	0	14	0	0
Olive	1 tbsp	14	125	0	0	14	0	0
Peanut	1 tbsp	14	125	0	0	14	0	0
Safflower	1 tbsp	14	125	0	0	14	0	0
Sunflower	1 tbsp	14	125	0	0	14	0	0
Salad dressings								
Blue cheese	1 tbsp	15	75	1	1	8	3	164
French								
Regular	1 tbsp	16	85	Tr	1	9	0	188
Low-calorie	1 tbsp	16	25	Tr	2	2	0	306
Italian								
Regular	1 tbsp	15	80	Tr	1	9	0	162
Low-calorie	1 tbsp	15	5	Tr	2	Tr	0	136
Mayonnaise								
Regular	1 tbsp	14	100	Tr	Tr	11	8	80
Thousand island								
Regular	1 tbsp	16	60	Tr	2	6	4	112
Low-calorie	1 tbsp	15	25	Tr	2	2	2	150
Fish and shellfish								
Crab meat, canned	1 cup	135	135	23	1	3	135	1350
Fish sticks, frozen, reheated (stick, 4 by 1 by ½ in)	1 stick	28	70	6	4	3	26	53
Flounder or sole, baked, with lemon juice and butter	3 oz	85	120	16	Tr	6	68	145
Ocean perch, breaded, fried[e]	1 fillet	85	185	16	7	11	66	138
Salmon								
Baked (red)	3 oz	85	140	21	0	5	60	55
Smoked	3 oz	85	150	18	0	8	51	1700
Scallops, breaded, frozen, reheated	6 scallops	90	195	15	10	10	70	298

[c]For salted butter; unsalted butter contains 12 mg sodium per stick, 2 mg per tbsp, or 12 mg per pat.

[d]For salted margarine.

[e]Dipped in egg, milk, and bread crumbs; fried in vegetable shortening.

Food item	Serving size	Grams	Calories	Protein (g)	Carbohydrate (g)	Fat (g)	Cholesterol (mg)	Sodium (mg)
Fish and shellfish *(continued)*								
Shrimp, french fried (7 medium)[f]	3 oz	85	200	16	11	10	168	384
Trout, broiled, with butter and lemon juice	3 oz	85	175	21	Tr	9	71	122
Tuna, canned, drained solids								
Oil pack, chunk light	3 oz	85	165	24	0	7	55	303
Water pack, solid white	3 oz	85	135	30	0	1	48	468
Tuna salad[g]	1 cup	205	375	33	19	19	80	877
Fruits and fruit juices								
Apples								
Raw								
Unpeeled, without cores, 3¼-in diam (about 2 per lb with cores)	1 apple	212	125	Tr	32	1	0	Tr
Peeled, sliced	1 cup	110	65	Tr	16	Tr	0	Tr
Apple juice, bottled or canned	1 cup	248	115	Tr	29	Tr	0	7
Apricots								
Raw, without pits (about 12 per lb with pits)	3 apricots	106	50	1	12	Tr	0	1
Bananas, raw, without peel								
Whole (about 2½ per lb with peel)	1 banana	114	105	1	27	1	0	1
Sliced	1 cup	150	140	2	35	1	0	2
Blueberries, raw	1 cup	145	80	1	20	1	0	9
Cherries, sweet, raw, without pits and stems	10 cherries	68	50	1	11	1	0	Tr
Grapefruit, raw, without peel, membrane, and seeds (3¾-in diam. 1 lb 1 oz, whole, with refuse)	½ grapefruit	120	40	1	10	Tr	0	Tr
Grapes, European type (adherent skin) raw, Thompson seedless	10 grapes	50	35	Tr	9	Tr	0	1

[f]Dipped in egg, milk, and bread crumbs; fried in vegetable shortening.

[g]Made with drained, chunk light tuna, celery, onion, pickle relish, and mayonnaise-type salad dressing.

Food item	Serving size	Grams	Calories	Protein (g)	Carbohydrate (g)	Fat (g)	Cholesterol (mg)	Sodium (mg)
Fruits and fruit juices *(continued)*								
Melons, raw, without rind and cavity contents								
Cantaloupe, orange-fleshed (5-in diam, 2⅓ lb, whole, with rind and cavity contents)	½ melon	267	95	2	22	1	0	24
Honeydew (6½-in diam, 5¼ lb, whole, with rind and cavity contents)	⅒ melon	129	45	1	12	Tr	0	13
Nectarines, raw, without pits (about 3 per lb with pits)	1 nectarine	136	65	1	16	1	0	Tr
Oranges, raw, whole, without peel and seeds (2⅝-in diam, about 2½ per lb, with peel and seeds)	1 orange	131	60	1	15	Tr	0	Tr
Orange juice								
Raw, all varieties	1 cup	248	110	2	26	Tr	0	2
Canned, unsweetened	1 cup	249	105	1	25	Tr	0	5
Peaches, raw								
Whole, 2½-in diam, peeled, pitted (about 4 per lb with peels and pits)	1 peach	87	35	1	10	Tr	0	Tr
Sliced	1 cup	170	75	1	19	Tr	0	Tr
Pears, raw, with skin, cored, Bartlett, 2½-in diam (about 2½ per lb with cores and stems)	1 pear	166	100	1	25	1	0	Tr
Pineapple, raw, diced	1 cup	155	75	1	19	1	0	2
Pineapple juice, unsweetened, canned	1 cup	250	140	1	34	Tr	0	3
Plums, without pits, raw, 2⅛-in diam (about 6½ per lb with pits)	1 plum	66	35	1	9	Tr	0	Tr
Raisins, seedless, cup, not pressed down	1 cup	145	435	5	115	1	0	17
Raspberries, raw	1 cup	123	60	1	14	1	0	Tr
Strawberries, raw, capped, whole	1 cup	149	45	1	10	1	0	1

FOOD ITEM	SERVING SIZE	GRAMS	CALORIES	PROTEIN (G)	CARBOHYDRATE (G)	FAT (G)	CHOLESTEROL (MG)	SODIUM (MG)
Fruits and fruit juices (*continued*)								
Watermelon, raw, without rind and seeds, piece (4 by 8-in wedge with rind and seeds; 1/16 of 32 2/3-lb melon, 10 by 16 in)	1 piece	482	155	3	35	2	0	10
Grain products								
Bagels, plain or water, enriched, 3½-in diam[h]	1 bagel	68	200	7	38	2	0	245
Breads								
French or vienna bread, enriched[i]								
Slice								
French, 5 by 2½ by 1 in	1 slice	35	100	3	18	1	0	203
Vienna, 4¾ by 4 by ½ in	1 slice	25	70	2	13	1	0	145
Italian bread, enriched								
Slice, 4½ by 3¼ by ¾ in	1 slice	30	85	3	17	Tr	0	176
Mixed grain bread, enriched[i]								
Slice (18 per loaf)	1 slice	25	65	2	12	1	0	106
Pita bread, enriched, white, 6½-in diam	1 pita	60	165	6	33	1	0	339
Pumpernickel (2/3 rye flour, 1/3 enriched wheat flour)[i]								
Slice, 5 by 4 by 3/8 in	1 slice	32	80	3	16	1	0	177
Rye bread, light (2/3 enriched wheat flour, 1/3 rye flour)[i]								
Slice, 4¾ by 3¾ by 7/16 in	1 slice	25	65	2	12	1	0	175
Wheat bread, enriched[i]								
Slice (16 per loaf)	1 slice	25	65	2	12	1	0	138
Whole-wheat bread[i]								
Slice (18 per loaf)	1 slice	28	70	3	13	1	0	180
Breakfast cereals								
All-Bran (about 1/3 cup)	1 oz	28	70	4	21	1	0	320
Cap'n Crunch (about ¾ cup)	1 oz	28	120	1	23	3	0	213

[h]Egg bagels have 44 mg cholesterol and 22 IU or 7 RE vitamin A per bagel.
[i]Made with vegetable shortening.

Food item	Serving size	Grams	Calories	Protein (g)	Carbohydrate (g)	Fat (g)	Cholesterol (mg)	Sodium (mg)
Grain products *(continued)*								
Cheerios (about 1¼ cup)	1 oz	28	110	4	20	2	0	307
Corn Flakes (about 1¼ cup)								
Kellogg's	1 oz	28	110	2	24	Tr	0	351
Toasties	1 oz	28	110	2	24	Tr	0	297
40% Bran Flakes								
Kellogg's (about ¾ cup)	1 oz	28	90	4	22	1	0	264
Post (about ⅔ cup)	1 oz	28	90	3	22	Tr	0	260
Froot Loops (about 1 cup)	1 oz	28	110	2	25	1	0	145
Lucky Charms (about 1 cup)	1 oz	28	110	3	23	1	0	201
100% Natural Cereal (about ¼ cup)	1 oz	28	135	3	18	6	Tr	12
Product 19 (about ¾ cup)	1 oz	28	110	3	24	Tr	0	325
Raisin Bran								
Kellogg's (about ¾ cup)	1 oz	28	90	3	21	1	0	207
Post (about ½ cup)	1 oz	28	85	3	21	1	0	185
Special K (about 1⅓ cup)	1 oz	28	110	6	21	Tr	Tr	265
Sugar Frosted Flakes, Kellogg's (about ¾ cup)	1 oz	28	110	1	26	Tr	0	230
Wheaties (about 1 cup)	1 oz	28	100	3	23	Tr	0	354
Cakes prepared from cake mixes with enriched flour[j]								
Angel food, piece, ¹/₁₂ of cake	1 piece	53	125	3	29	Tr	0	269
Devil's food with chocolate frosting								
Piece, ¹/₁₆ of cake	1 piece	69	235	3	40	8	37	181
Cupcake, 2½-in diam	1 cupcake	35	120	2	20	4	19	92
Cakes prepared from home recipes using enriched flour								
Carrot, with cream cheese frosting[k]								
Piece, ¹/₁₆ of cake	1 piece	96	385	4	48	21	74	279
Pound								
Slice, ¹/₁₇ of loaf	1 slice	30	120	2	15	5	32	96
Cheesecake								
Piece, ¹/₁₂ of cake	1 piece	92	280	5	26	18	170	204

[j]Excepting angel food cake, cakes were made from mixes containing vegetable shortening and frostings were made with margarine.
[k]Made with vegetable oil.

Food item	Serving size	Grams	Calories	Protein (g)	Carbohydrate (g)	Fat (g)	Cholesterol (mg)	Sodium (mg)
Grain products *(continued)*								
Cookies made with enriched flour								
Brownies with nuts, commercial, with frosting, 1½ by 1¾ by ⅞ in	1 brownie	25	100	1	16	4	14	59
Chocolate chip, commercial, 2¼-in diam, ⅜ in thick	4 cookies	42	180	2	28	9	5	140
Oatmeal with raisins, 2⅝-in diam, ¼ in thick	4 cookies	52	245	3	36	10	2	148
Peanut butter cookie, from home recipe 2⅝-in diam[l]	4 cookies	48	245	4	28	14	22	142
Corn chips	1-oz package	28	155	2	16	9	0	233
Crackers[m]								
Graham, plain, 2½-in square	2 crackers	14	60	1	11	1	0	86
Melba toast, plain	1 piece	5	20	1	4	Tr	0	44
Saltines[n]	4 crackers	12	50	1	9	1	4	165
Wheat, thin	4 crackers	8	35	1	5	1	0	69
Croissants, made with enriched flour, 4½ by 4 by 1¾ in	1 croissant	57	235	5	27	12	13	452
Doughnuts, made with enriched flour								
Cake type, plain, 3¼-in diam, 1 in high	1 doughnut	50	210	3	24	12	20	192
Yeast-leavened, glazed, 3¾-in diam, 1¼ in high	1 doughnut	60	235	4	26	13	21	222
English muffins, plain, enriched	1 muffin	57	140	5	27	1	0	378
French toast, from home recipe	1 slice	65	155	6	17	7	112	257

[l]Made with vegetable shortening.

[m]Crackers made with enriched flour except for rye wafers and whole-wheat wafers.

[n]Made with lard.

FOOD ITEM	SERVING SIZE	GRAMS	CALORIES	PROTEIN (G)	CARBOHYDRATE (G)	FAT (G)	CHOLESTEROL (MG)	SODIUM (MG)
Grain products *(continued)*								
Macaroni, enriched, cooked (cut lengths, elbows, shells), firm stage (hot)	1 cup	130	190	7	39	1	0	1
Muffins made with enriched flour, 2½-in diam, 1½ in high, from home recipe								
Blueberry°	1 muffin	45	135	3	20	5	19	198
Bran	1 muffin	45	125	3	19	6	24	189
Corn	1 muffin	45	145	3	21	5	23	169
Noodles (egg noodles), enriched, cooked	1 cup	160	200	7	37	2	50	3
Noodles, chow mein, canned	1 cup	45	220	6	26	11	5	450
Pancakes, 4-in diam								
Buckwheat, from mix (with buckwheat and enriched flours), egg and milk added	1 pancake	27	55	2	6	2	20	125
Plain								
From home recipe using enriched flour	1 pancake	27	60	2	9	2	16	115
From mix (with enriched flour), egg, milk, and oil added	1 pancake	27	60	2	8	2	16	160
Pies, pie crust made with enriched flour, vegetable shortening, 9-in diam								
Apple, piece, ⅙ of pie	1 piece	158	405	3	60	18	0	476
Blueberry, piece, ⅙ of pie	1 piece	158	380	4	55	17	0	423
Cherry, piece, ⅙ of pie	1 piece	158	410	4	61	18	0	480
Lemon meringue, piece, ⅙ of pie	1 piece	140	355	5	53	14	143	395
Pecan, piece, ⅙ of pie	1 piece	138	575	7	71	32	95	305

°Made with vegetable shortening.

FOOD ITEM	SERVING SIZE	GRAMS	CALORIES	PROTEIN (G)	CARBOHYDRATE (G)	FAT (G)	CHOLESTEROL (MG)	SODIUM (MG)
Grain products *(continued)*								
Popcorn, popped								
Airpopped, unsalted	1 cup	8	30	1	6	Tr	0	Tr
Popped in vegetable oil, salted	1 cup	11	55	1	6	3	0	86
Sugar syrup coated	1 cup	35	135	2	30	1	0	Tr
Pretzels, made with enriched flour								
Stick, 2¼ in long	10 pretzels	3	10	Tr	2	Tr	0	48
Twisted, dutch, 2¾ by 2⅝ in	1 pretzel	16	65	2	13	1	0	258
Rice								
Brown, cooked, served hot	1 cup	195	230	5	50	1	0	0
White, enriched								
Cooked, served hot	1 cup	205	225	4	50	Tr	0	0
Instant, ready-to-serve, hot	1 cup	165	180	4	40	0	0	0
Rolls, enriched								
Commercial								
Dinner, 2½-in diam, 2 in high	1 roll	28	85	2	14	2	Tr	155
Frankfurter and hamburger (8 per 11½-oz pkg.)	1 roll	40	115	3	20	2	Tr	241
Hard, 3¾-in diam, 2 in high	1 roll	50	155	5	30	2	Tr	313
Hoagie or submarine, 11½ by 3 by 2½ in	1 roll	135	400	11	72	8	Tr	683
Spaghetti, enriched, cooked								
Firm stage, "al dente," served hot	1 cup	130	190	7	39	1	0	1
Tender stage, served hot	1 cup	140	155	5	32	1	0	1
Tortillas, corn	1 tortilla	30	65	2	13	1	0	1
Waffles, made with enriched flour, 7-in diam								
From home recipe	1 waffle	75	245	7	26	13	102	445
From mix, egg and milk added	1 waffle	75	205	7	27	8	59	515
Legumes, nuts, and seeds								
Almonds, shelled								
Whole	1 oz	28	165	6	6	15	0	3
Beans, dry								
Black	1 cup	171	225	15	41	1	0	1
Lima	1 cup	190	260	16	49	1	0	4
Pea (navy)	1 cup	190	225	15	40	1	0	13
Pinto	1 cup	180	265	15	49	1	0	3

FOOD ITEM	SERVING SIZE	GRAMS	CALORIES	PROTEIN (G)	CARBOHYDRATE (G)	FAT (G)	CHOLESTEROL (MG)	SODIUM (MG)
Legumes, nuts, and seeds *(continued)*								
Black-eyed peas, dry, cooked (with residual cooking liquid)	1 cup	250	190	13	35	1	0	20
Brazil nuts, shelled	1 oz	28	185	4	4	19	0	1
Cashew nuts, salted								
Dry roasted	1 oz	28	165	4	9	13	0	181[p]
Roasted in oil	1 oz	28	165	5	8	14	0	177[q]
Lentils, dry, cooked	1 cup	200	215	16	38	1	0	26
Mixed nuts, with peanuts, salted								
Dry roasted	1 oz	28	170	5	7	15	0	190[r]
Roasted in oil	1 oz	28	175	5	6	16	0	185[r]
Peanuts, roasted in oil, salted	1 oz	28	165	8	5	14	0	122[s]
Peanut butter	1 tbsp	16	95	5	3	8	0	75
Peas, split, dry, cooked	1 cup	200	230	16	42	1	0	26
Pistachio nuts, dried, shelled	1 oz	28	165	6	7	14	0	2
Refried beans, canned	1 cup	290	295	18	5 1	3	0	1228
Sesame seeds, dry, hulled	1 tbsp	8	45	2	1	4	0	3
Sunflower seeds, dry, hulled	1 oz	28	160	6	5	14	0	1
Meat and meat products								
Beef, cooked[t]								
Cuts braised, simmered, or pot roasted								
Relatively fat, such as chuck blade								
Lean and fat, piece, 2½ by 2½ by ¾ in	3 oz	85	325	22	0	26	87	53
Relatively lean, such as bottom round								
Lean and fat, piece, 4⅛ by 2¼ by ½ in	3 oz	85	220	25	0	13	81	43
Ground beef, broiled, patty, 3 by ⅝ in								
Lean	3 oz	85	230	21	0	16	74	65
Regular	3 oz	85	245	20	0	18	76	70

[p]Cashews without salt contain 21 mg sodium per cup or 4 mg per oz.

[q]Cashews without salt contain 22 mg sodium per cup or 5 mg per oz.

[r]Mixed nuts without salt contain 3 mg sodium per oz.

[s]Peanuts without salt contain 22 mg sodium per cup or 4 mg per oz.

[t]Outer layer of fat was removed to within approximately ½ inch of lean. Deposits of fat within the cut were not removed.

Food item	Serving size	Grams	Calories	Protein (g)	Carbohydrate (g)	Fat (g)	Cholesterol (mg)	Sodium (mg)
Meat and meat products *(continued)*								
Roast, oven cooked, no liquid added								
Relatively fat, such as rib								
Lean and fat, 2 pieces, 4⅛ by 2¼ in	3 oz	85	315	19	0	26	72	54
Relatively lean, such as eye of round								
Lean and fat, 2 pieces, 2½ by 2½ by ⅜ in	3 oz	85	205	23	0	12	62	50
Steak								
Sirloin, broiled								
Lean and fat, piece, 2½ by 2½ by ¾ in	3 oz	85	240	23	0	15	77	53
Lamb, cooked								
Chops (3 per lb with bone)								
Arm, braised								
Lean and fat	2.2 oz	63	220	20	0	15	77	46
Loin, broiled								
Lean and fat	2.8 oz	80	235	20	0	16	78	62
Leg, roasted								
Lean and fat, 2 pieces, 4⅛ by 2¼ by ¼ in	3 oz	85	205	22	0	13	78	57
Rib, roasted								
Lean and fat, 3 pieces, 2½ by 2½ by ¼ in	3 oz	85	315	18	0	26	77	60
Pork, cured, cooked								
Bacon								
Regular	3 medium slices	19	110	6	Tr	9	16	303
Canadian-style	2 slices	46	85	11	1	4	27	711
Ham, light cured, roasted								
Lean and fat, 2 pieces, 4⅛ by 2¼ by ¼ in	3 oz	85	205	18	0	14	53	1009
Luncheon meat								
Canned, spiced or unspiced, slice, 3 by 2 by ½ in	2 slices	42	140	5	1	13	26	541
Chopped ham (8 slices per 6-oz pkg)	2 slices	42	95	7	0	7	21	576

FOOD ITEM	SERVING SIZE	GRAMS	CALORIES	PROTEIN (G)	CARBOHYDRATE (G)	FAT (G)	CHOLESTEROL (MG)	SODIUM (MG)
Meat and meat products *(continued)*								
Cooked ham (8 slices per 8-oz pkg)								
Regular	2 slices	57	105	10	2	6	32	751
Extra lean	2 slices	57	75	11	1	3	27	815
Pork, fresh, cooked								
Chop, loin (cut 3 per lb with bone)								
Broiled								
Lean and fat	3.1 oz	87	275	24	0	19	84	61
Ham (leg), roasted Lean and fat, piece, 2½ by 2½ by ¾ in	3 oz	85	250	21	0	18	79	50
Rib, roasted Lean and fat, piece, 2½ by ¾ in	3 oz	85	270	21	0	20	69	37
Shoulder cut, braised Lean and fat, 3 pieces, 2½ by 2½ by ¼ in	3 oz	85	295	23	0	22	93	75
Sausages								
Bologna	2 slices	57	180	7	2	16	31	581
Frankfurter	1 frank	45	145	5	1	13	23	504
Pork link	1 link	13	50	3	Tr	4	11	168
Salami								
Cooked type, slice (8 per 8-oz pkg)	2 slices	57	145	8	1	11	37	607
Veal, medium fat, cooked, bone removed								
Cutlet, 4⅛ by 2¼ by ½ in, braised or broiled	3 oz	85	185	23	0	9	109	56
Rib, 2 pieces, 4⅛ by 2¼ by ¼ in, roasted	3 oz	85	230	23	0	14	109	57
Mixed dishes and fast foods								
Mixed dishes								
Beef and vegetable stew, from home recipe	1 cup	245	220	16	15	11	71	292
Beef potpie, from home recipe, baked, piece, ⅓ of 9-in diam pie	1 piece	210	515	21	39	30	42	596
Chicken á la king, cooked, from home recipe	1 cup	245	470	27	12	34	221	760

Food item	Serving size	Grams	Calories	Protein (g)	Carbohydrate (g)	Fat (g)	Cholesterol (mg)	Sodium (mg)
Mixed dishes and fast foods (*continued*)								
Chicken and noodles, cooked, from home recipe	1 cup	240	365	22	26	18	103	600
Chicken chow mein								
Canned	1 cup	250	95	7	18	Tr	8	725
From home recipe	1 cup	250	255	31	10	10	75	718
Chicken potpie, from home recipe, baked, piece, ⅓ of 9-in diam pie	1 piece	232	545	23	42	31	56	594
Chili con carne with beans, canned	1 cup	255	340	19	31	16	28	1354
Chop suey with beef and pork, from home recipe	1 cup	250	300	26	13	17	68	1053
Macaroni (enriched) and cheese								
Canned	1 cup	240	230	9	26	10	24	730
From home recipe[u]	1 cup	200	430	17	40	22	44	1086
Spaghetti (enriched) in tomato sauce with cheese								
Canned	1 cup	250	190	6	39	2	3	955
From home recipe[u]	1 cup	250	260	9	37	9	8	955
Spaghetti (enriched) with meatballs and tomato sauce								
From home recipe	1 cup	248	330	19	39	12	89	1009
Poultry and poultry products								
Chicken								
Fried, flesh, with skin[v]								
Batter dipped								
Breast, ½ breast (5.6 oz with bones)	4.9 oz	140	365	35	13	18	119	385
Drumstick (3.4 oz with bones)	2.5 oz	72	195	16	6	11	62	194
Flour coated								
Breast, ½ breast (4.2 oz with bones)	3.5 oz	98	220	31	2	9	87	74
Drumstick (2.6 oz with bones)	1.7 oz	49	120	13	1	7	44	44
Roasted, flesh only								
Breast, ½ breast (4.2 oz with bones and skin)	3.0 oz	86	140	27	0	3	73	64

[u]Made with margarine.

[v]Fried in vegetable shortening.

FOOD ITEM	SERVING SIZE	GRAMS	CALORIES	PROTEIN (G)	CARBOHYDRATE (G)	FAT (G)	CHOLESTEROL (MG)	SODIUM (MG)
Poultry and poultry products *(continued)*								
Drumstick (2.9 oz with bones and skin)	1.6 oz	44	75	12	0	2	41	42
Turkey, roasted, flesh only								
Dark meat, piece, 2½ by 1⅝ by ¼ in	4 pieces	85	160	24	0	6	72	67
Light meat, piece, 4 by 2 by ¼ in	2 pieces	85	135	25	0	3	59	54
Light and dark meat								
Chopped or diced	1 cup	140	240	41	0	7	106	98
Pieces (1 slice white meat, 4 by 2 by ¼ in and 2 slices dark meat, 2½ by 1⅝ by ¼ in)	3 pieces	85	145	25	0	4	65	60
Soups, sauces, and gravies								
Soups								
Canned, condensed								
Prepared with equal volume of milk								
Clam chowder, New England	1 cup	248	165	9	17	7	22	992
Cream of chicken	1 cup	248	190	7	15	11	27	1047
Cream of mushroom	1 cup	248	205	6	15	14	20	1076
Tomato	1 cup	248	160	6	22	6	17	932
Prepared with equal volume of water								
Bean with bacon	1 cup	253	170	8	23	6	3	951
Beef noodle	1 cup	244	85	5	9	3	5	952
Chicken noodle	1 cup	241	75	4	9	2	7	1106
Chicken rice	1 cup	241	60	4	7	2	7	815
Clam chowder, Manhattan	1 cup	244	80	4	12	2	2	1808
Cream of chicken	1 cup	244	115	3	9	7	10	986
Cream of mushroom	1 cup	244	130	2	9	9	2	1032
Minestrone	1 cup	241	80	4	11	3	2	911
Pea, green	1 cup	250	165	9	27	3	0	988
Tomato	1 cup	244	85	2	17	2	0	871
Vegetable beef	1 cup	244	80	6	10	2	5	956

Food item	Serving size	Grams	Calories	Protein (g)	Carbohydrate (g)	Fat (g)	Cholesterol (mg)	Sodium (mg)
Soups, sauces, and gravies (*continued*)								
Sauces								
From dry mix								
Cheese, prepared with milk	1 cup	279	305	16	23	17	53	1565
Hollandaise, prepared with water	1 cup	259	240	5	14	20	52	1564
Gravies								
Canned								
Beef	1 cup	233	125	9	11	5	7	1305
Chicken	1 cup	238	190	5	13	14	5	1373
Mushroom	1 cup	238	120	3	13	6	0	1357
Sugars and sweets								
Candy								
Caramels, plain or chocolate	1 oz	28	115	1	22	3	1	64
Chocolate								
Milk, plain	1 oz	28	145	2	16	9	6	23
Milk, with almonds	1 oz	28	150	3	15	10	5	23
Milk, with peanuts	1 oz	28	155	4	13	11	5	19
Milk, with rice cereal	1 oz	28	140	2	18	7	6	46
Fudge, chocolate, plain	1 oz	28	115	1	21	3	1	54
Gum drops	1 oz	28	100	Tr	25	Tr	0	10
Hard candy	1 oz	28	110	0	28	0	0	7
Jelly beans	1 oz	28	105	Tr	26	Tr	0	7
Marshmallows	1 oz	28	90	1	23	0	0	25
Custard, baked	1 cup	265	305	14	29	15	278	209
Honey, strained or extracted	1 cup	339	1030	1	279	0	0	17
	1 tbsp	21	65	Tr	17	0	0	1
Jams and preserves	1 tbsp	20	55	Tr	14	Tr	0	2
	1 packet	14	40	Tr	10	Tr	0	2
Jellies	1 tbsp	18	50	Tr	13	Tr	0	5
	1 packet	14	40	Tr	10	Tr	0	4
Popsicle, 3-fl-oz size	1 popsicle	95	70	0	18	0	0	11
Puddings								
Canned								
Chocolate	5-oz can	142	205	3	30	11	1	285
Tapioca	5-oz can	142	160	3	28	5	Tr	252
Vanilla	5-oz can	142	220	2	33	10	1	305
Dry mix, prepared with whole milk								
Chocolate								
Instant	½ cup	130	155	4	27	4	14	440
Regular (cooked)	½ cup	130	150	4	25	4	15	167
Rice	½ cup	132	155	4	27	4	15	140
Tapioca	½ cup	130	145	4	25	4	15	152

FOOD ITEM	SERVING SIZE	GRAMS	CALORIES	PROTEIN (G)	CARBOHYDRATE (G)	FAT (G)	CHOLESTEROL (MG)	SODIUM (MG)
Sugars and sweets *(continued)*								
Vanilla								
Instant	½ cup	130	150	4	27	4	15	375
Regular (cooked)	½ cup	130	145	4	25	4	15	178
Sugars								
Brown, pressed down	1 cup	220	820	0	212	0	0	97
White, granulated	1 cup	200	770	0	199	0	0	5
	1 tbsp	12	45	0	12	0	0	Tr
	1 packet	6	25	0	6	0	0	Tr
Syrups								
Chocolate-flavored syrup or topping								
Thin type	2 tbsp	38	85	1	22	Tr	0	36
Fudge type	2 tbsp	38	125	2	21	5	0	42
Vegetables and vegetable products								
Asparagus, green, cooked, drained								
From raw, cuts and tips	1 cup	180	45	5	8	1	0	7
From frozen, cuts and tips	1 cup	180	50	5	9	1	0	7
Beans								
Lima, immature seeds, frozen, cooked, drained, thick-seeded types (Ford hooks)	1 cup	170	170	10	32	1	0	90
Beets, cooked, drained, diced or sliced	1 cup	170	55	2	11	Tr	0	83
Black-eyed peas, immature seeds, cooked and drained, from raw	1 cup	165	180	13	30	1	0	7
Broccoli, raw	1 spear	151	40	4	8	1	0	41
Spears, cut into ½-in pieces	1 cup	155	45	5	9	Tr	0	17
Brussels sprouts, cooked, drained, from raw, 7–8 sprouts, 1¼ to 1½-in diam	1 cup	155	60	4	13	1	0	33
Cabbage, common varieties, raw, coarsely shredded or sliced	1 cup	70	15	1	4	Tr	0	13
Carrots, Raw, without crowns and tips, scraped, whole, 7½ by 1⅛ in, or strips, 2½ to 3 in long	1 carrot or 18 strips	72	30	1	7	Tr	0	25

Food item	Serving size	Grams	Calories	Protein (g)	Carbohydrate (g)	Fat (g)	Cholesterol (mg)	Sodium (mg)
Vegetables and vegetable products *(continued)*								
Carrots								
Cooked, sliced, drained, from raw	1 cup	156	70	2	16	Tr	0	103
Cauliflower								
Raw (flowerets)	1 cup	100	25	2	5	Tr	0	15
Cooked, drained From raw (flowerets)	1 cup	125	30	2	6	Tr	0	8
Celery, pascal type, raw								
Stalk, large outer, 8 by 1½ in (at root end)	1 stalk	40	5	Tr	1	Tr	0	35
Corn, sweet, cooked, drained								
From raw, ear 5 by 1¾ in	1 ear	77	85	3	19	1	0	13
From frozen	1 ear	63	60	2	14	Tr	0	3
Cucumber, with peel, slices, ⅛ in thick (large, 2⅛-in diam; small, 1¾-in diam)	6 large or 8 small slices	28	5	Tr	1	Tr	0	1
Eggplant, cooked, steamed	1 cup	96	25	1	6	Tr	0	3
Lettuce, raw								
Butterhead, as Boston types:								
Head, 5-in diam	1 head	163	20	2	4	Tr	0	8
Leaves	1 outer or 2 inner leaves	15	Tr	Tr	Tr	Tr	0	1
Crisphead, as iceberg								
Pieces, chopped or shredded	1 cup	55	5	1	1	Tr	0	5
Loose leaf (bunching varieties including romaine or cos), chopped or shredded pieces	1 cup	56	10	1	2	Tr	0	5
Mushrooms								
Raw, sliced or chopped	1 cup	70	20	1	3	Tr	0	
Cooked, drained	1 cup	156	40	3	8	1	0	3
Onions								
Raw, chopped	1 cup	160	55	2	12	Tr	0	3
Cooked (whole or sliced), drained	1 cup	210	60	2	13	Tr	0	17
Peas, edible pod, cooked, drained	1 cup	160	65	5	11	Tr	0	6

FOOD ITEM	SERVING SIZE	GRAMS	CALORIES	PROTEIN (G)	CARBOHYDRATE (G)	FAT (G)	CHOLESTEROL (MG)	SODIUM (MG)
Vegetables and vegetable products *(continued)*								
Peas, green								
Canned, drained solids	1 cup	170	115	8	21	1	0	372w
Frozen, cooked, drained	1 cup	160	125	8	23	Tr	0	139
Potatoes, cooked								
Baked (about 2 per lb, raw)								
With skin	1 potato	202	220	5	51	Tr	0	16
Flesh only	1 potato	156	145	3	34	Tr	0	8
Boiled (about 3 per 1b, raw)								
Peeled after boiling	1 potato	136	120	3	27	Tr	0	5
Peeled before boiling	1 potato	135	115	2	27	Tr	0	7
French fried, strip, 2 to 3½ in long, frozen								
Oven heated	10 strips	50	110	2	17	4	0	16
Fried in vegetable oil	10 strips	50	160	2	20	8	0	108
Potato products, prepared								
Au gratin								
From dry mix	1 cup	245	230	6	31	10	12	1076
From home recipe	1 cup	245	325	12	28	19	56	1061
Hashed brown, from frozen	1 cup	156	340	5	44	18	0	53
Mashed								
From home recipe								
Milk added	1 cup	210	160	4	37	1	4	636
Milk and margarine added	1 cup	210	225	4	35	9	4	620
Potato salad, made with mayonnaise	1 cup	250	360	7	28	21	170	1323
Scalloped								
From dry mix	1 cup	245	230	5	31	11	27	835
From home recipe	1 cup	245	210	7	26	9	29	821
Potato chips	10 chips	20	105	1	10	7	0	94
Pumpkin, cooked from raw, mashed	1 cup	245	50	2	12	Tr	0	2
Radishes, raw, stem ends, rootlets cut off	4 radishes	18	5	Tr	1	Tr	0	4
Sauerkraut, canned, solids and liquid	1 cup	236	45	2	10	Tr	0	1560

wFor regular pack; special dietary pack contains 3 mg sodium.

FOOD ITEM	SERVING SIZE	GRAMS	CALORIES	PROTEIN (G)	CARBOHYDRATE (G)	FAT (G)	CHOLESTEROL (MG)	SODIUM (MG)
Vegetables and vegetable product *(continued)*								
Spinach								
Raw, chopped	1 cup	55	10	2	2	Tr	0	43
Cooked, drained								
From raw	1 cup	180	40	5	7	Tr	0	126
From frozen (leaf)	1 cup	190	55	6	10	Tr	0	163
Sweet potatoes								
Cooked (raw, 5 by 2 in; about 2½ per lb)								
Baked in skin, peeled	1 potato	114	115	2	28	Tr	0	11
Boiled, without skin	1 potato	151	160	2	37	Tr	0	20
Tomatoes								
Raw, 2⅗-in diam (3 per 12-oz pkg)	1 tomato	123	25	1	5	Tr	0	10
Tomato juice, canned	1 cup	244	40	2	10	Tr	0	881[x]
Tomato products, canned								
Paste	1 cup	262	220	10	49	2	0	170[y]
Sauce	1 cup	245	75	3	18	Tr	0	1482[z]
Vegetable juice cocktail, canned	1 cup	242	45	2	11	Tr	0	883
Miscellaneous items								
Catsup	1 cup	273	290	5	69	1	0	2845
	1 tbsp	15	15	Tr	4	Tr	0	156
Chili powder	1 tsp	2.6	10	Tr	1	Tr	0	26
Mustard, prepared, yellow	1 tsp or individual packet	5	5	Tr	Tr	Tr	0	63
Olives, canned								
Green	4 medium or 3 extra large	13	15	Tr	Tr	2	0	312
Ripe, Mission, pitted	3 small or 2 large	9	15	Tr	Tr	2	0	68
Pickles, cucumber								
Dill	1 pickle	65	5	Tr	1	Tr	0	928
Sweet	1 pickle	15	20	Tr	5	Tr	0	107
Salt	1 tsp	5.5	0	0	0	0	0	2132

[x]For added salt, if none is added, sodium content is 24 mg.

[y]With no added salt; if salt is added, sodium content is 2070 mg.

[z]With no added salt; if salt is added, sodium content is 998 mg.